NET **ZERO** ENERGY DESIGN

NET **ZERO** ENERGY DESIGN

A GUIDE FOR COMMERCIAL ARCHITECTURE

Tom Hootman

John Wiley & Sons, Inc.

Cover image: NREL/PIX 17613; photograph by Dennis Schroeder

This book is printed on acid-free paper. 

Published by John Wiley & Sons, Inc., Hoboken, New Jersey

Published simultaneously in Canada

Library of Congress Cataloging-in-Publication Data:

Hootman, Thomas.
  Net zero energy design : a guide for commercial architecture / Thomas Hootman.
    p. cm.
  Includes bibliographical references and index.
  ISBN 978-1-118-01854-5 (cloth); ISBN 978-1-118-34516-0 (ebk); ISBN 978-1-118-34517-7 (ebk); ISBN 978-1-118-34848-2 (ebk); ISBN 978-1-118-34849-9 (ebk); ISBN 978-1-118-34850-5 (ebk)
  1. Commercial buildings—Energy conservation. 2. Commercial buildings—Environmental aspects. 3. Architecture and energy conservation. I. Title.
  TJ163.5.B84H66 2013
  690'.520286—dc23

2012002033

Printed in the United States of America

10 9 8 7 6 5 4 3 2 1

To Jackson and Ray Hootman, for their—

and our world's—net zero energy future. Here comes the sun.

TABLE OF CONTENTS

ACKNOWLEDGMENTS

This book is important to me. I believe it can play a meaningful role in moving our industry toward a new way of designing and delivering buildings—toward net zero energy architecture. In the process of writing *Net Zero Energy Design: A Guide for Commercial Architecture*, I was fortunate to be supported by a remarkable network of like-minded, passionate individuals—colleagues, friends, and family—who also believe in the book and the objective of achieving net zero energy buildings.

I would first like to thank my wife, Deonne Hootman, for being the ultimate support system. She not only took up all of the slack around the house, enabling me to work countless hours without worry or distractions, she also served as a fantastic sounding board for my ideas, and often had just the cure for any case of writer's block. Thanks also to my two children, Jackson and Ray, and to my parents and sister for their support, and for understanding my crazy writing schedule.

I would next like to thank my contributing authors, Shanti Pless, from the National Renewable Energy Laboratory (NREL), and David Okada, who worked at Stantec while contributing to this book and is now with Integral Group. Both were instrumental in the success of the Department of Energy/National Renewable Energy Laboratory (DOE/NREL) Research Support Facility (RSF); they are also passionate and accomplished leaders and experts in net zero energy buildings. This book would not have been possible without their contributions. I am grateful for their hard work and the sacrifices they made to help make this book a reality.

I am fortunate to work at RNL, where net zero energy architecture has become part of our daily practice, and where there is a strong focus on developing the next generation of architecture. I would like to thank everyone at the firm for being supportive of the book and my process of writing it, and specifically, for fostering the kind of creative culture that inspires such undertakings. Thanks to RNL's CEO, Josh Gould, for his enthusiasm and encouragement during the production of this book, as well as for his tolerance of the demanding schedule I had to maintain to complete the manuscript. Thanks as well to Leslie Alpert and Sarah Rege for their personal support; they stepped in when necessary to keep my projects moving forward when I took time off from them to work on the book. Thanks also to Lisa Glass, for her always-keen writing advice and help in pulling together some of the images for this book. And to Tom Wuertz, for his assistance in providing content from the Eastside Human

Services Buildings, a net zero energy-ready building, which could be one of our next zero energy buildings.

I am also grateful to Alecia Huck of Maverick & Company, who has worked with me as a leadership and presentation consultant. She has helped me hone and craft the net zero energy story, particularly in regard to the Research Support Facility project. She has also helped me recognize, and embrace, the important leadership role required to get this message out.

The experience of delivering the Research Support Facility sparked the inspiration for this book. The entire project team, while not all listed here, was made up of some of the most talented and hard-working professionals I have ever worked with. I would like to thank the entire team, and then single out the following individuals from RNL's internal team of architects, interior designers, and landscape architects: Rich von Luhrte, Craig Randock (now with HDR Architecture), Michael Simpson, Allison Menke, Nathan Gulash, Rachel Petro, Wendy Weiskopf, Michelle Richter, Brian Nicholson, and Steve Breitzka. From Stantec I thank David Okada (now with Integral Group), John Andary (now with Integral Group), Porus Antia, and Lloyd Mariner. From Haselden Construction, I thank Phil Macey, Byron Haselden, Brian Livingston, and Jerry Blocher; and Dana Villeneuve, from Architectural Energy Corporation.

There is a tremendous amount of truth in the saying that it takes a great client to design a great building. The DOE/NREL has been an exceptional client. The professionals there have a strong vision for the future of high-performance buildings, and they wanted their project to show the way to this future. We were fortunate to partner with them along this journey. In the process of delivering the Research Support Facility, I came to be friends with many of the talented staff in the NREL Advanced Commercial Buildings Research Group, many of whom have been instrumental in the development of this book. Thanks to everyone at DOE/NREL, not only for making the Research Support Facility a reality, but for your ongoing research and the development of tools and resources needed by the industry to make a net zero energy future possible. Specifically, I am grateful to Jeff Baker, Bill Glover, Drew Detamore, Ron Judkoff, Paul Torcellini, Shanti Pless, Eric Telesmanich, Bret Cummock, Peter McMillin, Nancy Carlisle, Karen Leitner, Jennifer Scheib, Nicki Johnson, Michelle Slovensky, Frank Rukavina, Rob Guglielmetti, Chad Lobato, Greg Stark, Nick Long, and David Goldwasser.

I thank, too, all of the professionals in the industry who are working hard to make net zero energy buildings a mainstream reality. I interviewed several key individuals from both the owner and developer perspective, as well as from an energy modeling viewpoint. Highlights from these interviews are featured throughout the book. Thanks to Donald Horn of the General Services Administration, Richard Kidd of the U.S. Army, Chris Rogers of Point32, Linda Morrison of Ambient Energy, and Porus Antia of Stantec.

I also conducted many informal interviews, and had numerous discussions and exchanges with various experts in the field, all of which helped me develop specific content areas of the book. It is through their generosity, their willingness to spend time with me and share their knowledge, that I was able to gather the most current and innovative ideas about the myriad challenges and opportunities inherent in any net zero energy project. In this regard, I thank Rachel Petro of RNL, Dean Stanberry of Jones Lang LaSalle, Paul Means of Davis Graham & Stubbs, Ken Urbanek of

MKK Consulting Engineers, Cathy Higgins of the New Buildings Institute, and David Lehrer of the Center for the Built Environment.

I want to express appreciation, as well, to everyone who provided the remarkable photographs and images in the book, which do so much to tell the net zero energy story. Notably, Frank Ooms and Ron Pollard, two of the most talented architectural photographers RNL has worked with, graciously granted permission to include many of their exquisite photographs of the DOE/NREL Research Support Facility; Tania Salgado and Pat McKelvey, friends and coworkers at RNL, shared a few of their personal architectural photographs, taken during their extensive travels; and Lisette Lebaillif, a photographer from Dallas/Fort Worth, captured a stunning image of the Kimbell Art Museum, designed by Louis Kahn. Thanks also to all of the talented staff and contract photographers at NREL, and to Mike Linenberger and Shanti Pless for facilitating the use of many photographs from the NREL PIX collection.

I am grateful also to the many firms and individuals who contributed photos and images of their own work. They include Erin Lawrence of The Kubala Washatko Architects, Dawn Porcellato and Ray Sinclair of RWDI, Erin Gehlr of BNIM, Tiffany Lee of Buro Happold, Kevin Nance of Adrian Smith + Gordon Gill Architecture, Doug Spuler of the Beck Group, Jill Badenhop of Westlake Reed Leskosky, Manfred Starlinger, and Martin Read of Colt International and Mike Allen of AWV Architectural, Porus Antia and Liesel Wallace of Stantec, Linda Morrison of Ambient Energy, Tracy Becker and Steve Comstock of ASHRAE, Molly Canales of Weber Shandwick for Bloom Energy, Chris Rogers of Point32, Matt Ellis and Nick Alexander of U.S. Army Corps of Engineers at Fort Carson, Dr. Murray Peel of the University of Melbourne, Michael Holtz of LightLouver, and Gavin Platt of Lucid Design Group. I appreciate both your commitment to contributing quality work and your willingness to share it with me for this book.

In many ways, *Net Zero Energy Design* began with a coincidental airport reunion I had in 2010, with Jim Leggitt, an architect and Wiley author whom I have known for years. We were both traveling to Miami for the AIA convention and he encouraged me to consider writing a book. He also introduced me to John Czarnecki, who was, at the time, an editor at Wiley and in Miami for the convention. Subsequently, I began writing my book proposal, for which I enlisted help and feedback from Jim Leggitt, Daniel Tal, and Annette Stelmack, all friends and Wiley authors. Thanks to all of you, for your support, encouragement, and great advice.

Finally, I thank John Wiley & Sons, specifically publisher Amanda Miller, for seeing the value and need for this book within the industry, and for making it a reality. I'm grateful to Kathryn Bourgoine, who stepped in when John Czarnecki left Wiley to become the editor-in-chief at *Contract* magazine. She did a fabulous job as I was putting the finishing touches on the manuscript. I'm also grateful to Mike New and Danielle Giordano for helping me through the publishing process. And finally, thanks to Donna Conte, the senior production editor, who masterfully guided the manuscript and artwork through production of the book.

Image courtesy of RNL; photograph by Frank Ooms.

In INTRODUCTION

MY NET ZERO ENERGY JOURNEY

In my role as director of sustainability at RNL, I have been very fortunate to be involved in a world-changing architectural project. It is the project that inspired the writing of *Net Zero Energy Design,* and the project that sharply focused the commercial building industry on the goal of achieving net zero energy buildings. This project has been profiled by and featured in building industry conferences across the nation, and covered by building industry media, as well as national publications such as the *Wall Street Journal* and the *New York Times. Metropolis* magazine defined it as a game-changer for 2011, by taking net zero energy to scale. The project I am referring to is the Department of Energy's (DOE) Research Support Facility (RSF) at the National Renewable Energy Laboratory (NREL), shown in Figure I.1.

This project demonstrated not only that net zero energy is viable for large-scale commercial buildings, but that it also adds unique value to them. Furthermore, the project revealed the gaps in current conventional building delivery processes, gaps we will need to fill if we are to develop net zero energy solutions. It is one aim of this book is to help fill these gaps in our process—specifically, to answer the question: How do we deliver a net zero energy commercial building?

■ **FIGURE I.1** DOE/NREL Research Support Facility. *Image courtesy of RNL; photograph by Frank Ooms.*

My involvement in the DOE/NREL Research Support Facility project influenced me greatly; and the "fingerprints" of this project can be seen throughout this book, whether in specific examples from the project or in the form of a general influence on how the delivery process must be retooled. I have been inspired by the amazing results achieved by the project, especially by all the extraordinary individuals on the delivery team who made them all happen. That team included talented professionals from RNL, Stantec, Haselden Construction, and a host of capable and quality design consultants and subcontractors. As you can imagine, having the Department of Energy and the National Renewable Energy Laboratory as a client pursuing net zero energy in a large office building was a profound experience (see Figure I.2). NREL is a remarkable resource for low-energy and net zero energy buildings, supporting some of the best research and thinking in the world. I have come to believe that NREL is one of the nation's best-kept secrets. In sharing the story of this project with thousands of people in the building industry, I was always surprised by how many were unaware of NREL, one our greatest energy resources. I am certain the DOE/NREL Research Support Facility will do remarkable work in advancing the mission of DOE and NREL, and I sincerely hope that this book will do its part to move our industry to net zero energy.

HOW TO USE THIS BOOK

The purpose of *Net Zero Energy Design* is to serve as a design and delivery guide for net zero energy commercial buildings. What distinguishes this book from other sustainable design guides is its singular focus on reaching net zero, coupled with a dedication to the entire comprehensive process it takes to get there. Success for a net zero energy building is rooted in the holistic process, from the conception of the project to its ongoing operation. It's not just a design problem; it's an entire delivery problem, one that includes the building's occupancy and operation. Therefore, this book is meant to advance the most important aspects of each part of the delivery process as it relates to achieving net zero energy. Thus, because the focus is on the *entire* delivery process, *Net Zero Energy Design* is not intended to serve as a highly detailed technical guide to specific issues within the delivery process; there are many excellent books and resources available that offer focused guidance on the individual efforts needed to execute the numerous individual net zero energy decisions within the process.

Net zero energy buildings are challenging to complete, and each project has unique issues that must be wrestled with. This book does not aspire to address all conditions and circumstances that a net zero energy building might face. In this sense, then, the book is not an instruction manual; it does not offer a process that guarantees a net zero energy building. Nor is the content of this book meant to replace the expert judgment of design professionals. The book is based on my personal project experience and my ongoing research into the net zero energy process, supplemented by the valuable contributions of my invited contributors, Shanti Pless and David Okada, who share my driving desire to advance a net zero energy building practice. It is written from the point of view of a practitioner, and meant to convey information useful in practice.

Therefore, in it, I have made a conscious effort to introduce tools and resources that I use and am familiar with; I also attempt to set them within the context of their implementation in actual practice. I also mention several software programs that have been valuable to me and, I believe, might be useful to others. Such mention

■ **FIGURE I.2** DOE/NREL Research Support Facility. *Image courtesy of RNL; photograph by Frank Ooms.*

is not, however, intended as an endorsement, or meant to imply that there are not other applications available that satisfy the same need. I also include content on software tools, though I recognize that this information will be outdated at some point in the near future—to be superseded, I hope, by more powerful and capable programs than those currently available.

As an architect I have come to realize that we in the profession have a unique role in making net zero energy architecture possible; we must assume a leadership role in order to transform our industry and the built environment. Furthermore, as a profession, we have some changes to make. Most important, we need to take ownership of the energy design problems inherent in our projects, rather than relegating them to the engineers and energy modelers. As such, though this book is targeted in large part at architects, it is also meant as a guide for all those involved in the entire process of delivering a net zero energy building. My goal is that the content will have value for everyone in the building industry. Thus, while focused primarily on the commercial building sector, many of the ideas and principles presented can be readily applied to the residential sector as well.

And to ensure that the book has something to offer those who are new to the field, as well as those who have substantial experience, I have intentionally provided key introductory concepts as primers for more detailed understanding and project application, and to assist new practitioners in expanding their net zero energy knowledge base. The seasoned practitioner will benefit from the perspective I offer on the delivery process. For the reader's convenience, I have also compiled essential resources for net zero energy building delivery, to serve as an ongoing project reference.

The book is organized around the net zero energy project delivery process, hence can be used as a road map to help each practitioner develop his or her own process. The chapters address, in turn, each stage in the process, and are generally sequential in terms of the overall delivery process of a net zero energy project.

Chapter 1: Net Zero Energy Building Overview
Chapter 1 provides an overview of net zero energy buildings. It defines them, makes the case for them, and discusses the current trends in the building industry.

Chapter 2: Project Conception and Delivery
Chapter 2 captures the owner's perspective on net zero energy buildings and explains how the net zero energy objective can be integrated into the early conception of a project. It also addresses the variety of delivery methods available in the industry, and the impact they can have on this objective.

Chapter 3: Integrated Process
Chapter 3 presents the delivery team's perspective on delivering a net zero energy project and introduces the specific issues in the integrated process that can assist in delivering the project.

En

Chapter 4: Energy

Chapter 4 is a primer on energy concepts. Having a strong foundation on energy principles is a prerequisite to designing and delivering a net zero energy project. This chapter also focuses on the practical application of energy in the process, including setting an energy target.

DF

Chapter 5: Design Fundamentals

Chapter 5 describes the fundamental principles that need to be established and understood before the design of a net zero energy project can begin. It offers a perspective on climate analysis and site assessment, and explains building geometry, massing, and building typology, as related to the pursuit of net zero energy.

PA

Chapter 6: Passive Architecture

Chapter 6 stipulates that net zero energy design starts with the architecture. It explores the role passive design strategies play in reducing energy loads in a building.

EE

Chapter 7: Energy-Efficient Building Systems

Chapter 7 offers guidance on how to efficiently meet the reduced loads of a passively designed building with low-energy building systems.

RE

Chapter 8: Renewable Energy

Chapter 8 introduces the various renewable energy systems available for a project and explains how they can be integrated with the design of a net zero energy project.

Ec

Chapter 9: Economics

Chapter 9 takes a close look at the economics behind net zero energy buildings. The focus is on understanding and analyzing energy efficiency and renewable energy systems.

OO

Chapter 10: Operations and Occupancy

Chapter 10 tackles one of the most important aspects of a net zero energy building: its operation and use. Because a net zero energy building is measured in actual operation, thoughtful consideration of this factor is critical. This chapter works to bridge the gap between design intent and the realities of building operation.

NZ

Chapter 11: Net Zero Energy

Chapter 11 serves to synthesize the preceding chapters, in order to derive a final calculation methodology for measuring a project's net zero energy balance. The chapter also provides a framework for understanding and evaluating carbon neutrality for a building project.

CS

Chapter 12: Case Study: DOE/NREL Research Support Facility

Recognizing that, often, an actual example is the best way to learn about and advance the practice of net zero energy delivery, Chapter 12 presents the DOE/NREL Research Support Facility project as a case study.

Of course, in practice, the delivery process is not strictly sequential, but rather may be iterative and cyclical in nature. Therefore, the book may be approached in much the same way: It may be read from start to finish, or approached from a number of different pathways through the book. The chapter "road map" shown in Figure I.3 suggests how the chapters may be organized based on their focus on guidance, design issues, or process issues.

- Chapters 1, 4, 11, and 12 are dedicated to overall guidance for net zero energy; they provide definitions, fundamental concepts, and an overall synthesis of concepts.
- Chapters 5, 6, 7, and 8 provide design guidance; as such, they may be regarded as the core chapters of the book.
- Chapters 2, 3, 9, and 10 give process guidance for net zero energy commercial buildings.

One of the ways I have found effective to introduce net zero energy as a concept to new audiences is through a simple conceptual equation, which states that net zero energy equals the accumulation of passive design plus energy-efficient building systems plus renewable energy systems, all over an integrated process. The chapters of this book then may be seen as the building blocks of this conceptual equation, which is shown Figure 1.4.

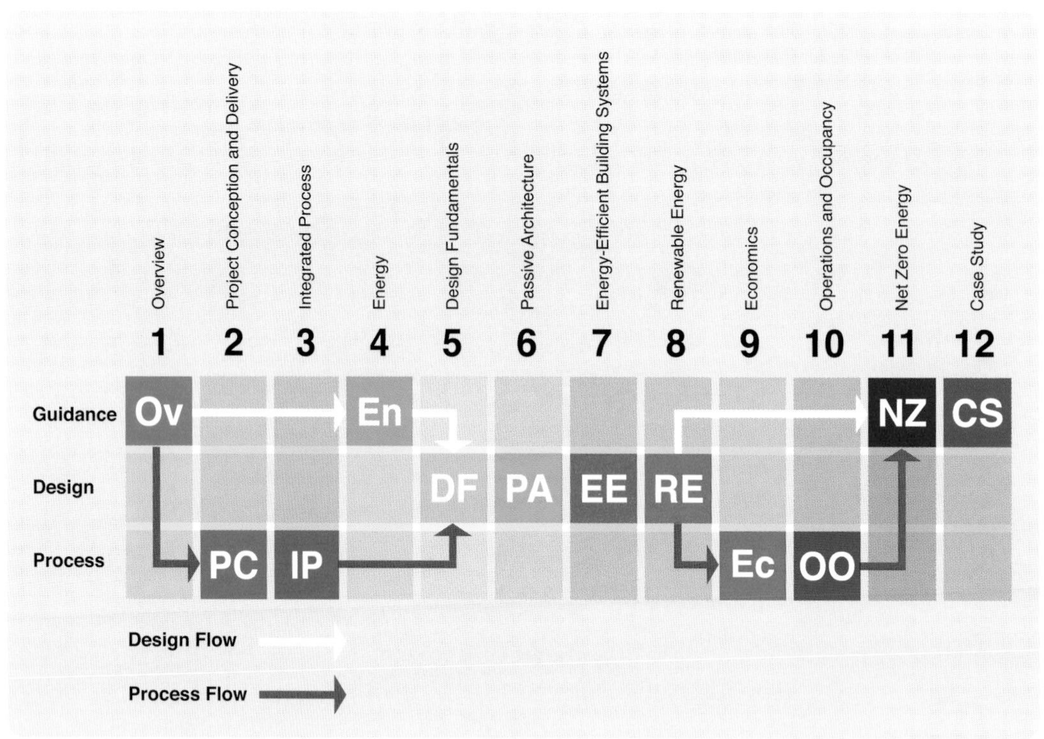

■ **FIGURE I.3** Chapter Road Map.

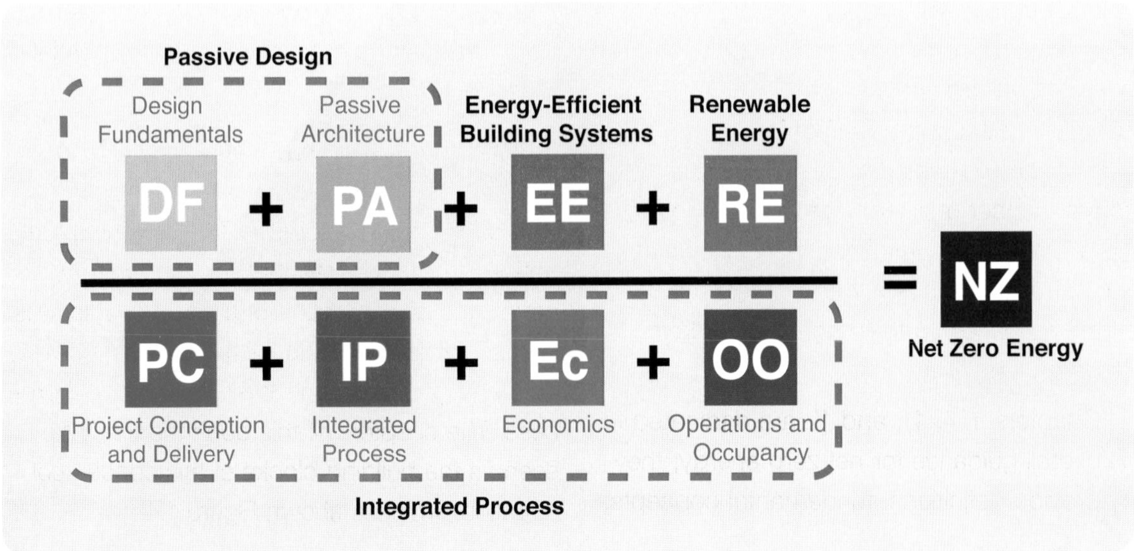

■ **FIGURE I.4** Net Zero Energy Concept as an Equation.

Ov

CHAPTER 1
NET ZERO ENERGY BUILDING OVERVIEW

THE CASE FOR NET ZERO ENERGY BUILDINGS

A Global Solution

The twenty-first century is shaping up to be a transitional era for the way humanity dwells on this earth. The pressure we are placing on the planet's resources has become increasingly unsustainable. The resulting problems we face, such as water and resource scarcity, increasing energy demands and costs, shrinking fossil fuel reserves, and a changing climate, have sounded a wakeup call heard round the world. Those who are heeding the call and embracing the need for change are finding in the necessary solutions opportunities not only to address this global set of problems but to advance and improve humanity's relationship with the living world, and improve our quality of life.

Much of the stress we impose on the earth is manifested in the way we design, construct, and use our built environments; that means buildings and cities must play a vital role in shaping our sustainable future. Net zero energy buildings are tools in shaping this future. The buildings themselves offer significant environmental, social, and economic value. They are as much representatives of a global approach to our built environment as they are exemplary buildings (see Figure 1.1). The lessons they can teach us about the power of integrated design and delivery, and about the true interconnectivity between our built environment and the natural world, can be applied to a diverse range of sustainable solutions, such as net zero waste and sustainable water balances in buildings and communities.

There is a powerful synergy between net zero energy objectives and other holistic sustainable goals. They all require a focus on performance and an integrated delivery process. The benefits of a holistic approach are, themselves, synergistic. Many strategies that reduce energy use can also have a positive impact on indoor environmental quality and, thus, the health and well-being of occupants. The net zero energy approach can be taken to any scale and positively affect the way we build and live in communities and cities.

A Vision for the Future

Net zero energy buildings offer a compelling vision for the future, a vision that can be seen as a new direction in architecture. The pursuit of this vision can be technically rigorous; moreover, it requires tremendous creativity and innovation in design. As such, it offers an opportunity for new expressions of form to elegantly resolve energy solutions with program, site, and climate. Net energy design is an architecture that rediscovers the passive strategies of our architectural history and then integrates them into current ideas about contemporary design. It also embraces the best of state-of-the-art technology and renewable energy systems to provide solutions that set new standards for building and occupant performance.

Net zero energy architecture is also about process, one that requires genuine and intense integration, and takes a long view of the idea of building delivery. The integrated process can lead to the creation of truly holistic buildings, for net zero energy buildings should be more than just exemplary energy performers; they should embrace sustainability, performance, and beauty as well. They should actively work to enhance the human experience and, by connecting to the larger systems of nature, enhance all life. Net zero energy architecture is part of a larger movement to design regenerative buildings, buildings that are part of our living world.

■ **FIGURE 1.1** View of New York City skyline, with 4 Times Square in the center. This building was an early adopter of integrated renewable energy systems in a high-rise.

As a new architecture, net zero energy uses data-driven and performance-oriented innovation to yield new forms. It also explores innovative, living connections to a building's place, its climate, and the people who occupy it. It offers an opportunity to create beauty and meaning in our lives and in our communities. Beauty is particularly important for net zero energy buildings, because beautiful buildings tend to endure and be preserved, in addition to adding cultural and social richness. Net zero energy architecture must, therefore, be as beautiful and meaningful as it is pragmatic and high-performing; most important, it must have a higher purpose. In sum, net zero energy architecture presents a vision for building a better and more sustainable future (see Figure 1.2).

The Time Is Now

Net zero energy architecture is not an idea for the distant future; it is an idea whose time is now. We have the technology and the knowledge to delivery net zero energy commercial buildings today. What we lack, more than anything, is the collective imagination to make it happen. It is an objective of this book to spark the reader's imagination and to help industry professionals adopt a net zero energy approach to buildings.

The fact that net zero energy buildings are possible today does not mean there are not challenges. Perhaps the greatest *perceived* challenge is cost; but I would argue that the greatest actual challenge is the process to achieve a net zero energy building, as it is rigorous and requires change across the industry. Change is always difficult, particularly for such a change-resistant industry as the building industry.

■ **FIGURE 1.2** DOE/NREL's Research Support Facility provides a blueprint for a net zero energy future. *NREL/PIX 17613; photograph by Dennis Schroeder.*

Yes, cost can be a hurdle, but cost can be effectively managed with the right integrated delivery process. While it is possible to pay the way to net zero energy by purchasing more renewable energy and layering in more expensive and cutting-edge technology, it is also possible to manage costs effectively by integrating simple solutions that address multiple problems and do the hard work of reducing a building's loads, thereby minimizing the investment needed in renewable energy systems.

The many benefits of pursuing net zero energy buildings make the challenges worth taking on. Net zero energy buildings have economic, social, and environmental benefits, and represent a new standard for high-performing buildings, offering the greatest building and market value and, at the same time, the lowest life-cycle costs. These buildings can offer higher-quality interior environments that enhance quality of life for their occupants. They also lead to profound environmental benefits related to energy and resource conservation and the dramatic reduction of greenhouse gas emissions. Not only are these benefits tangible today, they also make the case for a solution that addresses humanity's larger global challenges, and hence point to a better future (see Figure 1.3).

Needless to say, net zero energy buildings do not appear overnight. Because net zero energy is such a long-term goal and process, the industry to date has recorded very few buildings with verifiable data of one year or more of net zero energy performance. But the number of proven examples will grow over time and add to our knowledge of how to achieve this challenging goal. At the same time, net zero energy is an idea bigger than a narrow group of exemplary, high-performing buildings. Net zero energy should, therefore, be adopted as an approach to delivering all buildings, Whether or not they hit the zero target over time may be less important than the energy performance and the integrated on-site renewable energy solutions that can consistently be developed as part of our built environment. Ultimately, all buildings, including existing buildings, have the potential for net zero energy future.

■ **FIGURE 1.3** The Omega Center for Sustainable Living is net zero energy and one of the world's first certified Living Buildings. *Image courtesy of BNIM; photograph © 2009, Assassi.*

DEFINING NET ZERO ENERGY

At its core, net zero energy is a measure of a building's energy performance, whereby it produces as much or more renewable energy as it uses over the course of a year in operation. Two key concepts make up this definition of net zero energy. First, *net* means that nonrenewable energy sources (fossil fuel and nuclear) may be used; but over the course of a year, enough renewable energy must be generated so that the project can offset or exceed the use of nonrenewable energy. The concept *zero energy* does not mean that the building uses no energy; rather, it refers to reaching a net zero energy position for buildings that have full program demands. The second key concept is *operation*. Net zero energy is an operational goal. The period for measuring performance is one year of operation, to include all seasonal variations. It is possible to demonstrate a net zero energy in design. In fact, this is part of the process to achieve net zero energy. But a true net zero energy building must be achieved through actual measured operation.

The use of the word *operation* in the definition changes the approach to net zero energy, indicating that it involves delivery of the project, not just design. At the same time this expands the process, it also enforces a more integrated process overall by aligning owner, occupants, operations, and construction and design professionals around delivery. Designing for net zero energy is only one stage; actually operating as a net zero energy building is the real objective. *Operation* also means that the performance results in actual, quantifiable benefits—real carbon emission reductions and real cost savings.

Net zero energy buildings are, first and foremost, very low-energy buildings. The emphasis on this point is important. The intent of reaching net zero energy is not to secure enough renewable energy for a project regardless of energy efficiency. This is an inelegant and extremely expensive solution. A net zero energy building is a very low-energy building with enough dedicated renewable energy generation to meet its energy requirements over the course of a year.

The National Renewable Energy Laboratory (NREL) has defined four ways of measuring and defining net zero energy for buildings: *net zero site energy*, *net zero source energy*, *net zero energy emissions,* and *net zero energy cost* (see Figure 1.4). The NREL paper, "Zero Energy Buildings: A Critical Look at the Definition," by Paul Torcellini, Shanti Pless, Michael Deru, and Drury Crawley, published in 2006, introduced these standardized definitions. Having an established definition and methodology for measuring net zero energy is key if the industry is to be able promote and communicate the metric in a unified way. (A more detailed explanation of site energy versus source energy is provided in Chapter 4, along with other energy terms used in net zero energy definitions. The calculation methodologies for net zero energy buildings and the concept of carbon neutrality are explored in Chapter 11.)

Net Zero Site Energy Building

A *net zero site energy* building produces at least as much renewable energy as it uses over the course of a year, when accounted for at the site. The measurement at the site is quite literal; that is, if a boundary is drawn around a building site, and all of the energy within the site boundary is measured and added up, the result is a site energy measurement (see Figure 1.5). This is the most commonly used and understood measure of net zero energy, because it reflects what would be recorded at the meter, and is easier to account for because it does not need the

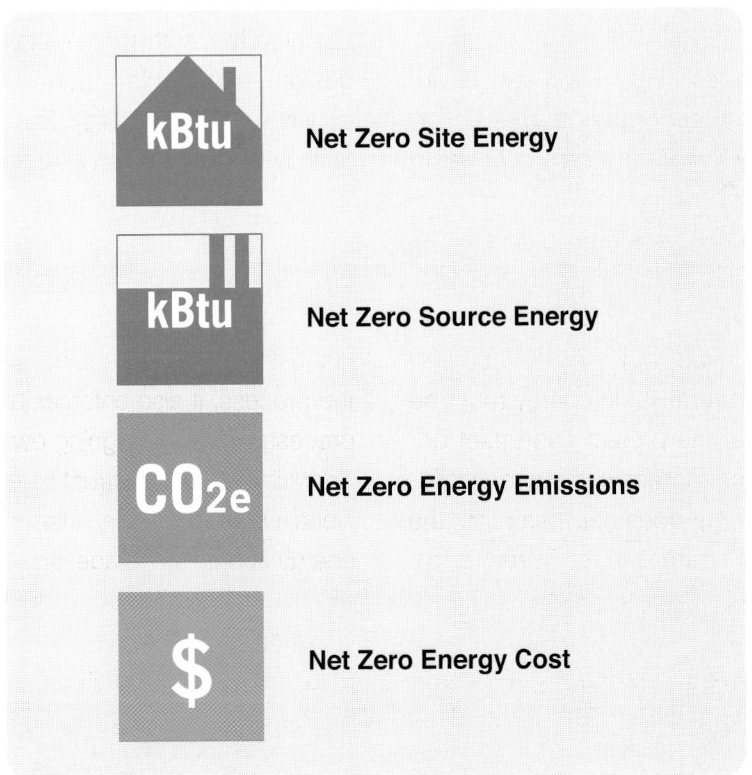

■ **FIGURE 1.4** Net Zero Energy Building Definitions.

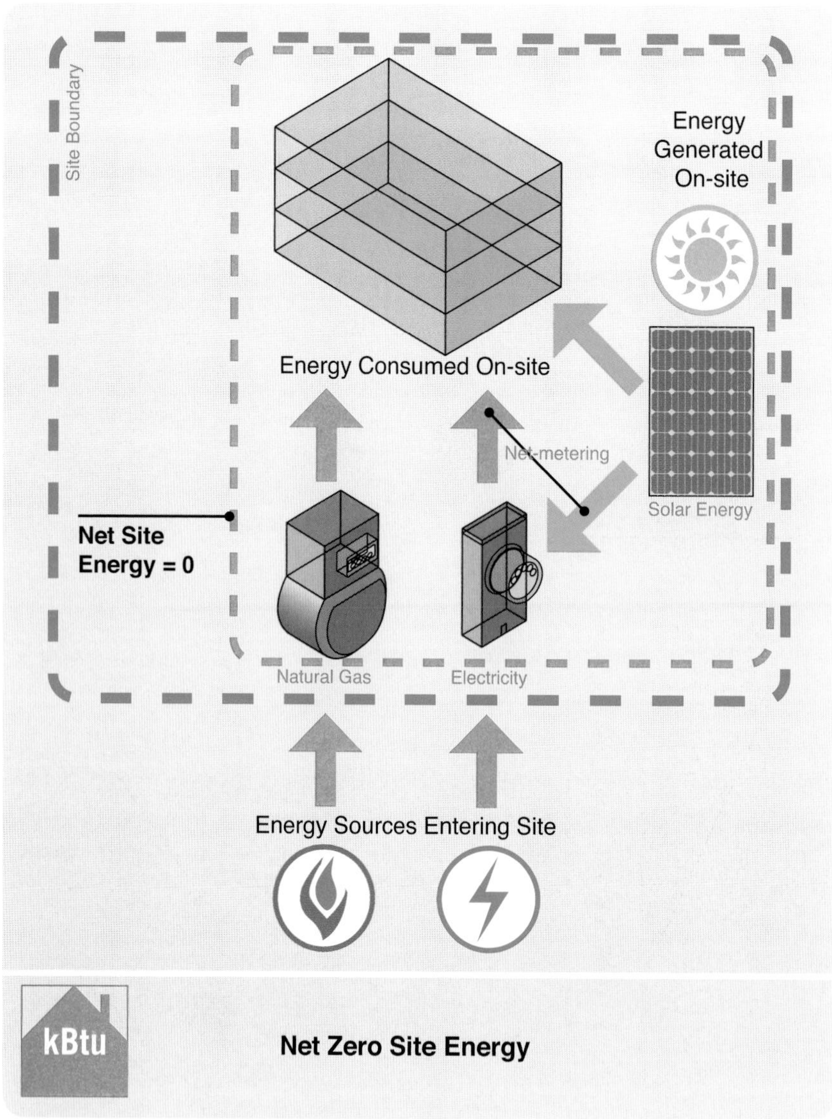

■ **FIGURE 1.5** Net Zero Site Energy Diagram.

additional factors required of the other measures of net zero energy. That said, net zero site energy can be one of the most difficult of the four definitions to achieve, which makes it a good standard for measuring performance.

Net Zero Source Energy Building

A *net zero source energy* building produces or purchases at least as much renewable energy as it uses over the course of a year, when accounted for at the energy source. This measure includes factors related to providing energy to a site. For example, it takes about three times the energy, in terms of coal-fired, grid-based electricity, measured at the source as compared to what is actually delivered and measured at the site. Why? Because numerous losses result from generating and transporting electricity, as shown in Figure 1.6. Thus, source energy gives a more complete picture of energy use. In order to estimate source energy use, however, a site-to-source energy factor must be determined for each energy source used and applied to the site energy value.

Net Zero Energy Emissions Building

A *net zero energy emissions* building produces or purchases enough emissions-free

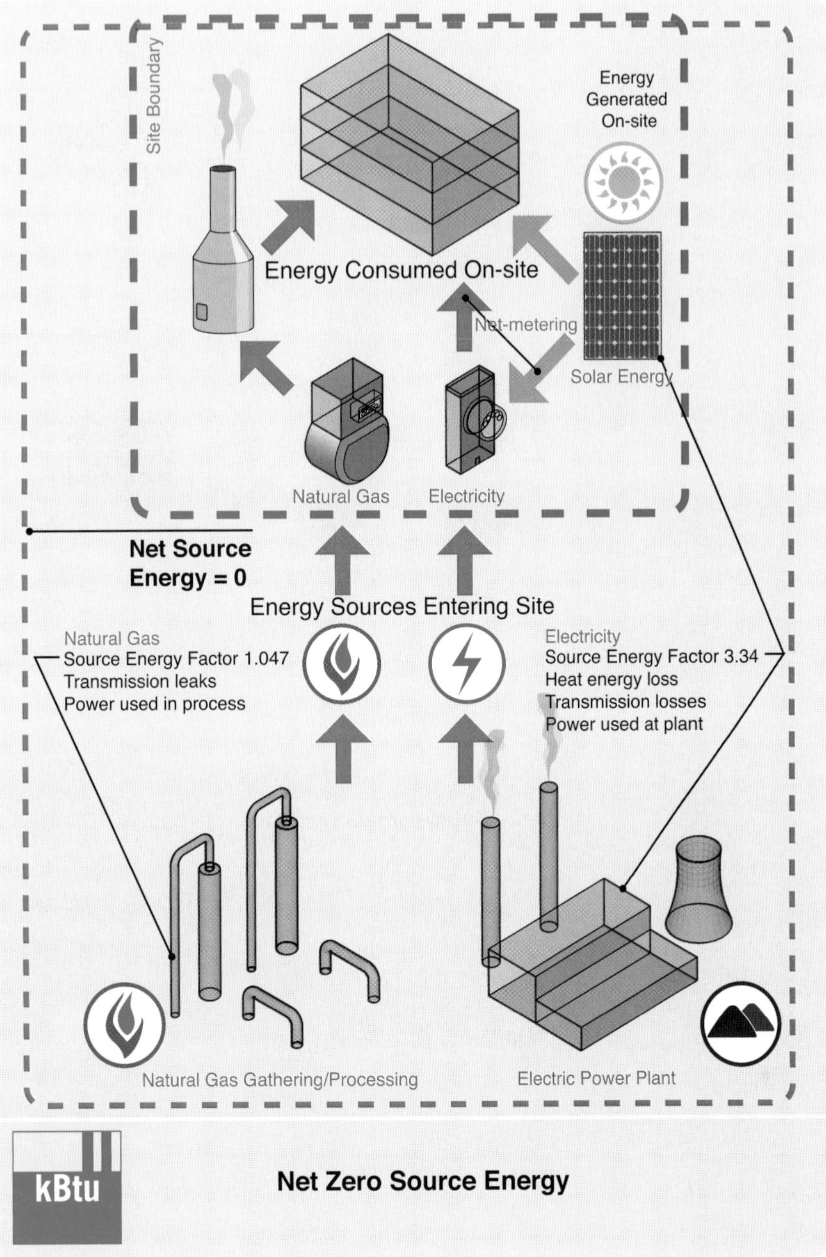

■ **FIGURE 1.6** Net Zero Source Energy Diagram.

renewable energy to offset emissions from all energy used in the building over the course of a year. Whereas site and source energy are measured in energy units, energy emissions is measured in mass of carbon-equivalent greenhouse gas emissions related to the energy use of the building. To determine the quantity of energy emissions, a carbon emission factor must be applied to the site energy use for each energy source or fuel used for the project, as shown in Figure 1.7. In this calculation, renewable energy generation can offset emissions from fossil fuel.

The definition of *net zero energy emission* is an important one because it quantifies the key value of a net zero energy building: the elimination of greenhouse gas emissions from building operational energy. This definition provides one way to consider a building carbon-neutral for building energy operation. (A more detailed

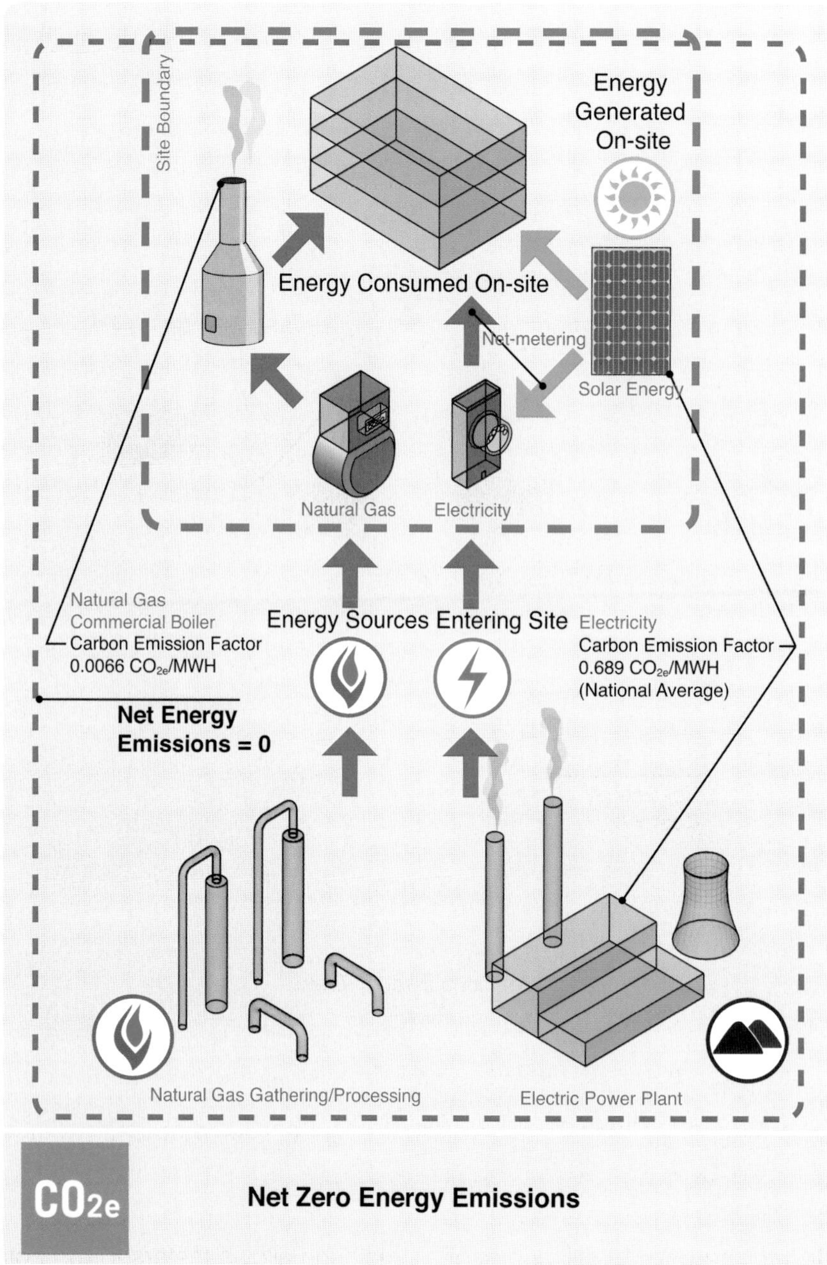

■ **FIGURE 1.7** Net Zero Energy Emissions Diagram.

discussion about carbon neutrality is presented in Chapter 11.)

Net Zero Energy Cost Building

A *net zero energy cost* building receives at least as much financial credit for exported renewable energy as it is charged for energy and energy services by the utility over the course of a year (see Figure 1.8). There are several parameters that need to be tracked to adhere to this definition. On the utility cost side, there are the rate structure for energy use, peak demand charges, fees, and taxes. Some utilities charge using rate structures based on time of use, which also would need to be factored in. In short, to arrive at this measure, all energy and energy service charges on the utility bill should be

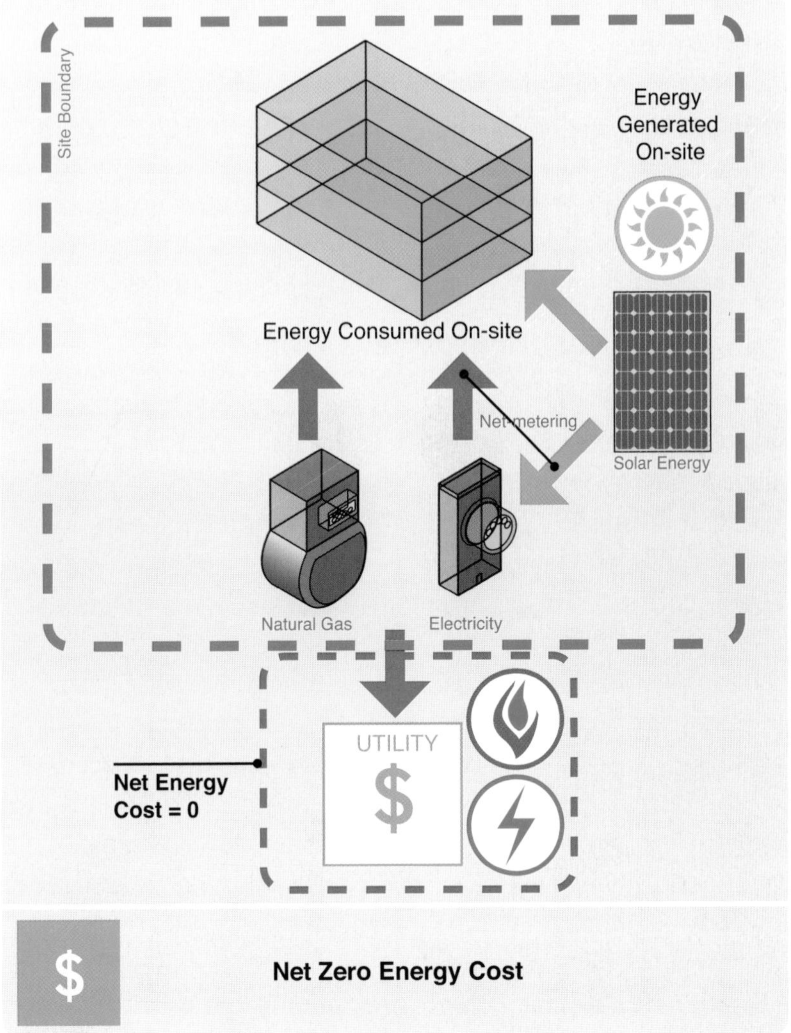

■ **FIGURE 1.8** Net Zero Energy Costs Diagram.

included. The parameter that needs to be tracked on the credit side is the value credited by the utility company for any renewable energy exported to the grid. Ideally, on-site renewable energy would offset a significant portion of the energy use before grid-based electricity is used, and would also offset peak demand. However, renewable energy generation is highly variable and so may not match up consistently in real time with energy use and peak demand. To achieve this definition, it is likely that the project will need to implement effective demand reduction strategies and demand management systems.

Each utility company will have its own net-metering policies that define how on-site renewable energy generation is credited. Net metering allows meters to run both forward and backward, depending on whether the building is importing grid-based electricity or exporting on-site renewable energy. True net metering permits a one-to-one exchange of imported and exported electricity, thereby crediting renewable energy at the same retail rate charged for electricity imported from the grid. However, some utilities will switch from crediting at retail rates to wholesale rates for any excess renewable energy exported on an annual basis, or sometimes on a monthly basis.

Ultimately, the way to demonstrate net zero energy cost is through actual utility bills. In fact, this cost can be relatively simple to verify, because the utility company makes the calculation. On the other hand, it can be hard to predictably meet this measure from month to month or year to year because of changes in utility rates and variations in monthly power demand. These variations also make the measure hard to plan for and to estimate, as discussed in Chapter 11. It also makes it challenging to properly design a renewable energy system that makes it possible to consistently meet this measure, year after year.

It's also important to point out that the definition of *net zero energy cost* does not give the entire economic picture of a net zero building. The measure accounts strictly for the net cost of nonrenewable energy use. One important element outside of this measure is the investment in the renewable energy systems. Just as a net zero energy building still uses energy, a net zero energy cost building will still incur renewable energy costs. (Chapter 9 focuses on the economic analysis of a net zero energy building.) One of the main values of this measure is that it identifies a key value of a net zero energy building: energy cost savings. Moreover, it focuses attention on management of peak demand as part of the overall strategy, which the other three definitions do not address.

CLASSIFYING NET ZERO ENERGY BUILDINGS

Having standardized definitions and methodologies for measuring net zero energy in a building is essential for giving the industry a unified approach to designing these buildings and then measuring the results of their actual operation. That said, there are many ways of getting to a net zero energy building within all four of the definitions given in the previous section, and they are not equitable or often even comparable. How, for example, do you compare a building that achieves net zero energy with renewable energy generated by on-site systems to one that achieves this objective using renewable energy generated off-site or through purchased renewable energy certificates?

Anticipating this issue, NREL, after publishing the four definitions of net zero energy buildings, followed up in 2010 with a technical report outlining a classification system for net zero energy buildings, titled "Net-Zero Energy Buildings: A Classification System Based on Renewable Energy Supply Options," by Shanti Pless and Paul Torcellini.

NREL's classification system has four classes, A through D, and prioritizes the application of renewable energy to place a greater value on high-priority renewable energy applications. The system also grants buildings that may have difficulty achieving net zero energy the option to reach it at some level. The NREL system, which should be used in conjunction with the four definitions, enables a building to achieve one or more at a specific classification level per definition achieved.

Furthermore, the NREL classification system emphasizes demand-side reduction as a prerequisite, to reflect the important necessity of a net zero energy building to be a very low-energy building. The system then prioritizes the application of renewable energy based on its type and location relative to the building. The classifications also generally quantify the difficulty of meeting net zero energy with the renewable energy application under consideration.

Renewable energy applications range from providing all needed renewable energy systems within the building footprint (Classification A, or NZEB:A) to supplementing on-site renewable energy with purchased renewable energy certificates to satisfy a net zero energy building definition (Classification D or NZEB:D). Note that NZEB stands for "net zero energy building," and the notation "NZEB:classification" is used

Net Zero Energy Classification System

Classification A

Summary: A low-energy building with enough renewable energy generation from sources located within the footprint of the building to achieve one or more of the four definitions for net zero energy. This classification applies only to individual buildings.

Example Scenarios

- Photovoltaic systems mounted on the building roof or façade.
- Solar thermal systems mounted on the building roof or façade.
- Wind turbines mounted to, or integrated into, the building.

Classification B

Summary: A low-energy building with enough renewable energy generation from sources located within the project's site to achieve one or more of the four definitions for net zero energy. The definition of *site boundary* is to include campus scenarios where the renewable energy systems are located on commonly owned contiguous property (easements are permitted to separate commonly owned property). This classification may apply to individual or multiple buildings.

Example Scenarios

- Photovoltaic systems mounted over parking areas, or ground-mounted.
- Solar thermal systems ground-mounted on the site.
- Wind turbines on towers mounted on the site.
- Biomass harvested on-site and used to generate energy on-site.

Classification C

Summary: A low-energy building that first utilizes renewable energy sources within the footprint of the building and on-site, to the extent feasible, then imports enough off-site renewable energy used to generate energy on-site to achieve one or more of the four definitions for net zero energy. This classification may apply to individual or multiple buildings.

Example Scenarios

- Biomass imported on-site and used for electricity generation.
- Biomass imported on-site and used for thermal energy generation.

Classification D

Summary: A low-energy building that first utilizes renewable energy sources within the footprint of the building and on-site to the extent feasible, then optionally imports off-site renewable energy used to generate energy on-site, but purchases off-site renewable energy to achieve a source or emission definition for net zero energy. This classification cannot achieve a site or cost definition of net zero energy. This classification may apply to individual or multiple buildings.

Example Scenarios

- Purchased renewable energy certificates (RECs).

within NREL's classification system. A number of different renewable energy applications are available between these two extremes. Perhaps, for example, the renewable energy system is installed on-site or on a campus, not on the building itself (Classification B, or NZEB:B). Or an off-site renewable energy source such as biomass is imported (Classification C, or NZEB:C). Classification A is the most challenging because it requires a net zero energy building to manage all of its needed renewable energy within its own footprint. It is worth the effort, however, because earning this Classification A designation has intrinsic value, in that the renewable energy systems are integrated into the building and will likely serve the structure for the life of the renewable energy system. Such may not be the case for renewable energy systems installed on a site, which can be removed or may end up shaded when new buildings or additions are added to the site.

The highest classification earned by the project's renewable energy resources becomes the designation used for the project. Renewable energy resources from higher classifications may, however, be used to contribute to meeting a lower classification designation. For example, if the project does not have enough building mounting photovoltaics to meet a net zero energy definition for classification A, the combination of site-mounted and building-mounted photovoltaics may be used to meet a net zero energy definition for classification B. A more detailed summary of the system follows.

ALTERNATIVE APPROACHES TO NET ZERO ENERGY

Off-Grid Net Zero Energy Buildings

Off-grid net zero energy buildings represent a unique application, and as such can be difficult and, often, impractical to achieve for a commercial building. However, in cases where conventional utilities are unavailable or very costly to bring to a project site, an off-grid solution may be very appropriate. Off-grid net zero energy buildings are prohibited from using fossil-fuel-based energy sources because they have no way of offsetting such use by exporting renewable energy to the grid. And because an off-grid net zero energy building relies completely on on-site renewables, it meets all four definitions of net zero energy and, hence, exceeds the requirements of the various classifications.

The challenge with the off-grid net zero energy building approach is that because of the dynamic and variable nature of on-site renewable energy, some type of energy storage would be required to maintain building operation when renewable energy generation is lower than needed. Furthermore, off-grid net zero energy buildings may need additional renewable energy systems to handle peak loads. Finally, the combination of extra renewable energy capacity and on-site storage must be carefully managed, as both extra capacity and storage are significant cost issues.

Using the grid (if available and feasible) to manage the surplus and shortage of energy needs for operating a net zero energy building has some distinct advantages. It reduces first cost and the need for batteries or other forms of energy storage, along with their related environmental and maintenance issues. It also allows the export and use of excess renewable energy within the grid, resulting in an increase in distributed renewable energy available to the grid as more net zero energy buildings are brought online. This also has implications for smart-grid applications, which could add other benefits in regard to how on-site renewable energy, as well as energy use and peak load, are managed. Ultimately, as energy storage becomes more sophisticated and cost-effective, it may play a key role in energy management and backup energy in grid-connected buildings.

Partial Net Zero Energy Buildings

There are several versions, or hybrids, of net zero energy buildings that do not meet the actual operational objective but are driven by the same goals and have very low energy use and a substantial infrastructure of renewable energy systems. Partial net zero energy buildings, while lacking the prestige of fully meeting the net zero objective, are still notable achievements, as they require the same integrated process to develop, and result in a large number of the same benefits.

NEAR NET ZERO ENERGY BUILDINGS

As noted previously, the net zero energy objective is challenging to meet. It has an absolute measure and can be verified year after year. With a factor as absolute as zero, it is either met or it isn't. That said, *approaching* net zero also has tremendous value, and falling short of absolute zero should not be considered a failure. Buildings that come close, or fail to achieve the status every year, should nevertheless be recognized as outstanding energy performers. Some in the industry call these buildings *near net zero energy buildings*.

NET ZERO ELECTRICITY BUILDING

A hybrid of net zero energy is the *net zero electricity* building. This type of building has a number of environmental and cost benefits even though it does not qualify as a net zero energy building. In a net zero electricity building, the nonrenewable electricity use is zero or less over the course of a year, while other nonrenewable energy sources are not offset through renewable energy. The various measures of site energy, source energy, energy emissions, and energy cost can be used to define a net zero electricity position.

NET ZERO ENERGY-READY BUILDING

A net zero energy-ready building, or net zero capable, is a building designed as a net zero energy project but with the renewable energy systems deferred; they are not installed as part of the project. Without question, the financing and procurement of the renewable energy system adds new challenges to the entire process of procuring a building or undertaking a major renovation of an existing building; and in some cases, it may be desirable, though not feasible, to procure the renewable energy systems. In such cases, the project can be designed for future integration of renewable energy systems. That means the systems should be planned to meet the net zero energy goal when installed, and the building should be designed for easy addition of the new systems by installing the necessary infrastructure, such as conduits, equipment areas, and structural capacity. If renewable energy systems cannot be installed initially, there is still tremendous value in making the project renewable energy-ready (see Figure 1.9).

Net Zero Energy for Multiple Buildings, Campuses, and Communities

Sometimes, the right scale for net zero energy is not an individual building, but multiple buildings with a net zero energy solution. There are a variety of circumstances where this could be advantageous. Every building has its own obstacles and challenges to achieving net zero energy. It may be that the building has a high energy use intensity (EUI), or lacks a roof and site area for renewable energy systems such as photovoltaic (PV) (see Figure 1.10). Grouping adjacent buildings together may make it possible to balance out individual obstacles. In this way, a building with a high EUI can be grouped with neighboring lower EUI buildings; and an available area for renewable energy systems can be shared as well. Such a strategy is ideal for moving more challenging buildings into a net zero energy position. (Chapter 4 defines and details the uses of the EUI metric.)

There are additional synergies for grouping multiple buildings for the purpose of meeting net zero energy and other performance objectives. On mixed-use projects there may be opportunities to balance energy and thermal loads between uses. Scaling for multiple buildings can also make a district-level sustainable infrastructure more efficient and economically feasible. Often, the project scope does not include multiple buildings; nevertheless, it may present a good opportunity to influence future master planning and to evaluate neighboring existing buildings for renovation opportunities and possible inclusion in the net zero energy objective.

Master planning and urban design projects for communities, neighborhoods, or cities can also take advantage of a net zero energy approach. In fact, planning for energy and renewable energy at this scale can reap many benefits. By taking advantage of the economies of scale, all building in the plan can achieve a net energy position. In this way, an entire net zero energy district can be created. At this scale, a diverse range of strategies can be employed. District energy services can be provided efficiently, through central plants or *cogeneration* (combined heat and power) systems. *Trigeneration* systems that add absorption chillers for cooling with heating and power can also be considered. From a net zero energy perspective, the drawback to cogeneration or trigeneration is that the systems typically operate on fossil fuels, such as natural gas. So, while these systems offer significant energy efficiencies, particularly from a source energy perspective, they need to be planned accordingly. Depending on the needs of the planned development, the systems can be sized to meet heating needs rather than electricity needs; or a system that utilizes biomass

■ **FIGURE 1.9** The Eastside Human Services building in Denver, Colorado, is net zero energy-ready, designed as a low-energy building with open roof space for a future photovoltaic system installation. *Image courtesy of RNL.*

could be considered. Large-scale renewable energy systems, such as solar farms and community wind farms, are major opportunities for large-scale developments (see Figure 1.11). The renewable energy systems can be further distributed through smaller-scale systems located on buildings within the development.

When looking at net zero energy on a community scale, there exists an opportunity to look at net zero energy within a larger scope of interest. This can include accounting for the energy of transportation associated with the community and the energy associated with the community's infrastructure, and industry energy in addition to the energy associated with building operation. As NREL has worked to define and classify net zero energy buildings, in 2009 NREL published "Definition of a Zero Net Energy Community" by Nancy Carlisle, Otto Van Geet, and Shanti Pless to further the definition and classification system in communities.

CERTIFYING NET ZERO ENERGY BUILDINGS

At the time of this writing, there was no market-accepted standard for certifying a net zero energy building. Although the metric is not difficult to measure, the multiple definitions and classifications developed by NREL do indicate there are many ways to do so. Thus, currently, net zero energy achievement is typically self-reported or self-promoted. Unfortunately, most self-reported claims lack any significant detail as to how the objective was measured and met. This situation points to the need in the industry for a third-party certification program for achieving net zero energy buildings.

The current top energy-related building label and certification programs in the United States

■ **FIGURE 1.10** The net zero energy campus planned for the Sacramento Municipal Utilities District utilizes single-axis tracking photovoltaic canopies over the main parking lot. *Image courtesy of Stantec Consulting Services Inc. and RNL.*

are ENERGY STAR and LEED, and neither is set up to measure and rank this level of performance. They could perhaps be retooled for this purpose. The International Living Future Institute launched the first-of-its-kind net zero energy certification program in October 2011, based on the institute's Living Building Challenge certification program, discussed later in this chapter.

The Department of Energy (DOE) is dedicated to promoting low-energy and net zero energy buildings, and at the time of this writing, it was developing a commercial building energy asset rating program as a standard way of evaluating as-built energy efficiency for buildings across the nation.

ASHRAE has a new building energy labeling program for energy performance, called the "Building Energy Quotient," or "Building EQ" (www.buildingeq.com). It is set up to provide an operational rating based on an appraisal and application from a certified assessor. The actual label is very simple for the general public to understand; it features a grade from A+ to F (see Figure 1.12). A project must be net zero energy to be graded A+. Behind the simple label, however, is detailed certification and support documentation, which add value to both the building and real estate industries. Building EQ is voluntary but is designed in anticipation of mandatory building energy labeling programs, now proposed in locations across the United States, and similar to the system used in the United Kingdom. While Building EQ is not strictly a net zero energy certification, it does include this feature.

BUILDING INDUSTRY RESEARCH AND TRENDS

Much of the current interest and focus on energy and sustainable building practices can be attributed to the success of the U.S. Green Building Council's (USGBC's) LEED rating system. Today, the green building market and industry expertise are becoming very sophisticated; a broad diversity of green building standards and programs

■ **FIGURE 1.11** After being devastated by a tornado in 2007, the town of Greensburg, Kansas, was reconstructed with LEED Platinum buildings and community wind power. An interior view of the new Kiowa County Schools looks out toward a wind turbine on the horizon. Image courtesy of BNIM; photograph © 2010, Assassi.

have emerged and continue to grow. And although most of the current programs are neither tailored to nor focused on net zero energy, a few are, and it seems that all roads are leading to a net zero energy future.

Department of Energy

The Department of Energy and the National Renewable Energy Laboratory have developed extensive resources and conducted wide-ranging research on energy efficiency, renewable energy technologies, and the development of net zero energy buildings. Many of these resources are referenced throughout this book. The primary web portal for the DOE's resources is through its Office of Energy Efficiency & Renewable Energy (EERE), at www.eere.energy.gov. The NREL website, which contains a searchable publication database, can be found at www.nrel.gov. As another resource, DOE also provides very detailed case studies on high-performing buildings (http://eere.buildinggreen.com) and maintains an online database on net zero energy buildings (http://zeb.buildinggreen.com).

Zero Energy Commercial Buildings Consortium

The Zero Energy Commercial Buildings Consortium (CBC) is a public/private entity working with the DOE to develop and deliver technologies, policies, and practices to aid the industry in realizing economically viable net zero energy buildings by 2030. This initiative supports the measures set forth in the 2007 Energy Independence and Security Act. The CBC, created in 2009, is open to membership across the industry; as of late 2011, more than 500 organizations had joined.

In early 2011, the CBC published two major reports focused on challenges and recommendations for the advancement of net zero energy building practices. The reports, "Next Generation Technologies Barriers and Industry Recommendations" and "Analysis of Cost & Non-Cost Barriers and Policy Solutions," are both available for download from the CBC website, www.zeroenergycbc.org. These reports address both the technical and the market barriers for net zero energy solutions.

New Buildings Institute

The New Buildings Institute (NBI) is a nonprofit organization focused on providing the building industry resources and research for improved energy performance in commercial buildings. NBI has released a first-of-its-kind research paper on the current status of net zero energy buildings in the U.S. market. The report, "Getting to Zero 2012 Status Update: A First Look at the Costs and Features of Zero Energy Commercial Buildings," can be downloaded from the NBI website, www.newbuildings.org. For this research paper, NBI searched for a reasonably sized study group of net zero energy buildings in the United States. It found 21 with sufficient data on design,

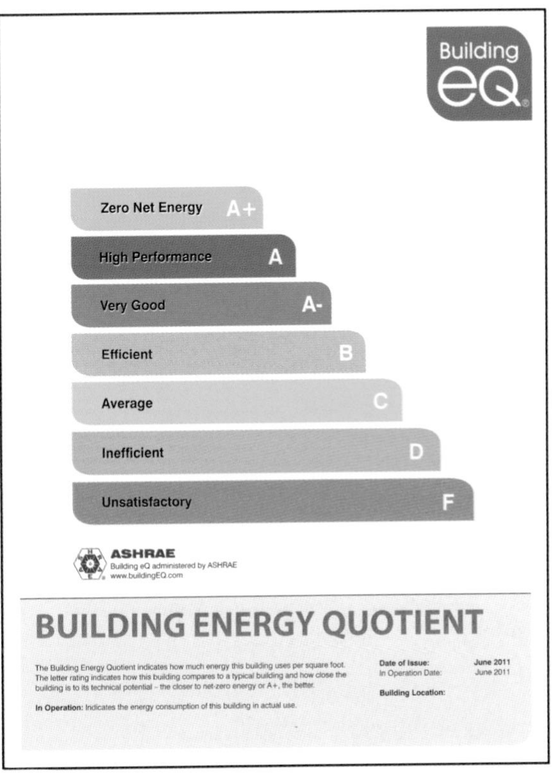

■ **FIGURE 1.12** Generic Label from ASHRAE's Building Energy Quotient Program. *Image courtesy of ASHRAE.*

technologies, and measured energy use to analyze (see Figures 1.13 and 1.14). NBI also identified 39 cases of emerging or potential net zero energy projects, which were still under construction or recently completed but without sufficient data for review. The institute reviewed another 39 buildings that had low-enough energy use for practical consideration of adding renewables to reach net zero. For the purpose of the report, these zero energy-capable (ZEC) buildings were

Net Zero Energy Buildings Studied in NBI's "Getting to Zero" Report

Year	Building	Type	Location	Square Feet	Purchased EUI	Total EUI	Data Source
2000	Oberlin College Lewis Center	Higher Education	Oberlin, OH	13,600	0	32.2	Measured
2001	Environmental Tech. Center Sonoma State	Higher Education	Rohnert Park, CA	2,200	0	2.3	Measured
2002	Challengers Tennis Club	Recreation	Los Angeles, CA	3,500	0	9.1	Modeled
2002	Leslie Shao-Ming Sun Field Station	Higher Education	Woodside, CA	13,200	3.8*	9.5*	Measured
2003	Audubon Center at Debs Park	Interpretive Center	Los Angeles, CA	5,000	0	17.1	Modeled
2003	Science House	Interpretive Center	St Paul, MN	1,530	0	17.6	Measured
2005	Hawaii Gateway Energy Center	Office, Interp. Center	Kailua-Kona, HI	3,600	0	27.7	Measured
2007	Aldo Leopold Legacy Center	Office, Interp. Center	Baraboo, WI	11,900	0	15.6	Modeled
2007	IDeAs Z2	Office	San Jose, CA	6,600	0	24.6	Modeled
2008	Camden Friends Meeting House	Assembly	Camden, DE	3,000	0	na	Measured
2008	Environmental Nature Center	Assembly	Newport, CA	8,535	0	17.6	Measured
2008	Hudson Valley Clean Energy HQ	Warehouse, Office	Rhinebeck, NY	4,100	0	13	Measured
2009	Chrisney Library	Library	Chrisney, IN	2,400	0	15.3	Measured
2009	Living Learning Center (Tyson Research Ctr)	Higher Education	Eureka, MO	2,968	0	24.5	Measured
2009	Omega Center for Sustainable Living	Interpretive Center	Rhinebeck, NY	6,246	0	21	Measured
2009	Pringle Creek Painter's Hall	Assembly	Salem, OR	3,600	0	9.5	Measured
2009	Putney Field House	Recreation	Putney, VT	16,800	0	9.7	Measured
2010	Energy Lab at Hawaii Preparatory Academy	Education	Kamuela, HI	5,902	0	11	Measured
2010	Magnify Credit Union	Office	Lakeland, FL	4,151	3.5	45	Measured
2010	Richardsville Elementary	K-12	Bowling Green, KY	77,000	0	18	Modeled
2010	NREL Research Support Facility	Office	Golden, CO	222,000	35**	35	Modeled

Notes:
EUI is kBtu/sf/yr.
Total EUI includes both renewable and purchased energy.

■ **FIGURE 1.13** Net Zero Energy Buildings in the NBI Study. *Data source: New Buildings Institute, "Getting to Zero 2012 Status Update: A First Look at the Costs and Features of Zero Energy Commercial Buildings," March 2012. Refer to www.newbuildings.org for complete report.*

defined as having total site EUI not exceeding 35 kBtu/square foot, the maximum found in the group of documented net zero energy buildings (with the exception of the Magnify Credit Union). Inclusion of these buildings increased NBI's total data set to 99 buildings.

NBI's report revealed some important trends for net zero energy buildings. A few of the notable trends from the report include:

- Net zero energy buildings have been built in most climate zones of the United States.
- Early net zero energy commercial buildings are small in size and within a limited range of building types, but the trend is toward larger net zero energy buildings and more building types.
- Photovoltaic systems are the primary source for on-site renewable energy. Daylighting control was the most common technology used throughout the building data set.
- Net zero energy buildings typically utilize readily available technologies and an integrated design approach.
- The limited number of current net zero energy buildings makes it difficult to identify any specific cost trends. However, based on the limited data set, it appears that making trade-offs within the overall construction budget can minimize cost premium.

The table in Figure 1.13 is a summary of the 21 net zero energy buildings included in the NBI's "Getting to Zero" report.

BUILDING INDUSTRY PROGRAMS

The 2030 Challenge

If all roads lead to net zero energy, the estimated time for achieving this goal as standard practice within the building industry seems to be the year 2030. The 2030 Challenge (www.architecture2030.org), developed by Edward Mazria and his nonprofit organization Architecture 2030, is a voluntary program intended to challenge architects to achieve carbon-neutral buildings by that decade. Launched in 2006, the 2030 Challenge calls for escalating rates of carbon reduction in the built environment.

The 2030 Challenge defines *carbon-neutral* as using no fossil fuel greenhouse-gas-emitting

■ **FIGURE 1.14** The Hawaii Gateway Energy Center is one of the net zero energy buildings in the NBI study.

energy to operate. The challenge accounts for significant energy efficiency and the incorporation of renewable energy. There are no limits to the amount of on-site renewable energy that can be used in calculating the 2030 Challenge. However, if green power is purchased, it may be claimed for only up to 20 percent of the required reduction (based on year).

2030 Challenge

Proposed reductions in fossil fuel energy use in new buildings, developments, and major renovations:

- Up to 2009: 50 percent reduction
- 2010–2014: 60 percent reduction
- 2015–2019: 70 percent reduction
- 2020–2024: 80 percent reduction
- 2025–2029: 90 percent reduction
- 2030: carbon-neutral

Existing buildings marked for renovation are called on to achieve a 60 percent reduction in fossil fuel energy use.

The timeline for reductions is based on the expected building completion date. The reductions in fossil fuel energy use are based on comparisons to a baseline representing the regional or national average energy use for the building type being evaluated. This energy use baseline can be established using energy data from the 2003 Commercial Building Energy Consumption Survey (CBECS). There are numerous ways of accessing energy data derived from this survey; the most common is through ENERGY STAR Target Finder. (Chapter 4 provides detailed guidance on establishing a 2030 Challenge baseline and target and using the benchmarking tools.) It is interesting to note that the 2003 CBECS database is becoming acknowledged as a valuable and reliable baseline metric, and will likely continue to gain recognition in the future. Architecture 2030 plans to keep the 2003 version of the database as its consistent baseline.

The 2030 Challenge operates literally as a challenge; as such, it works to inspire change within the industry, not one building at a time, but firm by firm and city by city. Thus, the challenge is adopted not at the project level, but at the organizational level. The adopting organization makes a commitment to pursue the challenge milestones on all of its projects. No formal evaluation or third-party certification exists for the 2030 Challenge. In this sense, the program lacks the rigor of building rating or labeling systems. However, the program has been effective at raising awareness and advocating for policy changes to support the mission. It has also inspired, in unique fashion, architects and the design community, its original target audience.

ASHRAE Vision 2020

ASHRAE, a strong supporter of net zero energy buildings, has developed many resources that have moved the industry in this direction. In 2008, it published a report called "ASHRAE Vision 2020." A few of the recommended developments include a rating system (now, Building EQ), partnership across industry organizations, targeted education, improvement of ASHRAE standards, improvement of design tools, and certification of sustainable design and NZEB design professionals. One interesting aspect of the report is the promotion of a single definition for a net zero energy building as one that produces as much energy as it uses, when measured at the site.

BUILDING INDUSTRY CODES AND REGULATIONS

Energy Independence and Security Act of 2007

The federal government is, in many ways, an early adopter of green building practices, and is poised to lead the way to the adoption and implementation of net zero energy buildings. In 2007, it passed the Energy Independence and Security Act (EISA), aimed at providing greater energy independence and energy security for our nation by improving energy efficiency for buildings and vehicles and increasing the availability of renewable energy. With regard to the commercial sector, the act established a zero energy commercial building initiative, with a national goal for new commercial buildings built after 2025 and existing buildings to achieve net zero energy by 2050. EISA also set dramatically high energy performance thresholds for new federal buildings and major renovations of existing federal buildings. The thresholds call for a reduction in fossil fuel energy use, with an increased required reduction over time. The reductions are based on 2003 CBECS, and the requirements have a lot in common with the 2030 Challenge.

Energy Independence and Security Act

Proposed reductions in fossil fuel energy use for new federal buildings and major renovations to existing federal buildings:

- 2010: 55 percent reduction
- 2015: 65 percent reduction
- 2020: 80 percent reduction
- 2025: 90 percent reduction
- 2030: 100 percent reduction

EISA has highlighted the need for net zero energy buildings in the federal sector. And while achieving 100 percent reduction in fossil fuel energy use is still in the distant future, it is a reasonable-enough goal, with significant milestones leading up to it, and many in the federal sector are beginning to act on it.

The 2030 goal got a major boost in 2009, when President Obama signed Executive Order 13514, requiring federal agencies to implement net zero energy requirements by the year 2030.

California Public Utilities Commission

In September 2010, the California Public Utilities Commission launched a Zero Net Energy Action Plan, calling for net zero energy residential buildings by 2020 and net zero energy commercial buildings by 2030. Leveraging a network of diverse stakeholders, the action plan defines net zero energy as an aggressive and necessary goal, rather than as a mandate. In order to meet the goal, the commission and its public- and private-sector partners have put in motion a diverse set of specific actions and strategies to move the California market to net zero energy buildings. The actions include addressing code, policies, financial tools, incentives, and integrated design practices. They are accompanied by a plan to raise awareness and provide education through a "Path to Zero" campaign. In addition, the action plan outlines a goal to achieve net zero energy on 50 percent of existing buildings by 2030.

Massachusetts Zero Net Energy Buildings Task Force

The State of Massachusetts, under the direction of Governor Patrick, formed a Zero Net Energy Building Task Force to develop recommendations for universal adoption by commercial and residential buildings by 2030. The task force published its final plan in March 2009. It addresses the broad range of barriers to net zero energy adoption, and supplies specific actions to overcome these barriers in commercial, residential, and state-owned buildings. The actions include the development of energy performance standards and energy use labeling for buildings; addressing financial hurdles and regulatory hurdles; increasing the capabilities of the workforce through education; and inspiring innovation within the state's building industry.

Massachusetts has formed two groups to shepherd the adoption of the plan's recommendations. One is an internal group composed of state agencies; the other is a council represented by stakeholders in private industry. The state has made progress in starting net zero energy pilot projects; it has adopted the 2009 International Energy Conservation Code and started an energy labeling program for buildings.

European Union

In 2009, the European Parliament passed a recommendation to update the European Energy Performance of Buildings Directive (EPBD) to achieve net zero energy for all new buildings by 2019. This was viewed as an important, albeit extremely challenging, requirement; the subsequent update of the EPBD, adopted by the European Parliament in 2010, includes provisions for each EU member state to develop national plans to achieve nearly net zero energy for all new buildings by 2020, and for all new public buildings to achieve this goal by 2018. Although the directive does not fully define *nearly net zero energy,* it does state that a nearly net zero energy building has a very high-energy performance and that an on-site or nearby renewable energy supply should cover a significant portion of its energy needs.

Several European countries have been simultaneously developing their own aggressive energy efficiency and carbon reduction policies and plans for buildings. Much of their effort has been focused on the residential sector, rather than on commercial buildings.

- The United Kingdom has a zero carbon homes initiative by 2016; it includes a public/private partnership called Zero Carbon Hub.
- Germany is promoting its very popular Passivhaus initiative.
- The Netherlands has signed an agreement with representatives of its building industry, listing goals to increase energy efficiency in buildings. The ultimate goal is for new buildings to be energy-neutral by 2020.
- France is targeting energy-positive buildings by 2020.

Building Codes

Building codes as adopted by local jurisdictions are mandatory requirements. Until recently, green building and energy efficiency requirements have not been particularly demanding in these codes. The widespread adoption of LEED and other green building rating systems and programs have transformed the building market, making it ready for more comprehensive and mandatory green building code requirements.

Some of the new green building codes include:

- CALGreen: California Green Building Standards Code
- IgCC: International Green Construction Code by the International Code Council (ICC)
- Standard 189: Standard for the Design of High-Performance Green Buildings Except Low-Rise Residential Buildings by ASHRAE, USGBC, and IES

These codes address a wide range of green building issues, in addition to stricter energy efficiency measures. Energy-specific codes and standards such as ANSI/ASHRAE/IESNA 90.1 and the International Energy Conservation Code by ICC, have dramatically raised minimum performance requirements in recent years.

There is also a new trend marked by the introduction and adoption of *stretch codes* by states and jurisdictions. Stretch goals are additional requirements beyond baseline code; they are typically voluntary but may be adopted by jurisdictions so that they can customize their energy or green building codes with higher standards while still adhering to a common baseline code that has been adopted statewide. Another trend is toward performance-based code compliance options, rather than strictly prescriptive methods. Higher-energy and green building standards become more challenging to dictate with prescriptive measures and so are better met with a performance-based approach.

The current and proposed green building codes do not at this time require near net zero energy performance, but they represent an important foundational step to reaching lower-energy buildings. Raising the minimum baseline for energy will continue to play a role in setting the level of performance required for net zero energy. Energy and green building codes will increase thresholds in subsequent versions, and thereby continue to advance higher standard stretch goals. If the current momentum within the industry continues, it is possible that future code requirements may get to net zero energy or near net zero.

BUILDING RATING AND ENERGY LABELING SYSTEMS

ENERGY STAR

ENERGY STAR is an energy labeling program of the Environmental Protection Agency (EPA) and the Department of Energy (DOE). It provides labeling for energy-efficient products, homes, and commercial buildings. The ENERGY STAR program for commercial buildings scores facilities based on their actual energy performance as compared with peer buildings of the same type and location/climate.

ENERGY STAR performance is scored on a scale of 1 to 100, where 100 signifies a top-performing building. A score of 50 represents average building performance or a building in the fiftieth percentile. It takes a score of 75 or greater to earn the ENERGY STAR rating. ENERGY STAR has expanded beyond labeling and scoring existing buildings to also recognize buildings at the design phase, with a program called "Designed to Earn ENERGY STAR."

ENERGY STAR's Target Finder is an extremely valuable tool for building design professionals and building owners. (Chapter 4 describes the tool in terms of setting a CBECS baseline for a project.) Comparing a building to its peers in terms of energy performance is where ENERGY STAR shines. ENERGY STAR and its Portfolio Manager also now enable the incorporation of on-site renewable energy, specifically solar and wind. Because the score is based on energy use, rather than net energy use, ENERGY STAR does not specifically recognize net zero energy buildings. ENERGY STAR is based on source energy, and the use of on-site renewable energy has a major impact on the source energy calculation. Typically, a net zero energy building would do fairly very well in the ENERGY STAR program, most likely earning a score in the high 90s or 100, because a net zero energy building is also a very low source energy building, which is precisely what ENERGY STAR measures.

LEED

The U.S. Green Building Council's LEED green building rating system has had tremendous impact on green building in the United States and around the world. Because it is a widely recognized standard for green building, it would make sense for a net zero energy building to also pursue LEED certification at a high level, such as Platinum (see Figure 1.15). Following LEED assists the team and owner in developing a whole green building, with efficient use of resources and attention to indoor environmental quality.

While LEED recognizes, rewards, and prioritizes energy performance and the use of on-site renewable energy, it does leave a number of points on the table when it comes to recognizing a net zero energy building. For example, according to "LEED for New Construction, 2009," a new building maximizes points in the Optimize Energy Performance credit (EA Credit 1) at 48 percent energy cost reduction, compared with ASHRAE 90.1-2007. Hitting a 50 percent reduction can provide an exemplary credit through Innovation in Design. While meeting a 50 percent energy reduction over ASHRAE 90.1-2007, without accounting for on-site renewable energy, would be a considerable achievement for any building, the credit does allow for the inclusion of on-site renewable energy as part of the energy performance calculation. A net zero energy building with a very low base energy use and 100 percent on-site renewable energy far exceeds the top threshold. More importantly, the On-Site Renewable Energy credit (EA Credit 2) only has a top point threshold of 13 percent, with the energy cost being offset by on-site renewable energy. An exemplary performance credit can be achieved at a 15 percent level. These thresholds do not recognize the performance and investment in on-site renewable energy of a net zero energy building.

"LEED for Building Design and Construction, 2012" was being developed at the time of this writing, and according to the third public draft, the Optimize Energy Performance credit and the On-Site Renewable Energy credit thresholds were similar to 2009 levels. However, it is likely that as LEED develops and grows it will better align with net zero energy buildings.

Living Building Challenge

The International Living Future Institute's Living Building Challenge is a green building certification program that seeks to promote and define the highest level of sustainability for the built environment. Version 2.0 of the program includes seven performance areas, which encompass a total of 20 possible imperatives (or perquisites). In contrast to LEED, the Living Building Challenge is based on a simple but challenging set of required strategies, called "imperatives," that must all be met to earn the certification. Version 2.0 also introduced a project typology overlay, and allows projects of different scales (neighborhood, building, landscape/infrastructure, and renovation) to be assigned specific imperatives from the set of 20 that define the challenge.

The Living Building Challenge embraces the objective of net zero energy buildings. The seventh imperative, Net Zero Energy, is

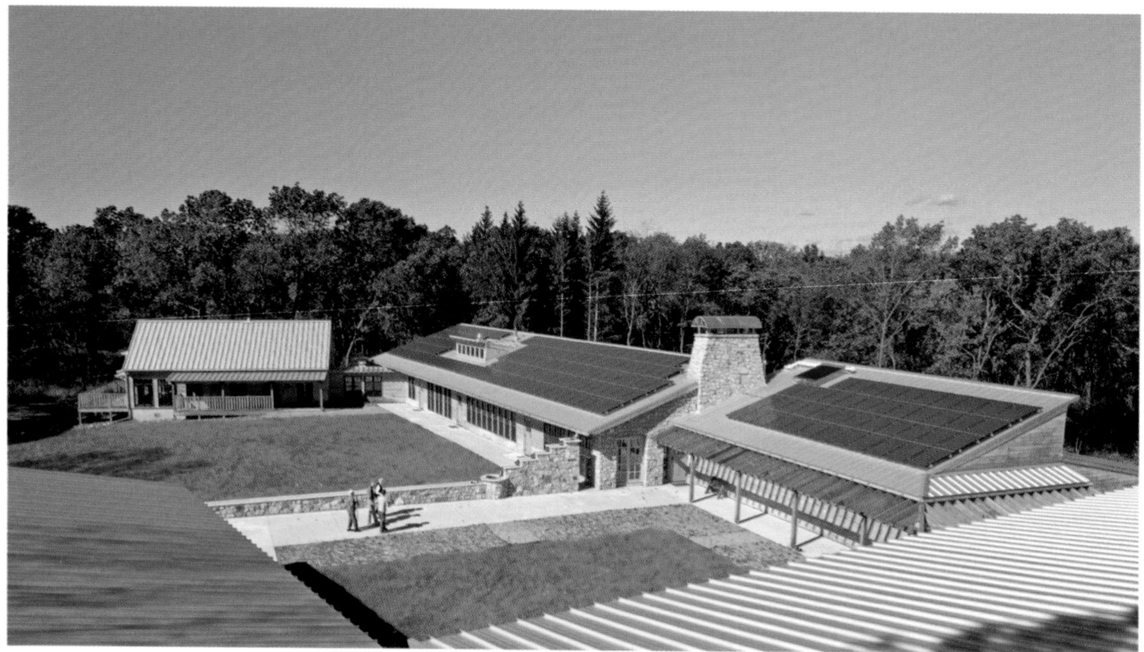

■ **FIGURE 1.15** The Aldo Leopold Legacy Center, LEED Platinum (61 points) and Net Zero Energy. *The Kubala Washatko Architects, Inc./Mark F. Heffron.*

required for project typologies. There are no other lower thresholds. If the project does not meet net zero energy, then it is ineligible to be certified as a Living Building (see Figure 1.16). The Net Zero Energy imperative has a rigorous definition for on-site renewable energy. It allows photovoltaics, wind turbines, water-powered microturbines, and direct geothermal. It excludes biomass, and does not allow combustion of any kind. Fuel cells may be used if powered by hydrogen that has been generated with renewable energy. The project may be off-grid or grid-connected.

Leveraging the net zero energy imperative, the International Living Future Institute launched the industry's first net zero energy certification program in October 2011. It uses the Net Zero Energy imperative as the basis for certification. However, a project must also meet three other Living Building Challenge imperatives to achieve the net zero energy certification:

- Energy Imperative: Net Zero Energy
- Site Imperative: Limits to Growth (sites restricted to grayfields and brownfields)
- Equity Imperative: Rights to Nature (buildings must not block access to or diminish fresh air, sunlight, and natural waterways for others)
- Beauty Imperatives: Beauty + Spirit, Inspiration + Education

Time will tell how the market responds to this new certification program. The addition of requirements through the use of multiple Living Building Challenge imperatives is commendable, for the simple reason that a net zero energy building should be more than just a high-performing energy building. However, the exclusion of any on-site combustion will make only a subset of net zero energy buildings eligible for this program, leaving a need in industry for a wider-focused and more comprehensive certification program.

To learn more about the International Living Future Institute's position on on-site combustion, refer to "Burning Questions—The Role of Combustion in Living Buildings: Why Prometheus Was Wrong," by Jason McLennan, published in *Trim Tab* magazine, summer 2010.

■ **FIGURE 1.16** The Hawaii Preparatory Energy Lab is a certified Living Building and net zero energy building. *Image courtesy of Buro Happold and Flansburgh Architects; photograph by Matthew Millman.*

PC

CHAPTER 2 PROJECT CONCEPTION AND DELIVERY

THE NET ZERO ENERGY OBJECTIVE

Ultimately, net zero energy is a building owner objective and commitment. The commitment must be expressed in earnest at the beginning of a project delivery process, throughout the process, and then through the building's occupancy. The main reason net zero energy is fundamentally an owner objective is that a net zero energy building is measured in actual operation, year after year. This is not to say that net zero energy is not an important design and construction objective; it certainly is. Because the building operation is so closely linked with a net zero energy goal, the planning, design, construction, and occupancy stages are best thought of as a completely integrated delivery process.

There has been a lot of talk of late in the industry about an integrated process, and for good reason. With an increase in owner and industry expectations for building performance and sustainability, it is not enough to design and construct a building in the conventional fragmented process that currently dominates the industry. The whole process, from procurement to occupancy, needs to be integrated with the performance requirements and objectives of the project (see Figure 2.1). Termed the *integrated delivery process*, it refers not just to the integrated design of a building but also to the integrated delivery of building and building performance objectives. The integrated delivery process is absolutely essential for net zero energy projects because they represent the apex of sustainable energy design and operation, with both challenges and opportunities that exceed the typical LEED projects of today.

The process and journey of a net zero energy building begins when building owners commit to net zero energy as one of their key objectives. Therefore, this chapter starts at this point, exploring the owner's role in defining the objective and making the commitment to it.

Owners should consider the implications of their net zero energy objective in the early days of project planning and definition. They then need to assemble a project delivery team whose members share this commitment and are aligned with this objective. The team should be comprehensive, made up not only of the professionals required to design, construct, and commission the building; the owner(s), user groups, and building operators are also key project delivery team members. Choosing the right project delivery team and committing to an integrated delivery process requires careful attention to the procurement process and how the various contractual relationships of the team members are defined.

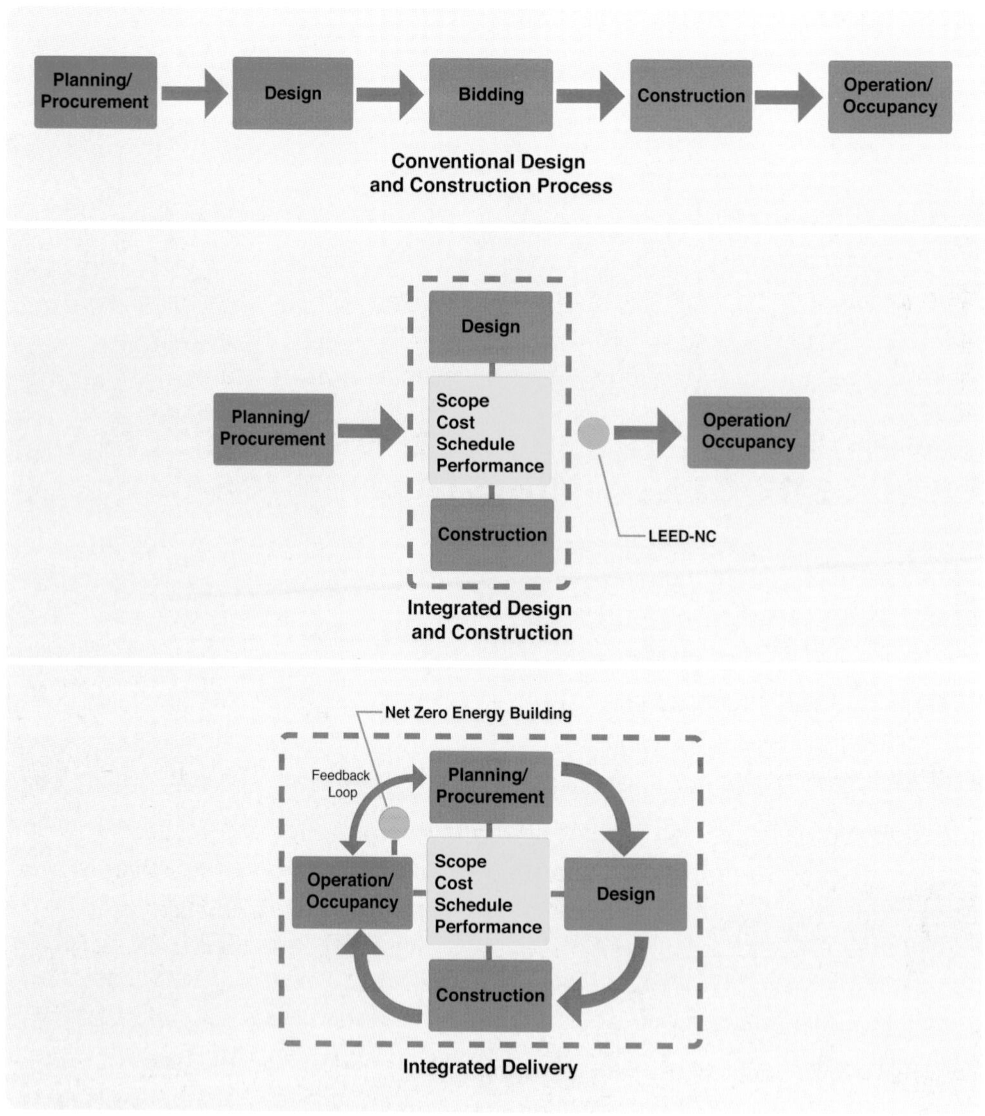

■ **FIGURE 2.1** Delivery Process Comparison.

NOTE

This chapter is not intended as a detailed guide to procuring a building; rather, it offers an overview of the implications of procuring a net zero energy building through an integrated delivery process. Chapter 3 provides guidance on the integrated process, and Chapter 10 explains the operation and occupancy of a net zero energy building.

Owner Perspectives

The commitment by owners to construct and operate net zero energy buildings stems from their unique perspectives, which are based on factors such as the type of building they own, the objectives for the building, and the mission of their organizations. Building owner perspectives may, therefore, vary significantly; likewise, their reasons for pursuing a net zero energy project will also vary. Keep in mind that net zero energy buildings are relatively new to the industry and so most owners do not yet have direct working experience with this type of building. That said, the implications of net zero energy buildings are understood by owners; moreover, the desire to explore them is growing.

Because the success of a net zero energy project hinges on the commitment of building owners to the objective, it is useful to further understand their underlying perspectives, which are the foundation for this commitment, and how a net zero energy building might help them achieve their larger organizational mission. To that end, I interviewed several building owners, and found their perspectives on net zero energy buildings to be enlightening, in particular regarding the value of net zero energy buildings. Summary points from these interviews are featured here.

BUILDING OWNER PERSPECTIVE: UNITED STATES GENERAL SERVICES ADMINISTRATION (GSA)

CASE STUDY

The GSA provides general services to the federal agencies of the U.S. government, including real estate and building services. The agency holds leases in more than 8,600 buildings and counts more than 1,500 government-owned buildings in its portfolio.

Interviewee

Donald Horn, AIA, LEED AP, Assistant Director of the General Service Administration's Office of Federal High-Performance Green Buildings

One of the biggest challenges we face as an industry moving toward net zero energy buildings is changing our mind-set. Most people are comfortable with the way things have always been done. The simple but enormous shift is getting people thinking it is possible.

—Donald Horn

Value and Need for Net Zero Energy Buildings

- The federal government has regulations in place, including Executive Order 13514 and the Energy Independence and Security Act of 2007. The Energy Independence and Security Act stipulates a tiered approach to fossil fuel energy reduction in federal buildings, reaching a 100 percent reduction by 2030. Executive Order 13514 stipulates that, beginning in 2020, all new federal building projects entering the planning process are to be designed to achieve net zero energy by 2030.
- Net zero energy buildings will generate value by reducing operating costs. This is significant for the GSA because of its large portfolio of buildings.
- There are several types of federal buildings that could have enhanced value as net zero energy buildings. Buildings that are remote and/or perform important security functions can potentially benefit from being off-grid or using only on-site renewable energy. Further, the use of on-site renewable energy is one strategy enabling these projects to move toward passive survivability, meaning they can maintain function in the event of disruption of conventional utilities. Border stations are one federal building type that can gain enhanced value through net zero energy applications.

Challenges Facing Net Zero Energy Buildings

- The GSA has established protocols for how buildings are to be procured by the federal government. Many of the new procurement and delivery methods, such as performance-based design-build or integrated project delivery, which enhance integration, do not fit the current procurement and budgeting procedures. These federal procedures are complex and impose many important protections for the use of public funds, hence will take time to adapt.
- The GSA notes the need for advancements in building-scale renewable energy systems. Its building portfolio spans a wide variety of building types and locations, and increased efficiency in photovoltaic systems would add tremendous flexibility in space-constrained sites. Further, a more diverse offering of technologies, such as improved urban wind power applications and improved energy storage systems, are seen as filling an important gap.
- The GSA faces one of the most universal challenges for moving toward net zero energy buildings: occupant expectations. It is widely noted that net zero energy and low-energy buildings that rely on passive strategies can achieve thermal comfort within a wider range of interior temperatures. Energy savings and thermal comfort can be enhanced through occupant behavior and aligned expectations, including dressing for climate conditions and actively using passive strategies such as operable windows for natural ventilation. While these occupant expectations are commonplace in other countries, the United States has yet to make the cultural shift.

Current Progress toward Net Zero Energy Buildings

- Tenant education is vitally important to making the shift to net zero energy buildings. To meet that need, the GSA instituted the Client Solutions group to work directly with tenants, providing a variety of workplace training and guidelines, including how to support energy goals. Some have called this approach "commissioning the occupants."
- Recognizing that it is necessary to work one's way up to the goal of net zero energy, and learn along the way, the GSA currently chooses at least three projects a year to work toward net zero energy.
- Looking at net zero energy is having an impact on the way the GSA building portfolio is managed, with energy performance becoming a very important part of the process. The GSA is identifying which buildings can be retrofitted to best meet all expectations. Existing buildings present major challenges, but opportunities as well in many cases. A current GSA net zero energy project is the renovation of the Wayne Aspinall Federal Office Building and U.S. Courthouse, a historic building in Grand Junction, Colorado.

Project Highlight

Wayne Aspinall Federal Building and U.S. Courthouse Building Preservation & Modernization (Figure 2.2) located in Grand Junction, Colorado.

The GSA is undertaking a modernization and preservation project for the historic Wayne Aspinall Federal Building and Courthouse, currently on track to become the nation's first net zero energy historic building. The Aspinall building is being designed by Westlake Reed Leskosky and the Beck Group. A few of the key energy strategies for the project include a geothermal heating and cooling system and a state-of-the-art fluorescent lighting system with daylight controls and storm windows with solar control film. A photovoltaic array is being integrated into the existing structure to offset the building's electrical demand. The project is scheduled for completion in January 2013.

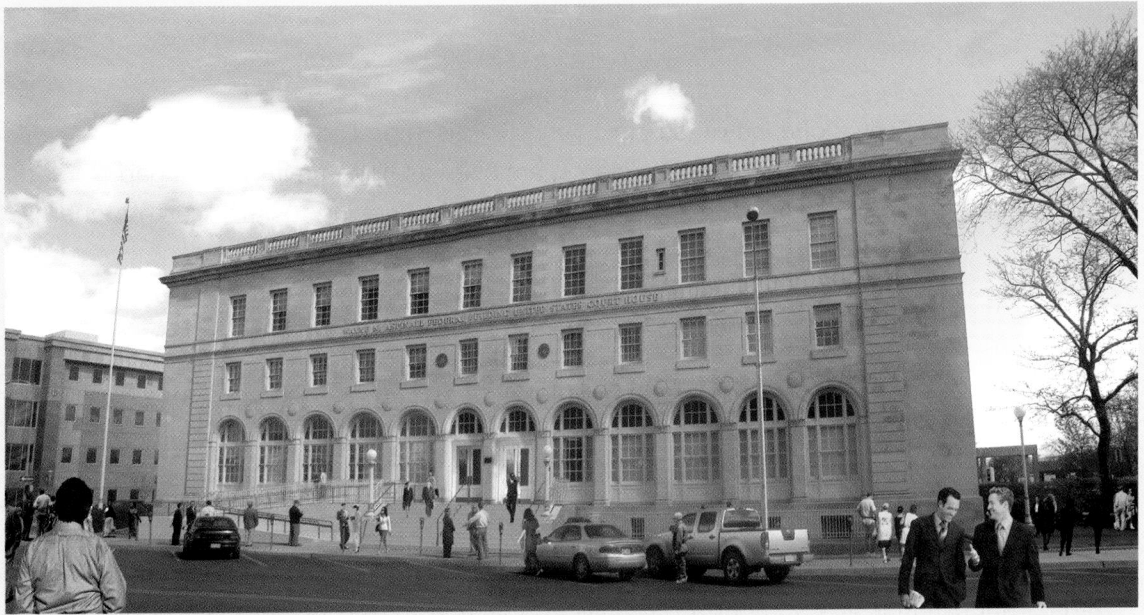

■ **FIGURE 2.2** Wayne Aspinall Federal Building and U.S. Courthouse is a historic building being renovated to meet net zero energy objectives. *Image courtesy of the Beck Group and Westlake Reed Leskosky.*

BUILDING OWNER PERSPECTIVE: UNITED STATES ARMY

CASE STUDY

The United States Army is the largest of the nation's armed forces. Its operations around the world add up to a global footprint of 158 installations and more than 1 billion square feet of building space. In 2010, the annual energy cost for Army building facilities totaled $1.2 billion. In the same year, the Army had 126 renewable energy projects in operation.

Interviewee

Richard G. Kidd IV, Deputy of Assistant Secretary of the Army (Energy & Sustainability), Office of the Assistant Secretary of the Army Installations, Energy & Environment

The Army has an important leadership role in the building industry regarding net zero energy. However, we use that leadership position and our purchasing power cautiously. We do not see ourselves as the test bed for bleeding-edge technologies; we see ourselves as utilizing the best and most cost-effective tools available to meet our mission.

—Richard Kidd

Value and Need for Net Zero Energy Buildings

- Federal statutory requirements are driving changes in sustainable building practices across the federal government. Executive Orders 13514 and 13423 require all new federal buildings and major renovations to comply with the Federal Energy Management Program's guiding principles, and provide similar guidance on sustainability initiatives for existing buildings. Further, by 2015, 15 percent of federal building inventory is to comply with these guiding principles.

  The Guiding Principles for Sustainable New Construction and Major Renovation include:

  1. Employ integrated design principles.
  2. Optimize energy performance.
  3. Protect and conserve water.
  4. Enhance indoor environmental quality.
  5. Reduce environmental impact of materials.

- The Energy Independence and Security Act of 2007 requires zero fossil fuel use in federal buildings by 2030. This is stimulating an interest in net zero energy buildings today.
- In light of the U.S. Army's global footprint and considerable annual energy expenses, the energy cost savings gained from high-performing and net zero energy buildings make them a strong value proposition. Simply put, it is cheaper to save energy than to buy it.
- Energy security is a high-priority objective for the U.S. Army and the Department of Defense. Assured access to reliable energy supplies is critical to the Army's mission and operational needs. The twofold first step toward energy security is to reduce demand and improve energy efficiency. The second step is to meet this reduced energy demand with power on the installations. On-site renewable energy sources offer excellent opportunities to provide energy security and are less vulnerable to outages caused by natural disasters, accidents, and attacks.

Challenges Facing Net Zero Energy Buildings

- The U.S. Army faces a cultural process challenge in pursuing net zero energy; it is an ambitious goal and requires new ways of doing things. Change does not come easily to any large organization and the Army is no exception. Evolving the military culture to overcome this natural resistance is an important part of the Army's approach to energy use reduction.
- Based on current technologies, the variety of building types, and the wide range of climates in its locations, the U.S. Army understands that not every one of its buildings can be a net zero energy building. At the same time, the Army recognizes the powerful advantage of scale, and so is focusing on net zero energy campuses and installations.
- While increased knowledge of technologies within the industry is important in pursuing net zero energy, it is more important to the U.S. Army to adopt a systems approach. Designing at a systems level, whether at a whole building level or at campus scale, is more effective than focusing too narrowly on individual additive technologies to reach net zero energy objectives.

- The U.S. Army is raising its standards for building energy performance, specifically seeking a 60 percent improvement over the current standard of a 30 percent energy reduction, compared to a baseline building, per ASHRAE 90.1. The Army has also recently adopted the highest standard for green building in the federal government: Standard 189.1, "Standard for the Design of High-Performance Green Buildings Except Low-Rise Residential Buildings."
- In 2011, the U.S. Army announced a major net zero initiative, and selected seven pilot installations. The initiative focuses on the campus or installation scale, rather than individual buildings. The Army is more interested in installations that meet its mission than building marquee buildings. What makes this initiative even more interesting is that it is not just net zero energy. For the Army, *net zero* means net zero energy, net zero water, and net zero waste, because it needs energy, water, and land to meet its mission. Therefore, in addition to addressing these mission-critical areas, the Army's net zero strategy provides for a way to steward natural resources in a sustainable way, manage operating costs, and maintain resilience into the future. The Army refers to these net zero benefits as a "force multiplier."

Installation Highlight

Fort Carson, Colorado (Figure 2.3)

Fort Carson is an Army post located along the front range of Colorado. The installation, which has a large concentration of LEED-certified buildings, has been a leader in the federal government and the armed forces for advancing sustainable design practices. It was designated a net zero pilot installation by the U.S. Army in April 2011, as part of its net zero pilot program focusing on net zero energy, water, and waste. Of its 18 pilot installations, Fort Carson is one of only two attempting to achieve all three net zero initiatives.

As a primary strategy, Fort Carson is focusing intently on resource use reductions and energy efficiency. The installation already has renewable energy projects in operation, such as a 2MW ground-mounted solar array, and is planning to bring on more renewable energy plants, as funding and energy economics allow. Additional technologies under consideration include solar, wind, geothermal, and biomass. The U.S. Army's approach demonstrates the power and opportunities of entire community scales when working toward a net zero energy goal.

■ **FIGURE 2.3** January 14, 2011, ribbon-cutting ceremony for Fort Carson's new 2MW solar array. *Photo courtesy of U.S. Army; photograph by Michael J. Pach.*

CASE STUDY DEVELOPER PERSPECTIVE: POINT32, SEATTLE, WASHINGTON

Point32 is a Seattle-based real estate development company that is serving as the development partner for the Bullitt Foundation's new Bullitt Center project. The Bullitt Foundation is an influential nonprofit whose mission is to safeguard the natural environment by promoting responsible human activities and sustainable communities in the Pacific Northwest. Its website boldly states: "The Foundation looks for high-risk, high-potential payoff opportunities to exert unusual leverage. It has a special interest in demonstrating innovative approaches that promise to solve multiple problems simultaneously."

Point32 led the Bullitt Foundation through site selection, entitlement work, design team selection, project management, financing, and construction oversight for the Bullitt Center project.

Interviewee

Chris Rogers, Partner, Point32

We need projects that challenge us to live within our means. This may be difficult, but now is the time for leadership.

—Chris Rogers

Value and Need for Net Zero Energy Buildings

- The Bullitt Center is a multitenant commercial office building being constructed and partially occupied by the Bullitt Foundation, a leading environmental nonprofit. Its mission and purpose are strong drivers for this project to pursue net zero energy. The project is pursuing the Living Building Challenge, and if it succeeds will likely be the first commercial office building to achieve such a distinction. The foundation was not only interested in meeting its own commitment to sustainable development, it wanted to fulfill its larger mission and create an international showcase for other commercial projects to learn from and follow.
- The Living Building Challenge and net zero energy are clearly mission-based benefits for the Bullitt Foundation. The Bullitt Center is also a commercial real estate asset and is striving to lead the market in making a case for net zero energy office buildings. From a real estate perspective, this project is being positioned to be the greenest commercial building in the world. By meeting the net zero energy goal, it is anticipated that tenants will not have energy bills. The center has initially attracted tenants who desire offices in a very high-performing green building and are attracted to the net zero energy objective.
- The development team is investing in high-performance building systems and materials, and actively managing the costs so the building can be competitive in the Class A office market. Unfortunately, the current economic climate is making the financial model very challenging. A net zero energy office building is a very new product in the commercial real estate market and so it may take time for the market to understand the unique value of the Bullitt Center project. One hope is to capture the growing interest of office tenants

in both building performance and human health benefits that can be gained from high-performance green buildings.

Challenges Facing Net Zero Energy Buildings

- The Bullitt Center project is being constructed in an urban context and must adhere to multiple regulatory requirements, which make it difficult to meet net zero energy objectives and the Living Building Challenge. Regulatory hurdles include health code issues related to the management of graywater systems, as well as fundamental zoning issues such as building height and percentage of roof area that can be dedicated to photovoltaic array coverage. The project was fortunate to be part of Seattle's new Living Building Pilot Program, which allows for flexibility in how the city's land use code is applied, in order to incentivize projects to achieve higher sustainability benchmarks. This enabled the project to have higher floor-to-floor heights and a narrower footprint, which help with the project's passive strategies, such as daylighting.
- Designing for net zero energy and the Living Building Challenge is a more complex and demanding process than for a typical commercial office building project. The Bullitt Center is meeting many required high-level performance goals, in addition to all other key concerns like program, cost, and aesthetics. The energy modeling effort, in particular, was extensive. However, the benefit of making the investment in up-front design will be a payoff in building performance, year after year.
- Tenant behavior and tenant buy-in within the context of a net zero energy multitenant office building is critical in achieving the energy performance objective. The building owners are proposing an energy budget approach whereby each tenant will have an energy budget to work within. Tenants that use less energy will have the opportunity to trade energy with other tenants that need more energy than their budgets allow—a sort of cap-and-trade program that can benefit energy-conserving tenants.

Current Progress toward Net Zero Energy Buildings

- The Bullitt Center is Point32's first venture into net zero energy development. The firm has already begun to incorporate lessons learned and best practices from the Bullitt Center into other projects; and there will likely be more net zero energy projects in the company's future. Their future looks positive for these types of developments because they address not only the economic constraints but also the environmental and social imperatives.

Project Highlight

The Bullitt Center, Seattle, Washington (Figure 2.4)

The Bullitt Center is poised to become the greenest, most energy-efficient commercial building in the world, firmly placing Seattle at the forefront of the green building movement. This 6-story, 50,000-square-foot building will be located at the intersection of Capitol Hill and the Central District in the city. The building is currently scheduled to be completed in 2012.

■ **FIGURE 2.4** Rendering of the Bullitt Center, Seattle, Washington. *Image courtesy of the Bullitt Foundation, Seattle, Washington, Miller Hull and Point32.*

The goal of the Bullitt Center is to change the way buildings are designed, built, and operated, to improve long-term environmental performance, and to promote broader implementation of energy efficiency, renewable energy, and other green building technologies in the Northwest. The building is seeking to meet the ambitious goals of the Living Building Challenge, the world's most strenuous benchmark for sustainability. For example, a solar array will generate as much electricity as the building uses, and rain will supply as much water, with all wastewater treated on-site. By creating a structure where every worker has access to fresh air and daylight, the Bullitt Center will provide a healthy, human environment, one that is more pleasant and more productive than most commercial buildings.

PROJECT CONCEPTION

Project Definition

A project begins when an owner determines a need for a building. Considerable planning is involved to take a building from conception through procurement. The owner will conduct feasibility and due diligence studies for the potential facility. The owner will also develop a project definition for the potential building, which includes essential planning components such as scope, budget, schedule, quality, and objectives.

This phase is the ideal time for an owner to consider the net zero energy objective, because it has implications for the project definition and planning process. Beginning a project with net zero energy in mind is advantageous, but it does require a reasonably thorough and detailed project definition by the owner in order to optimize it within the context of the net zero energy goal. Defining at this level of detail is often specialized and so may not be part of the owner's internal expertise; therefore, it is not uncommon for the project definition phase to be finalized once the owner has procured the project delivery team. Another option is to supplement in-house capabilities with outside consultants to complete the project definition phase. In either case, success is derived from early and continuous owner commitment, the ability of the owner to align the project delivery team around the net zero energy objective, and a clear project definition that reinforces the objective.

Defining the Objective

"If you don't ask, you don't get." This Stevie Wonder quote tells the story of many building projects. After all, high performance does not just happen; it starts with a clearly defined and stated objective. I am regularly surprised that more building owners do not demand greater performance from their buildings when they are procuring design and construction services. There are two common obstacles. The first is that building owners tend to choose cost and schedule as the drivers for project procurement of a given scope (program and function) and then hope for the best quality they can get within these parameters. The second is that many building owners do not know how to effectively define performance requirements for a project. It is easy to see how these two obstacles can reinforce one another, with the result that many projects fail to live up to their performance potential, regardless of budget or schedule.

This dilemma plays into an old adage widely held within the building industry: "There is cost, quality, and schedule: Pick two." In fact, this is a false choice and shows that sometimes conventional wisdom can lead us astray. There is no doubt that the three objectives are interdependent; but they are not exclusionary. The goal is to find ways to align them so they become inclusionary. With a net zero energy building and other highly sustainable buildings, a fourth objective is added: performance, and in particular, energy performance. The diagram in Figure 2.5 illustrates the conceptual difference between the conventional project objective "triangle" and the integrated project objective "spoke and hub." Procuring and delivering a net zero energy building requires prioritizing building performance so that it is on par with cost, schedule, and quality as drivers for the project. All four must be met, and all four need to be considered when evaluating project decisions. This can be accomplished with an integrated delivery process.

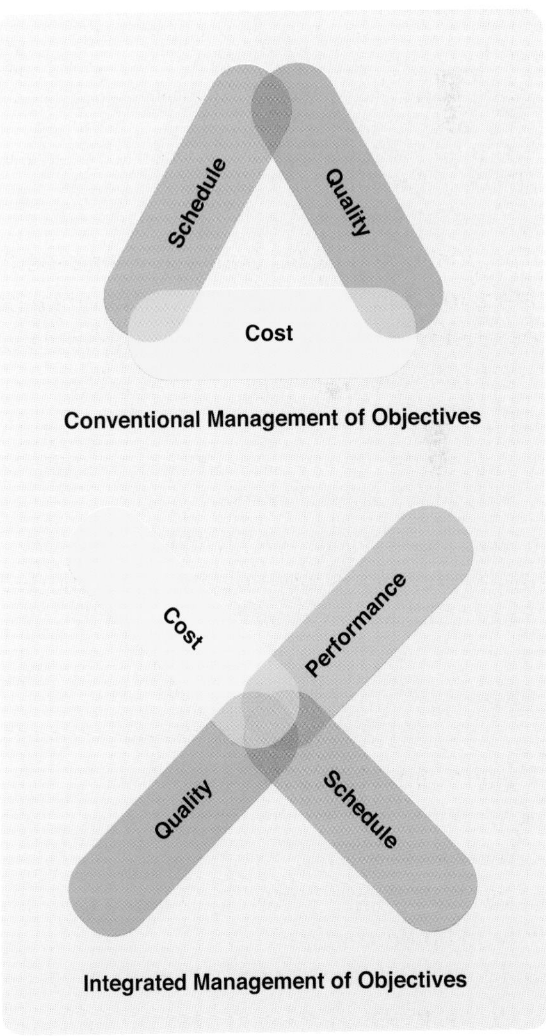

■ **FIGURE 2.5** Managing Project Objectives.

LEED AND NET ZERO ENERGY PERFORMANCE OBJECTIVES

USGBC's LEED rating system has had a positive effect on the ability of building owners to define performance requirements for a project and achieve holistic results. Because LEED is based on a variety of performance-based standards, simply by selecting a desired LEED certification level, a building owner should be able to complete a project that is designed and built to a higher standard, compared to a conventional approach. Some building owners leverage the individual credits within LEED and specify that certain credits be earned in addition to the desired rating. This is a valuable approach, in that owners can decide which performance standards are most important to them; they can also target a specific energy-efficiency goal.

Expanding on the industry's experience working with LEED as a set of performance criteria, net zero energy buildings take owner performance requirements to a new level. First, though setting an energy-efficiency target, such as 30 percent better than energy code, is an important step, it is not enough. A savvy owner will specify an *energy use target*, or how much energy the building should use in the course of a year, which becomes the basis for achieving net zero energy. An energy use target is directly related to actual operational energy. Put another way, the utility meter does not measure "percent better than energy code." This is a very different outcome compared to "LEED for Building Design and Construction," where energy is measured at the end of design and is based on the design energy model, reporting results in terms of a percent energy cost savings over energy code.

SETTING AN ENERGY PERFORMANCE OBJECTIVE

A single annual energy use number as a target for a project is a very straightforward factor for designers and builders to understand, design, and build for. It is also more meaningful than relying on an energy-efficiency percentage as the main energy objective, because it is a direct, measurable, and verifiable outcome. The actual process of establishing an energy use target will also inform building owners whether net zero energy is feasible, given their building program, location, and current on-site renewable energy technology. Setting an energy use target also establishes the owner's internal operational energy goals for the project, which requires buy-in and commitment throughout the owner's organization. Remember that net zero energy is ultimately a building owner's goal, and is measured in actual operation.

However, establishing a meaningful and feasible energy use target for a net zero energy building is not always straightforward. An effective target will be low enough to spur innovation on the part of the delivery team, but not so low that it is unattainable. For example, the DOE/NREL Research Support Facility had an energy target of 25 kBtu/ft^2/year in the project's request for proposals (RFP). This target was well vetted, using energy modeling (NREL has in-house energy modeling capabilities and experience). NREL also developed a sliding scale for the energy target, recognizing that some variables, such as final occupancy density and the final data center load, would influence the final target.

One approach is to set the overarching goal for a project as net zero energy and rely on the delivery team to define the appropriate energy use target. The advantage of this approach is that it outsources the technical analysis of the energy objective when it is not within the building owner's expertise or comfort zone. It also has the advantage of gaining early buy-in for the net zero energy objective from the project delivery team. On the other hand, this approach does not allow owners to fully assess the feasibility of net zero energy for their project before they select a team or proceed with design services. Without the net zero energy objective defined, it may be difficult to competitively select a design team and negotiate the proper scope of services.

It may be advantageous for a building owner to develop some energy expertise in-house or utilize appropriate outside consultants in the early project feasibility and definition stages. Even with a well-defined net zero energy project, however, the owner should revisit the definition and planning assumptions with the project delivery team ultimately selected. This is a key step for ensuring team alignment and helps to flush out possible issues within the project assumptions. (Chapter 4 provides detailed guidance on setting energy targets for a net zero energy project.)

Measuring the Energy Objective

The net zero energy objective involves more than establishing an energy use target goal. The objective also has to make clear how and when it is to be measured, and thus how the delivery team will be evaluated against this objective. There is no single answer as to when and how to measure a design team's performance against the energy target, but it is a more useful quality control measure when it is assessed at regular milestones. In addition, a performance-based incentive program attached to energy performance reviews can be a powerful motivator for team performance.

Net zero energy is ultimately a measure of actual operational energy use. Therefore, the ideal time to measure whether the target is met is during building occupancy and operation. The operational energy measurement is one every net zero energy project will make, but it can be problematic to tie the delivery team's performance to this outcome alone. The most pronounced challenges to linking actual measured annual building performance to the evaluation of the delivery team is that, typically, the delivery team does not play a major role during occupancy and operation, and that even the best designed and constructed building may be operated in ways never intended, resulting in lower-than-expected performance levels. Two common examples of this are plug load management and lighting schedules. Occupant behavior and operational policies have marked impact on plug loads and lighting use, such as the use of personal appliances at a workstation or leaving lights on during the night or unoccupied hours.

All that said, a net zero energy building is not a typical building, and the delivery team should be actively involved in postoccupancy services, to assist the owner in meeting the energy goal. Further, a net zero energy building cannot operate as a typical building; it must effectively manage plug and process loads, as well as lighting schedules. (Chapter 10 enumerates the strategies behind operating and occupying a net zero energy building.)

In addition to the measurement and assessment of the energy goal during building operation, evaluating the delivery team's energy model at key milestones in the delivery process is an important phase in the pursuit of the net zero energy goal. The milestones for energy model and energy goal evaluation would typically coincide with those for design reviews. Two important milestones are an as-designed energy model and an as-built energy model, completed at the end of construction.

Evaluating a design energy model against an energy goal requires additional scrutiny on the part of the owner, and so it may be wise to obtain a third-party or peer review of the design energy model. The energy model needs to be as close a representation of the actual construction and owner-intended operation as possible. All building construction assembly inputs and operational and occupancy schedule inputs to an energy model should be verified against actual data.

PROJECT PLANNING

It is clear that defining net zero energy as a principal performance objective profoundly affects the planning of a new project by a building owner; it has implications for many planning components, including the building's program, site selection, budget, and schedule.

Another important consideration is to assure that the building ownership or client team is organized so that they can effectively deliver on the owner's responsibilities for a net zero energy building. The client leadership should keep energy performance as a top priority, and make decisions based on energy consequences as a key consideration. Because a net zero energy building is a highly integrated solution, any major changes that happen as the project progresses raise the risk of causing a snowball effect; and, usually, the later the change, the bigger the snowball. Making good decisions up front and sticking to them is crucial to the delivery of a net zero energy project. However, when changes must be made, an owner who is aware of the integrated nature of the change will be better positioned to work with the team to successfully integrate the changes while maintaining overall project objectives.

Site Selection

A vast number of factors influence site selection. From a sustainable design point of view, the LEED rating system offers useful guidance on site selection. In addition to the priorities listed in LEED, a few other factors should be considered specifically for net zero energy buildings. While these factors will be analyzed in detail by the project design team once the site is selected, it is important that they be considered at some level of detail during site selection. Keep in mind, a large part of constructing a successful net zero energy building is working with what is available at the site and from the climate. A project site should offer as many opportunities as possible. (Chapter 5 offers a more detailed assessment of site considerations for a net zero energy building.)

Program

The building program addresses the primary need for the structure and its intended uses. If you need a school, the program defines the type of school, the population it will serve, and the types of spaces and functions required to meet the educational mission of the school. It is important to note that the building program also defines a large portion of the energy used by the proposed building. While the program may not be entirely flexible, it is still useful to explore opportunities to reduce energy through careful programming.

The place to start is also the place to make one of the most sustainable decisions you can at the beginning of a building project. Do not build more than you need. Find ways to make spaces serve multiple purposes, and then find ways to make them adaptable and expandable to accommodate future changes without rebuilding. In programming, identify spaces that have proportionally large energy uses, such as data centers, commercial kitchens, and certain process loads. Identify ways to right-size these functions, and plan to invest in the most efficient equipment you can justify.

The building program is also an opportunity to define the energy-related characteristics of a space, in addition to the functional requirements. For a net zero energy building, it is important to explore energy characteristics in the program that can result in a reduction of energy use.

Site Selection Guidelines for Net Zero Energy Projects

- **Solar access:** This is important for placement of photovoltaic modules and solar thermal collectors and for implementing passive strategies such as daylighting. Keep in mind that in very hot climates some well-placed shading can be a benefit, but it should not cover solar energy systems. Sites that allow building orientations to maximize south- and north-facing façades, and minimize east- and west-facing façades, can offer advantages for solar access, solar control, and daylighting.
- **Renewable resources:** Assess whether the site has access to renewable energy and passive design resources such as solar, wind, small-scale hydro, geothermal, and locally available biomass. If the project is part of a campus or multiple building site, consider opportunities for district-scale solutions to renewable energy.
- **Site size:** The size of the lot, as well as zoning regulations, influences the number of stories and massing of a building, as well as potential parking configurations. The two most common locations for photovoltaic arrays are the building roof and shade canopies over parking.
- **Existing buildings:** The same site selection considerations should be reviewed when doing major renovations to and/or expanding an existing building. However, the existing building fixes many of the variables. A feasibility assessment should be completed on the existing building, with special focus on energy efficiency, energy systems, and building envelope. Look for opportunities to utilize passive energy strategies. Keep in mind that if an existing building was constructed in the first half of the twentieth century or earlier, it likely was originally designed to provide thermal comfort without air conditioning and to provide daylit spaces. Can the original design intent be leveraged?

The program guidelines offered here specify a number of the energy-related characteristics for spaces that can be incorporated into a building program.

A well-written building program is instrumental to the success of any project; its importance for a net zero energy building should not be underestimated. Because much of the planning around energy happens at the beginning of a project, and there is usually a close balance between planned on-site renewable energy and the energy use target, changes in the program that come about later in the process can have a disastrous effect for net zero energy buildings. Imagine the impact of adding a cafeteria to a net zero energy school project, or a data center to an office building, during mid-design. A well-written building program gives clarity and assurance to a project and helps minimize risk. A building program can be even more valuable when it also addresses the energy implications of the space uses.

Because the program is so important, it is critical to have the design team conduct a program verification analysis, if the same design team did not develop the original building program.

Schedule

Net zero energy buildings do not necessarily take longer to deliver than conventional

Program Guidelines for Net Zero Energy Projects

- **Thermal requirements:** Define the temperature and thermal comfort requirements and opportunities for each space.
- **Lighting and daylighting requirements:** Note the application or priority for daylight for each space; remember that virtually any space that requires lighting can benefit from daylighting. Determine working light luminance levels in terms of general ambient light and task light at defined work areas.
- **Equipment and plug load requirements:** It is important to identify the equipment used within the building in terms of energy as well as space and power requirements. Begin a plug load management plan. (Chapter 10 describes plug load management and outlines steps for conducting a plug load inventory.)
- **Occupancy requirements:** The number of people occupying spaces influences ventilation rates and people-related heat gains. In addition, the occupancy schedule should be defined for each space.

buildings. In fact, they can take less time to deliver if they follow an integrated process. They do require spending more time on certain tasks, and spending time in different ways. Net zero energy buildings also necessitate a larger up-front investment in design. This is common with integrated design processes for delivering sustainable design projects of all types, but it is particularly the case for net zero energy designs because, in order to deliver energy performance, all design decisions must consider energy as well as cost, schedule, and quality. Thus, the process for low-energy and net zero energy buildings tends to be innovative and iterative, and requires more time up front to research, test strategies, and integrate solutions. There is also a need to perform detailed and frequent energy modeling throughout the process. If done right, this up-front investment in smart design can save time and money later in the process—not to mention the long-term payoff over years of improved building operation.

It is important to note that many aspects of energy performance, and even cost aspects of a building, are locked in when early design decisions are made. This gives greater credence to the idea of front-loading a project with smart design. *Front-loading design* does not mean advancing to construction documents faster. It means taking the time to make integrated and validated fundamental design decisions that clearly articulate the design intent needed to meet the program, cost, and performance requirements of a project. Part of this process also involves soliciting input from all project team members early in the process so that the early design is truly integrated. (Refer to Chapter 3 for detailed guidance on the integrated process.)

Certainly, speed of delivery can impact the cost and quality of any building project, and net zero energy buildings are no exception. Following an integrated process is critical to maintaining quality, controlling cost, and delivering performance under a tight schedule—so much so that integrated design has become a necessity in today's building industry, where ever-shorter delivery schedules are the norm. In this sense, there is some synergy between integrated fast-track projects and high-performance or net zero energy project delivery. Both require a strong commitment to integrated delivery.

Schedule Guidelines for Net Zero Energy Projects

- **Front-load design:** Integrated design requires an innovative and iterative process that invests design effort up front in order to derive cost-effective and integrated solutions.
- **Team continuity:** With front-loaded design, the multidisciplinary delivery team needs to be present from the very beginning of the project. Entire team continuity during the entire delivery process ensures retention of integrated project knowledge through to project completion.
- **Energy modeling:** Energy modeling is a more intense and iterative process in a net zero energy project and must be planned accordingly. In addition, energy modeling is one of the primary means to evaluate the delivery team's progress toward meeting the net zero energy objective; therefore, energy modeling review milestones should be added to the schedule.
- **Continuous design and construction:** In an integrated delivery process, design and construction become one fluid process. This enables design and construction activities to happen synchronously, which can free up more time for design, and allow construction to start and, therefore, finish earlier.

Budget

A net zero energy building, like green buildings in general, need not cost any more to build than a conventional high-quality project. This consideration assumes that the renewable energy systems comprise a separate budget item from the construction costs, while renewable energy systems should ideally be part of the overall delivery team's scope. That said, net zero energy buildings are certainly not a lowest first-cost solution. They are a low life-cycle cost solution, and not without their unique challenges. Comparing costs of a net zero energy building to other high-quality buildings is an important caveat, because you can always build cheaper if you are willing to lower quality and performance. I see high-performing green buildings completed within their budgets all the time. Sure, they tend to have some systems, such as daylighting controls or an improved exterior envelope, that may have an individual cost premium over lower-performing alternatives, but the overall cost is managed within the construction budget. In addition, these features can be fully integrated, and so reduce cost in other areas.

Integrated design is not only a good strategy to help manage schedules for complex projects, it is also a powerful tool for controlling costs. There is a distinct difference between design strategies and technologies that are *integrative* rather than *additive*. Additive approaches tend also to be additive in terms of cost. Integrative approaches may include the same features or technologies as those in an additive approach, but their benefits contribute to the building as a whole, and are integrated into the cost as well, allowing strategic cost trade-offs while managing the overall budget. Its objective is to invest in architecture to reduce load and reduce mechanical equipment size and cost, which in turn will reduce energy and the size and cost of the renewable energy system. (Refer to Chapter 9 for more detailed guidance on the economics of net zero energy buildings.)

Budget Guidelines for Net Zero Energy Projects

- **Life-cycle value:** Seek long-term, life-cycle value and budget for quality and performance, keeping in mind that net zero energy buildings are all about exemplary energy performance and value.
- **Selection and pricing:** Project team selection and pricing methods used for the project are as important as the budget for overall cost control. (The pros and cons of selection and pricing methods are addressed later in this chapter.)
- **Soft costs:** It is important to budget for additional soft costs, which include the effort and investment in smart design required during the front end of the design phase. Along with the investment in smart design comes the investment in a more rigorous energy modeling process. The additional soft costs also fund participation of all project delivery team members, to ensure an integrated project delivery.
- **Renewable energy:** Consider the cost of renewable energy systems as a separate investment from the construction cost. They can be a sizable investment, but one that virtually buys the future energy for the building up front. In this sense, it is also a financial investment and should be analyzed as such. (Refer to Chapter 9 for more on financial analysis of renewable energy systems.)

PROJECT TEAM SELECTION

All construction projects need a team of diverse experts to deliver the building; this may include architects, engineers, designers, landscape architects, planners, contractors, subcontractors, commissioning agents, and others. Also keep in mind that on a net zero energy project, the owner must be an integral member of the delivery team.

There are many ways of selecting a team to design and produce a net zero energy building. Each method has advantages and disadvantages with regard to meeting the objective of net zero energy. There are also many formal tools used by building owners to engage the market and solicit delivery teams, and these tools need to be embedded and aligned with the owner's net zero energy performance objective. The selection of a high-quality team, and the ability of the owner to adopt an integrated delivery approach, is instrumental to the success of a net zero energy building. These methods also work in tandem with the different contractual relationships, discussed in the next section of this chapter, "Delivery Methods."

Relationship-Based Selection

Relationship-based selection emphasizes the importance of a strong working relationship to build the team culture that is needed for a successful net zero energy building. While this type of selection is often sole-source, based on an existing relationship, it can be used as criteria with other selection methods. It can even be fostered in teams without strong existing relationships.

Qualifications-Based Selection

Qualifications-based selection emphasizes the importance of expertise in delivering net zero energy projects. No matter which selection method or hybrid of methods is used, qualifications should be a foundation of the process. With this selection method, the cost and fees are typically negotiated. This selection method is commonplace in the industry for architects

Relationship-Based Selection

Advantages

- Established relationships foster trust and team alignment.
- Trust-based relationships can improve risk management.
- Improved risk management can help control costs.

Disadvantages

- Lacks cost competition.
- Does not emphasize team qualifications.

and the design team, but it can also be used to select the entire delivery team.

Look for professionals who have experience with an integrated process and the appropriate level of technical expertise. A few key technical roles and characteristics to specify include the following: a creative and innovative mechanical engineer, a highly experienced energy and daylight modeler, an architect who is familiar with passive design strategies and systems integration, and a contractor who is experienced in developing quality cost models during conceptual design.

Qualifications-Based Selection

Advantages

- Useful when the project budget, schedule, and other elements of project definition have not been fully defined by the owner.
- An experienced team will avoid the learning curve for net zero energy delivery.

Disadvantages

- Lacks cost competition, but in a design-build scenario a portion of the work can be competitively bid.
- May be difficult to find teams with net zero energy experience.

Price-Based Selection

Price-based selection is typically analogous to low-bid selection. Selecting a project delivery team for a net zero energy project based on low bid or only on price is ill-advised. Low price may be an appropriate way to buy a commodity item, but a net zero energy building, and the services required to deliver it, are highly specialized—a far cry from a commodity purchase.

Price-Based Selection

Advantages

- Cost competition.
- Can pre-qualify bidders.

Disadvantages

- Assumes a "perfect" set of bidding or bridging documents.
- Initial low price often eroded by change orders.
- The bidder is in no position to buy into the owner's project objectives.
- Can create adversarial relationships rather than fostering trust or building team alignment.

Value-Based Selection

Value-based selection is a hybrid solution that attempts to balance cost, qualifications, relationships, and any other factors important to the building owner into an expression of best value. One common method for making a more comprehensive value-based selection is to set a fixed cost and ask competitors to provide solutions that provide the greatest value for that fixed cost in terms of scope, schedule, quality, and performance.

Value-Based Selection

Advantages

- The evaluation factors, such as cost, schedule, and qualifications, can be weighted based on the priority they hold for the owner.
- Can be cost competitive.
- Opportunity to optimize project performance and scope with the lowest life-cycle cost.

Disadvantages

- Owner needs to set clear criteria for team selection.
- Often involves a competition, which has its own advantages and disadvantages. (See the discussion on competitions in the upcoming "Project Team Selection Tools" section.)

Project Team Selection Tools

REQUEST FOR QUALIFICATIONS

A request for qualifications, or RFQ, is a tool used to solicit project delivery teams and develop a shortlist based on their qualifications related to an owner's project needs and requirements. This is a very useful process for procuring a net zero energy building because it is a straightforward way of including a qualifications-based selection method in the overall process. The RFQ is also one of the first announcements owners make about their projects to the architecture, engineering, and construction (AEC) marketplace. It also offers a great opportunity to express the objective of a net zero energy project, because it will attract many high-quality firms that actively seek clients that align with their goal for high-performance design and construction.

RFQ Guidelines for Net Zero Energy Projects

- Express the objective of a net zero energy building.
- Express the intended selection process and delivery method and its purpose of selecting an integrated delivery team.
- Look for project experience related to the successful delivery of net zero energy buildings and other high-performance projects.
- Look for a team whose members have established trust-based relationships.
- Look for a team whose members have experience working in a highly integrated fashion and with performance-based objectives.
- Look for a holistic team, with key expertise in design and construction around energy design.
- Look for demonstrated design and industry leadership and the capacity to innovate.

REQUEST FOR PROPOSALS

A request for proposal, or RFP, is perhaps the most widely used tool in procuring a building project; it is issued for all types of delivery methods and selection processes. The RFP is a key document in properly setting up the delivery process for a net zero energy building. The RFP and the RFQ, if used, combine to establish the selection process, the intended contractual relationship of design team members, the delivery method, and a well-crafted project definition. A well-written RFP for a net zero energy project will also successfully link the elements required for successful delivery, all in support of a clear performance objective.

RFP Guidelines for Net Zero Energy Projects

- Establish net zero energy as one of the key project objectives.
- Set an annual energy use target appropriate for the net zero energy objective.
- Clarify whether or not on-site renewable energy systems will be part of the RFP; in either case, consider how they will be coordinated with building design and construction.
- Provide a well-crafted project definition, one that takes into account the opportunities and challenges of net zero energy.
- If a separate RFQ is not used prior to the RFP, integrate the guidelines for RFQs stated in the previous RFQ section.
- Establish the selection process and delivery method in support of forming a trust-based, integrated delivery team, whose members are aligned with the project objectives.

INTERVIEWS AND REFERENCES

Conducting interviews and checking project and personal references are extremely commonplace phases of the selection process. Together, they comprise a good way to develop a more detailed understanding of the individual team members who will actually work on the project, the results they have achieved, and the relationships they have established on prior projects. Ultimately, it is the capabilities and mind-sets of the individual team members that make integration work for a net zero energy project.

The interview is one effective way to evaluate the individuals who will be delivering the project. The interview should allow plenty of time for meaningful dialog about the project to ascertain each team member's communication style and depth of knowledge. An innovative approach is to use a design charrette format for the interview or to include a short problem-solving exercise. This makes it possible to evaluate the team members' ability to think on their feet, collaborate, listen, facilitate, and innovate.

References are important, too; they can be used to inquire specifically about the actual energy performance of the projects that candidates have worked on. Find out whether the delivery team members have kept in touch with the owner after occupancy, to follow up on energy and building performance. Try to determine how proactive the team has been.

COMPETITIONS

Competitions can be an effective part of the process of selecting a team to deliver a net zero energy building. The downside is that they can be expensive, for both the owner and the competitors, hence should be undertaken only on projects that can support the cost. Because the owner is not present as part of the team during the competition design, a well-crafted RFP, with a clear project definition and project performance requirements and objectives, will need to be developed. In short, competitions are best suited to clients who have the resources to develop a comprehensive RFP and to projects that require highly innovative solutions.

One of the most important benefits of a competition is the innovation that emerges from the process. A very compelling project challenge, such as net zero energy, can really stimulate creativity among competitors. Competitions also give an owner the chance to use a comprehensive value-based approach to selecting a project team. Further, an owner gains unparalleled insight into the way a potential project team works and thinks, and serves as a strong indicator of the nature of the final building.

It's important to note, however, that not all competition formats are appropriate. To be effective, a competition should include delivery components, not just design. A design without cost and schedule information as part of the competition response lacks the early integration needed to ensure a successful final project. Further, a design without a cost proposal behind it amplifies the risk on the owner side.

On the other hand, providing a cost proposal with a competition-level design amplifies the risk for the project team. One way of managing risk in a competitive selection environment is for the owner to allow for a cost true-up and design development period by the winning team before final pricing is determined. This two-phase approach has a twofold benefit: It gives a project team valuable time to further develop the design and better understand the cost implications, and gives the owner a valuable period of input on the design before it is finalized. This type of two-phase approach was used to manage the competition risk for the DOE/NREL Research Support Facility project.

A competition used as the basis to select a project team should start with a qualifications-based phase, resulting in a shortlist of firms. This is critical, because many qualified teams will not invest in the effort if there is too much competition—often, no more than three total competitors. Owners should be fully aware that competitions typically require a very large investment from competing project teams, and should be prepared to pay stipends to responsive but unsuccessful competitors. Unfortunately, the lack of adequate stipends has begun to give the competition selection process a bad name, despite its many benefits.

BRIDGING DOCUMENTS

Bridging documents are a tool used to procure a design-build team, typically with a price-based selection process. An owner contracts with a separate design team to prepare a set of bridging documents, which the owner uses to solicit bids from design-builders. Bridging documents are design documents developed to a preliminary or schematic level, and articulate the owner's scope, quality, and performance requirements. The selected design-build delivery team then completes the design and construction of the project based on the bridging documents.

Competition Guidelines for Net Zero Energy Projects

- Conduct a competition that requires an integrated delivery response, not just a design response. The resulting delivery method should be integrated, such as design-build or integrated project delivery.
- Conduct a competition with a qualifications-based shortlist of no more three competitors.
- Provide a well-crafted performance-based RFP that serves to speak for the owner during the competition phase, and allows for innovative rather than prescribed solutions.
- Allow for a design and cost true-up period after the selection of the project team, to reduce both owner and project team risk.
- Budget for a reasonable stipend to unsuccessful competitors.

Bridging documents are normally an inappropriate tool for the procurement of a net zero energy building. They work against the goal of an integrated delivery process, because the design concept is developed without input from the delivery team, and does not benefit from early, integrated cost control. This prevents buy-in from and deeper understanding on the part of the delivery team. While the initial development of the bridging documents can be focused on performance, the documents themselves ultimately become prescriptive. Prescriptive measures will limit innovation and integration on the delivery team side. Further, the bridging documents may not even prescribe the best solution, which may be realized only through a truly integrated delivery process.

This gap in integration can be a difficult obstacle to overcome, and often leads to disputes among all parties. Further, if bridging documents are used in a low-bid scenario, all of the issues of low-bid pricing can compound the challenges of delivery and amplify problems related to any inconsistencies or omissions in the bridging documents.

Despite their many disadvantages, bridging documents can be used in an innovative manner. In this case, a small group of short-listed, qualified design-build competitors bid a set of bridging documents but are required to include the cost of the on-site renewable energy systems for a net zero energy project. This interesting twist tips the scale enough to incentivize bidders to invest in energy efficiency and lowest life-cycle energy cost. It is typically less expensive to save energy through energy-efficient design than it is to purchase a renewable energy system to generate the same amount of energy. Therefore, a team that makes an investment in energy efficiency will need to purchase a smaller renewable energy system, giving it a distinct competitive advantage in providing a low-cost bid. While this innovative low-bid approach can drive cost innovations around a net zero energy solution, it does carry with it many of the disadvantages of bridging documents and a low-bid process.

DELIVERY METHODS

The building industry has several methods and method hybrids available for procuring and delivering buildings. They are not all created equal, however, and have a variety of advantages and disadvantages for delivering a net zero energy building. Fortunately, a positive trend has been growing toward more integrated and performance-oriented delivery methods and contractual relationships.

The contractual relationships that bind all members of the project team influence the entire process of delivering a net zero energy project. And because a net zero energy project has some unique requirements in regard to its delivery method, selecting the appropriate one, in concert with establishing contractual relationships, is a key to success. As a general rule, procurement and delivery methods that reward performance, promote a fully integrated process, and create alignment among all project partners are highly desirable for net zero energy buildings.

The delivery mechanism also establishes the contractual requirements related to the project definition, such as scope, cost, schedule, quality, and performance. This is essential, too, because it is important on a net zero energy project to leverage contract language and delivery method to establish performance requirements. Including performance requirements in the contract will elevate their priority level, to ensure they are met along with cost and schedule requirements. This prioritization also begins the process of aligning the team members around the objective. An appropriate risk management and reward structure should accompany the inclusion of performance objectives in a contract.

Establishing an incentive award fee based on meeting performance requirements is another powerful tool. A bonus structure can be very flexible, and be based on meeting a final objective, multiple objectives, milestones, or even on the percent improvement over a baseline performance level. An incentive award fee can be a powerful motivator for the delivery team, and potentially offset the risk related to performance requirements.

Design-Bid-Build

The design-bid-build delivery method is characterized by separate contracts between the owner and architect, and the owner and the general contractor. This delivery method begins with the relationship of the owner and the architect and design team. The design is developed through a complete set of construction documents, which are used to establish the contractual relationship between the owner and the general contractor.

Design-bid-build is the traditional delivery method within the building industry; its purpose is to exploit the competitive nature of the market to determine the lowest price for a given project scope. With the late arrival of the general contractor, and thus the late arrival of the actual cost, this delivery method has institutionalized the fragmented process that still plagues the industry, often leading to adversarial relationships between key team members.

The use of design-bid-build raises many daunting challenges for net zero energy projects. Even when the design team follows an integrated design process with front-loaded design, the absence of the general contractor makes full delivery integration impossible. An enormous amount of design information and design decisions have to be accumulated by the team over many months, leading to the completion of construction documents. With a net zero energy building, these design decisions are linked to achieving the performance objective, making the whole building an integrated system. However, all the decisions and development lack the cost, schedule, and constructability inputs from the entity that will be building the project.

The general contractor is typically given a few short weeks to evaluate and understand the design, which may represent as much as a year of embedded design information and complex interactions. Further, it can be extremely challenging to assign an accurate cost to a net zero energy building during a short bidding process. This can deter value, because without the time to understand and buy into a unique or innovative solution, there can be a lot of uncertainty regarding actual cost. One of the options for a contractor or subcontractor to mitigate risk is to add contingency to a bid. Another option is to find opportunities for change orders after the project is awarded. Typically, the result is a combination of the two, and in any case, is not an effective way to manage risks and integrate cost implications into innovative solutions.

Design-build-bid is clearly a delivery method that has the potential to undermine innovation and undercut the performance potential of a project. One of the key strategies to ensure the project delivery team meets performance objectives is through the inclusion of performance requirements in the contract language. The issue with design-bid-build is the separation by contract of the delivery portions of the project: the design and the construction. This makes the inclusion of performance requirements problematic. How can the project design team be obligated to meet performance requirements if they are not integrated into the construction process; and how can the project construction team be obligated to meet performance requirements if they are not integrated into the design process? This creates a situation where it is difficult to centrally manage the performance requirement risks, and makes it all too easy to point fingers when performance objectives are not met.

Construction Management

The role of the construction manager is to provide construction management guidance to the owner throughout the entire process. This is particularly important during the design phases. Remember that one of the main disadvantages of the traditional design-bid-build method is the lack of integration of construction expertise during the design.

There are two roles a construction manager can play: *adviser* and *general contractor*.

- **Construction manager as adviser:** The construction manager as adviser delivery method is characterized by three separate contracts with the owner: owner-architect, owner-general contractor, and owner-construction manager/adviser.
- **Construction manager as general contractor (GMGC):** The construction manager as general contractor delivery method is characterized by two separate contracts with the owner: owner-architect and owner-construction manager/general contractor.

The construction manager as adviser, also known as *construction manager at-fee*, is hired solely in an advisory capacity. The construction manager as adviser method can also work in conjunction with other delivery methods, to provide continuity and construction guidance throughout the process. Unfortunately, it has several liabilities for net zero energy buildings and other high-performance buildings. A construction manager as adviser does not share the risk experienced by the rest of the team, a discrepancy that can undermine the risk management needed in a performance-oriented integrated delivery process. In addition, since the construction manager as adviser is not the entity contracted to build the project, the general contractor has limited opportunity for early integration into the project team.

The CMGC is also known as *construction manager at-risk*. In this case, the construction manager not only serves as a construction management adviser, but is also responsible for the construction of the building. CMGCs are usually selected based on qualifications, relationships, and/or a competitive proposal outlining their fees. The construction can be completed using a variety of pricing mechanisms, including fixed price, unit pricing, cost-plus-fee, and guaranteed maximum price. This delivery method may also include a variety of built-in incentives, such as saving and cost-sharing mechanisms to help manage cost and performance risks. Ultimately, the construction cost is negotiated, but a good deal of bidding may be used to obtain subcontractor pricing. In this case, care must be taken to ensure that key subcontractors are integrated into the process, and not selected based solely on price. The key is to separate out scope that can benefit from commodity pricing for bidding purposes, and develop cost in a negotiated fashion for the highly integrated scope of the building project.

The clear advantage of the CMGC delivery method for net zero energy projects is having an integrated constructor throughout the entire delivery process. In addition, the determination of construction costs can be managed using an integrated approach, which can add value and lower risks. One challenge to the CMGC delivery approach is that there are separate contracts for the design team and the construction team. This raises some of the same issues inherent in the design-bid-build structure—in particular, embedding performance requirements into the contract, and the adversarial relationships that can develop if things go wrong.

Design-Build

The design-build delivery method is characterized by a single contract for the design and construction of the project. The relationship between the architect and contractor is, therefore, integrated and contractually established in this delivery method.

A single contract between the owner and the design-build team does not mean there is only one way to organize the design-build entity; it may, in fact, be structured in a variety of ways. Often, a design-build entity is led by one of the design-build partners, such as the designer or builder. In some cases, a developer leads it. The lead firm holds a prime contract with the owner, while relationships with other team members are established in the form of subcontracts under the main prime contract. The prime contractor, thus, is ultimately responsible for the full delivery of the project; and the general contractor typically fills the lead role because of the GC's bonding capacity and experience managing construction and cost risks. However, designer-led design-build projects also can be successful, particularly when design, quality, and performance are priorities.

The design-build entity may also be structured under a joint venture or similar business structure, where the design team and construction team create a new separate entity that enters into a contract with the owner. The joint venture arrangement allows for more equity between delivery partners, which can help balance between the different strengths of the members.

Design-build has many of the traits necessary to deliver a successful net zero energy project. The opportunity exists for true integration, early cost control, front-loading of the design process, and effective risk management. Design-build is not, however, necessarily performance oriented by default. In fact, the typical contractor-led design-build delivery can be very effective at cost and schedule control, with great track records of "being on time and on budget." A new breed of design-build, called *performance-based design-build*, is currently evolving in the market.

PERFORMANCE-BASED DESIGN-BUILD

The addition of performance objectives, performance specifications, and performance-based contract language changes the dynamic of the typical design-build delivery process. Design-build is well suited to this language because of the single contract with the owner and the single point of responsibility for delivery. Design-build teams can leverage the highly integrative structure of this delivery method to create a project-centered team that is aligned with the net zero energy objective and optimizes the talent and resources of the team to meet the objective.

Performance-based contracts may give building owners a sense that they will lose control over the project. In fact, the owner does give control to the delivery team, under specific conditions, to deliver a building that meets all of the owner's project objectives. The owner defines what the building will do, not how it will do it or what it will look like. Setting performance-based objectives, performance specifications, and performance-based incentives is critical for promoting integration and innovation within the delivery team, giving them freedom to optimize the building around the performance objectives. The owner can manage the risks associated with the transfer of control to the team by requiring documentation from the delivery team for review and approval at key milestones that substantiates that all objectives and performance specifications are being met.

Integrated Project Delivery

The integrated project delivery (IPD) method is characterized by the creation of a single organization made up of the primary project team members whose purpose is to deliver the project as diagrammed in Figure 2.6. This organization can be established in a number of ways, including a single multiparty agreement between primary team members, or the establishment of a temporary, legal, single-purpose entity composed of the same team members.

IPD is a new type of contractual mechanism that promotes an integrated delivery process.

This approach is distinct from other delivery methods in that it joins the building owner with the other primary team members into a single entity around the successful delivery of a project. This increases the involvement of the owner in the process and results in a less hierarchical organization than other delivery methods. IPD creates a temporary enterprise that aligns the objectives, compensation, and processes of all team members around a business model for the delivery process for the building. It minimizes inefficiencies and waste in the process and allows for effective management of risks and contingencies, all of which can have tremendous cost-saving benefits.

The clear intent of IPD is to restructure the delivery process and contractual relationships to promote improved integrated working methods and higher-performing buildings. With it comes a culture that nurtures innovation and collaboration—both essential traits in a successful integrated process. However, it is still a very new and largely untested legal framework. As IPD methods evolve as the building industry embraces higher levels of integration and building performance, they are likely to be preferred in the future. Simply put, IPD seems ideal for the delivery of net zero energy buildings and other high-performing buildings.

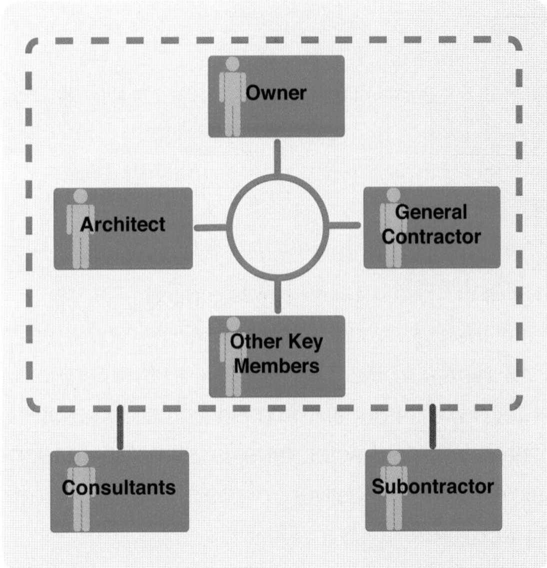

■ **FIGURE 2.6** Integrated Project Delivery.

RISKS AND REWARDS

Building projects are very complex endeavors with many inherent risks. Wherever there is uncertainty, there is risk; and there are many levels and types of risks. Some of the most serious revolve around life safety, construction safety, building defects, and building failures. These risks are present for net zero energy buildings as well, but are the not the focus of this section. In addition, net zero energy buildings do have an impact on such business risks as cost and schedule overruns. At the same time net zero energy buildings can alter the risk factors for a project, they also represent an opportunity for enhanced risk management, which can lead to lower costs and higher profits.

Risks can be opportunities. The opportunity for rewards comes with a certain degree of risk; and, often, the greater the risk, the greater the reward. The ability to take strategic risks and manage them is the key to success for a project and for all team members.

Risk and Net Zero Energy Projects

PERFORMANCE AND RISK

Net zero energy projects add a notable new performance risk to a building project. Does the building achieve its goal of net zero energy in actual operation? If not, what are the consequences to the owner? Operating and energy costs are a significant owner issue for the life of the building. The conventional, nonintegrated delivery process that was effective at managing the risks of cost and schedule largely leaves the risk of building performance unaddressed. Traditionally, performance risk has never been properly identified, transferred, and managed. The building owner has been bearing much of the risk related to performance, with little ability to mitigate it. A net zero energy building is not possible without managing performance risk, which is why the use of integrated project delivery methods, contracts, and performance-based incentives plays such a critical role.

INNOVATION AND RISK

Part of the inherent risk of net zero energy buildings is the objective itself. As noted, net zero energy buildings are relatively new, and few projects have been completed, meaning there is not a significant number of industry precedents. Trying something new almost always increases risk. There is risk associated with innovation, yet innovation is a vital part of a net zero energy delivery process. It often leads to the integration of a new idea, technology, or product application in order to achieve a higher-performance outcome or add project value. New and untested applications also present higher risks, compared to common, well-established applications. Innovation, as well, requires an iterative, high-effort design process, which can lead to business risks on the part of the delivery team, especially if design fees are not equitable to the true scope of work. In sum, innovation plays a vital role in delivering high-performing projects, such as net zero energy buildings, and should not be readily dismissed because of the risks involved. Conversely, innovation should not be approached capriciously, but undertaken in an interdisciplinary way that actively identifies and manages the risks associated with it.

COST, SCHEDULE, AND RISK

Net zero energy buildings also add pressure to budgets and schedules, which increase cost and schedule risks. A high-performance building often requires high-quality systems and/or additional design time and effort. If these costs and schedule impacts are not managed in an integrated way, they can result in potential cost or schedule overruns. Schedule and cost can also be positively impacted by two traits common to integrated delivery methods, and which go hand in hand with net zero energy projects. One, integrated delivery, allows for the continuous overlapping of design and construction activities, which can reduce overall project time. Because of this advantage, integrated delivery is often used on fast-track-type project schedules and to help manage scheduling risks. Two, early involvement of the contractor offers the owner the advantage of an early price commitment by the delivery team. This is one of the largest risks the delivery team will take on. The owner will naturally want to establish the project cost contractually as early as possible. This transfers the risk of cost overruns to the delivery team, who are managing the many decisions that impact final cost. The delivery team would significantly reduce their risk by providing a contract price as late as possible, when they will have much more accurate and complete project information in regard to price. There is no simple answer to this important risk transfer, but it always requires communication, trust, and an appropriate balance between owner and delivery team risks.

Risk Management Process

RISKS AND INTEGRATED DELIVERY

An integrated delivery team, particularly with an involved owner, offers unique opportunities to identify and manage risks, because of the enhanced levels of communication and trust building that occur within the team. Creating a culture of active risk management is certainly a best practice for integrated delivery teams pursuing a net zero energy objective. Whereas the integrated delivery process may seem to multiply risks, it in fact consolidates the risks that had been fragmented and distributed across the delivery team. In this way, IPD makes it easier to identify and quantify the risks that were already there, while also giving the team an effective way to manage them in an integrated way.

Risks, as noted earlier, are often manifested in the form of contingencies. Contingencies take many forms, but cost contingencies are of primary interest because they have the most influence on project cost. Often these contingencies will unintentionally overlap and compound where multiple team members interface over a solution or project scope. While some risks warrant a contingency as part of the management strategy, many result in additional contingencies simply because the team lacked the communication and integration required to manage them in a more direct and open manner. Integrated delivery and an open, trust-based culture can leverage risk management and serve as an effective cost management tool by eliminating unnecessary cost contingencies.

RISK IDENTIFICATION

The main project risks associated with cost, schedule, and performance are transferred to the delivery team through the contractual relationship with the owner. The delivery team is in a better tactical position than the owner to identify and manage these risks. This is the first step in an integrated risk management process. It allows the entire team to fully assess the complete risk picture of the project and make the fundamental decisions about and commitments to delivery in regard to the owner's cost, schedule, and performance requirements. The next step is for the delivery team to understand how the contractual risks result in unique risk factors across the team and project.

Detailed risk identification and quantification has an important role at the very beginning of a project, and should be part of the team's initial partnering efforts and early charrettes. Early risk identification does not typically happen without intention. It may even warrant special team workshops devoted to risk identification and management. It is extremely powerful to have a team share their concerns, fears, and perspectives regarding project risks. Doing so rapidly builds trust and cooperation across the team. It may also be useful to revisit risk across the team as the project develops, and the strategies, systems, and technologies to be utilized in the project are identified, as they may introduce new risks to the project. An unidentified and unmanaged risk is the greatest risk of all.

RISK MANAGEMENT

The risk management process moves from identifying and quantifying the project risks to transferring and sharing risks across the team. Most risks are not owned by a single team member; they are most effectively managed when shared appropriately. The transfer of risks should come with the authority to manage them and with the support of an integrated and trust-based team culture.

Risk transfers and responsibility assignments must be accompanied by an appropriate reward for successful risk management. Of course, the primary benefit of managing risk is the avoidance of penalties or additional costs. Negative consequences, too, are powerful motivators, but positive reinforcement through shared rewards can be even more motivational.

Net zero energy projects are inherently more complex than conventional, nonperformance-based projects, making the engagement of appropriate legal and insurance advisers essential. This book is by no means intended to offer such legal or insurance advice. The intricacies of performance-based contracts require customized and high-level legal and insurance expertise. And, as with all aspects of the innovative process for achieving net zero energy buildings, it is critical to find legal and insurance professionals who also take an innovative approach to their work and understand the power of the integrated delivery process to effectively manage risk.

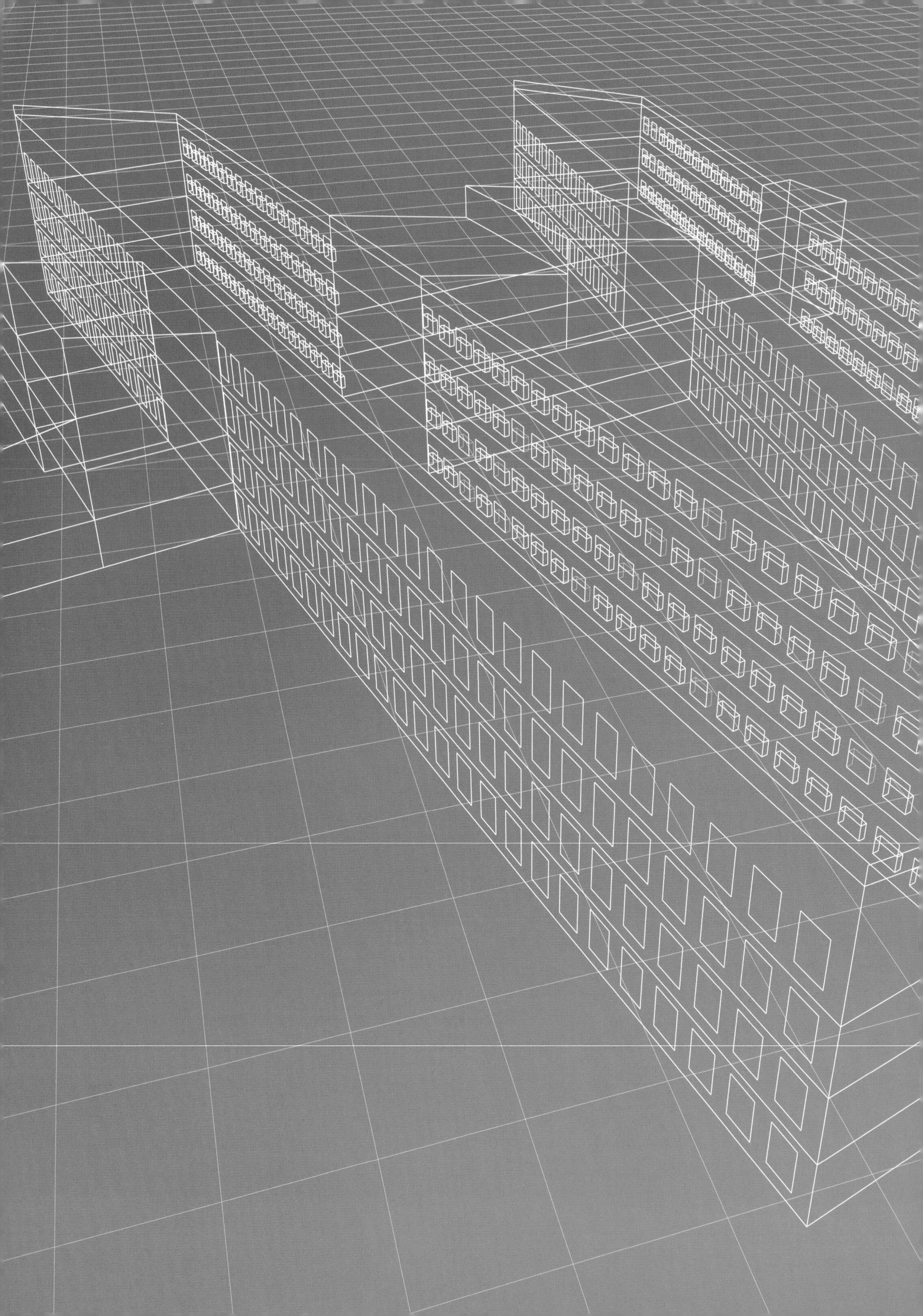

CHAPTER 3 INTEGRATED PROCESS

INTEGRATED DELIVERY AND MANAGEMENT

Integrated Delivery

A delivery team should follow a highly integrated process, to ensure successful delivery of a net zero energy project. The integrated process is becoming more widely understood and adopted throughout the industry, and there are a number of good resources dedicated to it. This chapter focuses on the important and/or unique aspects of this process as it relates to net zero energy buildings. Where Chapter 2 emphasized the necessary contractual foundations, and focused on the project conception, procurement, and delivery process of a net zero energy building from the owner's point of view, this chapter examines the process from the delivery team's perspective.

The energy objective is central to the integrated process, because it defines one of the owner's primary performance objectives and becomes a critical and driving force for the project delivery team. The delivery team must prioritize performance at a level equal to cost, schedule, and quality. This is not a common approach, which is why it distinguishes a truly integrated process. Prioritizing it in this way also impacts project management and influences team culture, which must align around achieving net zero energy.

An integrated process can be difficult to define because there are many different shades of it, and most teams practice a blend of integrated and traditional elements within their process. An integrated process does, however, mark a distinct move away from the traditional fragmented design and construction processes. This chapter discusses core elements of the integrated process, which is characterized by a relentless project-centered focus and is conducted by a team built on trust, collaboration, transparency, equity, and effective leadership. An integrated process is necessary for a net zero energy building because the building solution itself must be highly integrated to achieve such a high level of performance.

The Integrated Delivery Team

PROJECT-CENTERED TEAMS

The team is organized around the contractual obligations set forth by the owner. The various delivery models discussed in Chapter 2 define the basic organizational structure of the core team and influence the contractual relationships among all additional partners. These contracts should maintain the same level of focus on integrated project delivery as the prime contract, to ensure that the net zero energy objective (including risks and rewards) is clearly conveyed to the entire team network. Taking cues from the newest delivery methods, focused on integrated project delivery, it is clear that a project-centered team organization has many notable advantages in delivering a net zero energy project.

Project teams that are centered on a clearly defined objective are far more likely to be successful taking an integrated project delivery approach rather than a conventional one. Because net zero energy is such a significant and challenging project objective, it can serve as a powerful catalyst for team integration; this means that the commitment to net zero energy has an influential role in the overall success of a project team.

There is some hierarchy in a project-centered team, based on contractual relationships, but it is a mistake to assume that contractual lines drawn on an organization chart also represent the lines of communication and level of decision-making authority for a project-centered team. In practice, project-centered team structures tend to have a flatter hierarchy, and are more flexible and resilient than conventional team structures. The siloed and hierarchal structure of a conventional team, as diagrammed in Figure 3.1, results in a fragmented view of the project, in which team members have their own perspective of the project and what defines success for the project. A collective definition of the project is a project-centered structure, as diagrammed in Figure 3.2. The project-centered team tends to be more self-managed, and operates with greater autonomy from the "parent" firms

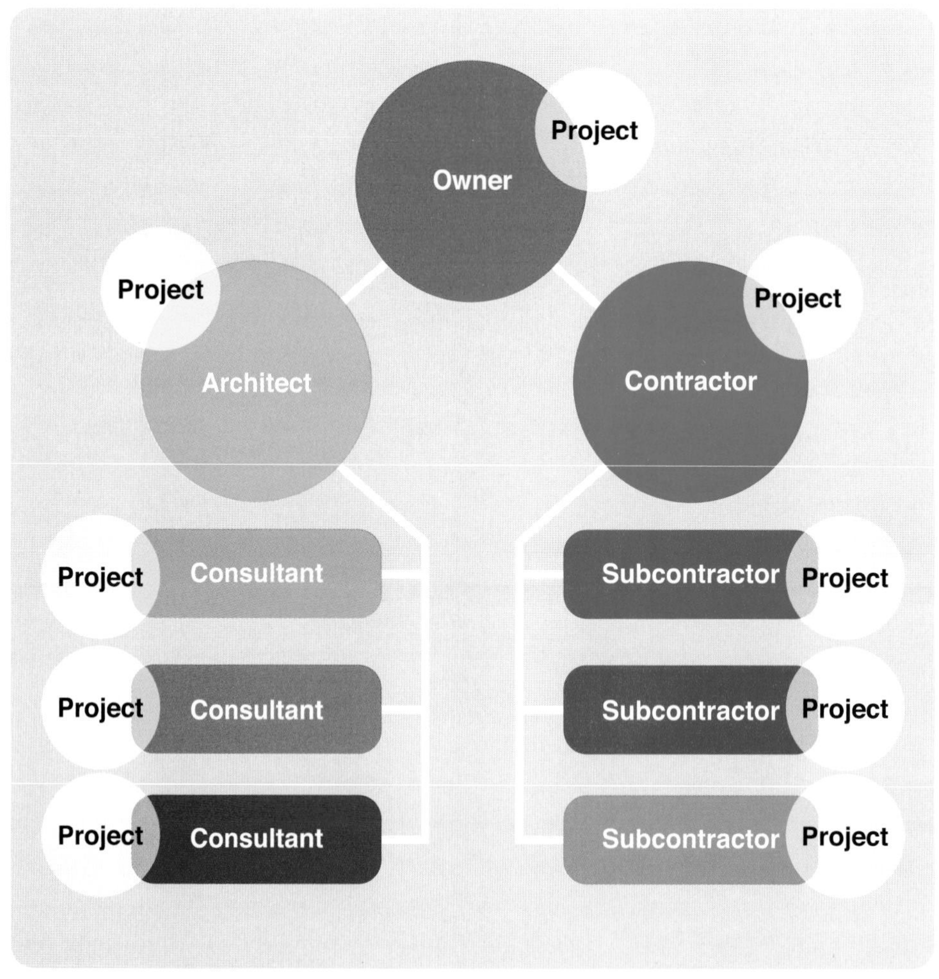

■ **FIGURE 3.1** Conventional Project Team Organization.

overseeing the team. One way to visualize a project-centered team is as a network structure centered on the project itself. The goal is to keep everyone connected rather than siloed, clearly define roles, and encourage active collaboration, to keep the team effective.

ALIGNING THE TEAM

Part of assembling a well-functioning project-centered team is aligning its members with the net zero energy objective. All team members come to a project with their own unique agendas regarding their work. You can imagine how difficult it would be to achieve high-level objectives if everyone on the team were pursuing their own agendas; yet this is precisely what often happens on a conventional building project.

Although agendas will vary according to individual team members and companies, they all stem from similar roots—purpose and mission, risk avoidance, and reward systems. Perhaps an architect's agenda is aesthetics, propelled by a desire to create a strong portfolio or gain recognition from peers, or simply by a passion for his or her craft. A contractor's agenda might be motivated by cost control, driven by the responsibility to meet profit and financial goals, keep the project under budget and the client happy, or manage risks and their deep cost implications. Consider the predicament in which we in the industry put engineers. Often, the reward system for an engineer is based on the construction cost of the system being designed. This can lead to an agenda that runs counter to a cost-effective,

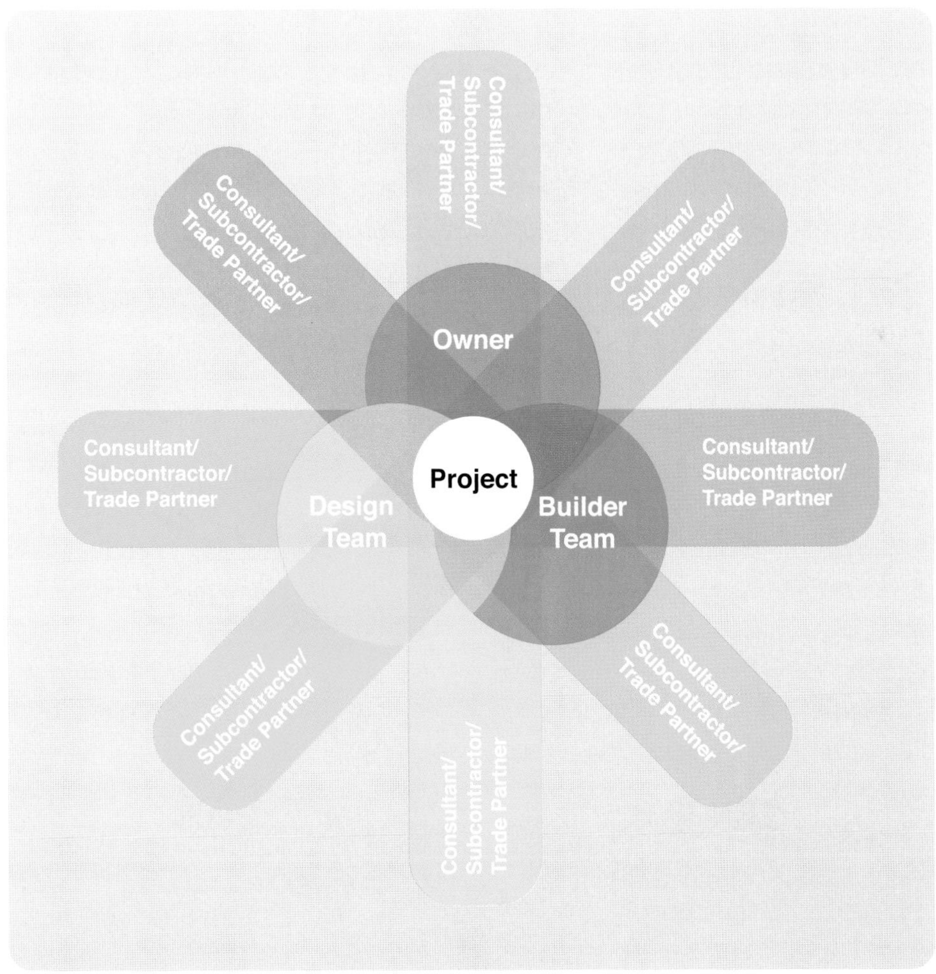

■ **FIGURE 3.2** Project-Centered Team Organization.

high-performance building because it rewards larger, rather than right-sized, systems.

The goal of aligning team members is not to eliminate agendas; that is impractical, if not impossible. Rather, the purpose is to add common objectives to everyone's agenda. Imagine a team where the designer's agenda includes aesthetics driven by energy and passive architectural solutions. Or a team where the contractor's agenda includes delivering net zero energy performance within the construction budget. Is it feasible to reward the team's mechanical engineer for high-performance and right-sized HVAC systems without the inequitable risks?

Modifying risk and reward factors can bring out positive agendas. (Managing risks and utilizing reward incentives were presented in Chapter 2 as essential elements of integrated design and cost control.) It is also a powerful way to create alignment across a delivery team. Often, the resistance to a net zero energy objective is rooted in uncertainty or risk. Once the risk has been identified and managed as a team, those barriers begin to fall down. In addition, nothing will align a team like an incentive reward that is shared by the team for meeting performance objectives.

Creating a positive team environment, where integrative and collaborative team behavior is the norm, is a function of many variables, including trust, the fluid sharing of information, and exemplary project leadership. One solution to developing trust and an integrated working relationship within the team is through a process called *partnering*. This is a facilitated process that gains alignment around the common goals of the project and marks the beginning of open communication among all members. The partnering process typically involves holding a partnering workshop at the outset of the project, followed by strategically timed check-ins with the team and update meetings to keep the partnering agreement on track. Partnering and other types of team-building exercises and workshops are extremely useful for net zero energy projects. As noted, the net zero energy objective is challenging, requiring an integrated solution, one that requires the best communication, risk management, and goal alignment tools the owner and project delivery team can utilize.

Trust is integral to the leadership within the team and the decision-making process the team follows. Team leaders need to be the strongest proponents of the net zero energy objective, and model integrated behavior for the entire team. On a trust-based team, it is important for leaders to develop and foster relationships, and avoid micromanaging tasks. The ideal decision-making process is a collective one, involving the team members who are stakeholders in the decision. Leadership lays the foundation for collective decision-making processes, as opposed to being the decision-making point at the top. It is critical that leadership create transparency across the team—transparency into project finances, risks, agendas, communication, and the decision-making process.

Managing the Energy Objective

Managing a project with a net zero energy objective means a balance must be maintained between the high-priority objectives: cost, schedule, quality, and performance. All project decisions require unique trade-offs, involving negative, neutral, and, ideally, positive impacts on these four objectives. A solid decision-making process can be a powerful tool for effectively managing multiple project objectives. Project management should also support innovation within the team, and encourage the development of solutions that address multiple objectives at once.

Each objective—cost, schedule, quality, and performance—has its own process and model for evaluating project decisions. The primary evaluation process for energy performance uses the energy model, in conjunction with all supporting analysis and modeling. Keep in mind, however, that net zero energy performance as an objective does have an impact on the typical project controls of cost, schedule, and quality. It is not adequate to consider these controls as isolated management tools; they need to be integrated as tools for managing multiple objectives, and in doing so, can yield improvements in cost, schedule, and quality control.

The traditional project delivery process is rife with examples of evaluations made too late for effective decision making and optimization of objectives. For one: Completing the first energy model at the end of construction documents, to document the building energy performance for LEED, offers little value to the design process or to the effort of balancing cost with energy performance. Another classic example is the design-bid-build process, which establishes the true construction cost and schedule of the project after the design is complete and all the quality and performance related decisions have been made.

Quality Control

Quality control during the delivery process reduces costly and time-consuming errors and can lead to better building performance. Several quality control activities that are important to meeting a net zero energy objective can be added to a project's quality control program.

Often, during design and after documentation, plans and drawings are reviewed for quality control, to check for completeness, accuracy, and coordination. This review should also include a check of the energy-related features of the project and include a review of the energy model at key project milestones. The energy quality control activity should compare building envelope design, mechanical, and electrical systems to the written basis of design statement and the project's current energy model report. The review of the building envelope should evaluate the potential for thermal bridging in exterior assemblies, as well as identify possible solutions.

In a fully commissioned project, the commissioning agent offers a valuable independent review of the drawings and specifications. This will certainly facilitate the fundamental commissioning of the building during construction. The commissioning agent should be a representative of the building owner, and independent of the delivery team. The commissioning process is an important part of the quality assurance for a project. It is discussed in Chapter 10.

Quality control for energy performance during construction is not just the commissioning agent's responsibility. Each trade needs to integrate energy-related quality control into their work. General contractors, with their broader understanding of the energy design intent, should provide coordination and oversight of energy issues within their project quality control plan. Details matter for properly performing systems and assemblies.

Cost Control

Net zero energy projects may require unique and innovative solutions to meet challenging objectives. Unfortunately, such solutions can come at a higher cost if not effectively managed. The main driver of cost for innovative solutions is the associated risk and the lack of understanding of the intended solution. Sharing project information across the team, coupled with collaborative decision making, helps reach higher levels of understanding, especially of complex or unique solutions and strategies. Dispelling misunderstandings or misconceptions, and actively managing risks, are important cost control techniques for net zero energy projects.

Integrated delivery can also lead to superior risk management, which goes a long way toward lowering costs of the project. Integrated delivery has another powerful way of lowering cost while raising performance. In their book, *Natural Capitalism: Creating the Next Industrial Revolution,* authors Paul Hawkens, Amory Lovins, and L. Hunter Lovins call this phenomenon "tunneling through the cost barrier." Several things happen in an integrated delivery process. Often, solutions solve multiple problems, and there are inherent cost savings in multifaceted solutions. However, the important breakthrough is to track investments in energy efficiency to reductions in energy load, which in turn minimize mechanical and electrical system sizes. Reducing energy load first and then right-sizing energy systems can result in significant savings. For example, investing in a better building envelope can reduce both heating and cooling loads, resulting in smaller systems. An integrated process can account for this transfer of cost between two distinct trades.

Cost control and cost modeling must begin at the outset of the design process to fully capture the benefits of integrated delivery, and must be continuous throughout the delivery phases. Project decisions cannot be made in isolation from cost, and the design decision-making process relies on rapid cost feedback from the contractor. There is certainly an art to early cost estimating, and a contractor fully integrated with the design process is in a much better position to translate early design concepts and intent into projected construction costs. Likewise, the early adoption of building information modeling (BIM) can facilitate the speed and accuracy of doing quantity takeoffs, leading to a more effective cost feedback loop during design.

Early involvement of key trade partners is yet another powerful tool to manage cost. For a net zero energy project, it is often essential to get early involvement of subcontractors whose work scopes have a significant impact on energy, such as mechanical and electrical contractors. Furthermore, it is often beneficial to engage manufacturers and suppliers directly, to help customize and optimize product offerings for a specific project. Early involvement by key trade partners can help to arrive at more accurate costs, and to lower costs by improving constructability, deepening understanding of design intent, managing risk, minimizing contingencies, and optimizing the overall system.

Schedule Control

Integrated delivery is an important tool for delivering projects on today's ever-shorter project schedules. Net zero energy buildings require a deep commitment to an integrated process, allowing both the schedule and the energy performance objectives to be managed proficiently. A key strategy for working on an integrated project schedule is to overlap activities (not just compress them all), spending time on those that add the most value, and saving time by not working on redundant or nonproductive activities. The idea of eliminating waste in the delivery process is a primary tenet of Lean Project Delivery, developed by the Lean Construction Institute (LCI). Lean Project Delivery has many synergies with integrated delivery processes, in that it focuses on eliminating waste and enhancing the value stream.

The net zero energy objective has the most dramatic effect on the design schedule. Time management during design should prioritize the value added by using a front-loaded process, to start a project in an integrated way. The beginning of an integrated design process is iterative and can test many different design solutions, but it is the initial investment in a highly integrated and well-tested design concept that can save a great deal of time and redesign effort during the rest of the project delivery phases. Early design integration is another important cost management strategy. Design strategies can be integrated early and cost-effectively, whereas the cost to make changes tends to increase as the project moves forward.

Another significant investment is in energy modeling, throughout the entire delivery process. It is important to plan in advance for the use of energy modeling, and to factor in a feedback cycle that informs the process. (The effective use of energy modeling is discussed later in this chapter.)

One of the advantages of a well-coordinated integrated project delivery process is the ability to overlap activities and minimize redundancy. The design, documentation, and construction of the various work scopes of the building can proceed according to different schedules, resulting in a shorter overall schedule while allowing certain work scopes of the project to stay in design longer (see Figure 3.3). For instance, the site, foundation, and structure of a project can start the documentation and construction phases while design of the architecture and mechanical systems is ongoing, to gain valuable design time but without adding more time to the schedule. Moreover, close coordination between the design and construction teams can minimize redundancy in the documentation phase and streamline the process of construction documents to submittal to installation.

PROJECT DELIVERY PHASES

The delivery of a net zero energy building occurs by following a sequence of work phases, beginning with the project definition and moving through a series of design and construction

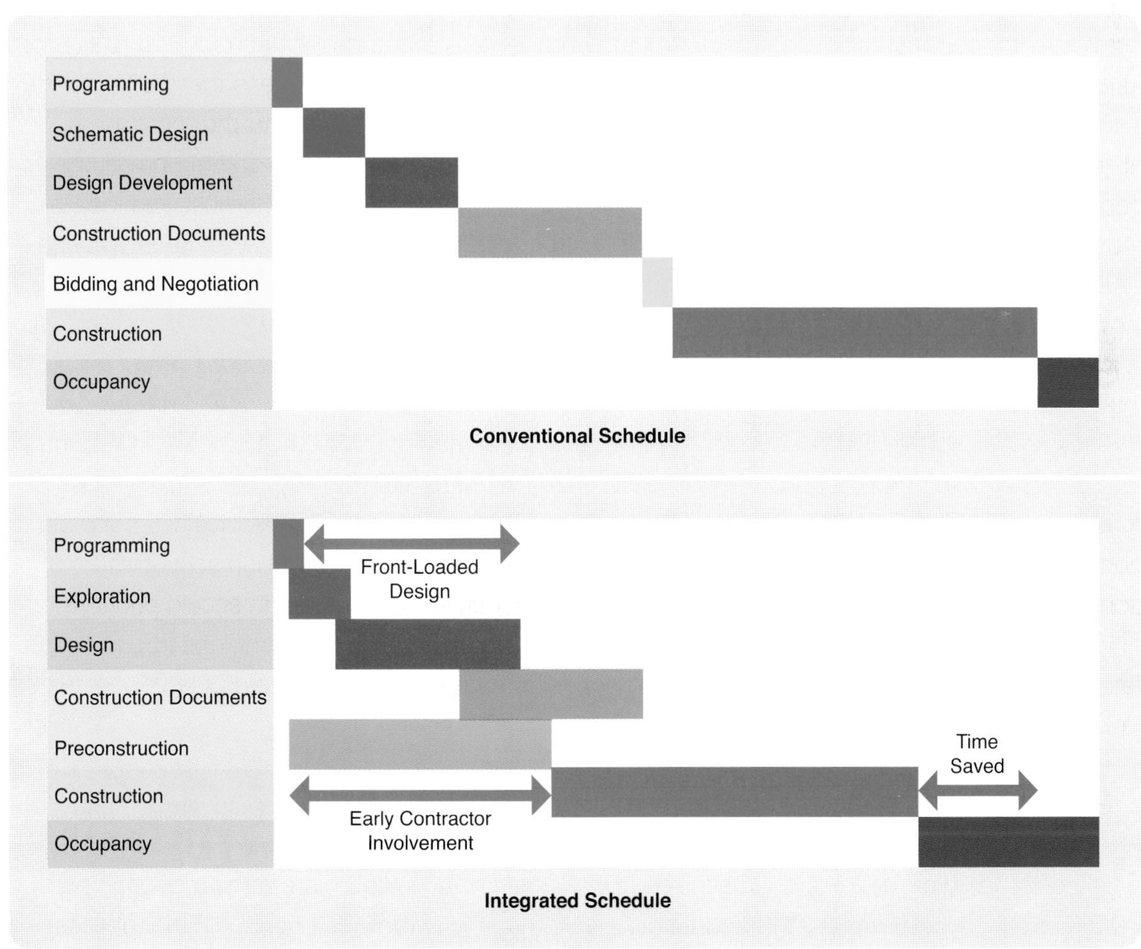

■ **FIGURE 3.3** Fast-Track Schedule through Integration.

activities, resulting in a project that operates at net zero energy on an annual basis. I reiterate that net zero energy is a very challenging project performance objective to meet. Thus, it must be considered from the very beginning and, thereafter, be a constant guide as the project is developed, delivered, and occupied. And because it is an outcome that is ultimately measured in actual operation, it is critical to include the operation and occupancy phases as part of the delivery process. More, it is important to bridge the gap that typically exists between design and construction and the actual operation of the building.

There are several models that organize project delivery into discrete phases of activity. The conventional model includes: predesign, schematic design, design development, construction documents, bidding and negotiations, and construction phases. The emerging integrated project delivery (IPD) model features a redefined and renamed set of the phases: conceptualization, criteria design, detailed design, implementation documents, agency coordination, final buyout, construction, and closeout. The phases of project delivery will also be influenced by the structure dictated in the project contracts and in the breakout of fees throughout the delivery process.

To keep things simple and flexible, and to avoid getting caught up in semantics, the following basic delivery phases will be used in this book to describe the key activities for a net zero energy project:

1. Conception
2. Exploration
3. Design
4. Construction
5. Occupancy and operation

The exploration phase may stand out on this list as new or unconventional. It is, in fact, part of design, and includes the predesign research and project setup required for a successful integrated project. Exploration is delineated as a distinct phase for the purpose of focusing on the importance of front-loading project delivery. The design phase also includes the documentation activity, rather than identifying a distinct documentation phase. Documentation, while critical, is not unique to a net zero energy building approach; the activities can often merge with construction in an integrated project delivery method. The importance of the occupancy and operation phases is emphasized in this model. In contrast to most delivery phase models, which consider the construction phase the *realization* or the closeout the *conclusion* of the delivery process, a net zero energy project treats the successful operation at net zero energy as the realization.

The delivery phases are both fluid and interconnected, resulting in activities that take place concurrently. With this in mind, the phases could be diagrammed as a circle or closed loop, where the net zero energy objective is both the start and end points, working as a feedback mechanism, influencing each other. Feedback from the entire process is then used as lessons learned, to serve as a way to improve the next building project cycle (or future building renovations) for the owner and/or delivery team. Figure 3.4 illustrates the cyclical and fluid quality of a net zero energy integrated delivery process.

Conception

A project begins when an owner decides to build to meet a specific set of needs. A net zero energy project starts when the building owner makes net zero energy a key objective for the desired building. (Chapter 2 provided detailed guidance on the project conception and definition phases, and described the procurement and integrated delivery process for net zero energy projects from the perspective of the owner.) The owner's role cannot be underestimated in terms of understanding and establishing the contractual framework for a performance-based integrated delivery process. With the negotiation and signing of the contract, the delivery team enters into an integrated process, with the purpose of meeting the many project objectives and delivering a building that operates at net zero energy over the course of its occupancy.

Exploration

To ensure a successful integrated design and delivery process, time must be taken before design begins to explore the parameters that will inform the design and delivery of the project. In particular, the net zero energy objective needs to be understood and explored by the owner and team, as it will influence the final definition, redefinition, and/or verification of the project parameters.

The exploration phase is the time to conduct project-based research, and explore a divergent range of ideas before design begins. It is also the time to ask questions that help the team develop a deeper understanding of the project. This lays the foundation for an innovative process. Although the issues studied during this phase will be varied, since the goal is to identify a holistic

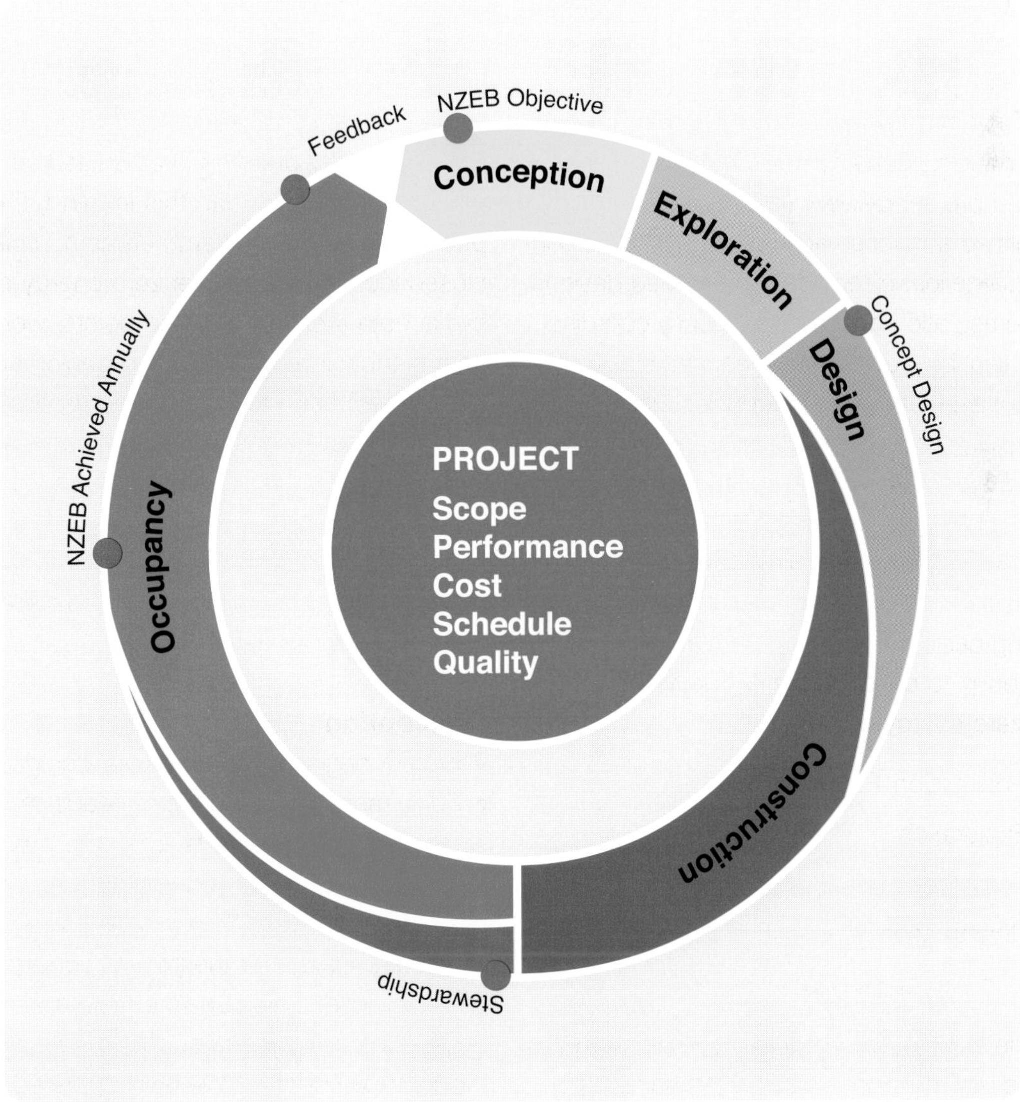

■ **FIGURE 3.4** Phases of a Net Zero Energy Integrated Delivery Process.

Key Net Zero Energy Exploration Activities

- State the net zero energy objective and clarify how it will be defined and measured. (Refer to Chapters 1 and 11.)
- Collect weather data and complete a climate analysis for the project. (Refer to Chapter 5.)
- Study the site to identify available resources and potential constraints. (Refer to Chapter 5.)
- Establish baseline energy use. (Refer to Chapter 4.)
- Establish a net zero energy use target. (Refer to Chapter 4.)
- Establish an on-site renewable energy generation target. (Refer to Chapter 4.)
- Establish likely energy end uses and energy load details based on building type, weather data file, and a simple energy model. (Refer to Chapters 3 and 4.)
- Identify and learn from relevant case studies and precedents. (Refer to Chapters 1 and 4.)
- Brainstorm potential passive design and low-energy system strategies. (Refer to Chapters 6 and 7.)
- Explore the relationship of program, building use, and occupancy with energy use and the net zero energy objective. (Refer to Chapters 2, 5, and 10.)

building solution, there are specific pieces to the energy picture that should be researched.

Design

The integrated design process emerges from the intensive and critical work done in the exploration phase. It starts with many rapid iterations and tests of multiple strategies, to learn from different design scenarios. Once the key strategies that will be used have been identified, the process synthesizes gradually, or ideas and strategies converge into an integrated whole. Highly integrative designs typically have simple, singular solutions that are used to address as many problems as possible. (The "Integrated Design Methods" section, next, provides more detailed guidance on the design phase of a net zero energy project.)

It is useful to consider the milestones in the integrated design process, starting with conceptual design. Conceptual design is the synthesis resulting from the initial design iterations and, as such, should embody the vision of the project, the various project parameters, and key integrated net zero energy strategies. A successful conceptual design can be thought of as the DNA for the project, strongly guiding its future development and evolution. Ideally, all essential net zero energy strategies and concepts are represented in the conceptual design. Although new strategies may be added to the design as it is developed, it becomes more challenging to integrate big new moves into the design as it progresses. In many ways, the conceptual design solution for a net zero project is one of the most important phases because it establishes the project's basic foundation for success as a net zero energy building.

The next step is to develop the design, whereby the various net zero energy strategies are refined through more detailed design studies, calculations, cost analyses, constructability reviews, energy modeling, and other performance simulations. This refinement process leads to a highly tuned and integrated building solution. The interim design milestones present opportunities for formal reviews and assessments on the path toward achieving the net zero energy objective. As the design develops, the amount of project information grows and becomes more detailed and complex. This is where using BIM and sharing a model and information across the team can help to make collaboration and decision making more effective.

It may be useful to view the design synthesis process as an inverted pyramid, as illustrated in Figure 3.5, first considering the widest range of options and strategies at the base and then moving downward into a convergence of strategies to reach a singular solution. Unlike the inverted pyramid of design synthesis, the decision-making process model can be drawn as an upright pyramid. For example, the flow of energy design information may start with a net zero energy objective and energy target and then move through a progressively detailed decision-making process that results in an accumulation of project energy information. It is important not to confuse the accumulation of project information with the design process itself, which needs to be focused on synthesis and convergence to achieve the best singular solution.

The next step is to document the design for construction. This step is, literally, the development of documents used to communicate the design intent for use in construction and by the contractor and all trades. The process can blur with the construction phase, as integrated delivery methods can now streamline the flow of project information from construction documents to shop drawings. Further, with an integrated team, it is possible to fully document discrete parts of the building independently, so the construction activity can happen concurrently with design. One of the most important activities during the construction documents phase of a net zero energy project is to ensure the inclusion of all of the technical details developed in the design for energy performance. It is also critical to review and resolve all exterior building assembly details for thermal bridging *before*

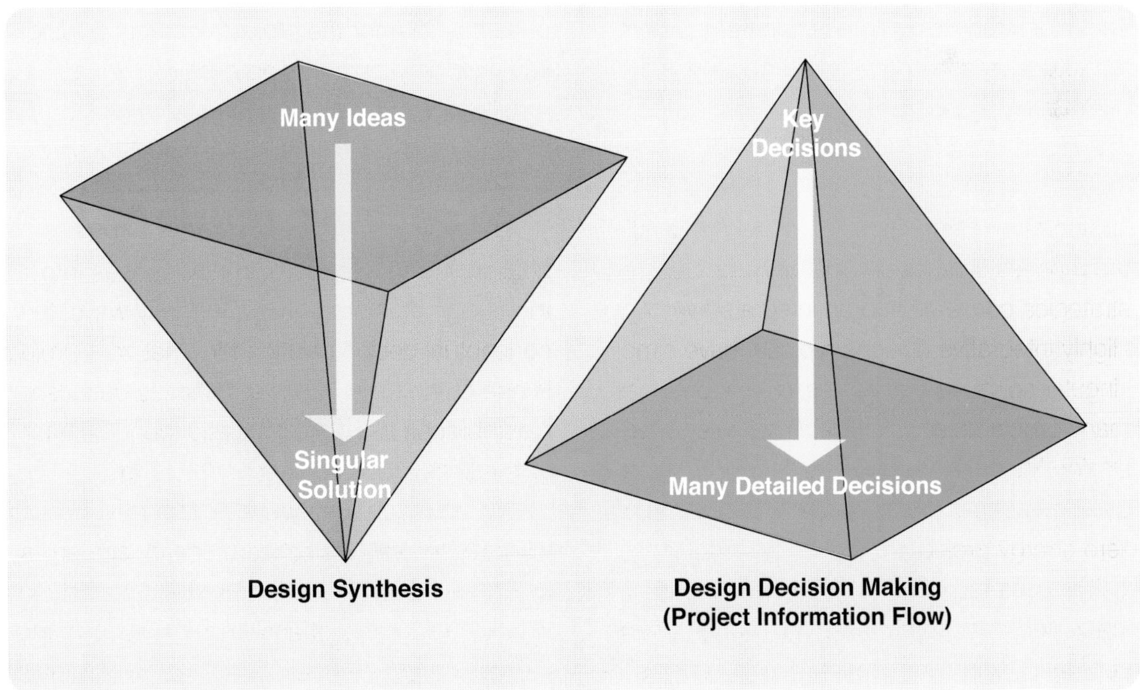

■ **FIGURE 3.5** Design and Project Information Flow.

the documents are issued for construction. The energy model should be used during this phase to assess any changes to the project's details and specifications.

Construction

A successful construction phase for a net zero energy project hinges on two factors: effective communication of project information, and a contractor fully engaged with the net zero energy objective. It follows, then, that one of the most important construction activities for a net zero energy project is the preconstruction services provided by the contractor during the exploration and design phases. The preconstruction services enable the contractor to gain a deeper understanding of the project, which aids immensely in the construction process and future communication with all trade partners. Preconstruction services are the beginning of the cost model and cost control, and can ensure constructability as well as schedule compliance.

Construction is a complex process, during which the delivery team size swells tremendously to include all of the trades and vendors that integrate into the project. Successfully maintaining the flow of project information, and ensuring it is understood by the network of subcontractors, suppliers, and manufacturers, is crucial to getting the details right and managing both risk and cost. It is important to transmit the net zero energy objective throughout the entire delivery network. Likewise, it is vital to get key trade partners—those that will have the greatest impact on the net zero energy objective—on board early and engaged in the preconstruction services. These principal partners may include mechanical, electrical, lighting systems, renewable energy systems, and building envelope systems

As with the documentation phase of design, the details are indispensable throughout the construction process. The building envelope is rife with construction details, all of which have a direct bearing on the energy performance of the building. Ensuring tight construction to minimize infiltration, proper insulation installation, and the elimination of thermal bridges are all fundamental components to producing a quality envelope. Thermographic photography can be a valuable tool for identifying thermal issues in the building envelope. An infrared camera is sensitive to infrared light, rather than visible light waves, and can produce a thermal image that uses false color mapping to depict surface temperatures, thus detecting thermal weak spots in a building envelope.

A simple and revealing story from the construction of the DOE/NREL Research Support Facility highlights the importance of craft and the dedication of every trade on the job. Paul Torcellini, principal group manager for Commercial Buildings Research at the National Renewable Energy Laboratory, was walking the job site with a group from the general contractor, Haselden Construction. Paul stopped to talk to a tradesman who was insulating a king stud at an exterior wall opening, and asked what he was working on. The tradesman, unaware that Paul was part of the ownership team for the project, began to express how important his job was and how carefully he was installing the insulation. "Energy efficiency is very important to the owner," he concluded.

It is important that all the trades and workers be committed to the net zero energy mission; meeting it then becomes a source of pride, which elevates the quality of work. The details, coordination, and integration of the various energy-related building systems are also instrumental to delivery of a net zero energy building. Extra coordination and dedicated project engineers on the side of the general contractor help facilitate quality control and the integration of complex systems.

Occupancy and Operation

The operation of the building is the context wherein a net zero energy building is measured and the objective is ultimately met. Yet most buildings experience a gap between the best of intentions in design and the actual use of the building. (Chapter 10 offers guidance on bridging that gap for net zero energy performance.) In keeping with an integrated process, there are important benefits to having the operations team and users involved early in the design, and the delivery team staying involved into postoccupancy. This planned-for continuity should be paired with a net zero energy performance plan that outlines key activities and responsibilities that help make the net zero energy objective an operational reality.

INTEGRATED DESIGN METHODS

Integrated design for net zero energy buildings is part of an evolving design approach that has industry professionals rethinking the methods and purpose of design. Through this new approach, based on innovation, they seek to derive value and purpose-driven outcomes in response to research and data-driven inputs. You could say that designing a net zero energy building requires an optimal balance of art and science. Net zero energy architecture offers an opportunity for simple and elegant design, full of purpose and meaning—to make beautiful the measured and thoughtful interaction of the building with the environment and the people who occupy it. And because the process is collaborative, rather than relying on a single source, innovation and integration begin with design leadership. Simply put, architectural professionals today need to rediscover energy and building science as a foundation for design; they need to reinvent the design process and use it as a powerful tool for the synthesis and integration of ideas from all disciplines.

The process should also embrace a holistic view of sustainable design. There are many models and methods for approaching design as an integrated and innovation-based process, several of which are discussed in this section.

Holistic Design

At the same time net zero energy buildings represent exemplary energy use, they should also be considered whole, or complete, green buildings; that means pursuing a holistic approach to sustainable design. The good news is that the integrated approach to achieving net zero energy is the same basic method for meeting a wide variety of sustainability and project objectives.

Holistic design works to optimize the three main priorities of sustainability, often defined as the *triple bottom line*: environmental, economic, and social concerns. Said another way, holistic design works to create buildings that eliminate negative impacts on the environment; more, it aims to produce buildings that are regenerative within the environment. That is, they are economically prosperous; they are healthy and beautiful places for people to live and work. Net zero energy objectives—most notably, energy use reduction—have a strong connection to all three of these concerns. Energy efficiency and renewable energy offer an important environmental benefit in terms of carbon emission reduction. The economic benefits emerge from both energy use reduction and the added market value of net zero energy buildings. More, net zero energy buildings are, typically, great "people spaces," in that they enhance human well-being and health by providing high-quality indoor environments and implementing techniques such as daylighting and natural ventilation.

Another way to think of holistic buildings is the living building model. In this holistic approach, nature is the model, and the objective of the building or community is to function as an ecosystem or part of the natural ecosystem. In the natural environment, nature's energy measure is clear—it runs on renewable energy. This seems to be a basic tenet for deeply holistic sustainability frameworks. In the late 1960s, architect Malcolm Wells developed a simple rating system to evaluate sites and buildings and compare them to wilderness. Among the points of evaluation were: "uses solar energy" and "stores solar energy," versus "wastes solar energy" and "stores no solar energy." Today, rating systems such as the Living Building Challenge, introduced by the International Living Building Institute, incorporate net zero energy as a requirement.

Systems Thinking

Systems thinking is highly valuable to the integrated design process necessary to produce a successful net zero energy project, in that it leverages the power of whole systems thinking over individual component design. Developing system flow diagrams facilitates this process. System diagrams aid designers as they explore how a whole system can be designed and optimized.

This type of thinking can be applied to any system flow of the building and site. Figure 3.6 illustrates the basic elements of a system diagram. As shown, all systems have a *stock* (energy for an energy system diagram), a *boundary* to evaluate the system, *flows* with in-flows and out-flows from the boundary conditions, *modifiers*, and *feedback loops*.

Generally, it is appropriate to define the boundary of a system diagram as the project site, as this boundary defines the scope of design and influence. At the same time, it is useful, and sometimes necessary, to at least consider how a system flows at different scales. For energy systems, this change in scale can reveal opportunities for energy solutions at a districtwide or community scale. If a single building cannot achieve net zero energy, can it be achieved at the community scale? An exploration of system scales reveals where human technology systems have characteristics similar to natural systems and ecosystems. In fact, a profound way to think of the systems of a building is as an ecosystem. Natural systems tend to work toward balance; they exhibit closed-loop behavior at the right scale—for example, the global water cycle is a large closed loop with a finite stock. Also,

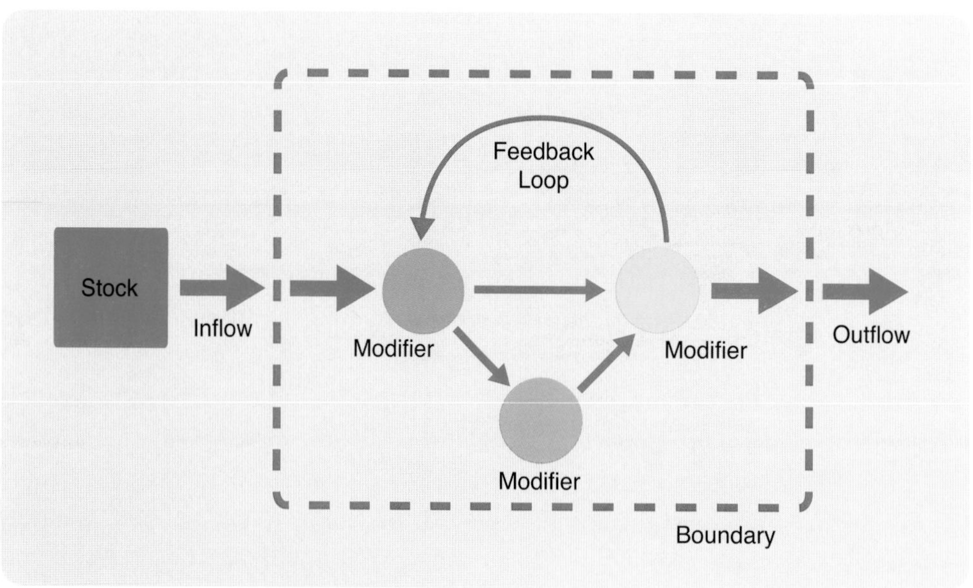

■ **FIGURE 3.6** Basics of System Flow Diagrams.

because natural systems are closed-looped, they produce no resulting waste. If a system boundary is drawn at a small scale within a larger system, it will be difficult to see the behavior of the system as a whole. A closed-loop system may appear as a simple linear in/out system when examined at a small scale.

Energy system diagrams for a net zero energy building can also help design professionals explore, analyze, and communicate many detailed elements in the energy system flow (see Figure 3.7). The energy flow is the basic stock in an energy system diagram and, as such, can include any number of energy sources and passive energy resources that flow in and out of a building and site boundary. Within the project boundary are many modifiers: the loads that need to be met by the energy stock. The loads can be categorized in terms of lighting, heating, cooling, ventilation, and plug or process loads. The loads and the energy flow through the system are altered based on feedback loops by the occupants, who respond to needs for thermal comfort, or follow their patterns and schedules of building use (lighting, equipment, etc.). The loads are also altered by weather patterns. The feedback loops may be realized through the use of thermostats, sensors, and the building management system. The goal of energy system diagrams is to first see and then design energy as a whole system. Diagrams may, as well, help reveal potential design solutions that may not be apparent when considering each individual component.

Design Decision Making

NREL's Paul Torcellini, introduced earlier in this chapter, often cites this adage about energy: "Every design decision has an energy impact."

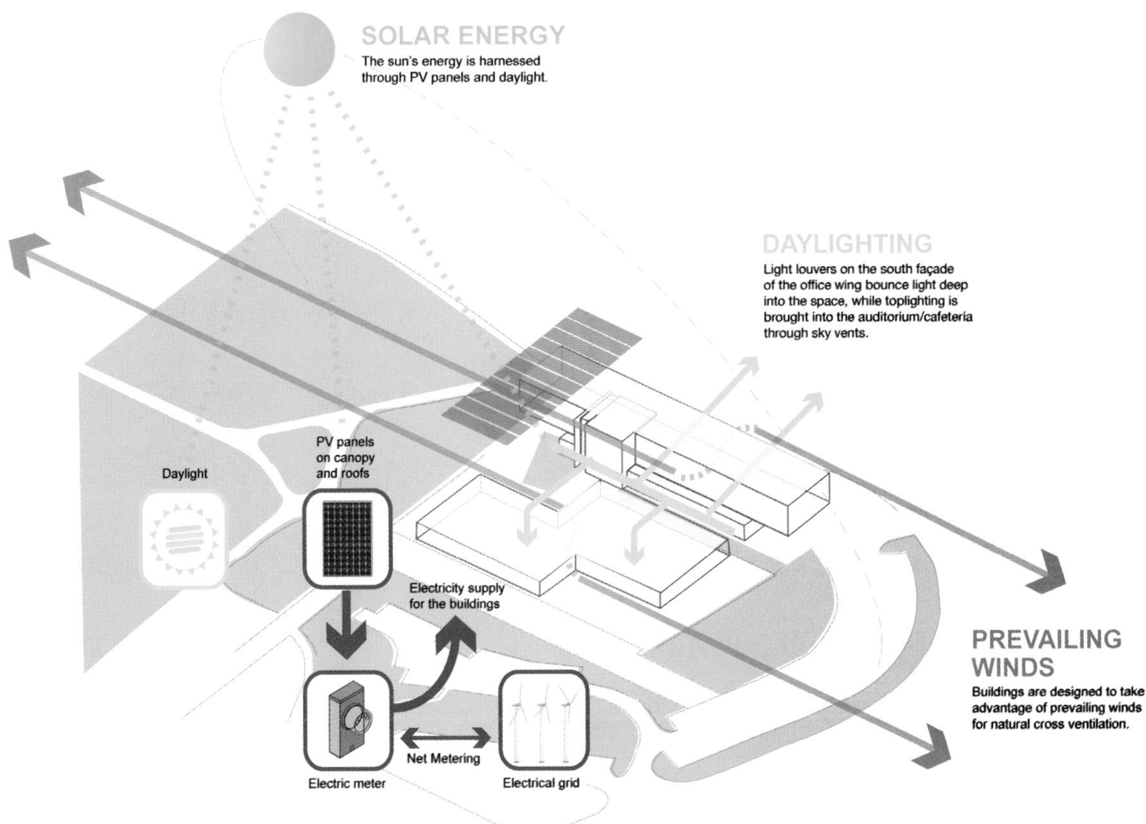

■ **FIGURE 3.7** Energy System Diagram for a Net Zero Energy Competition. *Image courtesy of RNL.*

The implication is clear: To deliver a successful net zero energy building, you need an integrated way of evaluating and reconciling the energy consequence of each project decision. Of course, the energy impact can vary considerably, based on the design decision being made, but even small decisions begin to add up. The point is, energy evaluation is, in general, an excellent filter to use during the decision-making process. It exemplifies one of the truths about net zero energy buildings: that details matter.

The elements of successful design decision making are embedded in the dynamics of the team organization; they include team leadership, hierarchy, trust, and communication. Paramount to decisions made about energy is to add energy performance as a high-level decision-making filter (along with cost, schedule, and quality) and make the information available to evaluate the energy impact. It may not be particularly difficult to add energy performance as a primary decision-making filter; it may, however, be challenging to gather relevant information on a timely basis to make decisions. One reason is that, because there are many factors that go into every decision, the necessary information will likely be spread throughout the team. But keep in mind, the quality of a design decision is only as good as the information used to make it. This underscores the importance of implementing a collaborative, nonhierarchical decision-making process.

The diagram in Figure 3.8 illustrates the basic design decision-making process for energy in a net zero energy building. It is consistent with the principle that design information grows in quantity and level of detail, in an effort to

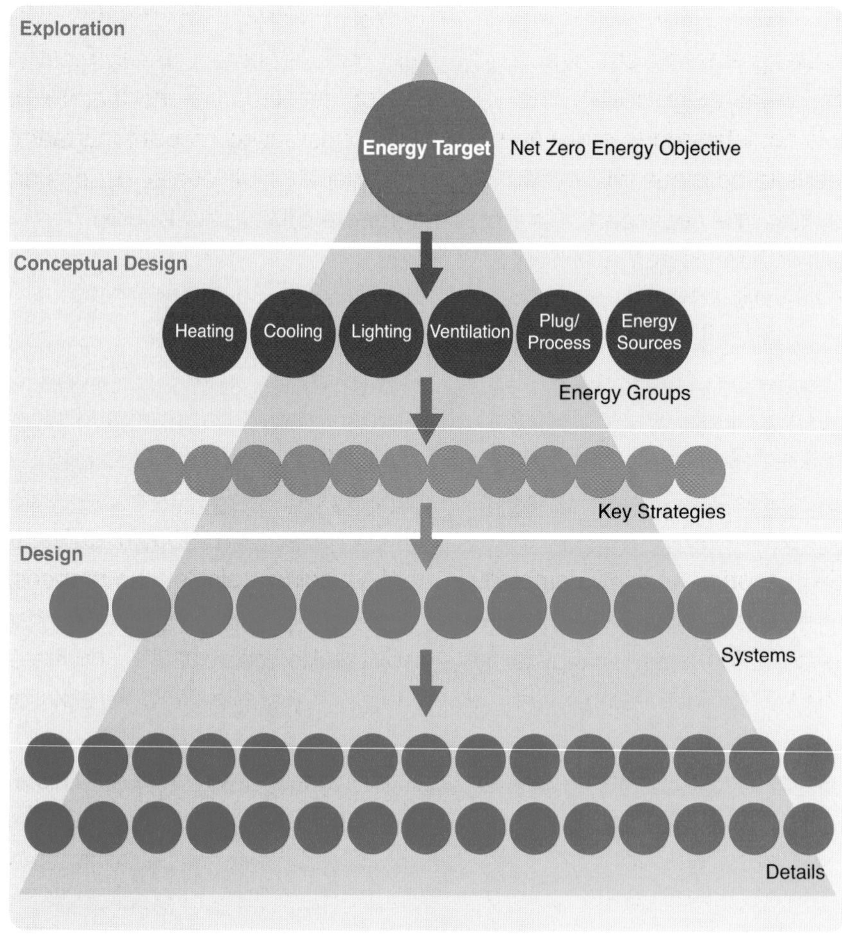

■ **FIGURE 3.8** Energy Design Decision-Making Process.

synthesize the project into a singular solution. Design is, simply, the integration and synthesis of all the many decisions that need to be made to ensure a successful project outcome. The basic design-making flow starts at the beginning of the project, with the net zero energy objective and energy target. During concept design, the various energy end uses and energy sources (utility-based and on-site renewable) are considered as key energy groups. Each energy end use or energy source would also have an energy budget, based on meeting the overall target. Strategies are developed to address each of the energy groups and their budgets into the conceptual design. Systems are then designed to carry out the agreed-upon strategies. As the design advances, the systems and assemblies are fully detailed and specified to meet system performance requirements.

The diagram in Figure 3.9 shows a detailed view of how this design-making process works for one of the major energy groups—in this case, lighting. It is not intended to show every decision that needs to be made, but to convey the hierarchy and interdependence of the design-making flow. This diagram also serves to illustrate how the many detailed decisions made at the end of design, which might appear small or isolated, are in fact made within the context of the overall energy target. The decisions are connected in a chain of decisions, starting with the energy goal, which is divided into major energy end uses. Each detailed decision is made in support of the parameters established in the preceding decision phase, which in turn supports the overall energy target and advances the key design strategies and concepts established in conceptual design.

The decision-making process for a net zero energy project must be supported by a sound problem-solving process, which is driven by the energy criteria. The problem-solving process used during design is focused on synthesis and revolves around a process of definition, analysis, evaluation, and refinement. Figure 3.10 illustrates this basic process.

Identifying solutions and strategies takes collaboration, experience, and research. Analyzing and assessing solutions require data and evaluation criteria. The use of simulation tools and design studies are important aids for developing design data and testing solutions. In particular, the energy model should be the core problem-solving tool in a net zero energy project. The evaluation criteria are based on meeting and supporting the project objectives. Specifically, the project objectives should influence the identification of potential options. Understanding the desired result (project objectives) and making an analytical comparison should reveal the best option among all those considered. It may also demonstrate that the best option needs further development to fully meet the project objectives. Keep in mind that the quality of the solution is based on both the team's ability to, first, identify high-quality options and, second, compare options analytically.

BUILDING ENERGY MODELING

The Virtual Net Zero Energy Building

Net zero energy design, construction, and operation benefit from simulating and modeling the building in each of the design phases. As computer technology matures, the potential for leveraging a single, comprehensive virtual model of the building during all phases of the project's life will greatly enhance the delivery process, by aiding design integration, fostering collaboration, and streamlining performance simulations. The virtual building is a fundamental principle of building information modeling (BIM). The idea is to construct the building virtually before it is actually built. The coordination and communication benefits of "test

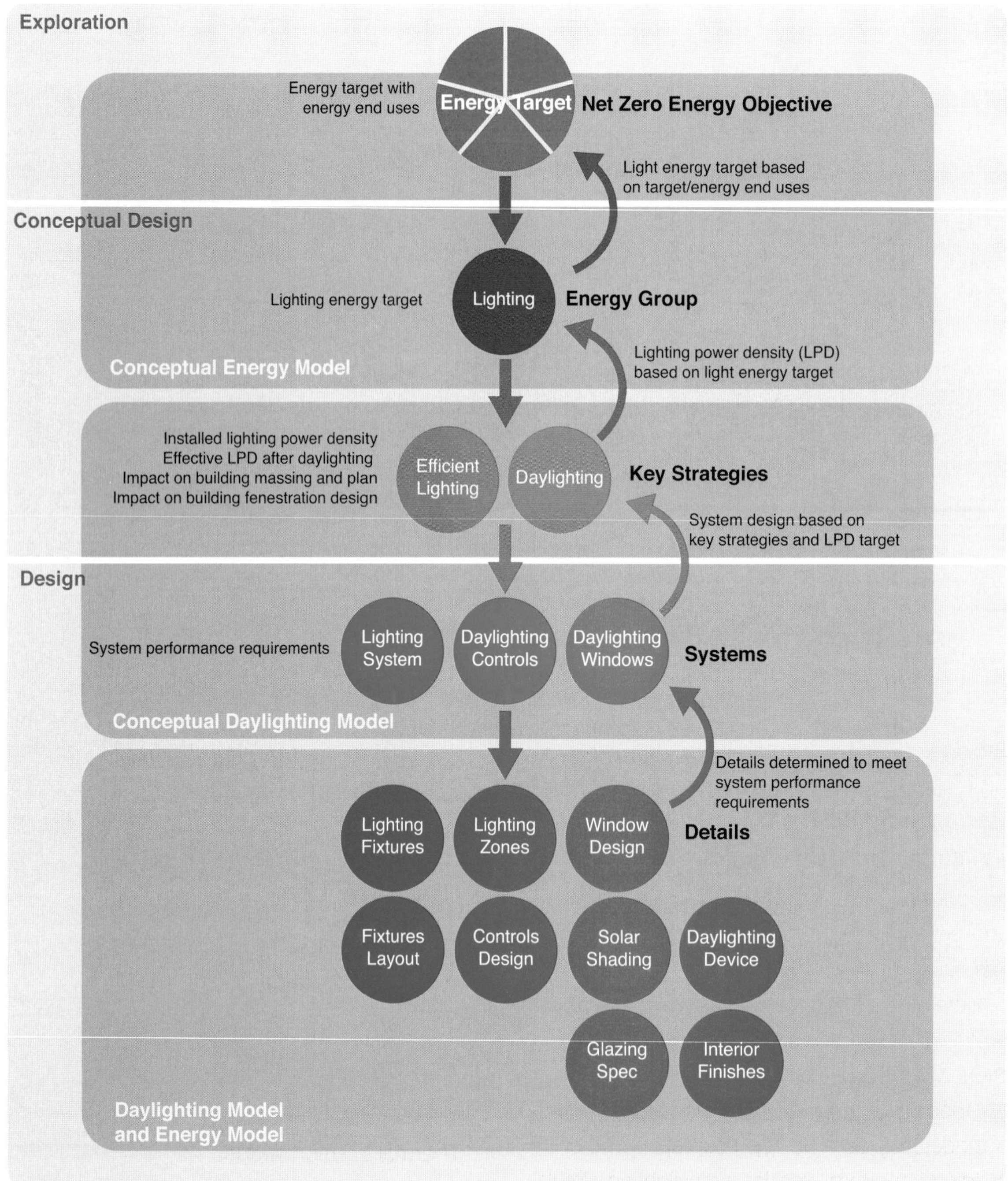

■ **FIGURE 3.9** Energy Design Decision-Making Process Detail: Lighting Example.

building" and "collision testing" projects are obvious, and are realized today by many integrated project teams effectively utilizing BIM.

While the goal, and the technological trend, is to develop a *single* virtual model, one that can also process the performance and energy simulations, the reality is that most building performance simulations are processed in a wide variety of modeling applications, each with its own model. At best, today's vision of a virtual building is a composite of different models used together to understand and communicate the building virtually. The industry is focusing on interoperability, and is making

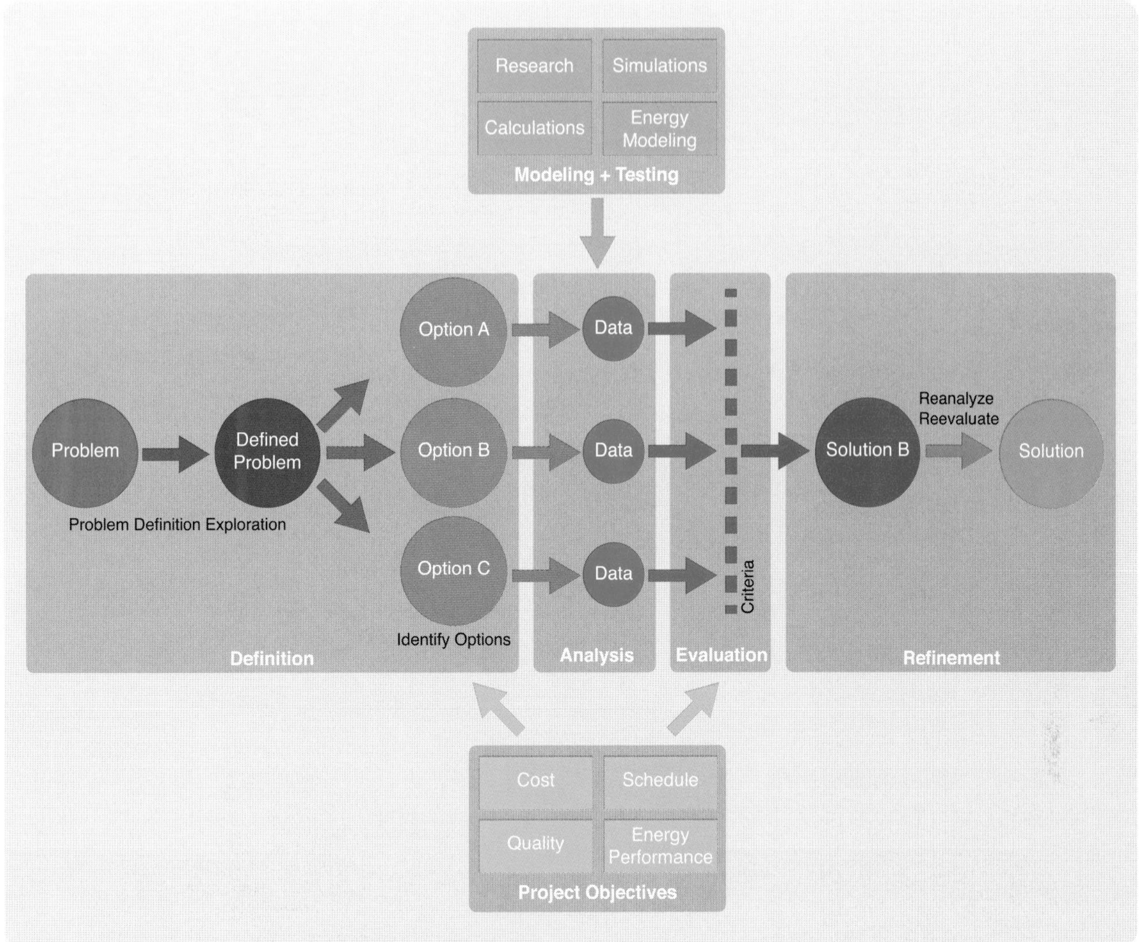

■ **FIGURE 3.10** Energy Design Problem-Solving Process.

good strides toward developing file platforms and protocols that work across multiple modeling programs.

Note that the term *model* here is used rather broadly, to refer to a set of analytical data or information that simulates the building or a component of the building or its performance. A model may be a 3D representation of the building, an energy model, a daylighting simulation, or even an Excel spreadsheet. Consider some of the simulations and individual models that may comprise a composite virtual net zero energy building model over the course of the delivery process (also see Figure 3.11).

- Climate study model
- Massing and design study models
- 3D visualization model
- Design and construction BIM model
- Energy model
- Daylighting and lighting model
- Natural ventilation model
- Thermal transfer and thermal bridging study model
- Thermal comfort model
- Cost model
- Schedule model and 4D model

Role of Modeling

The best way to make informed design decisions in the net zero energy design process is by simulating the impact those decisions will have on the resulting building. This powerful approach should start even before design

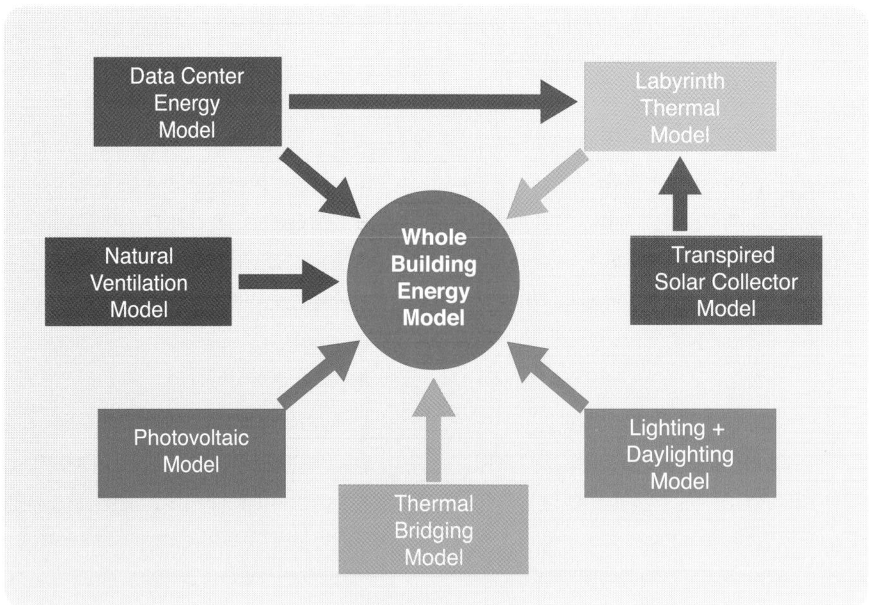

■ **FIGURE 3.11** Composite Energy Model: This example shows the basic composite energy model structure for the NREL Research Support Facility.

begins and then continue throughout the process, as appropriate, either to further test, add detail, or evaluate results. In this way, the entire building energy model becomes the central decision-making representation of the net zero energy delivery process—although many other models or simulations may be used to inform specific decisions and contribute to the inputs on the energy model.

Building energy models and performance simulations serve many purposes, but the two fundamental ones are for decision making and verification. These two activities occur at different times and have very specific objectives. Using the energy model as a decision-making tool happens throughout the process, but it is most important and most effective during the earlier stages of design. During the exploration and early design phases, a variety of models may be used to study broader and bigger-picture strategies. During later stages of design, when the primary energy model has a good level of detail, it can be used to test discrete components or component bundle selections. For example, glazing specs or wall insulation levels can be isolated in the model and altered between various design options to determine the energy-saving potential. This will also lead to understanding the cost-effectiveness of various options because the cost difference between the options can be analyzed.

Using the building energy model as a verification tool is important at key milestones in the delivery process. This is the fundamental process to determine whether the project as a whole is meeting the established energy target; consequently, it enables an evaluation of its potential to meet net zero energy in operation. Milestone verification models should be tied to the net zero energy balance calculations (refer to Chapter 11). In this sense, the energy model as an assessment tool is meant to be a predictive model, with the goal of developing it into a close representation of the actual building. Using an energy model as a predictive tool may seem unwise in light of the recent reports of buildings failing to perform as predicted by the design energy model. Certainly, there are many variables that influence the actual building energy use compared to an energy model prediction, such as occupant behavior, building schedules, weather, and construction deficiencies. However, the goal of a net zero energy building is met in actual building operation, meaning that if the energy model is to inform the design and application of renewable energy for the building, it must be as predictive as possible. This also means more careful attention is required to either reduce, or at least quantify, the potential for variation between reality and the model—or minimize the assumptions. Finally, it means managing the expectations of the model so that the building owner understands where variations can occur.

Another verification role that the energy model fulfills is to comply with the LEED rating system and document energy performance. A typical LEED compliance model is governed by "ASHRAE Standard 90.1, Energy Standard for Buildings Except Low-Rise Residential Buildings" and uses the performance rating method in its "Informative Appendix G." Unfortunately, the process of energy modeling for LEED is an adjunct to that for modeling for net zero energy. The two models assess two different goals using two different criteria. The ASHRAE 90.1 model uses a baseline energy model for comparison, and the metric is the percent energy cost savings of the proposed design over the baseline. Ultimately, for a net zero energy model, there is no baseline, just an absolute energy target. The absolute net zero energy target represents a new process and purpose for energy modeling.

Effective Modeling

THE ENERGY MODELER

The primary energy model should be built, maintained, and analyzed by an experienced energy modeler. This skill, which is a blend of art and science, takes a great deal of experience and creativity to master. A talented energy modeler will be capable of understanding the pros and cons of different modeling software and approaches, and know how to effectively translate the design intent (and its many complexities) into the framework of the energy model, and, thereafter, use it as an effective tool to analyze the model to derive useful results.

The energy modeler must also have a deep knowledge base in building physics in order to use the energy model to, first, ask the right questions and, second, successfully interpret and use the results. As building energy modeling software technology improves, it becomes more tightly integrated with the project's BIM platform, and certain tasks become more automated; but it does not, nor can it, replace the expertise of the energy modeler. Improvements in software or in the tools can only help to make experienced energy modelers even more effective in their work on net zero energy project teams.

Energy Modeler Certification

No program for professional certification of energy modelers existed until early 2010, when ASHRAE introduced Building Energy Modeling Professional (BEMP) certification. This program makes it possible to identify energy modeling professionals who have demonstrated competency in applying energy modeling techniques and software to assess building and system energy performance, economics, and building physics.

The energy modeler must be well integrated into the team, to ensure a steady and fluid flow of project information, which assures the model is up to date in terms of design, construction, and occupancy decisions, and that the design process is informed by timely energy modeling results. Furthermore, it can be beneficial to use energy modelers who are independent of the mechanical engineer (or other team members with crucial design or management responsibilities). In their role as specialized independent consultants, with the practical experience needed to guide a complex energy modeling process, energy modelers can focus on the modeling process, which is extensive for net zero energy projects, instead of being pulled back and forth between design and energy modeling roles. As independents, modelers also can serve as a valuable check-and-balance between design and engineering and energy analysis.

The preceding is not to say that energy modeling should be only the realm of the energy modeler. Although the energy modeler is the developer and manager of the primary energy model and other modeling and simulation efforts that need to be coordinated with the primary model, others on the design team, including mechanical engineers, lighting designers, and architects, also have valuable roles to play in a variety of design simulations.

ACCURACY

The saying "garbage in, garbage out" is very true for energy modeling—which does not mean that "perfect" information is needed for the inputs into an energy model. It does mean that the "right" information inputs need to be used for the types of questions being asked. In addition, it's important to fully understand any assumptions and limitations of the information when evaluating energy modeling results.

The issue of accuracy in a model really comes down to the specific need to be fulfilled. When using the energy model as a decision-making tool, accuracy is often not that important. Further, the details needed to make the model accurate can be more cumbersome than they are worth, and can even delay or prohibit effective design decisions. In decision-making mode, it is critical to understand the important variables related to the design decision and set up the model query around them. For certain design decisions, it may be enough to know which option offers the best energy performance and, perhaps, the order of magnitude of energy. A highly accurate assessment of actual energy savings often is not needed to make a solid decision.

Accuracy has much greater importance when using the model to evaluate and predict the energy performance of the building. The goal is for the model to become more detailed over the course of design and construction, resulting in a faithful representation of the actual construction and intended operation. In this sense, the model results should also grow more accurate as it develops. For a net zero energy project, the goal is to develop a predictive model and tool that can be used in building operation.

Typically, the energy modeling software itself can, however, be extremely accurate. It is the variability of the input, and whether it accurately captures the future building operation, that has the greatest influence on how well the model predicts energy results. Quality control steps should be taken to make sure the model accurately represents the design and construction. Measures include ensuring there is a common understanding and expectation about how the building will be used—for example, programmatic elements, installed equipment, building use schedules, and occupant behavior.

During early phases of design, it is challenging to understand the entire energy problem and to identify all of the details that make up a complete and predictive energy model. The solution to this problem is the strategic use of contingency. Maintain an energy contingency, or extra energy use in reserve, during the early stages of design. At the owner's and team's discretion it can be gradually released as the energy model becomes more detailed. Establishing an energy contingency is a useful tool for net zero energy projects because the energy use target and the planned on-site renewable energy systems are tightly linked. Falling short on either side will mean falling short of the objective.

TIMING

One of the most important influences on the effectiveness of energy modeling is the timing of the modeling activity in relation to the core design activity. It is a common problem to start energy modeling too late to have an impact on the underlying design of the building—its program, orientation, massing, form, and window-to-wall ratio are all developed very early in the process. Timing can be a major issue even later in design if the modeling phases are not in sync with the design decisions, such as those affecting wall assemblies, glazing selections, and system selections. It may help to think of the energy model as the pulse of a net zero energy project, and that ongoing monitoring and use of the energy model will keep the project on track toward its objective.

The energy modeling effort should be planned throughout the entire delivery process, to include specific milestones for tracking against the net zero energy objective. Some key milestones include: conceptual design, design models appropriate for each phase of design (including an as-designed model), an as-built energy model at the end of construction, and the model used in the measurement and verification process and building operations (see Figure 3.12).

COORDINATION

The entire team should interface with the energy model. This includes coordinating the inputs used in the model with the design, to help ensure accuracy. For example, the thermal properties of the building envelope should be carefully coordinated, not just assumed. Other coordinated inputs include schedules,

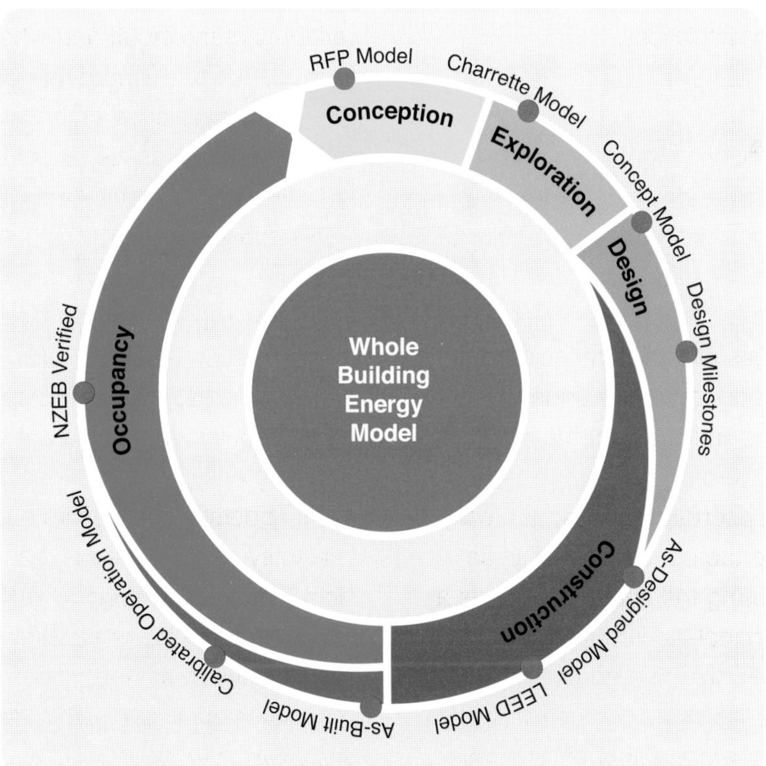

■ **FIGURE 3.12** Energy Modeling as Part of the Delivery Process.

loads, temperature set points, and details about the various systems. The team should be fully integrated around both the inputs and results of the energy model, as a means of helping to make better design decisions.

Good communication is the basis of coordination between the design and the energy model. Several important pieces of information should be clearly communicated and coordinated across the team: model inputs, model results, limitations and assumptions, and an analysis of the results. The model is only as good as its inputs; therefore, it is critical that they represent the design intent and the owner's intended occupancy and operation. It is also imperative that inputs be kept up to date and regularly reviewed. The energy modeling report is an essential communication device the team can use for this purpose. It is vital for the team to understand the components of the energy model and be able to leverage the modeling results.

COST-EFFECTIVE MODELING

The level of energy modeling and other design simulations that I advocate here for a net zero energy design process go far beyond the scope of typical green building projects pursuing LEED certification. Extensive modeling should be viewed as an investment, one that adds value to the project and long-term value to the building, rather than as an added cost. To make this investment wisely, it is important to estimate the modeling process and scope up front and then build these estimates into the project schedule, project fees, and fee negotiation.

Fortunately, the extensive effort described here will become more streamlined and cost-effective over time, as modeling and BIM integration tools improve. Much of the cost associated with the energy modeling process is due to the need to build new models for each simulation program used. The future evolution toward a single virtual model, discussed earlier, minimizes this time-consuming effort of building multiple models that also introduce the potential for discrepancies. In the meantime, we have to depend on experienced energy modelers who are efficient at building models and know how to match simulation needs with design needs.

White-Box Modeling

I use the term *white-box modeling* to describe very simple energy and daylighting models built by the architect, engineer, energy modeler, or other team member. I am an enthusiastic advocate of the architect using this type of model. A white-box model is a simple decision-making tool and, accordingly, should be thought of as a design tool, one used creatively to help solve design problems. The term *white box*, as opposed to *black box*, implies an open system or model that you can see *into*—not just the inputs and outputs. *White box* also describes the visual appearance of some of these model studies, because one of the best tools for building a white-box model is Google SketchUp, whose default color for objects is white (see Figure 3.13).

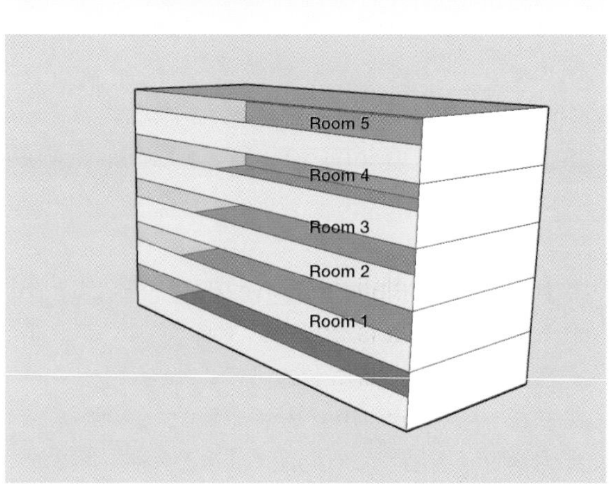

■ **FIGURE 3.13** Simple SketchUp Baseline Model for a Five-Story Building with Rooms Identified for IES VE.

SketchUp, in and of itself, is not an energy or daylighting modeling program. It is, however, useful for developing shading and solar access studies. There are new sets of plug-ins available for SketchUp that now allow energy and other simulation software to interface with, and run the model generated in, SketchUp. Generally, energy modeling software programs do not excel at generating building geometry. SketchUp, however, does—which is one of the reasons it is such a widely used tool among architects and designers. (Note that, currently, a free version of the SketchUp is available from Google.)

Currently, the two leading energy modeling programs that have plug-ins available for SketchUp are IES Virtual Environment (IES VE) and EnergyPlus through its OpenStudio plug-in. EnergyPlus and OpenStudio, developed by the Department of Energy and the National Renewable Energy Laboratory, are available for free download. IES also makes a free version of its software and plug-in, called IES VE-Ware. More robust and full-featured versions of VE are available for purchase through IES.

TYPES AND USES OF WHITE-BOX MODELS

A net zero energy project should start with a simple white-box model, to begin defining an energy baseline. While a baseline is not necessary for setting and achieving a net zero energy goal—because net zero is absolute and ultimately independent of a baseline—it does add value to the energy target process. With a baseline model, it is possible to query the model for relative energy end uses, as well as quantify what is contributing to the energy loads of the building (see Figures 3.14 and 3.15). Remember, this type of model is not necessarily a good gauge of the total energy; it is really meant to convey important information about what is driving energy use in the project. One way to develop a simple baseline model is to use basic construction assemblies and building systems that are set to default code minimums.

It is possible with simple models to study alternative massing, as well as window-to-wall ratios. In addition, the default values or model parameters can be adjusted to begin to

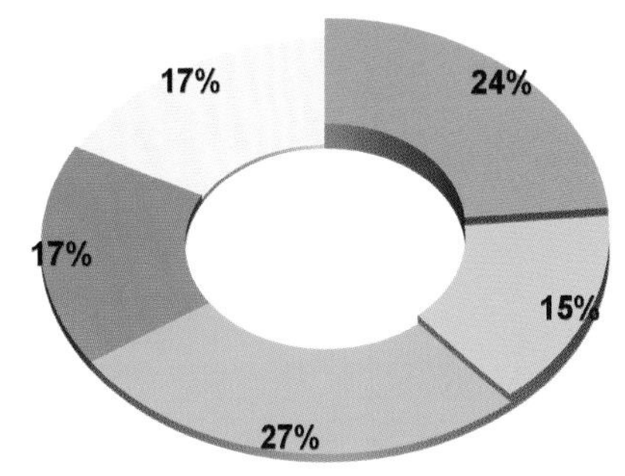

■ **FIGURE 3.14** Energy Pie Chart Report from IES VE's Architectural Toolkit.

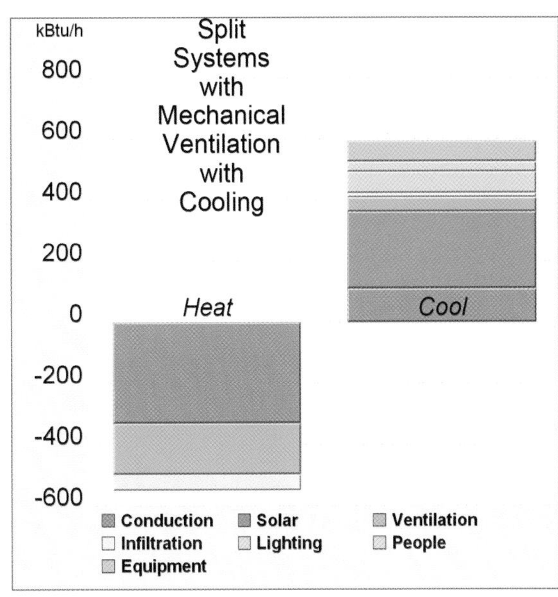

■ **FIGURE 3.15** Heating and Cooling Load Chart Report from IES VE's Architectural Toolkit.

determine the relative impact different assemblies and systems will have on building performance. White-box modeling can help rapidly evaluate decisions during early design, but the process must be paired with solid judgment of building physics and energy strategies. Energy results from simple white-box models can serve to help make relative comparisons, but should not be interpreted as conclusive results.

Another simple and effective type of white-box model is a single-space or unit model that studies an area of interest or a building bay that repeats in the design. This type of streamlined model can be used to assess many space-specific performance parameters, such as daylighting, temperatures, thermal transmittance, and solar heat gain (see Figures 3.16 and 3.17). It can be used to discretely test different glazing designs, shading solutions, window-to-wall ratios, and building assemblies, as well as architectural form and mass.

In conclusion, white-box models are only meant to be conceptual in nature. They are made quickly and simply to address the needs of the early design process. More detailed models will have to be developed as the project moves forward. The energy modeler may be able to utilize aspects of the white-box model in developing a more detailed whole building model. The goal is to have the building energy modeling process mirror the design process, characterized by early experimentation and innovation, followed by development and refinement of the synergies and systems of the conceptual design into a successful design for a net zero energy project.

Energy Modeler Perspective

A couple of nationally recognized and deeply experienced energy modelers with experience in modeling for net zero energy buildings were interviewed for this book. The following represents a brief summary of their perspectives on building energy modeling for net zero energy buildings. The perspectives include considerations for the process of modeling for net zero energy and future trends that will impact this process. The energy modelers also reveal their favorite analysis tools and allow a look into their modeling toolbox.

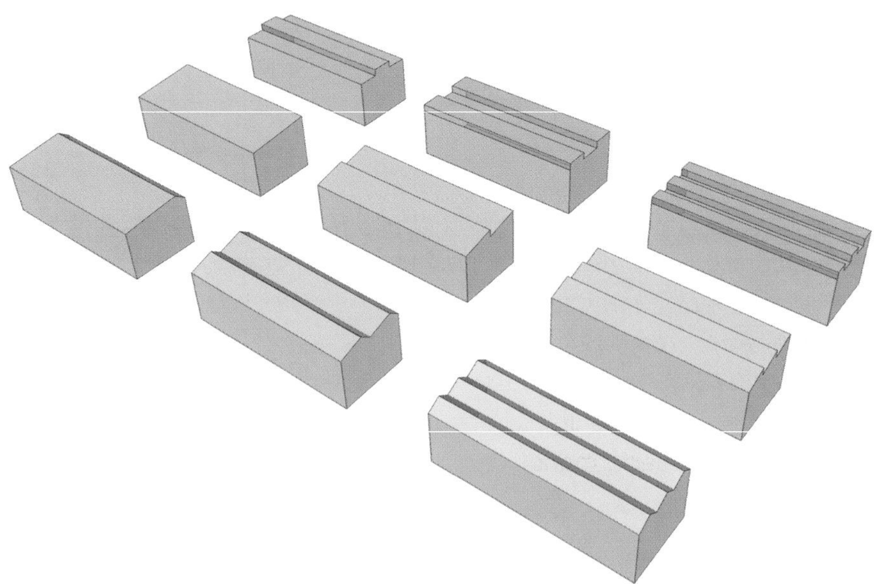

■ **FIGURE 3.16** SketchUp model incorporates multiple toplighting strategies for a typical maintenance facility bay. *Image courtesy of RNL.*

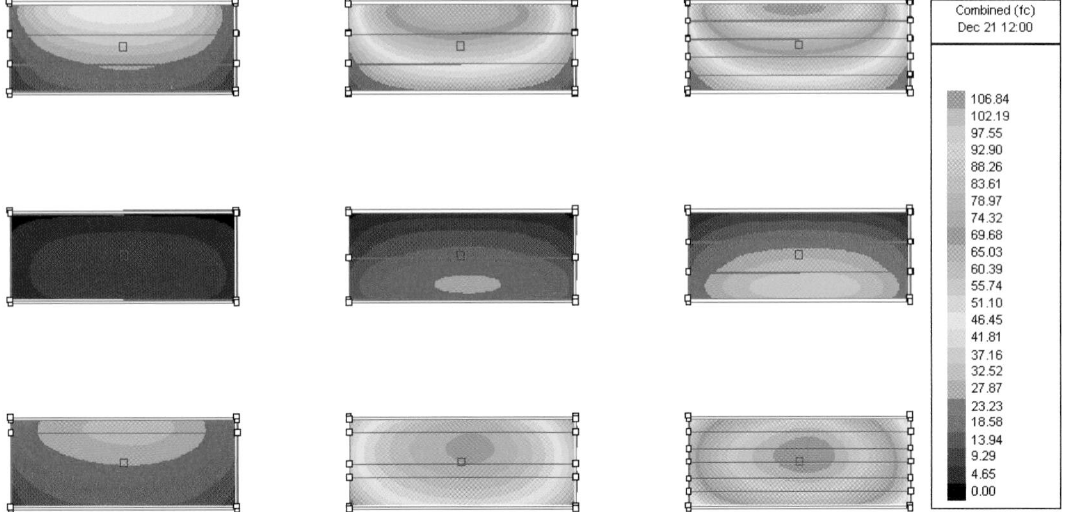

■ **FIGURE 3.17** IES VE Daylighting results compare the different strategies at December 21, noon. *Image courtesy of RNL.*

ENERGY MODELING PERSPECTIVE

CASE STUDY

I interviewed two nationally recognized and highly experienced energy modelers with expertise in modeling for net zero energy buildings. The following represents a brief summary of their individual perspectives on building energy modeling for net zero energy buildings. They include considerations for the process of modeling for net zero energy and future trends that will impact this process. The energy modelers also reveal their favorite analysis tools and allow a look into their modeling toolboxes.

Interviewee

Linda Morrison, PE, BEMP, LEED AP, CEM
Building Performance Engineer Team Leader, Ambient Energy

Process

There are many variables and assumptions that go into an energy model. To improve the usefulness and accuracy of the results, a benchmarking process is recommended as a step for quality control and as a sanity check. This includes benchmarking that is top-down, bottom-up, and sideways. Top-down benchmarking is whole-building benchmarking, such as ENERGY STAR or CBECS; bottom-up benchmarking compares a specific end use with historic submetered data, such as lighting, process loads, or HVAC; and sideways uses industry metrics for typical performance and comparison of each model in the series for reasonableness (base case versus option A, option B, etc.).

To develop a predictive energy model, instead of a comparative model (option A versus option B, or design case versus ASHRAE Standard 90.1 code-compliant base case), it is important to bracket the results with sensitivity and error tolerance. While this sounds awfully statistical, it should be informative because any prediction of the future needs to assess a number of potential possibilities. Early in the process the range of bracketing will be larger, to account for more unknowns. As the project develops and uncertainty decreases, the range of bracketing can also decrease. Further, sensitivity analysis can be conducted on certain model variables to understand how strongly they influence the final results.

Bracketing helps manage risk and uncertainty, but it should also be part of a process of transparency with the delivery team and owner. It is an opportunity to communicate which elements of the energy model need further definition, and the level of safety factor applied. This communication can help the entire design and operations teams understand not only what to expect from the modeling results, but how their decisions and the information they provide helps develop the accuracy of the model, and, ultimately, how closely the model and actual results will track.

Future Trends

Predicting thermal comfort, not just energy use, is an important feedback result. Some performance modeling software, such as IES VE, can do this today. This metric will be used more in the future as we get more sophisticated about reporting and sharing energy model results with teams and owners. It is a great way to identify potential issues and to maintain a dialog with the owner and occupants about their expectations for thermal comfort.

Using thermal comfort modeling can facilitate the use of energy modeling in an innovative way. The energy model can be used to understand the part load conditions of a building, which in turn can be used as a tool to right-size mechanical equipment. Current practice is to size equipment to meet the design condition. However, right-sizing can lead to significant first-cost savings and life-cycle energy cost savings. Thermal comfort analysis can determine the comfort implications of failing to meet the worst-case design load, and how many hours during the year thermal comfort may be challenged. This can lead to making an educated decision about equipment sizing that considers cost, energy, and comfort.

Toolbox

- eQUEST
- Miscellaneous Autodesk tools, as they are available
- IES Virtual Environment (VE)
- Energy Pro
- PVWatts
- Retscreen
- Proprietary tools

Modeler Screenshots

Figures 3.18 through 3.20 are three examples of Ambient Energy's workflow from Revit to IES VE to understand a natural ventilation scheme.

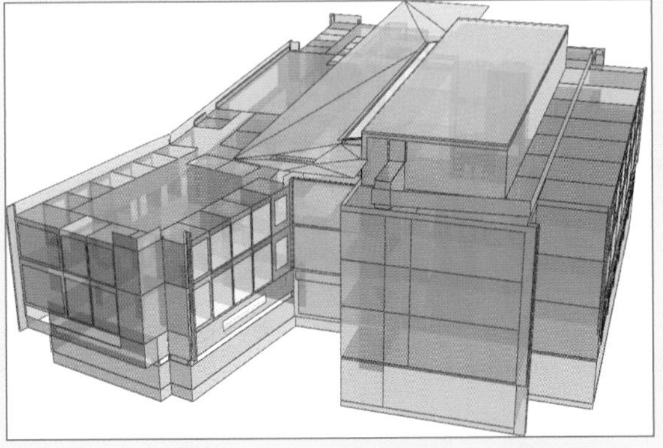

■ **FIGURE 3.18** Natural Ventilation Study for Atrium at the CSU Engineering II Building. Import from Revit to IES VE. *Image courtesy of Ambient Energy.*

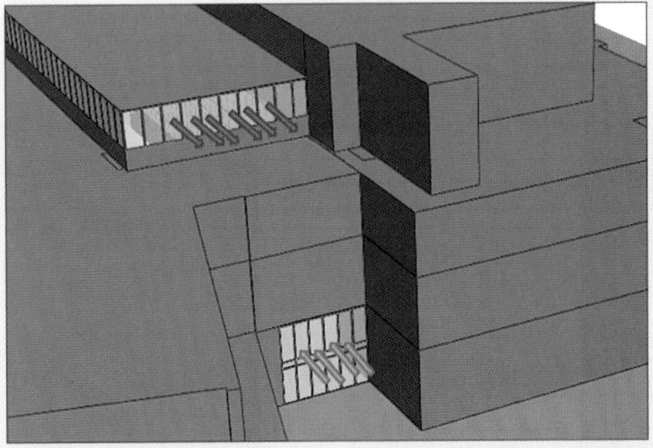

■ **FIGURE 3.19** IES VE Natural Ventilation Analysis. *Image courtesy of Ambient Energy.*

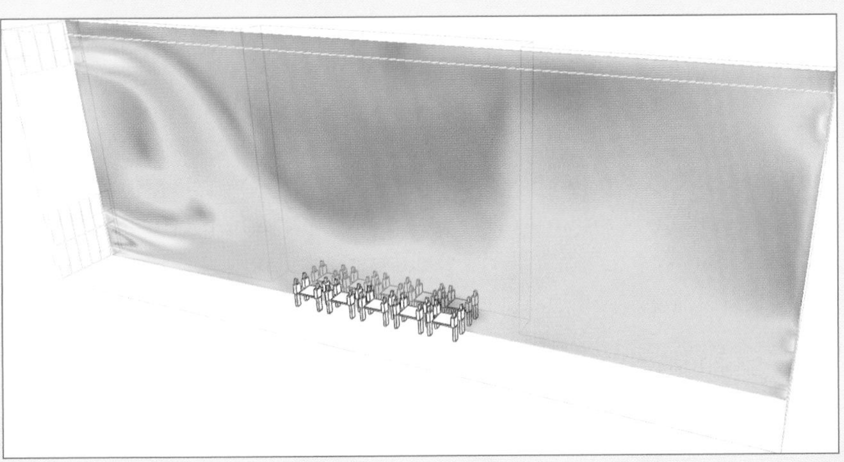

■ **FIGURE 3.20** Section through Lobby Showing Airflow Results from IES VE. *Image courtesy of Ambient Energy.*

ENERGY MODELING PERSPECTIVE

Interviewee

Porus Sam Antia, LEED AP
Project Manager, Building Simulation, Stantec

Process

Net zero energy projects require detailed energy modeling in order to accurately size the renewable energy source. Compared with compliance-based energy models, such as those for California T-24 compliance, the plug load inputs for predictive models are critical. The internal/plug loads are perhaps the most challenging to get right, and have historically not been accurately accounted for in energy models. Typical office equipment such as computers and monitors comprise only a small portion of the entire plug load of an office building.

UPS's, transformers, telecom switches, security equipment, AV equipment, and exit lights all can add up fast and significantly impact the size and cost of a renewable energy plant.

Once all of the equipment is identified, the greatest challenge is to understand the schedule of operation for each particular piece of equipment. With predictive modeling there is a lot of risk. If the energy is overestimated, it could cost the owner and/or design-build team in larger renewable energy systems, such as PV. If the energy is underestimated, the project could fail to meet the net zero energy goal.

Future Trends

The industry would benefit tremendously from a seamless integration of energy modeling with BIM. We are still a few years away from gaining this capability. Also, with more robust energy modeling should come a more diverse tool set within a single software package. Currently, many different tools need to be employed, depending on the problems to be solved. However, the most important improvement we could see in the future is a dramatic increase in simulation speed. Many of the most powerful tools have run times that are too long to be viable in a typical commercial project schedule and process. Net zero energy and high-performing buildings often require passive and hybrid systems with a fair level of complexity. Leveraging BIM for building geometry and component parameters, along with complete modeling tool sets and fast run times, will go a long way toward supporting the design of net zero energy buildings.

There is a trend among energy modeling software developers to position their products at architects and designers. They are using graphical and user-friendly interfaces and new concept design tool sets to bring energy modeling to a wider market. There are pros and cons to widening the group of energy modelers:

- **Pros:** Getting more people in the industry familiar with the tools and processes would help everyone understand why energy modeling is important to the design process, and would help design teams come up with effective design solutions. Also, it would help designers shift away from the black-box perception of energy modeling, which has traditionally kept it as a fringe service in the design process.
- **Cons:** One of the central problems is that users of new interfaces and tools do not necessarily have the proper knowledge and experience to use them effectively. It takes experience to understand energy modeling results, and to draw the correct conclusions, which is the key to the successful deployment of ideas on a project.

Toolbox

- Weather Maker
- SketchUp
- eQUEST
- IES Virtual Environment (VE)
- TRNSYS
- THERM
- Window 6.2

Modeler Screenshots

Figures 3.21 through 3.23 illustrate Stantec's use of multiple modeling softwares to evaluate the design of the DOE/NREL Research Support Facility.

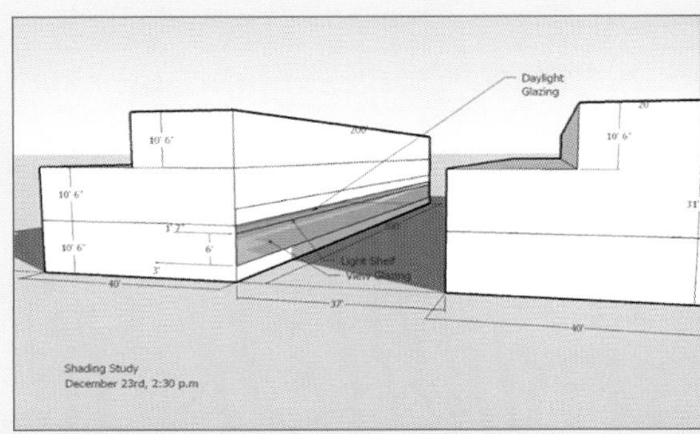

■ **FIGURE 3.21** Early shading study made in SketchUp for the DOE/NREL Research Support Facility. *Image courtesy of Stantec Consulting Services Inc.*

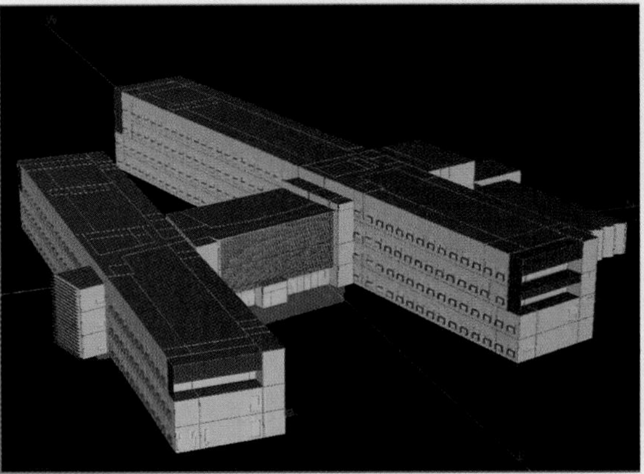

■ **FIGURE 3.22** The central energy model made in eQuest for the DOE NREL Research Support Facility. *Image courtesy of Stantec Consulting Services Inc.*

■ **FIGURE 3.23** IES VE used to study natural ventilation. *Image courtesy of Stantec Consulting Services Inc.*

En

CHAPTER 4
ENERGY

ENERGY BASICS

Energy and architecture have always been intertwined. Architecture has always been formed by energy; it has been used to both mediate and harness the energy of the world. But Luis Fernández-Galiano is one of the few to explore the importance of energy in architectural history. In his book *Fire and Memory: On Architecture and Energy*, he refers to two fundamental interactions of energy and architecture: "regulation of free energy through construction" and "exploitation of accumulated energy through combustion"—or, more simply, sun and fire. He further exemplifies Le Corbusier's use of the *brise-soleil* as architectural interaction with the sun (see Figure 4.1), and Frank Lloyd Wright's use of the hearth as architectural interaction with fire (see Figure 4.2).

More recently, energy has become primarily the realm of the engineer. It should not remain so. All those who develop and use buildings should have some degree of fluency in energy. This is particularly true of the architect, whose design interest in energy has gradually been displaced because of the dominance of cheap fossil fuel energy and mechanical and electrical systems that can make any design solution work in any climate. Net zero energy design offers architects an opportunity to reengage in one of the fundamentals of architectural

■ **FIGURE 4.1** Le Corbusier's Unité d'Habitation, in Berlin, Germany.

■ **FIGURE 4.2** Frank Lloyd Wright's Fallingwater, in Mill Run, Pennsylvania.

design, which combines the rigors of building science and the expression of the purpose and meaning of energy in architecture.

Defining Energy

There are two types of energy: *kinetic* and *potential*. Kinetic energy is energy doing work. Potential energy is stored energy. Within the two types are several forms of energy, listed in Figure 4.3. Energy can change form, but it is always conserved. Energy also can be harnessed and transformed to do useful work. For example, solar cells convert sunlight into electrical energy, but also produce waste thermal energy (see Figure 4.4).

Work and power are related to the concept of energy. Work is the transfer of energy. Kinetic energy is mechanical work, and potential energy is work-store. Work is expressed as force acted over a distance, or $W = F \times D$. Work is also expressed as power over a period of time, or $W = P \times T$. Power is the rate of doing work or the energy transferred per unit of time, or $P = \frac{W}{T}$.

Energy, work, and power are expressed in units. Both work and energy share the International System of Units (SI) unit of a joule (J), named after James Prescott Joule. Joule, a brewer, began applying his experience with industrial processes to scientific experiments to explore the mechanical energy equivalent of heat. His work is a precursor to the law of conservation of energy. A joule is a newton of force applied over a meter of distance. A joule is also 1 watt of power for one second. To conceptualize the unit of a joule: It is approximately equal to the energy it takes to lift a small apple the height of 1 meter.

Potential Energy	Kinetic Energy
Mechanical Energy	Motion Energy
Gravitational Energy	Thermal Energy
Nuclear Energy	Radiant Energy
Chemical Energy	Sound Energy
Electrical Energy	

■ **FIGURE 4.3** Forms of Energy.

Energy Is the Capacity to Do Work

Energy is a fundamental building block of life. The universe is made from energy and matter. Energy may be derived from matter through nuclear fission or fusion. It can also be harnessed by living organisms to grow. Albert Einstein defined the relationship of energy and matter by the now-familiar equation $E = mc^2$.

To understand the nature of energy, it is useful to review the first two laws of thermodynamics.

First Law of Thermodynamics

The first law of thermodynamics is that energy cannot be created or destroyed. The total amount of energy in the universe always remains the same. This is also called the *law of conservation of energy*. However, though overall energy remains constant, energy can change form.

Second Law of Thermodynamics

The second law of thermodynamics is that closed systems move toward states of greater disorder over time. This is also known as the *law of entropy*. This law also states that heat flows from a hot body to a cold body.

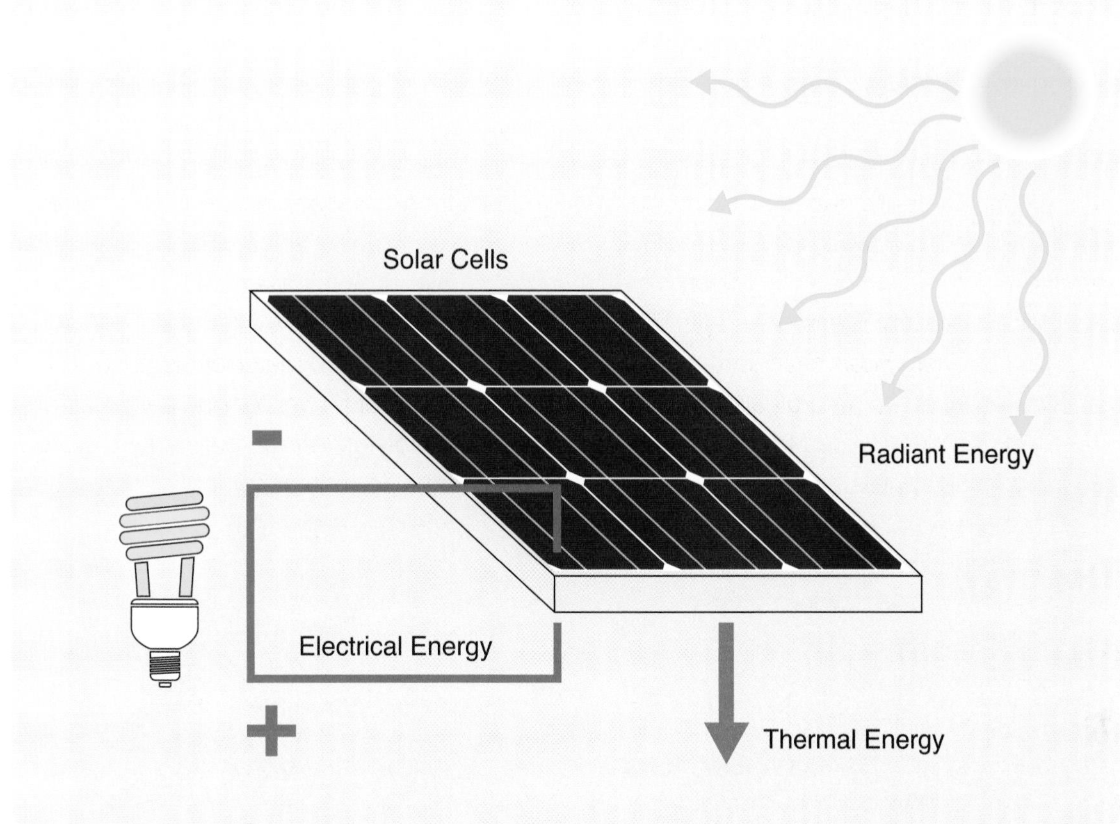

■ **FIGURE 4.4** Example of Transformation of Energy Forms in Photovoltaics.

Power is the rate of energy transfer. It is energy divided by time and, therefore, is an instantaneous measure, whether measured at any given point in time or as an average over a period of time. The SI unit for power is joule per second, which is a watt (W). The lightbulb is the classic example of the relationship of power and energy. If a 1 watt light-emitting diode (LED) is illuminated for one hour, it consumes 1 watt-hour of energy. Power ratings are used to quantify mechanical and electrical power for equipment in a building. Electrical power is measured in watts. Horsepower and a variety of other units are used to measure mechanical power.

Two common units of energy in building design are the British thermal unit (Btu)—or, more appropriately, the MBtu (million Btu)—and the megawatt-hour (MWh). There are many other units of energy that have more specific application to certain fuels, or have application outside of building design. A Btu is equal to the heat energy required to raise the temperature of 1 pound of water 1 degree Fahrenheit. (See Figures 4.5 and 4.6 for basic conversions.) The MBtu is, therefore, associated with heating and cooling energy in buildings; it is also the common unit to describe total energy use of a building in the United States. The SI unit of energy, megawatt-hour, is associated with electrical energy and is a common unit, along with the gigajoule (GJ), to describe total energy use in buildings in countries that have adopted SI units.

Measuring Energy in the Built Environment

SITE ENERGY

Site energy is the energy as measured at the site. This relatively straightforward measure of energy is the one most people are familiar with and commonly use, as it is the energy measured by a building's utility meter and listed on utility bills. Site energy also is the energy represented in energy modeling software during building design.

For example, for an all-electric office building that receives 100 percent of its electricity from the grid, the site energy is the same as the energy use measured at the electricity meter or listed on a utility bill. In this case, there is only one energy source and one meter. If the building also uses natural gas, the measure at the natural gas meter would likewise constitute site energy and be added to the electrical site energy to arrive at the total site energy. The site energy, then, is the total energy used from all energy sources as measured at the site (see Figure 4.7).

	Btu	kBtu	MBtu	Wh	kWh	MWh	J	MJ	GJ
1 Btu	1	1.0×10^{-3}	1.0×10^{-6}	0.293	2.93×10^{-4}	2.93×10^{-7}	1,055	1.06×10^{-3}	1.06×10^{-6}
1 kBtu	1,000	1	1.0×10^{-3}	293.1	0.293	2.93×10^{-4}	1.06×10^{6}	1.055	1.06×10^{-3}
1 MBtu	1.0×10^{6}	1,000	1	2.93×10^{5}	293.1	0.293	1.06×10^{9}	1,055	1.055
1 Wh	3.412	3.41×10^{-3}	3.41×10^{-6}	1	1.0×10^{-3}	1.0×10^{-6}	3,600	3.6×10^{-3}	3.6×10^{-6}
1 kWh	3,412	3.412	3.41×10^{-3}	1,000	1	1.0×10^{-3}	3.6×10^{6}	3.60	3.6×10^{-3}
1 MWh	3.41×10^{6}	3,412	3.412	1.0×10^{6}	1,000	1	3.6×10^{9}	3,600	3.60
1 J	9.48×10^{-4}	9.48×10^{-7}	9.48×10^{-10}	2.78×10^{-4}	2.78×10^{-7}	2.78×10^{-10}	1	1.0×10^{-6}	1.0×10^{-9}
1 MJ	947.8	0.948	9.48×10^{-4}	278	0.278	2.78×10^{-4}	1.0×10^{6}	1	1.0×10^{-3}
1 GJ	9.48×10^{5}	947.8	0.948	2.78×10^{5}	278	0.278	1.0×10^{9}	1,000	1

■ **FIGURE 4.5** Basic Energy Unit Conversions.

	Unit	1 kBtu	1 kWh	1 MJ
Natural Gas	Cubic Feet	1.03	0.30	1.09
	Hundred Cubic Feet	102.90	30.15	108.56
	Cubic Meters	36.33	10.64	38.33
	Therms	100.00	29.30	105.50
Propane	Cubic Feet	2.52	0.74	2.66
	Gallons	91.65	26.85	96.69
	Liters	23.83	6.98	25.14
Fuel Oil + Diesel	Gallons	138.69	40.64	146.32
	Liters	36.03	10.57	38.04
Coal (Anthracite)	Pounds	12.54	3.67	13.23
Coal (Bituminous)	Pounds	12.46	3.65	13.15
Wood	Tons	15,380.00	4,506.34	16,225.90
District (Chilled Water)	Ton Hours	12.00	3.52	12.66
District (Hot Water)	Therms	100.00	29.30	105.50
District (Steam)	Therms	100.00	29.30	105.50
	Pounds	1.19	0.35	1.26

■ **FIGURE 4.6** Fuel and Energy Use Conversions.

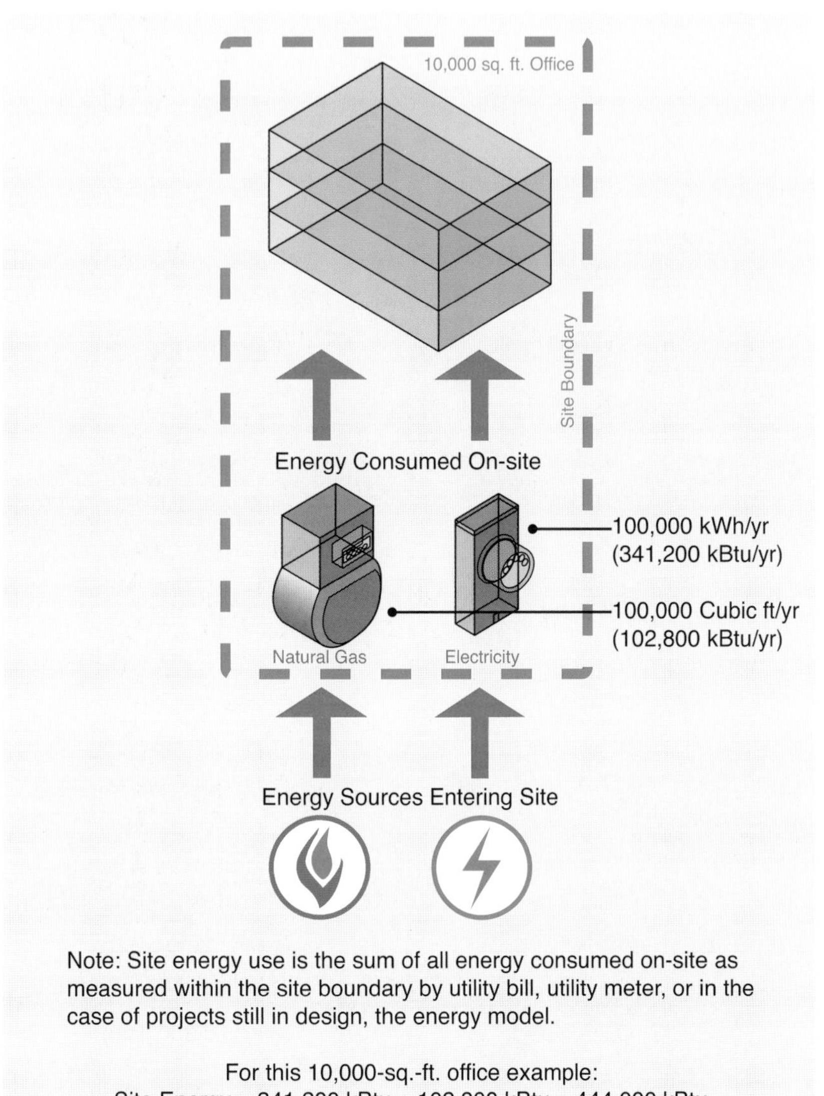
10,000 sq. ft. Office
Site Boundary
Energy Consumed On-site
100,000 kWh/yr
(341,200 kBtu/yr)
100,000 Cubic ft/yr
(102,800 kBtu/yr)
Natural Gas
Electricity
Energy Sources Entering Site
Note: Site energy use is the sum of all energy consumed on-site as measured within the site boundary by utility bill, utility meter, or in the case of projects still in design, the energy model.
For this 10,000-sq.-ft. office example:
Site Energy = 341,200 kBtu + 102,800 kBtu = 444,000 kBtu

■ **FIGURE 4.7** Site Energy Example.

SOURCE ENERGY

Source energy, also called primary energy, is energy measured at the source. Source energy accounts for all additional energy and energy losses required to deliver energy to a site. Continuing with the example of the all-electric office building, the source energy would be measured at the power plant (see Figure 4.8). In this example, the source energy would be approximately three times the site energy—in fact, in 2009, the average ratio in the United States was 3.11, according to the *U.S. EIA Annual Energy Review, 2009.* The high ratio of source-to-site energy for electricity is primarily due to heat loss in the typical coal-fired power plant. In the United States, again for the year 2009, this heat loss accounted for 63 percent of the energy generated. In contrast, transmission losses accounted for almost 3 percent of the energy generated, and power plant electricity use accounted for 2 percent of the energy generated.

Electricity is generated by a variety of primary energy sources, each of which has its own rate of efficiency. Whereas coal is characterized by high heat losses, hydroelectric generation has no combustion and a high efficiency rate. The fuel mix of grid electricity determines the ratio of source-to-site energy for electricity, and this ratio varies by region and even by time of day.

Source energy is a more accurate way of understanding total energy use in a building and for comparing efficiencies of different systems.

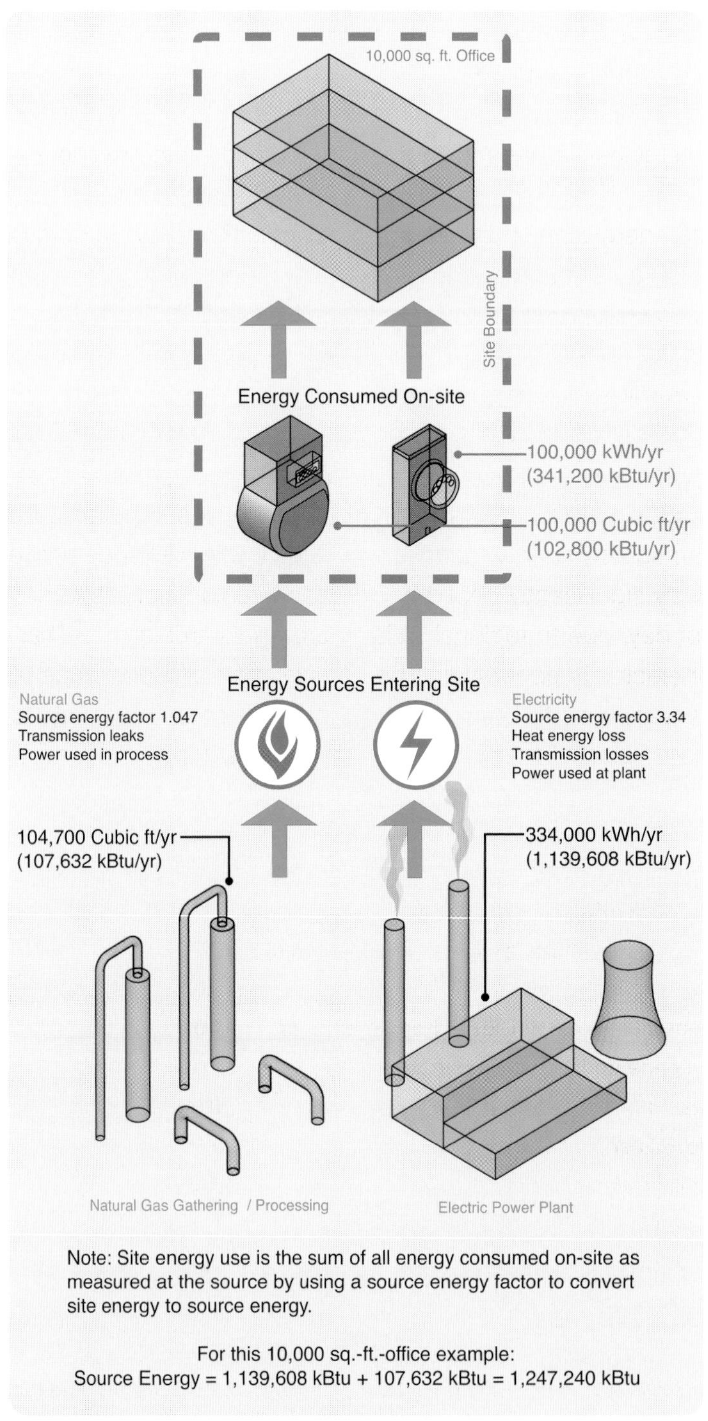

■ **FIGURE 4.8** Source Energy Example.

Source energy is important, as well, for understanding the total resource consumption issue of energy source choices; therefore, it is central in evaluating their environmental impact. Consider that greenhouse gas emissions are generated at the source of combustion, which is not necessarily the point of energy use. Many energy assessment programs, such as the Department of Energy's (DOE's) and the Environmental Protection Agency's (EPA's) ENERGY STAR program, use source energy as the basis for building energy evaluation.

In contrast to site energy, which is easily and accurately measured through metering at the site, source energy is difficult to measure accurately; it has to be estimated after first measuring site energy. A *source energy factor* can be applied to site energy to convert it to source energy. There is a unique source energy factor for each type of energy source (see Figure 4.9). The source energy factor for electricity can vary significantly based on location and time of day, due to regional variations in fuel mix for electricity generation. The ENERGY STAR program uses the national average source energy factor for electricity for all building so that projects can be consistently compared across the United States.

Using a national average for electricity's source energy factor is appropriate in certain contexts. However, determining the specific source energy factor for a project location can lead to a more accurate picture of energy use. The nation's grid is divided into three main grid interconnections, with the exception of Hawaii and Alaska, which are independent of them. The three grid interconnections—Western, Texas, and Eastern—are managed by the North American Electric Reliability Corporation. They are further divided into eight regions and extend into Canada and Mexico. Source energy factors can be determined for any of these grid scales and regions. They can also be determined by state.

One challenge to arriving at an accurate source energy factor is that electricity can move freely between states. At the same time, there is very little exchange between the three main grid interconnections, even though their borders are a little ambiguous. Therefore, in states that import a high percentage of their electricity, it may be more appropriate to use the source energy factor at the grid interconnection level.

Fuel Type	Source Energy Factor
Electricity (Grid Purchase)	3.340
Electricity (On-Site Solar or Wind Installation)	1.0
Natural Gas	1.047
Fuel Oil (1,2,4,5,6, Diesel, Kerosene)	1.01
Propane and Liquid Propane	1.01
Steam	1.45
Hot Water	0.35
Chilled Water	0.05
Wood	1.0
Coal/Coke	1.0
Other	1.0

■ **FIGURE 4.9** Source Energy Factors for the EPA's ENERGY STAR Program.
Source: "ENERGY STAR Performance Ratings Methodology for Incorporating Energy Use," Table 1, Source-Site Ratios for All Portfolio Manager Fuels.

Refer to the maps shown in Figures 4.10 and 4.11 for grid electricity source energy factors. Note that these values also include a precombustion factor that accounts for extracting, processing, and delivering fuel used in the generation of electricity.

The classic example that demonstrates the importance of source energy compares the efficiency of electric resistance heating to a high-efficiency natural boiler. While the rated efficiency of mechanical equipment is part of the story, including the efficiency of the energy source completes the evaluation. Efficiency is the ratio of energy out to energy in. The efficiency of some mechanical equipment is expressed as a coefficient of performance (COP). COP is the ratio of heat energy added to or removed from (cooling) a space per unit of energy consumed; the higher the COP, the more efficient the equipment.

The example shown in Figure 4.12 compares different heating equipment using conventional utility-based energy sources. It exposes the inefficiencies that are part of the electricity grid. Here, even very efficient mechanical systems like ground-source heat pumps are only slightly more efficient than commercial natural gas boilers when measured at the source.

The example in Figure 4.13 illustrates how the introduction of on-site renewable energy leads to very different conclusions. Because the site-to-source factor for on-site renewable energy, such as photovoltaics, is 1.0, rather than 3.34, as used in the preceding example, the true efficiencies of electricity-based ground-source heat pumps can be realized. Note that the measure of site energy (and the efficiency of the equipment) does not change between these two examples.

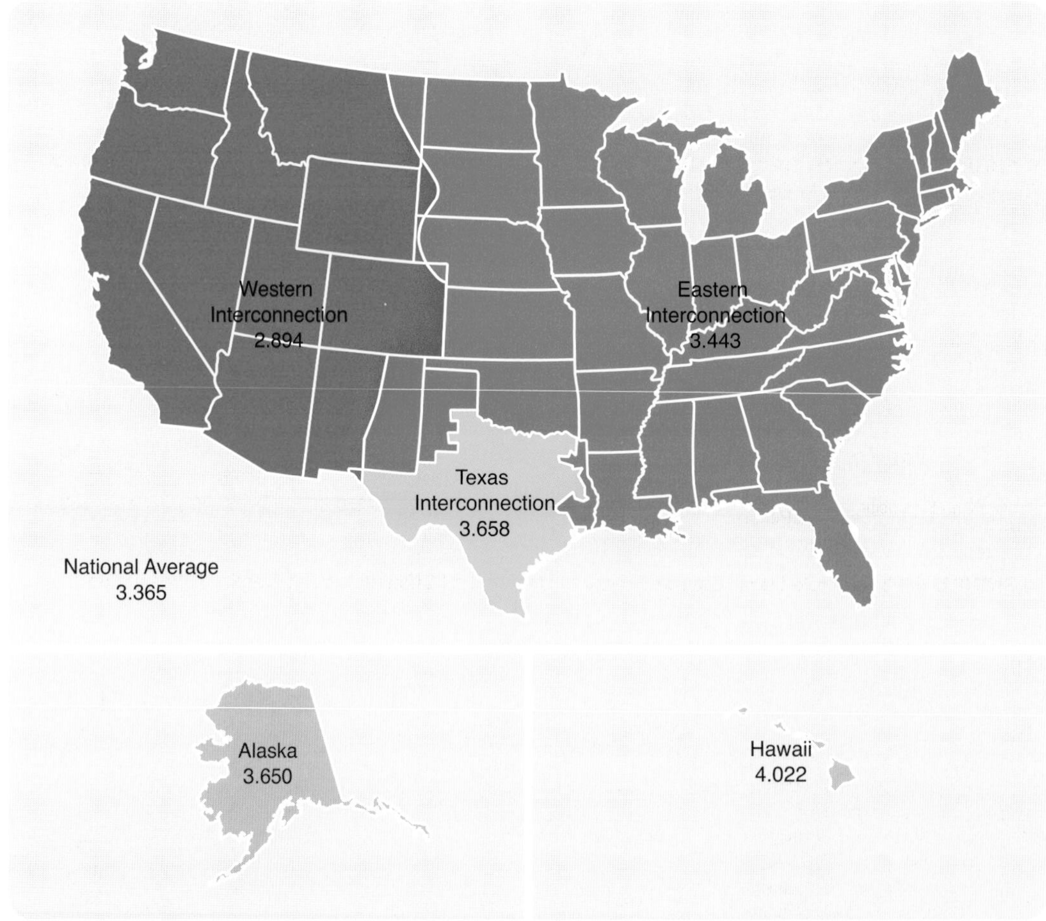

■ **FIGURE 4.10** Source Energy Factors for Electricity by Grid Interconnections (2004). *Sources: M. Deru and P. Torcellini, "Source Energy and Emission Factors for Energy Use in Buildings," Table 2; www.ercot.com; www.wecc.biz.*

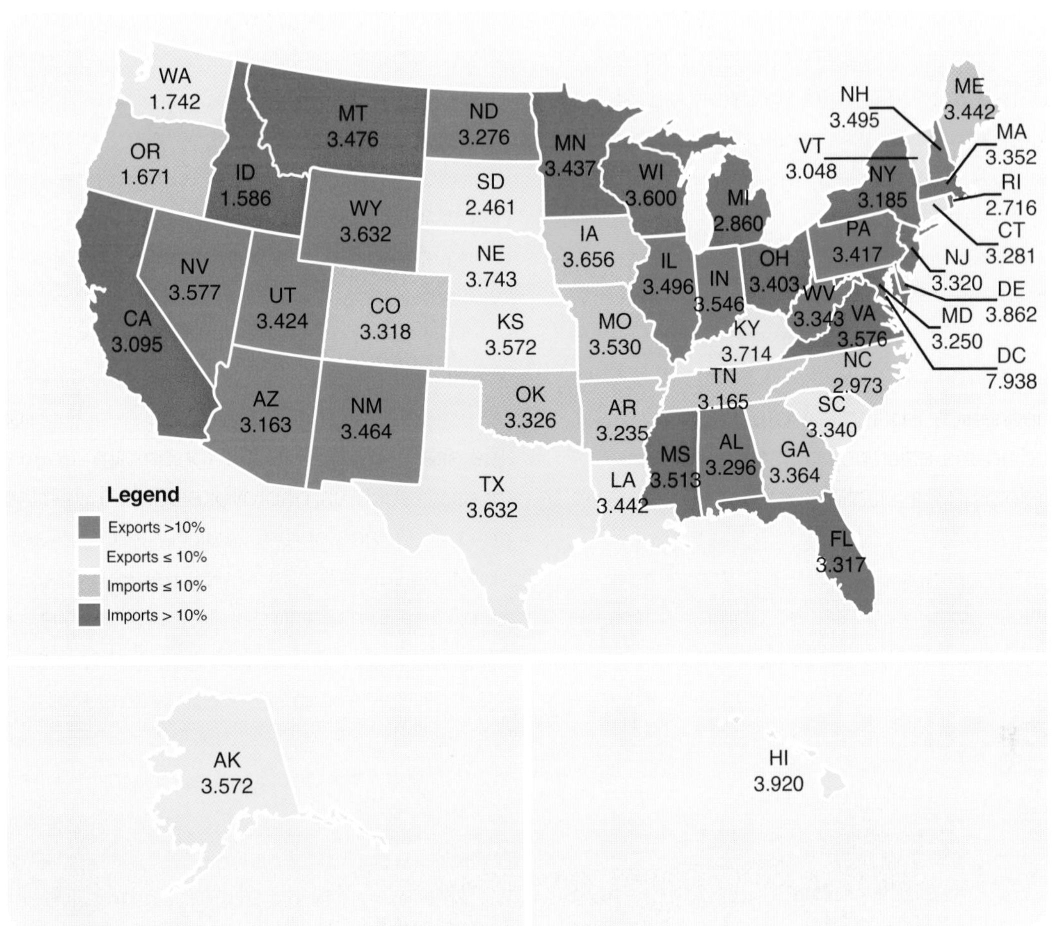

■ **FIGURE 4.11** Source Energy Factors for Electricity by State (2004). *Source: M. Deru and P. Torcellini, "Source Energy and Emission Factors for Energy Use in Buildings," Table B-9 and Table B-7.*

Energy Source	Heating System	Heat Energy (kBtu)	Efficiency or COP	Site Energy (kBtu)	Source Energy Factor	Source Energy (kBtu)
Natural Gas	Condensing Boiler	1,000	85%	1,176	1.047	1,232
Grid Electricity	Electric Resistance	1,000	100%	1,000	3.340	3,340
Grid Electricity	Ground Source Heat Pump	1,000	4.0 (COP)	250	3.340	835

■ **FIGURE 4.12** Example Using Source Energy to Understand Efficiency of Conventional Energy Sources.

Energy Source	Heating System	Heat Energy (kBtu)	Efficiency or COP	Site Energy (kBtu)	Source Energy Factor	Source Energy (kBtu)
Natural Gas	Condensing Boiler	1,000	85%	1,176	1.047	1,232
On-site RE Electricity	Electric Resistance	1,000	100%	1,000	1.0	1,000
On-Site RE Electricity	Ground Source Heat Pump	1,000	4.0 (COP)	250	1.0	250

■ **FIGURE 4.13** Example Using Source Energy to Understand Efficiency of On-site Renewable Electricity Table.

Energy Sources

Fuels are materials that can be consumed to produce energy. They are sources of energy, as well as forms of energy storage or energy carriers. The term *energy sources*, rather than *fuels*, is a broader and more meaningful way to refer to energy production; it is inclusive of fuels and includes nonfuel sources of energy and secondary energy sources such as electricity or hydrogen (see Figure 4.14). The energy source is an important consideration for net zero energy buildings because it impacts source energy, energy emissions, and energy costs, which are three of the four methods for measuring net zero energy. Put more simply, the energy source plays an important role in delivering a net zero energy building. Net zero energy buildings are essentially net zero nonrenewable energy buildings (or 100 percent net renewable energy), but that doesn't preclude them from utilizing a nonrenewable based source of energy—at least in the near term.

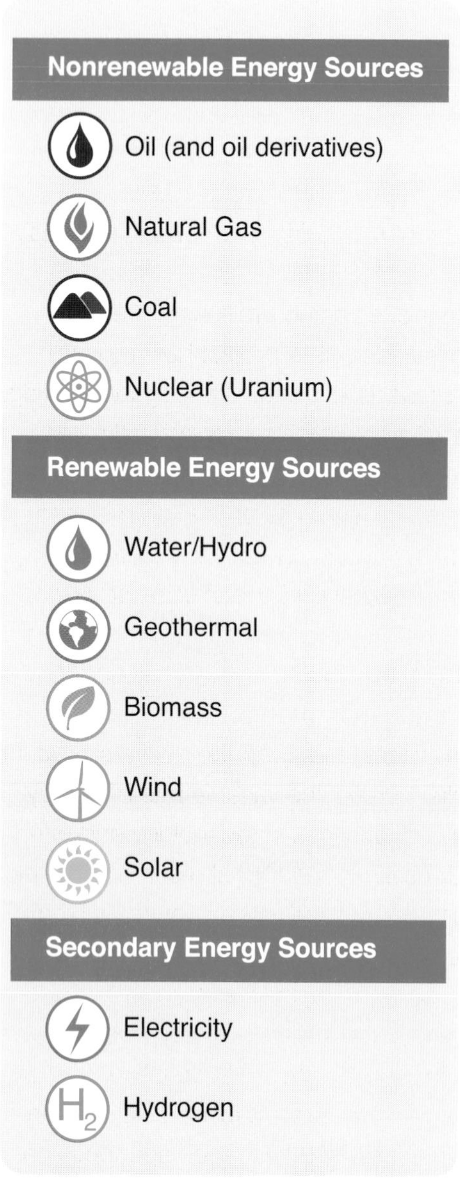

Nonrenewable energy sources are finite; they cannot be replenished. Fossil fuels, such as coal, natural gas, and oil are nonrenewable. Fossil fuels produce greenhouse gas emissions when consumed. The disadvantages of fossil fuel energy sources are among the primary reasons that net zero energy buildings are so important for our future. In addition to being finite, fossil fuels are also geographically constrained. These two factors lead to significant economic and geopolitical instability. In addition, the extraction of fossil fuels has detrimental environmental impacts. The three-month-long deep-water oil spill in the Gulf of Mexico in the spring of 2010 made the environmental consequences of fossil fuel extraction prime-time news. However, it is the contribution to global climate change that is the greatest disadvantage to the use of fossil fuel energy.

Uranium, the fuel for nuclear energy, is also a finite, nonrenewable energy source. This metallic element, used to generate energy through nuclear fission, does not directly result in greenhouse gas emissions. The disadvantages of nuclear power include the production of radioactive waste and the potential for an uncontrolled reaction at the plant. The world was made acutely aware of this danger with the nuclear plant disaster in Japan following the severe tsunami and earthquake on March 11, 2011.

Renewable energy sources are those that are continually replenished, such as solar,

Nonrenewable Energy Sources

- Oil (and oil derivatives)
- Natural Gas
- Coal
- Nuclear (Uranium)

Renewable Energy Sources

- Water/Hydro
- Geothermal
- Biomass
- Wind
- Solar

Secondary Energy Sources

- Electricity
- Hydrogen

■ **FIGURE 4.14** Energy Sources.

wind, and hydro, or those that replenish fast enough that, when managed properly, can be sustained indefinitely, such as biomass. Certain renewable energy sources, such as solar and wind, are not constant over time. Renewable energy also tends to be unevenly distributed and, often, sparsely distributed. For example, solar energy resources vary, depending on time of year, time of day (not available at night), and cloud cover, and generally are not highly concentrated. These dynamic characteristics are among the primary challenges to utilizing certain renewable energy sources. These sources are considered "clean," because they emit no greenhouse gases or are carbon-neutral. Even biomass in some applications may be considered carbon-neutral because the carbon emission from combustion is balanced against the carbon it sequestered when growing. The true carbon balance of biomass includes additional processing and transportation issues, and should be evaluated on a life-cycle basis. (Refer to Chapter 8, "Renewable Energy," for detailed guidance on renewable energy applications in the built environment.)

Energy sources for buildings are typically either 100 percent electricity or a combination of electricity and a fuel consumed on-site to generate heat. The two leading primary fuels used for building energy are coal (used to generate electricity) and natural gas (used to heat buildings and generate electricity at a utility scale). Replacing electricity with renewably generated electricity, and replacing fossil fuel heating fuels with renewable fuels, is a good starting point when moving from nonrenewable to renewable energy sources. Because photovoltaic systems comprise the most versatile and common approach to on-site renewable energy systems, all-electric buildings make net zero energy buildings relatively straightforward, from an energy source point of view. However, there are a variety of renewable energy sources available, depending on a project's site and location, and opportunities for developing renewable energy system at a multiple building scale. Therefore, net zero energy buildings often require creative and resourceful thinking about energy sources to achieve a net zero energy balance. (Chapter 8 provides detailed guidance on integrating renewable energy sources into commercial buildings.)

It's clear that the serious disadvantages of fossil fuel use make moving to a renewable-energy-based society essential; at the same time, it is important to keep in mind the important role fossil fuels have played in our history. These extremely effective and easy-to-use fuels are responsible for our development through the industrial age and into the information age. More specifically, they are responsible for our current standard of living, and form the basis of our economy.

Fossil fuels, as noted previously, are finite; however, it is difficult to predict how much of each fossil fuel is left, and how long the existing reserves will last. Based on recent estimates of proved reserves and current fuel consumption for coal, oil, and natural gas, both oil and natural gas could be depleted in half a century (see Figure 4.15). In contrast, the United States alone has enough coal to last a couple of centuries. There are numerous complex variables that come into play when considering the depletion of fossil fuels and the conversion to renewable sources: the variable rate of energy consumption, changes in technology and efficiency, discovery of additional reserves, and the advancement of renewable energy technology. The economic position of renewable energy continues to improve, thanks to advancements in technology, and increase in market share. Perhaps the most powerful force influencing the future transition away from fossil fuels is when renewable energy sources reach economic parity with nonrenewable energy sources.

Fuel	Reserves	Units	Consumptions	Units	Years Remaining*
Coal — World	930,423	Million Short Tons	7,238	Million Short Tons	129
Coal — U.S.	263,781	Million Short Tons	1,121	Million Short Tons	235
Crude Oil — World	1,354	Billion Barrels	31	Billion Barrels	43
Crude Oil — U.S.	19	Billion Barrels	7	Billion Barrels	3
Natural Gas — World	6,609	Trillion Cubic Feet	110	Trillion Cubic Feet	60
Natural Gas — U.S.	245	Trillion Cubic Feet	23	Trillion Cubic Feet	11

* Years Remaining is based only on author's calculation of reserves divided by rate of consumption, and is only meant to compare reserves and consumption for the geographic scope designated.

■ **FIGURE 4.15** Current Rate of Consumption and Reserves for Fossil Fuels. *Data source: U.S. Energy Information, 2008 data, accessed on December 6, 2010.*

Although the use of fossil fuels helped to rapidly advance our culture, economy, and technology, in context of the history of the human species, the dominance of fossil fuels represents a very small window of time. We have been living on 100 percent renewable energy for the vast majority of human history, and the choice of fuel has been biomass, or more specifically, wood. The earliest record of a controlled wood fire is 790,000 years old. The history of architecture is also marked by capitalizing on energy sources to create comfort and amenity. Ancient cultures on every continent developed architectural form and city-making in tune with the climate and to take advantage of solar resources. The introduction and evolution of fuel to heat buildings is a major factor in the shaping of architecture—from open fires to chimneys to central heaters. Heating involved the combustion of fuel within buildings, which required the introduction of combustion air and the exhaust of the products of combustion.

A return to renewable energy sources is part of the continuous trend toward shifting energy sources, developing technologies, and evolving architectural form. Fortunately, we have a long history of precedents for climate- and solar-responsive architectural design. While net zero energy architecture represents a new way of building, compared to practices of today, it is, in fact, a reintegration of energy into architecture. It is a step in the ongoing evolution of building systems technology, rapid advancement of renewable energy systems, and a reassessment of building form to respond to climate and take advantage of passive energy.

Energy and Carbon

One of the primary benefits of net zero energy buildings is the reduction of greenhouse gas emissions related to the building industry. The building industry is a major contributor to greenhouse gas emissions. Greenhouse gases (GHG) are those that contribute to the retention of heat in the atmosphere through the greenhouse effect. The Kyoto Protocol identifies six greenhouse gases for inventory reporting: carbon dioxide (CO_2), methane (CH_4), nitrous oxide (N_2O), hydrofluorocarbons (HFCs), perfluorocarbons (PFCs), and sulfur hexafluoride (SF_6). (See Figures 4.16 and 4.17.)

Of the six greenhouse gases, carbon dioxide (CO_2) has weaker global warming potential on a molecule-by-molecule basis. However, carbon dioxide dominates the other greenhouse gases in terms of amount of emissions and, therefore, in terms of overall global warming potential. For this reason, greenhouse gases are often simply referred to as *carbon emissions*. A special notation for this simplification has been developed,

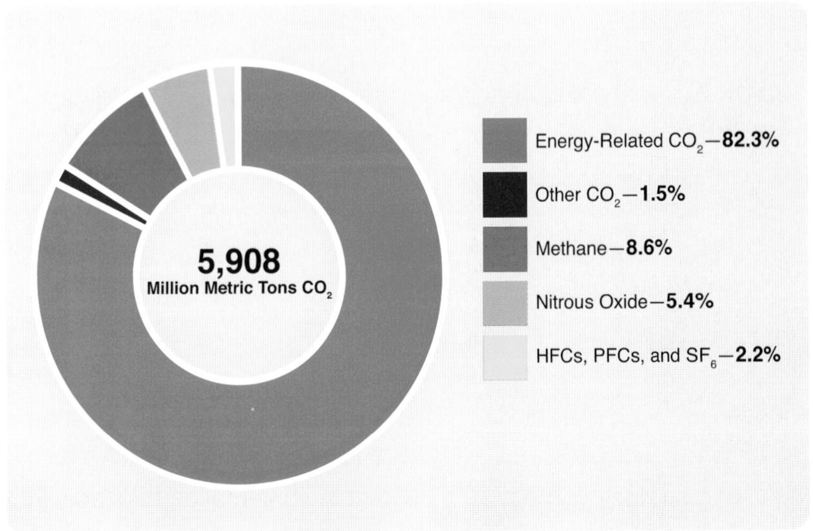

■ **FIGURE 4.16** U.S. Greenhouse Gas Emissions (2006). *Data source: U.S. Energy Information Administration, 2006.*

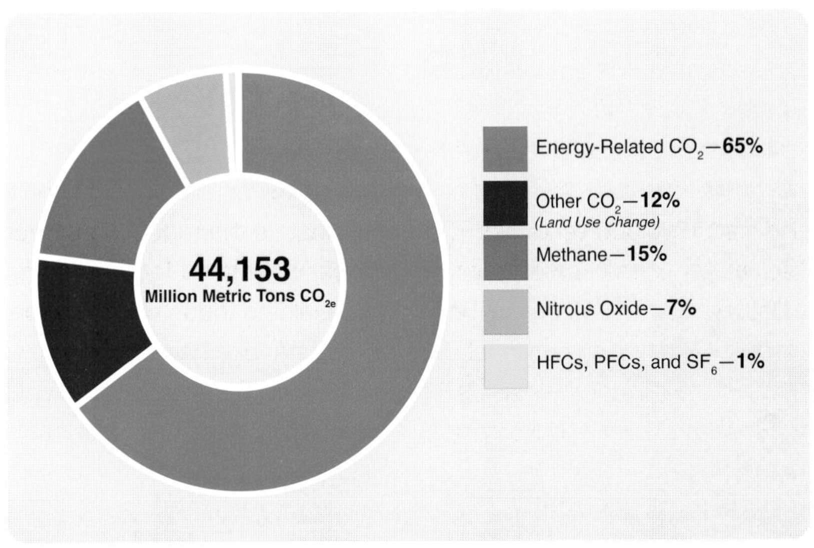

■ **FIGURE 4.17** Global Greenhouse Gas Emissions (2005). *Data source: World Resources Institute; www.wri.org/chart/world-greenhouse-gas-emissions-2005.*

called *equivalent carbon dioxide*, or CO_{2e}. Equivalent carbon dioxide is meant to express the global warming potential of all greenhouse gases in terms of a quantity of carbon dioxide.

The building industry has now become aware of the important role buildings play in terms of carbon emissions. Groups such as Edward Mazria's Architecture 2030 are educating the industry on the impacts of buildings; in particular, Architecture 2030 is inspiring transformation with its 2030 Challenge, which is set on incrementally eliminating fossil fuel emissions in buildings to a goal of carbon-neutral by the year 2030. The impact of the built environment as a whole is not necessarily communicated clearly in government statistics in terms of carbon emissions per industry sector. Typically, the U.S. statistics separate residential and commercial buildings into two distinct sectors. This organizational model positions commercial buildings as the smallest contributor to carbon emissions; however, the building industry comprises both commercial and residential buildings. Combining these sectors, as shown in Figure 4.18, immediately makes the impact clear. In addition, buildings have embodied carbon emissions from the manufacture and transportation of materials. To take this argument even further, it is possible to point to the role buildings and land use planning have in transportation intensity and patterns.

There can be no doubt that the building industry is responsible for a large portion of carbon emissions; what is also unquestionable is that the building industry offers one of the most important solutions and opportunities we have for addressing the problem. Net zero energy buildings offer a framework for transforming our built environment and addressing climate change. In addition, energy emissions present a method for measuring a net zero energy building. (Chapter 11 offers guidance on net zero energy emissions, carbon neutrality, carbon emission factors, and carbon footprint calculations.)

ENERGY USE INTENSITY

Uses and Limitations of Energy Use Intensity

Energy use intensity (EUI) is perhaps one of the most important and useful metrics employed in the design of net zero energy buildings. EUI is a measure of total annual building energy use divided by the gross building floor area. This can be expressed in terms of site energy or source energy. Common EUI units include kBtu/ft^2, kWh/ft^2, kWh/m^2, and MJ/m^2. In the United States, kBtu/ft^2 is the EUI unit most commonly used.

What makes the EUI metric so useful is that it serves as a way to compare energy performance of buildings, or compare energy performance with established baselines. EUI is a measure of energy performance, not of overall energy use. A good analogy for EUI is the miles-per-gallon (mpg) fuel efficiency measure for vehicles, except that, with EUI, the lower the number, the better the energy performance for the building (see Figure 4.19).

As a performance metric, EUI has many uses. During the design of a building, an

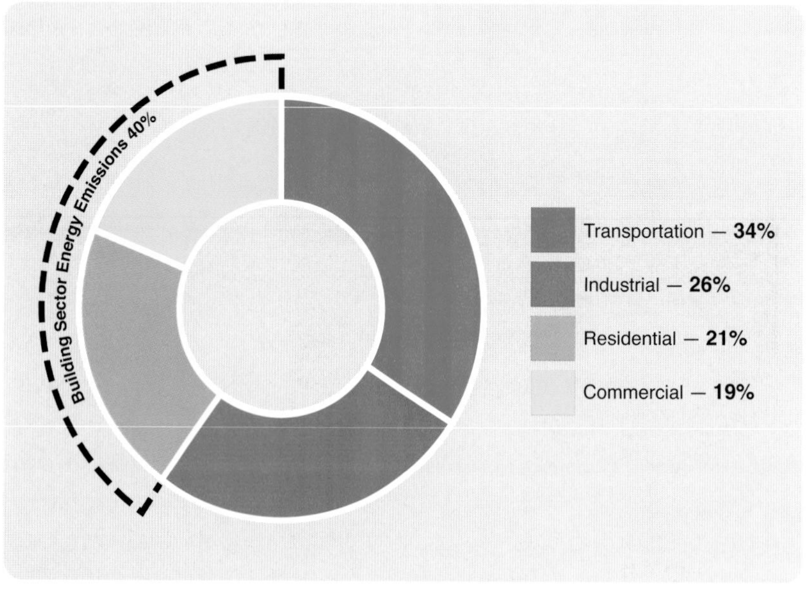

■ **FIGURE 4.18** U.S. Greenhouse Gas Emissions by Sector (2009). *Data source: U.S. Energy Information Administration, 2009.*

energy performance EUI target can be set and compared to EUI performance baselines. It can also be used to understand and communicate existing building energy performance. This is particularly beneficial with regard to building energy performance labeling. At the root of the EPA's ENERGY STAR score is the EUI metric. ASHRAE's emerging energy performance label, Building Energy Quotient (Building EQ), likewise uses EUI as the basis for measurement.

EUI is also useful as a planning tool. It can help manage energy performance across multiple building assets or a large commercial building portfolio. In a similar way, EUI has value in master-planning future projects, as a way to quantify projected energy performance and use through a wide set of mixed uses and building types. An excellent example of implementing EUI in a large-scale planning effort is the Chicago Central Area DeCarbonization Plan, completed by Adrian Smith + Gordon Gill Architecture. This plan for revitalizing Chicago's loop area focuses on assessment, strategies, and investment in a diverse range of urban design metrics, with a primary goal of energy and carbon reductions (see Figure 4.20).

It is best to think of the EUI metric as a tool that makes possible relative comparisons—to compare energy performance between buildings. That said, it is important to keep in mind the limitations of such comparisons. An EUI comparison is less helpful when comparing buildings in different climates or of different types. Variations in climate and program can result in dramatically different energy use. Therefore, it is more meaningful to compare buildings of the same type and in the same climate. That is not to say, however, that no important differences will exist between buildings of the same type and climate. Consider two office buildings in the same city: If they have different occupancy densities, their EUIs will vary accordingly. There are many such building program characteristics that affect energy use in commercial buildings of all types; but by being aware of these nuances, you will be able to exercise sound judgment in comparing and understanding EUI values.

Another potential limitation of EUI to keep in mind is that it is a measure based on the gross building floor area. ANSI/ASHRAE/IESNA 90.1, "Energy Standard for Buildings Except Low-Rise Residential Buildings," includes a definition of gross floor area, which

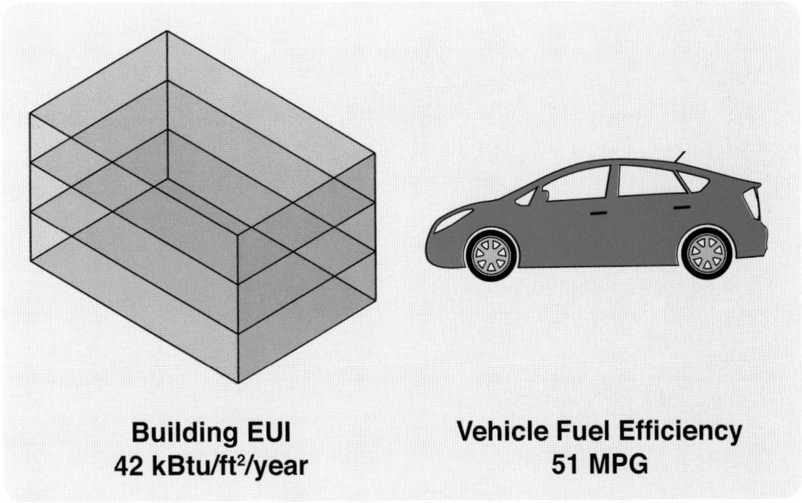

■ **FIGURE 4.19** Comparing EUI for Buildings and MPG for Vehicles.

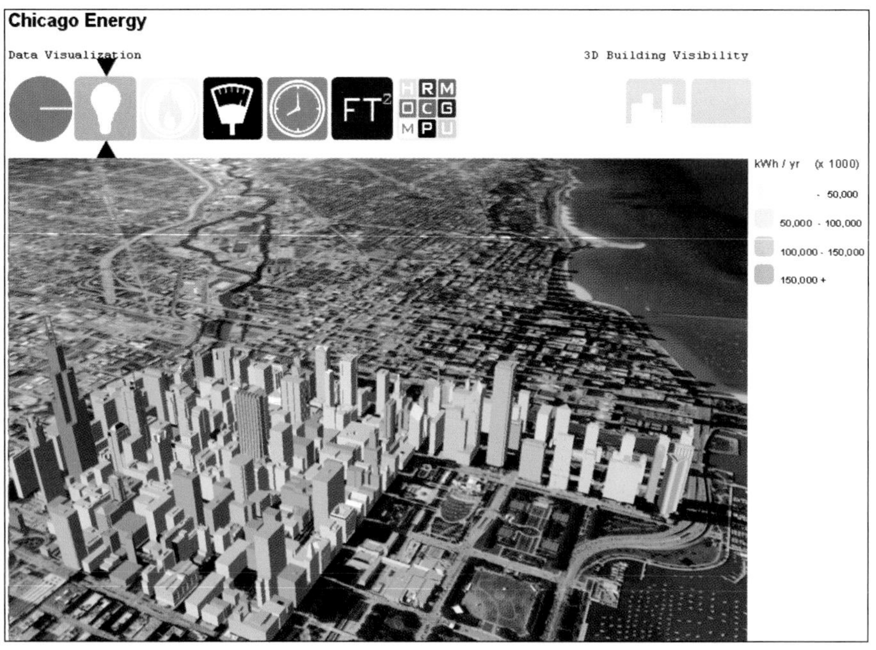

■ **FIGURE 4.20** The parametric model of Chicago's Loop allows large-scale analysis of energy, carbon, and other urban design metrics. *© 2010, Adrian Smith + Gordon Gill Architecture.*

factors in the area of exterior walls, among other details. Building codes and other building and real estate standards all have their own unique definitions of how to measure floor area. Even more noteworthy than minor differences in calculating gross floor area is the potential inclusion or exclusion of auxiliary spaces, such as enclosed parking. A wide variation in EUI can be calculated for the same building depending on whether the energy and/or the area of these auxiliary spaces are included or excluded. For example, should an office building EUI include the area or energy of an attached parking garage? Typically, the parking garage energy is included but the area is not. The decision should be based on how you are using the EUI calculation. The goal is to maintain an apples-to-apples comparison.

Because of some of the limitations of using simple EUI in terms of annual energy use per building area, there is increased interest among building industry professionals to explore building type-specific EUI metrics that allow for comparisons of energy use to a meaningful measure of production for each building type. For example, an office building could be measured by kBtu/occupant hour/year, rather than, or in addition to, kBtu/ft^2/year. Alternative EUI metrics might include kBtu/guest nights/year for a hotel, or kBtu/meals served/year for a restaurant, as examples. These metrics would likely best supplement standard EUI definitions and make it possible to explore multiple ways of minimizing energy use while maximizing building use and benefit.

While keeping the limitations of the EUI in mind, it can still be a very valuable tool. One reason is that there is a growing database on EUI values for use in benchmarking a building. In addition, the use of EUI metrics is growing within the industry. The source of most existing commercial building energy use and EUI metrics in the United States comes from a comprehensive nationwide survey of existing buildings, called the Commercial Building Energy Consumption Survey (CBECS). CBECS-derived EUI values constitute the average performance of current existing building stock, as represented by the

5,215 buildings sampled in the 2003 survey. At the time of this writing, a 2012 CBECS version is being planned by the U.S. Energy Information Administration, being the first update since the 2003 survey. The anticipated release of the 2012 data is in the spring of 2014. CBECS 2003 forms the basis for ENERGY STAR baselines and, therefore, 2030 Challenge baselines.

Energy and Climate

Climate dictates the heating and cooling loads at the building envelope. Thermal energy transfer at the building envelope load can account for a large portion of the overall energy use of a building, particularly in severe climates. Understanding the climate of a project locale is one of the first steps to understanding its energy problem(s).

The Climate Zone Definitions, established by the Department of Energy, and used by ASHRAE and the International Code Council (ICC), divide the United States into eight climate zones, based on heating degree-days and cooling degree-days, and distinctions between major climate types: moist (A), dry (B), and marine (C) (see Figures 4.21 and 4.22). Heating degree-days (HDD) is a measure of the difference between the mean daily temperature and a base temperature (for example, 65°F) when the mean temperature is below the base temperature and heating is required). For example, for a day with a 24-hour mean temperature of 30°F, the number of HDDs would be 35, using a base of 65°F. The annual heating degree-days constitute the sum of heating degree-days over the course of a year; the total is an indicator of the heating load related to a climate, while the total of cooling degree-days (CDDs) is the indicator of the cooling load related to a climate. CDDs measure the difference between the mean daily temperature and a base temperature (for example, 65°F) when

Zone No.	Climate Zone Type	Degree-days Criteria
1A	Very Hot-Humid	9000 < CDD50°F
1B	Very Hot-Dry	9000 < CDD50°F
2A	Hot-Humid	6300 < CCD50°F ≤ 9000
2B	Hot-Dry	6300 < CCD50°F ≤ 9000
3A	Warm-Humid	4500 < CDD50°F ≤ 6300
3B	Warm-Dry	4500 < CDD50°F ≤ 6300
3C	Warm-Marine	HDD65°F ≤ 3600
4A	Mixed-Humid	CDD50°F ≤ 4500 and HDD65°F ≤ 5400
4B	Mixed-Dry	CDD50°F ≤ 4500 and HDD65°F ≤ 5400
4C	Mixed-Marine	3600 < HDD65°F ≤ 5400
5	Cool-Humid	5400 < HDD65°F ≤ 7200
5B	Cool-Dry	5400 < HDD65°F ≤ 7200
5C	Cool-Marine	5400 < HDD65°F ≤ 7200
6A	Cold-Humid	7200 < HDD65°F ≤ 9000
6B	Cold-Dry	7200 < HDD65°F ≤ 9000
7	Very Cold	9000 < HDD65°F ≤ 12600
8	Subarctic	12600 < HDD65°F

■ **FIGURE 4.21** Climate Zone Definitions. *Data source: Briggs, R. S., Lucas, R. G., Taylor, Z. T., 2003, Climate Classification for Building Energy Codes and Standards: Part 1—Development Process. Richland, WA (PNNL/DOE).*

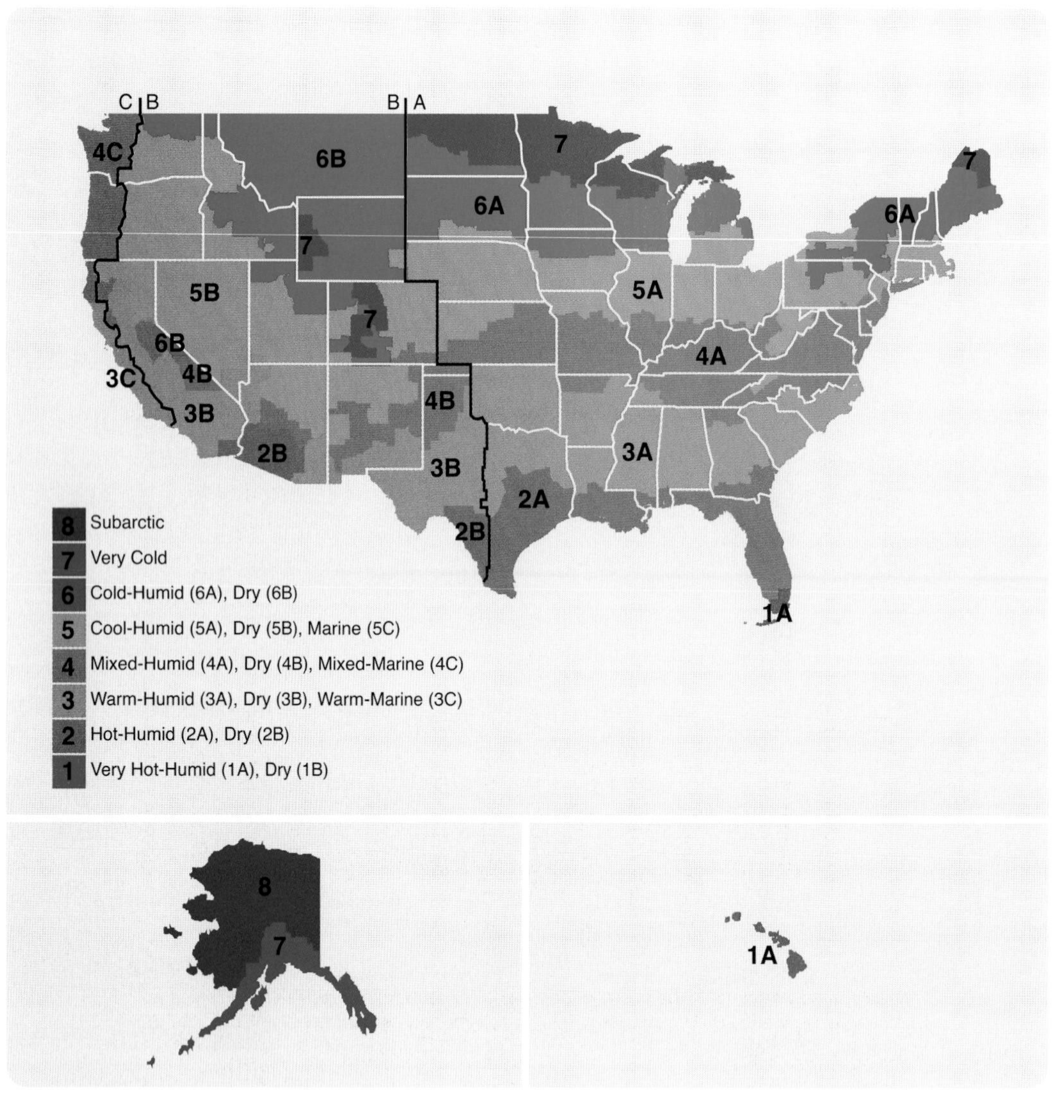

■ **FIGURE 4.22** U.S. Climate Zone Map. *Data sources: DOE, 2005, "Map of DOE's Proposed Climate Zones"; Briggs, R. S., Lucas, R. G., Taylor, Z. T., 2003, Climate Classification for Building Energy Codes and Standards: Part 1—Development Process. Richland, WA (PNNL/DOE).*

the mean temperature is above the base temperature and cooling is required).

The two primary climate-related factors that influence energy use are temperature and humidity. These translate into two types of heating and cooling loads: The *sensible heat load* is related to dry bulb temperature and the energy to add or remove heat to change dry bulb temperature. The *latent heat load* is related to wet bulb temperature and the energy to cause a phase change in the moisture content of the air, or to humidify or dehumidify the air.

Some generalities can be made about the impact of climate on energy use in a building. Humid climates tend to have higher energy use than dry climates, because of the latent heat load. The other generality is that the larger the sensible heat load is, due to more heating or cooling degree-days, the higher the resulting energy use. The colder climate zones—6A, 7, and 8—exhibit the highest EUI; the lowest EUI is in the mild climate zones of 3B and 3C. Refer to the EUI Climate Comparison table in Figure 4.23 for an analysis of commercial building energy use intensity

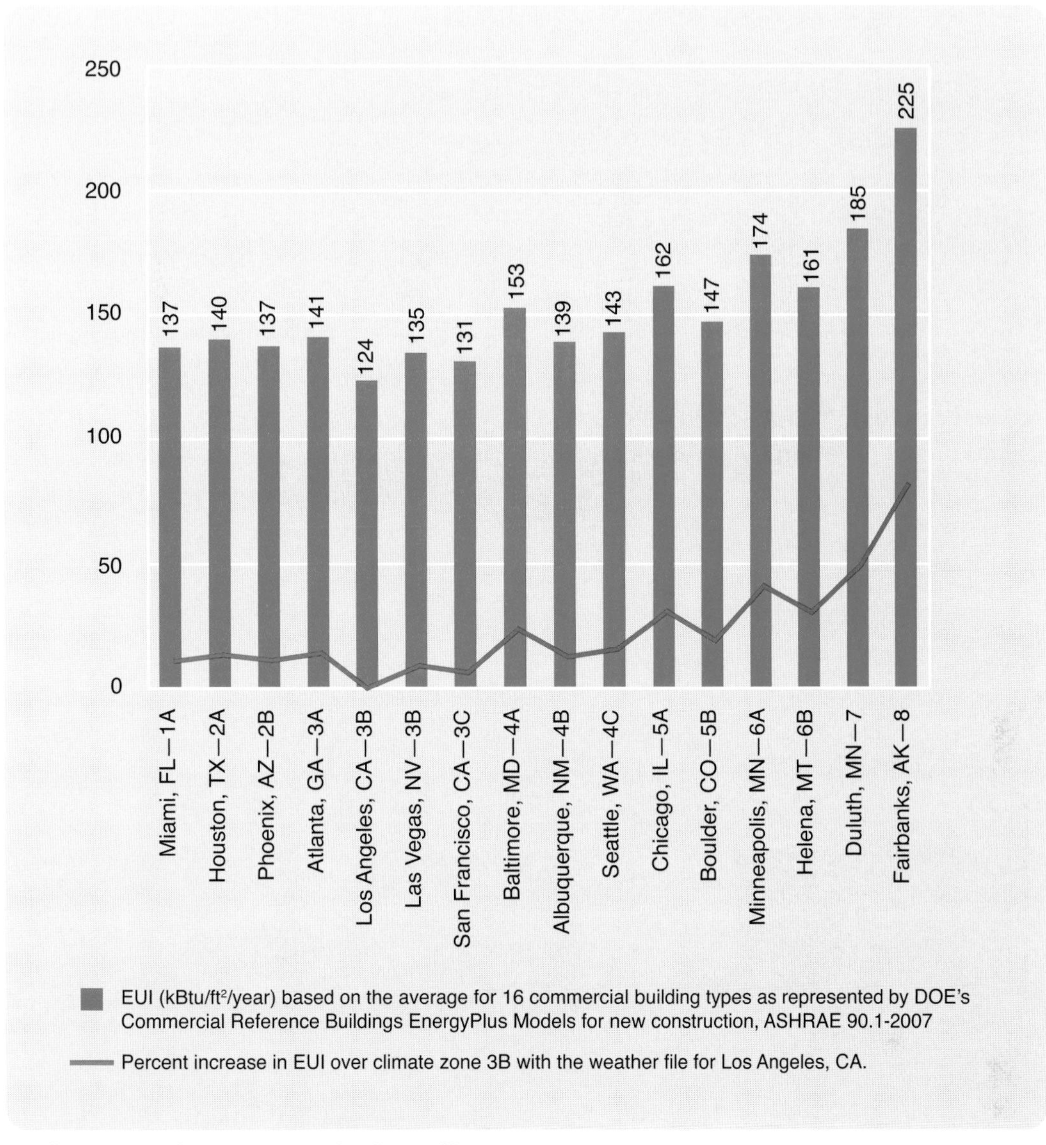

■ **FIGURE 4.23** Comparing EUI of Different Climates.

across 15 climate zones in the United States, using 16 weather files. The EUI values are from DOE Commercial Reference Buildings modeled in EnergyPlus. Sixteen different commercial building types are represented in the reference building models.

Climate as a factor of energy use in a building offers tremendous resources and the potential for free energy to buildings. Identifying these resources, as well as a climate's impact on energy loads, is key to achieving net zero and low-energy design. (Chapters 5 and 6 provide detailed guidance on designing with climate for low and net zero energy.)

Energy and Building Type

Just as climate dictates the energy loads at the building envelope, the building type dictates the internal loads. The building type or principal building activity determines schedules, occupancy densities, types of plug and process loads, domestic hot water and cooling loads from equipment, and lighting internal heat gain. These loads have a marked impact on the energy use of a building. Overall, building type can have a far greater effect on energy use than climate. Further, whereas climate can generally be addressed in the design of the exterior envelope, the loads related to building type can be more problematic.

Refer to the EUI Building Type Comparison table in Figure 4.24 for a comparison of 16 different commercial building types. The EUI values, taken from DOE Commercial Reference Buildings modeled in EnergyPlus, are averaged for 16 different weather files representing 15 climate zones. The majority of building types fall into a low to moderate energy use intensity category. Building types such as large hotels, supermarkets, and hospital uses have high EUIs, while restaurants have very high EUIs.

Building type is a major influence on the feasibility of and approach to a net zero energy building. Most apparent is the wide range of energy use intensities. In general, the higher the EUI, the more challenging the net zero energy building will be. The other notable influence is that building types often take

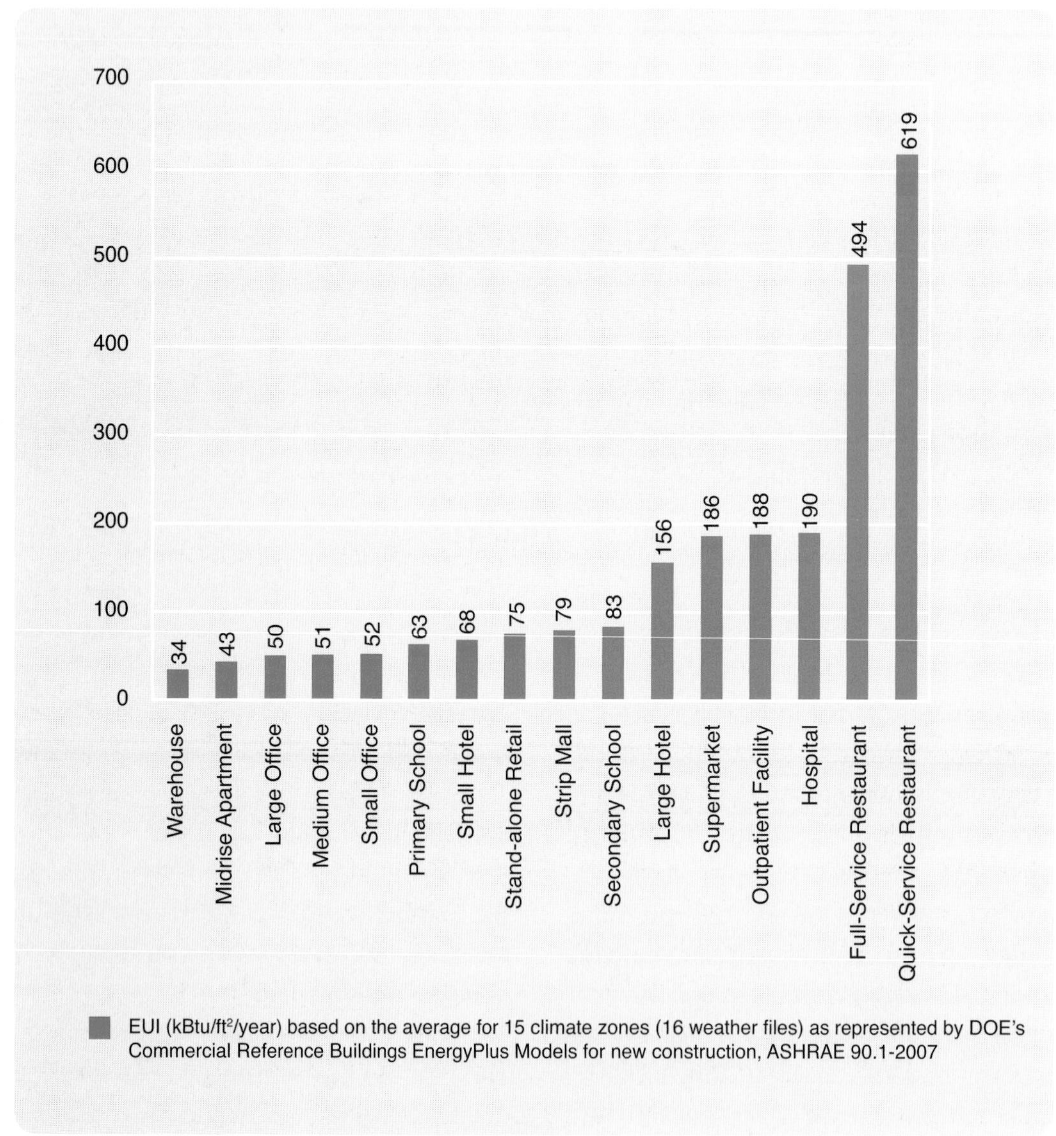

■ **FIGURE 4.24** Comparing the EUI of Different Building Types.

typical architectural form and massing based on function and precedents. For example, a supermarket, big-box retailer, or warehouse will commonly be single-story with a large footprint. This type of massing has a large roof area per floor area ratio. The advantage of large roof areas is the potential for larger roof photovoltaic systems. Other building types, such as large office buildings, hotels, and hospitals tend to be multistory buildings and have a lower roof area to floor area ratio. (Chapter 5 offers detailed guidance on the relationship between building massing and net zero energy design.)

ENERGY TARGETS

Energy Baseline

Energy use intensity targets are powerful tools for the design of low-energy and net zero energy buildings because in setting these targets, a project team and building owner can establish energy performance objectives that can then be used to guide and inform a design process. One unique quality of a net zero energy building is that it does not rely on the comparison of a baseline energy use to quantify its objective. Net zero energy is an absolute energy measure, as opposed to the common approach of "percent better" than an accepted baseline. Nonetheless, it is helpful to develop and interpret conventional energy baselines for a net zero energy project, to provide additional ways of understanding and communicating the energy efficiency of the building, with the ultimate goal being to successfully set and hit the net zero energy target.

The first step in establishing an energy target is to develop EUI baselines for the project, as this leads to the development of an energy target or group of bracketed targets against the baselines. Two common energy baselines are developed for projects: CBECS and ASHRAE 90.1. (Note: ASHRAE 90.1 refers to ANSI/ASHRAE/IESNA 90.1, "Energy Standard for Buildings Except Low-Rise Residential Buildings," used in commercial building energy codes and as the energy reference standard for LEED.)

A CBECS (reference year 2003) baseline is used for the 2030 Challenge and for ENERGY STAR. It establishes the energy performance level of the average existing building of the specified type and allows the comparison of a new building design (or an existing building) against a sampling of similar existing buildings. As discussed in the previous section, the CBECS survey data forms the basis for defining a CBECS baseline. Unfortunately, the CBECS database is very large and not very user-friendly. Fortunately, several published tables are available that consolidate and normalize the data. There are also very useful, and free, web-based interfaces that can provide a CBECS database. Software, too, is available, such as IES Virtual Environment, that can generate a CBECS baseline (as well as the ASHRAE 90.1 baseline).

The ASHRAE 90.1 baseline establishes a minimum code performance standard for the specific building under consideration. And although it does not provide a comparison with other peer buildings, it enables a comparison with different versions of the same building. With ASHRAE 90.1, a baseline, or code-minimum version, of a project is simulated using energy modeling. This baseline model includes defined code default building parameters, such as insulation levels and mechanical systems, and combines the effects of rotating the building in all four orientations.

One of the difficulties of setting an ASHRAE 90.1 baseline at the beginning of a project is that an energy model will need to be developed—a very rigorous undertaking. Typically, the final baseline model isn't created until the end of design. However, it may be possible to use a simplified model to establish an early baseline. The ASHRAE 90.1 baseline may have only limited value in setting an absolute energy target because it is a prescriptive, and abstract as a metric, and is fundamentally different from an absolute energy target metric. Nevertheless, it is another filter through which to view the energy problem, and as such can add value for teams with experience using ASHRAE 90.1 metrics. Further, it is very likely that LEED certification will be pursued for a net zero energy process, so developing an ASHRAE 90.1 baseline and target will, in any case, have to be part of the process.

Clearly, CBECS and ASHRAE 90.1 have distinctly different meanings and value for establishing energy baselines, and so it is useful to look at the energy baseline from multiple perspectives. There may be other code-comparative baselines that can add value to a project, such as Title 24 for projects in California. In addition to CBECS and code-based baselines, another method of establishing energy baselines for a project is to research building precedents. This could include gathering energy performance data on the best-performing peer buildings or on a set of existing similar buildings with the same owner, or completed by the same design team.

ENERGY STAR TARGET FINDER

Perhaps the best and easiest-to-use baseline and target-setting tool is the web-based ENERGY STAR Target Finder (www.energystar.gov/targetfinder). The ENERGY STAR program and website have many resources that are valuable to the building industry. In addition to Target Finder, it offers a Portfolio Manager, education programs, award and recognition programs, partnership opportunities, and ENERGY STAR-labeled buildings (the latter at the heart of the program).

With just some basic project information and a few minutes of time, the Target Finder website can provide a CBECS baseline, ENERGY STAR Targets, and useful information about energy use for a building project, such as carbon emissions and energy costs. Target Finder normalizes the data from CBECS to generate a specific target for the zip code and project parameters entered into the website. One caveat, however: Target Finder works only for a limited group of building types and uses. But within these predefined uses, you can customize a mixed-use project and add auxiliary spaces such as parking garages and swimming pools.

By selecting ENERGY STAR's Target Rating or Energy Reduction Target option, Target Finder can be used to determine both an energy baseline and target. The Target Rating, called the "EPA Energy Performance Rating," is a score from 1 to 100, where 100 represents the equivalent of an energy performance in the hundredth percentile of the CBECS sample group, or the top performing in the group. A score of 50 represents the fiftieth percentile, or the average building performance. To set a baseline energy target equivalent to a CBECS EUI target, select a Target Rating of 50. Note that this target is also used for the 2030 Challenge. Setting a higher performance target, either a score of 95 or better or an Energy Reduction Target of 60 percent or greater, might be a good starting point in defining a net zero energy EUI target. (Refer to the "Net Zero Energy Target" section later in this chapter for more information.)

Note that Target Finder also allows the input of "Estimated Design Energy." This step is not required to develop a baseline or energy target; if left blank, the program fills in default values for fuel types and energy costs. The purpose of this step is to input results from a design energy analysis for the purpose of comparing design energy against the selected target. This feature is then used to develop a "Statement of Energy Design Intent," which can be used to apply for the EPA's excellent Designed to Earn ENERGY STAR program, which allows projects to be certified at the end of design and to include a special certification logo on construction drawings.

Figure 4.25 is a sample page from the Target Finder performance results report. This report supplies a lot of valuable information in addition to baseline and/or target EUI and annual energy use, including fuel mix, EPA Energy Performance Rating, energy costs, and carbon-equivalent emissions. The report also has an Edit button, which, when clicked, will take you back to the project's

Target Energy Performance Results

The design **must** achieve a rating of 75 or higher to be eligible for "Designed to Earn the ENERGY STAR".

View Statement of Energy Design Intent

NOTE: Assumptions are 45% Electricity - Grid Purchase and 55% Natural Gas. The Target & Average Building energy use for this facility are calculated based on the typical fuel mix in the zip code specified.

Target Energy Performance Results (estimated)			
Energy	**Design**	**Target**	**Average Building**
Energy Performance Rating (1-100)	N/A	50	50
Energy Reduction (%)	N/A	0	0
Source Energy Use Intensity (kBtu/Sq. Ft./yr)	N/A	168	168
Site Energy Use Intensity (kBtu/Sq. Ft./yr)	N/A	81	81
Total Annual Source Energy (kBtu)	N/A	12,585,902	12,585,902
Total Annual Site Energy (kBtu)	N/A	6,054,262	6,054,262
Total Annual Energy Cost ($)	N/A	$ 125,011	$ 125,011
Pollution Emissions			
CO2-eq Emissions (metric tons/year)	N/A	441	441
CO2-eq Emissions Reduction (%)	N/A	0%	0%

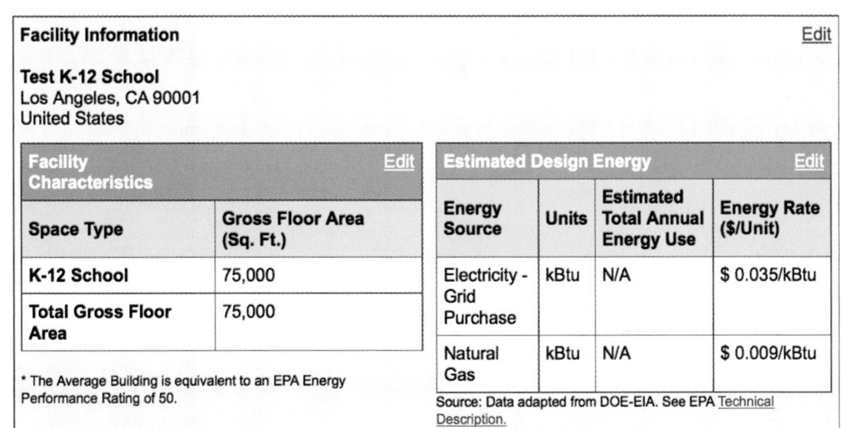

Facility Information Edit

Test K-12 School
Los Angeles, CA 90001
United States

Facility Characteristics Edit	
Space Type	**Gross Floor Area (Sq. Ft.)**
K-12 School	75,000
Total Gross Floor Area	75,000

* The Average Building is equivalent to an EPA Energy Performance Rating of 50.

Estimated Design Energy Edit			
Energy Source	**Units**	**Estimated Total Annual Energy Use**	**Energy Rate ($/Unit)**
Electricity - Grid Purchase	kBtu	N/A	$ 0.035/kBtu
Natural Gas	kBtu	N/A	$ 0.009/kBtu

Source: Data adapted from DOE-EIA. See EPA Technical Description.

■ **FIGURE 4.25** ENERGY STAR Target Finder Performance Results Report for Example Elementary School in Los Angeles. *Screen capture from ENERGY STAR Target Finder website.*

input screen, where you can change inputs if desired. This example shows Target Finder results for a 75,000-square-foot elementary school located in Los Angeles, California. In this case, an ENERGY STAR target of 50 was selected; no estimated design energy was input, as the goal was to determine the CBECS baseline for the project. As shown, the CBECS baseline EUI for annual site energy is 81 kBtu/ft^2, and the annual source energy is 168 kBtu/ft^2.

EnergyIQ

The Lawrence Berkeley National Laboratory in Berkeley, California, has developed a web-based energy baseline tool called EnergyIQ (www.energyiq.lbl.gov), to perform what it calls *action-oriented energy benchmarking.* EnergyIQ utilizes two databases, the California Commercial End-Use Survey (CEUS) and CBECS. The CBECS database allows for considerable customization, including building type, climate zone or region, building vintage, and building area. The CEUS database offers an expanded list of features for projects in California. What distinguishes EnergyIQ from ENERGY STAR is the ability to customize the output and work directly with the CBECS data. With EnergyIQ, it is possible to examine energy use in multiple ways, including total energy use, energy end uses, and type of fuel. Results can be displayed in a variety of units and graphical formats.

Figure 4.26 shows a sample page from an EnergyIQ report. It uses the same 75,000-square-foot elementary school cited in Figure 4.25. Here, the CBECS (national) data was used, rather than the CEUS (California) data, to be more consistent with the preceding example. EnergyIQ generates a median EUI for annual site energy of 59.6 kBtu/ft^2 for the example project. This differs from the ENERGY STAR result, mainly because EnergyIQ uses raw CBECS building results, whereas ENERGY STAR normalizes for location and specific project parameters. EnergyIQ

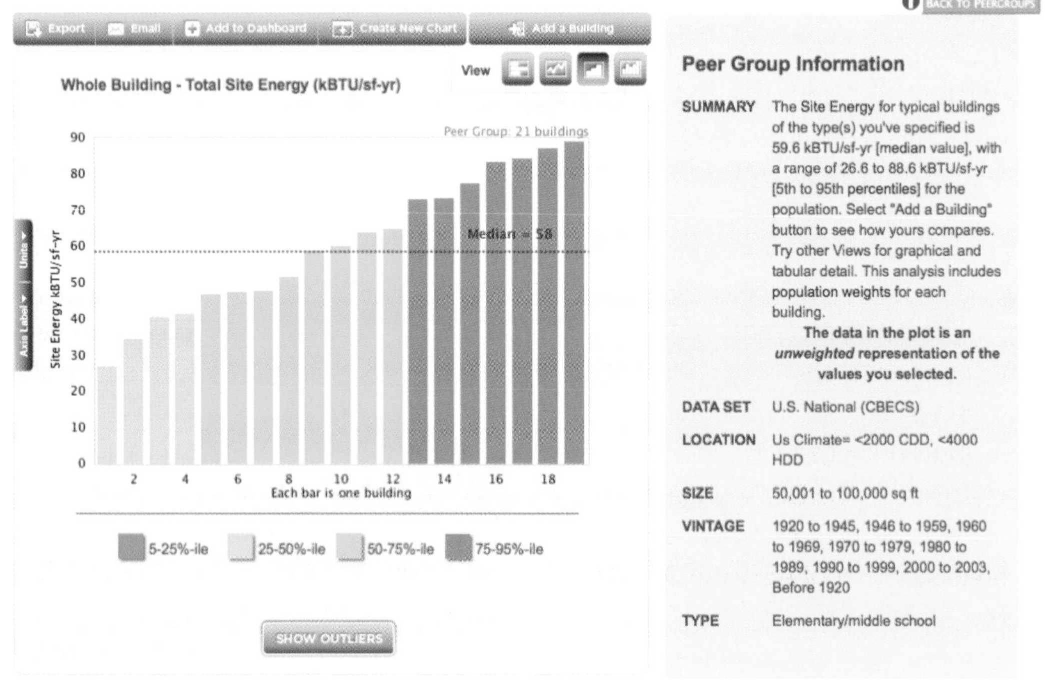

■ **FIGURE 4.26** EnergyIQ Performance Results Report for Example Elementary School in Los Angeles.
Screen capture from EnergyIQ website.

found 21 peer buildings in the selected climate zone, size range, and vintage. It is interesting to note the wide range of EUI values for the 21 peer buildings. EnergyIQ also allows for the export of data into Excel format, for further analysis.

CBECS-BASED BASELINE TABLES

There are several sources of published CBECS-based energy baseline tables. The 2030 Challenge is one. The 2030 Challenge target table for commercial buildings in the United States, along with a residential table and tables for projects in Canada, can be found at the Architecture 2030 website (www.architecture2030.org). The 2030 Challenge target table provides baseline data on building types that are not available with ENERGY STAR Target Finder. For those building types that are available in Target Finder, the 2030 Challenge defaults back to Target Finder. There is, however, one notable disadvantage to using the 2030 Challenge table: The EUIs are national averages, and not based on climate zones.

The DOE, through its national laboratories, has developed an assortment of benchmark modeling tools, among them published tables that summarize and analyze CBECS data by building type and climate zone. This effort includes the creation of a set of EnergyPlus models by DOE/NREL that represent the CBECS database of buildings. These models were analyzed in EnergyPlus and compared to the CBECS database; more important, the analysis allowed the CBECS projects to be normalized around the DOE-defined climate zones for the United States. DOE and NREL also developed a set of ASHRAE 90.1–2004 baselines from this set of models. The results of both studies have been compiled in the DOE/NREL Baseline Energy Use Intensities table (see Figure 4.27).

Again using the 75,000-square-foot elementary school in Los Angeles, which is climate zone 3B, a CBECS and ASHRAE 90.1–2004 baseline can be derived from the DOE/NREL table. The CBECS EUI baseline for the project is 74 kBtu/ft^2 annual site energy; the ASHRAE 90.1 preliminary EUI baseline is 41 kBtu/ft^2. Note that an ASHRAE 90.1 baseline must be developed through energy modeling that is specific to each individual project; but this table also can be used as a guide before the actual baseline is modeled. Also note that these ASHRAE 90.1 baseline tables were developed using the 2004 standard, and that subsequent updates have raised the performance requirements.

SOFTWARE-BASED ENERGY BASELINES

DOE and NREL have developed the next generation of energy modeling software, called EnergyPlus, and a number of supporting tools and resources, including a Google SketchUp plug-in called OpenStudio. DOE has created a library of reference for commercial building EnergyPlus model files for use by the building industry.

Using EnergyPlus modeling software and DOE's published commercial reference building models is one way to develop energy baselines; in addition to utilizing these preset EnergyPlus files, DOE has developed a web-based interface called the EnergyPlus Example File Generator (http://apps1.eere.energy.gov/buildings/energyplus/cfm/inputs). NREL also has a web interface for the EnergyPlus Example File Generator, called "Model Maker" (http://modelmaker.nrel.gov). Note that using these EnergyPlus modeling methods will not result in a CBECS EUI baseline, but they can generate a baseline for a more specific peer building definition, or approximate an ASHRAE 90.1 baseline during the early stages of design. Other

Building Type	Climate Zone																													
	All		1A		2A		2B		3A		3B		3C		4A		4B		4C		5A		5B		6A		6B		7	
All	90	71	74	82	72	68	114	73	89	78	70	58	62	62	95	70	108	55	99	56	104	75	87	64	89	76	97	74	71	74
Office	93	57	42	55	82	61	72	65	88	52	70	46	58	44	97	60	143	58	95	53	107	60	66	48	110	62	114	61	68	68
Education	83	52	52	52	73	49	160	57	62	42	74	41	105	54	102	60	38	34	58	43	87	53	79	44	90	60	90	64	84	64
Public Assembly	94	62	75	66	60	66	N/A	66	112	72	48	52	45	52	110	54	44	48	249	77	103	68	97	50	88	66	102	51	97	70
Public Order and Safety	116	67	N/A	54	91	54	N/A	54	160	67	79	67	N/A	67	129	60	N/A	60	N/A	60	108	78	94	78	126	73	148	87	N/A	87
Religious Worship	44	44	N/A	40	31	40	N/A	40	28	29	31	29	N/A	29	47	44	56	59	N/A	59	52	51	39	35	53	57	34	39	N/A	44
Service	77	83	60	83	53	78	N/A	78	49	60	61	63	27	63	82	79	83	52	N/A	52	80	92	101	76	88	102	99	86	65	108
Retail (Other Than Malls)	74	68	61	68	63	66	129	66	60	63	50	54	31	54	65	68	100	58	N/A	58	88	73	80	71	93	76	97	91	102	100
Food Sales	200	181	N/A	200	166	200	N/A	200	212	190	183	151	120	151	242	188	N/A	188	N/A	188	203	173	147	182	242	208	N/A	208	199	181
Food Services	258	354	393	354	208	354	N/A	354	423	380	393	375	82	375	234	368	N/A	368	260	368	258	336	228	283	203	341	236	341	192	354
Lodging	94	55	81	65	91	51	N/A	51	98	52	57	40	N/A	40	92	57	264	61	545	61	89	55	65	51	108	60	93	64	68	63
Skilled Nursing	125	131	N/A	132	71	132	N/A	132	84	113	85	102	N/A	103	148	145	N/A	145	N/A	145	148	142	153	106	118	132	134	132	N/A	132
Inpatient Health Care	249	111	200	108	246	108	360	108	205	118	257	98	204	97	248	106	163	106	N/A	106	294	115	245	106	240	113	235	116	256	116
Outpatient Health Care	95	76	19	76	77	80	N/A	80	55	64	106	79	N/A	79	70	66	190	66	N/A	66	111	90	120	76	112	82	91	78	166	107
Laboratory	305	323	N/A	323	N/A	323	N/A	323	242	323	170	369	N/A	369	600	272	N/A	272	N/A	272	370	313	N/A	313	268	323	115	323	N/A	323
Refrigerated Warehouse	99	86	N/A	86	N/A	86	N/A	86	N/A	86	N/A	86	N/A	86	120	88	N/A	86	N/A	86	68	85	51	86	62	86	N/A	86	N/A	86
Nonrefrigerated Warehouse	42	41	22	27	16	31	N/A	31	22	37	21	30	20	30	39	42	29	49	37	30	79	47	60	51	37	50	58	47	33	45
Vacant	21	30	N/A	30	4	23	47	23	4	30	6	20	0	20	40	41	3	41	60	41	21	21	93	21	22	40	N/A	40	55	40
Other	79	58	N/A	73	48	73	N/A	73	100	58	175	58	N/A	58	71	57	26	57	N/A	57	94	61	92	61	69	63	85	63	57	63

2003 CBECS Weighted Mean Energy Use Intensities Source: *DOE/NREL, B. Griffith, N. Long, P. Torcellini, R. Judkoff, D. Crawley, J. Ryan, Methodology for Modeling Building Energy Performance Across the Commercial Sector, March 2008, Table 4-1 (Note that CBECS samples sizes vary between different building types and climate zones. N/A denotes no samples in specific category.)*

ASHRAE 90.1-2004 Minimally Compliant Mean Energy Use Intensities Source: *DOE/NREL, B. Griffith, N. Long, P. Torcellini, R. Judkoff, D. Crawley, J. Ryan, Assessment of the Technical Potential for Achieving Net Zero-Energy Buildings in the Commercial Sector, December 2007, Table 4-10 (Note that EUI values are derived from EnergyPlus simulations of 2003 CBECS samples. Many categories have less than 5 CBECS samples and in such cases modeling results are carried across adjacent climate zones)*

For building type definitions, refer to: www.eia.doe.gov/emeu/cbecs/building_types.html.

FIGURE 4.27 Baseline Energy Use Intensities in kBu/ft2/year(DOE/NREL).

energy-modeling software, such as eQUEST Autodesk Vasari and IES Virtual Environment (VE), can be used to develop baseline building models and studies. (Refer back to Chapter 3 for guidance on using energy and simulation tools, with an emphasis on the designer and/or architect for early design simulations.)

Using the EnergyPlus Example File generator, our example elementary school project would result in an ASHRAE 90.1–2004 baseline of 32.1 kBtu/ft²/year and an ASHRAE 90.1–2007 baseline of 30.5 kBtu/ft²/year.

PEER BUILDING BASELINES

Researching precedents of buildings of similar use, size, and climate can result in another useful type of energy baseline. A peer building baseline can offer a tangible comparison of, and serve as learning tool for, understanding the energy potential of a project. It might be beneficial, and appropriate, to develop peer building baselines based on an owner's existing facilities using utility data. In addition, a number of high-performance building databases can be searched for exemplary performing peer projects. The DOE's High Performance Building Database is one such tool, and can be found at http://eere.buildinggreen.com.

Using the DOE building database, a relevant peer building was found to baseline against our 75,000-square-foot elementary school: a 69,600-square-foot elementary school in Long Beach, California, built in 2004 with an energy use intensity of 33.5 kBtu/ft²/year, based on 2007 utility bills.

BASELINE EXAMPLE

Continuing with our 75,000-square-foot elementary school in Los Angeles, we will determine what the appropriate energy baselines are, using the examples and baseline sources discussed throughout this section.

A variety of CBECS and ASHRAE 90.1 sources and techniques were used to gain a multiperspective view of the energy baseline. The following example analysis summarizes the results of the energy baseline research conducted on our elementary school.

Example CBECS and ASHRAE 90.1 Baseline Analysis for 75,000-Square-Foot Elementary School in Los Angeles, CA

The full range of energy baselines researched are useful for understanding the energy problem and for setting a net zero energy target. In addition to a net zero energy target, a project may also have a 2030 Challenge and LEED target and baseline. Based on the research summarized here, this project would have a CBECS (2030 Challenge) baseline of 81 kBtu/ft²/year because the 2030 Challenge prioritizes results from ENERGY STAR; the preliminary ASHRAE 90.1 baseline for LEED would be 31 kBtu/ft²/year (see Figure 4.28).

CBECS from ENERGY STAR Target Finder (Figure 4.25)

- 81 kBtu/ft²/year site energy baseline
- 168 kBtu/ft²/year source energy baseline

CBECS from EnergyIQ (Figure 4.26)

- 60 kBtu/ft²/year site energy baseline
- Note a range from 27 to 89 kBtu/ft²/year.

CBECS from DOE/NREL Table (Figure 4.27)

- 74 kBtu/ft²/year site energy baseline

ASHRAE 90.1–2004 from DOE/NREL Table (Figure 4.27)

- 41 kBtu/ft^2/year site energy baseline

ASHRAE 90.1–2004 from EnergyPlus Example File Generator

- 32 kBtu/ft^2/year site energy baseline

ASHRAE 90.1–2007 from EnergyPlus Example File Generator

- 31 kBtu/ft^2/year site energy baseline

Peer Building Baseline

- 34 kBtu/ft^2/year site energy baseline

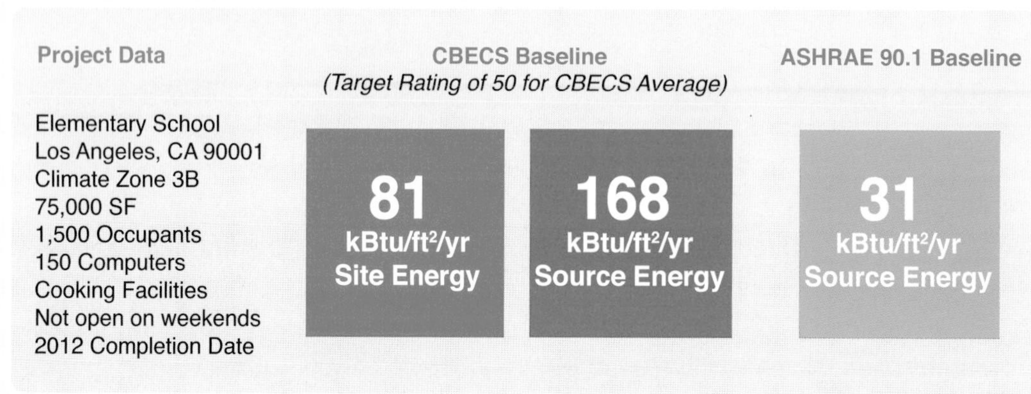

Project Data
Elementary School
Los Angeles, CA 90001
Climate Zone 3B
75,000 SF
1,500 Occupants
150 Computers
Cooking Facilities
Not open on weekends
2012 Completion Date
CBECS Baseline
(Target Rating of 50 for CBECS Average)
81
kBtu/ft²/yr
Site Energy
168
kBtu/ft²/yr
Source Energy
ASHRAE 90.1 Baseline
31
kBtu/ft²/yr
Source Energy

■ **FIGURE 4.28** Example Project Baselines.

Setting Targets

Perhaps the most difficult part of establishing an energy target is establishing a realistic and relevant energy baseline. As noted previously, it is good practice to develop both a CBECS baseline and ASHRAE 90.1 baseline and to examine a variety of sources for baseline data.

Before tackling the energy target for net zero energy, let us look at setting targets based on the two most common performance metric criteria in the United States today: LEED and the 2030 Challenge. Setting these targets provides calibrated gauges against which to evaluate the net zero energy target.

2030 CHALLENGE TARGET

The 2030 Challenge energy target is, in general, relatively straightforward to establish. Simply apply the scheduled percent reduction of fossil

NOTE

It is important to note that this book defines the *energy target* to be the energy use of the building, either in total energy or as a EUI. The energy target does not include a reduction for renewable energy. Net zero buildings continue to use energy, so their energy targets should reflect this accurately. It is likewise important to quantify the building performance before renewable energy is applied. Renewable energy goals are stated separately from energy targets. There are cases in both the 2030 Challenge and LEED that will warrant special clarification around this definition of energy targets.

fuel consumption to the project's CBECS baseline. For example, if a project is to be complete in 2014, the appropriate reduction would be 60 percent and hence the target would equal 40 percent of the baseline. (The details of the 2030 Challenge were outlined in Chapter 1.)

There is, however, one potential complication with setting the 2030 Challenge target. The target is communicated as the net fossil fuel energy target, and can incorporate unlimited renewable energy offsets and green power up to 20 percent. For example, in the year 2020, the fossil fuel reduction is scheduled to be 80 percent. If the baseline is 60 kBtu/ft^2/year, the target will be 12 kBtu/ft^2/year. However, the actual energy use of the building may be 22 kBtu/ft^2/year, with renewable energy offsetting 10 kBtu/ft^2/year to reach the goal. The 12 kBtu/ft^2/year metric reflects the goal of the challenge, but not the actual energy use target of the building. The point is, it is best to clearly define the 2030 Challenge target as including renewable energy and then move forward to set a net zero energy use target, with separate targets for energy use and renewable energy generation.

2030 Challenge Target Example

Still using the 75,000-square-foot elementary school project, the diagram in Figure 4.29 shows the 2030 Challenge target of 32.4 kBtu/ft^2 for annual site energy, assuming the project is to be completed in the year 2012. Since the baseline was derived from ENERGY STAR Target Finder, a preliminary EPA Energy Performance Rating (1–100 scale) was also determined.

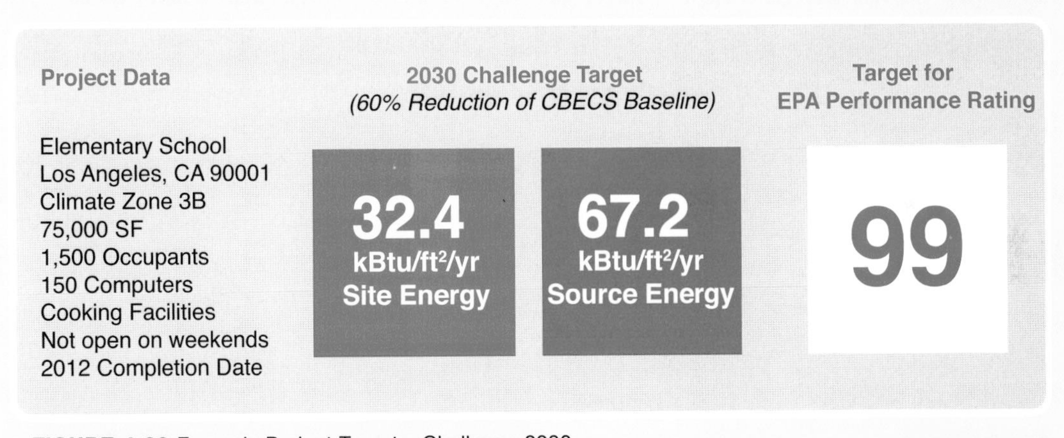

■ **FIGURE 4.29** Example Project Targets: Challenge 2030.

LEED TARGET

A LEED energy target is based on how many Energy & Atmosphere, Optimize Energy Performance (EAc1) credits the owner and design team plan to pursue. LEED EAc1 is based on energy cost savings compared to the ASHRAE 90.1 baseline. At the beginning of design, when the energy target is established, the ASHRAE 90.1 baseline will only be a preliminary estimate. Further, it is unlikely that energy cost savings will be used as a baseline metric. To keep things simple when developing a LEED energy target, apply the desired energy reduction for LEED EAc1 as a percent of energy use (rather than energy cost savings). (Note that because of different fuel mixes in a building, energy cost savings are rarely the same as energy savings.)

Renewable energy merits special consideration in LEED EAc1; and on-site renewable

ASHRAE 90.1 Target Example

Note that this is an example of setting a LEED target, *not* the net zero energy target.

A common LEED goal for energy performance is 30 percent better than ASHRAE 90.1. In LEED "Building Design and Construction, EAc1," a 30 percent performance improvement in new buildings is worth 10 points. For the 75,000-square-foot Los Angeles elementary school project, a 30 percent reduction in energy (not energy cost) would yield an EUI target of 22 kBtu/ft^2/year for annual site energy (see Figure 4.30). (Note the baseline was established earlier in this chapter as 31 kBtu/ft^2/year based on ASHRAE 90.1–2007.)

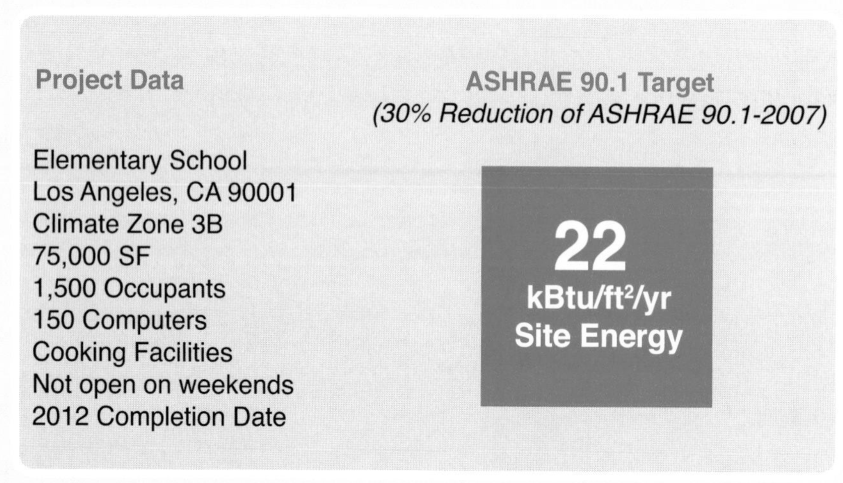

■ **FIGURE 4.30** Example Project Targets: ASHRAE 901.

energy generation can be taken off the bottom line in the energy cost savings calculation for LEED EAc1. Again, following the advice outlined in the 2030 Challenge target section, it is useful to set separate energy use and renewable energy generation targets.

NET ZERO ENERGY TARGET

For net zero energy buildings, it is still useful to set and understand the building's 2030 Challenge and LEED energy targets. Likely, both systems will be used to assess the project, in addition to the building's net zero energy goal. These two targets also serve as useful points of reference while establishing a net zero energy use target.

Setting the energy target is an important part of the process of delivering a net zero energy building, in that it helps quantify the objective of net zero. It is remarkably powerful to have a tangible target to strive for; and in that sense, it can help align an entire project team around achieving net zero energy.

When setting a net zero energy target, the goal is to establish the lowest feasible energy use budget for a project. By "feasible," I mean that cost and budget, as well as status of current technology, must be strongly considered. This can be a daunting proposition, and experience is perhaps the best guide. High-performance peer building baselines can prove very valuable in this effort, at least in researching what has been accomplished by the best-of-class. It may also be possible to "build up" a net zero energy target, if enough is known about the anticipated energy end uses of the project. (Determining energy end uses is discussed next in this chapter.)

Another approach for zeroing in on the target is to use aggressive percent reductions for the established CBECS and ASHRAE 90.1 baselines. As a rule of thumb, a reduction of 60 percent or better than a CBECS baseline, and 40 percent or better than ASHRAE 90.1–2007, might represent an appropriate net zero energy target. Note that there is a practical limit to how low of an energy target can be reached based on climate, building type, and project-specific variables (see Figure 4.31).

Another way to define a net zero energy target is to consider the potential for on-site renewable energy generation and then cap the net zero energy use target at this value. Keep in mind that increasing energy efficiency is more cost-effective than purchasing larger renewable energy systems. So the priority goal is to establish an energy use target that is as low as feasible. That said, a renewable energy target, or cap, is a useful accompaniment to a net zero energy use target. (Chapter 8 provides guidance on estimating renewable energy capacity.)

The following example uses planning techniques discussed in Chapter 8 to determine a renewable energy target for the hypothetical Los Angeles elementary school being used throughout this chapter as an example project.

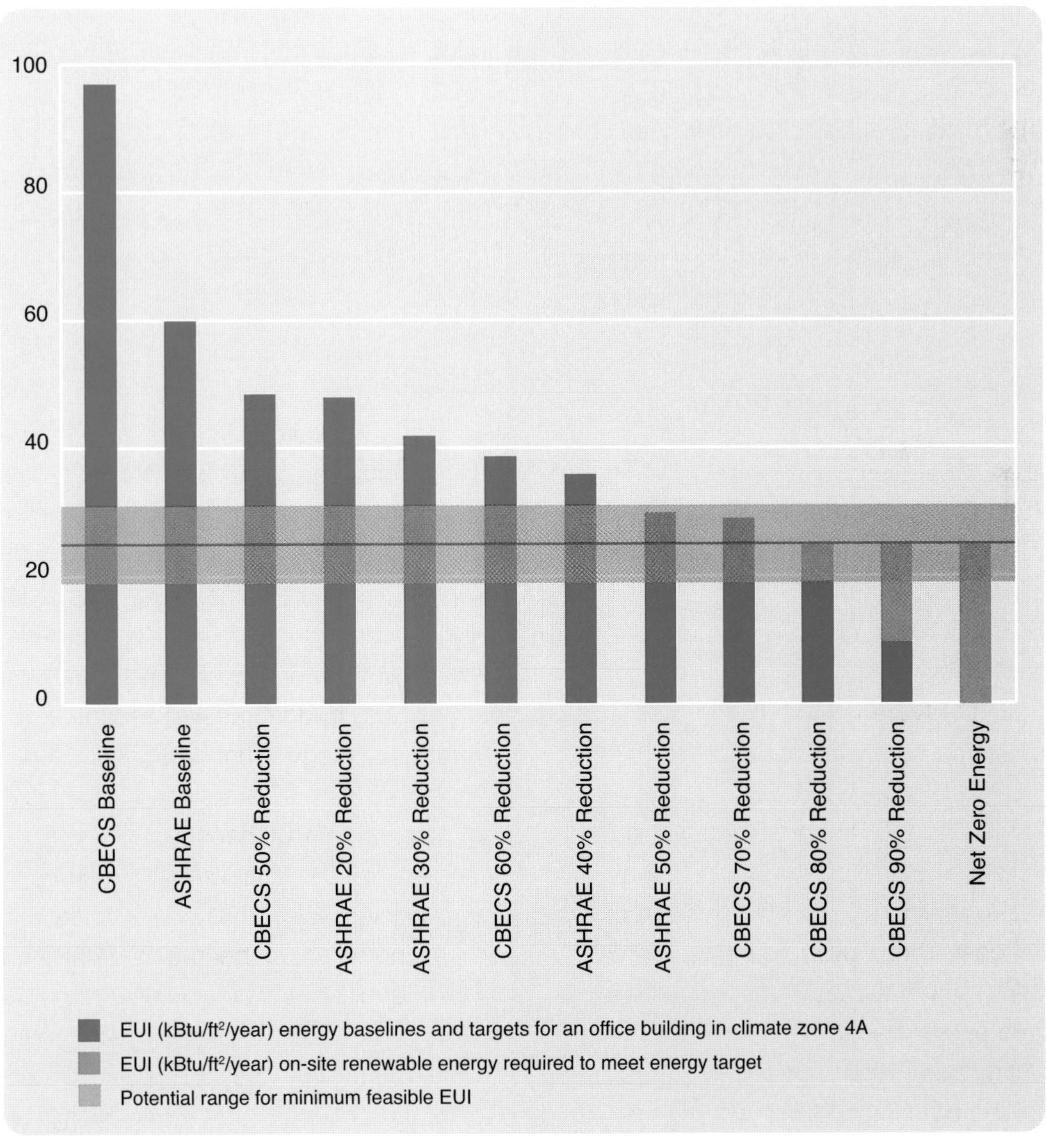

■ **FIGURE 4.31** EUI Target Comparison (Based on a Typical Office in Climate Zone 4A).

Net Zero Energy Target Example

Developing a net zero energy target requires further analysis of the energy baseline data gathered for a project. Using aggressive percent reductions from the CBECS and ASHRAE 90.1 baselines is a good place to start.

CBECS Analysis

- 65 percent of 81 kBtu/ft^2/year is 28 kBtu/ft^2/year
- 75 percent of 81 kBtu/ft^2/year is 20 kBtu/ft^2/year

ASHRAE 90.1 Analysis

- 40 percent of 31 kBtu/ft^2/year is 19 kBtu/ft^2/year
- 50 percent of 31 kBtu/ft^2/year is 16 kBtu/ft^2/year

It also helpful to look at peer building baselines; and in this case, a similar peer building was found in the DOE's High-Performance Building Database. The analysis, performed using the web-based tool EnergyIQ, makes it possible to identify the peer building with the lowest energy use from among the 21 in CBECS at 27 kBtu/ft^2/year. EnergyIQ can also be used to examine individual buildings and define peer groups from the California End-Use Survey (CEUS). An EnergyIQ query for elementary schools between 25,000 and 150,000 square feet, located on the southern coast of California, resulted in five peer buildings. The lowest peer building energy use was 20 kBtu/ft^2/year, and the highest, 34 kBtu/ft^2/year.

Peer Building Analysis

- DOE High-Performance Building Database Peer at 34 kBtu/ft^2/year
- EnergyIQ CBECS Lowest Energy Peer Building at 27 kBtu/ft^2/year
- EnergyIQ CEUS Lowest Energy Peer Building at 20 kBtu/ft^2/year

Based on this baseline analysis, a net zero energy target can be set. Note, there is no single correct answer; rather, the conclusion is based on professional judgment, using the baseline analysis to support it. The lowest peer building achieved 20 kBtu/ft^2/year, whereas the CBECS and ASHRAE baseline and target analysis yielded values trending toward 20 kBtu/ft^2/year. In this example, a net zero energy target of 20 kBtu/ft^2/year would be a reasonable goal (see Figure 4.32).

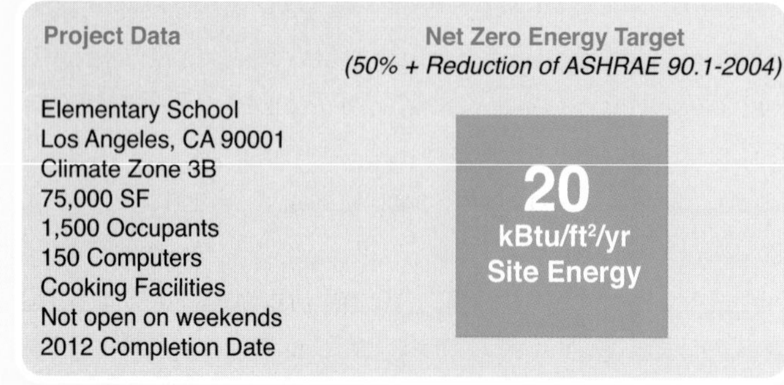

■ **FIGURE 4.32** Example Project Targets: Net Zero Energy.

Renewable Energy Target Example

Assume that the 75,000-square-foot school building is one story, with an area of 40,000 square feet available on the roof for a photovoltaic system. Assuming no tilt to the photovoltaic modules, and planning for a range of module efficiencies, the potential renewable energy system size and generation for the project would be determined as follows:

- High-efficiency modules at 18 watts/ft^2 × 40,000 ft^2 yields a system size of 720 kW.
- Medium-efficiency modules at 15 watts/ft^2 × 40,000 ft^2 yields a system size of 600 kW.
- Low-efficiency modules at 12 watts/ft^2 × 40,000 ft^2 yields a system size of 480 kW.
- Performance factor for modules located in Los Angeles with no tilt = 1,293 kWh/kW, or 4,412 kBtu/kW (PVWatts website, http://rredc.nrel.gov/solar/calculators/PVWATTS/version1/).
- High-efficiency modules' generation potential is 42 kBtu/ft^2/year.
- Medium-efficiency modules' generation potential is 35 kBtu/ft^2/year.
- Low-efficiency modules' generation potential is 28 kBtu/ft^2/year.

Because the renewable energy generation of the low-efficiency modules at 28 kBtu/ft^2/year exceeds the net zero energy target of 20 kBtu/ft^2/year, the project has a good buffer for achieving its net zero energy goal, hence could slightly relax the energy target, or, better yet, install a smaller renewable energy system (see Figure 4.33).

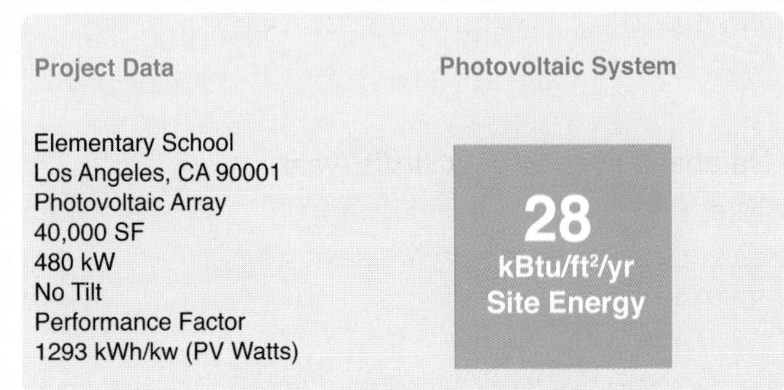

Project Data
Photovoltaic System
Elementary School
Los Angeles, CA 90001
Photovoltaic Array
40,000 SF
480 kW
No Tilt
Performance Factor
1293 kWh/kw (PV Watts)
28
kBtu/ft²/yr
Site Energy

FIGURE 4.33 Example Project Renewable Energy Target.

Ideally, the estimated potential for on-site renewable energy will exceed the estimated minimum possible energy use target. The wider the spread, the more options and flexibility are available to meet a net zero energy goal. When the estimated minimum energy use target exceeds the estimated potential for on-site renewable energy, the energy use target must be lowered to match the renewable energy capacity or further study must be conducted to determine additional renewable energy options.

Energy by End Use

After developing the appropriate EUI baselines and net zero energy target for a project, the next step is to figure out what contributes to the energy use in the building. *Energy end use* is the term used to describe the range of building uses, processes, and functions that contribute to energy use. Identifying which functions contribute to energy use in a building, and the proportion of each end use to the total energy use, will make managing energy use and reduction far more effective.

A thorough understanding of energy end uses is critical for targeting appropriate strategies for energy reduction; and in a net zero energy building, every end use is an opportunity for energy use reduction.

Most commercial buildings have a similar set of energy end uses. These can be grouped in different ways, but include the following types:

- Interior and exterior lighting
- Space heating
- Space cooling
- Ventilation
- Water heating
- Equipment (including office equipment)
- Cooking
- Refrigeration

The Department of Energy tracks energy use data across the commercial building sector, categorized according to specific end uses. The chart in Figure 4.34 summarizes average commercial building energy end use splits from 2006, for an overview of how energy is commonly used in the commercial sector.

Both principal building activities and climate have an impact on energy end uses. Therefore, it is essential to examine energy end uses in greater detail. However, this undertaking is beyond the scope and capability of ENERGY STAR and most energy target databases, so it will require either some form of preliminary energy modeling, or experience with the same building type in the same climate. (Refer back to Chapter 3 for guidance on integrating energy modeling into early design.) Alternatively, the web-based EnergyIQ tool allows the examination of peer building groups in terms of energy end uses. This can be a quick method to set a starting point for energy end use splits. Figure 4.35 shows an example of an energy end use breakdown report based on the CEUS database from EnergyIQ using the elementary school example cited throughout this chapter.

To illustrate the impact of just climate on energy end uses, let's look at a different example—a 25,000-square-foot, stand-alone

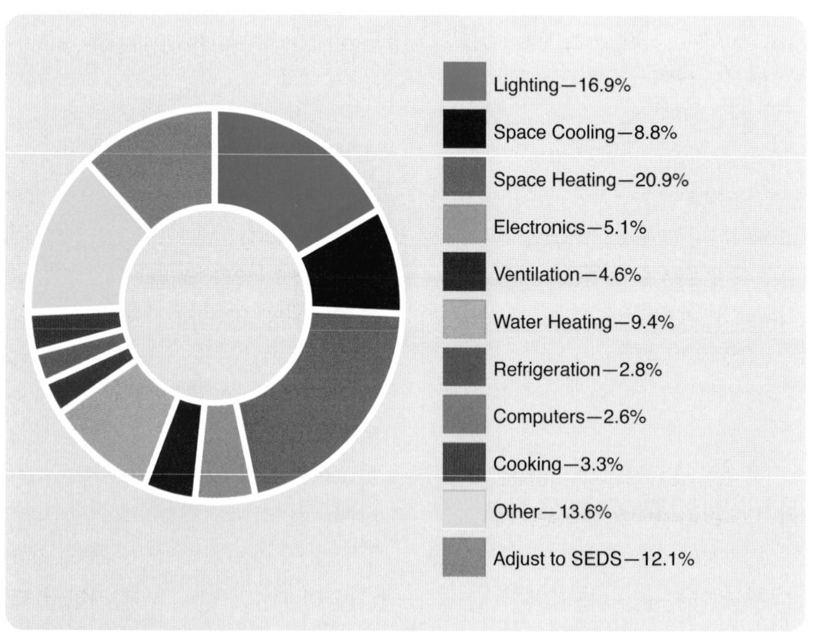

■ **FIGURE 4.34** Commercial Building Energy End-Use Splits Pie Chart (2006). *Data source: Department of Energy, 2009 Building Energy Data Book, Table 3.1.4, Site Energy.*

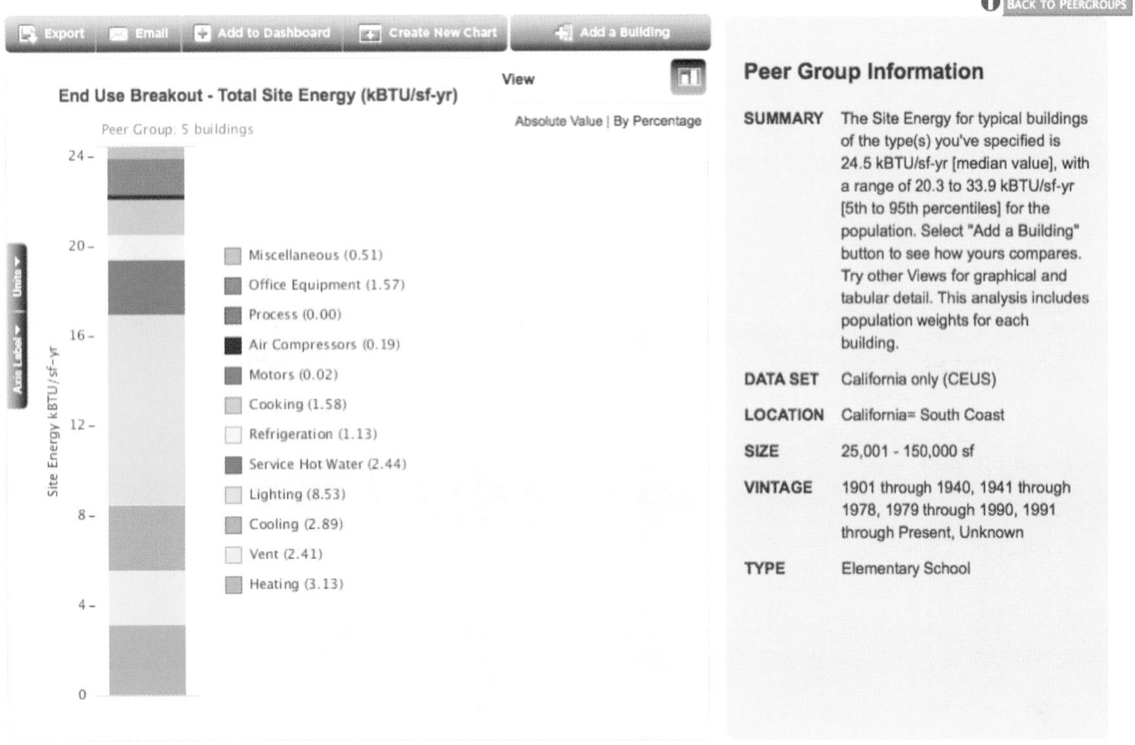

■ **FIGURE 4.35** EnergyIQ Energy End-Use Report for Hypothetical Elementary School in Los Angeles. *Screen capture from EnergyIQ website.*

retail building in two very different climates: zones 1A and 6A. Using the DOE's commercial reference building EnergyPlus model file, we can compare the dramatically different results for zones 1A and 6A in Figures 4.36 and 4.37, respectively. Note that the overall energy use is much higher in the building in climate zone 6A; also note that interior and exterior lighting and equipment energy end uses, measured in total energy rather than as a percentage, are the same in both climate zones. The building in zone 6A, a cold climate, is dominated by a high heat load.

Power Density

Once you have set an EUI energy target, and understand the energy end uses of the building, as well as the their proportion to the total energy use, the next step is to examine energy use intensities, or power densities, of individual end uses.

The most common and useful metric tied to end use is power density of installed equipment and lighting. Power density budgets are helpful because they allow you to plan and manage energy reduction goals for equipment and lighting.

Lighting power density is a commonly used metric in the building industry and is integrated into energy codes and ANSI/ASHRAE/IESNA 90.1, "Energy Standard for Buildings Except Low-Rise Residential Buildings." It is the sum of installed lighting fixture power (watts) divided by floor area. It is good practice to establish individual lighting power densities for the different types of space in a building, as well as an overall lighting power density for the entire building.

Lighting power density is only an expression of installed power, not energy. However, it is an indicator of the energy efficiency of the lighting system and so can be used to

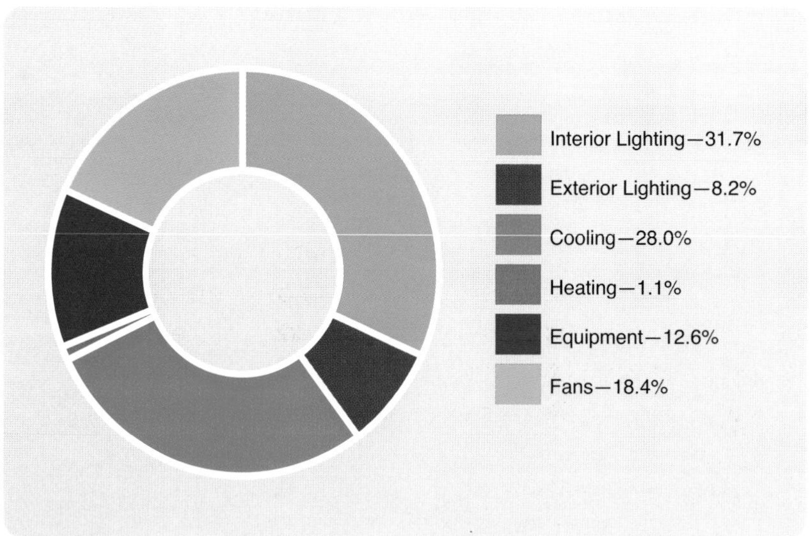

■ **FIGURE 4.36** Energy End-Use Splits Pie Chart for a Stand-alone Retail Store in Climate Zone 1A. *Data source: EnergyPlus modeling results from DOE commercial reference building model file.*

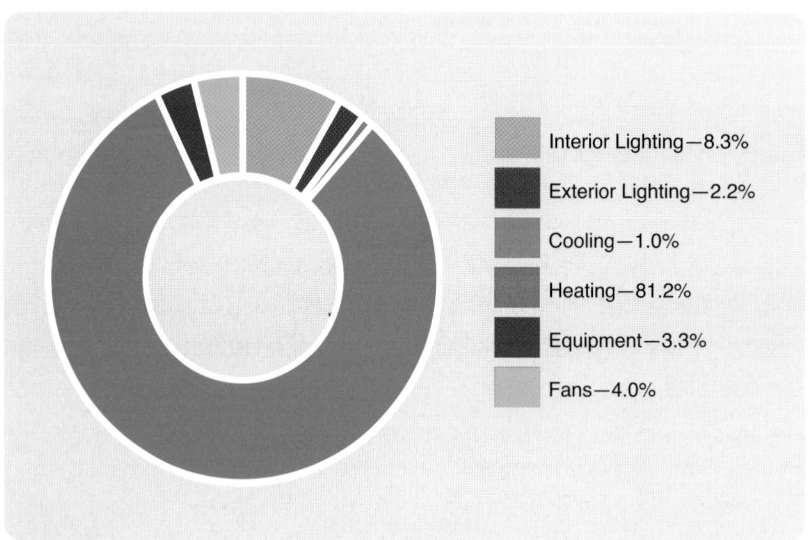

■ **FIGURE 4.37** Energy End-Use Splits Pie Chart for a Stand-alone Retail Store in Climate Zone 6A. *Data source: EnergyPlus modeling results from DOE commercial reference building model file.*

develop an EUI for lighting. Following a lighting schedule, and accounting for daylighting and occupancy sensors, it is possible to convert power in watts to energy in watt-hours.

In the same way that a lighting power density budget can be developed for a building design, equipment load density budgets can also be planned to manage plug load and process load energy reduction. Plug load density can be established for commercial buildings, but is particularly important for building types such as offices where a large quantity of computer and office equipment is in use. For building types with specific process loads, such as a commercial kitchen in a restaurant, a process load density budget should be developed. Data centers are very energy-intensive and should be planned using a data center load density budget—keeping in mind that the installed equipment power for data centers is only half the story. Another metric, called power usage effectiveness (PUE), is a measure of the total data center energy use, including cooling and power distribution, divided by the installed power of the data center equipment. (Chapter 10 offers detailed guidance on plug and process load management and operations for net zero energy buildings.)

ENERGY AND THERMAL COMFORT

Thermal Comfort Opportunities

A substantial portion of building energy use is dedicated to the important function of thermal comfort, one of the most complex interactions in a building. Passive architectural design and efficient building systems have dramatic impact on the energy use and the quality of thermal comfort. In addition to the complex science involved in understanding how humans experience comfort, many cultural and personal idiosyncrasies also come into play.

Thermal comfort presents an often-overlooked opportunity in architecture. Lisa Heschong, in her book *Thermal Delight in Architecture*, explores the profound human connection to architecture through thermal senses and experience. Thermal qualities can be as beautiful, meaningful, and important as visual or acoustical qualities. Part of their beauty comes from some thermal diversity and contrast, rather than a homogeneous 72°F interior environment. In addition to aesthetic advantages, there are also energy savings advantages to be gained from thermal diversity.

By *thermal diversity*, I am referring to a wide range of strategies that can impact thermal comfort, such as air movement, humidity, and radiant temperature, not just air temperature. These factors can make it possible to achieve thermal comfort while allowing for greater daily and seasonal variation in indoor air temperature. The General Services Administration (GSA) study, "Energy Savings and Performance Gains in GSA Buildings: Seven Cost-Effective Strategies," estimates that raising the thermostat by 2°F in the summer would reduce air conditioning energy by 4 percent in most federal facilities.

Consider that the human body has a remarkable ability to adapt thermally to environments; however, contemporary Americans have been acclimatized to a constant 72°F environment. But recently, a trend toward using adaptive thermal comfort models in the design of buildings has been gaining momentum. ASHRAE Standard 55, "Thermal Environmental Conditions for Human Occupancy," is the benchmark for thermal comfort in buildings for the United States. The 2004 version of this standard incorporates the addition of an adaptive thermal comfort approach, which recognizes that thermal control and natural ventilation shift occupants' expectations so that they can be comfortable in a wider range of indoor temperatures.

Net zero energy buildings need to take advantage of the energy savings potential of adaptive thermal comfort design. There is a strong synergy with adaptive thermal comfort and net zero energy buildings, because they tend to be designed with numerous passive energy strategies such as natural ventilation and thermal mass, which not only aid in providing thermal comfort, but also create an environment that raises awareness, changes expectations, and allows occupants to participate in the control and adaptation of their personal thermal comfort.

The primary goal is to reduce energy use and improve thermal comfort by taking advantage of the many ways humans experience the thermal environment. This is important, because thermal comfort has been strongly linked to productivity in office buildings; in short, it has a direct impact on human performance and well-being. Building owners and occupants should be consulted, educated, and involved when using adaptive thermal comfort approaches. Adaptive thermal comfort may be seen as a long-term, gradual goal. People take time to adapt both physically and psychologically to the thermal environment, such as the time it takes them to adjust to the heat of summer and the cold of winter. Accordingly, thermal comfort standards can be adjusted over time in a building, easing occupants into new thermal comfort conditions and strategies. Perhaps, as more people become exposed to new approaches to thermal comfort, a more far-reaching goal would be to shift societal expectations of thermal comfort in buildings. These approaches are not really new at all; it is just that humanity has only very recently come to expect the homogeneous interior environments of sealed, air-conditioned boxes.

Basics of Heat Flow

The second law of thermodynamics, the law of entropy, dictates that heat flows from a body of higher temperature to a body of lower temperature. Thermal comfort and the heating and cooling of buildings are governed by the building science of heat flow (see Figure 4.38).

Heat flows in three ways:

1. Conduction
2. Convection
3. Radiation

Conduction is heat transferred through and between bodies by direct contact, and thermal energy transferred from warmer particles to cooler particles. For example, heat flow by conduction occurs through a building wall when the outside temperature differs from the inside temperature. Hence, walls and roofs with high thermal resistance can help maintain interior temperatures. *Convection* is heat transferred by the movement of liquids and gases. Air is a poor thermal conductor, but it can transfer thermal energy through movement. Air movement is enhanced as air warms and rises. *Radiation* or radiant heat flow does not occur by contact or movement of liquid or gases; rather, heat is transferred through electromagnetic waves. A body can radiate heat to a colder body, as long as the two bodies are in direct line of sight of each other. Electromagnetic waves move in straight lines

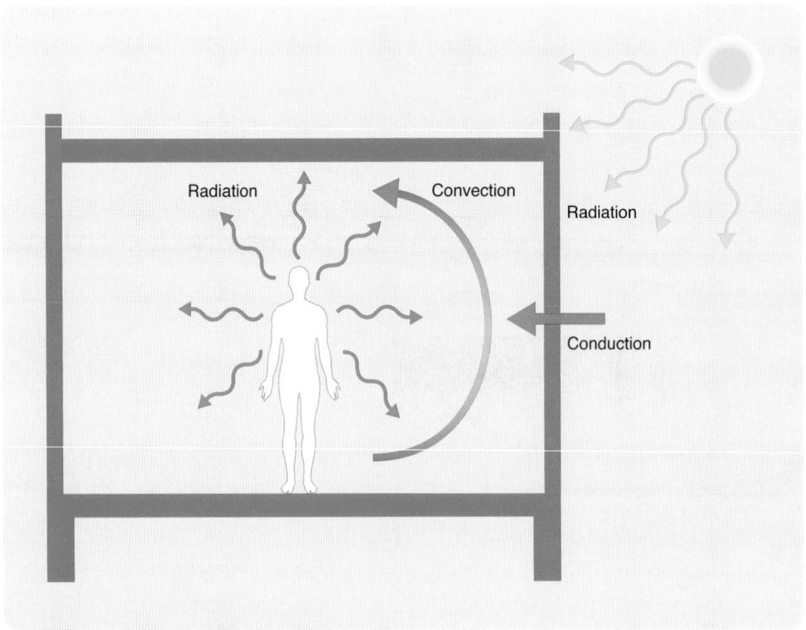

■ **FIGURE 4.38** Heat Flows in Buildings.

and in all directions. The sun is the classic example of heat flow by radiation.

Human Factors and Thermal Comfort

A basic understanding of how the human body regulates temperature is the foundation for the successful design for thermal comfort in buildings. The thermal design of the human body is centered on keeping the core body temperature at 98.6°F. We humans continually generate heat as we burn calories from food. Depending on a number of environmental, behavioral, and personal factors, we need to regulate the amount of heat loss from our body in order to maintain our core temperature.

Heat loss is regulated primarily through the surface of our skin, and blood is the primary heat transfer medium through the body. Blood flow to the skin can be reduced as the surrounding temperature grows cooler and less heat loss through the skin is needed; or blood flow can increase to the skin as the surrounding temperature warms up and the rejection of more heat is needed. While our internal body temperature operates at a narrow range, our skin temperature can function at a very wide range of temperatures.

There are four ways the body can transfer heat with the surrounding environment (see Figure 4.39):

1. Conduction.
2. Convection
3. Radiation
4. Evaporation

Conduction occurs through contact with warmer or cooler bodies, such as contact with the earth. *Convection* and *radiation* are effective means of losing heat when the surrounding temperature is cool. As the surrounding temperature becomes warmer, *evaporation* in the form of perspiration becomes more effective. Perspiration uses latent energy to transfer heat away from the skin—that is, the evaporation of sweat. Latent heat transfer through perspiration is a highly effective method of regulating heat in a body, although it can be impeded in hot and humid climates.

BEHAVIORAL FACTORS

There are three behavioral factors that also influence thermal comfort:

1. Activity level or metabolic rate
2. Clothing level
3. Migration

As our activity level rises, we generate more heat, which will need to be regulated to maintain thermal comfort. Most people have common experience with this phenomenon in a variety of forms. Exercise and strenuous work will elevate body temperatures to such a point that sweating becomes the only effective means of rejecting heat. Even subtle shifts in activity levels can result in heat generation and

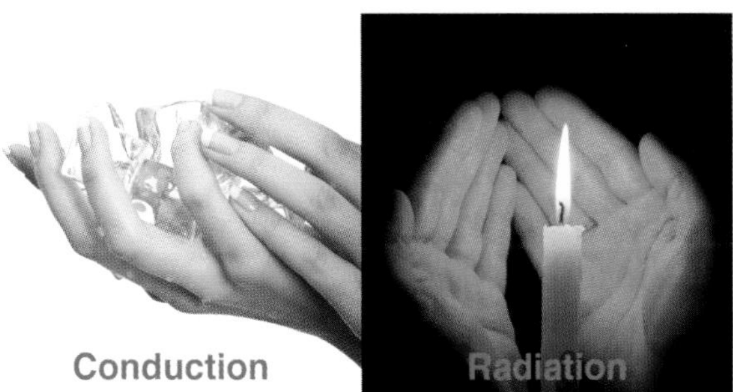

■ **FIGURE 4.39** Methods of Heat Transfer from the Human Body.

can be used to adapt to thermal conditions. Shivering, for example, is a natural response to cold temperatures; it generates heat through reflexive muscle contractions. The amount of heat generated by the body can vary by more than a factor of 10. While sleeping, an adult may produce about 245 Btu/h of heat; in contrast, while exercising strenuously, such as in a game of basketball, the body may produce up to 3,000 Btu/h or more (see Figure 4.40).

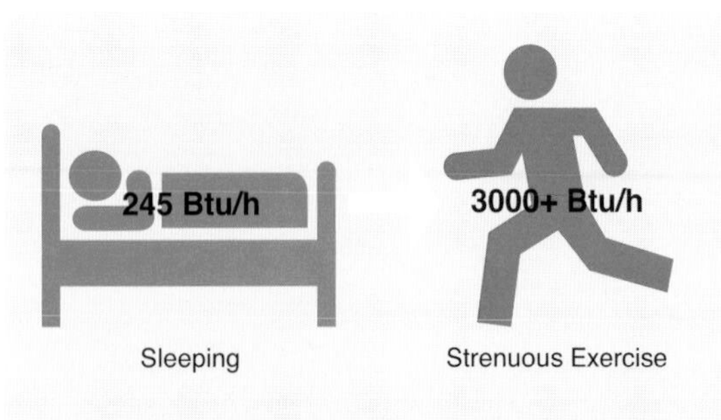

■ **FIGURE 4.40** Approximate Range of Body Heat by Activity Level.

Our "second skin" is our clothing layer. When matched to environmental conditions, clothing can be a very effective thermal adaptation strategy; conversely, when not matched to environmental conditions, clothing can be a hindrance to thermal comfort. Dressing for the climate and seasons can be an effective thermal comfort strategy. Social norms and trends play a major role in the clothing choices people make. Recently, certain of these norms have been shifting, in a positive way. For example, the traditional business attire for men, the suit and tie, is thermally inappropriate during summers and in hot climates, leading to more casual business attire. A notable example is the Cool Biz campaign in Japan. In 2005, the Japanese government bucked strong cultural norms when it turned up the thermostats in office buildings, in the summer, to 28°C (82.4°F) and instituted a new business dress code that encouraged workers to leave their ties and jackets at home. The program tracked substantial energy and carbon emission savings as a result of the campaign. In fact, in 2011, following Japan's March 11 earthquake that took much of the country's electricity generation off-line, the Japanese government stepped up the campaign, calling it "Super Cool Biz" in hopes of reducing energy demand.

In some cultures, long-standing fashion traditions are based on climate-appropriate attire. A good example is the dishdasha, the traditional Arabic attire for men. During the summer, this white cotton, lightweight, loose-fitting one-piece dress tunic reflects heat away from the body and allows air circulation, for an additional cooling effect. The color, weight, and material of the dishdasha is changed in the winter months. Even the traditional Arabic head covering allows thermal adaptation during summer and winter temperatures.

At times, the best behavioral adaptation for thermal comfort is to migrate, or relocate, to a place with more favorable thermal conditions. This is a classic seasonal adaptation strategy in the animal kingdom, but some people, too, take on migration patterns; they spend summers in cooler climates and move to warm climates in the winter. However, most of us have a lifestyle that has us fixed in one location year-round. Yet, everyone does migrate, if only temporarily. For instance, if you are outside in the summer and getting too warm, you might choose to relocate to a place that offers shade. This strategy can be implemented in the built environment, and can work in interior environments with varying thermal conditions to provide additional opportunities for thermal adaptation.

ENVIRONMENTAL FACTORS

There are four environmental factors that influence thermal comfort:

1. Air temperature
2. Humidity
3. Radiant temperature
4. Air movement

Air temperature is a primary environmental factor that influences thermal comfort. Most people can relate the temperature shown on a thermostat to a certain expectation of thermal comfort. *Humidity* impacts thermal comfort because as relative humidity—the amount of water vapor present in air compared to how much water vapor it can hold—increases, the capability of the body to perspire effectively decreases. Humidity is a concern because it takes a significant amount of energy to remove latent heat from the air and, thus, condense the moisture from the air. The sensible heat to warm 1 pound of water at 1°F is 1 Btu. Compare this to the 970 Btu of latent heat needed to transform a pound of water between liquid and gas form at 212°F. This is the energy required to boil water, or the latent heat of vaporization.

Often in interior environments, air movement is at a low velocity, and *radiant temperature* varies very little compared to air temperature. In this condition, air temperature and humidity are the primary factors affecting thermal comfort. That said, radiant temperature can be a major influence on thermal comfort when the mean radiant temperature experienced by a body is different from the surrounding air temperature. Think of the warming effect of a fireplace or the undesirable warming effect of an adjacent window that permits solar radiation gain during the summer. During the winter, the cold interior surface temperature of glazing can have an undesirable radiant effect on thermal comfort as well.

Air movement and its speed can also have a marked impact on thermal comfort. Air movement transfers heat through convection and enhances evaporation and perspiration. Airspeeds from 50 to 150 feet per minute can provide a cooling sensation equivalent to a 1°F to 5°F difference. ASHRAE Standard 55, which gives detailed guidance on using airspeed to provide thermal comfort, limits airspeed to 160 feet per minute and the maximum temperature offset to 5.4°F if the air movement is controllable by the occupant. The benefit of airspeed is enhanced by the relationship of mean radiant temperature and air temperature. As mean radiant temperature increases over air temperature, air movement becomes more effective. Air movement can improve comfort dramatically when cooling is needed, but is a liability in cold temperatures. Cold drafts in buildings and the wind chill experienced in cold, windy climates are examples of this negative effect.

Psychrometry

Psychrometry is the study of the thermodynamic characteristics of moist air. The psychrometric chart (Figure 4.41) is a useful tool for understanding the role of temperature and humidity in thermal comfort. It is also a very valuable design tool for evaluating the effectiveness of design strategies in providing thermal comfort. The chart is particularly good when it comes to the evaluation of passive design strategies, which should be the foundation of a net zero energy design.

A psychrometric chart includes, and can define, many variables related to the thermodynamics of moist air, including:

- Dry bulb temperature (horizontal axis)
- Absolute humidity (vertical axis)
- Relative humidity
- Wet bulb temperature
- Dew point
- Specific volume
- Sensible heat
- Latent heat
- Enthalpy (combined latent and sensible heat)

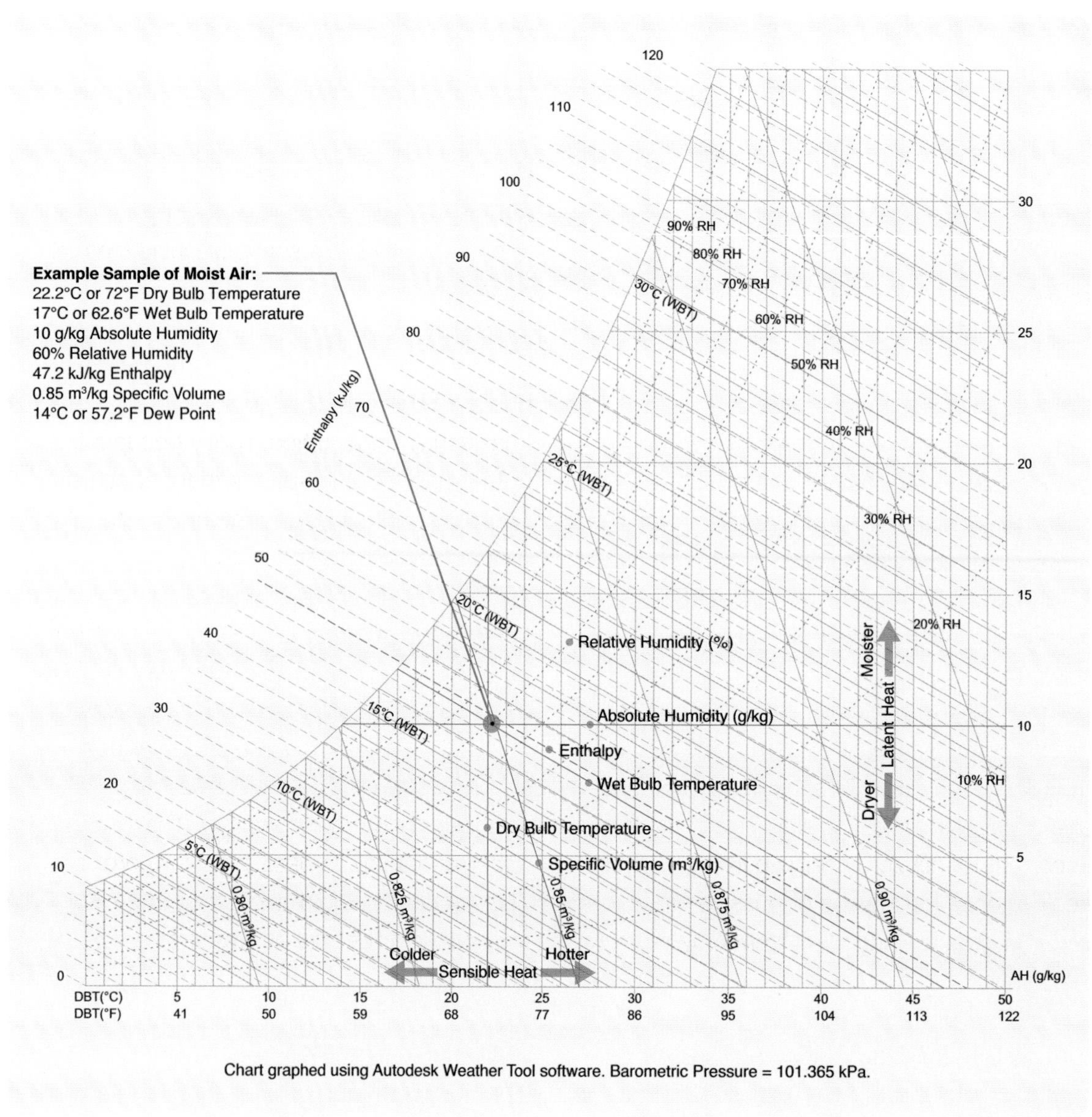

■ **FIGURE 4.41** Reading a Psychrometric Chart.

The first step in using a psychrometric chart is to mark the zone that defines thermal comfort. The thermal comfort zone becomes the primary target for design strategies related to thermal comfort. The next step is to map the conditions of the climate for the specific project location. Using a weather data file and a psychrometric analysis software tool, such as Weather Tool, can expedite this mapping and further analysis. Comparing the comfort zone to the range of temperatures and humidity levels found in the climate year-round can be very informative regarding the issues to be tackled in the building design to create thermal comfort. (Chapter 5 further explores the use of psychrometric charts in relation to climate, comfort, and passive design strategies.)

Thermal Control and Adaption

We humans use a wide range of physiological and behavioral adaptation strategies to maintain thermal comfort, yet we still rely on the built environment as a primary method of thermal control and adaptation. The most common way building occupants achieve thermal control is through a thermostat, which can be adjusted to meet individual thermal comfort needs. The goal of adapted thermal comfort is to use a variety of adaptation strategies to provide thermal control in order to reduce the energy used to condition the space conventionally. Additionally, adaptive strategies can give occupants more control options. Thermal control is an important variable in providing thermal comfort, and can raise occupant satisfaction with a space.

Thermal zoning is an important concept in the design of HVAC systems because a building will have a variety of thermal loads and exterior exposures depending on the location of the zones within the building. For example, a building may have a zone of interior space along each of the four orientations (i.e., north, south, east, and west) and a zone for internal loads (see Figure 4.42).

Thermal zoning can also be useful in the design of the architectural plan; it can impact the program of the building and the use of passive design strategies, as well. This is particularly important for net zero energy buildings, which seek to optimize the use of passive strategies. Within a building plan, there may be many spaces that should or could be maintained at different thermal conditions. Using the program of the building, identify the thermal requirements and opportunities for each space, including the activity type of the space, special thermal loads, and the use schedule of the space. Couple this with thermal zones based on building orientation to begin to develop a space planning thermal zoning strategy.

Thermal zoning can also include strategies such as thermal buffer spaces and microclimates. Thermal buffers spaces are typically transitional, unoccupied, lightly occupied, or thermally flexible spaces that act as buffer zones between more thermally controlled spaces and the exterior; or they may provide thermal benefit to adjacent spaces, such as a sunroom. Creating microclimates around the exterior of a building is one way of directly impacting the thermal loads on the exterior of the building, such as deciduous trees that shade in the summer but allow passive solar energy during the winter. The goal of a thermally zoned space plan is to provide both enhanced thermal comfort and reduced energy use. (Thermal zoning strategies are explored in more detail in Chapter 5.)

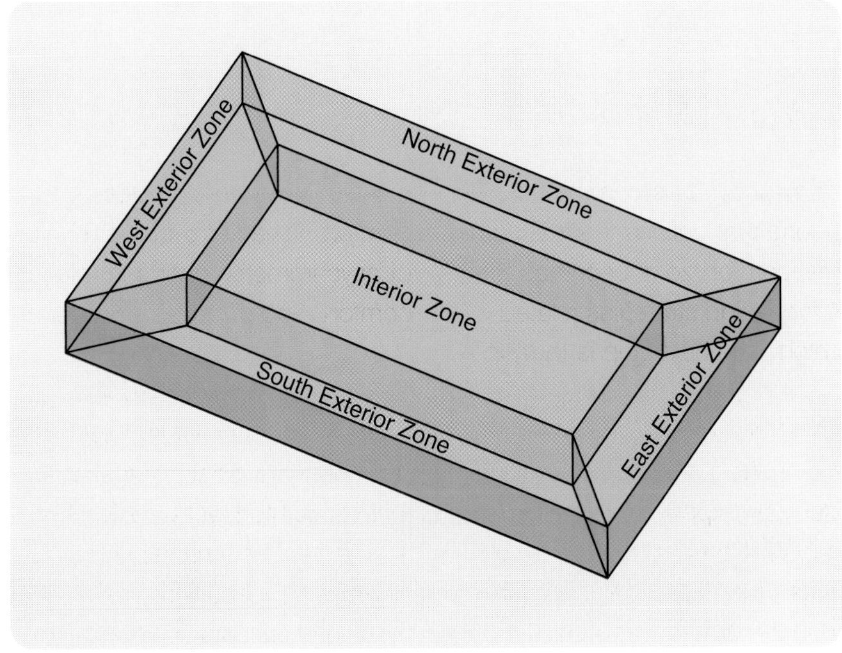

■ **FIGURE 4.42** Basic Thermal Zones in Buildings.

CHAPTER 5 DESIGN FUNDAMENTALS

ENERGY DESIGN CONDITIONS

During the exploration phase of a net zero energy project, as discussed in Chapter 3, it is important to establish the fundamental energy design conditions for the project before beginning the design phase in earnest. This is a critical research and assessment activity, which will supply the design process with relevant design data and lay the ground rules for achieving net zero energy. The energy design conditions include an understanding of the project's climate; site resources and constraints; building typology, massing, and orientation; and building program and building occupancy.

These fundamentals frame a big-picture view of the energy problem of any project by elucidating the forces that result in external energy loads, internal energy loads, and access to energy resources. It is also important to understand how the requirements of the building typology influence and mediate the energy flow through the project and site. The exploration of building massing and orientation from an energy perspective enables the first translation of the energy design research into design propositions.

The energy design conditions or design fundamentals of climate, site, massing, and program comprise the foundation for passive design development, discussed in Chapter 6. They also serve as a basis for the design of energy-efficient building systems, addressed in Chapter 7, and the planning for on-site renewable energy systems, covered in Chapter 8.

CLIMATE ASSESSMENT

Climate is a critical variable in the design of a net zero energy project. It influences the external thermal loads of a project, and is also a source of free energy. This gift of free energy is available in any climate, in different forms and quantities. Simply put, a net zero energy project must be climate-responsive. It must be capable of passively mitigating the thermal loads while taking advantage of all the free energy of the climate and site.

Although climate has a significant impact on energy use, it is not necessarily the dominant factor in achieving net zero energy. Often, the building program typology and program have a more profound influence on meeting this objective. Net zero energy buildings are possible in any climate, but achieving net zero energy for all building types is a much more difficult challenge.

Climate Definitions

Mark Twain gets to the heart of the distinction between climate and weather when he said, "Climate is what we expect; weather is what we get." Climate is defined as the predominant weather conditions of a place as averaged over a long period of time. It is a major input to the process of defining the qualities and characteristics of place beyond the weather, in terms of the natural and human responses to climate, as evident in the prevailing architecture (at least, the vernacular architecture), city planning, and the ecosystem of the place. If climate has such a dominant role in defining the ecosystem of a place, if it influences the form of life in a place, then it follows that it should be a fundamental driver of architectural form.

Just as climate influences the character of a place, the place—or, more specifically, the location on earth—in turn, directly influences climate. Latitude and altitude directly affect climate. As you move away from the equator in latitude, the solar altitude angle decreases, resulting in reduced solar radiation. When you move higher in elevation, air pressure decreases and, with it, air temperature. Geographic features, too, such as terrain, mountains, bodies of water, and in particular oceans, have a dynamic effect on climate. Globally, the interaction of atmospheric patterns and ocean currents plays a leading role in determining overall climate characteristics.

To understand climate in a global context, it is helpful to refer to a climate classification system. One of the most common is the Köppen

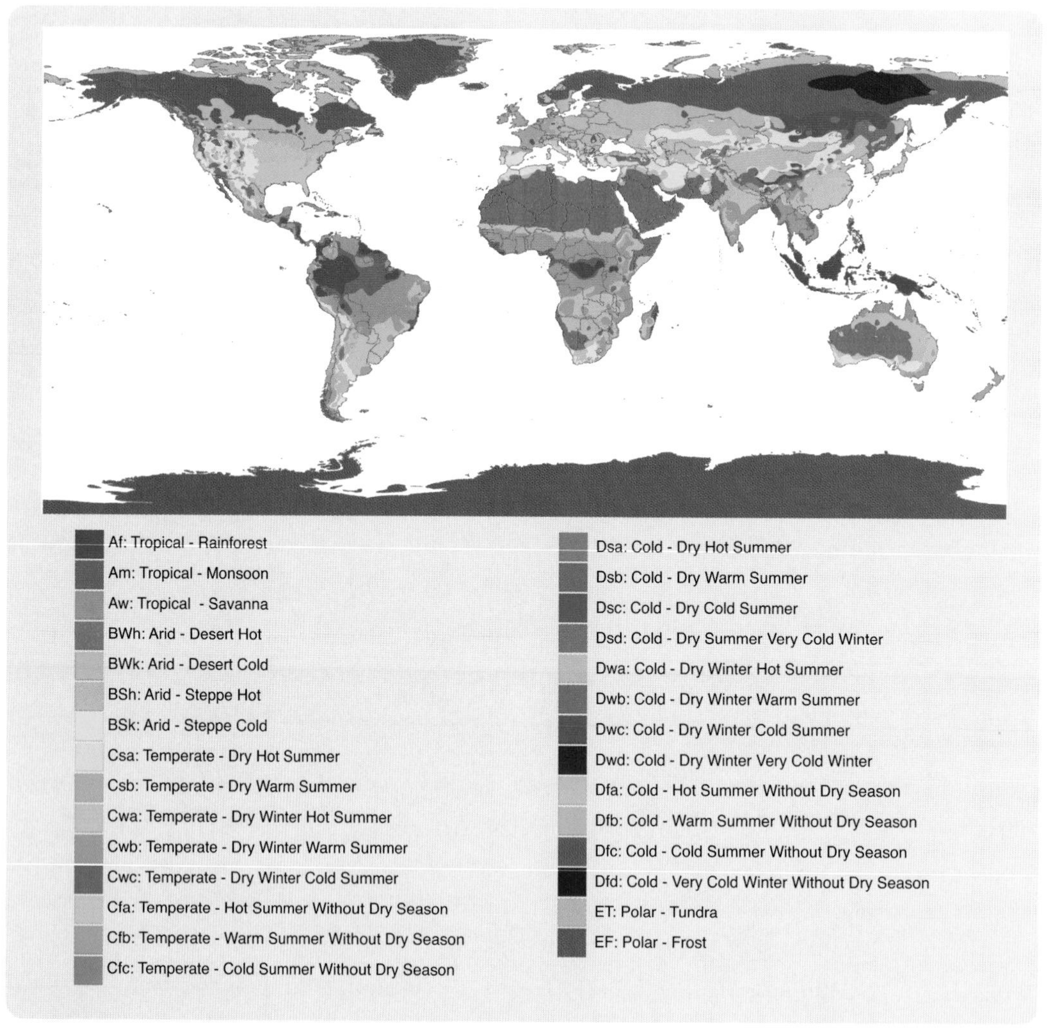

■ **FIGURE 5.1** Köppen Climate Classification Map. *Map graphic and data sources: Peel, M. C., Finlayson, B. L., and McMahon, T. A., 2007, Updated world map of the Köppen-Geiger climate classification, Hydrology and Earth System Sciences, 11, 1633–1644.*

climate classification system (see Figure 5.1). First published in 1918, this system has been improved over time and is still used to this day. The scheme is based on five primary climate classes (identified using the uppercase letters A though E), which are then subdivided into types and subtypes (using lowercase letters). A sixth primary climate class, H, for highland climates of mountainous areas, is used in some versions of the Köppen system. The highland classification is also at times used as a type of E climate, designated as EH. The five primary classes are:

A: Tropical

B: Arid

C: Temperate

D: Cold

E: Polar

Climate Classifications and Design Responses

Below are brief summaries of the five main Köppen climate classifications and typical passive and low-energy design responses. For detailed information about the climate classification criteria, refer to "Updated World Map of the Köppen-Geiger Climate Classification, *Hydrology and Earth System Sciences,* 11, 1633–1644" by Peel, M.C., Finlayson, B. L. and McMahon, T. A., 2007.

Climate Classification A: Tropical

Climate Characteristics

Tropical climates are characterized by year-long hot and moist weather with significant rainfall and humidity. Tropical climates are located along the equator and experience limited to no seasonal variation (except seasonal precipitation levels, in some cases).

Example Location: Miami, Florida, USA (Tropical-Monsoon; see Figure 5.2)

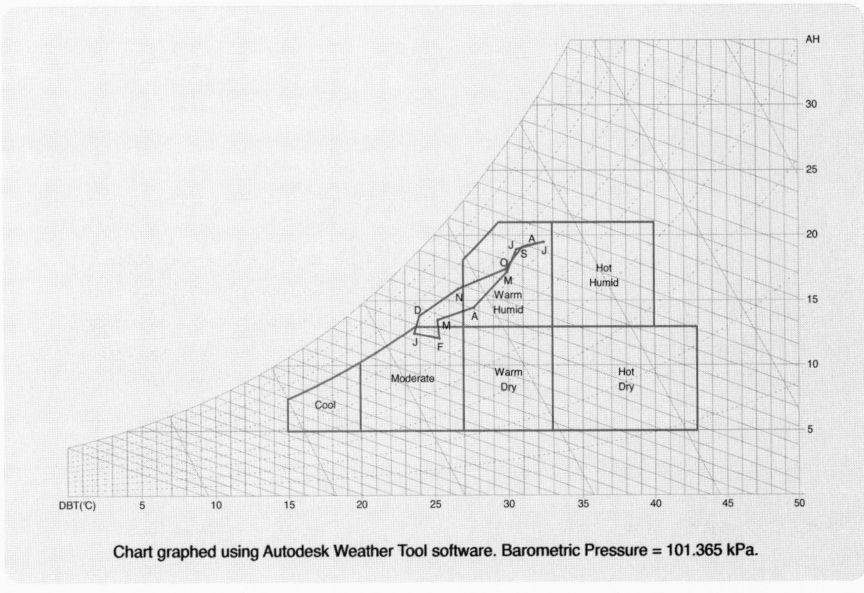

■ **FIGURE 5.2** Psychrometric Climate Classification A: Tropical Example, Miami, Florida.

Passive Design Responses

- The primary concern is to reduce cooling load with passive strategies, such as minimizing solar radiation through 100 percent solar shading, reducing thermal conduction through the envelope, and lowering internal heat gain through lighting and equipment load reductions. Locations are near the equator, so the high solar altitude makes shading the roof a potentially good strategy.
- Due to the abundance of water and year-long growing season, vegetated shading elements outside of or integrated within the building envelope can be an effective means of providing shading.
- Light colors for exterior surfaces reflect rather than absorb solar radiation. This can be very beneficial for roofs, due to the high solar altitude all year long.
- Natural ventilation can be useful in some tropical climates and at certain periods of the day or year, depending on the mechanical system selection.
- Daylighting lowers lighting energy use and internal heat gain. Daylighting should be carefully coordinated with shading strategies.
- Passive desiccant dehumidification can be used to control interior humidity levels and allow air to be cooled with nonconventional and refrigerant-free cooling, such as evaporative cooling. Passive solar or waste heat desiccant drying or recharging should be considered.

Climate Classification B: Arid

Climate Characteristics

Arid climates are characterized by lack of precipitation. Arid and semiarid climates can be cold or hot.

Example Location: Cairo, Egypt (Arid-Desert, Hot; see Figure 5.3)

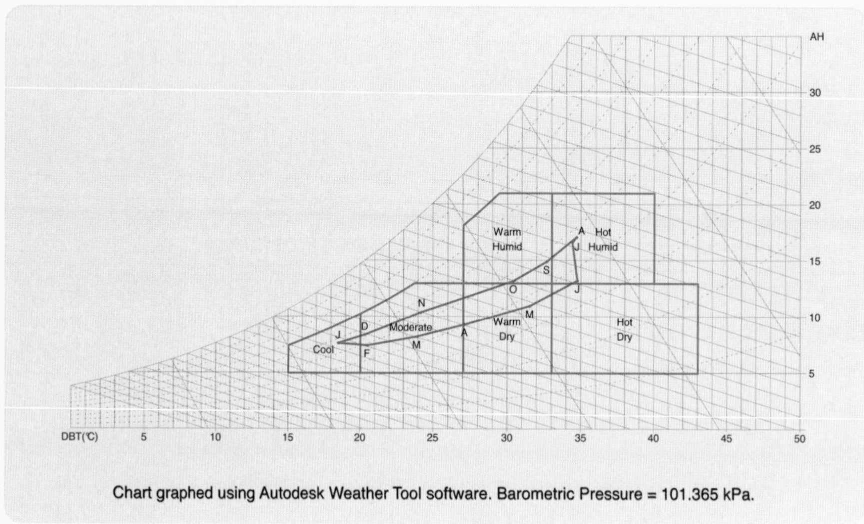

■ **FIGURE 5.3** Psychrometric Climate Classification B: Arid Example, Cairo, Egypt.

Passive Design Responses

- Hot arid climates will be cooling dominated, whereas cold arid climates will be heating dominated.
- Wide diurnal swings allow for the effective use of thermal mass with night flushing.
- Thermal mass without night flushing can also be effective for moderate cooling.
- Provide solar shading during cooling season.
- Provide natural ventilation during cooling season.
- The generally low levels of humidity allow for nonconventional cooling, such as evaporative cooling.
- Passive solar during heating season: Be careful not to overheat with solar gain during heating periods.
- Daylighting lowers lighting energy use and internal heat gain.
- Reduce heat transfer through conduction with a well-insulated building envelope.

Climate Classification C: Temperate

Climate Characteristics

Temperate climates are characterized by mild to very mild temperatures (compared to other classifications), including warm summers and cool winters. They can exhibit a considerable range of precipitation and humidity. Many locations in temperate climates are influenced by the climate-tempering impacts of the ocean.

Example Location: San Francisco, California, USA (Temperate-Dry and Warm Summer; see Figure 5.4)

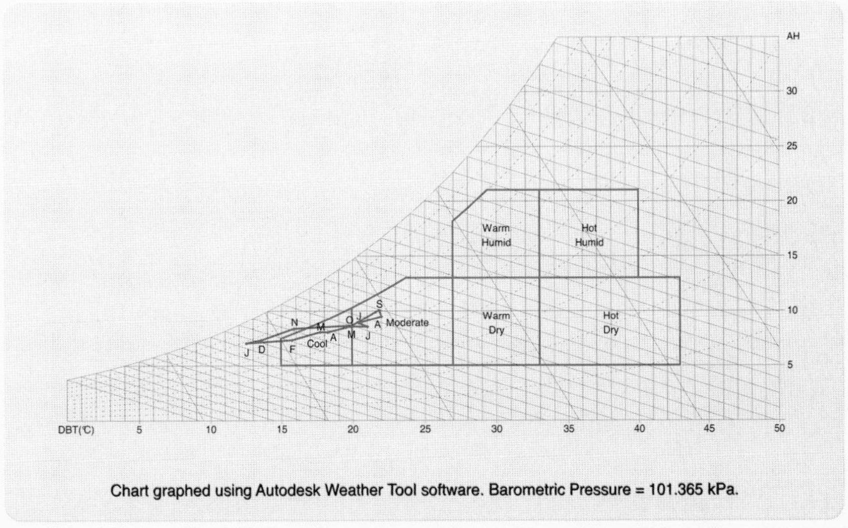

■ **FIGURE 5.4** Psychrometric Climate Classification C: Temperate Example, San Francisco, California.

Passive Design Responses

- Temperate climates vary considerably. Although they do not have extreme hot or cold periods, they typically have both heating and cooling seasons. Humidity levels vary and can be high in climates with hot summers.
- Wide diurnal swings allow for the effective use of thermal mass with night flushing.
- Thermal mass without night flushing can also be effective for moderate cooling.
- Provide solar shading during cooling season.
- Provide natural ventilation during cooling season.
- Passive solar during heating season: Be careful not to overheat with solar gain during heating periods.
- Daylighting lowers lighting energy use and internal heat gain.
- Reduce heat transfer through conduction with a well-insulated building envelope.

Climate Classification D: Cold

Climate Characteristics

Cold climates exhibit a wide range of seasonal temperatures but are characterized by cold winters with snow. Locations in cold climates are often interior to continental landmasses.

Example Location: Anchorage, Alaska, USA (Cold-Cold Summer Without Dry Season; see Figure 5.5)

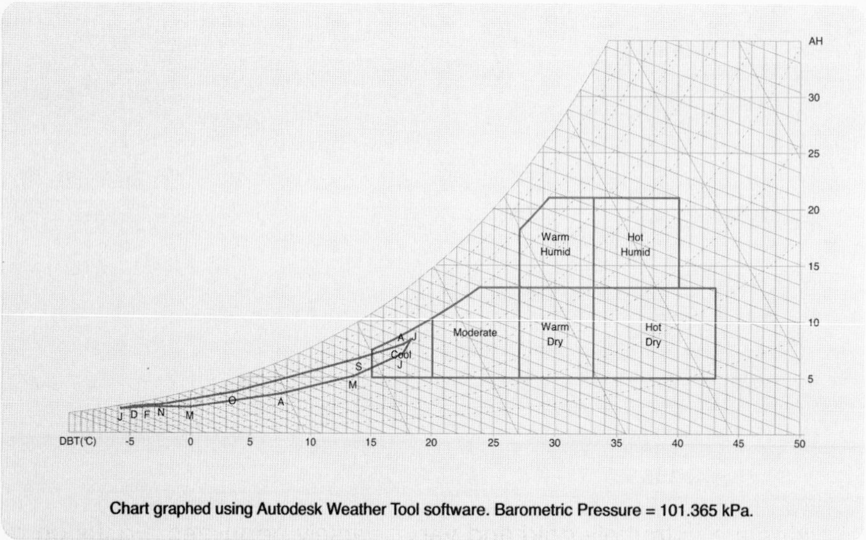

Chart graphed using Autodesk Weather Tool software. Barometric Pressure = 101.365 kPa.

■ **FIGURE 5.5** Psychrometric Climate Classification D: Cold Example, Anchorage, Alaska.

Passive Design Responses

- Cold climates with cold summers are very heating dominant.
- Humidity levels vary but can be high in climates with hot summers.

- Reduce heat transfer through conduction with a well-insulated building envelope.
- Wide diurnal swings allow for the effective use of thermal mass with night flushing for cooling during warm or hot summers.
- Provide solar shading during cooling season if summers are hot.
- Provide natural ventilation during cooling season.
- Passive solar during heating season: Thermal mass can be used to store passive heat gain. Be careful not to overheat with solar gain.
- Daylighting lowers lighting energy use and internal heat gain. Northern locations have drastically reduced daylit hours, annually.

Climate Classification E: Polar

Climate Characteristics

Polar climates are characterized by extremely cold temperatures, often with no summer season, and are typically treeless.

Example Location: Arctic (Nanisivik Airport) (Polar-Tundra; see Figure 5.6)

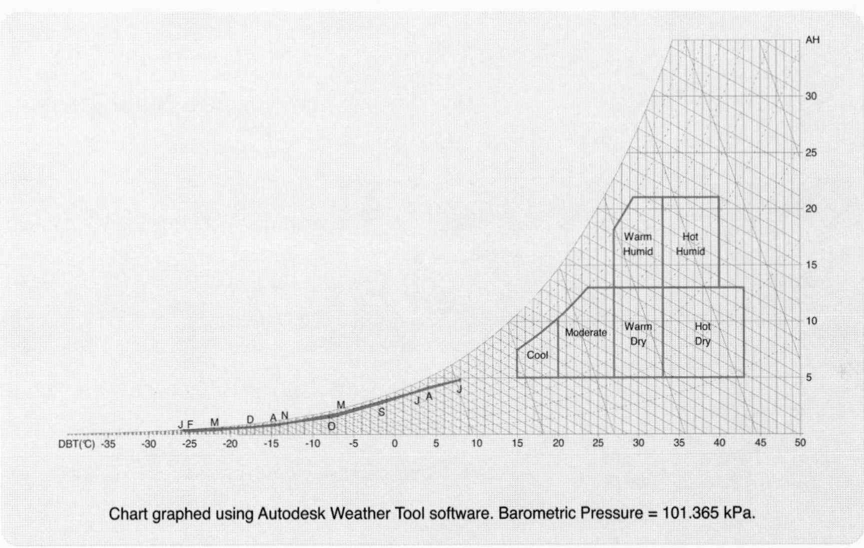

■ **FIGURE 5.6** Psychrometric Climate Classification E: Polar Example, Nanisivik Airport.

Passive Design Responses

- Polar climates are extremely cold and very sparsely populated. Focus on reducing heat loss through convection with a well-insulated building envelope.

The Köppen climate classification system inspired and influenced the current climate zone classifications used in the United States today. Chapter 4 provided details and a climate zone map for the United States based on the Climate Zone Definitions assigned by the Department of Energy and used by ASHRAE and the International Code Council.

These definitions are important for use in energy codes and in a wide variety of building energy-efficiency resources provided by the Department of Energy. The 17 climate zones in the Department of Energy Climate Zone Definitions have correlations to the Köppen system, making it possible to utilize some of these resources in the context of projects outside of the United States (see Figure 5.7).

Zone No.	Climate Zone Type	Köppen Classification
1A	Very Hot-Humid	Aw
1B	Very Hot-Dry	BWh
2A	Hot-Humid	Cfa
2B	Hot-Dry	BWh
3A	Warm-Humid	Cfa
3B	Warm-Dry	BSk/BWh/H
3C	Warm-Marine	Cs
4A	Mixed-Humid	Cfa/Dfa
4B	Mixed-Dry	BSk/BWh/H
4C	Mixed-Marine	Cb
5	Cool-Humid	Dfa
5B	Cool-Dry	BSk/H
5C	Cool-Marine	Cfb
6A	Cold-Humidd	Dfa/Dfb
6B	Cold-Dry	BSk/H
7	Very Cold	Dfb
8	Subarctic	Dfc

■ **FIGURE 5.7** Climate Zone Definitions and Köppen Classification. *Data source: Briggs, R. S., Lucas, R. G., Taylor, Z. T., 2003, Climate Classification for Building Energy Codes and Standards: Part 1—Development Process. Richland, WA (PNNL/DOE).*

Classifying a project location by climate zone is a useful first step for both learning about the project's climate and beginning the research into a climate-responsive net zero energy building. Understanding the broader climate zone and its characteristics can help identify climate-responsive building precedents in other locations with similar climates.

Climate Data

In addition to understanding the general climate classification for a project, it is important to investigate deeper, to develop a comprehensive set of climate data for the project and inform a climate-responsive design.

There are many parameters that make up climate and weather definitions. The best sources for climate data are the weather data files used for energy modeling. Common formats for weather files include CZ, CZ2, WYEC, WYEC2, TMY, TMY2, TMY3, and EPW. WYEC, which stands for Weather Year for Energy Calculations, is a weather data set developed by ASHRAE. CZ is a California-based weather data standard. TMY, which stands for Typical Meteorological Year, uses comprehensive weather data over several decades to determine a "typical" year in hourly weather data. EPW is the weather file format used by the Department of Energy's EnergyPlus software; it is widely compatible, or can be converted with climate analysis software and energy modeling software. The DOE's EnergyPlus website is an excellent source for weather files; it includes 2,100 locations worldwide, available for free download. In addition to the EPW weather file, each station has a summary data STAT file.

To begin climate research and analysis of weather data, you will need a software program that is capable of reading the weather file format and provides an interface to access, compile, visually display, and study the weather data. Several programs are available that feature useful interfaces to weather file data sets.

- Climate Consultant is a free program for Windows and Mac, available from the University of California, Los Angeles, and developed by the UCLA Energy Design Tools Group.
- Commercially available climate analysis software includes Autodesk's Ecotect Weather Tool and Meteotest's METEONORM, among others.

Weather Tools and Data Links

- Climate Consultant: www.energy-design-tools.aud.ucla.edu
- Autodesk Ecotect Weather Tool: http://usa.autodesk.com
- METEONORM: www.meteonorm.com
- EnergyPlus Weather Files: http://apps1.eere.energy.gov/buildings/energyplus/cfm/weather_data.cfm

The weather files used to develop a climate study and energy model are compiled from weather stations across the globe. Often, these weather stations are located at airports. In most circumstances, it may be appropriate to assume that the weather from a nearby station is approximately the same as that experienced at the actual project site. Think of the weather file for a given city or location as the general weather condition that persists in that area. Fortunately, weather files for most cities are available. However, when a weather file for a project site location is not available from a nearby weather station, the climate and energy analysis can be a challenge to conduct. In some cases, it may be acceptable to use the nearest available weather station, or extrapolate from nearby weather stations.

METEONORM

METEONORM has an extensive database of climatological data from locations around the globe. One of METEONORM's most useful features is its capability to generate a custom weather file for any location on the planet by automatically extrapolating data from nearby weather stations. Output files from METEONORM can be used for further climate and energy analysis with other software programs. The program produces its own graphic results, showing a few simple climate data graphs (see Figure 5.8); another of its core capabilities is to calculate solar radiation

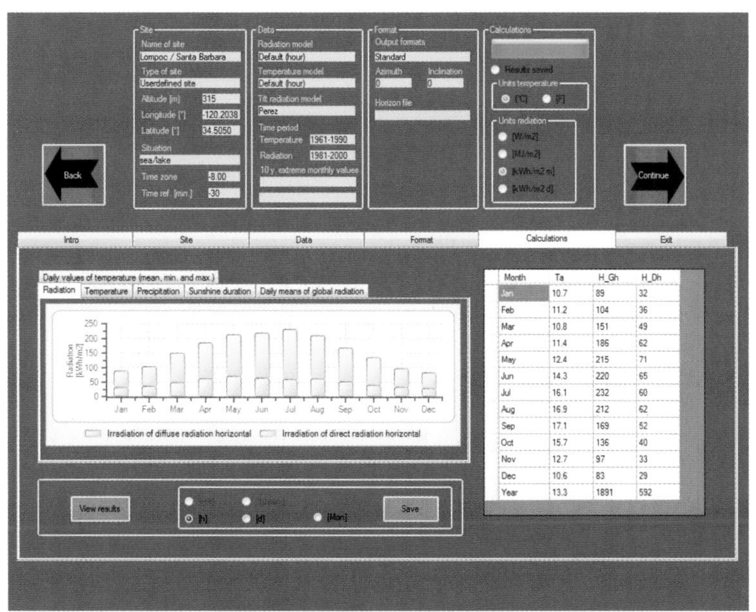

■ **FIGURE 5.8** METEONORM Example: Typical Results Screen.

data for arbitrarily oriented surfaces anywhere on the globe.

Sites near notable topographic features or water features will experience variations in weather data compared with a weather station location further removed from this location. Also, adjacent buildings can have an impact on sites located in dense urban areas. Wind and solar access are particularly variable. Sites with any of these features may require additional site-specific analysis to evaluate their impacts on passive design strategies. METEONORM has the capability to define site terrain parameters and set a custom site horizon, to account for building skylines or prominent topographic features (see Figure 5.9).

Climate Change

There is growing interest in assessing the impact of climate change on future weather data, and how future weather could affect energy use in buildings. For example, to assess the risk of undersizing cooling systems, renewable energy systems, or other energy-related systems, there is a need to determine the effect climate change could have on the typical meteorological year. In addition, as exemplary sustainable buildings, net zero energy buildings should have a long service life and so will face the realities of climate change over the course of their existence. Future weather files can be created for several decades into the future. Several universities in the United Kingdom are leading the way with research on using climate change models to morph weather data files. The University of Exeter, for one, offers future weather data files for locations in the United Kingdom; and the University of Southampton has developed tools for converting present-day weather files into future weather files using IPCC DDC Hadley CM3 climate scenario data. The psychrometric chart in Figure 5.10 shows climate classification for London with current weather, compared with two of many climate change scenarios: one for the year 2050 and the other for the year 2080.

METEONORM also has the capability to generate a future weather file for locations across the globe. The software uses a Hadley CM3 model, using a business-as-usual scenario to generate the data. Reference years corresponding to each decade between 2010 and 2100 are available for analysis.

The goal of energy modeling for net zero energy building is to be as predictive as possible. But a word of caution is in order here:

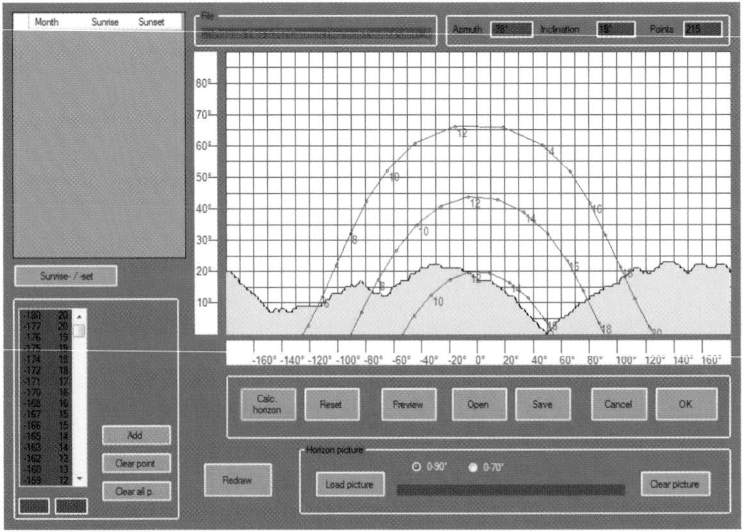

■ **FIGURE 5.9** METEONORM Example: Showing a Site Horizon.

Using morphed future weather files for the primary energy simulation of the building could be problematic. Future weather files are based on modeled predictions rather than historical data, meaning that there will be a fair amount of uncertainty in using a morphed future weather data file. In addition, future weather files will not be appropriate for estimating present-day and near-future energy use. It may be difficult to justify oversizing mechanical and energy-related systems to address an uncertain future weather, especially given the importance of right-sizing equipment. Mechanical and energy systems of a building do require upgrades and replacement over time, which may allow for sizing based on estimated service life of individual systems, and provide the opportunity to enhance system sizes during future upgrades.

The use of future weather files is still a new phenomenon within the building industry; hence, consensus has not been reached on the most effective way to design for future climate change. It may be best to conduct comparative energy and climate studies between present-day weather and multiple future weather files to understand the severity of the potential impact of climate change over time. It would also be important to hypothesize how passive strategies might need to change in response to climate change. Given that they are typically part of the architecture, passive strategies may not permit easy future upgrades, so considering a range of climate scenarios when developing passive strategies could be a resilient approach to design.

Another resilient design approach is to provide for future building system upgrades by designing for simple future upgrades and, if needed, upsizing. Perhaps one of the most important resilient strategies for designing to accommodate climate change is, simply, to realize that climate change is unpredictable and will likely result in greater extremes and severity in weather events. *Designing for passive survivability* captures the idea that a building is resourceful and resilient enough to weather the storm and any accompanying power outages and interruption of public utilities. Net zero energy buildings, with a unique blend of passive energy strategies and renewable energy

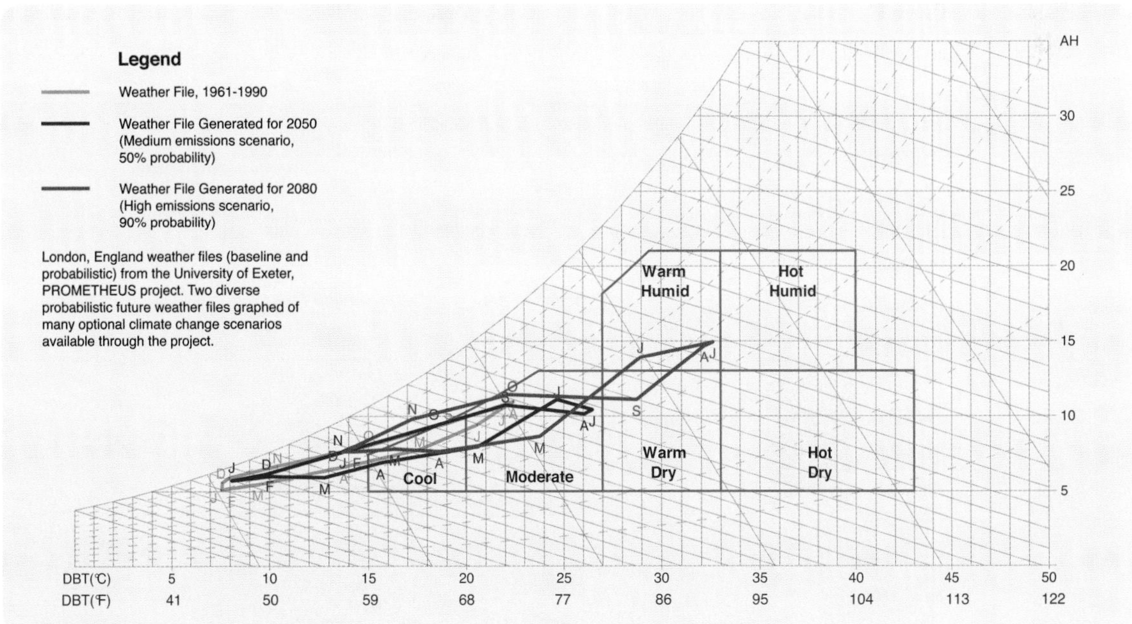

■ **FIGURE 5.10** Assessing Probabilistic Future Weather in London, England.

systems, are inherently apt for passive survivability. In fact, net zero energy buildings are, in many ways, the building industry's ultimate response to climate change.

Climate Analysis

Once an appropriate weather data file is acquired, it can be used to perform climate analysis for the project. Climate analysis includes developing a general comprehension of the climate parameters for a project site and then using it to generate and test passive design and renewable energy strategies. Climate responsiveness is of central importance to designing for net zero energy buildings, as this is one of the most effective ways of reducing energy loads for buildings. The weather data file is also used for all energy and daylight simulations. Climate Consultant, Weather Tool, or other climate analysis software tools can be used to create graphical studies of the various climate parameters.

CLIMATE CONSULTANT

UCLA Energy Design Tools Group's Climate Consultant is a simple and quick way to catalog the climate data for a project. To start, have the weather data file in EPW file format and then choose to proceed with Imperial or SI units. After the EPW weather file is loaded, the opening screen provides a valuable overview of the climate parameters based on monthly means. In the example in Figure 5.11, a weather file for Portland, Oregon, was used.

Proceeding to the next screen in Climate Consultant, choose the thermal comfort model for the analysis. Choices include the California Energy Code Comfort Model, ASHRAE Handbook of Fundamentals Comfort Model, ASHRAE Standard 55 PMV Model, and ASHRAE Standard 55 Adaptive Comfort Model. After you select the thermal comfort model desired for the design of the project, Climate Consultant overlays those specific comfort criteria into the climate analysis; it also prepopulates the next screen, which defines the design criteria for the climate analysis (see Figure 5.12). The User Help section of Climate Consultant offers valuable guidance on the variables for the criteria, and explains how to use and interpret the graphed charts. Note that the internal heat gain criterion is really a function of building type. The outdoor temperature balance point is the estimated outdoor temperature at which the internal heat gains can provide comfort, or the lowest outdoor temperature at which heating will

Climate Consultant 5.0 (Build 3, Oct 19, 2010)

WEATHER DATA SUMMARY

LOCATION: Portland International Ap, OR, USA
Latitude/Longitude: 45.6° North, 122.62° West, Time Zone from Greenwich -8
Data Source: TMY3 726980 WMO Station Number, Elevation 19 ft

MONTHLY MEANS	JAN	FEB	MAR	APR	MAY	JUN	JUL	AUG	SEP	OCT	NOV	DEC	
Global Horiz Radiation (Avg Hourly)	52	72	98	111	129	143	150	145	118	82	56	45	Btu/sq.ft
Direct Normal Radiation (Avg Hourly)	58	70	82	83	97	109	132	136	131	85	45	53	Btu/sq.ft
Diffuse Radiation (Avg Hourly)	32	43	53	59	64	66	59	55	43	41	39	30	Btu/sq.ft
Global Horiz Radiation (Max Hourly)	135	174	241	280	299	319	300	276	264	203	140	114	Btu/sq.ft
Direct Normal Radiation (Max Hourly)	269	290	301	279	302	290	293	272	292	266	247	270	Btu/sq.ft
Diffuse Radiation (Max Hourly)	68	94	134	161	158	143	147	130	145	102	88	71	Btu/sq.ft
Global Horiz Radiation (Avg Daily Total)	386	608	986	1270	1700	1901	1983	1736	1267	751	434	337	Btu/sq.ft
Direct Normal Radiation (Avg Daily Total)	462	615	859	972	1298	1467	1773	1673	1425	828	349	394	Btu/sq.ft
Diffuse Radiation (Avg Daily Total)	244	369	541	690	849	889	791	664	472	381	306	225	Btu/sq.ft
Global Horiz Illumination (Avg Hourly)	1657	2305	3132	3556	4116	4550	4724	4539	3698	2588	1796	1455	footcandles
Direct Normal Illumination (Avg Hourly)	1555	1960	2373	2429	2839	3197	3853	3994	3777	2428	1237	1357	footcandles
Dry Bulb Temperature (Avg Monthly)	41	44	47	53	57	63	68	68	63	55	47	39	degrees F
Dew Point Temperature (Avg Monthly)	36	37	38	44	47	51	54	55	52	45	41	35	degrees F
Relative Humidity (Avg Monthly)	83	77	74	73	71	67	64	66	72	74	82	87	percent
Wind Direction (Avg Monthly)	150	149	186	167	226	241	276	251	217	167	172	144	degrees
Wind Speed (Avg Monthly)	8	9	7	8	7	7	8	6	6	6	7	6	mph
Snow Depth (Avg Monthly)													inches
Ground Temperature (Avg Monthly of 3 Depths)	44	44	47	50	57	61	63	62	59	54	49	45	degrees F

Back Next

■ **FIGURE 5.11** Climate Consultant Example: Portland, Oregon Weather Data Summary.

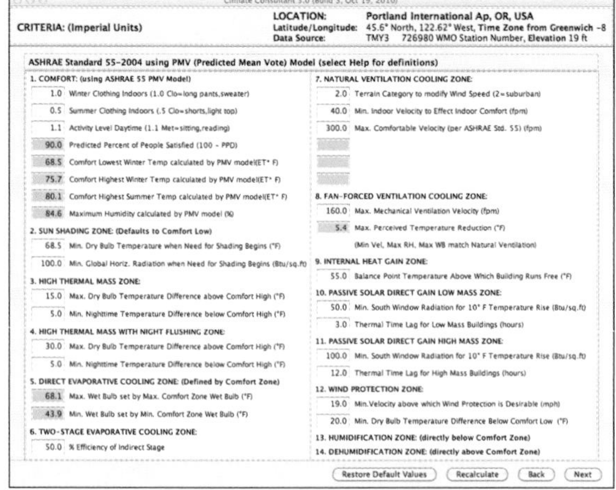

■ **FIGURE 5.12** Climate Consultant Example: Portland Thermal Comfort Criteria, ASHRAE 55 PMV.

not be required. The outdoor temperature balance point can be decreased for buildings with higher internal gains from people and equipment, and should be increased for buildings with low internal gains. The balance point temperature is also a function of building mass and thermal performance of the envelope.

With the thermal comfort model and the climate design criteria selected, Climate Consultant can create a wide variety of graphic representations of climate data. See Figure 5.13 as an example of the type of data that can be graphed in Climate Consultant.

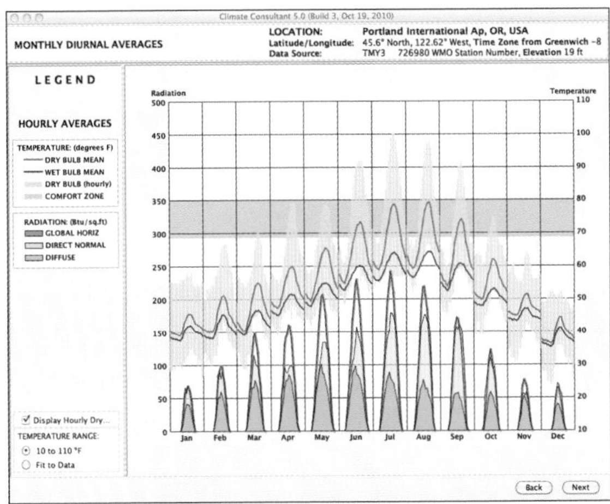

■ **FIGURE 5.13** Climate Consultant Example: Portland Monthly Diurnal Averages.

WEATHER TOOL

Another useful tool for generating graphic plots of weather data is Autodesk's Ecotect Weather Tool. Weather Tool's native weather file format is WEA. However, it can convert and use an EPW file. Once the EPW file is converted and opened, it can be saved as a WEA file. When a weather file is opened in Weather Tool, a summary page is generated that provides simple charts of daylight hours, solar radiation, temperature, precipitation, heating/cooling/solar degree-days, and wind, over the course of the year. If certain summary data are absent from the imported weather file, monthly data can be manually input via the monthly data tab. Units in Weather Tool are metric. For the example in Figure 5.14, a weather file for Phoenix, Arizona, was used.

Weather Tool has a number of graphic analysis options for the weather data. One advantage of Weather Tool is that by printing results to a PDF, the file retains vector information, making it highly customizable for a wide set of graphic and presentation needs. The options for analysis are arranged in a vertical menu along the left side of the window.

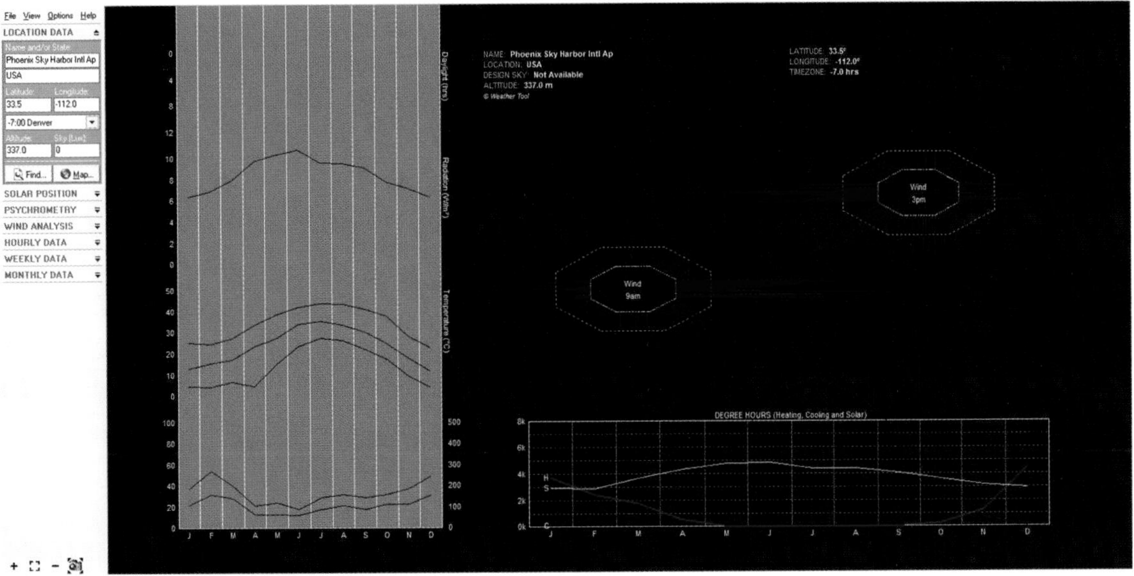

■ **FIGURE 5.14** Weather Tool Example: Phoenix, Arizona, Weather Summary.

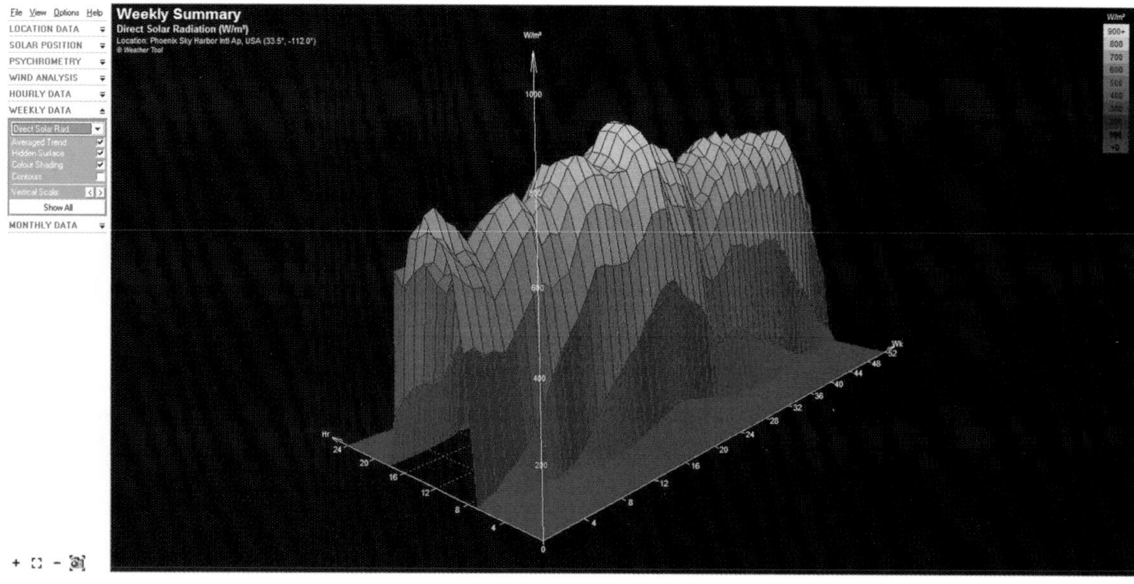

■ **FIGURE 5.15** Weather Tool Example: Phoenix Direct Solar Radiation in 3D Time Plot.

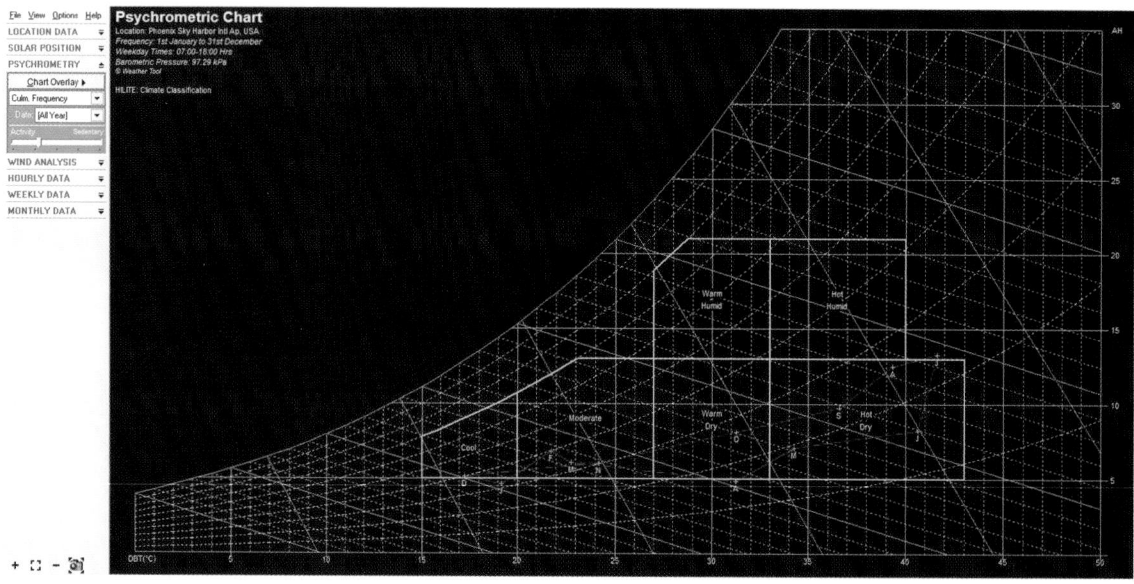

■ **FIGURE 5.16** Weather Tool Example: Phoenix Climate Classification Plotted on a Psychrometric Chart.

Each menu option provides customization of the data. Figure 5.15 is an example of the type of graphical climate analysis available with the Weather Tool.

The thermal comfort model is *not* adjustable in Weather Tool, as it is in Climate Consultant. Weather Tool uses a monthly *thermal neutrality* range model. (Thermal neutrality is the indoor temperature that is needed for comfort based on the average outdoor temperature each month for a specific location.) Based on studies of perceived comfort in free-running buildings in a variety of locations, the thermal neutrality model is valuable for considering the effectiveness of passive strategies.

The options under the psychrometry tab allow for analysis of passive strategies based on the hourly climate data for the year or for different months and seasons. Additional user inputs are possible when conducting a psychrometric analysis in Weather Tool:

- The default settings for the chart can be adjusted, and the barometric pressure default setting (based on sea level) can be changed for a specific location.
- The hours of operation can be set from the default 24 hours a day, 7 days a week, to the appropriate schedule, using the passive design analysis dialog box.
- The occupant's typical activity level can be adjusted on a sliding scale.

Weather Tool's psychrometric chart function contains a passive design analysis tool that can plot the benefits of passive strategies on a psychrometric chart or create a comfort percentages bar chart for each passive strategy, showing the effect on comfort for each month of the year. The chart can also be set up to give a climate classification, using a simple plot of monthly average conditions (see Figure 5.16).

Climate Evaluation

Studying climate data will help inform and evaluate the design of passive strategies, and assist in the planning of renewable energy resources and systems. There are primary sets of climate data that should be compiled and evaluated to aid this process. The following guide itemizes how to develop a comprehensive climate evaluation for a net zero energy project and arrive at recommendations for passive design, efficient building systems, and renewable energy systems.

Climate Data Sets

Temperature

Terminology

- **Dry bulb temperature:** Air temperature measured with a standard thermometer without exposure to direct solar radiation or moisture.
- **Diurnal temperatures:** A 24-hour temperature cycle.
- **Heating degree-days (HDD):** A measure of the difference between the mean daily temperature and a base temperature at which heating should not be required (for example, 65°F), when the mean temperature is below the base temperature. The annual HDD is the sum of each daily measure.
- **Cooling degree-days (CDD):** A measure of the difference between the mean daily temperature and a base temperature at which cooling should not be required (for example, 50°F), when the mean temperature is above the base temperature. The annual CDD is the sum of each daily measure.

Steps

1. Collect and plot on a graph:
   - Comfort zone temperature range
   - Dry bulb temperatures—monthly high, low, and mean
   - Dry bulb temperatures—monthly diurnal averages
   - Time of daily and monthly dry bulb temperatures
   - Heating degree-days and cooling degree-days for site's climate zone

2. Conduct analysis:
   A. Develop an overall understanding of the thermal conditions of the site's climate (see Figure 5.17).
   B. Compare the relationship of the thermal comfort range with the annual temperature ranges (see Figure 5.17).
   C. Evaluate the depth of diurnal temperature swings. Deep swings, particularly in excess of 15°F, may indicate the beneficial use of thermal mass. Diurnal swings that dip below the comfort zone during summer nights may indicate the beneficial use of night purging with thermal mass (see Figure 5.17).

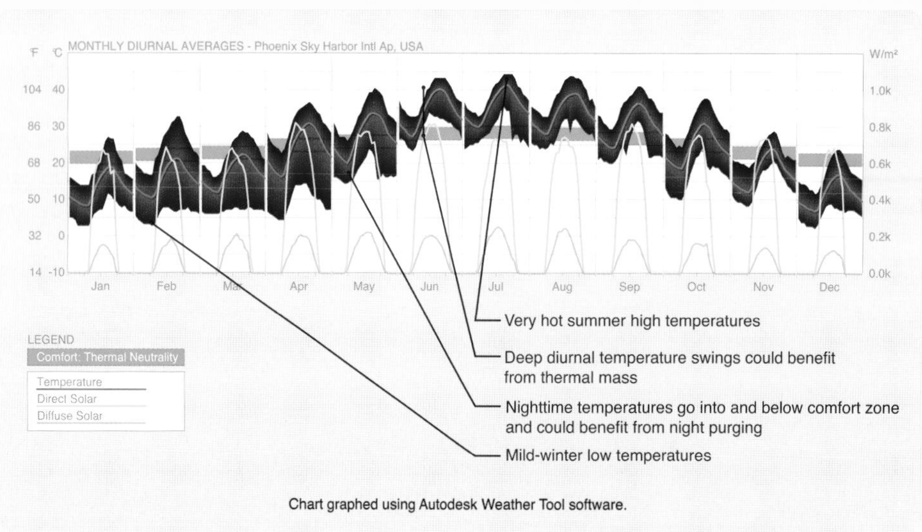

■ **FIGURE 5.17** Climate Data Set Temperature—Average Monthly Diurnal Temperature.

Humidity

Terminology

- **Relative humidity:** The percent of water in air compared to the maximum amount of water the air can hold at a given temperature.
- **Wet bulb temperature:** The temperature measured with a wet bulb thermometer (a bulb wrapped in a wet cloth with freely evaporating water). Wet bulb temperature represents the minimum temperature of air through the effect of evaporation or evaporative cooling.
- **Wet bulb depression:** The difference between dry bulb temperature and wet bulb temperature.

Steps

1. Collect and plot on a graph:
   - Time of daily and monthly relative humidity levels
   - Time of daily and monthly wet bulb depression
   - Time of daily and monthly wet bulb temperatures

2. Conduct analysis:
   A. Develop an overall understanding of the general relative humidity levels of the site's climate.
   B. Evaluate the relationship of humidity levels to temperature levels, to determine whether humidity is a thermal comfort and latent energy concern.
   C. Evaluate and graph the wet bulb depression. A deep wet bulb depression during cooling season may indicate the beneficial use of evaporative cooling (see Figure 5.18).

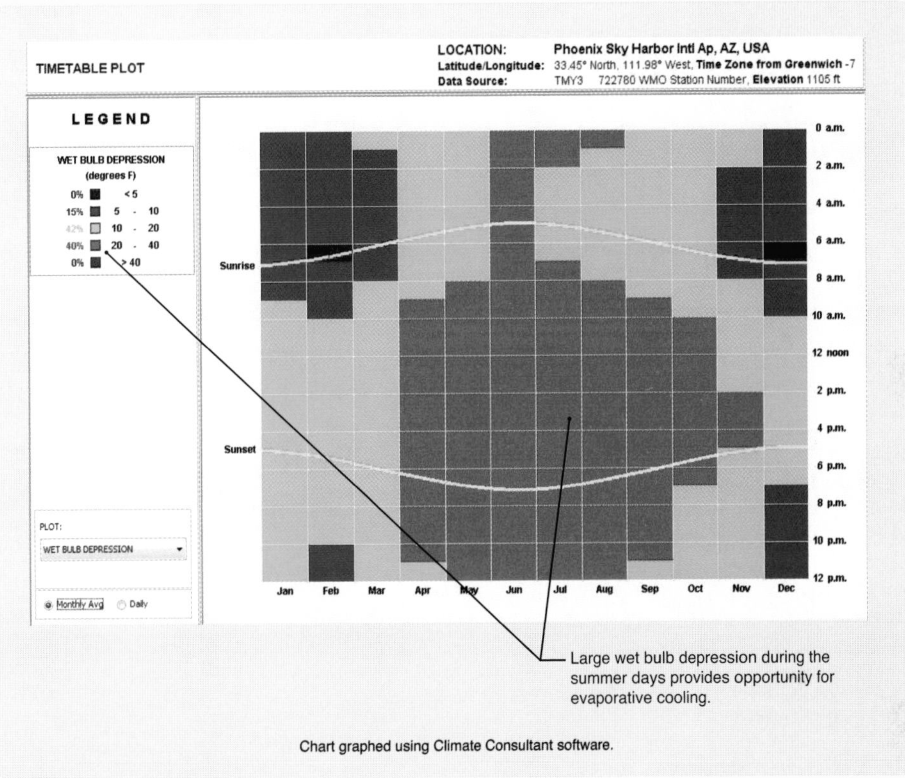

■ **FIGURE 5.18** Climate Data Set—Wet Bulb Depression.

Wind Rose

Terminology

- **Wind Rose:** A graph characterizing wind data, such as wind speed, wind direction, and wind frequency, for a specific period of time. Wind roses plot the direction wind is blowing from.

Steps

1. Collect and plot on a graph:
   - Seasonal wind roses, which include speed, direction, and frequency, with time-of-day variations if present

2. Conduct analysis:
   A. Develop an overall understanding of the wind direction and speed as characterized over the course of a year.
   B. Evaluate wind direction and speed during times of potential passive cooling through natural ventilation (day and night) (see Figure 5.19).
   C. Evaluate wind direction and speed during times when wind protection is desired (strong winds and/or cold temperatures).
   D. Evaluate wind speed over the course of the year for potential for renewable electricity generation using site or building-integrated wind turbines. (Estimating and planning renewable energy generation is discussed in Chapter 8.)

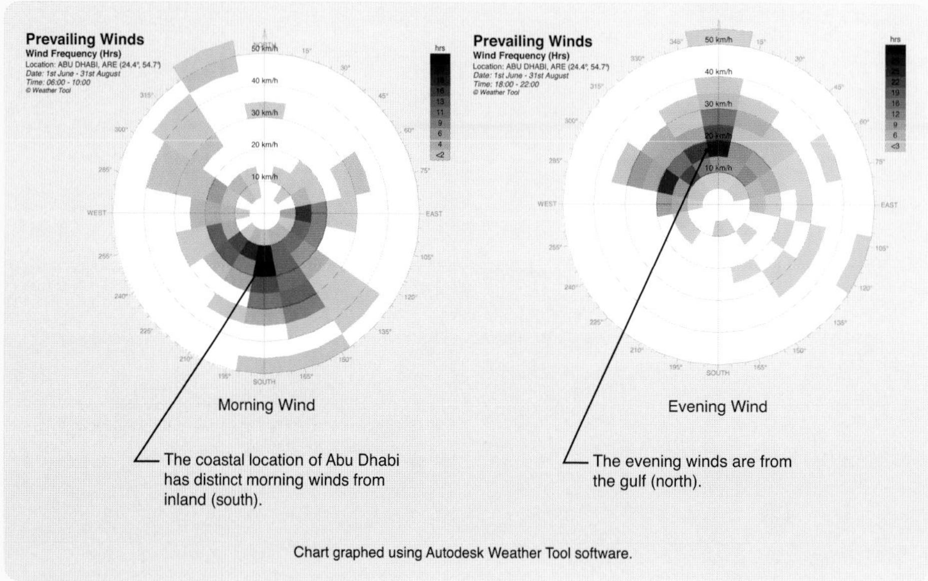

■ **FIGURE 5.19** Climate Data Set—Wind.

Ground Temperature

Terminology

- **Ground Temperature:** The temperature of the soil at a specific depth.

Steps

1. Collect and plot on a graph:
   - Monthly average ground temperatures over the course of a year at different ground depths
2. Conduct analysis:
   A. Evaluate the temperature swings and temperature range for different ground depths. Determine the depth at which the ground temperature swings become relatively flat (see Figure 5.20). This condition reveals the greater difference between ground temperature and outside air temperature during winter and summer.

B. Compare ground temperature to outside air temperature over the course of a year. Significant temperature differences during heating and cooling seasons may indicate the beneficial use of earth-coupling strategies such as earth tubes, earth sheltering, and ground-source heat pumps.

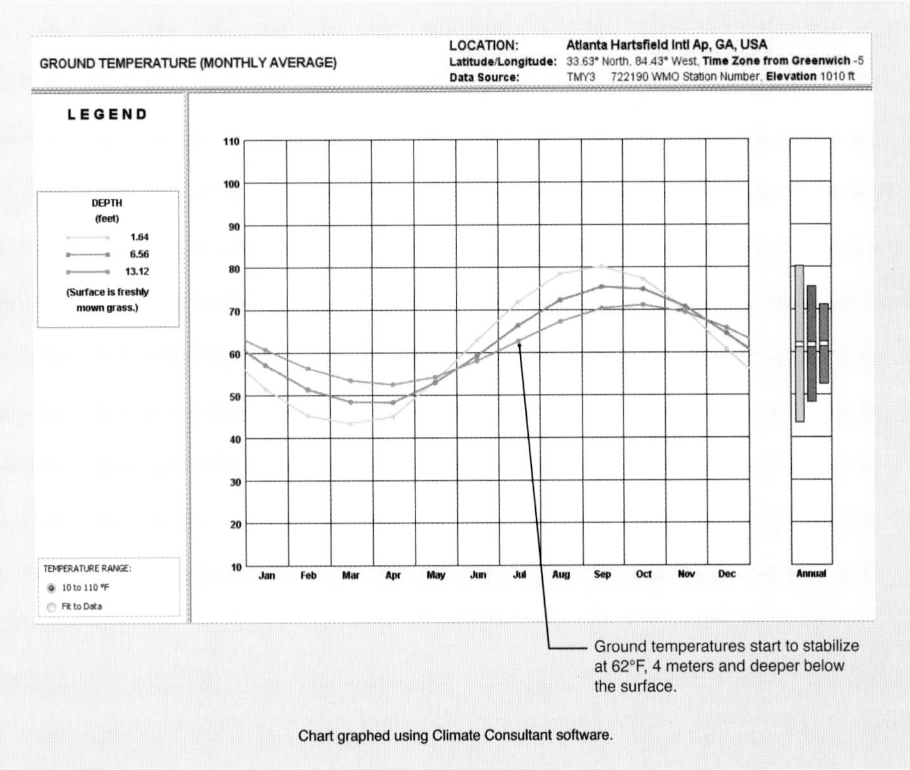

■ **FIGURE 5.20** Climate Data Set—Ground Temperature.

Solar Radiation

Terminology

- **Direct normal solar radiation:** The direct solar radiation measured on a surface perpendicular to the direct beam.
- **Global horizontal solar radiation:** The combined direct and diffuse solar radiation measured on a horizontal surface.
- **Diffuse radiation:** The measure of radiation resulting from the reflecting and scattering of direct beam radiation.
- **Global incident solar radiation:** The combined direct and diffuse solar radiation measured on a tilted surface. The angle of incident is the difference between the angle of tilt for the surface and a line perpendicular to the sun's rays.
- **Irradiance:** A measure of radiation in the units of power per area, or W/m^2, or Btu/h · ft^2.
- **Insolation:** A measure of radiation in the units of energy (or power over a specific time exposure) per area, or Wh/m^2, J/m^2, or Btu/ft^2. These are often expressed per day or per year.

Steps

1. Collect and plot on a graph:
   - Direct normal solar radiation by hourly average per month and annually
   - Global horizontal solar radiation by hourly average per month and annually
   - Diffuse solar radiation by hourly average per month and annually
   - Global incident solar radiation for key building or solar energy technology orientations by hourly average per month and annually
2. Conduct analysis:
   A. Develop an overall understanding of the solar radiation levels over the course of the year, and note seasonal variations.
   B. Compare global horizontal solar radiation levels, direct normal solar radiation, and diffuse radiation over the course of a year, to determine the relative contributions of diffuse radiation and direct beam radiation.
   C. Compare global horizontal solar radiation to the outdoor temperatures over the course of a year, to assess the liability of solar radiation during the cooling season and estimate the value of solar radiation during the heating season.
   D. Evaluate monthly and annual global incident solar radiation for key building orientations, to determine impact on solar gain and glazing design (see Figure 5.21).
   E. Evaluate monthly and annual global incident solar radiation for renewable energy strategies such as photovoltaics and solar thermal. (Estimating and planning renewable energy generation is discussed in Chapter 8.)

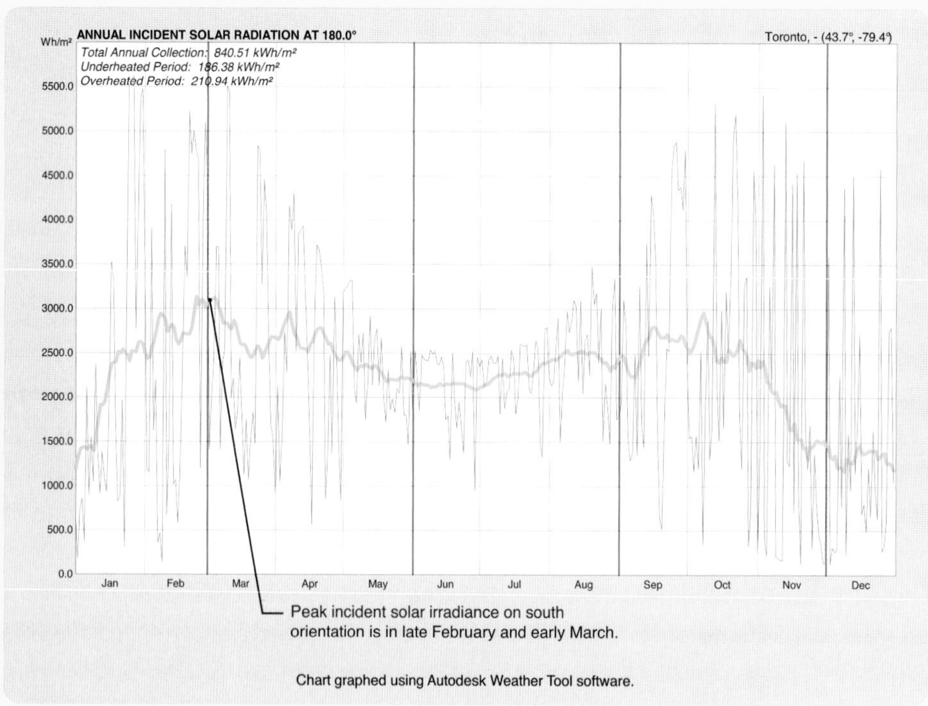

■ **FIGURE 5.21** Climate Data Set—Solar Radiation.

Solar Geometry

Terminology

- **Solar azimuth:** The horizontal angle of the sun's direct beam in reference to north or south.
- **Solar altitude:** The vertical angle of the sun's direct beam to the horizontal.
- **Design solar shading dates:** The time and date on which the design of shading of all glazed surfaces in each orientation is based. The date is the earliest and latest in the year when full shading of glazing is deemed important to limit solar radiation gain in the building. Include the start time and end time of the day on the design dates.
- **Solar shading cutoff angles:** The solar altitude and azimuth angles of the sun to be shaded from building glazing, based on the design solar shading dates for each façade. These shading cutoff angles guide the depth and geometric design of shading on each façade.

Steps

1. Collect and plot on a graph:
   - Sun path diagram that captures the sun's azimuth (horizontal angle) and the sun's altitude (vertical angle) plotted hourly for each month of the year
   - Solar radiation comparisons over the course of the year (monthly and hourly) with the sun path diagram
   - Temperature comparisons over the course of the year (monthly and hourly) with the sun path diagram
2. Conduct analysis:
   - **A.** Develop an overall understanding of the solar path over the course of a year, notably seasonal differences and extremes (see Figure 5.22).
   - **B.** Determine design solar shading dates based on the earliest or latest date that full shading of glazing is deemed important to limit solar heat gain in the building. Establish the times during the design solar shading dates that shading is to be provided.
   - **C.** Determine solar shading cutoff angles for each façade for design solar shading dates using a sun path diagram.
   - **D.** Use the solar shading cutoff angles to determine the shading plane geometry needed for each glazing configuration per façade. The design solar dates will generally influence the required depth of shading device, while the start and end time of the shading date greatly influence the length of horizontal shading devices or the use of vertical shading devices.
   - **E.** The use of computer simulation software, such as Autodesk Ecotect, can help resolve building geometry and solar geometry for effective solar shading design.

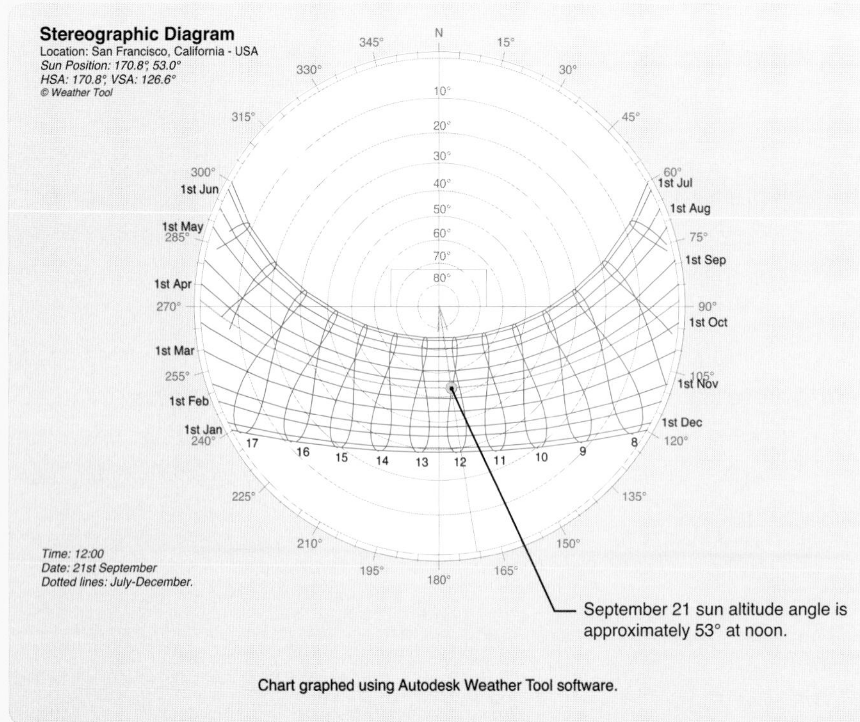

■ **FIGURE 5.22** Climate Data Set—Solar Geometry.

Sky Cover

Terminology

- **CIE:** International Commission on Illumination.
- **Clear sky:** Completely cloudless sky.
- **Overcast sky:** Completely overcast, with highest sky illumination at the zenith (top of sky dome) and lowest sky illumination at the horizon.
- **Intermediate sky:** Based on a clear sky with the addition of atmospheric haze.
- **Uniform sky:** A theoretical sky condition defined by uniform illumination across the entire sky dome.

Steps

1. Collect and plot on a graph:
   - Percent cloud cover over the course of a year
2. Conduct analysis:
   A. Develop an overall understanding of the sky cover conditions over the course of a year. Note any daily or seasonal characteristics (see Figure 5.23).
   B. Determine the sky condition or set of conditions to use in daylighting analysis, based on CIE definitions of *clear*, *overcast*, and *intermediate* skies. Note: The CIE definition of overcast sky will represent the worst-case condition for daylight, and is used for analyzing daylight factor; but predominantly overcast sky conditions also require markedly different daylight strategies, which may not be appropriate for climates with predominantly sunny conditions.

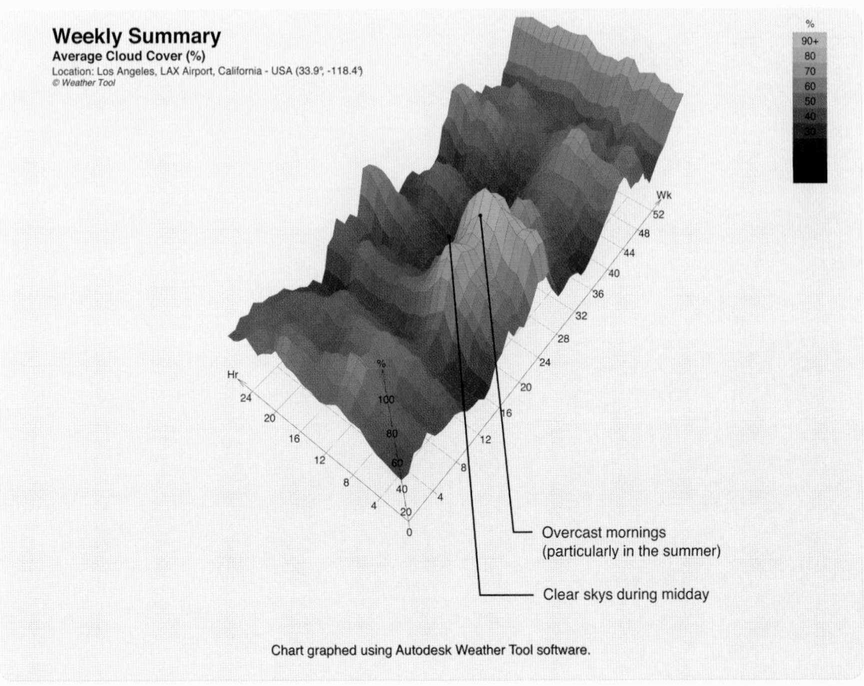

■ **FIGURE 5.23** Climate Data Set—Cloud Cover.

Illumination

Terminology

- **Direct normal illumination:** The direct exterior illuminance measured on a surface perpendicular to the direct sunbeam. Units are in footcandles (lumens per square foot) or lux (lumens per square meter).
- **Global horizontal illumination:** The total exterior direct and diffuse sky illuminance measured on a horizontal surface. Units are in footcandles (lumens per square foot) or lux (lumens per square meter).
- **Daylight factor:** The indoor illumination at any particular point in a building as a percentage of outdoor illumination level at that time and sky condition.

Steps

1. Collect and plot on a graph:
   - Direct normal illumination by hourly average per month and annually
   - Global horizontal illumination by hourly average per month and annually
2. Conduct analysis:
   - **A.** Develop an overall understanding of the exterior illumination levels over the course of the year, and note seasonal variations (see Figure 5.24).
   - **B.** Compare global horizontal illumination levels with direct normal illumination over the course of a year, to ascertain the relative contributions of diffuse illuminance and direct beam illuminance.

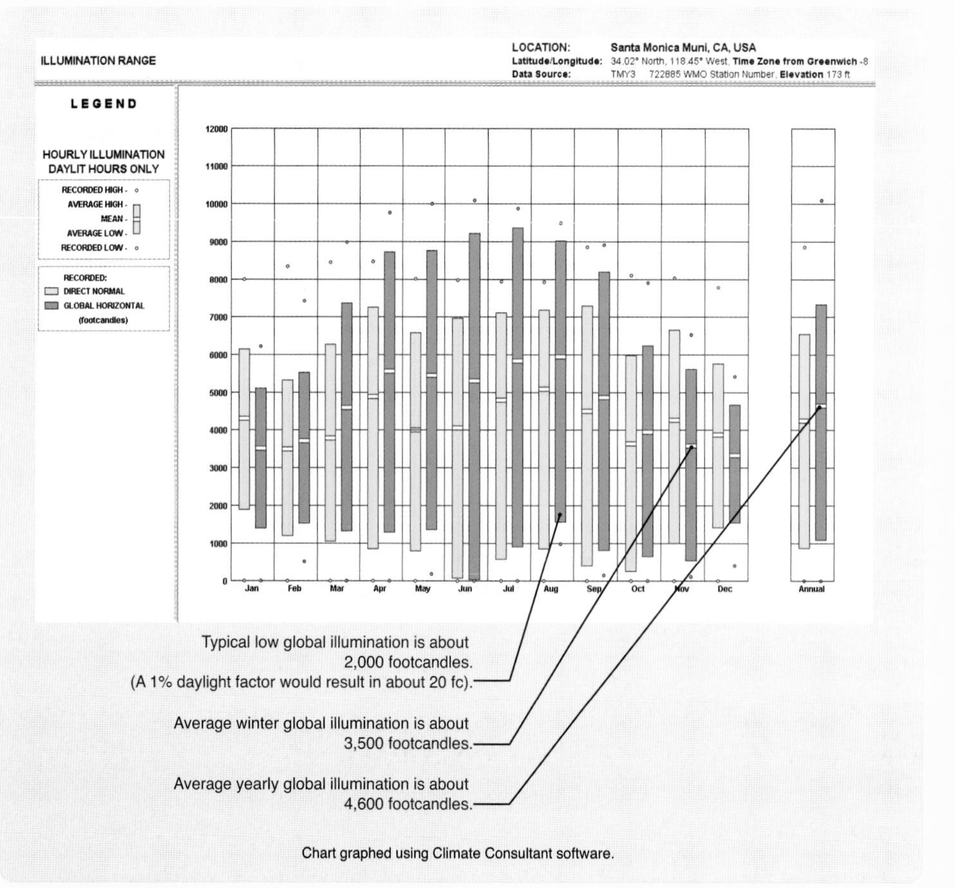

■ **FIGURE 5.24** Climate Data Set—Illumination.

C. Correlate sky cover conditions with exterior illumination levels, to understand design sky conditions for worst, best, and typical cases, and how the sky conditions change with the seasons.

D. Estimate design daylight factors by dividing the desired interior illumination levels or requirements by the worst-case overcast exterior illumination level. (Chapter 6 provides guidance on daylight factors and daylighting.)

E. Evaluate daylight hours, monthly or seasonally, to determine application of daylighting.

Psychrometric Chart

Terminology

- **Psychrometry:** The study of the thermodynamic characteristics of moist air.

Steps

1. Collect and plot on a graph:

- Psychrometric chart with plots of annual hourly thermodynamic air properties for the climate based on the weather data file for the project. The psychrometric chart should also plot the conditions for thermal comfort based on the project's thermal comfort criteria.

- Thermal comfort zone extensions based on passive design strategies. For example:
  - Solar shading of windows
  - High thermal mass
  - High thermal mass with night flush
  - Direct evaporative cooling
  - Indirect evaporative cooling
  - Natural ventilation
  - Internal heat gain
  - Passive solar direct gain
  - Wind protection
- Seasonal and/or monthly averages for thermodynamic air properties, to isolate seasonal variations

2. Conduct analysis:

A. Develop an overall understanding of the project's climate based on time plots of the air conditions of the climate over the course of a year.

B. Develop time plots using monthly or seasonal averages, to illustrate the seasonal variation in air conditions.

C. Evaluate the potential increase in the thermal comfort zone after applying passive design strategies, to determine which passive design strategies are most beneficial for the project (see Figure 5.25).

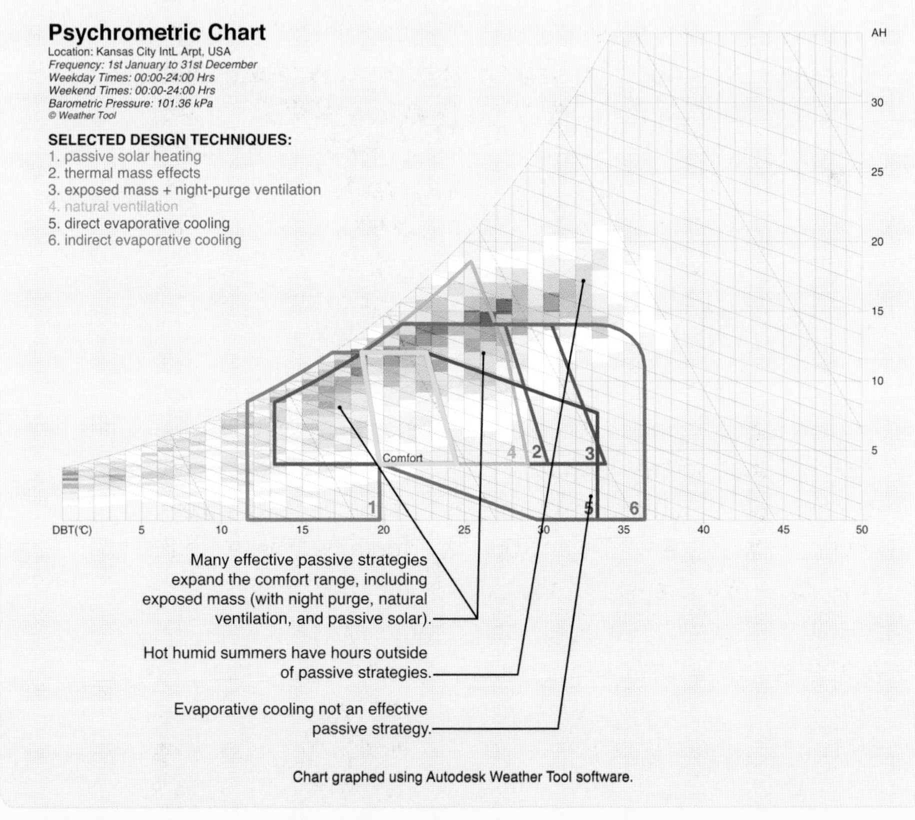

FIGURE 5.25 Climate Data Set—Psychrometric.

THINKING IN SEASONS

Organizing climate data by season can be a useful way of structuring, analyzing, and communicating the data. Seasonal organization can consolidate monthly data into meaningful units of time, which also tend to distinguish the basic heating, cooling, or shoulder seasons (the transition months between heating and cooling seasons) for a climate. This begins the process of thinking about the design of a net zero energy project in terms of seasons. Seasonal organization also allows for the identification of noteworthy seasonal characteristics, which can aid in the development of climatic responses, and starts the rational integration of passive design strategies and renewable energy systems. See Figure 5.26.

SITE ASSESSMENT

Site assessment for a net zero energy project builds on the information collected during the climate analysis. Often, the parameters of a climate study need to be analyzed in more detail within the specificity of the site. In fact, building sites can have, or be designed for, unique microclimates. The site also needs to be evaluated to discover both constraints and opportunities as they relate to energy use and energy flow through the site. The goal is to assess the types and flow of free energy that can be incorporated into the design. Evaluating the site leads to understanding how the building could be placed within it. Issues of orientation and massing should be analyzed within the parameters developed for the site assessment.

Further, the general organization and development of the building program expands the use of climate and site data when creating a climate-responsive building. Applying climate data and renewable energy resource data to the site and building planning process is essential for informing the design of net zero energy architecture.

Opportunities and Constraints

All project sites have their own unique sets of opportunities and constraints. The types of opportunities and constraints to analyze depend on the project objectives. They could range from economic, real estate, and land use issues to various sustainable design parameters, such as carbon, energy, water, materials, waste, or habitat. All of these are

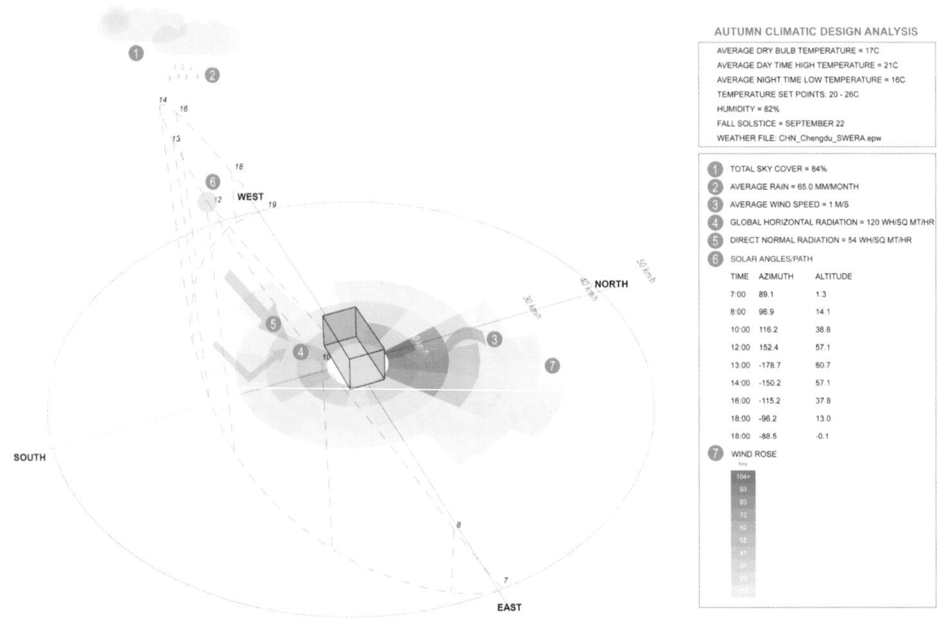

■ **FIGURE 5.26** Seasonal Summary Diagram for Autumn in Chengdu, China. *Image courtesy of RNL.*

essential to a successful holistic building, but it is the analysis of energy that is key to the development of a net zero energy architecture; it is, therefore, the focus of this section.

INVENTORY

Begin a site energy analysis with an inventory of the site features that can influence energy design. The inventory process involves development of site plans and computer site models, photography, diagrams, and data collection. The energy-related inventory is typically combined with or made part of a larger site inventory process that is a function of the holistic site assessment.

Site Inventory for Energy and Climate Design

- Site boundary/property line
- Topography
- Landscaping/geography/surrounding development
- Adjacent buildings
- Conventional energy sources/utilities
- Climate data sets/evaluation

It is important to identify the site boundary, as this essentially demarcates the limit of work. However, it is also important to take the inventory and site analysis well beyond the borders of the property line or site boundary. From an energy and climate perspective, many features in the surrounding area impact the site.

The topography of a site is a fundamental feature, but the topography at the horizon can also be critical for solar access for a site. The surrounding landscape and geography can influence microclimates of a site. Notable features and the characteristics of the surrounding development, such as bodies of water and large landscaped areas, should be recorded. Breezes flowing into a site from an adjacent park or landscaped area could translate into a welcome cooling benefit, whereas a large adjacent asphalt parking lot or major vehicular thoroughfare could be a liability. The surrounding buildings directly influence solar access, but also create unique wind patterns through a site.

From a site inventory perspective, the availability of conventional energy sources through the local utilities must be determined, as well. Also ascertain whether there is access to energy sources through a central plant or district energy system, and whether there are any issues with available capacity; and estimate the expense of bringing a conventional energy source to the site. Net zero energy buildings need not be off-grid; they can use conventional energy as a way to balance the dynamic availability of renewable energy generation on-site. Access to grid electricity, with the capability to net-meter, is an effective strategy for net zero energy buildings.

SITE ANALYSIS

Using the site plan, site inventory, and climate data, the site can be analyzed, and opportunities and constraints regarding energy flows evaluated. This process makes the climate analysis project-specific and establishes the evaluation of climate parameters at a site and building level. The process also enhances the evaluation of passive energy and renewable energy strategies. From a passive design and renewable energy perspective, site evaluation of both the opportunities and constraints presented by the sun and wind define many of the primary design drivers.

Site analysis should also include an assessment of other renewable energy strategies, as discussed in Chapter 8. If a project has access to a waterway appropriate for micro or small hydropower, or is in a region with good geothermal or biomass resources, these opportunities should be explored and leveraged.

Site Opportunities and Constraints Analysis

Solar and Daylight

Diagram and Model

- Plot seasonal solar path over site plan.
- On a stereographic sun path diagram, plot landforms, buildings, and other obstructions that make up the site's horizon. Overlaying a photograph of the site's sky, taken with a circular fisheye lens, onto the stereographic sun path diagram is an effective method of plotting obstructions on the horizon. The horizon can also be manually plotted by measuring the azimuth (horizontal) and altitude (vertical) angles of the horizon at a range of points across the site's horizon.
- Conduct annual shadow studies from adjacent buildings or notable features. Note summer solstice, winter solstice, and equinox shadows.
- Plot solar access on-site on winter solstice (the day of the year with the lowest solar altitude, typically December 21st or 22nd), from 9:00 am to 3:00 pm.
- Plot seasonal solar radiation on the ground surface of the site, and on a simple massing/white-box model at potential building location(s).
- Plot seasonal surface temperatures on the ground surface of the site, and on a simple white-box model at potential building location(s). Note corresponding seasonal air temperatures.
- Plot optimal orientation on the site for solar control and daylight harvesting, and identify site-specific orientation issues.

Opportunities and Constraints Assessment

Daylighting

- Does the site's horizon limit solar access during any time of day and year? Does this change the hours of sunshine available, seasonally and annually? What are the seasonal daylit hours at the site?
- What sky conditions and exterior global horizontal illumination represent the average seasonal condition, the average annual condition, and the worst-case daylighting design scenario?
- Which areas of the site are in shadow from on-site or adjacent buildings and other site features? What times of the year is the shading present?

Solar Control and Passive Solar

- What are the times of the year when overheating is likely, and when should solar shading be utilized? Does existing shading offer any benefits during these times?
- What are the times of the year when heating is needed and passive solar could be a benefit?
- Which areas of the site have solar access during periods when heating is needed?

Solar Renewable Energy

- How much of the site receives solar access on winter solstice from 9:00 am to 3:00 pm, which is a guide for location of solar thermal panels and PV?
- Determine the site's annual solar insolation per square foot, and the feasibility for solar energy.

Wind

Diagram and Model

- Position wind rose data on the site plan. Include seasonal or even day and night wind roses if they reveal important wind patterns.
- Determine direction, frequency, and speed of beneficial winds. Beneficial winds can be used to naturally ventilate a building and provide pedestrian comfort for exterior spaces during warm or hot periods.
- Determine direction, frequency, and speed of detrimental winds, defined as unwelcome during periods of cool or cold temperatures.
- Diagram potential wind modifiers (urban or natural terrain and features).
- Plot optimal or range of orientations for access to wind for natural ventilation.
- Plot orientations that should be protected from wind during heating periods.

Opportunities and Constraints Assessment

Natural Ventilation

- What times of the year would the project (building and site) benefit from natural ventilation cooling?
- Is there a wide diurnal temperature swing during the summer that would make night flushing a beneficial strategy? Night purging is a viable strategy even during the hottest summer days, when daytime temperatures are too high for effective natural daytime ventilation.
- Which direction, and at what frequency and speed, does the wind flow during the cooling period (day and/or night)?

Wind Protection

- What times of the year would the project need to provide wind protection? Identify winds that coincide with cool or cold temperatures, and those that are high-speed or gusts and thus are liabilities for human comfort all year long.
- Which direction, and at what frequency and speed, does the wind flow during the heating period?

Wind Renewable Energy

- What is the average annual wind speed? How much variation in wind speed occurs over the course of the year?
- Do adjacent buildings or site features have the potential to cause wind turbulence in areas of the site?

General

- Do adjacent or nearby landforms or bodies of water impact wind movement or temperature at the site?
- Does adjacent or nearby development impact wind movement or temperature at the site?

Figures 5.27 through 5.29 show three project site and weather analyses, first diagramming key climate data on a site plan and then quantifying the effects of solar and wind, respectively.

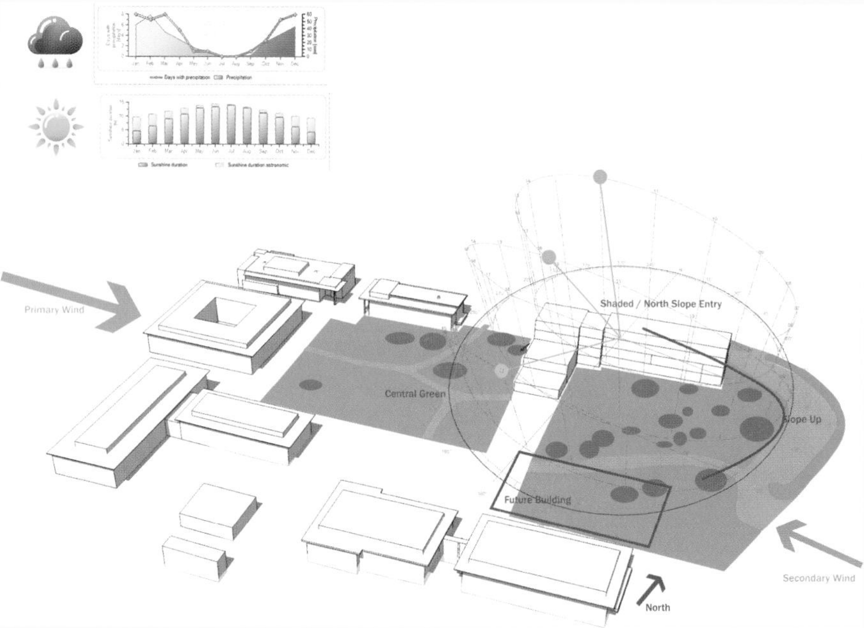

■ **FIGURE 5.27** Example Project Site Climate Diagram. *Image courtesy of RNL.*

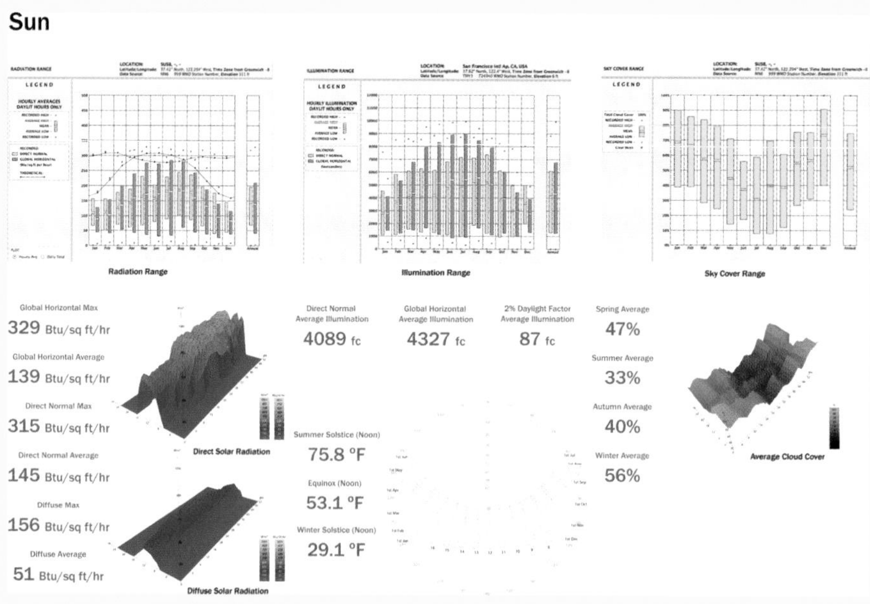

■ **FIGURE 5.28** Example Project Site Solar and Daylighting Analysis. *Image courtesy of RNL.*

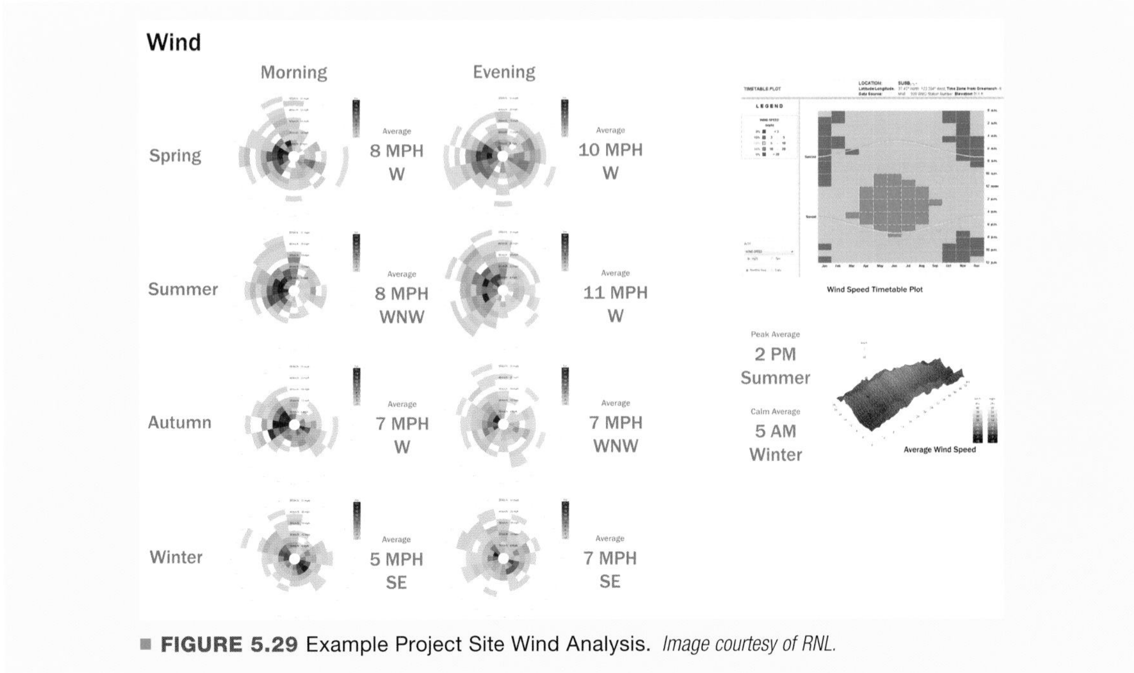

■ **FIGURE 5.29** Example Project Site Wind Analysis. *Image courtesy of RNL.*

Microclimate

Climate data derived from weather data files enable an important and useful assessment of the general or baseline climate conditions for a location. Keep in mind, however, that actual climate conditions vary, based on the characteristics of a specific place. *Microclimate* is the term used to describe the localized climate parameters based on the characteristics of a specific place. The analysis of a site reveals the many features that can affect a microclimate, such as natural and built features that impact solar access, wind patterns, and temperatures. One of the purposes of the site analysis is to define the site's existing microclimates. Another is to identify potential microclimate design strategies that can be developed within the project and explored during the design process.

Developing optimized or tuned microclimates involves control of the sun and wind, in concert with the design of landscape elements and the design and form of building elements. A simple and effective example of designing for microclimate at the site is to implement strategies that reduce the urban heat island effect. Urban and highly developed areas are often characterized by a large number of surfaces that absorb solar radiation, such as asphalt roads, asphalt parking lots, and black roofs. These stores of solar radiation raise air temperatures in urbanized areas and should, therefore, be considered in the site analysis. Incorporating high-albedo paving, landscaping, shade trees, green roofs, and cool roofs prevents solar radiation absorption and the temperature rise caused by the urban heat island effect.

Microclimate design for a site involves a thoughtful and effective integration of architecture, landscape architecture, and urban design. It creates opportunities for free energy, and can greatly enhance the passive thermal comfort of a site and building. It can also reduce thermal loads of a building and, therefore, lower energy use. Microclimate design for a site should respond to the seasonal climate analysis and program for the site and building. Microclimates can be created at a variety of scales and in a number of configurations, from open sites to enclosed courtyards, and even against the exterior envelopes of buildings. When designing for microclimates, it may be useful to divide the site into microclimate zones, each with its own set of strategies, to optimize the benefits throughout the site.

COOLING MICROCLIMATES

During periods of warm or hot weather, creating cooling microclimates can be advantageous for the site and building. Providing solar shade, solar reflectance, cooling breezes, water, and evapotranspiration from vegetation all contribute to a cooling microclimate. Cooling microclimates can be developed for areas such as courtyards and plazas, frequented by pedestrians during the summer (see Figure 5.30). These exterior areas can reduce thermal loads on the building and can be used to cool and direct breezes into the building. There are numerous techniques for developing cooling microclimates; often, the options are limited only by the degree of creativity applied to solution.

Providing shade is a fundamental strategy. It is clear from direct tangible experience that being able to find shade when temperatures are too warm can dramatically lower temperatures and increase thermal comfort. Shading as a cooling microclimate strategy can be accomplished with the building form providing shading and by adding shading elements to exterior spaces. Shade structures can serve this purpose, as can strategically located trees. One word of warning is in order here, however: Make sure shading does not disrupt daylighting strategies, and that solar access is maintained to all solar panels.

Reducing the amount of solar radiation absorbed by exterior surfaces of the building and hardscape also lowers ambient temperature. Using surfaces with high solar reflectance, or high albedo, is a common method to minimize absorption of solar radiation. The LEED rating system has useful guidelines regarding solar reflectance for both roofs and hardscape areas.

Harnessing breezes can have a dramatic effect on pedestrian comfort in exterior

■ **FIGURE 5.30** Creating a microclimate in a courtyard can enhance outdoor and indoor comfort in hot climates such as the Middle East. *Image courtesy of RNL.*

areas, creating cooler microclimates. Building massing and orientation can be used to promote the flow of low-speed winds in desired areas. Wind, though it has highly complex behaviors, can nonetheless be understood through science; rules of thumb can be followed to approximate conditions, and detailed analyses by wind specialists can be conducted to develop detailed design responses and quantify expected results for pedestrian comfort. An exterior microclimate with comfortable breezes could also be used to provide natural ventilation for adjacent buildings.

Trees do more than provide shade; they, and other vegetation, also actively evapotranspire moisture into the air, creating a cooling effect, especially in dryer climates where evaporation is an effective means of cooling (see Figure 5.31). Landscape design is one of the most important elements of successful microclimate design because vegetation influences solar reflectance, shade, and evapotranspiration. Landscape design may also incorporate either natural or manmade water features. Water can be used in a number of ways to create a cooling microclimate. Regional water resources and water conservation should always be considered when planning site water features.

The design of the exterior envelope can include a secondary assembly to create a specialized microclimate right next to the building envelope. Many of these strategies are also considered good passive building design strategies; they are summarized here because it is important to understand that the reason they are effective is because they alter the climate directly adjacent to the building.

Thinking about creating a microclimate directly adjacent to the building can produce potentially creative solutions to cooling or heating problems. The same techniques that can be used to create successful cooling microclimates at a site scale can be employed adjacent to buildings. Exterior shading structures not only shade solar radiation at window locations, but larger-scale exterior shading structures can shade whole exterior building surfaces to lower surface

■ **FIGURE 5.31** The landscaped courtyard at the New York Times Building in New York, by Renzo Piano Building Workshop.

temperatures and reduce both solar radiation and conduction loads at the envelope. This type of supershading strategy is more appropriate in hot climates that experience cooling demands all year long. High-albedo and high-solar-reflective surfaces also can have a positive cooling effect and reduce conduction cooling loads. Vegetation and water have been used to create microclimates for both exterior wall and roof surfaces. Green roofs and roof ponds are common examples. The BCA Academy in Singapore retrofitted an existing building as a net zero energy building, where one of the strategies for energy reduction was the development of a cooling microclimate at the building façade, utilizing vegetated walls and louvered shades with built-in photovoltaics (see Figure 5.32).

WARMING MICROCLIMATES

During periods of cool or cold weather, creating warming microclimates can be advantageous for the site and building. Providing solar access, solar absorption, and wind protection all contribute to a warming microclimate. Often, strategies that promote warming in the winter are at odds with promoting cooling during the summer, so care should be taken to consider the primary objective of the microclimate and design of the exterior space. There are, of course, exceptions: Deciduous trees can shade in the summer and provide warming sun in the winter. Nevertheless, always exercise caution to keep daylight-specific windows shade-free year-round. Often, winter winds come from a different direction than summertime winds. When this is the case, the massing and orientation can be designed to accept the breezes in the summer but block winds during the winter. Wind protection is helpful for pedestrian comfort, as well as for minimizing infiltration losses at the building envelope, where both excessive positive and negative pressures move air through any leaks in the building.

■ **FIGURE 5.32** Close-up view of vegetated wall and BIPV shade louvers for the façade at BCA Academy in Singapore. *Photograph by Patrick M. McKelvey.*

BUILDING MASSING AND GEOMETRY

The available passive strategies for a project are informed by the climate analysis. The site analysis and design can help make the most of the climate. The next step is to decide how the building massing and geometry can be developed to optimize the identified passive strategies. Different passive strategies might warrant a different response to the massing and geometry of a building.

Orientation

Building orientation is one of the most fundamentally important decisions for most net zero energy buildings, because passive strategies and renewable energy rely on access and control of the climate. Orientation is also strongly influenced by many other urban design and site parameters, such as views, property boundaries, zoning regulations, access, topography, architectural and urban contexts, existing site features, and existing buildings. In the face of so many competing agendas, solving the building orientation issue for a net zero energy project can, at times, be extremely challenging, yet essential to get right.

SOLAR

From a climatic perspective, orientation needs to respond to both sun and wind. Wind is variable, but trends can be predicted, whereas the path of the sun is definitively known. The certainty of the sun's path takes the guesswork out of solar-appropriate design. Solar orientation is a high priority because daylight, control of solar radiation, and solar access for on-site photovoltaic or solar thermal systems are all dominant strategies that drive energy loads down and allow optimization of the passive and renewable energy strategies that are so important for net zero energy projects.

In locations in the northern hemisphere, the sun follows a range of seasonal paths from east to west in the southern sky (see Figure 5.33). The summer has the highest sun angles, and the winter the lowest. These solar

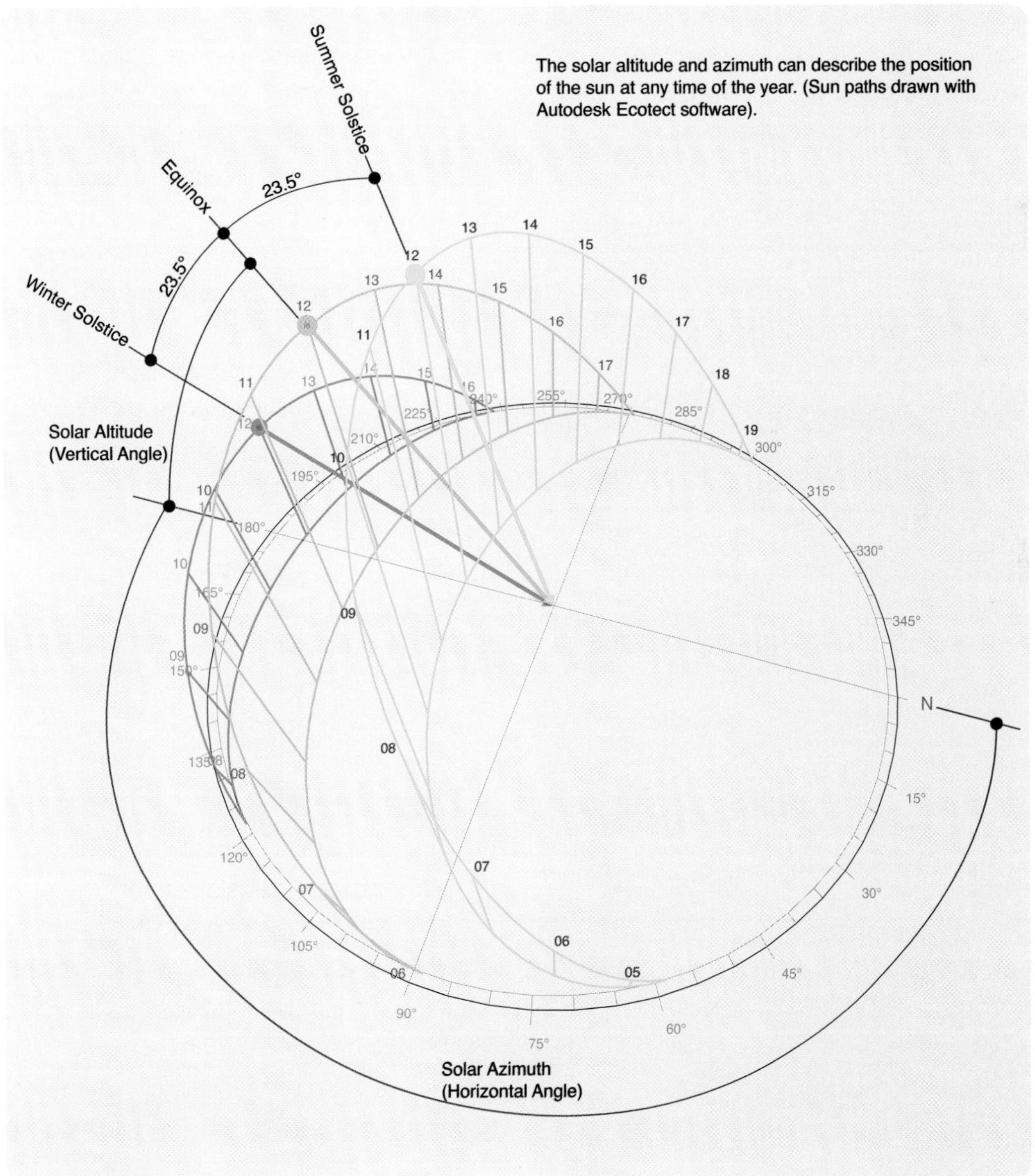

■ **FIGURE 5.33** Basic Solar Geometry.

angles directly influence the amount of solar radiation received on horizontal and vertical surfaces (see Figure 5.34). Low sun angles concentrate radiation on vertical surfaces, while high sun angles concentrate radiation on horizontal surfaces.

For most building applications, a long building form elongated along the east-west axis, with maximized south and north façades, is best practice for solar control. As a rule of thumb, the orientation can vary by as much as 15 degrees and still allow acceptable solar control. The sun in the southern sky is easier to shade than the rising and setting sun in the east/west, with very low sun angles. Western sun is the most problematic because it can add significant solar gain and heat at the end of the day when outside temperatures are near their highest. The solar radiation for east and west orientations can be higher than for the south orientation during the summer. In addition, the sun is highest in the summer, making south-oriented summer season shading architecturally feasible. The north orientations receive minimal direct sun (early mornings and late evenings), and under most circumstances do not require solar control.

WIND

Determining building orientation for the wind involves, first, deciding when and where wind is welcome and when it is unwelcome. Will natural ventilation be an effective strategy for the building and climate? Consider whether wind control is needed for developing pleasant outdoor spaces and microclimates and for protection of the building. Using a wind rose

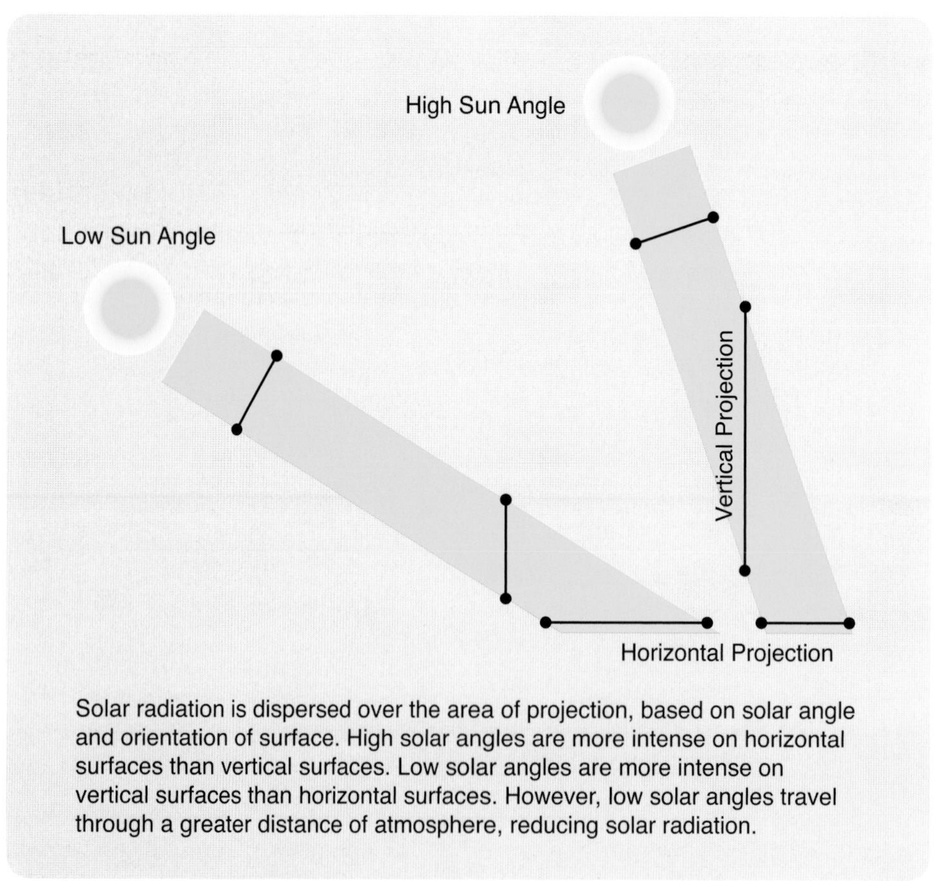

High Sun Angle
Low Sun Angle
Vertical Projection
Horizontal Projection
Solar radiation is dispersed over the area of projection, based on solar angle and orientation of surface. High solar angles are more intense on horizontal surfaces than vertical surfaces. Low solar angles are more intense on vertical surfaces than horizontal surfaces. However, low solar angles travel through a greater distance of atmosphere, reducing solar radiation.

■ **FIGURE 5.34** Solar Radiation and Sun Angle.

analysis, the building massing, orientation, and geometry can be studied to optimize wind as a resource. Building science and wind specialists can make a more detailed assessment of the interaction of building mass and orientation with wind using wind simulation software and wind tunnel testing (see Figure 5.35).

Wind speed and direction may be variable, but as noted previously, general trends can be identified. To design for natural ventilation, the orientation of the building should allow the narrow section of the building to be cross ventilated by orienting the long face of the building to the wind. Cross ventilation utilizes pressure differences to move air; it requires a positive wind pressure on the receiving (windward) building face and a negative pressure on the exiting (leeward) building face (see Figure 5.36). The orientation need not be directly perpendicular; as a rule of thumb, it can vary by about 30 degrees. Additionally, vertical fins on the façade can be used to direct breezes to operable windows. It is also important to consider sources of air turbulence, such as adjacent buildings or other site features.

Stack ventilation is another effective means to naturally ventilate a building. It utilizes air temperature differences to move air (see Figure 5.37). As air warms in the interior of a building, it rises. The massing and design of the building can include vertical ventilation paths that allow for effective stack ventilation. Natural ventilation can utilize both pressure and temperature differences, and can be supplemented and assisted by mechanical fans. Detailed analysis of natural ventilation through a building can be completed using computational fluid dynamics (CFD) modeling software (see Figure 5.38).

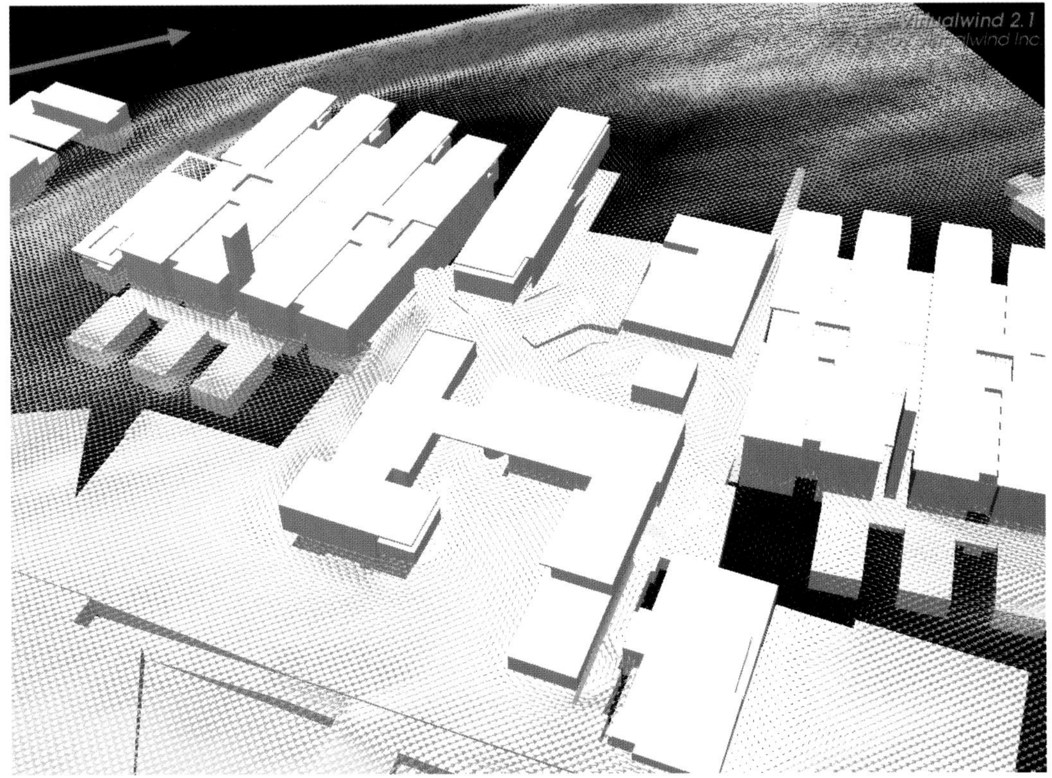

■ **FIGURE 5.35** RWDI wind analysis of the King Abdullah University of Science and Technology (KAUST), designed by HOK using Virtualwind to review building form and optimize wind flows and natural ventilation. *Image courtesy of RWDI.*

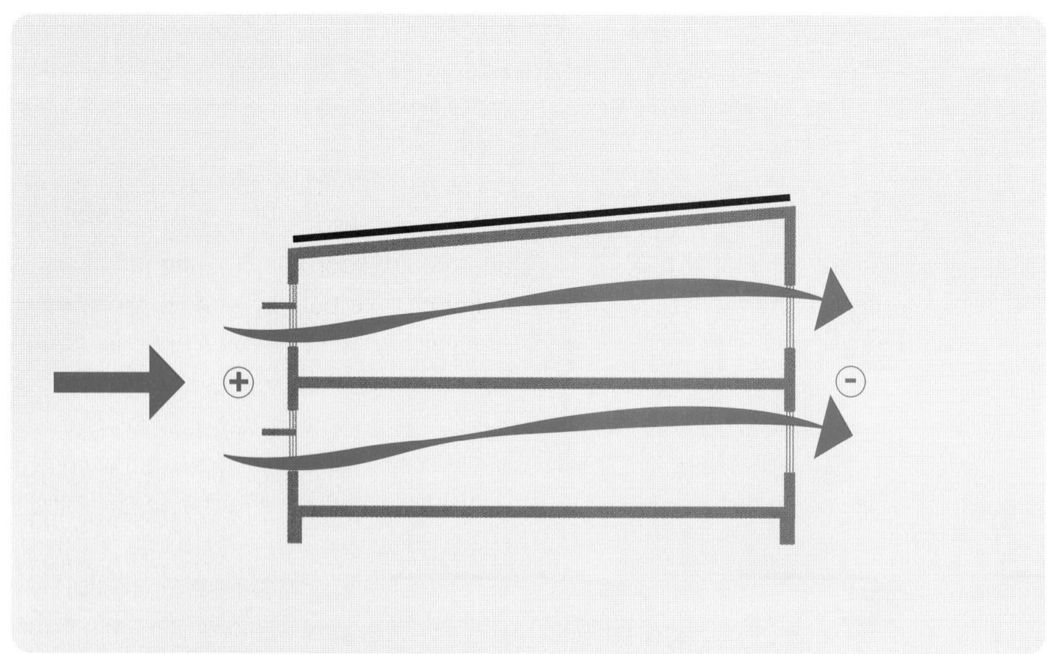

■ **FIGURE 5.36** Cross Ventilation Principle.

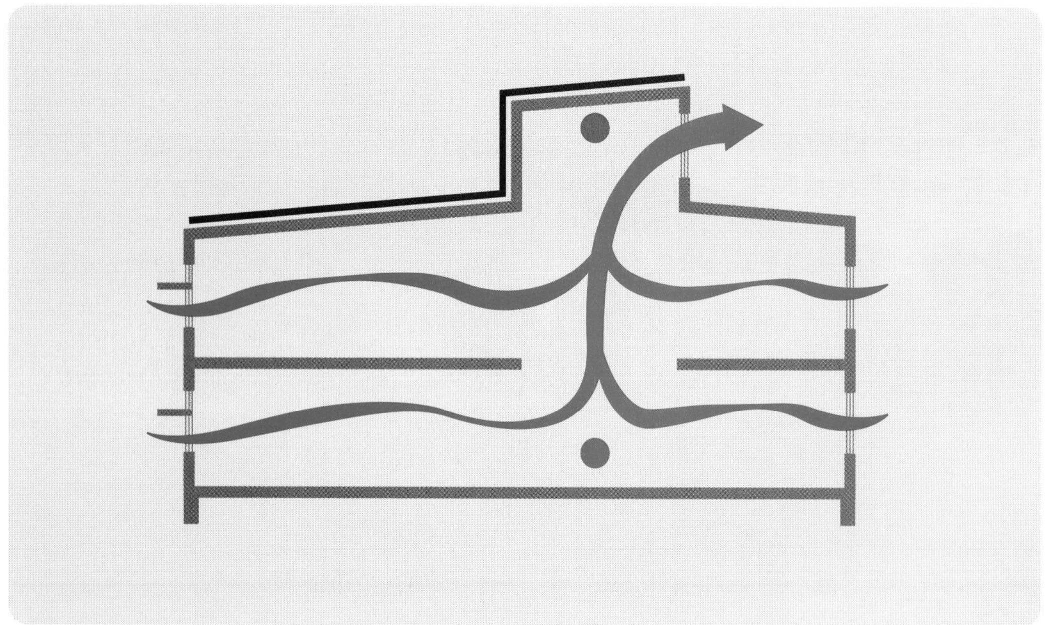

■ **FIGURE 5.37** Stack Ventilation Principle.

Exterior Wall to Floor Area Ratio

There are two competing ideas about the relationship of energy to the exterior envelope of a building. The first states that the exterior surface area to volume of enclosed space should be decreased to reduce thermal transfer through the envelope. After all, the building envelope and the exterior climate are key drivers to the thermal loads in a building. The second states that the exterior surface area to volume of enclosed space should be increased to expand the area where passive design strategies can be utilized and, therefore, satisfy thermal, ventilation, and lighting

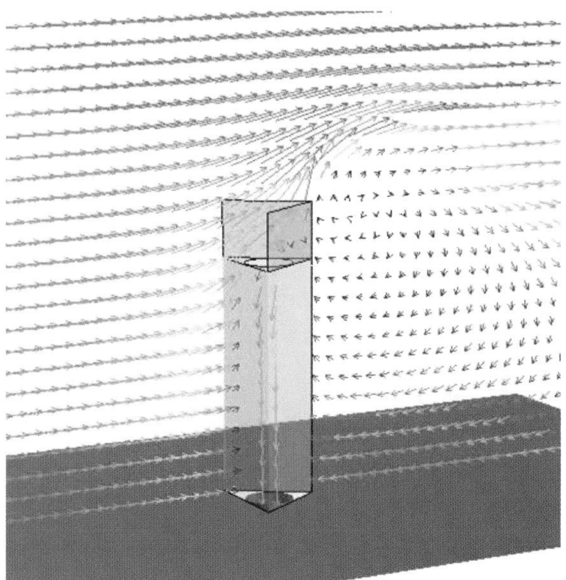

■ **FIGURE 5.38** Computational Fluid Dynamics (CFD) Analysis of a Wind Tower by RWDI. *Image courtesy of RWDI.*

conditions for the greatest area of interior space. Reducing the exterior envelope can conserve energy, while enlarging the exterior envelope can maximize free energy. In most cases, maximizing free energy has many advantages, so this approach should be the starting point for net zero energy projects. The key is to minimize the liabilities of a large surface area by neutralizing the envelope, or minimizing infiltration, conduction, and radiation thermal loads.

Surface area to volume ratio is a metric meant to convey the relative compactness of a building. The convention for the surface area to volume (S/V) ratio is typically given in SI units. To convert the ratio from ft^2/ft^3 to m^2/m^3, simply multiply by 3.28 ft/m. The ranges of S/V can vary, with a typical range of 0.10 to 0.60. A lower S/V ratio implies a more compact design. A higher ratio implies more exterior surface for taking advantage of passive strategies. The ratio can, however, be a misleading metric when quantifying the building form for the application of passive strategies. Whereas square buildings are compact, and result in a lower S/V ratio than narrow buildings, the number of stories dramatically impacts the metric. The higher the number of stories, the lower the resulting ratio. This would imply that single-story and low-rise buildings are optimal for passive strategies, but this is a result of factoring the large roof and ground floor area into the ratio.

For passive buildings, the exterior walls are typically more useful than roofs for implementing passive strategies. Further, minimizing roof area helps with heat loss and heat gain. Multiple-story buildings can have a clear advantage. (Note that roof area is an important parameter for solar energy.) Perhaps a better metric to gauge building geometry for passive strategies is to use an exterior wall area (exposed wall surface) to gross floor area ratio, or simply exterior wall to floor area (EW/F) ratio. This ratio also has the advantage of being identical in both empirical units and SI units. The matrix in Figure 5.39 offers a comparison of massing metrics for a range of massing options for a 25,000-square-foot building. In this example, the four-story thin mass has the highest EW/F ratio and would be optimized for passive strategies while also being among the most compact (lowest S/V ratio) in the matrix. The primary disadvantage is the high floor to roof area (F/R) ratio, which can limit the potential size of roof-installed photovoltaic systems.

Letter Buildings

An aerial view over a historic city such as Berlin (see Figure 5.40) or Paris reveals an approach to building massing and urban design that optimizes daylight and natural ventilation. Some have described the configuration of the buildings in plan as letter-shaped. Does the plan look like an L; maybe an H or an E? The negative shape between the buildings can also take on this type of letter shape. What is really going on is that the creation of narrow

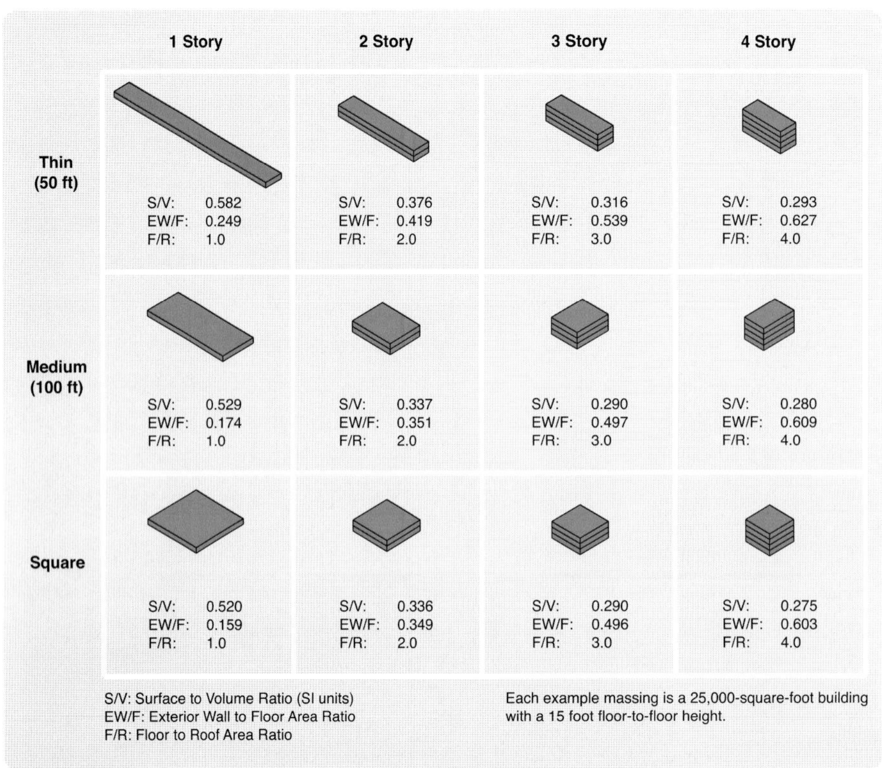

1 Story
2 Story
3 Story
4 Story
Thin (50 ft)
S/V: 0.582
EW/F: 0.249
F/R: 1.0
S/V: 0.376
EW/F: 0.419
F/R: 2.0
S/V: 0.316
EW/F: 0.539
F/R: 3.0
S/V: 0.293
EW/F: 0.627
F/R: 4.0
Medium (100 ft)
S/V: 0.529
EW/F: 0.174
F/R: 1.0
S/V: 0.337
EW/F: 0.351
F/R: 2.0
S/V: 0.290
EW/F: 0.497
F/R: 3.0
S/V: 0.280
EW/F: 0.609
F/R: 4.0
Square
S/V: 0.520
EW/F: 0.159
F/R: 1.0
S/V: 0.336
EW/F: 0.349
F/R: 2.0
S/V: 0.290
EW/F: 0.496
F/R: 3.0
S/V: 0.275
EW/F: 0.603
F/R: 4.0
S/V: Surface to Volume Ratio (SI units)
EW/F: Exterior Wall to Floor Area Ratio
F/R: Floor to Roof Area Ratio
Each example massing is a 25,000-square-foot building with a 15 foot floor-to-floor height.

■ **FIGURE 5.39** Massing Metrics Matrix.

floor plates with fingered wings and courtyard spaces allows for daylight and natural ventilation. These are common design features of buildings that predate electric lighting and air conditioning. These buildings follow a high exterior wall to floor area ratio and have geometry and massing built for passive strategies. It is interesting to note that existing buildings of these types can be good candidates for retrofitting as net zero energy buildings.

Massing and Geometry for Passive Strategies

We have already established a few key strategies for massing—specifically, proper orientation and increasing exterior wall to floor area ratio to expand the connection to the free energy of the climate. Many passive strategies such as daylighting and natural ventilation are effective only near the exterior perimeter. Daylight can penetrate just so deep into a space.

Building or floor plate depth is another important consideration for net zero energy buildings. Narrow buildings have an advantage for passive strategies. Achieving narrowness can be done in a variety of ways, and the ultimate solution will depend on other variables such as site and program. The most basic passive-responsive form is a simple, long, narrow, rectangular form that is properly oriented. It is, indeed, the workhorse for passive design, and most other forms are derived from it. Larger buildings may require multiple long narrow wings oriented along the east-west axis, connected by a central spine. There are as many variations on this as there are sites and building programs. These are the letter building forms discussed above, or hybrids of this type. Letter-form buildings work through the development of courtyards between wings for access to light, air, and view. Courtyards are also excellent ways to develop favorable microclimates (see Figure 5.41).

■ **FIGURE 5.40** Aerial view of Berlin, Germany, shows the many letter-shaped buildings typical of European cities.

■ **5.41** Courtyard at the DOE/NREL Research Support Facility. *Image courtesy of RNL; photograph by Frank Ooms.*

The idea of a designed microclimate courtyard can lead to another passive-driven form, the atrium building (see Figure 5.42). Atriums are essentially enclosed courtyards. They can be used to bring daylight or natural ventilation into the space. Atriums also can be an effective way to break up a deep floor plate, especially in building programs or sites that might lead to this type of building form.

While atriums may have the same passive design function as a courtyard, they are distinctly different because they are enclosed spaces. This introduces a wide variety of additional design concerns. For one, an atrium as enclosed space can have cost ramifications. It also adds building area, which may or may not be part of the building program. Depending on how the atrium spaces are conditioned, they may have energy consequences. Poorly designed atriums can add considerable solar gain. They also represent a significant volume of space for conditioning, yet they do need to be conditioned as typical occupied space, depending on the intended use.

The upside is that because they are enclosed, atriums provide unique opportunities to create specialized microclimates that can provide synergies for adjacent space or building-wide systems. They can also create opportunities for unique uses and spaces for building occupants.

A variation on the atrium building is the use of nonoccupied or semioccupied zones for providing daylight and natural ventilation throughout the building footprint. Light wells and natural ventilation shafts can be located strategically in a building form. Light wells, however, present their own inherent design

■ **FIGURE 5.42** The atrium and glass dome of the Reichstag in Berlin, by Foster + Partners, uses a series of mirrors to bring daylight to the Parliament space below. *Photograph by Tania Salgado.*

■ **FIGURE 5.43** Exterior view of 30 St. Mary Axe by Foster + Partners, with the spiraling light wells clearly visible.

challenges and so should be modeled carefully. The problem to solve is to determine how to effectively bring in a reasonable amount of daylight using a vertical volume with a restricted horizontal area. The depth, or the number of stories, to be served is another major factor. In addition to moving light, ventilation shafts can be used to move outside air entering the building through perimeter windows. The vertical shaft can have a positive stack effect on the movement of air.

Light wells and ventilation shafts can be a major design concept applied to an entire building, as in the case of Foster + Partner's 30 St. Mary Axe building in London, which uses six spiraling light and air wells to assist in the daylighting and ventilation of the office tower (see Figure 5.43). Light wells or ventilation shafts might also be applied strategically to passively challenged areas of a floor plate, rather than as a universal strategy.

Massing and Geometry for Renewable Energy

Several types of renewable energy systems can be mounted on or integrated into a net zero energy building, such as photovoltaic panels, solar thermal panels, and building-mounted wind turbines. When integrated, a renewable energy system, together with the building geometry and massing, are critical to the successful application and optimization of the energy systems.

SOLAR

Both photovoltaic modules and solar thermal collectors need access to solar. Since the sun's path is a highly dynamic but predictable variable, the use of solar analysis can help optimize solar panel placement. (A detailed discussion on planning solar energy systems is presented in Chapter 8.) One of the first determinations to make is the number of photovoltaic and solar thermal panels necessary to meet the project's net zero energy balance. A building that uses solar energy as its primary renewable energy system will typically require a large area of photovoltaic panels, and planning for panel locations begins with the massing.

The floor to roof area ratio is a critical determining factor in massing for a net zero energy building using solar energy; typically, it results in a relatively low-rise building mass. Each project has its own threshold, which depends on the building energy use intensity (EUI) and the efficiency of the photovoltaic panels. An office building in most climates might top out at three stories or less if the roof-mounted photovoltaics are the building's only renewable energy source. As panel efficiencies improve and the building energy use decreases, the floor to roof area ratio will be able to increase and allow higher-story buildings to achieve net zero energy. Note that there is a clear discrepancy between the advantage of a low floor to roof area ratio to maximize roof-mounted solar energy and the advantages of a multistory building, discussed previously in the exterior wall to floor area ratio section. Balancing these trade-offs is at the heart of designing a net zero energy building.

The orientation of the building is also a critical massing decision with regard to solar energy. Fixed solar panels are typically optimized for year-round production by orienting them south, with a tilt equal to the location's latitude (in the northern hemisphere). For northern locations, this can be a significant amount of tilt. If optimal tilt cannot be achieved, some tilt can, nevertheless, provide a worthwhile benefit. Each project has its own constraints, and the details of tilt should be analyzed on a project-by-project basis. If the roof is providing the tilt, or if the tilt is developed with the racking system of the solar panels, the orientation of the building should allow the tilted panels to face south. If the panels have no tilt, then the orientation is not a concern. It is also important to site a building for shade-free, solar access on roof surfaces.

Using a sawtooth pattern for solar panels can provide beneficial tilt on flat roof massing. This can be a good way to optimize energy production per panel when sloping the roof is not an option. However, sawtooth solar panel installation will likely not optimize the total energy production of a given roof area, compared with a horizontal panel installation. With a sawtooth installation, each row of panels must be positioned with an adequate gap, to prevent the panels from shading the next row of panels behind it. The higher the tilt, the larger the required spacing will need to be. (Refer to Chapter 8 for an analysis of this issue.)

A shading study should be conducted for the proposed massing design. It is critical to consider parapet heights, any roof-located mass, or any mass that could shade the roof. Mechanical equipment located on the roof is a major issue, as it can end up shading a large portion of a roof. Discussion about mechanical systems should occur during this building massing evaluation stage. This might also be a good time for the team to make a commitment *not* to locate mechanical equipment on the roof. If the team cannot make this commitment, then careful planning should be undertaken to determine location and estimated size of the mechanical equipment.

The design of a net zero energy building may require the use of additional site-installed photovoltaic panels to meet its energy balance. This has the advantage of enabling buildings with higher floor to roof area ratios (or other circumstances that might limit available roof area) to still hit their net zero energy targets. The same type of analysis should be conducted for site-located photovoltaics, to ensure optimized orientation and desired tilt, and to prevent the building or other elements from shading it.

WIND

The use of building-mounted wind turbines, despite the recent rise in interest in them, is a niche application for renewable energy systems (see Figure 5.44). There is considerable controversy over the application of building-mounted wind turbines on buildings due to their notable disadvantages. Typically, the energy generated by these turbines meets a very small portion of the energy needs of a building. There are also technical issues regarding the structure of the building and the impacts the building and neighboring buildings may have on the wind. Wind turbines can also make a lot of noise, which may disturb building occupants. In addition, wind speeds are favorable at higher elevations, as evident in the height of site-mounted turbines.

Perhaps the technical issues will be solved as the application evolves. One interesting solution is the integrated wind turbine. Examples of this application include the Bahrain World Trade Center (see Figure 5.45) and the Pearl River Tower (see Figure 5.46). The idea is to integrate the wind turbines into the building and design the form of the building to enhance wind flow into the turbines. This form-integrated application may be more feasible for towers or tall buildings, but may still generate only a small portion of a large building's total energy needs.

From a building mass perspective, consider the massing of the building and neighboring buildings and terrain, and the potential location of the turbines. Using general principles of wind movement around buildings can give some guidance on the application of wind

■ **FIGURE 5.44** Small Building-Integrated Wind Turbines at Arizona State University.

turbines on buildings. A specialist in wind design should complete a more rigorous analysis before the project advances too far with a building- or site-mounted wind turbine design. (Chapter 8 offers a more detailed discussion on the application of wind power for net zero energy buildings, with a focus on site-installed turbines and towers.)

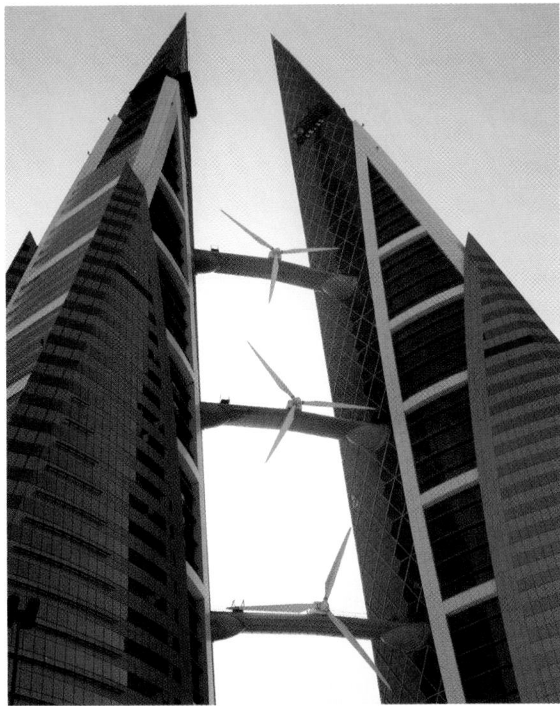

■ **FIGURE 5.45** Three 29-meter wind turbines integrated into the Bahrain World Trade Center, by Atkins.

■ **FIGURE 5.46** Wind analysis for integrated wind turbine at the Pearl River Tower in Guangzhou, China, by SOM; analysis by RWDI. *Image courtesy of RWDI.*

BUILDING TYPE AND ZONING

Building Type

All building types have a tendency toward certain massing characteristics, which are driven by program, code, and zoning regulations. In turn, this massing of a building also has significant impact on its net zero energy objective, as it affects energy loads, passive strategies, and renewable energy. While massing and stacking studies are undertaken to study how to effectively meet the programmatic requirements of a project, the energy and climate fundamentals discussed in this chapter should also be explored. This is an effective way to integrate programmatic requirements, early design concepts, and energy strategies into a singular solution.

Evaluating the building massing in terms of both exterior wall to floor area ratio and floor to roof area ratio against the massing and geometry conditions that satisfy the building typology and program should reveal the opportunities, as well as the limitations, in developing the architecture around net zero energy. The ideal solution arises when a conceptual building form begins to optimize passive strategies, renewable energy generation, and programmatic requirements simultaneously. In fact, this synthesis of form around function, energy, and beauty is at the heart of designing net zero energy architecture. It is the accumulation of inquiry and study of the project's climate, site, program, and energy, and the resulting architectural expression as a singular solution.

Many building types have common building massing conventions that can be adapted relatively easily to the massing needed for reaching net zero energy from roof-mounted photovoltaics. In fact, NREL has found that 62 percent of commercial buildings have the technical potential to reach net zero energy using currently available technologies and design practices. Many commercial building types are inherently low-rise and have relatively low EUIs, which makes reaching net zero energy less problematic. Building types that fall into this category include low-rise and midrise multifamily, low-rise office, schools, stand-alone and strip retail, and low-rise hotels and warehouses. In contrast, large hotels and hospitals are very challenging because they tend to be both high in EUI and multiple stories in height. Likewise, restaurants and foodservice, despite often being single-story, stand-alone buildings, are very challenging because of their extremely high EUIs. Supermarkets are difficult for the same reason.

Thermal Zoning

Thermal zoning within a building refers to the strategic arrangement of spaces to take advantage of the thermal synergies and qualities of spaces, and their relationship to other spaces. Just as exterior microclimates can be created to benefit exterior or even interior comfort, interior spaces or thermal zones can also be developed and arranged based on thermal requirements and the thermal relationship to the exterior as well as interior spaces. There are two basic approaches to planning for thermal zones. The first is to consider the thermal requirements of a space in relation to the exterior. The second is to consider the thermal requirements of a space in relation to other interior spaces.

From the building program, identify the desired or allowable range of thermal conditions of each space. Also identify the thermal loads of the space, based on use. From the climate analysis, identify the seasonal temperature ranges and solar radiation. These thermal conditions can be studied to determine optimal thermal zoning, to help reduce thermal transfer, create thermal buffers, and allow beneficial thermal transfer or storage. The thermal efficiency of the plan and massing of the building are effective passive means of reducing energy use through the reduction of thermal loads. There are many additional considerations for space planning and for developing adjacencies between program spaces, and thermal zoning should be included as one of them. It is also important not to short-circuit other passive design strategies being employed, such as daylighting and natural ventilation, which rely strongly on spaces being located adjacent to the building exterior perimeter.

Due to both adaptive thermal comfort and the various uses of spaces, the thermal conditions and air temperature set points of different interior spaces may be able to be varied. Rooms that can afford a wider range of thermal comfort, and can float between a wide range of temperatures, such as temporary spaces or circulation spaces, can serve as thermal buffers between more extreme exterior temperatures and interior spaces with tighter thermal comfort requirements and a narrower range of temperature set points (see Figure 5.47).

Some spaces have high internal heat gains, such as computer server rooms, data centers, mechanical rooms, and commercial kitchens. In some heating-dominated climates, these high heat gain spaces can be located at the perimeter (notably, the northern perimeter), where the space can be cooled more passively. These high heat gain rooms can be a source of heat for spaces that have a heating load. The heat can also be stored, if an appropriate thermal storage space is designed in the building (see Figure 5.48). A thermal storage space is most effective when it is a remote

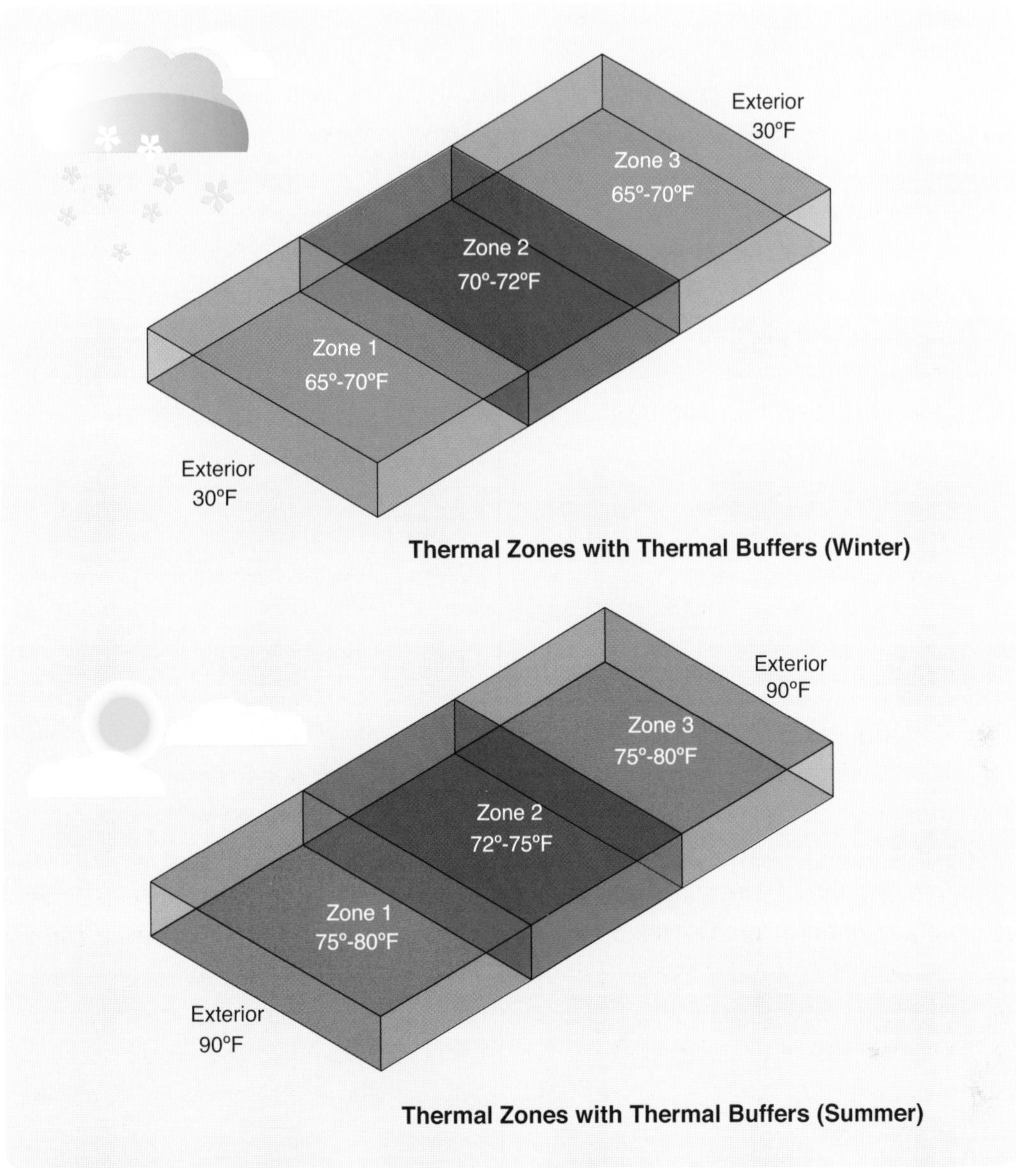

■ **FIGURE 5.47** Thermal Zones and Thermal Buffers.

thermal mass zone that is unoccupied and can store heat (or store coolth) for an extended period for use in other areas of the building and at various times of the day or night.

Sunrooms and sunspaces can be used in heating-dominated climates to provide a means of passively heating adjacent spaces. This technique involves the intentional creation of a high heat gain space, and is often more effective with the incorporation of thermal mass to store heat in the space for use during the evening or night. The thermal transfer needs to be controlled and adjusted between the sunspace and the adjacent space needing heat (see Figure 5.49). The sunspace should also have a means to prevent solar gain when heating in the building is not needed. Sunspaces need to be carefully designed and adequately controlled to be effective and to ensure they do not introduce thermal liabilities during the cooling season (see Figures 5.50 and 5.51).

Thermal zoning for optimizing thermal flows with the building plan also informs the zone planning for the mechanical systems, because the process tends to organize spaces with similar heat gain and thermal comfort requirements, and considers the location of spaces in relation to the building exterior and exterior thermal loads. The combination of thermal zoning and neutralizing the building envelope, as discussed in Chapter 6, can result in high-quality thermal comfort with reduced energy use.

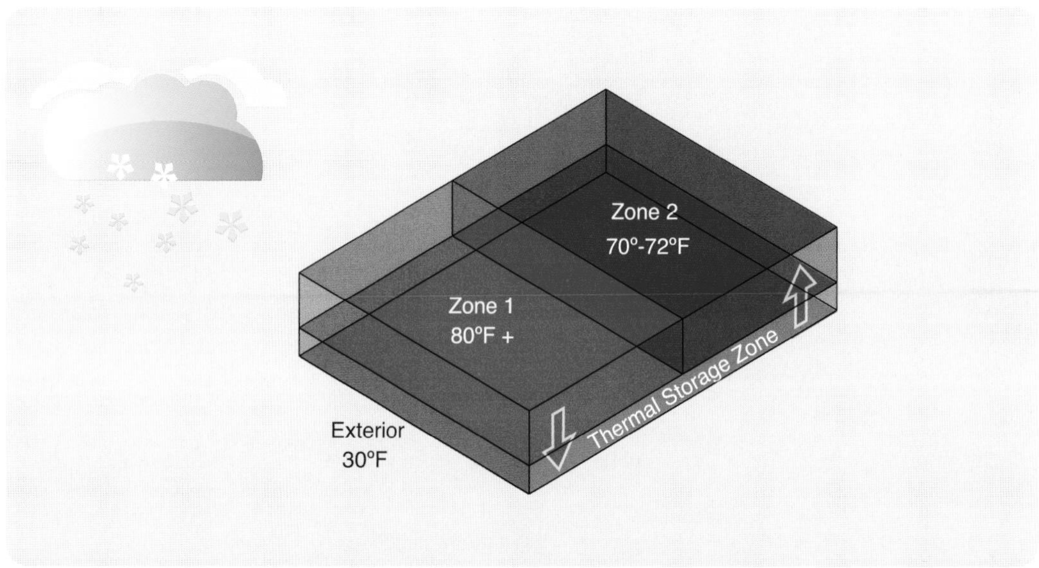

■ **FIGURE 5.48** High Internal Heat Gain Zone with Thermal Storage Zone (Winter).

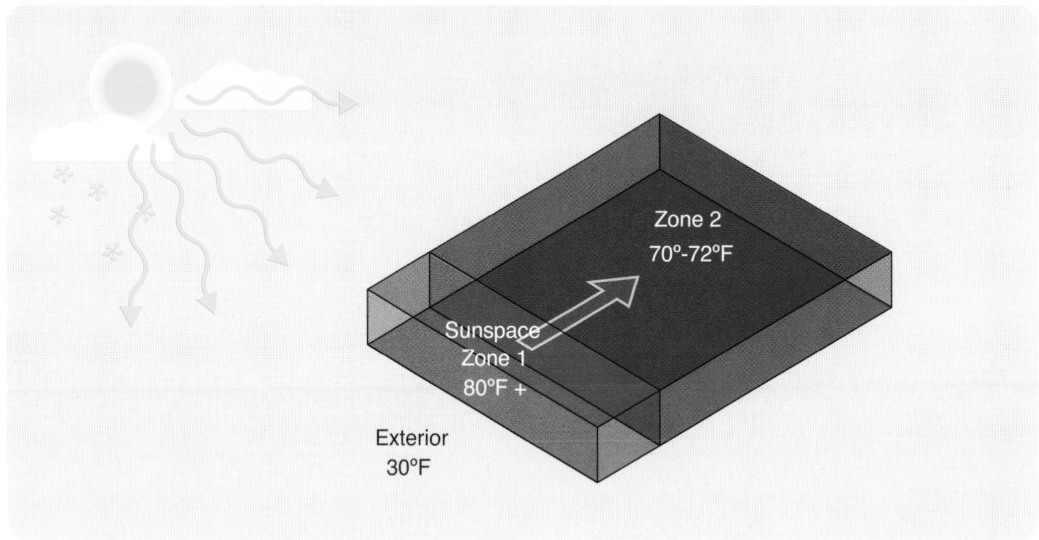

■ **FIGURE 5.49** Thermal Zones with Sunspace (Winter).

■ **FIGURE 5.50** The net zero energy Aldo Leopold Legacy Center's thermal flux space, with dividing doors closed. *The Kubala Washatko Architects, Inc./Mark F. Heffron.*

■ **FIGURE 5.51** The Aldo Leopold Legacy Center's thermal flux space, with dividing doors open. *The Kubala Washatko Architects, Inc./Mark F. Heffron.*

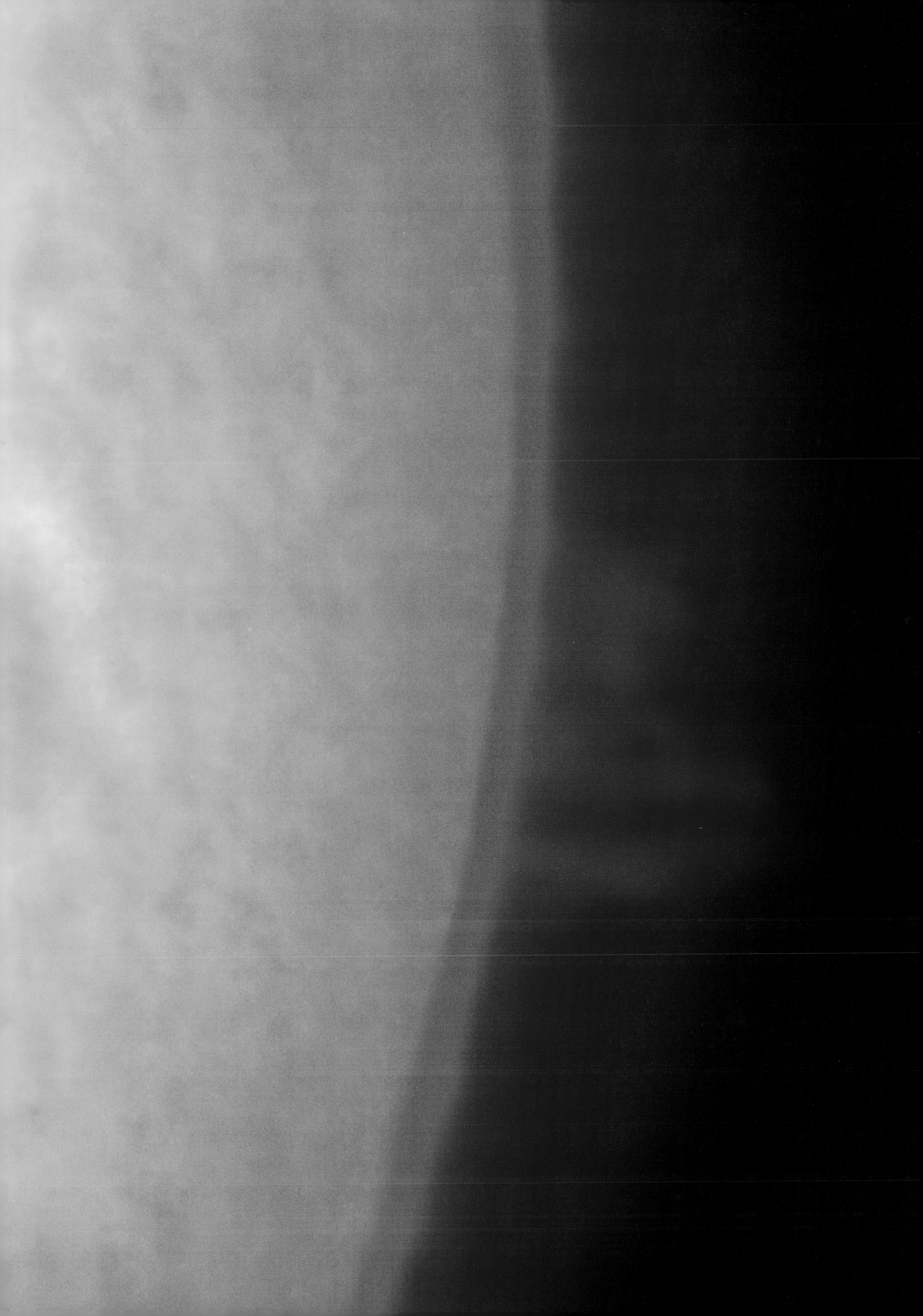

PA CHAPTER 6 PASSIVE ARCHITECTURE

PASSIVE DESIGN

A New Architecture

Passive architecture is a fundamental prerequisite for net zero energy buildings. It introduces a significant opportunity to build energy efficiency into the skin and bones of the building. Passive design has a strong influence on the form and details of the architecture. The passive strategies are responses to very project-specific parameters such as climate, microclimate, site, and program. In this sense, passive design is not only an energy opportunity; it is an architectural opportunity. It is an opportunity to express the connection of energy to place and program, and to make that connection beautiful, functional, and meaningful. This is the one of the distinguishing features of net zero energy architecture.

The current emphasis on the energy efficiency of buildings, and the role of the built environment in climate change, is a strong force for innovation. Today's most celebrated buildings are successfully adopting passive design strategies and, in the process, propelling the firms that have invested in this design approach into leadership positions in the industry. In answering the call today for energy-efficient buildings, the handful of leading practitioners offering compelling new precedents in low-energy passive design solutions are taking the industry to a tipping point (See Figure 6.1). This tipping point is critical for the mainstream adoption of a net zero energy building approach. It signals the formation of a new architecture.

■ **FIGURE 6.1** London's City Hall, by Foster + Partners, features a radically designed building form that minimizes solar radiation on the building envelope.

Historical Context

Passive strategies can found as fundamental characteristics of pre-midcentury architecture across the globe. In fact, most passive strategies have been commonplace in architecture for hundreds, if not thousands, of years. In this sense, the history of architecture is also a history of passive design. With the steady adoption of air conditioning and the ready supply of cheap energy over the course of the twentieth century, architecture no longer had to deal with the constraints of climate. The ability to artificially control the interior environment of a building to exacting standards made virtually any architectural solution possible. This, of course, led to new architectural explorations of form and materiality. At the same time, it also led to a loss of knowledge and process in the architectural profession about energy and passive design. Furthermore, it precipitated a change in the expectations of building occupants about the control and conditions of the interior environment. People have become accustomed to artificially uniform temperatures and lighting levels year-round. Perhaps the rediscovery of passive design and net zero energy will influence the next generation of architectural trends.

Often, ancient cultures serve as excellent examples of very simple approaches to thermal comfort through passive design—for example, the Anasazi cliff dwellings at Mesa Verde, Colorado (see Figure 6.2). These cliff dwellings, which were built and occupied from around 1100 to 1300 AD, consist of rooms and structures built from sandstone within naturally formed alcoves in the sides of cliffs. The overhanging cliffs provide shade in the summer, to keep the dwellings cool, but also allow sun penetration during the winter, to keep them warm. The cliff overhang and alcove provides protection from wind, rain, and snow. The stone cliff alcove and stone structures are thermally massive, which can help moderate temperature changes, and serve the important function of absorbing winter sun and reradiating the warmth into the dwellings. The dwelling walls are perforated with openings and passages that promote airflow through the rooms. It is not hard to imagine how such a dwelling managed to provide a microclimate that was considerably warmer than the outside winter temperatures and considerably cooler than the outside summer temperatures. It is a simple lesson that all architects can learn from.

■ **FIGURE 6.2** Spruce Tree House at Mesa Verde.

The vernacular architecture of a region can also offer clues on how to build in a climate-responsive way. Studying techniques used in vernacular architecture can be an effective way of learning about new project locations or even reexamining locations you already work in. Examples can be found in all regions. In the Middle East, where temperatures can get excessively hot, there is a long history of building traditions that maximize shade and optimize airflow. Courtyards and tightly spaced buildings create shaded microclimates and building surfaces, while also permitting natural ventilation. Ventilation is enhanced with tall wind towers that capture and redirect breezes from above the roofline (see Figure 6.3). Thermally massive building materials help buffer against the peak temperatures of the day.

Net zero energy architecture presents an excellent opportunity to rediscover and

■ **FIGURE 6.3** The courtyards and wind towers of Yazd, Iran.

incorporate the best strategies of the past; remember, it was not so long ago when all buildings were net zero energy, because they had no access to fossil fuel energy. Of course, the intent is not to replicate the buildings of the past, because contemporary ideas about architecture have evolved. Further, these buildings took advantage of passive design, but they did not necessarily always have the highest indoor environmental quality—certainly not when compared to today's standards. Net zero energy buildings give us the chance to apply the best of time-tested passive strategies and the best of today's technology to ensure our energy-secure future, as well as to set new standards for comfort, amenity, and building value.

Passive Design Defined

Passive design is defined as the use of architecture and climate to provide heating, cooling, ventilation, and lighting. Another way to define passive design is the use of architecture to harvest free energy from the environment. Passive design makes it possible to provide a high interior environmental quality coupled with low-energy requirements. The classic or technical definition of a passive system is a strategy that does not require any active system inputs or the addition of conventional energy to operate (heat, cool, ventilate, or light).

The goal for a passive net zero energy building is that it be *free-rolling* whenever feasible, based on building use and weather conditions. Free-rolling means that the traditional active systems are not employed and that the passive strategies alone are enough to satisfy the needs of building occupants. However, due to their dynamic nature, passive strategies generally cannot be counted on to always meet heating, cooling, ventilation, and/or lighting needs. Therefore, the building will still likely need active systems to supplement passive systems or to condition the building when passive strategies are not available. Passive strategies do not generally replace active building systems, but they do often work in place of or in tandem with active strategies for a large portion of the year. This hybrid of active and passive solutions results in a *mixed-mode building*. Mixed-mode buildings are designed to operate in a variety of modes that are meant to optimize the passive strategies. The basic modes include passive mode (free-rolling), active mode, or a mix of passive and active modes.

In reality, in good, low-energy, passive design, the line between passive and active systems is blurred all the time. Many of the passive design strategies discussed in this chapter include integration with active systems. I fall back on the definition of passive design as those strategies that require an architectural response to the climate to provide heating, cooling, ventilation, and lighting. While in some cases it may be hard to define some of the hybrid strategies as predominantly passive or active, the distinction is not very important. A successful net zero energy building will have an inseparable and, sometimes, indistinguishable integration between passive and active systems.

Designing a conventional building with only active systems is certainly easier than designing a mixed-mode building with both passive and active systems. Part of the reason is that there is less institutional knowledge about passive and mixed-mode design in the architectural profession today. This lack of passive design knowledge, coupled with the familiarity and ease of designing 100 percent active buildings, is certainly one of the highest barriers to adopting passive and hybrid buildings. Yet, it is a barrier we must overcome, for we have a valuable opportunity to dramatically improve the quality and efficiency of our buildings.

One of the most important and striking characteristics of passive architecture is that it seamlessly blends art and science. This, in fact, should be the foundation of architectural design. The repositioning of building design science as a foundation for architecture is instrumental in the advancement of passive design practices.

This chapter aims to serve as a primer for design science as a building block for passive strategies. The focus is on the building envelope as the primary architectural device for climate-responsive passive strategies. And because a great deal of quality literature already exists on the implementation of passive strategies, this chapter calls attention to the implications of passive strategies in developing a net zero energy building, in an effort to help establish a framework of design science concepts.

Recommended reading for passive design includes: *Sun, Wind & Light: Architectural Design Strategies*, by G. Z. Brown and Mark DeKay; and *Heating, Cooling, Lighting: Sustainable Design Methods for Architects*, by Norbert Lechner.

DESIGN SCIENCE

Thermal Energy Design Science

An understanding of the basic parameters and formulas that govern heat flows in building forms the basis for applying passive strategies and low-energy systems to net zero energy buildings. Most important, this information gives the designer a broad background in all the variables that will come into play during energy modeling and the design of the building systems. These concepts and simple calculations can be used to quickly test different design decisions, particularly those involving the building envelope. They can also be used to discover the relative magnitude of different heat flows in the building at various times and enumerate basic thermal energy design criteria.

The heat flows from transmission, solar radiation, infiltration, ventilation, and internal heat gain can be combined to determine total heat gain or heat loss for any time. Usually, this would be calculated by factoring in the design temperatures, or the near-extreme summer and winter temperatures, but it can be completed for any temperature of interest. Design temperatures and related heat flows are important to know because they represent the peak load and inform the sizing of systems. Winter peak heat loss is simpler to estimate, because solar radiation is assumed to be of no impact during the time of the coldest temperature. However, the overall heat flows during the winter will be impacted by solar radiation. Solar radiation is a leading factor in the summer design temperature, as it affects heat flow all year long, and is far more difficult to estimate using simple calculations. The solar irradiance on any surface is highly dynamic; it changes according to orientation of the surface and time of day.

In addition to the simple methods discussed in this book, several calculation methods have been developed for estimating heat flows that account for solar radiation, such as the sol-air temperature method. ASHRAE has developed the transfer function method and the cooling load temperature difference (CLTD) method as alternatives to the sol-air temperature method. Fortunately, energy modeling and load calculation software have made it easier to account for the dynamic nature of heat flow and do more accurate calculations of both peak thermal loads, as well as estimated annual energy use.

THERMAL ENERGY LOADS

The thermal energy loads for any building are a complex combination of exterior thermal conditions and internal thermal conditions, with the performance of the building envelope mitigating the two (see Figure 6.4). The exterior environment can generate thermal energy loads within a building in all modes of heat transfer—conduction, convection, and radiation. Thermal transmission through the building envelope, solar radiation gains through glazing, and air infiltration all create thermal loads at the perimeter zone of a building. Aside from perimeter loads, the interior's main heat source is internal heat gains from people, lighting, and equipment. Thermal energy design is about controlling the thermal loads at the perimeter, due to the exterior environment, and controlling the internal heat gain loads.

THERMAL TRANSMISSION

Heat flow through the envelope is a major factor in the overall energy use of a building. This is particularly true in buildings in locations with high heating or cooling degree-days, where there is a significant difference between interior and exterior temperatures. Thermal transmission through the building envelope includes the impacts from conduction, convection, and radiation. Note that this property excludes the impact of solar radiation through glazing, and of convection through air infiltration, which are quantified separately.

Thermal transmission is driven by conduction, convection, and radiation through building envelope materials. If the exterior is warmer than the interior, thermal transmission by conduction will move from the outside in through the building envelope materials, creating heat gain. If the interior is warmer than the outside temperature, thermal transmission becomes heat loss by conduction through the building envelope. Convection causes heat flow across air films and air cavities in the building envelope. Solar radiation can raise the exterior surface temperature well above the adjacent exterior air temperature and, therefore, increase thermal transmission through the envelope. A concept known as *sol-air temperature* is a representational outside air temperature that is meant to be equivalent to the added effect of solar radiation on the exterior surface, for the purposes of understanding heat flow through the envelope.

The primary factors influencing thermal transmission are the temperature difference between the interior and exterior surfaces of the building

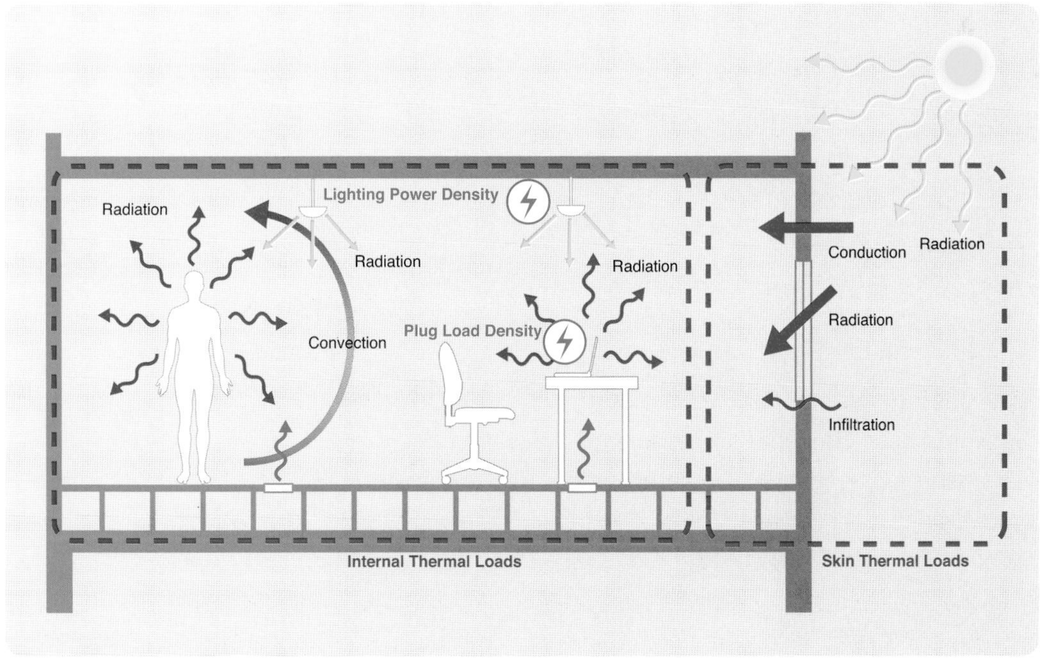

■ **FIGURE 6.4** Thermal Energy Loads in Buildings.

envelope and the capability of the building envelope to resist thermal energy flow. The resistance and transfer of heat through materials and assemblies is defined and quantified by three interrelated factors: thermal conductance, thermal resistance, and thermal transmittance.

Heat Flow Properties of Materials

- ***Thermal conductance (C-factor):*** *The measure of heat flow in Btu per hour through 1 square foot of the material at a stated thickness and with a temperature difference of 1°F between two surfaces of the material. C-factor is a measure of hourly Btu heat energy with the units of Btu/h·ft^2·°F or the SI units of W/m^2·°K (see Figure 6.5).*
- ***Thermal resistance (R-value):*** *The reciprocal of the C-factor and, therefore, a measure of hours needed for 1 Btu of heat energy transfer through 1 square foot of material at a stated thickness and with a temperature difference of 1°F. The units of R-value are h·ft^2·°F/Btu with SI units of m^2·°K/W (see Figure 6.5).*
- ***Thermal transmittance (U-factor):*** *The hourly Btu heat energy transmittance through an assembly of materials, including air films on both sides of the assembly. U-factor has the same units as C-factor and is measured through 1 square foot of construction assembly, with a temperature difference of 1°F. U-factor is calculated by taking the reciprocal of the sum of R-values through the assembly. Note that taking the sum of U-factors is not the same, and will result in an incorrect value for the assembly.*

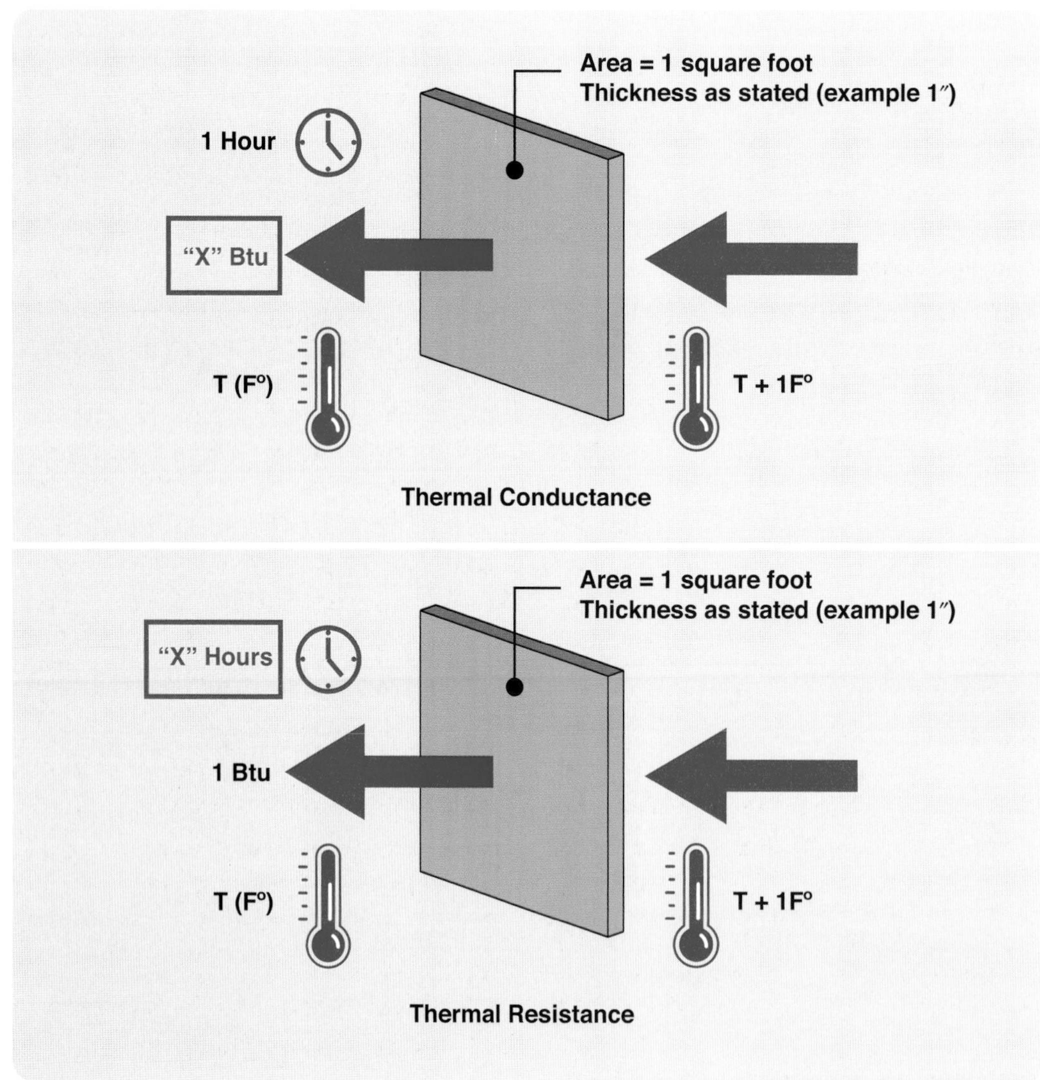

FIGURE 6.5 Heat Flow Properties of Materials.

Because the U-factor is the hourly Btu transmittance through 1 square foot of assembly with 1°F of temperature difference between inside and outside surfaces, the following basic equation can be used to quantify heat gain or heat loss through an assembly or component of the building envelope. In this equation, Q is the heat loss or gain in Btu per hour, U is the thermal transmittance (U-factor) for the assembly in Btu/h·ft^2·°F, A is the area of the assembly in square feet, and ΔT is the difference between inside and outside temperature in degrees Fahrenheit. If the sol-air temperature is known, it can be used as the outside temperature.

$$Q = U \times A \times \Delta T$$

The example in Figure 6.6 illustrates the heat loss through thermal transmission for 1 square foot of building envelope with an R-value of 10.0. The design temperature is based on winter in Denver, Colorado. The *ASHRAE Handbook—Fundamentals* is one source for design temperatures for different locations. The example is for a wall condition, but a roof condition would follow the same procedure.

The difference in temperature can reflect whatever condition is to be studied. It can be the design day for heating and cooling, which would provide the peak heating or cooling load. In addition, heating degree-hours or cooling degree-hours could be used to quantify the annual heating or cooling energy. To estimate degree-hours (DH), multiply the location's annual degree-days by 24 hours. Be sure to use a base temperature that is related to your project's balance point temperature. Cooling degree-hours do not reflect the impact of sol-air temperature and, therefore, should be used with caution.

$$Q = U \times A \times DH$$

Heating and cooling degree-days can be found in a number of sources, two of which are the *ASHRAE Handbook—Fundamentals* and the online resource at www.degreedays.net. The latter enables the calculation of degree-days with different base temperatures.

INFILTRATION AND VENTILATION

All occupied buildings need to supply fresh air to their occupants. To do so, the building

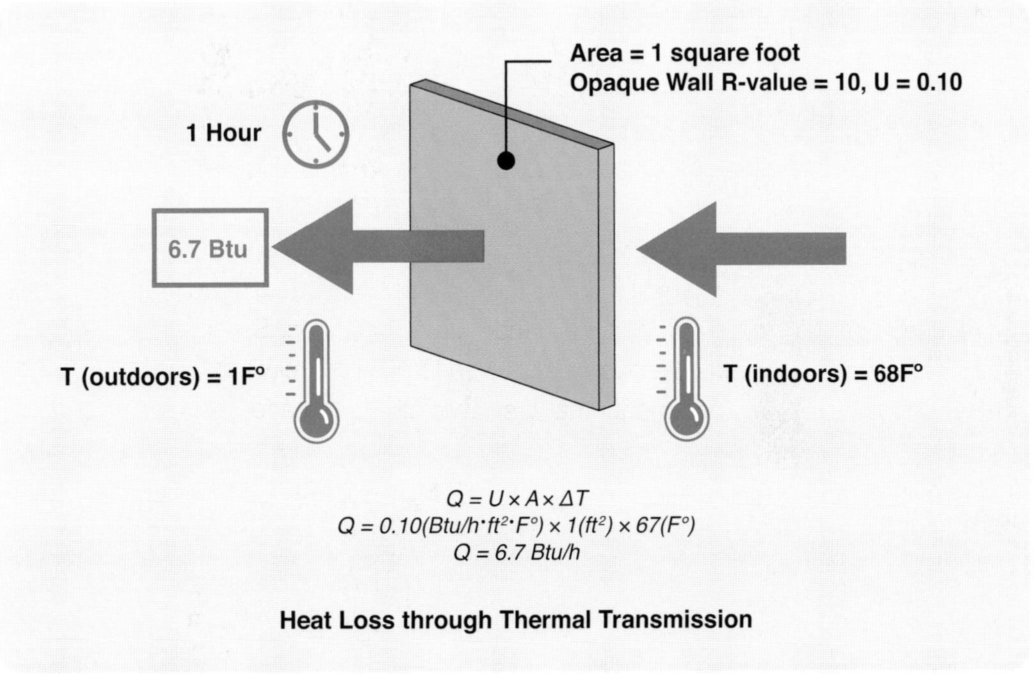

■ **FIGURE 6.6** Thermal Transmission Example.

must provide air changes with outside air. Outside air enters a building through infiltration and ventilation. Ventilation is the controlled introduction of outside air; infiltration is the uncontrolled introduction of outside air through the building envelope. Outside air entering the building in either case can become a thermal energy load when a difference in temperature exists between the outside air and the interior set point temperature.

It follows, then, that dramatically reducing infiltration, and optimizing ventilation for fresh air requirements, is an important strategy for low-energy and net zero energy buildings. Because ventilation air is controlled, there are numerous opportunities to reduce the energy load related to ventilation. First, outside air rates can be reduced to the minimum, providing that a healthy and comfortable interior environment is maintained. There is a delicate balance between energy use and increasing ventilation rates for increased indoor environmental quality, and it must be addressed on a per-project basis. Demand-controlled ventilation is a strategy that adjusts the rate of ventilation air based on CO_2 monitoring in spaces. For further energy savings, ventilation air can be passively heated or cooled, and heat recovery systems are common ways of limiting the heating requirements for ventilation air.

Another important impact of infiltration and ventilation is the latent heat that is also transferred into the building when humid outside air enters a space. In certain climates and during certain seasons, the introduction of humid outside air will be a liability. Infiltration, being an uncontrolled introduction of outside air, cannot be dehumidified. Controlled ventilation can be dehumidified, as needed, for thermal comfort and to reduce the amount of latent heat added to a space. When the ventilation air is decoupled from the primary heating and cooling system of a building, very high levels of energy reduction can be achieved. This approach involves the use of a dedicated outside air system (DOAS). Because the amount of air needed to provide for ventilation is markedly lower than a conventional air system sized to heat and cool a space, a DOAS has a reduced latent load, as well as a reduced sensible load, because the ventilation air does not need to be conditioned to the cooling and heating supply temperature extremes needed if it were also required to condition the space. (This is a low-energy concept, discussed further in Chapter 7.)

Ventilation rates can be quantified in either air changes per hour (ACH) for the entire volume of the building, or as cubic feet per minute (CFM) per square foot or area, or CFM per person. Air infiltration rates are quantified as cubic feet per minute per square feet of envelope. The next basic equation quantifies the rate of heat loss or gain through ventilation or infiltration, where Q is the rate of heat loss or gain in Btu/hour; *1.08* is a factor that represents the volumetric heat capacity of air under average conditions (0.018), multiplied by 60 minutes/hour, and in the units Btu · min/h · ft^3 · °F; *CFM* is the volume of ventilation or infiltration in cubic feet per minute (multiply the CFM rate per square feet by the area); and ΔT is the difference between inside and outside temperature in degrees Fahrenheit.

$$Q = 1.08 \times CFM \times \Delta T$$

The example in Figure 6.7 illustrates the heat loss through infiltration for 1 square foot of building envelope with an air infiltration rate of 0.40 CFM per square feet of envelope. The design temperature is based on winter for Denver, Colorado.

This equation can also be given based on air changes per hour. Note that air changes per hour times the volume of air is in terms of cubic feet per hour.

$$Q = 0.018 \times ACH \times V \times \Delta T$$

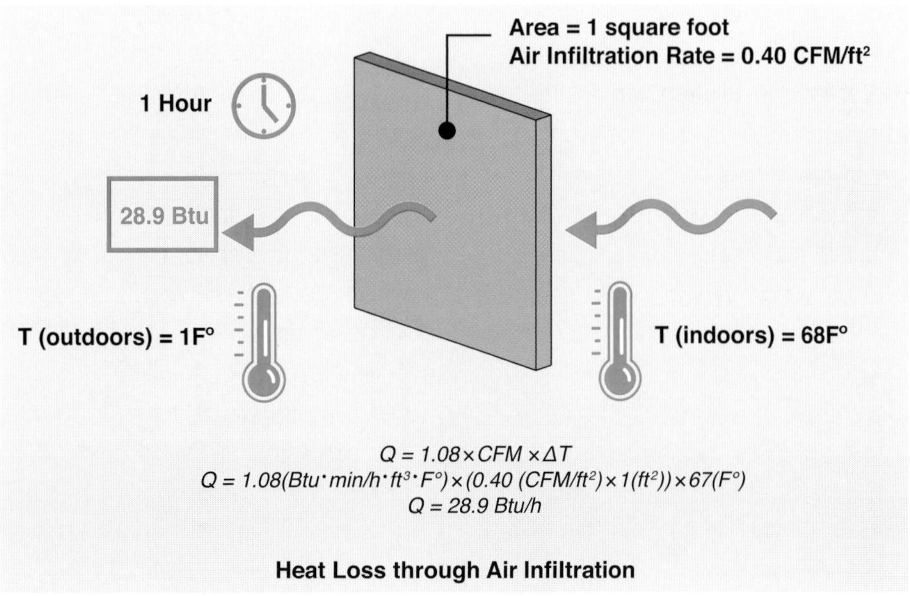

■ **FIGURE 6.7** Air Infiltration Example.

SOLAR RADIATION

Solar radiation through glazing can be a significant source of heat energy transferred to the interior of a building. While radiation can drive thermal transmission through all building envelope assemblies, including opaque and transparent constructions through the sol-air effect, the majority of the impact of solar radiation is from radiant transfer through glazing. Solar radiation through glazing systems creates heat gain in the interior, regardless of the difference between indoor and outdoor temperatures. When the building is in cooling mode, solar radiation adds more cooling load. When the building is in heating mode, solar radiation may be welcome, but needs to be carefully designed to prevent overheating.

Glass readily allows this transmission of solar radiation, and the glazing units can be designed to reduce the radiant transfer. The primary factors influencing heat gain through solar radiation through glazing are the amount of solar radiation striking the glazed surface and the properties of the glazing units, specifically the glazing unit's solar heat gain coefficient, or SHGC. SHGC is the decimal expression of the percentage of incident solar radiation transmitted through glazing. (Glazing system design is discussed in more detail in the "Building Envelope" section of this chapter.)

In addition to the tints and coatings that can be applied to glazing units to reduce the transfer of solar radiation, physical shading of the glazing can reduce or eliminate direct solar radiation gains. The effects of physical shading need to be considered, in combination with the effects of the glazing's SHGC, to determine how the glazing unit will perform in reducing total solar heat gain.

The following basic equation can be used to quantify solar heat gain through a window. Q is the rate of heat gain in Btu per hour, G is the global irradiance incident on the glazing surface in Btu/h · ft^2, and A is the area of the glazing.

$$Q = G \times A \times SHGC$$

The example in Figure 6.8 illustrates the solar heat gain through glazing for 1 square foot of building envelope with an SHGC of 0.30. The global incident solar radiation is for Denver, Colorado, in August, for a south-facing vertical window. NREL has published tables with solar radiation values for windows in Solar Radiation Data Manual for Buildings. It is available free, online at http://rredc.nrel.gov/solar/pubs/bluebook/bluebookindex.html. Climate analysis software such as METEONORM and Ecotect Weather Tool can also generate solar radiation values for different orientations.

INTERNAL HEAT LOADS

The building program impacts the sources of internal heat gain from occupants, lighting, and equipment. Each of these internal heat loads can be estimated separately; or they can be combined to quantify total heat gain. Note that the lighting and equipment loads result in electrical loads, in addition to thermal loads, and there are valuable energy reduction benefits to be gained from working to reduce these two loads.

Occupant Heat Gain

Heat gain from occupants is related to the number of occupants, or the occupancy density, and the nature of their physical activities. Occupants add both sensible heat and latent heat to the interior. Combining the sensible and latent heat gain will provide the total heat gain; but for passive strategies and certain low-energy strategies, such as evaporative cooling and radiant cooling, only sensible heat is removed.

Occupant heat gain is directly related to the program, and usually does not represent an opportunity for heat gain reduction or control, because in the big picture, lowering occupancy density would require a larger building for the same program population, and thus have a far greater negative impact on overall resource use.

The next three basic equations quantify the heat gain from occupants. Q_{os} is the sensible heat gain for a given number of occupants, *SHG* is the sensible heat gain per occupant, and *O* is the number of occupants. Q_{ol} is the latent heat gain for a given number of occupants, and *LHG* is the latent heat gain per occupant. Q_{ot} is the combined, or total, heat gain for a given number of occupants due to sensible and latent heat gain. Note that if the number of occupants is not known, it can be

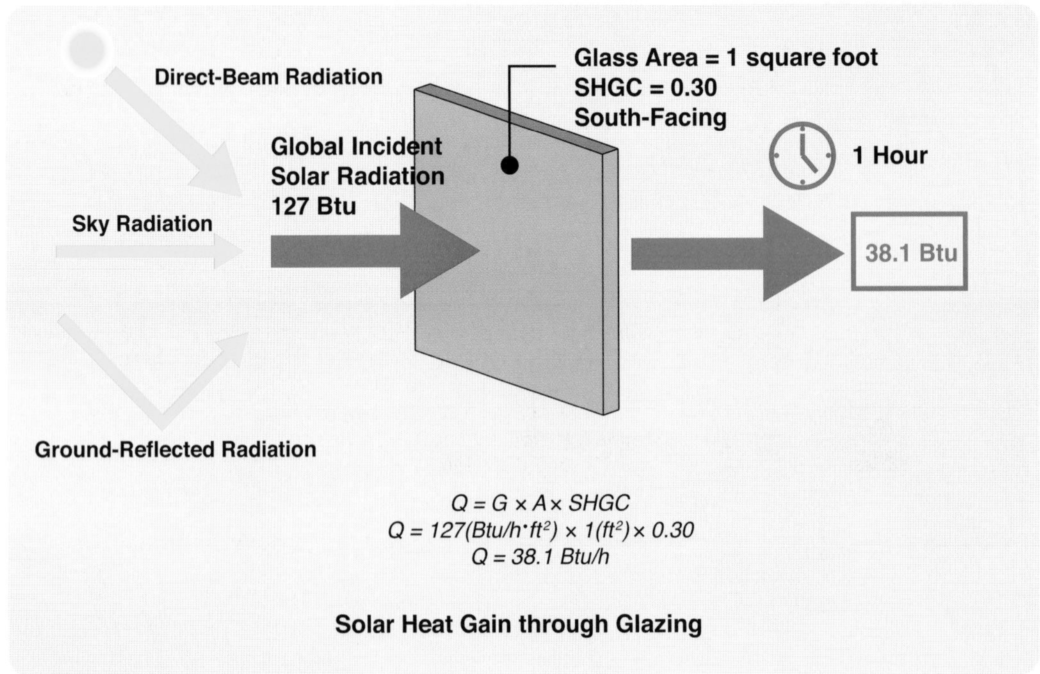

■ **FIGURE 6.8** Solar Radiation Example.

estimated by multiplying the anticipated occupancy density by the area. In addition, the equations could use the occupancy density (people per square foot) as *O* to determine occupant heat gain per square foot.

$$Q_{os} = SHG \times O$$
$$Q_{ol} = LHG \times O$$
$$Q_{ot} = Q_{os} + Q_{ol}$$

The example in Figure 6.9 illustrates the internal heat gain generated by people for 1 square foot of space. The example assumes an office-type occupancy density and seated, light work by the occupants. Sensible and latent heat gains for people based on activity level can be found in the *ASHRAE Handbook—Fundamentals*, as well as in *Mechanical and Electrical Equipment for Buildings*, by Walter T. Grondzik, Alison G. Kwok, Benjamin Stein, and John S. Reynolds.

Lighting Heat Gain

Lighting can be a major source of internal heat gain, and there is a direct correlation between the lighting power density and the internal heat gain. Heat gain from lighting can be dramatically reduced by installing more efficient lighting fixtures, resulting in a lower installed lighting power density. Further, utilizing control strategies that keep lights off or dimmed based on daylight availability or occupancy can also reduce heat gain. In short, saving lighting energy will also reduce internal heat gain.

To quantify internal heat gains from lighting, simply convert the watts of installed lighting for the building or space under consideration to Btu/hour, as shown in the next equation. Note that this results in a heat gain for the full lighting power density. The calculation can be adjusted to account for the lighting schedule and controls by applying an appropriate percentage, particularly when looking at this calculation over a longer period of time. Q_l is the rate of heat gain from lighting in Btu/hour, *LPD* is the lighting power density per square feet in watts (accounting for controls and daylighting if necessary), and *A* is the area in square feet.

$$Q_l = 3.412 \times LPD \times A$$

The example in Figure 6.10 illustrates the internal heat gain from lighting, assuming a lighting level for a typical office building.

Equipment Heat Gain

Equipment installed in building generates internal heat gain. The classic example is computer and server equipment in an office building.

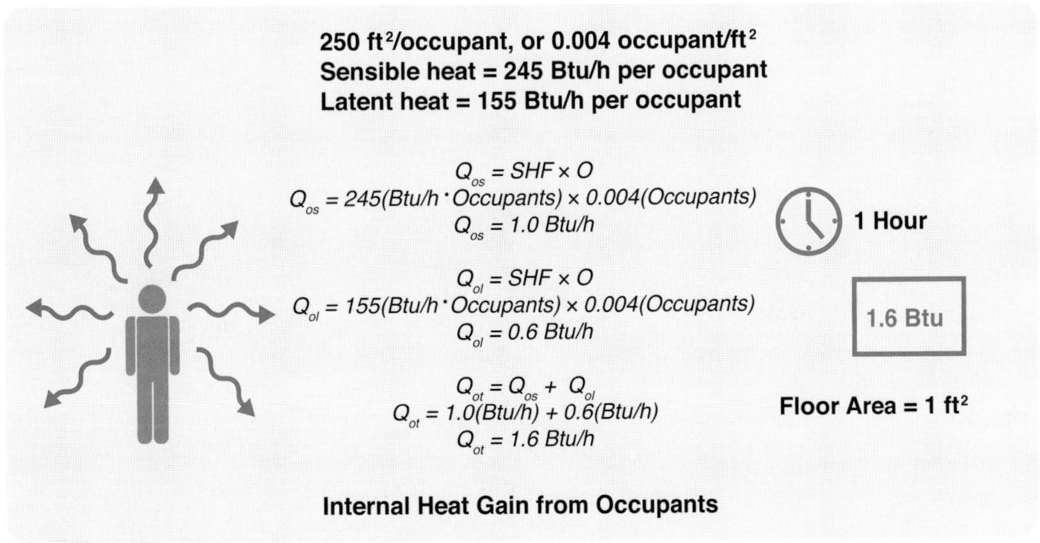

250 ft²/occupant, or 0.004 occupant/ft²
Sensible heat = 245 Btu/h per occupant
Latent heat = 155 Btu/h per occupant
$Q_{os} = SHF \times O$
$Q_{os} = 245(\text{Btu/h} \cdot \text{Occupants}) \times 0.004(\text{Occupants})$
$Q_{os} = 1.0$ Btu/h
$Q_{ol} = SHF \times O$
$Q_{ol} = 155(\text{Btu/h} \cdot \text{Occupants}) \times 0.004(\text{Occupants})$
$Q_{ol} = 0.6$ Btu/h
$Q_{ot} = Q_{os} + Q_{ol}$
$Q_{ot} = 1.0(\text{Btu/h}) + 0.6(\text{Btu/h})$
$Q_{ot} = 1.6$ Btu/h
1 Hour
1.6 Btu
Floor Area = 1 ft²
Internal Heat Gain from Occupants

■ **FIGURE 6.9** Internal Heat Gain by Occupants Example.

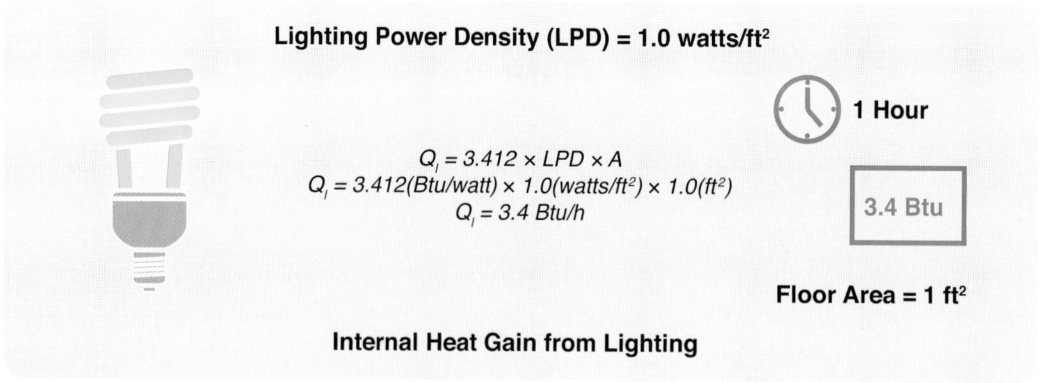

■ **FIGURE 6.10** Internal Heat Gain Lighting Example.

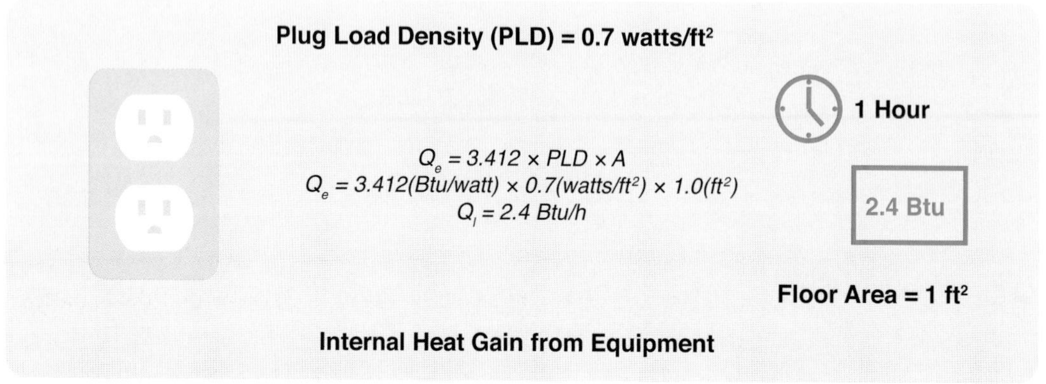

Plug Load Density (PLD) = 0.7 watts/ft²
1 Hour
Q_e = 3.412 × PLD × A
Q_e = 3.412(Btu/watt) × 0.7(watts/ft²) × 1.0(ft²)
Q_l = 2.4 Btu/h
2.4 Btu
Floor Area = 1 ft²
Internal Heat Gain from Equipment

■ **FIGURE 6.11** Internal Heat Gain Equipment Example.

The same logic about reducing power density for lighting can be applied to equipment. Reducing plug loads and process loads by selecting energy-efficient equipment and appliances, and keeping them off when not in use, will reduce internal heat gain. The calculation of heat gain for equipment and appliances is the same as for lighting, and requires quantifying the installed watts of equipment and estimating their schedule of use. A plug load density or total installed equipment and appliance load is used to quantify the load. In the next equation Q_e is the rate of heat gain from equipment and lighting in Btu/hour, *PLD* is the plug load density per square feet in watts, and *A* is the area in square feet.

$$Q_e = 3.412 \times PLD \times A$$

The example in Figure 6.11 illustrates the internal heat gain from equipment using a typical office building plug load density.

Total Internal Heat Gain

Total sensible internal heat gain (Q_i) for people, lighting, equipment, and appliances is the sum:

$$Q_i = Q_{os} + Q_l + Q_e$$

See Figure 6.12.

It can be valuable to compare the relative impact of the various sources of heat gain and heat loss in a building. Note that in the preceding examples each heat gain or loss was based on a different unit of area; for example: area of opaque wall area versus glazed area. If the respective areas are known, then the various heat gains and losses can be normalized for building floor area. Further, these examples look at points in time—perhaps, peak load times. The actual annual energy calculation includes many more variables. The value of this simple level of calculation is to understand the conceptual-level energy problem for a building and compare the relative

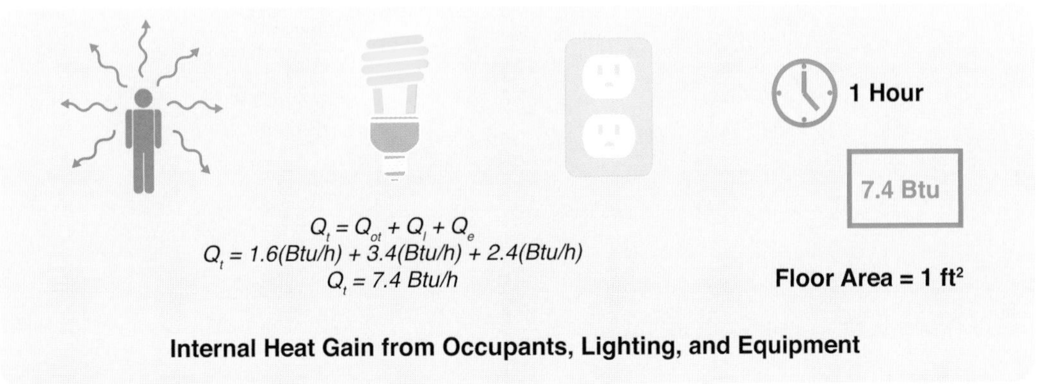

■ **FIGURE 6.12** Internal Heat Gain Total Example.

importance of different heat flows. This idea can be taken further when considering the balance point temperature of a building.

BALANCE POINT

The balance point temperature is the outside air temperature when the building is in transition between heating and cooling modes. As the outdoor temperature drops from the balance point, the building will go into heating; conversely, when the outdoor temperature rises from the balance point, the building will go into cooling. Said another way, the balance point temperature is the condition when the building does not need heating or cooling.

One interesting element of the balance point concept is that it essentially considers only the climate and the architecture. This can make it a useful concept for architects and designers to consider early in the design process, in that it can help them to define the thermal interactions of climate, program, and architecture. The balance point is dependent on the climate, building program, massing, and building envelope design. All of these factors influence the thermal energy flows in a building. And because many of the factors are variable, such as building use and weather, the balance point temperature is not static; it changes with these variables. Moreover, it is a thermal balance concept, so it can be used to test massing and building envelope decisions based on different weather and building use scenarios.

Balance point temperature is explored in more detail in *Sun, Wind & Light: Architectural Design Strategies*, by G. Z. Brown and Mark DeKay, and in a 1997 paper titled "Building Balance Point," by Michael Utzinger and James Wasley of the University of Wisconsin–Milwaukee. The paper was published as part of the University of California–Berkeley's Vital Signs series.

Luminous Energy Design Science

Luminous energy or light, as well as thermal energy, is central to building design science. Understanding the principal properties of light forms the basis for applying daylighting strategies and implementing energy-efficient lighting systems. In addition to knowing about the basic physics of light, it is important to have an understanding of the fundamental measures and metrics of light, and specifically daylight, in an architectural environment.

PROPERTIES OF LIGHT

Light is energy. Light is the visible spectrum of electromagnetic radiation. It is a narrow band within the full electromagnetic spectrum, consisting of wavelengths roughly between about 400 to 700 nanometers (see Figure 6.13). Within this range, all of the colors of light are produced. All visible-light wavelengths combined appear white, whereas the absence of visible-light wavelengths appears black. The relatively uniform color spectrum of daylight results in a high-quality (full-color) white light capable of rendering any color of the rainbow.

The color and wavelength of light is important for more than rendering surface colors correctly; it is also essential for controlling energy. Color is perceived by the eye when specific wavelengths, or colors, are reflected from a surface. The wavelengths not reflected are absorbed by the surface.

White surfaces reflect most of the light. The greater the range of wavelengths of light reflected, likewise the greater the amount of thermal energy reflected. The converse is true for black surfaces, which absorb most of the light, and hence absorb more thermal energy. This principle plays a role in the thermal loads of a building's exterior. Colors with high reflectance also play a role in distributing daylight.

Light interacts with surfaces and materials in a variety of quantifiable ways. The amount of light reflected from a surface as a ratio to the amount of incident light striking the surface is called *reflectance*, or reflectance factor, with values between 0 and 1, or between 0 and 100 percent. The light that is not reflected is absorbed. Light reflects at an angle equal to the angle of incidence, when striking a surface. However, the reflection itself can be specular, diffuse, or a combination of the two. See Figure 6.14. A rough

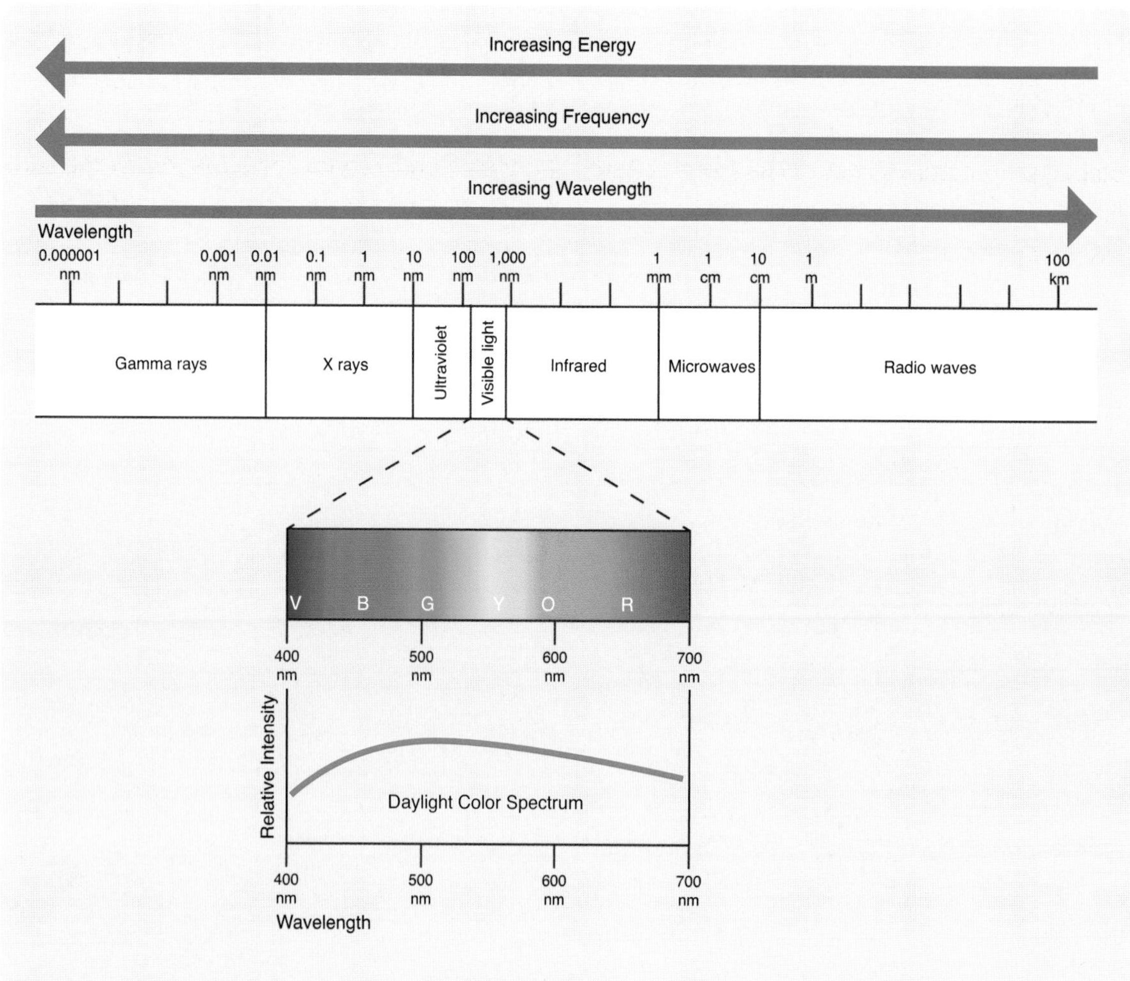

■ **FIGURE 6.13** Electromagnetic Spectrum.

or matte surface texture diffuses light because of the many small changes of surface angles, whereas a perfectly smooth and polished surface causes a direct specular reflection.

Materials can reflect and absorb light, but clear and translucent materials also transmit light. The *transmittance*, or transmittance factor, is equal to the ratio of the light transmitted through a material to the amount of incident light striking the surface of the material. Translucent materials diffuse the light as it transmits through, also obscuring the ability to see through the material.

In addition to defining the color and behavior of light, it is important to be able to define the quantity of light. Luminous energy is the visually perceived radiant energy, or quantity, of light measured in lumen-second (lm · s). The time rate, or flow, of luminous energy is luminous flux, measured in lumen-second per second, or simply lumen (lm). Luminous flux is also a measure of power, but it is not the same as radiant flux (the total power of electromagnetic radiation measured in watts). It is a measure of the power of light energy perceived by the human eye and is based on wavelength. For example, at a wavelength of 555 nanometers, 683 lumens equals 1 watt. The measure of efficiency of a light source is called *efficacy* and is a ratio of the luminous flux output for input of power in watts, or lumens per watt. Luminous intensity is the measure of luminous flux density based on direction. Light sources can distribute light or lumens narrowly (spot) with more density or broadly (flood) with less density. The unit of luminous intensity is candela, which is a lumen per steradian (solid angle). See Figure 6.15.

The concepts just described quantify the light emitting from a light source. In architectural lighting design, the measurement of light on surfaces is a primary concern. Illuminance is a measure of lumens per area of surface. Lux is 1 lumen per square meter, and footcandle (fc) is 1 lumen per square foot; 1 fc is equal to 10.76 lux. We can measure footcandles on a workplane surface, but the light that is reflected to the eye is measured as luminance. Luminance is the level of light we

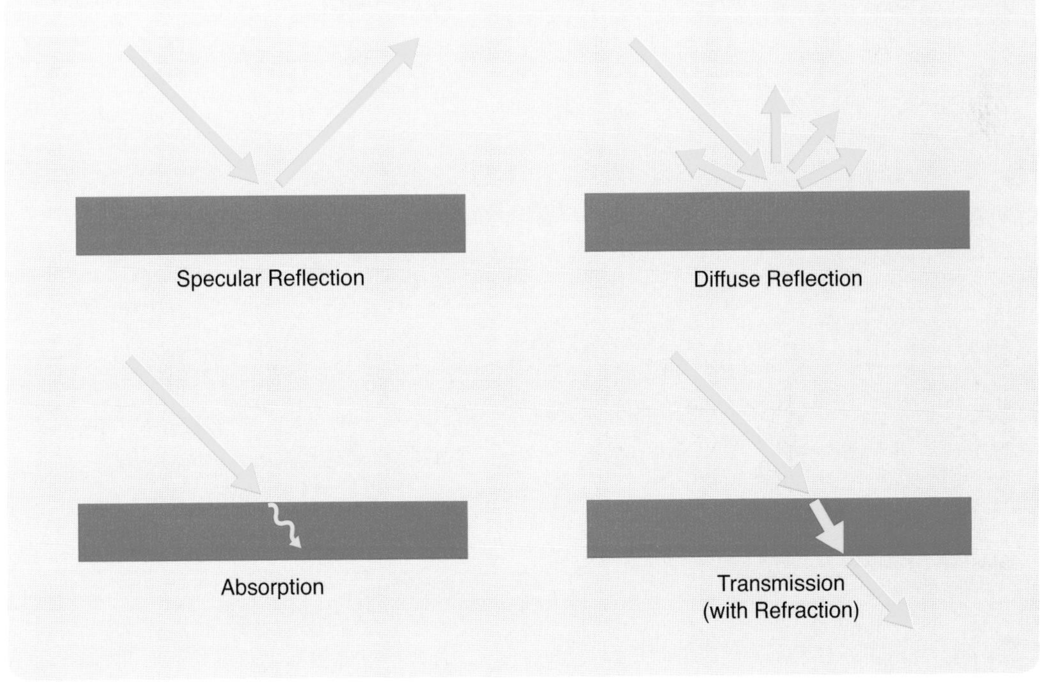

■ **FIGURE 6.14** Light Interaction with Surfaces.

perceive. It is a measure of luminous intensity per unit of area (see Figure 6.15).

Photometric Units

- Luminous energy: lumen second (lm · s)
- Luminous flux: lumen
- Efficacy: lumen/watt
- Luminous intensity: candela (cd) = lumen/steradian (lm/st)
- Illuminance: lumen/ft^2 = footcandle (fc), or lumen/m^2 = lux
- Luminance: cd/ft^2 or cd/m^2

DAYLIGHTING LEVELS

Daylighting design begins by understanding the lighting needs of the space to be daylit. Illuminance in footcandles (fc) or lux (SI units) is a measurement of lighting level. Illumination requirements can vary, depending on the space and type of activities taking place within it. Illumination requirements are also subjective, and individual needs may vary based on age and other personal factors. Other factors, such as contrast and glare, are also important design considerations for successful daylighting design.

One important design strategy for many spaces is to separate the illumination requirements for ambient lighting and task lighting. In spaces such as offices, the ambient light in the overall space can be lower than the light levels needed at the desk for task work. This provides a good opportunity to lower overall lighting levels and save energy, while facilitating the needs of the occupants at their desks with an individually controlled task light.

While targeting lighting levels based on space use and activity, keep in mind that light levels are highly subjective and can be expressed as a range of acceptable lighting

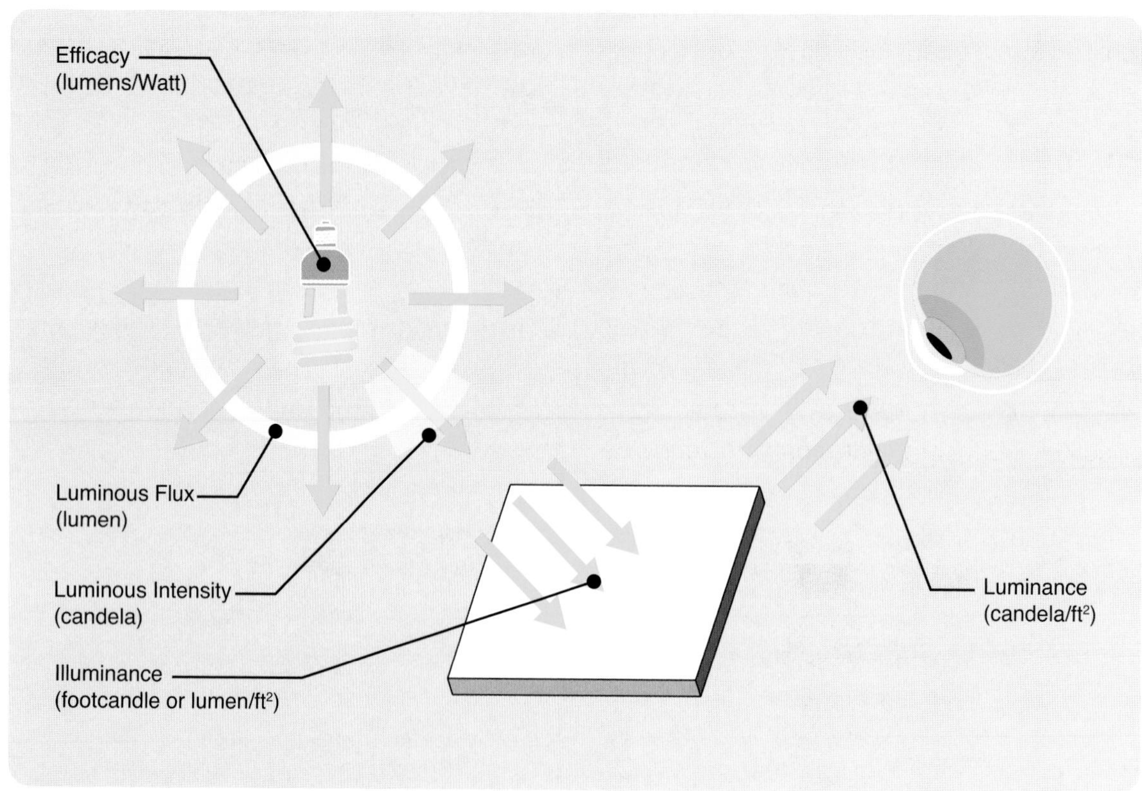

■ **FIGURE 6.15** Photometric Units.

levels. Daylighting is highly dynamic, and will vary hour by hour and day by day. Also, excessively high levels are unnecessary; high lighting levels should be reserved for areas with specific lighting needs. One of the best sources for illumination requirements and design standards for individual spaces comes from the Illuminating Engineering Society of North America (IESNA, or simply, IES). Figure 6.16 lists simplified recommended ranges of lighting levels, based on activity, which can guide daylighting design.

The requirements for the daylighting credit in LEED 2009, IEQ credit 8.1, are often used as a design requirement for daylit spaces. LEED 2009 requires that regularly occupied spaces achieve a minimum of 10 footcandles and a maximum of 500 footcandles daylight illuminance under clear-sky conditions on September 21 at 9:00 am and 3:00 pm. Note that the U.S. Green Building Council (USGBC) has only recently used the 10 footcandles minimum, replacing the previous requirement of 25 footcandles. The 25 footcandles level of interior illuminance is a good design target for office and similar space types. Ultimately, daylighting design should provide the lighting levels needed for any given space.

The quality of the daylight, in addition to the quantity of daylight, is another important design requirement. Bringing in too much daylight or uncontrolled daylight can lead to areas of high contrast and glare. Glare is a particularly problematic issue due to the veiling reflections from computer monitor screens. Control of glare should be an integrated part of any daylighting strategy.

EXTERIOR ILLUMINATION

The ranges of exterior illumination and sky conditions that characterize a location will inform the opportunities and strategies available for daylighting. Exterior illumination is highly variable, and depends on sky conditions, time of year, and time of day; it also varies based on latitude and corresponding solar angles (altitude and azimuth). On a clear, sunny day, exterior illumination can range from a few thousand to 10,000 thousand footcandles. The brightest region of a clear sky is intuitively toward the sun, and the horizon is brighter than the zenith by a factor of three to one. In an overcast sky, the zenith is the brightest region in the sky by a factor of about three to one. Overcast exterior illumination ranges from a few hundred to a few thousand footcandles.

Weather analysis software, such as Climate Consultant, as discussed in Chapter 5, is a convenient way to determine the range of exterior illumination for a given site and climate. Sky-cover ranges are also generally available from weather data files. Understanding the range in sky conditions and exterior illumination will aid in the development of a worst-case design sky and lead to the emergence of daylighting strategies that address the range of conditions. Daylight modeling software will make it possible to select design sky conditions for any given simulation run.

Activity	Footcandle Range
Orientation/Limited Detail/Occasional Use	3–10 fc
Basic Visual Tasks/Moderate Detail/Regular Use	20–30 fc
Basic Visual Tasks/High Detail/Regular Use	50 fc
Special Visual Tasks/Extremely High Detail	100–200 fc

■ **FIGURE 6.16** Recommended Interior Illuminance Levels.

DAYLIGHT FACTOR

Daylight factor (DF) is the ratio of the illumination level at a point in the interior of the building to the exterior illuminance under an overcast sky. It is expressed as a percentage. In the following equation, *DF* is the daylight factor, E_i is the interior horizontal illuminance at a given point, and E_o is the exterior horizontal illuminance under an overcast sky.

$$DF = \frac{E_i}{E_o} \times 100\%$$

For example, given a daylight factor of 5 percent at a desk in a classroom, and the exterior illumination with an overcast sky of 1,000 footcandles, the illumination at the desk will be 50 footcandles. The factor can be a measurement at a point in the building, or expressed as an average over the entire space. Daylight factor is a useful design metric because it quantifies the daylighting design performance of a space. Overcast sky illuminance will vary over time, whereas the daylight factor is fixed. Therefore, if desired interior lighting levels and the worst-case overcast exterior illuminance are known, the design target for daylight factor can be determined and used to test design options.

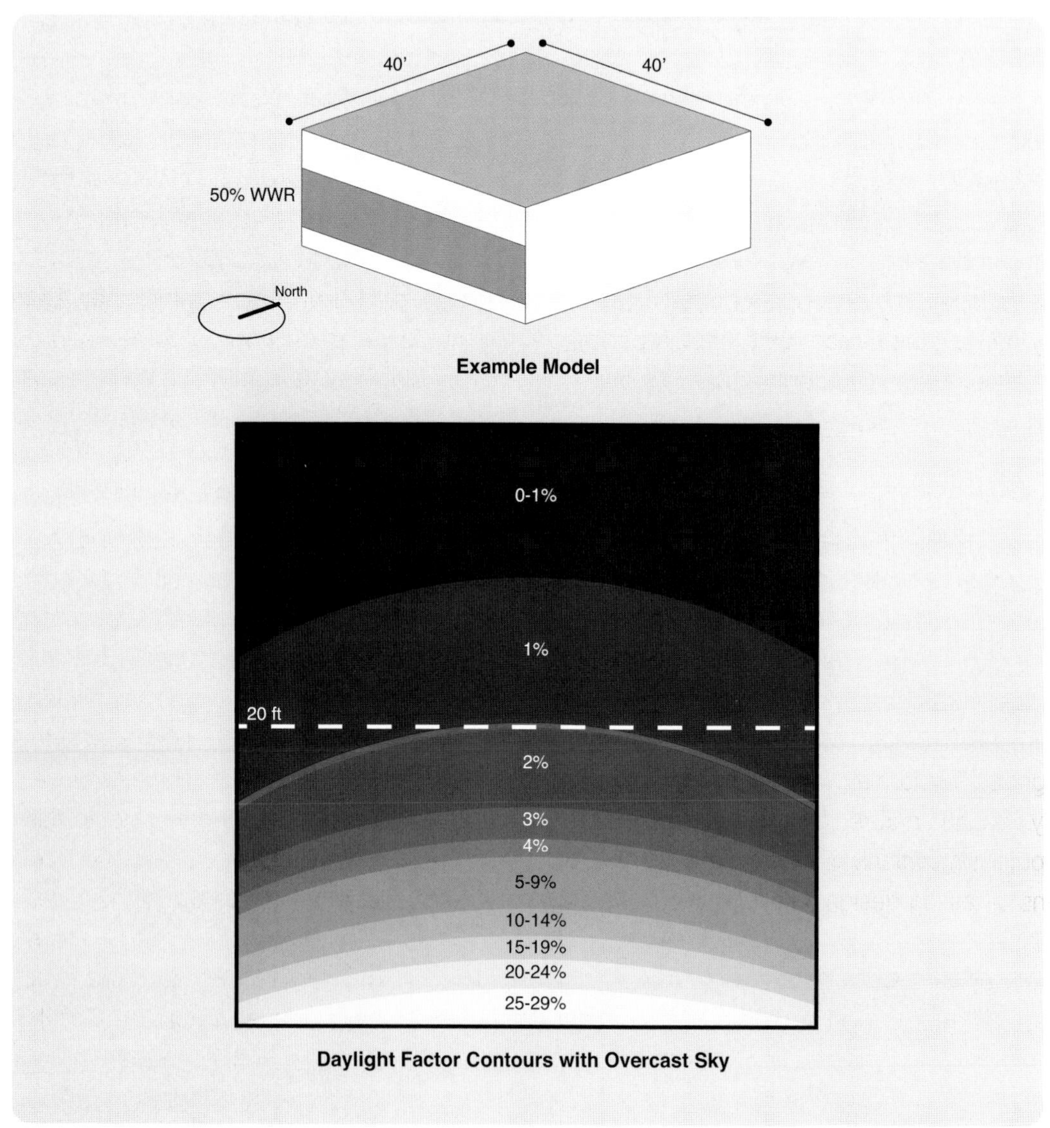

■ **FIGURE 6.17** Daylight Factor Example.

The daylight factor is the sum of the sky component, exterior-reflected component, and interior-reflected component. Many excellent books, including *Mechanical and Electrical Equipment for Buildings* by Grondzik et al., focus on daylighting design and provide methods for calculating and estimating the daylight factor. The use of daylight modeling software is becoming common practice for determining daylight factors, as well as illuminance, glare analysis, and other daylighting attributes. See Figure 6.17 for an example of daylight factors calculated using daylight modeling software.

One of the main drawbacks of the daylight factor is that it does not quantify the daylight strategies that utilize clear sky or controlled direct daylight. While a low solar altitude, winter, overcast sky condition will represent a worst-case sky condition for daylight minimum levels, clear-sky conditions and periods of direct sun penetration represent a worst-case scenario for glare and visual comfort. Relying solely on daylight factors as a design performance metric could potentially lead to overlighting and glare issues.

DYNAMIC DAYLIGHT PERFORMANCE

There are many dynamic variables that directly influence daylighting performance, including changing solar angles, sky conditions, occupancy patterns, and patterns of operable window shade use. Daylight factor provides a metric that is static over time. It is important to consider daylight performance over time. Because of the highly dynamic nature of daylight, the use of computer simulations has become the primary means of testing design solutions and assessing performance.

A common approach to assessing the annual performance of daylighting for a space is to test seasonal conditions. Doing so can give the designer an understanding of the annual variations in daylight performance for a design. Seasonal variations are typically tested on summer solstice, winter solstice, and spring or autumn equinox. These seasonal time periods should be tested with both overcast and clear-sky conditions. It is also useful to examine morning (9:00 am), noon, and afternoon (3:00 pm) conditions.

DAYLIGHT AUTONOMY

As noted, daylight factor is a static metric of daylight performance; but there are also a series of dynamic daylight performance metrics related to daylight autonomy that can provide a deeper understanding of daylight performance and energy savings over time.

Daylight autonomy is a metric that measures the percent of time that the design-level illuminance of space is met with only daylight. The measure is for a point in space; but multiple points can be aggregated for an entire space. Typically, the hours considered in the metric are occupied daylit hours, rather than 24 hours a day. However, the hours included can be modified to meet a specific project need.

A helpful modification to the basic daylight autonomy measure is to account for all daylight by prorating times when daylight is provided but under the design illuminance level. This metric, known as *continuous daylight autonomy*, was developed in 2006 by Zack Rogers, coauthor of "Dynamic Daylighting Performance Metrics for Sustainable Building Design." Another useful modification to the daylight autonomy metric is to consider a maximum daylight autonomy value. In this case, a maximum design illuminance threshold is evaluated based on the highest desired illuminance level in a space. This metric is calculated as a percent of time that the maximum design illuminance is exceeded with daylight, and is an indication of glare issues and direct sunbeam. LEED 2009 has established 500 footcandles as a maximum. Other experts, such as John Mardaljevic and Azza Nabil, suggest a maximum threshold as low as 2000 lux (approximately 200 fc). Another approach to setting a maximum lighting-level threshold is to use the desired contrast ratio, such as 1:10. In this case, if the design illuminance is 25 footcandles, then the maximum would be 250 footcandles.

BUILDING ENVELOPE

The building envelope is the front line of the building's interface with the exterior environment and climate. This means it plays a critical role in the implementation of passive strategies, and so should be integrated with decisions about orientation and massing, as well as with mechanical and electrical system design. The building envelope must balance the needs for passive strategies such as daylighting and natural ventilation that require the climate to permeate the interior, with the need for integrity and performance from a thermal energy perspective. The building envelope is a critical element in the energy performance of any building, but it is absolutely vital to the performance of net zero energy buildings.

Neutralize the Envelope

The concept of neutralizing the envelope means neutralizing the thermal loads of the envelope. This is a key element in the passive design approach to net zero energy buildings. The design of the building envelope needs to address and neutralize thermal energy conduction, convection, and radiation loads related to thermal transmission, solar radiation, and infiltration.

There is a dizzying array of technical issues to resolve in neutralizing the envelope in a net zero energy building, and an even greater number of technologies and emerging technologies that can provide solutions. One overall guideline would be to strive to design for building envelope neutralization as simply and directly as possible. It is important to be comprehensive and follow through on the details. Use technology very selectively, focusing on cost-effective and integrated solutions. Using the brute-force method of technology, with layers and layers of technologies added to the building, can result in an overly complex building, which will be costly to build, prone to problems, and difficult to maintain. This is not to say that innovation should be hampered; innovation is more about how to apply and integrate technologies than the technologies themselves.

Neutralizing the envelope begins with the optimization of building massing and orientation. The site's solar and wind conditions will impact thermal loads on the building based on orientation, envelope size, and site obstructions that shade solar radiation or impede wind penetration. The ability to shade glazing is also directly affected by orientation. In addition, the sol-air effect can be dramatic on surfaces in hot climates with high levels of solar radiation. In fact, in locations that also have high solar altitudes, the sol-air temperature on the roof can be extremely high, and the roof can, therefore, be a major source of heat gain in commercial buildings with large roof areas. Using cool roofs, green roofs, and shaded roofs will work to lower the sol-air temperature and resulting heat gain (see Figure 6.18).

Proper orientation, massing, and site planning can make the thermal loads less difficult to overcome; when paired with a well-designed and detailed building envelope, they are key to successfully neutralizing the envelope. Design envelope assemblies for low thermal transmittance (U-factor) by superinsulating the wall, which includes using high R-value insulating materials, as well as eliminating thermal bridging. The roof should have the highest R-value of the building envelope, because it represents a primary location for heat loss in heating-dominated climates. It also represents a location for high heat gain in cooling-dominated climates as related to the sol-air temperature impact of solar radiation.

Convection also contributes to heat loss and heat gain through a building envelope. Air infiltration through gaps in the building envelope can cause thermal leaks between the building and the exterior, causing heat gains during the cooling season and heat loss during the heating season. Winds and pressure differences between the interior and exterior can drive infiltration losses. Creating an airtight building envelope is the main approach to controlling thermal convection loads.

One of the most important design features on the building envelope are glazed openings. Thermally, glazing is the weakest link in the building envelope. Glazing and window frames have among the lowest thermal resistance of almost any material in a building assembly. Glazing, due to its transparency, also results in heat gain from solar radiation. Furthermore, windows and window openings can be a primary point of air leakage in a building envelope. At the same time, glazing is also one of the most important design elements in a building, providing many architectural, program, and performance benefits. Therefore, making the most of glazing, while working to minimize its associated thermal liabilities, is an essential part of neutralizing the envelope.

Multiple strategies for dealing with glazing are described in this chapter. Key among them is optimization of the glazing system's energy performance properties, such as low

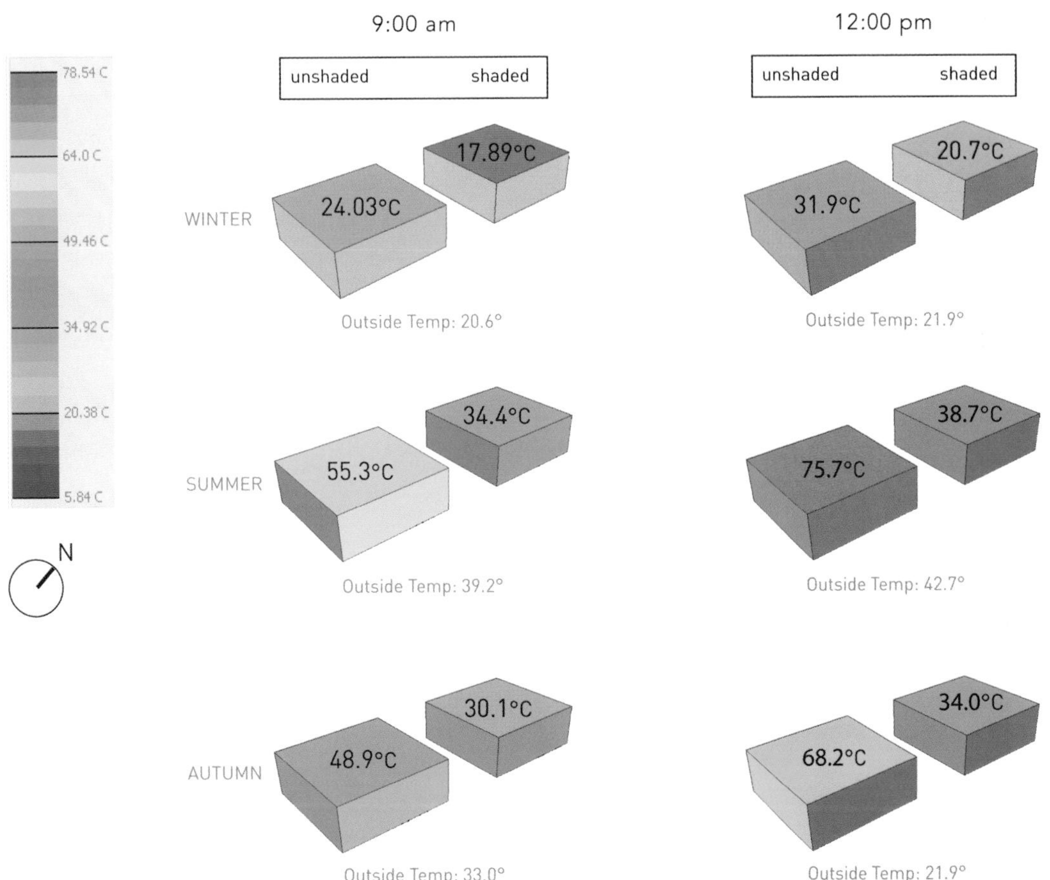

■ **FIGURE 6.18** Surface temperatures plotted on surfaces using OpenStudio to determine the impact of shading on roof temperature for a project in Abu Dhabi. *Image courtesy of RNL.*

thermal transmittance and low solar heat gain coefficient. The window to wall ratio (WWR) is a critical metric that helps balance thermal liabilities with performance benefits, such as daylight and views. Numerous shading strategies, daylight-enhancing devices, and window attachments are available that provide enhanced insulation, shading, and glare control. Overall window design is governed by orientation, climate, and building program, and responsive buildings will often incorporate a wide variety of glazing and shading solutions to address the specific need of each window location (see Figure 6.19).

Neutralizing the envelope results in the reduction of perimeter heating and cooling loads, which has several system and thermal comfort benefits. Neutralizing can eliminate the need for perimeter heating and cooling typical in buildings; in addition, because of the resulting minimal perimeter loads, it also permits the use of very low-energy mechanical system solutions, such as radiant heating and cooling. Neutralizing the façade also enhances thermal comfort, because high-performance glazing systems lower the interior surface temperature of glazing, which can cause discomfort in the winter, and reduce solar heat gain, which can cause discomfort in the summer.

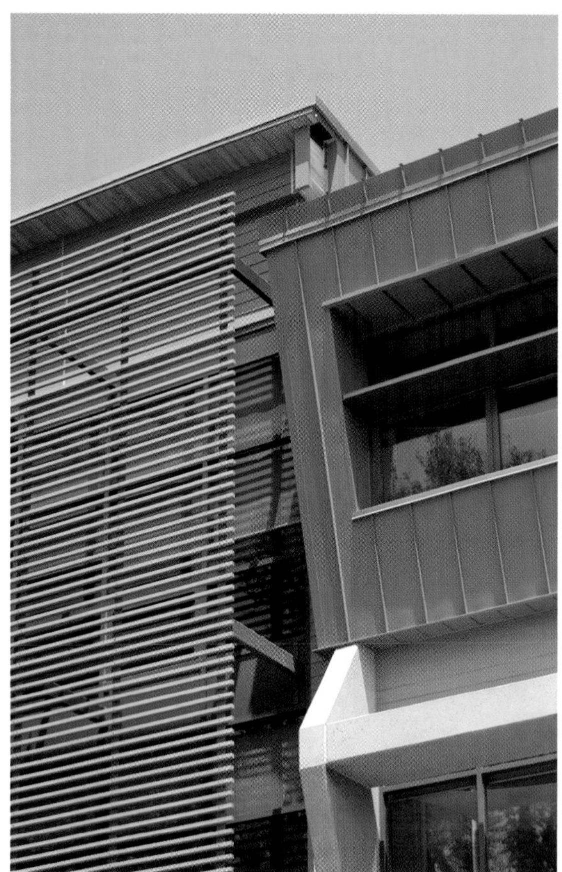

■ **FIGURE 6.19** Lewis and Clark State Office Building for the Missouri Department of Natural Resources has well-integrated solar control for glazing. *Image courtesy of BNIM; photograph © 2006, Assassi.*

As discussed in the next section on optimizing passive design, neutralizing the envelope is critical for net zero energy buildings that have large exterior wall area to floor area ratios, in order to maximize passive design strategies. This approach limits the thermal liability that can come with these types of buildings, and is part of the process of optimizing a net zero energy building for passive design.

PASSIVE DESIGN OPTIMIZATION

Several dichotomies must be addressed when designing and optimizing net zero energy and passive energy buildings. First, from a building massing perspective, a compact massing is optimized for active mechanical systems because of the reduced envelope loads. A thin, spread-out massing has a significant amount of envelope, or exterior wall area to floor area ratio, hence can have additional thermal loads. However, the additional envelope is an advantage for utilizing passive design strategies such as daylighting and natural ventilation. Small buildings may be able to maintain relatively compact masses, while still having a footprint that is easy to daylight and ventilate naturally. Large commercial buildings are more challenging because a compact massing will typically result in deep footprints that cannot be daylit and naturally ventilated. It follows that successful passive design for commercial buildings will incorporate a thin massing arrangement, but then seek to neutralize the building envelope to limit the liability it represents.

The next major dichotomy that must be addressed is the difference between a sealed versus an open or porous envelope. A highly insulated and airtight design is optimized for active mechanical system design; however, sealed buildings may limit the beneficial exchange with the environment when passive strategies can be leveraged in lieu of mechanical systems. The use of high-quality glazing with operable sections, in conjunction with an airtight, superinsulated envelope, can deliver an improved approach. In addition, the use of dynamic façade elements can further enhance the capability of a building envelope to be passively open when appropriate and sealed closed when appropriate.

Figure 6.20 shows the basic steps in optimizing a net zero energy building for passive energy strategies and further integrating low-energy active and renewable energy systems. Notice the diagrammatic energy pie chart to the side of each step, conceptualizing the incremental energy reduction and, ultimately, the addition of renewable energy to the building.

Building Envelope Design

THERMAL TRANSMITTANCE

The thermal transmittance, or U-factor, for the various assemblies in a building envelope is an important design consideration for a net zero energy building. A building envelope should be designed and constructed with low U-factor wall assemblies, foundation wall assemblies, roof assemblies, floor and slab assemblies, glazing assemblies, and doors and other openings. The "Design Science" section earlier in this chapter is meant to form the building science foundation for the guidance offered in this section on building envelope design. As previously noted, the assembly U-factors determine the heat gain or loss through an assembly.

There is a trend toward higher insulation levels in buildings, because they are cost-effective means of reducing thermal energy loads and neutralizing the envelope. The trend is resulting in a strategy often called *superinsulated buildings*. The Passive House standard is one of the primary initiatives that have spurred this strategy, at least in the residential market. However, the Passive House standard can also be used as a guide for commercial buildings. For example, a typical passive house wall R-value will be over 40, and roofs significantly higher than that over R-60. Although commercial energy codes do not match the very high requirements of the Passive House standard, they are raising the prescriptive measures around thermal transmittance of the building envelope. ASHRAE standard 90.1 provides a valuable guide for designers of commercial buildings by enumerating minimum building envelope requirements for roofs, walls, floors, slabs, doors, glazing, and skylights, based on climate zone. There is also a developing emphasis on continuous insulation to reduce thermal bridging, which can be accomplished in a variety of wall assemblies. For a net zero energy project, these values should be considered as starting points for establishing the energy performance of a building envelope.

In addition to the thermal transmittance properties of construction assemblies, the detailing of the building envelope and the elimination of thermal bridging also play critical roles in reducing heat flow through the envelope. Thermal bridges are thermally conductive material bridges that create discontinuity of the insulation layer of an assembly and connect the exterior and interior thermal environments through an assembly. Classic thermal bridges include metal window frames, steel studs in a typical batt-insulated wall, uninsulated parapet walls, and concrete slab edges or structure exposed to the exterior. The development of thermal bridging within an exterior assembly can appreciably derate the overall R-value of the assembly, resulting in higher thermal transmittance, or lower R-value. Even the best-intentioned assemblies with high levels of insulation can become poor-performing assemblies unless careful attention is paid to detailing and construction, to eliminate thermal bridging.

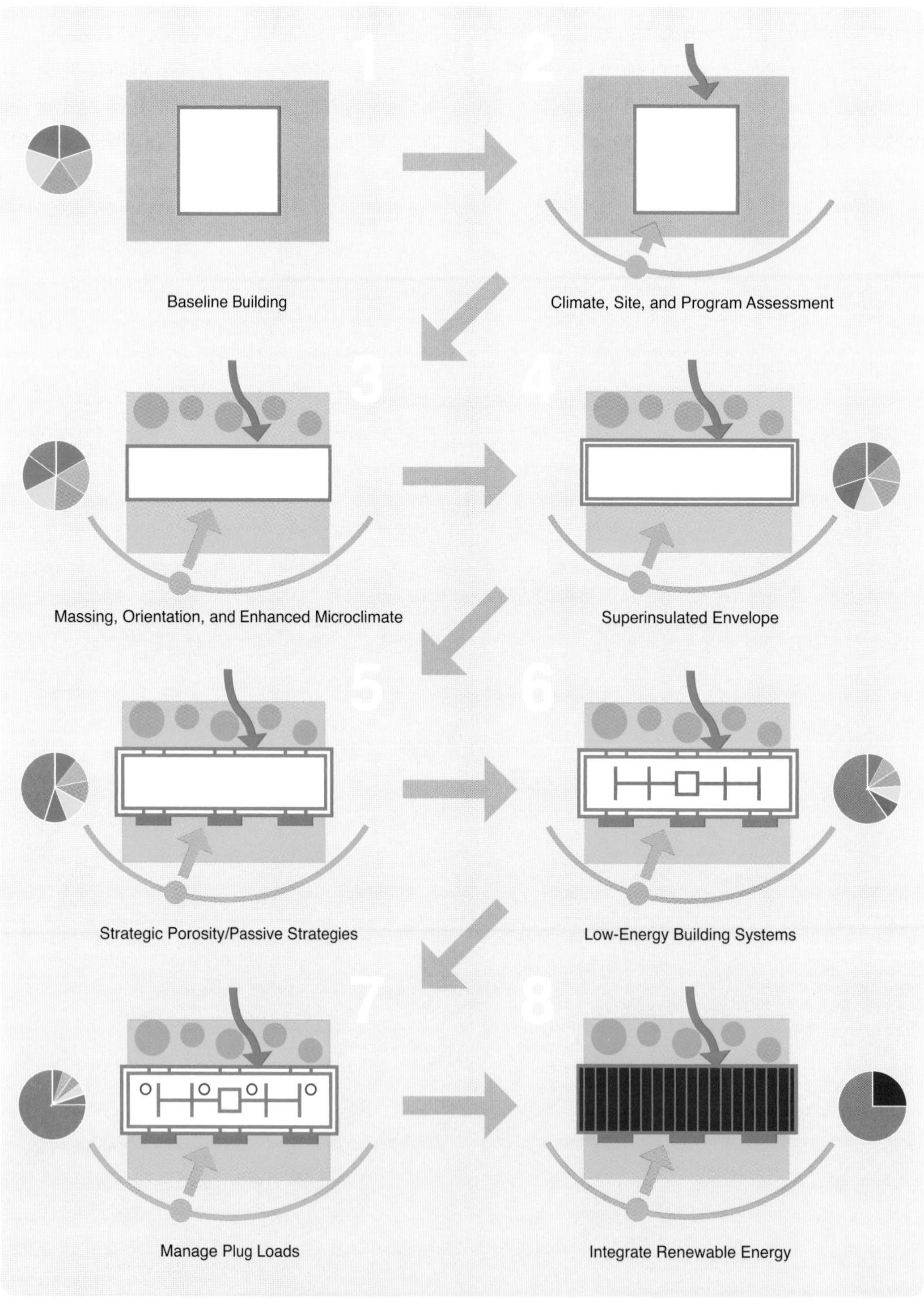

■ **FIGURE 6.20** Basic steps in optimizing a building for passive strategies, low-energy integration, and net zero energy.

It is important to note that the calculation for the true U-factor or total R-value for a building assembly is far more complex than simply adding the various individual R-values of materials together. It is necessary to also account for thermal bridges and discontinuities in the assembly. As shown in Figure 6.21, steel-stud-framed walls cause thermal bridging, which can dramatically derate the R-value of a basic clear wall assembly. This example used the Oak Ridge National Laboratory's online Modified Zone Method Calculator for determining clear wall R-values for steel-stud-framed walls.

The overall wall is also dramatically influenced and further derated by any disruption in the clear wall by openings for windows and doors, corners, and structural elements that are embedded in the wall. In addition to the derating caused by these framed-in elements, these interruptions are generally detailed with additional studs, which can further derate the assembly. Windows are usually the most significant factor in thermal derating for the exterior envelope, due to their relatively large area and typically poor thermal performance. Skylights on roofs are a similar liability.

Details that are repeated over and over, such as exterior metal wall studs, and framed openings in the exterior, such as windows and doors, are top priorities to address because of the magnitude of their scale. However, even small details, such as conduit penetrations through exterior walls, should be considered. Typically, a visual review of the drawings of exterior envelope assembly details can reveal problematic thermal bridges, and solutions can be directly developed to address each condition (see Figure 6.22).

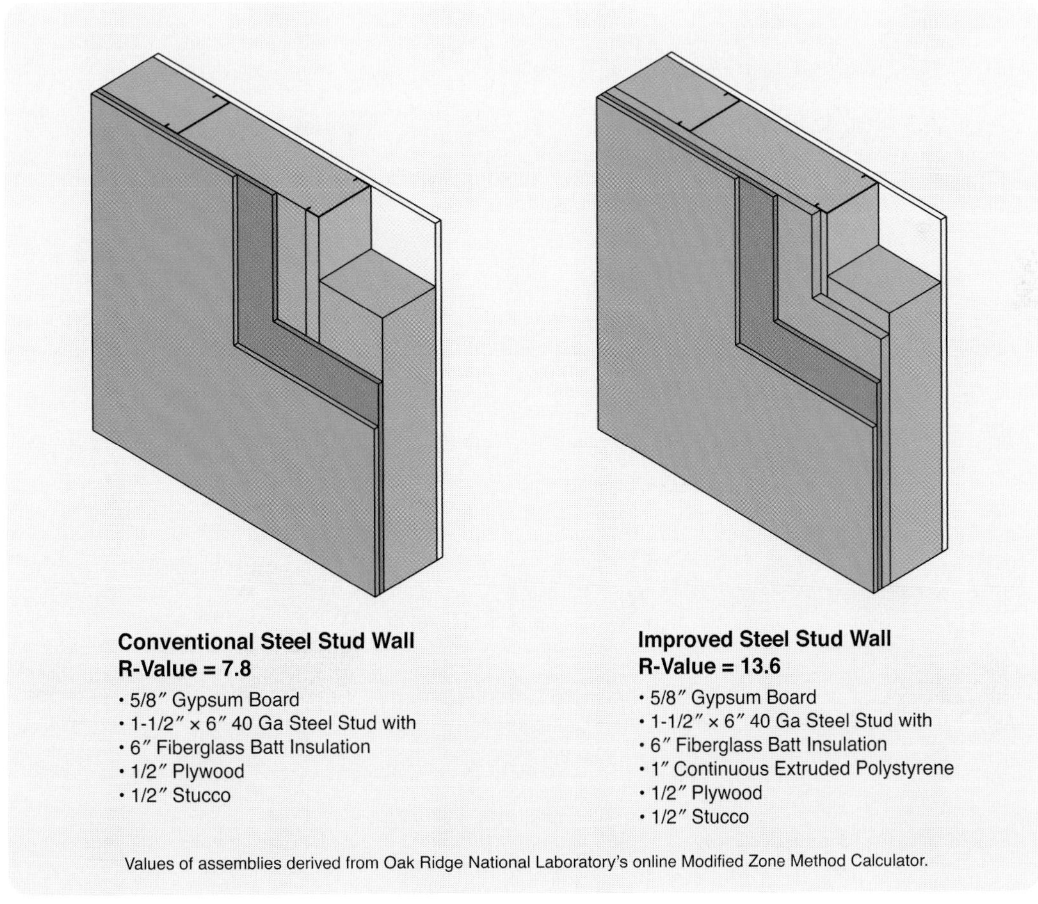

Conventional Steel Stud Wall
R-Value = 7.8
• 5/8″ Gypsum Board
• 1-1/2″ × 6″ 40 Ga Steel Stud with
• 6″ Fiberglass Batt Insulation
• 1/2″ Plywood
• 1/2″ Stucco
Improved Steel Stud Wall
R-Value = 13.6
• 5/8″ Gypsum Board
• 1-1/2″ × 6″ 40 Ga Steel Stud with
• 6″ Fiberglass Batt Insulation
• 1″ Continuous Extruded Polystyrene
• 1/2″ Plywood
• 1/2″ Stucco
Values of assemblies derived from Oak Ridge National Laboratory's online Modified Zone Method Calculator.

■ **FIGURE 6.21** Steel Stud Wall R-Value Comparison.

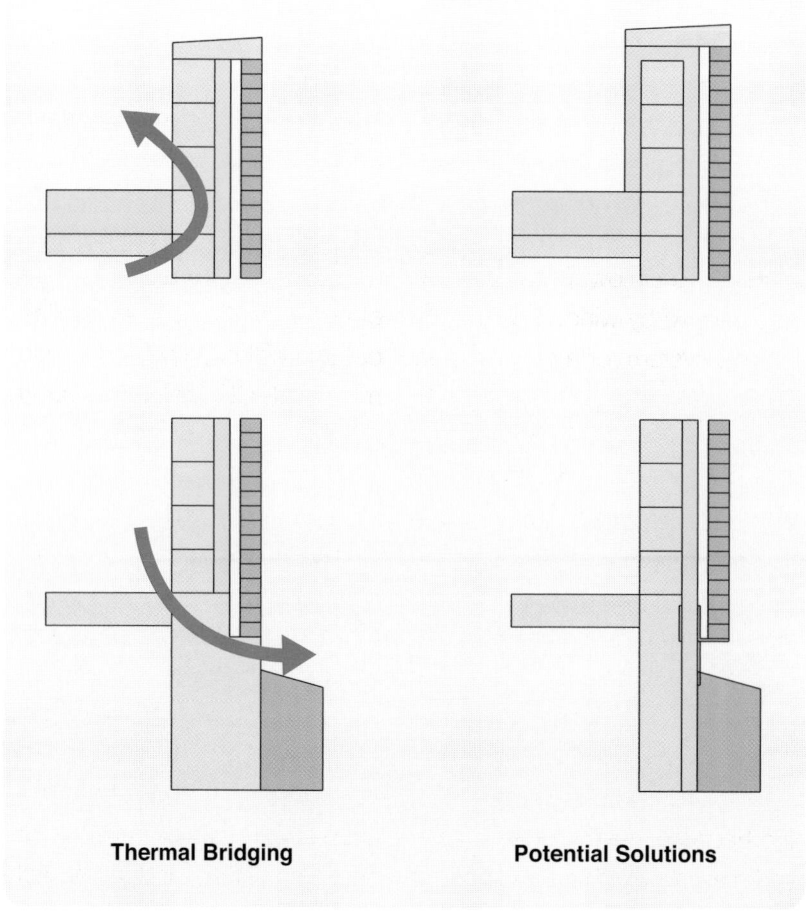

■ **FIGURE 6.22** Examples of Common Thermal Bridging and Potential Solutions.

Utilizing such thermal simulation software as THERM, developed by the Lawrence Berkeley National Laboratory, the implications of exterior assembly design and thermal bridges can be quantified, and solutions tested. The resulting quantification can be used to determine a true value for the U-factor of exterior assemblies. Figure 6.23 shows the result of a THERM analysis in identifying thermal bridging.

AIR INFILTRATION

Until relatively recently, air infiltration in commercial buildings had not received a great deal of attention. A 2005 National Institute of Standards and Technology (NIST) report, "Investigation of the Impact of Commercial Buildings Envelope Airtightness on HVAC Energy Use" by Steven Emmerich, Timothy McDowell, and Wagdy Anis, revealed that, commonly, commercial buildings are not airtight, and that proper detailing can result in energy cost savings of up to 36 percent for heating and cooling. Large temperature and air density differences and stronger winter winds drive air infiltration and exfiltration in the winter. The uncontrolled introduction of humidity and latent heat through infiltration is a concern in humid summer months.

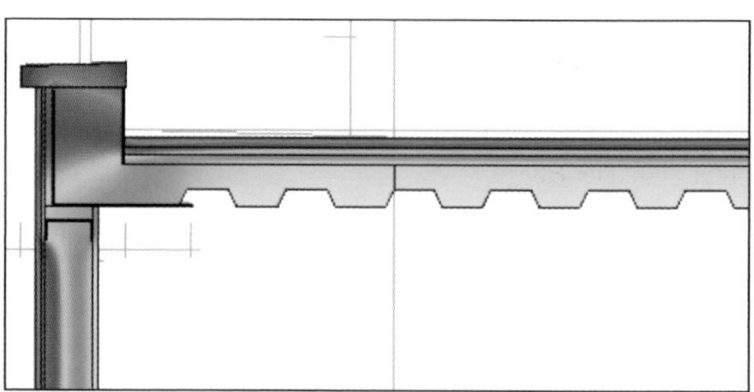

■ **FIGURE 6.23** Building Envelope Studies Using THERM to Analyze Thermal Bridging. *Image courtesy of Stantec Consulting Services Inc.*

Air infiltration, like thermal bridging, is essentially thermal holes in the exterior building envelope. In the case of air infiltration, small gaps in the envelope can allow air to pass directly between the interior and exterior environments, causing either heat gain or heat loss. Air movement through the envelope is caused by pressure differences that drive airflow. Pressure differences can be caused by wind, the stack effect, the mechanical system, or a combination of these effects.

Detailing and careful construction for airtightness can dramatically minimize the negative impacts of infiltration. The air barrier is one of the fundamental elements in any building enclosure that addresses airtightness. The air barrier must be designed and constructed as a complete, continuous system, extending over the entire exterior envelope. Particular attention to the joints between different envelope assemblies, such as wall to roof or at window and door openings in walls, is warranted because these interfaces are more complex and may involve different air barrier products. In general, all air barrier joints need to be durable, flexible, and airtight. Air barrier materials should have a maximum air permeability of 0.004 CFM/ft^2 of exterior area at a pressure differential of 0.3 inches of water, or 75Pa, as tested per ASTM E2178. The various assemblies in a building envelope, and their connection to the main air barrier system, should conform to ASTM E2357 and have a maximum air permeability of 0.04 CFM/ft^2 of exterior area at a pressure differential of 0.3 inches of water, or 75Pa.

As with thermal transmission, windows, skylights, and doors are also potential liabilities from an air infiltration perspective. In addition to the air barrier joint at the perimeter of each opening, the component itself should be designed for airtightness. Air leakage specifications should be considered for all fenestrations and doors. Doors can be a major source of infiltration, especially when they are used frequently. The introduction of vestibules and revolving doors can create thermal buffer zones that can limit infiltration.

The entire air barrier system should be tested with an air leakage test by fan pressurization, as per ASTM E779. The common standard for commercial buildings is a maximum air infiltration rate of 0.4 CFM/ft^2 of exterior area at a pressure differential of 0.3 inches of water, or 75Pa. The baseline for a typical commercial building is believed to be approximately 1.8 CFM/ft^2. However, the U.S. Army Corps of Engineers' standard for air infiltration is 0.25 CFM/ft^2, meaning that there is a lot of room for improved performance in all commercial buildings (see Figure 6.24).

Adherence to design standards for air leakage and fan pressurization testing of the building can ensure that high levels of airtightness are achieved. The design infiltration rate can be accounted for in the energy model. Also refer to the "Design Science" section earlier in this chapter for basic calculations of heat gain and heat loss through infiltration. Achieving high levels of airtightness must be done in unison with the design of an effective ventilation system, to ensure a healthy building with high indoor air quality.

GLAZING SYSTEMS

Glazing systems are absolutely essential for great architecture, and play a very important role in net zero energy buildings, because they are integral to many passive strategies, such as daylighting, natural ventilation, and passive solar. Further, glazing systems can be integrated with energy generation systems such as building-integrated photovoltaics. This section serves as a summary for basic glazing system design and a discussion of the energy performance of glazing. The primary focus here is on vertical glazing, but the principles can be applied to skylights as well.

In addition to its inherent beauty and expressiveness in architecture, glazing system design should consider the functional and passive performance of glazing in an integrated way. Glazing systems can have numerous functional elements, including daylighting, natural ventilation, passive solar heat, views, privacy, security, moisture control, and acoustics. It is useful to address each of these functions discretely, based on orientation and building program. In fact, good glazing design purposely integrates and optimizes each of these functions into the glazing systems of a building.

Glazing systems are assembled largely from conductive materials, such as glass and metal, which results in inherently high thermal transmission. However, the capability to form cavities of air or gas within a glazing unit of two or more panes dramatically decreases the U-factor of the glazing. The edge of the glazing unit is a different story. Glazing unit edges are sealed and made structurally stable with edge spaces, which are typically made of aluminum. However, edge spaces create a large thermally weak zone around the perimeter of a glazing unit. The window frame, likewise usually made of aluminum, extends this zone of thermal weakness at the perimeter. The smaller the glazing unit, the more impact the edge's thermal condition has on the overall window performance. Glazing is usually provided with a U-factor at the center of glass, which excludes the edge and frame effect. The overall U-factor for the whole window is a much better indicator of actual window performance.

The transparent quality of glass allows the introduction of visible light, but it also allows the introduction of thermal energy in the form of solar radiation into the building. Solar radiation must be carefully controlled to reduce its

■ **FIGURE 6.24** Air leakage test being conducted on a commercial building at Fort Carson, Colorado. *Credit: Nicholas K. Alexander, U.S. Army Corps of Engineers.*

impact on energy and thermal comfort. At the same time, solar radiation may be used as part of a passive solar heating strategy. Visible light transmittance is an important parameter for daylighting design. The selective control of light and solar radiation is one of the challenges of glazing system design.

Glazing Energy Performance Properties

- ***Visible light transmittance (VLT or VT):*** *The percentage of visible light transmitted through glazing.*
- ***Solar heat gain coefficient (SHGC):*** *The decimal expression of the percentage of incident solar radiation transmitted through glazing.*
- ***Light to solar gain ratio (LSG):*** *The ratio of visible light transmittance to solar heat gain coefficient (LSG = VLT/SHGC). This ratio is an expression of glazing performance, as these are properties that are difficult to optimize with respect to each other. Typically, VLT is to be maximized while SHGC is be minimized. The higher the LSG ratio, the more visible light transmittance per unit of solar heat gain. This performance ratio is particularly important for daylighting.*
- ***Thermal transmittance (U-factor):*** *The hourly Btu heat energy transmittance through a glazing assembly includes air films on both sides of the assembly. The U-factor has the units of Btu/h·ft^2·°F or the SI units of W/m^2·°K and is measured through 1 square foot of glazing assembly with a temperature difference of 1°F. The U-factor can be measured at the center of the glass (excluding the edge and frame effect) or as a whole window or overall U-factor, including edge and frame losses. The total R-value is the inverse of the U-factor.*
- ***U-factor summer:*** *Measure of thermal transmittance under summer conditions, which includes solar radiation.*
- ***U-factor winter:*** *Measure of thermal transmittance under winter conditions, which includes higher wind speeds and no solar radiation (nighttime).*

The "Design Science" section provides simple equations for calculating solar heat gain and loss through building assemblies. The energy performance properties of glazing can be used to compare the energy consequences of different glazing selections. The energy implications of glazing are complex. Fortunately, the Lawrence Berkeley National Laboratory has developed a free program, called COMFEN, to analyze the energy interactions of commercial fenestration.

COMFEN is a powerful tool for quantifying and comparing fenestration design scenarios for a project (see Figure 6.25). Many variables of fenestration design can be tested, such as glazing and frame types, window sizes and locations, shading devices, and window shades. COMFEN uses EnergyPlus to run the analysis on any given design scenario; and the program has a robust library of window components to choose from, as well as the capability to create custom window components and assemblies. The energy analysis of COMFEN 4.0 provides feedback on energy use, peak loads, heat gain, thermal comfort, visual comfort, and daylighting for any given scheme, and creates charts that can compare up to four scenarios side-by-side. COMFEN can be downloaded at http://windows.lbl.gov.

One of the key factors in glazing system design is the window to wall ratio (WWR) for the building, and its different orientations. This is illustrated in the COMFEN application shown in Figure 6.25. The WWR need be no larger than necessary to provide the required level of daylight and natural ventilation. It should also be designed for quality views and connections to the outdoors. Many high-performing buildings have WWRs of 25 to 35 percent. Ultimately, the climate drives the importance of a low ratio in a building. Additionally, orientations such as east- and west-facing glazing are sensitive to the window to wall ratio because the solar gain is more difficult to control with the low morning and low evening sun angles. In addition, east and west orientations can have a higher solar insolation than the south during summer months. North glazing is least sensitive to solar heat gain but more sensitive to thermal transmittance; and in some climates, the north can afford higher WWRs. Larger north-facing windows offer increased daylight performance. South-facing windows are prime locations for daylighting windows, and view windows can be effectively shaded. For south windows, the WWR is typically governed by daylight optimization and reduction of solar radiation.

Low WWRs help mitigate climates with a large number of heating and/or cooling degree-days and climates with high solar radiation levels. Further, low WWRs help mitigate typically poor window thermal performance, including air infiltration related to glazing systems. To top it off, reduced WWRs mean smaller total window areas, which can translate into lower construction cost. This cost savings can be appropriated back into the glazing system to further enhance its thermal performance, which can ultimately lower HVAC costs.

When looking at large areas of glass, and higher window to wall ratios, the design of the glazing systems takes on even greater importance, complexity, and cost. The design goal for large glazed areas is to establish thermal properties similar to an opaque wall, which means eliminating solar heat gain and developing a very low U-factor assembly. One strategy for neutralizing large glazed areas is to use a double skin façade (see Figures 6.26 and 6.27). The advantage of this strategy is that the cavity between the inner and outer glazed walls can facilitate solar control and develop high thermal resistance. Solar control can provide complete solar shading through a variety of approaches, including shading devices, sunshades, or automated shades. The large airspace between the glazed walls is a good insulator, because the air can be warmed when exposed to solar radiation, further resisting heat flow through the assembly.

■ **FIGURE 6.25** This COMFEN screen capture shows the analysis and comparison of four different window to wall ratios for a south-facing façade in Los Angeles.

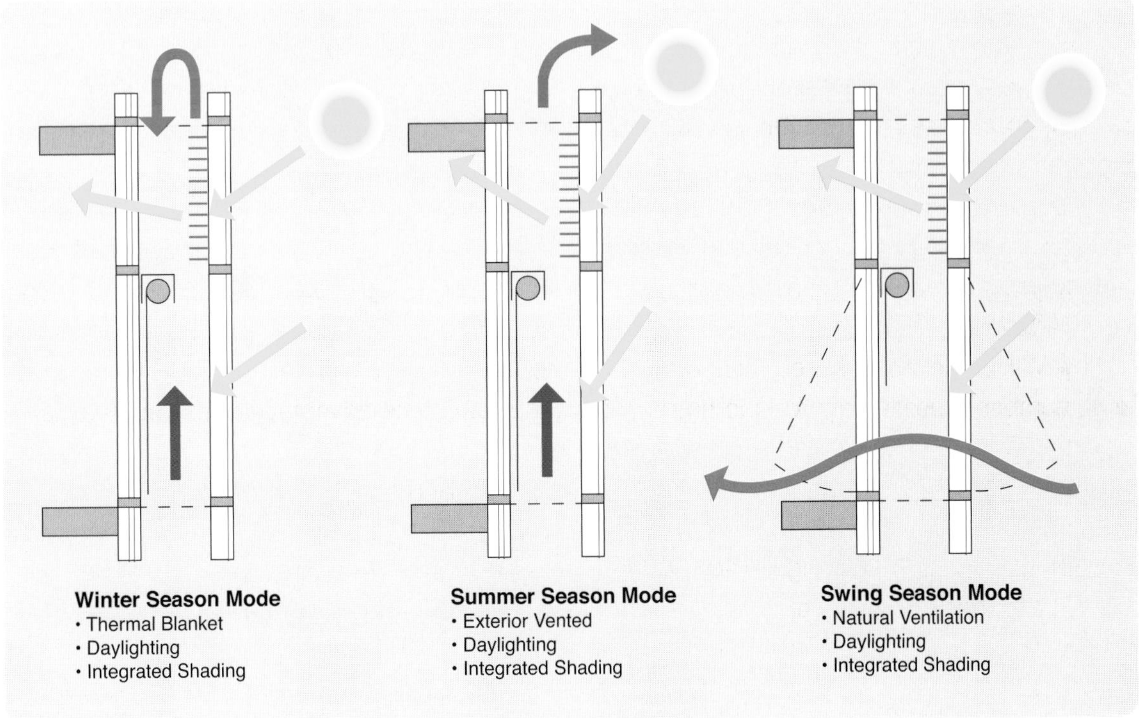

■ **FIGURE 6.26** Double Skin Façade Concept Showing Seasonal Operation.

Glazing and frame technologies are evolving quickly, in concert with higher performance standards. Insulated units are moving from double-pane to triple- or even quadruple-pane units. The panes can be created with additional layers of glass or thin films, which keep unit size and weight down. Low-e coatings are improving to be spectrally selective across a broader span of wavelengths, allowing more visible light transmittance but limiting UV and infrared radiation while improving the glazing's U-factor and solar heat gain coefficient. Materials and construction for both edge spacers and frames are improving, as well, in terms of thermal performance. Warm edge spacers are a newer generation of spacers that use less conductive material than the conventional aluminum bars. Aluminum frames, which are very commonplace in commercial buildings, are beginning to feature improved thermal break technology. The use of less conductive materials such as fiberglass is becoming more common, with notable thermal advantages.

■ **FIGURE 6.27** Double skin façades can be integrated into existing buildings to enhance energy performance and provide new architectural expression. *Photograph by Tania Salgado.*

In addition to these substantial enhancements of energy performance properties, there are a number of new and maturing technologies that are set to advance overall glazing performance and function. Many of these technologies can reduce the thermal liabilities of glazing, leading to opportunities for greater use of glazing in a building envelope.

Enhanced Glazing Technologies

- ***Chromogenic glass:*** *Also known as smart glass, chromogenic glass can change properties based on environmental stimulus. Types of chromogenic glazing include electrochromic, gasochromic, thermochromic, and photochromic.*
- ***Aerogel:*** *Aerogel is a next-generation insulation material that can allow light transmission while offering superior thermal transmittance performance. Aerogels can be applied to the airspace in a glazing unit, resulting in a translucent glass. Currently, glazing units with a U-factor up to 0.05 (R-20) are available.*
- ***Thermal mass:*** *Translucent phase-change materials can be added to glazing units to provide the benefits of thermal mass in a glazing system.*
- ***Dynamic shading:*** *Automated (and manual) shading devices can be included inside the glazing units or onto the interior or exterior of the glazing system. They offer the important advantage of providing complete shading when needed and relatively unobstructed views when shading is not needed (see Figure 6.28).*
- ***Daylighting devices:*** *A number of light-reflecting devices can be incorporated into the glazing unit or onto the interior or exterior of the glazing system. The newest generation of daylighting devices are reflective parabolic-shaped louver systems (see Figure 6.29).*
- ***Prismatic glazing:*** *Prismatic panes of glass or plastic (ribbed/sawtoothed surface) can be added to glazing units to redirect sunlight. Prismatic glazing has been historically used to redirect light deeper into a space, for improved daylight. It can also be configured to reflect high-angle sunlight while allowing lower-angle sunlight to enhance solar gain control during the summer.*
- ***Integrated photovoltaics:*** *A variety of photovoltaic technologies can be integrated into glazing systems, including crystalline panels and thin films. Various levels of transparency or opacity can be achieved, which can be tailored to shading and view requirements.*

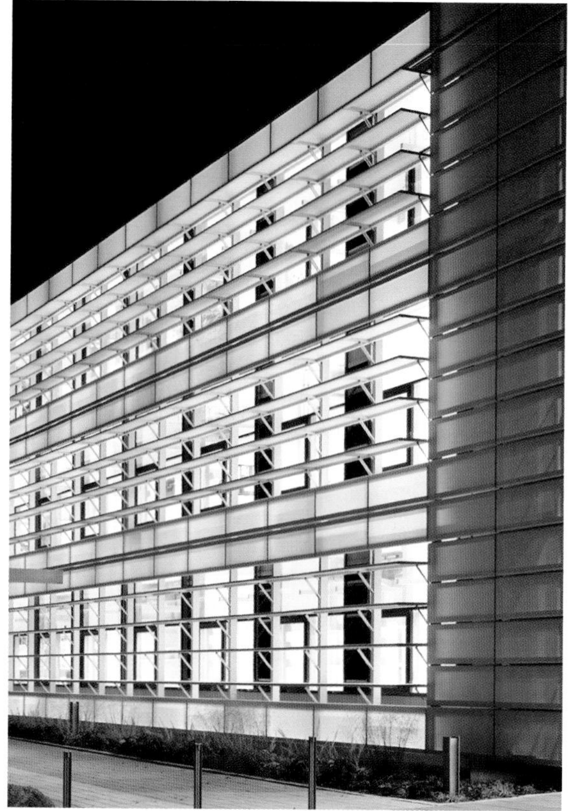

■ **FIGURE 6.28** Dynamic shading over glazing at the Science Center at Straubing, Germany, designed by Nickl & Partner. *Image courtesy of the Colt Group.*

■ **FIGURE 6.29** The LightLouver daylighting device can reflect light to the ceiling, providing enhanced daylight penetration. *Image courtesy of LightLouver LLC.*

PASSIVE STRATEGIES

Application

Passive design takes considerable integration and coordination across the entire process of delivering a net zero energy building. Furthermore, passive design strategies are tied to early architectural design decisions; therefore, the front-loaded delivery process that invests in early climate and programmatic energy research is necessary for proper building massing and orientation. Passive design cannot be effectively integrated as an afterthought; it must inform the very shape of the building. Thus, it is essential to consider mechanical and lighting systems that work with passive design strategies, and integrate this hybrid approach into the building control system. The construction of a passive building demands attention to detail, in particular, when it comes to the quality of the building envelope. Ultimately, the building operators and occupants need to understand the passive design strategies in order for them to be effective. To that end, prioritizing usability and simplicity of function, over complex control systems and onerous occupant demands, can ensure the successful application of passive strategies.

One of the primary challenges to the application of passive design strategies revolves around the fact that the free energy available from the climate is highly dynamic. Seasonal variations in climate can be significant, as can daily or even hourly shifts in weather patterns. Understanding the dynamic nature of the climate is key to designing passive strategies that are capable of responding to and optimizing the beneficial use of the climate when it is an asset, and limiting the detrimental effects of the climate when it is a liability. It is important to think of passive strategies as doing both—minimizing the negative impacts of the climate while taking advantage of its positive effects.

Developing appropriate passive design strategies for a project involves the assessment of multiple elements, starting with the climate and site, to identify the opportunities for passive strategies. The available strategies should be matched against the expected energy end uses of the project. It is also important to determine the times the strategy will be needed, as well as the times it will be available, based on the climate and site conditions.

The performance requirements of the building must be understood from multiple points of view: thermal comfort, ventilation requirements, and lighting levels. The performance requirements should also be understood in terms of how they might vary between different parts of the building program. Passive design strategies, just like active strategies, need to be designed to meet these performance requirements. But because passive strategies are dynamic, the performance requirements are best quantified as acceptable ranges within the minimum and maximum levels identified.

As noted, passive strategies are integrated into the the design process from the very beginning, and it is good practice to invoke simple and effective rules of thumb, and use appropriate tools at the formative stages of design, when decisions are being made fast and often are broad in implication. It is critical that the architect become familiar with the basic principles of passive design in order to be able to effectively inform those early design decisions. The analysis of passive strategies can increase in specificity as the design progresses, especially when the active systems are more fully developed and the energy model is refined.

Passive Strategy Types

There are many available passive strategies, as well as numerous variations and hybrids derived from common designs. Generally, passive strategies are employed to provide one or more of four basic building services: heating, cooling, ventilation, and lighting. The matrix in Figure 6.30 highlights some of the

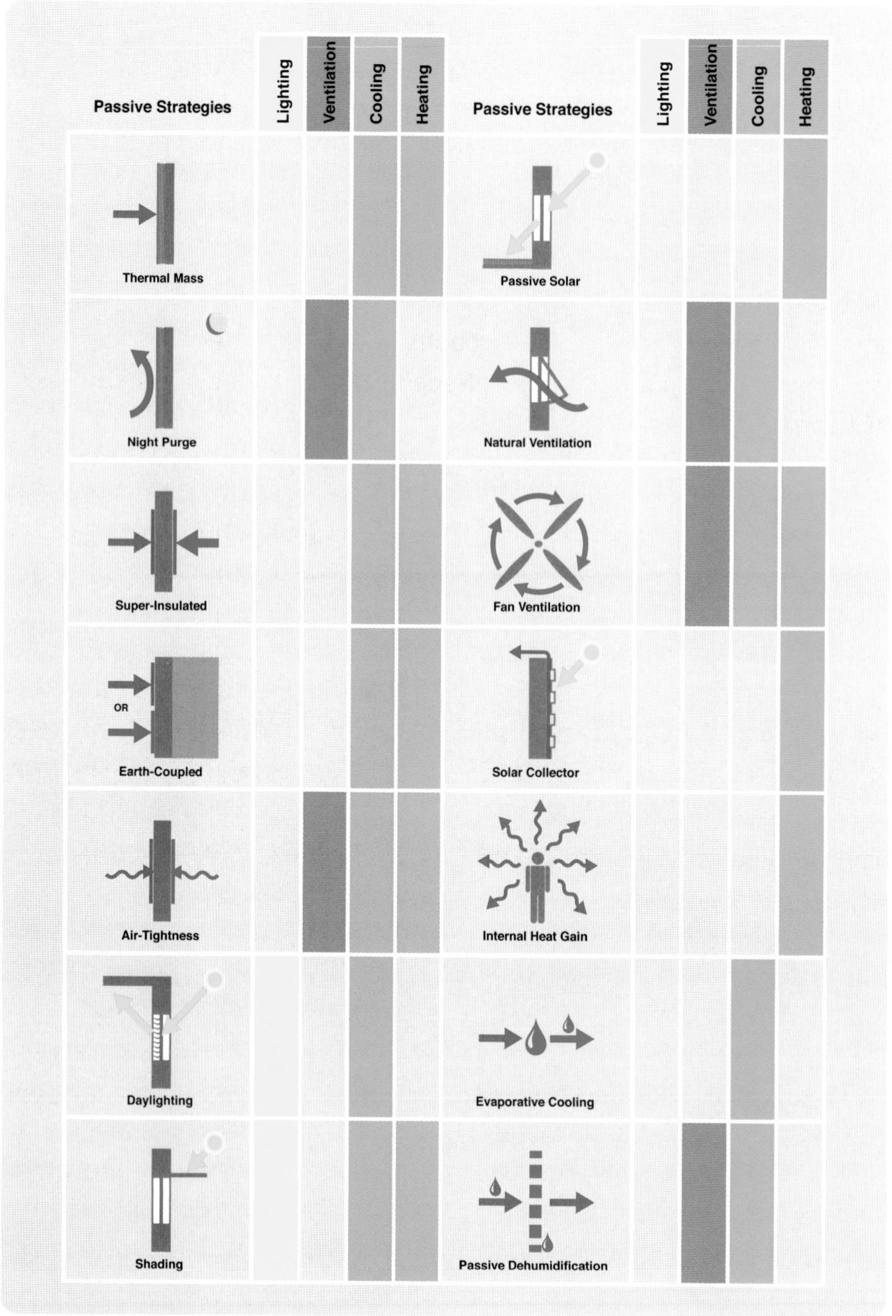

Passive Strategies	Lighting	Ventilation	Cooling	Heating
Thermal Mass			■	■
Night Purge		■	■	
Super-Insulated			■	■
Earth-Coupled			■	■
Air-Tightness		■	■	■
Daylighting	■		■	
Shading	■		■	■

Passive Strategies	Lighting	Ventilation	Cooling	Heating
Passive Solar				■
Natural Ventilation		■	■	
Fan Ventilation		■	■	■
Solar Collector				■
Internal Heat Gain				■
Evaporative Cooling			■	
Passive Dehumidification		■	■	

■ **FIGURE 6.30** Passive Design Matrix.

most common passive strategies used around the world, and classifies them in relation to the services of lighting, ventilation, cooling, and heating. It is not an exhaustive list, nor is it a list that can be applied generically to any climate. The climate and site of each project should be studied prior to evaluating potential passive design strategies.

Heating, Cooling, and Ventilation

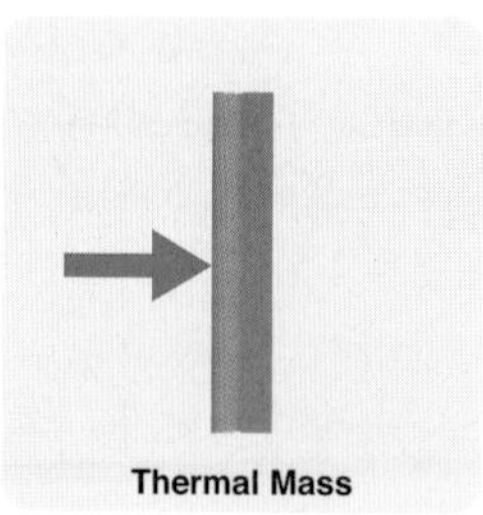

THERMAL MASS

Thermally massive materials have a high density and a high specific heat capacity. Materials such as

Passive Design Application

1. Evaluate the climate and site for available passive resources.
2. Determine building needs and performance requirements/metrics.
3. Research passive strategy options.
4. Assess available passive resources against performance requirements.
5. Test and refine building program, zoning, massing, and orientation approaches for passive design application.
6. Test and refine building envelope approaches for passive design application.
7. Develop, quantify, and integrate project-specific passive design strategies.
8. Integrate passive and active strategies.
9. Plan for occupant interaction and controls.

concrete, stone, masonry, and water have the capability to store heat, as well as release the heat back into the environment once the ambient temperature cools. This short-term thermal storage has many passive heating and cooling applications, and is implemented as part of several other passive strategies cataloged in this chapter.

One of the primary benefits of thermal mass is its capability to even out diurnal temperature swings in the interior environment. For thermal mass to be effective at regulating interior temperatures, the mass needs to be exposed to the interior environment. Thermal mass can also be used on the exterior envelope in hot climates as a means of slowing down temperature swings through the envelope.

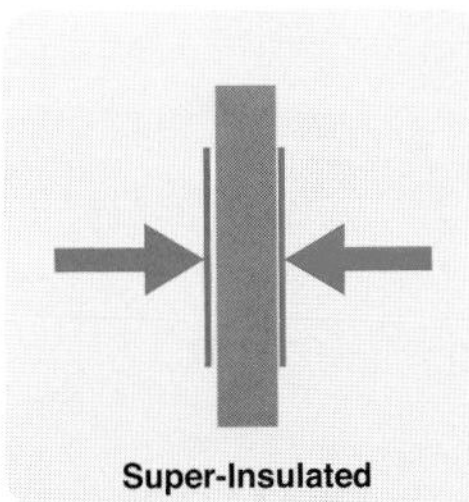

SUPERINSULATED

The design of the exterior envelope can profoundly reduce heat gains and losses through the building skin. The main approach to superinsulating is to develop very high R-value assemblies, but it is the integration and coordination of all elements of the exterior envelope that create a continuous high-integrity building skin. Reducing thermal bridges is as important as detailing high R-value components and assemblies. Superinsulating the envelope is vital in cold climates with high heating energy demands. It can also play a role in milder climates, for controlling the thermal exchange with the environment and manipulating the building's balance point temperature. (The "Building Envelope" section earlier in the chapter provides guidance on thermal transmittance and superinsulation of the building.)

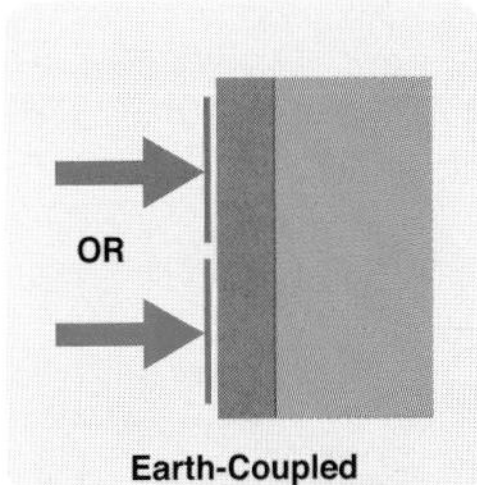

EARTH-COUPLED

The earth is a massive heat sink that can be leveraged for relatively consistent temperatures year-round. In fact, the temperatures of the earth are cooler than air temperatures during the summer, and warmer than air temperatures in the winter. Ground temperatures begin to stabilize as a function of soil depth beneath the surface. At some point, the temperature will be consistent year-round and approximately equal to the average annual air temperature of the location. The annual outside temperature extremes affect ground temperatures, as do the characteristics of the soil and ground surface.

Earth-coupling, or earth-sheltering, by burying or berming the building into the earth, can enable the building to take advantage of milder temperature differences between the interior and exterior. This can be part of a strategy to reduce thermal transmission into the building. Earth-coupling can also be used to cool spaces. Remote earth-coupling, achieved by creating long, buried earth tubes, is another way of leveraging ground temperature to cool air before entering a building. At the same time, care must be taken to address the potential liabilities of earth-coupling, such as water and moisture issues, structural issues, and the introduction of radon gas.

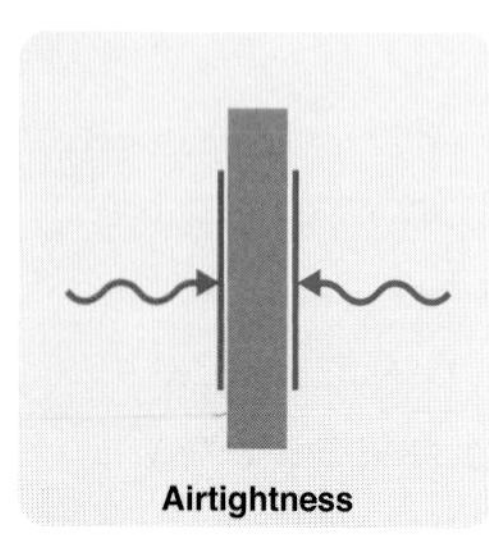
Airtightness

AIRTIGHTNESS

Airtightness goes hand in hand with superinsulating the building envelope. Eliminating uncontrolled air exchanges with the exterior environment is a key part of neutralizing the façade. (The "Building Envelope" section of this chapter also provides guidance on airtightness.)

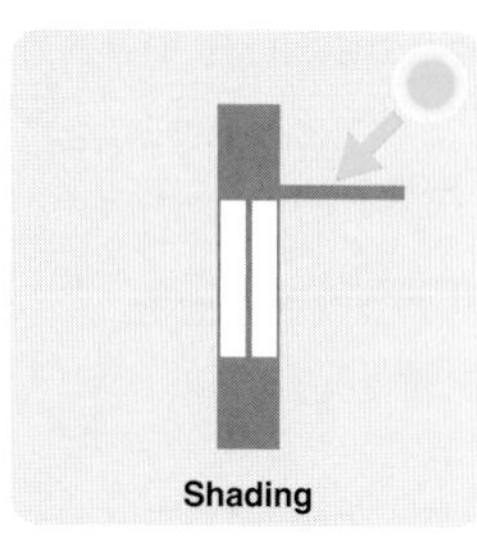
Shading

SHADING

Shading is one of the most basic and time-tested passive cooling strategies there is. Heat avoidance should always be the first priority for cooling. Shading is highly climate- and building-specific, meaning that shading design should respond to the seasonal cooling needs of a building, the building's orientation, and the sun's path throughout the year. Because glazing is the largest contributor to solar radiation gain, shading is primarily designed with the glazing systems. But shading also is integrated with many other passive strategies, such as daylighting, and should be implemented in a way that allows the daylighting techniques to remain fully functional year-round.

Shading the building and shading as an element of a site's microclimate are also valuable passive cooling strategies. Shading a building can be accomplished in a wide variety of ways; the approach chosen often becomes a part of the final architectural expression.

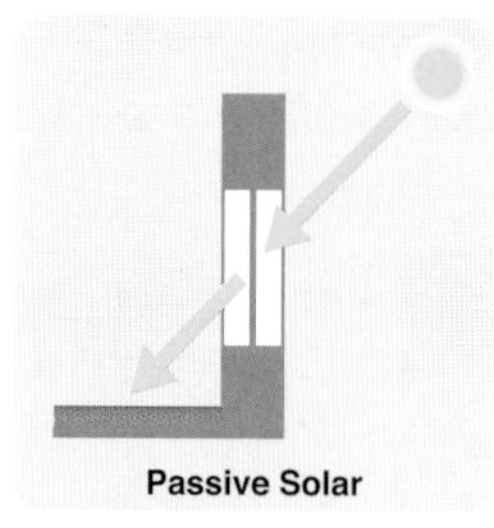
Passive Solar

PASSIVE SOLAR

The sun can be used to power and light the building; it can also be used to heat the building. Passive solar heat is common in sustainable residential construction, but not often incorporated into commercial projects. The reason is that commercial buildings tend to be large, internal-load-dominated, and in cooling mode much of the year. Nevertheless, passive architecture with higher exterior wall area to floor area ratios and reduced internal loads can result in skin-load-dominated buildings with modest internal gains, and in certain climates can have a substantial heating season.

Integrating passive solar techniques requires special attention, to avoid overheating, and should be carefully coordinated with thermal zoning strategies. Thermal mass is an important part of the passive solar strategy, as the space will need thermal storage. Passive solar can be used directly to heat a space, or can be used indirectly, such as with a Trombe wall in the space. It may also be possible to integrate remote thermal storage, such as a sunroom or a thermal labyrinth to collect and store heat for controlled distribution to other parts of the building.

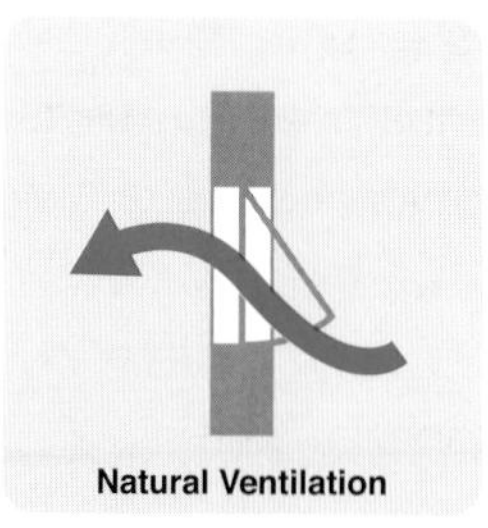
Natural Ventilation

NATURAL VENTILATION

Natural ventilation is a simple and effective means of providing cooling and fresh outside air to building occupants. Operable windows were once commonplace in commercial buildings, but now are quite rare. Today's commercial buildings generally have fully engineered environments, and operable windows interfere with the operation of many common air-based HVAC systems. Nevertheless, natural ventilation can work with many low-energy HVAC strategies, such as evaporative cooling, radiant cooling, and decoupled ventilation systems.

Natural ventilation is an effective cooling strategy whenever the building is in cooling mode and the outside air temperature is cool enough that it does not add heat gain to the space. It requires the motion of air through the building to produce a cooling effect, either for occupants as comfort ventilation or for the building structure as night purging. Achieving this calls for careful design of the building, to allow for appropriate ventilation paths using techniques such as cross ventilation and stack ventilation that rely on wind pressure and air temperature differences to move air. Operable windows are the most common technique, but other strategies also are possible to employ, such as vents and structured wind towers and solar chimneys. Natural ventilation is an important thermal comfort amenity for occupants, allowing for fresh air and control of their immediate environment.

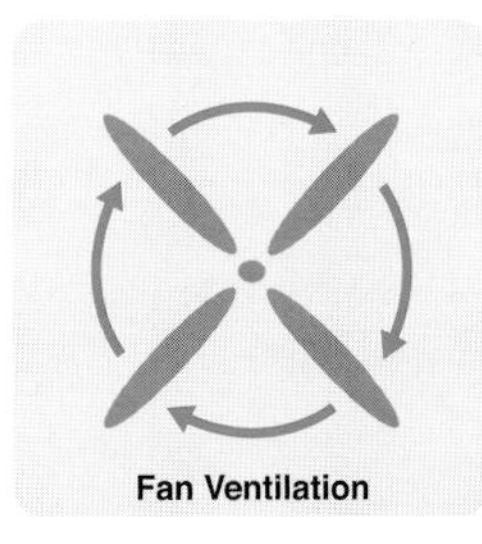

FAN VENTILATION

Although fan ventilation requires an energy input to function, it is a very low-energy way to create comfort and supplement natural ventilation techniques. Adequate wind speeds may not always be available for natural ventilation and night purging, and fans can extend the times when these strategies are effective. Fans help to control and maintain air movement, providing a cooling effect through increased evaporation. Fans can also be used to destratify air in tall spaces, to assist in heating by keeping heated air from quickly stratifying at the ceiling and exhausting through the return air system.

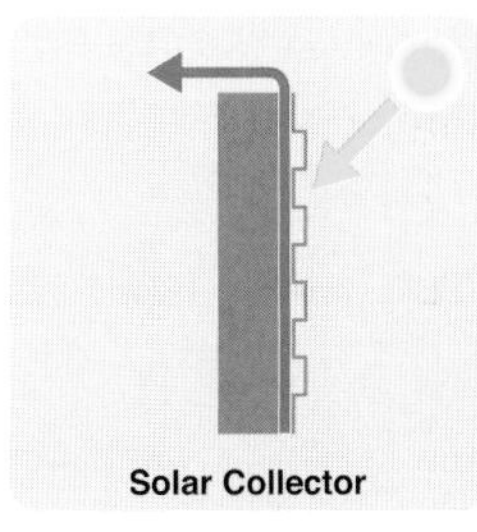

SOLAR COLLECTOR

Transpired solar collectors are a cost-effective technique for passively preheating outside air for use in a building's ventilation or heating system. A transpired solar collector consists of a corrugated dark metal panel with small perforations. It is typically oriented to the south, to optimize solar gain, while the metal panels are mounted with an air gap between the metal panel and the primary exterior wall of the building. Air is drawn into the small perforations and is heated by solar radiation. The preheated air can then be used for heating of ventilation air. As the heated air in the collector rises, it is common to collect the air at the top of the building; however, fans can be used to pull the air to any point of collection. During cooling periods, the transpired solar collector is vented to the outside at the top.

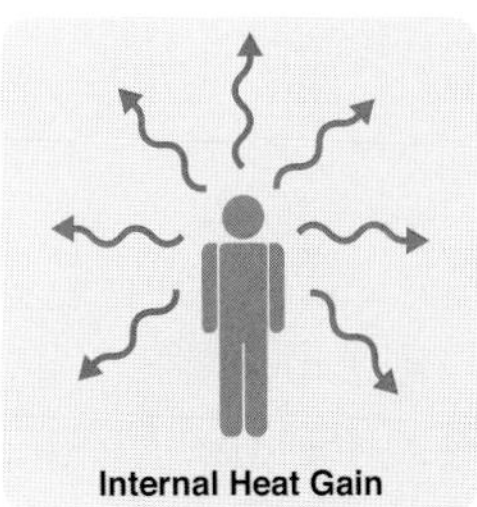

INTERNAL HEAT GAIN

Every building has internal heat gains from people, lighting, and equipment. Often, these heat gains become cooling loads. However, internal heat gains are not always a liability. When the building is in heating mode, the internal heat gain can be a useful strategy for passive heating, especially when paired with superinsulated and airtight building enclosures to retain the heat gain. With a high-quality building envelope, the heating loads will be very small, and so might largely be addressed by the internal heat gain of the building. This technique can be enhanced by recovering heat from return air through a heat recovery ventilation system. Of course, lighting and equipment loads must be aggressively reduced first, with the objective of putting any waste heat to beneficial use.

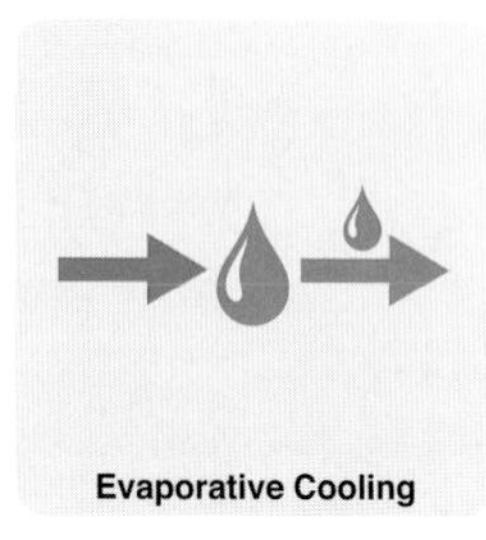

EVAPORATIVE COOLING

Evaporative cooling is effective in hot, dry climates with a large dry bulb depression (the difference between dry bulb and wet bulb temperature). Water is evaporated into a supply of outside air, and the process converts sensible heat in the air to latent heat as the water evaporates and is absorbed into the air. The reduction in sensible heat results in a lower temperature (it can approach the wet bulb temperature). The increase in latent heat adds humidity to the air.

Evaporative cooling can be a low-energy approach to mechanical cooling (as discussed in Chapter 7). It can also be used to passively cool spaces through the implementation of a cool tower, which introduces water to outside air at the top of a vented tower. The cool air then drops into the space below.

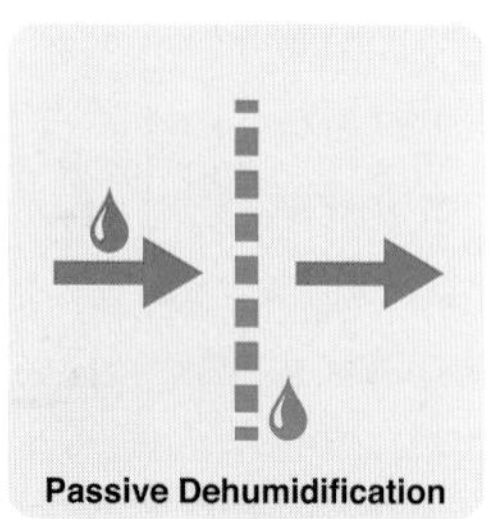

PASSIVE DEHUMIDIFICATION

In climates with high humidity, the humidity itself prevents thermal comfort and requires additional energy to address. Just as it is possible to passively cool hot dry air though the evaporation of water and addition of humidity, it is likewise possible to passively remove humidity from the air using a dessicant. The removal of moisture adds sensible heat while reducing latent heat, so the air temperature rises as the humidity decreases. Silica gel is a common dessicant, used in a variety of moisture-absorbing applications. The dessicant has to be dried after each cycle of dehumidification, however, ideally through a process that uses solar or waste heat. Passive dessicant dehumidification is still relatively uncommon, , but interest is growing in the technique.

Daylighting

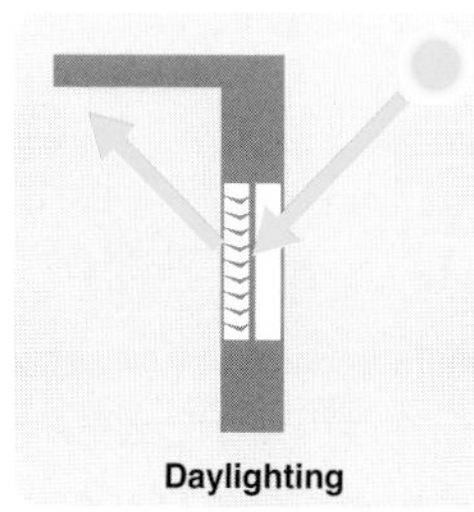

LIGHT AND NET ZERO ENERGY ARCHITECTURE

Light, and specifically daylight, has been the muse of many great architects. Alvar Aalto and Louis Kahn (see Figure 6.31), among others, spent their careers mastering the interaction of light and architecture. The quality of sunlight varies across the earth, and in its unique and dynamic properties adds visual beauty and complexity to architecture.

Daylight is a powerful architectural form driver for net zero energy architecture. It serves a poetic purpose, rendering the built form beautiful, at the same time it providing high-quality light to meet the functional needs of the architecture. To satisfy both beauty and utility, the building's orientation, massing, color, envelope, and interior planning all must be motivated by a deliberate response to daylight. The design of the building should be inspired as much by the response to the climate as it is by the site and the program. The architecture is the shaping of space, so it is optimized for daylight. The objective is to harness the exterior illumination from the sun, the sky, and reflected surfaces—in all its highly dynamic nature—to the best benefit of interior space illumination. The architecture is the interface between the natural lighting resource and the lighting need. In this way, architecture becomes the opening, the filter, the reflector, the diffuser, and the shaper of daylight.

Net zero energy architecture not only controls daylight for beauty and utility, it leverages daylight for energy. A net zero energy building hums to life as the first morning ray of sunlight strikes the building. The sun's energy provides more than light; it also can generate electricity and useful heat. Daylighting is more than free energy; it is a fundamental building block for energy use reduction in net zero energy buildings. This is an important distinguishing point about net zero energy buildings: They must be designed to leverage daylighting as a key energy reduction strategy. The reality of most daylit buildings is that the daylighting strategies do not lead to energy savings, because they are not successfully integrated into the architecture and the lighting systems and controls.

■ **FIGURE 6.31** The Kimball Art Museum, by Louis Kahn. *Credit: Lisette Lebaillif—Lebaillif Photography.*

Daylighting is one of the most important strategies for net zero energy buildings because, when done correctly, it can lead to substantial energy savings. Proper daylighting precipitates conditions whereby artificial lights can be turned off or dimmed. Proper daylighting also includes a control system to measure daylight and control artificial lighting levels accordingly.

Daylighting has many cascading benefits, as well. When the lights are turned down or off, large amounts of lighting energy will be saved. In addition, when done correctly, daylight provides cool light, compared to artificial light, so using daylight effectively in place of artificial lighting can reduce both the internal heat gain in a space and the energy to cool it. In comparison to fluorescent lighting, which produces roughly three-quarters heat and one-quarter light, daylighting can provide three-quarters light with only one-quarter heat.

According to the Department of Energy's *2009 Building Energy Data Book,* for energy end uses for commercial buildings across the United States, lighting is the second-highest energy end use, at an average of 16.9 percent of total building energy use. Lighting is an end use consistent across commercial building types and climate zones. Since virtually all buildings across all climate zones use lighting, daylighting can be considered for most every project.

SIDELIGHTING

Sidelighting is the technique of bringing daylight into a space through apertures in an exterior wall. It is a commonly used strategy because windows are also provided for views, and many spaces in a building have access to an exterior window. For most applications,

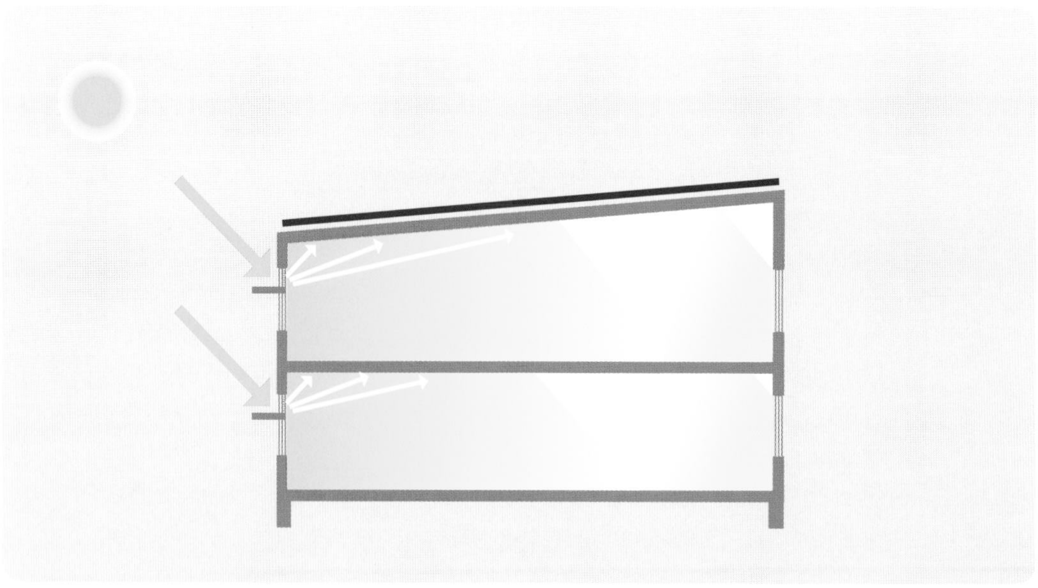

■ **FIGURE 6.32** Daylighting—Sidelighting.

sidelighting should be reflected to the ceiling or diffused, to prevent glare and direct sunbeam penetration (see Figure 6.32). Sidelighting strategies should seek to optimize daylight quality while reducing solar heat gain.

Building orientation has a dramatic impact on the techniques and successful application of sidelighting. East- and west-facing orientations are the most challenging because low morning and evening sun angles are difficult to control. The west orientation can contribute unwanted heat gains during the evening hours. The south and north are ideal orientations for sidelighting applications. The north (for the northern hemisphere) provides a diffuse, high-quality light (see Figure 6.33). Typically, north orientations do not need additional solar shading or control. The south provides controllable direct sun. The sun in the southern sky can be manipulated effectively by installing shading and light-reflecting devices. For a south-oriented sidelighting application, it is best to divide windows into view windows that are shaded to prevent solar heat gain, and daylight windows that always allow daylight to enter and be reflected toward the ceiling. Daylight windows need to be located high on the wall, to direct light toward the ceiling and prevent glare. High ceilings and open interior spaces benefit sidelighting applications.

■ **FIGURE 6.33** Sidelighting in a North Zone at the DOE/NREL Research Support Facility. *Image courtesy of RNL; photograph by Ron Pollard.*

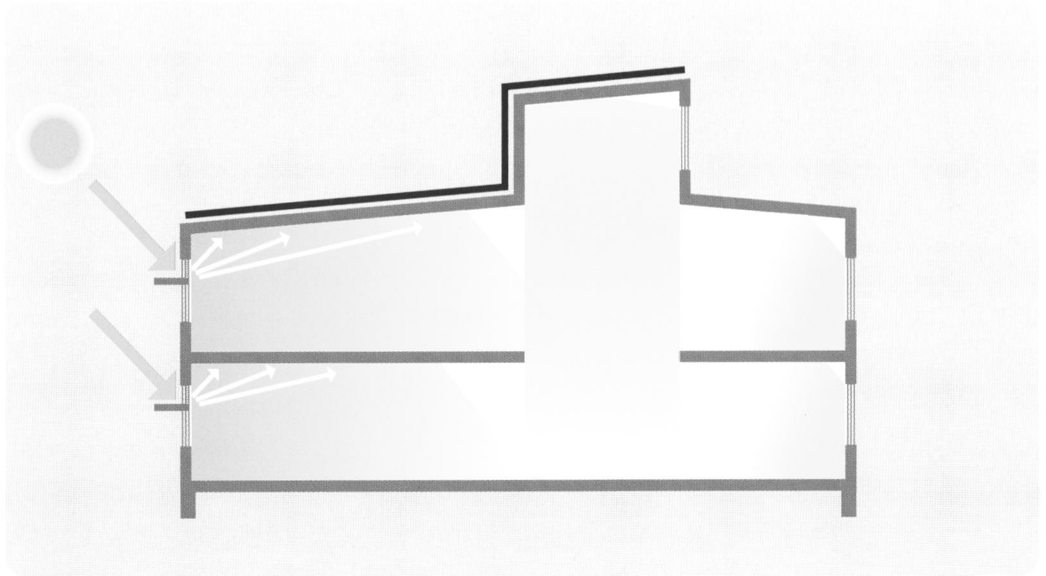

■ **FIGURE 6.34** Daylighting—Toplighting with Sidelighting.

TOPLIGHTING

Toplighting is a technique to bring daylight into a space from apertures on the roof. It is effective for spaces directly below roofs; but toplighting can also contribute to lower floor levels through the use of atriums, light wells, or other devices. Toplighting can distribute daylight evenly year-round, and can be particularly effective for deep floor plates (see Figures 6.34 and 6.35).

Toplighting can include glazed units that are horizontal, tilted, or vertical. Typical techniques include skylights, tubular devices, roof monitors, and clerestories. Control of direct sunbeam and solar gain is especially important in toplighting applications. Skylights, tubular devices, and horizontal glazing are generally not orientation-specific, whereas any tilted or horizontal glazing should be oriented according to the considerations described previously for sidelighting applications. Horizontal or tilted glazing systems may be distinctly problematic because high sun angles during the summer can allow intense direct-beam penetration. Toplighting applications often utilize translucent and insulated glazing units or skylights to diffuse the daylight and prevent heat loss. For clear glazing applications, reflecting and shading elements can be incorporated for solar control and light distribution. In climates with a predominantly overcast sky, toplighting (in particular, with a horizontal component) can be effective, because the exterior light is already diffuse and is brightest at the sky's zenith.

■ **FIGURE 6.35** Toplighting in the gymnasium of the Kiowa County Schools in Greensburg. *Image courtesy of BNIM; photograph © 2010, Assassi.*

DAYLIGHT DEVICES

An increasingly broad array of daylighting devices are available on the market today, aimed at solving many of the typical daylighting challenges faced in commercial buildings. A daylight device is an apparatus that manipulates and controls the delivery of daylight to enhance its performance or to distribute it a specific way or to a specific space.

Some daylight devices simply reflect or redistribute incoming daylight into a space. For example, light shelves are commonly used to bounce incoming light onto the ceiling and prevent direct sunbeams from penetrating occupied spaces. An improvement in the performance of a light shelf can be gained by setting a reflective louvered device into the entire frame or glazing unit of the daylighting window. The louvers are parabolic in shape and specular, to reflect light deep into a space; the spacing of the louver blades creates a cutoff for direct sunbeam penetration.

Daylighting devices can also be used to transport light further into a building or to different spaces. Mirrorlike reflective light pipes, ducts, and tubes can transport light reasonable distances, and even allow bends in the tube. The end of the light tube is fitted with a lens or fixture to distribute the light and limit glare. Tubular daylighting devices are one of the most common applications, featuring small circular skylights mounted on the roof.

Daylight can also be transported through fiber optics. In this case, sunlight is collected by an exterior receiver and distributed into fiber-optic cables, which feed and illuminate special fixtures. The fiber-optic cables are small and flexible and can be installed virtually anywhere in a building.

DAYLIGHT ZONING

Daylight zoning is a useful concept when evaluating different orientation, massing, and envelope options. Daylighting zones can be used to plan a range of daylighting design parameters, including lighting level zones, control zones, and daylight application or strategy zones. Zones can be categorized as fully daylit, partially daylit, and nondaylit. Thinking in terms of daylight zones during the early design phases is instrumental in successfully integrating daylighting into a net zero energy project.

The building program can be analyzed for lighting requirements based on space type and programmed activities. It may be beneficial to group together program elements with similar lighting level requirements. Be sure to focus primarily on overall illumination and ambient light, because certain task light functions are more difficult to provide with daylight. Also consider the appropriateness of each space for the use of daylight. Certain space types and uses will require special treatment, and may have the need for a high degree of control, or to darken the space. It is common to prioritize daylighting in regularly occupied spaces because of the human health benefits, but also because occupancy levels will require that lights stay on most of the day. Many nonregularly occupied spaces, such as storage rooms and restrooms, can also benefit from daylighting. However, these spaces can also save energy through occupancy controls; and the lights can remain off most of the time. When there are zones in the building that are challenging to daylight, these types of nonregularly occupied spaces should be located within those limited or nondaylit zones.

The more zones in a building that can be fully daylit, the greater the potential for energy savings from daylighting. With that in mind, designing with the goal of fully daylighting all zones is a good starting point (see Figure 6.36). In using daylight zones to design building massing and spaces, it is beneficial to consider how various daylighting strategies will either impact or create the actual zones. Daylight modeling is an ideal way to test a variety of daylighting strategies and determine effective zoning within the building. Daylight modeling can begin very simply, by studying basic massing ideas, and then continue with more refined studies of glazing sizes and glass types, to determine the details of the strategy.

Ultimately, daylight analysis will define and quantify the zones. However, there are some rules of thumb to follow in regard to establishing daylight zones, based on sidelighting and toplighting applications.

Sidelighting zones typically are not very deep, because it is difficult to bring daylight from exterior windows deep into a space. Typical south-facing zones are the deepest, typically in the 15- to 20-foot range. South zone depth can be greatly extended with effective daylight devices such as reflective louver devices, depending on the time of year and weather conditions. Typical north-facing zones are shallow and in the 10- to 15-foot range. See Figure 6.37. During overcast sky conditions, the zones are generally uniform, regardless of orientation.

Toplighting is very flexible, capable of creating zones of any depth, provided the zones are directly below the toplighting applications. Atriums and light wells can create interior daylight zones below them. Atriums also can be used to daylight horizontally adjacent spaces, but these zones can be narrow because the light reflected down an atrium becomes more diffuse and more challenging to redirect into adjacent spaces.

There are many building design variables that influence the depth of a daylight zone, including daylight aperture size, glazing visible light transmittance, window position, ceiling height, and color and reflectance of interior and exterior surfaces. The introduction of walls and high partitions can limit the depth of daylight zones,

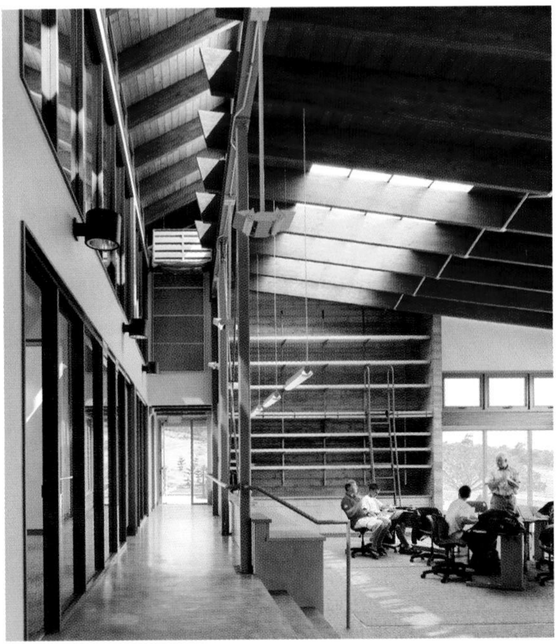

■ **FIGURE 6.36** Daylit interior of the net zero energy Hawaii Preparatory Energy Lab with sidelighting and toplighting zones. *Image courtesy of Buro Happold and Flansburgh Architects; photograph by Matthew Millman.*

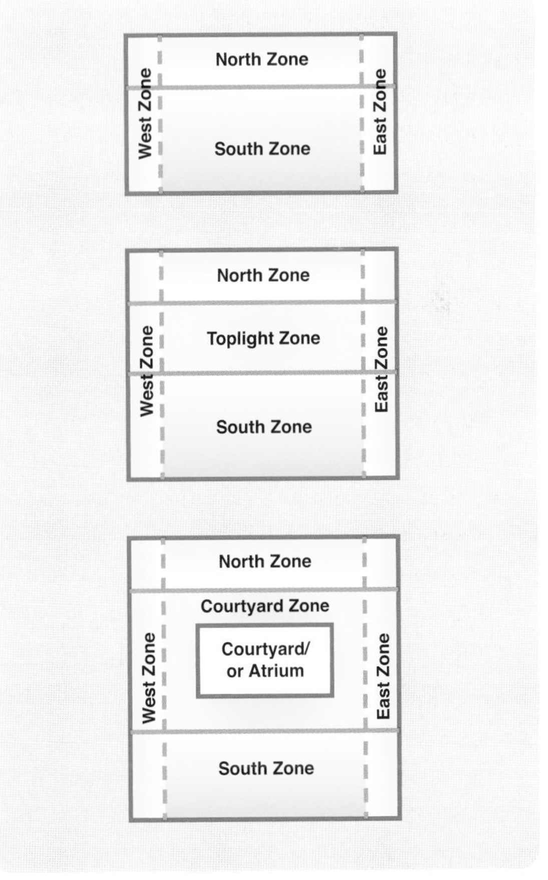

■ **FIGURE 6.37** Typical Daylighting Zoning Strategies.

as well. In sidelight applications, it can be very challenging to extend a daylight zone past a row of private offices along an exterior wall. Full or partially glazed office walls can help achieve this objective. A north sidelight zone is often the ideal location for private offices because it is typically the narrowest zone. The south zone is often ideal for open areas, where the daylight zone can be extended through the use of daylight devices, and remain unimpeded by internal partitions.

CONTROLS AND SENSORS

For daylighting to conserve energy, provisions must be made to turn off or dim the artificial lights when daylight is present. The key to daylight control is the use of sensors. These devices can be placed within the space being controlled or tied to a global exterior sensor that measures available daylight. Depending on the sensor reading and the control setting for illumination levels, the daylight controls will turn off/on, step down/up, or dim lighting fixtures. Typically, lighting in well-daylit zones, such as directly adjacent to south sidelighting applications, may need only simple switching or stepping controls. Zones with more daylight variation may be better served by dimming controls.

The daylight control and sensor must be integrated into the overall daylight controls for the lighting zones, and coordinated with other functions such as vacancy sensors and lighting schedules. Daylight sensors and controls are rapidly advancing in reliability, user-friendliness, and cost-effectiveness. All daylit zones need to be integrated with the lighting controls system to produce an effective energy reduction strategy.

Zones with similar lighting levels, occupancy rates, programs, and daylighting strategies are good choices for organizing lighting control zones. Since the daylighting controls are based on input from daylight sensors, creating control zones with similar daylight conditions yields strong synergies. Organizing control zones across spaces with different daylight conditions will be difficult to control effectively.

Future Trends

The future of passive design will see the evolution of dynamic façades and roofs. The potential for a building to adapt dynamically to changes in weather promises major advances in the way that architecture can take advantage of the free energy of the climate, compared to a more static, fixed approach. After all, seasonal, if not daily, weather conditions are highly dynamic. Dynamic façades and roofs will allow control over the way the exterior envelope interfaces with the climate, by adjusting elements such as shading, transparency, thermal transmittance, and ventilation openings. Further, dynamic façades and roofs can allow for active photovoltaic systems that incorporate tracking systems that adjust to follow the sun, greatly boosting energy generation (see Figure 6.38).

The two primary challenges of incorporating dynamic façades and roofs are the control of the system and the long-term maintenance that these types of technologies may require. System control can be very simple—manual, and accomplished by the occupants themselves in response to the environment or some other form of occupant feedback display. Many relatively static, passive technologies utilize simple occupant controls such opening and closing a window, shade, or shutter. This idea can be taken further by adding larger sliding or opening panels on the inside or outside of the façade. It can be taken further still by motorizing the operation, while allowing occupants to maintain control of the operation. Computerizing the system control yields the best optimization, however, because

■ **FIGURE 6.38** Dynamic BIPV wall moves 7.5 degrees every 30 minutes, tracking the sun at the EWE Arena in Oldenburg, Germany; designed by ASP Architekten. *Image courtesy of the Colt Group.*

the movement of the system can happen in real time, according to weather and building automation system data. Full automation may also offer the most convenience to occupants, while giving them override capabilities so the building can be customized to meet their needs.

The increase in automation does, however, come with a concomitant increase in complexity; thus, while greater automation offers important advantages, it has the disadvantage of potentially causing more system problems and maintenance issues. These are technological hurdles that can be overcome as dynamic façades and roofs become more commonplace and reliable (see Figures 6.39 and 6.40). Further, as dynamic façade and roof elements become capable of reducing the necessity for mechanical equipment in the building, the result could be a net decrease in maintenance requirements overall for buildings.

Already, phase-change materials and property-changing technologies are being used to develop the next generation of climate-responsive materials and components. This type of technology is being applied to smart glazing, to create electrochromic, gasochromic, photochromic, and thermochromic glass that can change properties in response to an environmental input.

Chromogenic Glass

- Electrochromic Glass
  - Active
  - Responds to low-voltage electrical charge
- Gasochromic Glass
  - Active
  - Responds to flow of hydrogen gas
- Photochromic Glass
  - Passive
  - Responds to exterior light level
- Thermochromic Glass
  - Passive
  - Responds to exterior temperature of glass

Electrochromic glass is, to date, the most suitable for architectural applications, and is the most advanced of the chromogenic glass technologies in the construction materials market. Electrochromic glass uses a low-voltage electrical charge to change the state of lithium or hydrogen ions, moving them from a storage layer to an electrochromic layer (such as tungsten oxide), to change the color and tint of glass (see Figure 6.41). The charge is conducted by two opposing, transparent, conducting layers, all within the glazing unit. The electrical charge can be switched on and off by the occupants, making it an active technology. It can also be set up to be triggered by a light-level sensor,

■ **FIGURE 6.39** Dynamic glass-louvered façade in closed position at Grunewald, in Bocholt, Germany; designed by Atelier Jörg Rügemer. *Image courtesy of the Colt Group.*

■ **FIGURE 6.40** Dynamic glass-louvered façade in open position at Grunewald, in Bocholt, Germany; designed by Atelier Jörg Rügemer. *Image courtesy of the Colt Group.*

making it function passively when responding directly to either exterior temperature or light levels. The solar heat gain coefficient can range from 0.48 when clear to 0.09 when tinted, according to one of the leading manufacturers of electrochromic glass. The units are available in double- or triple-glazed insulated units.

Phase-change materials are being incorporated into common building materials such as drywall, plaster, concrete blocks, and glazing;

there are also special membranes encapsulated with phase-change materials that can be applied within building assemblies. This technology holds great promise because it allows for the benefits of the important passive design strategy of thermal mass through the use of common building materials, rather than the traditional massive materials of concrete, masonry, and stone. Phase-change materials, typically wax- or salt-based, can absorb thermal energy and then release it later. When materials change phase, they absorb latent heat, while their temperature remains constant. Water is the classic phase-change material, remaining at its melting point temperature of 32°F while it either freezes into ice or melts into water. Ideal phase-change materials for buildings have a melting point similar to the upper comfort zone temperature of the interior.

■ **FIGURE 6.41** Sage electrochromic glass at the DOE/NREL Research Support Facility changes from tinted to clear. *Image courtesy of RNL; photograph by Frank Ooms.*

EE CHAPTER 7
ENERGY-EFFICIENT BUILDING SYSTEMS

ACTIVE SYSTEMS

The design of energy-efficient building systems or the active systems for a net zero energy project is completed in concert with the passive design strategies and climate-responsive architecture, as discussed in Chapters 5 and 6. The passive strategies serve as the foundation for heating, cooling, ventilation, and lighting for a project. Active systems are also integrated with the design of on-site renewable energy systems, addressed in Chapter 8.

For most commercial building types, we cannot expect climate-responsive architecture with passive strategies to meet all the desired interior functions of light, comfort, air quality, and hot water all the time. Active systems for lighting, heating ventilation and air conditioning (HVAC), and plumbing are required to provide these functions when passive strategies alone are insufficient.

Energy use from these active systems, referred to by the term *regulated energy use*, represents between 50 and 75 percent of energy in buildings. The remainder of energy use is referred to as *plug load energy* or *process energy* (addressed in Chapter 10). The term *regulated energy* use comes from the fact that these active systems have historically been regulated by electrical, mechanical, plumbing, fire, energy, and building codes, whereas plug load and process equipment have remained outside the scope of regulatory codes and permitting processes.

For a net zero energy project, it is necessary to dramatically reduce energy use by active systems. The target should be overall reduction of regulated energy use by 40 to 60 percent, compared to conventional practice or a CBECS baseline building, to make a net zero energy project cost-effective. To provide guidance on achieving this energy use reduction, this chapter presents general concepts, promising design strategies, and pitfall considerations for low-energy active systems.

Integration with Passive Architecture

THE CYCLING ANALOGY

Consider a bicyclist riding a path between hilltops. Starting down the first hill, the bicyclist instinctively tucks into the most aerodynamic and compact position to minimize the air drag that will slow her down as she picks up speed. The bicyclist looks up the second hill and thinks, "How far can I get up that slope before I have to start pedaling?" She reaches maximum speed at the bottom of the hill and starts to slow down as the path heads up the second hill. While the bicycle is still moving at a comfortable pedaling speed, she starts pedaling, first in high gear, then in increasingly lower gears to get to the top

Like this bicyclist getting the most out of gravity for her bike ride, active systems, to conserve energy, need to be secondary to and integrated with passive systems. The point is to use energy-consuming systems less of the time, and less power when they are on.

For the bicyclist, it is natural to minimize her energy use by prioritizing her passive resource and effectively integrating her active work; but in designing a building, this integration requires additional attention. Whereas an experienced bicyclist will not ride the brakes while going downhill, is not uncommon for a building to use mechanical cooling when it is colder outside than inside to handle solar and internal heat gain. Likewise, it would be senseless for the bicyclist to pedal frantically while the bike was cruising at top speed; but buildings frequently have lights on when there is plenty of sunlight in the space. Knowing "when to start pedaling" is perhaps the biggest challenge for building systems.

RELATIONSHIP OF PASSIVE AND ACTIVE SYSTEMS

A primary role of passive design strategies is in load avoidance, such as shading to reduce cooling load, or superinsulating a building envelope to reduce heating load. However, passive strategies also harness free energy from the climate to provide the services to heat, cool, ventilate, and light passively. Classic examples include daylighting, thermal mass, and natural ventilation. From a truly integrated perspective, the passive performance of the building architecture should be considered the first operating mode of the building systems. Active strategies must work with and complement passive strategies. As described in Chapter 6, this blending of passive and active systems should be typical for low-energy and net zero energy buildings; it leads to hybrid building systems. A mixed-mode building is a good example of utilizing a hybrid system approach; it uses both natural ventilation and active cooling and ventilation (see Figure 7.1).

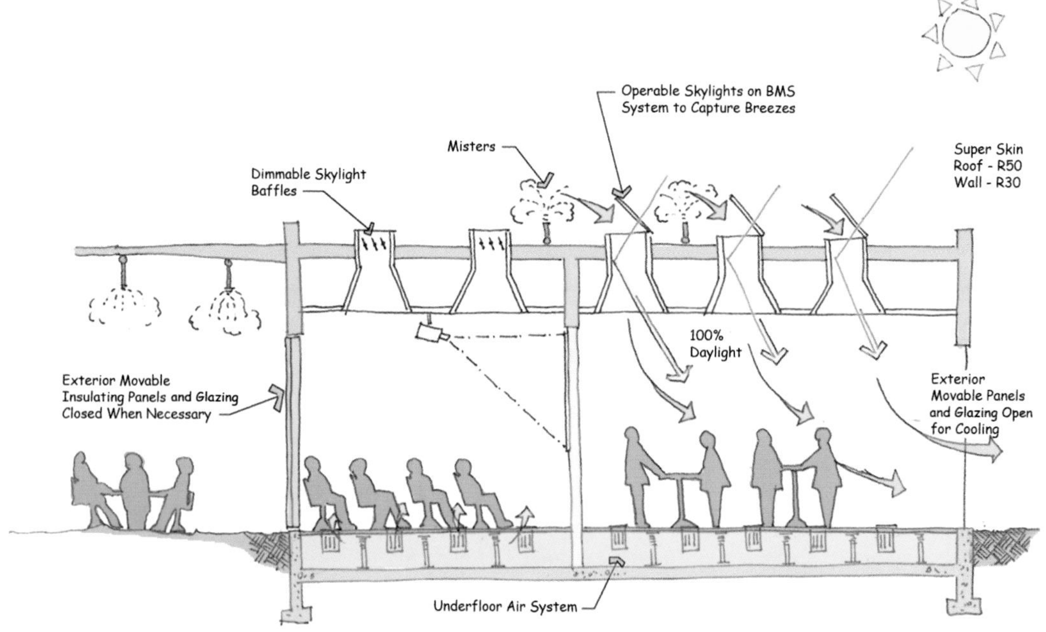

■ **FIGURE 7.1** Mixed-mode buildings can provide cooling and ventilation by natural ventilation and mechanical conditioning. *Image courtesy of Stantec Consulting Services Inc., drawing by Jim Burns.*

The successful introduction of passive design strategies has many notable implications for building design. Passive strategies may influence massing, building depth, orientation, and envelope design, all of which can move a building from internal-load dominated to skin-load dominated. The building's balance point temperature may shift as well. Certainly, thermal loads will be significantly reduced. In short, passive design changes the way the building behaves thermally. This means the active systems must be tailored to this new set of thermal design circumstances, opening the door to a wide range of innovative and low-energy solutions.

Perhaps the greatest benefit of integrating active systems with passive strategies is that the resulting reduced energy loads lead to more efficient options for the active system selection. A case in point is the use of radiant heating and cooling. Radiant systems are very energy-efficient, and also thermally effective; however, they are not quick reacting and may struggle under high thermal loads. The introduction of a high-performance envelope, internal thermal mass, and control of internal heat gains can make radiant systems a perfectly matched solution. (Radiant systems are discussed in more detail later in this chapter.)

Integration with Renewable Energy

MECHANICAL SYSTEM INTEGRATION

The integration of renewable energy systems and strategies in a net zero energy building can impact the design and selection of the building's active systems. One primary issue is the coordination of mechanical system and fuel and energy source selection. There are two very basic approaches. One is the all-electric building; the other is a building that uses electricity and fuel(s) for on-site combustion for heating. There are a variety of renewable and nonrenewable energy sources available for electricity and on-site combustion. A variation on this is the use of solar thermal energy for heating, which by itself requires no on-site combustion of fuel. As already discussed in Chapter 5 and elaborated on in Chapter 8, it is important to research the available energy resources for a project site.

The selection of systems for building heating and domestic and process water heating needs to be considered in close coordination with the selection of fuels for on-site combustion. The equipment selected needs to compatible with the planned fuel sources. For example, if a biomass fuel is available, but natural gas is also planned to supplement or back up the biomass fuel, then equipment selection and system design must accommodate multiple fuels. Note that if on-site combustion of nonrenewable energy sources such as natural gas is used, the building will have to be a net exporter of energy from a renewable energy source generator, to maintain a net zero energy balance—depending, of course, on the net-metering policies of the local utilities.

The electrical side of renewable energy integration with mechanical system coordination is relatively easy. The mechanical equipment makes no distinction between renewable electricity and grid-based electricity. That said, renewable electricity does have an impact on the source energy measures related to mechanical system selection, as outlined in Chapter 4. On-site renewable electricity can make electricity-based heating systems more efficient, from a source energy perspective, than on-site combustion options. Geoexchange systems, or ground-source heat pump systems, can have a very high coefficient of performance (COP), and are all-electric systems. Ground-source heat pump systems do require a site-specific study of soil conditions. (These pumps are discussed in more detail later in this chapter.)

Sometimes, the selection of active systems and equipment may have indirect effects on the on-site renewable energy systems. A very important example of this is the conflict that exists between roof-mounted equipment and roof-mounted solar energy systems (both photovoltaic and solar thermal). Rooftop equipment can be very detrimental to solar access on the roof, by shading large areas of roof space. The shadows are dynamic; they can move from the west side of the unit to the south and then to the east side throughout the course of the day. Further, the depth of the shadow during winter solstice, because of its low angle, can create shadows much taller than the height of the equipment. Based on the internal wiring of typical crystalline photovoltaic panels, it is common for this shading to actually deactivate more of the panels than just those where the shadow falls. The best way to address this issue is to avoid rooftop equipment, to keep the roof as clear of equipment as possible. If equipment is used on the roof, than careful shading studies should be undertaken to optimize locations.

ELECTRICAL SYSTEM INTEGRATION

On-site renewable energy systems have a number of integration impacts on and opportunities for the electrical power system for a building. One of the most obvious is the additional electrical service equipment, such as inverters and associated disconnects. Metering, and in particular the use of net metering and submetering for monitoring renewable energy systems, are important to coordinate when designing a net zero energy building. (Note: Design guidance on the electrical power system of a building is beyond the scope of this book, but basic system components for a wide range of renewable energy systems are discussed in Chapter 8.)

One characteristic of a net zero energy building is the dramatic reduction in electrical loads through decreased lighting use and effective plug load management. These whole-building reductions can lead to cutbacks in building power requirements, and result in both smaller electrical service equipment and transformer size, within the limits of the electrical code. One opportunity to keep in mind when evaluating the electrical service components of a net zero energy building is that the careful selection of a high-efficiency transformer can measurably decrease (by several percentage points) the electrical energy use for overall building. Efficiency can be enhanced when care is taken not to oversize the transformer—again, within the limits of the electrical code.

The integration of renewable energy systems in net zero energy buildings offers several emerging power-related opportunities, which are just beginning to raise interest in the industry. One of the most promising concepts is the integration of DC microgrids as a supplement to AC power within net zero energy buildings. The potential for energy savings can be substantial. First, photovoltaic systems produce DC power that is typically converted to AC with an inverter. This conversion is a source of inefficiency in the system. Second, it is remarkable how many devices in commercial buildings are DC-based and use a power adapter to convert AC to DC. Consider just the number and variety of "power bricks" attached to all the power cords in a building, converting the building's AC to DC. Energy is lost in this conversion as well. One major source of potential future innovation is DC-based lighting systems. LED technology, for example, is DC-based, and the drivers that convert AC to DC add up to a large part of LED system costs, and can diminish their efficiency.

While DC microgrids are small in scale relative to individual buildings or small groups of buildings, the development of large-scale smart grids will have an impact on net zero energy buildings and the electrical infrastructure that serves them. A smart grid is the integration of two-way communication over an electrical distribution grid. The addition of communication technology allows for a wide range of energy management applications, including enhanced and automated demand response, as well as management of distributed renewable energy systems. To interface with the smart grid, the building's energy-related systems will require a number of devices that can monitor and control equipment in response to the needs of the building and grid. With the growth of on-site renewable energy systems, distributed energy storage, and the development of smart grids and microgrids, the electrical landscape for buildings will change, offering net zero energy buildings greater efficiency and additional optimization capabilities.

BASIC CONCEPTS

Know Your Energy Pie

Experience with zero energy buildings shows that there is no silver bullet strategy to achieve the necessary energy efficiencies. All energy uses in the building must be examined and pared down, but where to start? The first step in this process is to determine how energy will be used in the building. As discussed in Chapters 3 and 4, the need to develop an understanding of the energy problem of a project, by analyzing energy end use, is the beginning of the integrated process toward hitting the energy target. The energy end-use analysis, or an energy pie chart, is also valuable at the start of design for low-energy building systems. The energy pie chart is useful to put energy issues into perspective. The relative importance of the various energy end uses, such as heating, cooling, or lighting, needs first to be understood and then strategically addressed. Particular attention should be focused on the biggest energy uses, to ensure they are addressed early in the design process. The diagram in Figure 7.2 shows an example breakdown of energy by end use in an office building.

The categories used in Figure 7.2 are fairly representative of most buildings; but for a given project, it may make sense to add specific categories or subcategories. For example, it may make sense to break out energy for specific program elements separately, such as kitchens and IT spaces. One recommendation is to break up heating and cooling energy use into

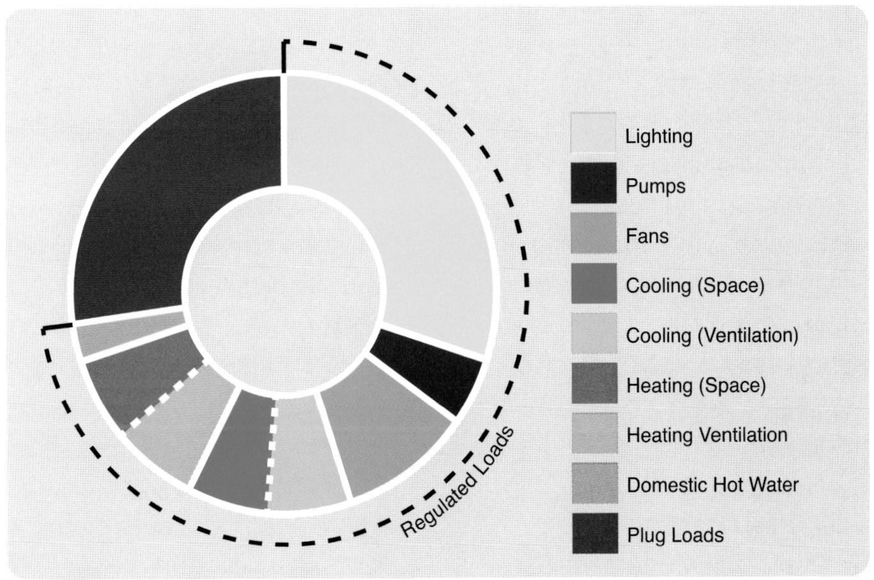

■ **FIGURE 7.2** Typical Commercial Office Building Energy Pie Chart.

ventilation and space subcategories, as shown. Splitting up this information is useful, because downstream of the primary heating and cooling equipment, different strategies are required to save energy, related to conditioning outside air brought into the building and maintaining temperatures of the occupied space itself. For office buildings, ventilation and space heating and cooling tend to be fairly balanced. For hospitals, laboratories, and foodservice facilities, heating and cooling tend to be dominated by ventilation. In contrast, residential applications tend to be dominated by space heating and cooling.

No two buildings will have the same breakdown in their energy pie chart. The general use of the building, the specific program, the local climate, and site constraints will each have an impact on the energy use of the building and the relative distribution of end uses. Of these end uses, the design team has substantial control over regulated energy uses: domestic hot water, heating, cooling, fan, pump, and lighting energy. The building owner and designers share responsibility for energy use of the miscellaneous or plug load category of equipment. To get to net zero energy, the team should expect to reduce energy use in the "regulated" energy uses as much as possible, as well as help the owner save energy with the plug loads.

The energy pie chart is an effective visual touchstone for the various project stakeholders, to help them understand how their work affects the building as a whole, and generate a sense of common purpose in reducing energy use. As the project develops and becomes more clearly defined, it is a good idea to update the energy pie chart, as a way to keep all project stakeholders in the loop about the overall design and their individual disciplines as each relates to energy.

Reduce, Reuse, Renewable

The slogan "Reduce, Reuse, Renewable" is a riff on the common recycling motto, "Reduce, Reuse, Recycle," serving to remind us of the greater priority of addressing consumption, and how to accomplish this. It also suggests an important hierarchy in the process of achieving a net zero energy balance for the project:

- Reduction must come first, ideally by load reduction or avoidance, followed by efficiency measures.
- Reuse comes next, with a focus on creatively putting energy waste in the system back into beneficial use.

These two steps comprise a low-energy solution that can then be offset with on-site renewable energy generation. It is important to keep in mind that setting the energy consumption budget also establishes the renewable energy generation requirement of a net zero energy building.

Energy Consumption = Energy Generation

Net zero energy buildings are not made simply by adding renewable energy systems to a typical building. To be cost-effective, energy consumption must be lowered to a point at which renewable generation becomes feasible—within both cost and space constraints. In terms of cost-effectiveness, many energy reduction and reuse strategies are better investments than adding renewable energy generation.

Reducing and reusing energy in active systems is the focus of this chapter. There are many ways to approach this objective, some of which are presented in the sections that follow. Treat these ideas as different angles from which to view the systems in your building, much as a sculptor examines his or her work from many sides, chipping away to reach the final form.

Start Downstream and Work Upstream

There are many steps involved when energy flows *to* and *through* active systems; and at each one, as the energy changes from one form to another, waste is associated with the inefficiency inherent to that step. For example, consider the diagram in Figure 7.3.

In the diagram, chemical energy (here, in the form of coal) is burned to produce steam, which turns a turbine, which rotates a generator, which produces electricity, which is distributed to a building, which is "stepped down" in voltage in the transformer, which powers a motor, which rotates a fan, which distributes cool air to condition a space. As a result of the inefficiencies, which compound at each step, 260 watts worth of chemical power in the form of coal must be expended to do 50 watts worth of work to move air in the building.

At any given step, a reduction in waste means that less power is required in all of the previous steps. This reduces the power wasted by all of the upstream equipment. If the fan efficiency increases from 60 to 70 percent, for example, the power requirement through all upstream equipment goes down by 27 percent. Efficiencies do not flow downstream in the same way. If the transformer becomes 3 percent more efficient, it reduces the power requirements on the electrical system upstream, but has no effect on the power at the fan. This means that the most effective approach to address energy efficiency is to focus on the function desired as far downstream as possible, then work upstream through the supporting equipment to the energy source.

Check Deep into Requirements

The question furthest downstream to answer is: What is this system supposed to do? Sometimes, waste is generated by solving the wrong problem. Energy is something we use all the time but rarely see, so it is easy to forget that all the decisions we make have energy implications. Thus, problems (arising from both unarticulated expectations and formal design criteria) are usually defined with energy waste built in.

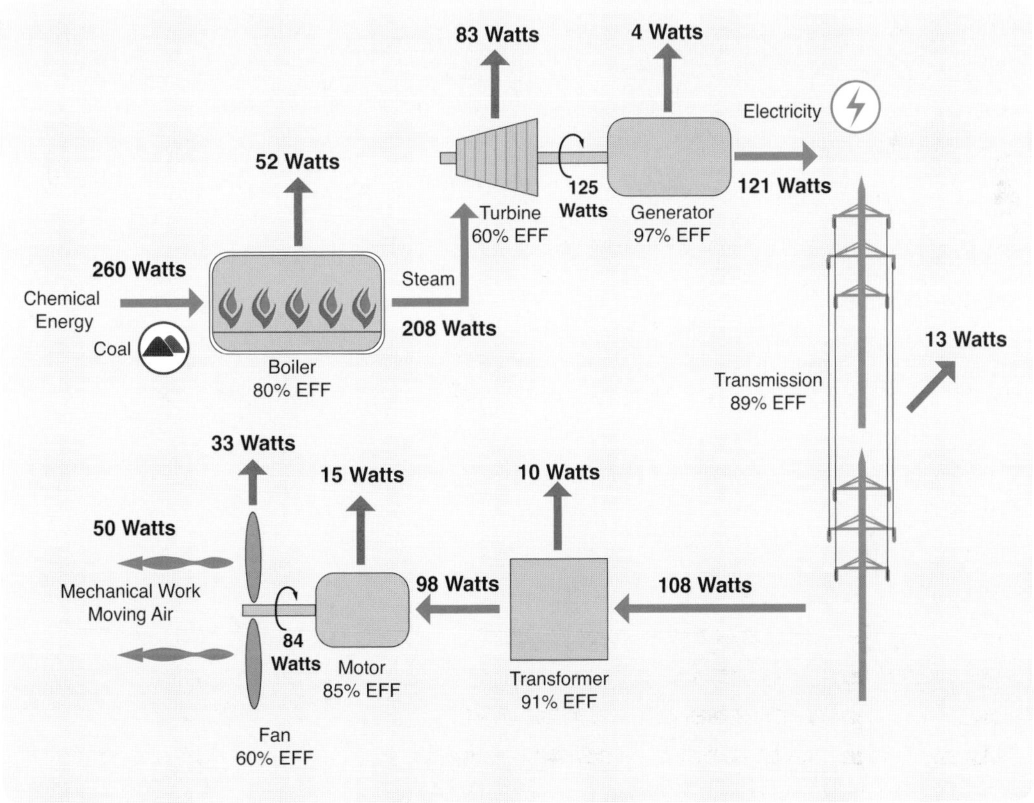

■ **FIGURE 7.3** Working Upstream to Understand Energy Flows.

Examining whether design criteria are the right fit for a net zero energy building is, therefore, the most cost-effective way to save energy on the project; and it must happen as early as possible, to set the project on a clearly defined net zero energy path. Often, subtle requirements can have glaring implications. For example, counting the comfort benefit of local air movement, rather than focusing on air temperature alone, may mean the difference between needing compressor-based cooling or not.

Part of examining project requirements is to help the building owner better interpret the design criteria—what they mean practically. For example, designing to a 1 percent outdoor design condition means that, on average, 88 hours in the year could be beyond the capacity of the system. Changing to a 2 percent design condition would mean that 88 more hours in the year would fall outside the equipment capacity. Is that acceptable? Another example would be to help the owner recognize the combined effect of radiant conditioning and air temperature for comfort if radiant systems or significant internal exposed thermal mass are used. But perhaps the best example revolves around examining the temperature requirements for IT equipment. Current industry standards provide a much wider envelope for temperature and humidity than common practice. Energy strategies like air and water economizers can save massive amounts of energy when these wider temperature conditions are invoked.

Another aspect of examining project requirements is to understand the specifics of the facility, and how it is going to be used. A great example of this issue is indoor comfort criteria. The indoor design temperature set points can make a substantial difference in energy use, and even in the type of systems required.

While it is always important to understand the likely use and function of different spaces within a building, it is even more important for a net zero energy building. Different use patterns, as well as thermal requirements and conditions, can be leveraged in planning active and passive strategies and systems. If particular spaces have distinctly different hours from the rest of the building, the system will need to efficiently accommodate the turndown of mechanical equipment to serve this space. If a building has large zones with widely different thermal and ventilation requirements, these zones might be better served by separate system approaches.

Last, it is critical to be able to ask the client: Do you really need that? All stakeholders involved in a net zero energy building need to embrace a less-is-more philosophy. The point here is not to deprive people of what they need, but to eliminate what they will not miss. Removing unnecessary equipment and functions creates a domino effect of energy savings upstream.

Right-Sizing Systems

Checking deep into the actual design requirements, as just discussed, and reducing or eliminating unnecessary requirements, are essential to right-sizing systems. The goal of right-sizing systems is twofold: one, to optimize the energy efficiency (especially running at part load); and two, to reduce equipment size and lower cost. Currently in the building industry, the concept of right-sizing is being reframed, as it is important to strike a balance between size and efficiency. Right-sizing is not always about choosing the smallest system size.

Right-sizing a system begins with downsizing it. Downsizing the system is a result of the load avoidance and load reduction built into the project—along with passive design strategies, a high-performance building envelope, and reduction of interior loads. Equipment sizing is focused on peak load (power) reduction, rather than overall energy use, because systems are sized to meet the peak, or design-case, loads. So, when developing energy reduction strategies for a project, it also important to keep in mind strategies that decrease peak load.

In addition to integrating load-reducing strategies, unrealistic peak load assumptions and factors of safety should be questioned. This is part of carefully defining the project requirements that are to be met with the active systems. It may be beneficial to question, too, conventional practices for determining peak loads, which assume improbable combinations of simultaneous loads. In fact, in a well daylit building, peak artificial lighting load should never occur simultaneously with peak solar heat gain load, because the lights should never be fully on when there is sufficient daylight for peak solar heat gain. In addition to being strategic when defining the peak load, it is important to use reasonable safety factors, and work hard to minimize assumptions or uncertainties in the load.

Right-sizing systems can result in smaller systems and, therefore, in lower system costs. Right-sizing is part of managing the overall construction budget of a net zero energy project. The reduced cost can be used to offset other investments in passive strategies; or the savings can be reinvested into the system, allowing for an upgraded, higher-efficiency system while still managing first cost.

One critical aspect of right-sizing systems is designing for efficiency at part load. Notably, conventional systems often run at half-peak capacity, or less; and some system components do not run efficiently at part load. Fortunately, efficiency can be improved by using adjustable speed drives and parallel units, which can be staged to operate efficiently at full or part load. Variable speed pumps and fans take full advantage of the relationships between flow, pressure, and power, referred to as *affinity laws*. According to these laws, the power of pumps or fans is a function of the flow or speed cubed, meaning reduced flow has an exponential reduction in power. In the relationship shown in the following equation, P_1 and P_2 represent the power of two different pumps/fans, based on the flow (F_1 or F_2) or speed (S_1 or S_2) of the pumps/fans.

$$\frac{P_1}{P_2} = \left(\frac{F_1}{F_2}\right)^3 = \left(\frac{S_1}{S_2}\right)^3$$

The last part of right-sizing is knowing what to upsize. Distribution elements, like ducts, and heat transfer elements, like cooling towers and radiant panels, typically enhance system efficiency as their size gets larger. Ultimately, right-sizing will be a balance of efficiency and cost, which must be addressed on a project-by-project basis.

Energy Reuse

Energy reuse can be considered a subset of energy reduction. With reuse, energy reduction is achieved by using "waste" energy in one system to serve a productive function in another system. Techniques include heat exchangers, heat pumps, and transfer air (using waste heat for space heating or ventilation preheat).

In considering energy use and reuse, the ideal is to create an energy ecosystem within a building. In a biological ecosystem, energy enters as sunlight and is converted to chemical energy in plants. Plants are eaten by herbivores, which live out their lives and provide energy for their predators. Eventually, all creatures become an energy source for scavengers and decomposers, which serve their own vital functions in the ecosystem. In a stable biological ecosystem, the amount of energy entering in the form of sunlight is equal to the amount of energy leaving; in between, it is used for countless functions. In buildings, energy enters as sunlight, electricity, and heating fuels. Energy inevitably leaves the system as heat, but there is potential to use it more than once before it does.

Another idea to think about is that energy has a quality or usefulness, in addition to its quantity. This is the heart of the second law of thermodynamics. For example, in a heat exchanger, 100 gallons of water at 160°F can be used to heat 100 gallons of 50°F water up to 90°F. In this process, 4,000 Btu of thermal energy are transferred to the cold water, and the 160°F water will be cooled down to 120°F. Heat naturally flows from the higher-temperature (higher-quality) source to the lower-temperature (lower-quality) source. While it would take the same quantity (4,000 Btu) of thermal energy to heat the 100 gallons of 160°F water up to 200°F, we cannot simply transfer this heat from the 50°F water. In reusing energy, we want to make sure to use our highest-quality source for the highest-quality need first, and then reuse it for the next-highest use possible.

For example, in the DOE/NREL Research Support Facility, electricity (our highest-quality energy) is used to power data center equipment; and per the first law of thermodynamics, heat (lower-quality energy) is released from the data center equipment in an equal amount, in the form of hot air, at approximately 95°F. This heat is used to warm ventilation air to approximately 55°F (lowest-quality).

Considering how to reuse energy within the building can be some of the most creative work on a project, and exemplifies the integrated approach to design. (More specific strategies to reuse energy—heat exchangers, heat pumps, and transfer air—are discussed later in this chapter.)

HVAC OVERVIEW

Thermal Comfort and Air Quality

The purpose of HVAC systems is to ensure adequate comfort and air quality in the space. It is important to recognize that both thermal comfort and air quality are subjective issues. The complex dynamics of individual physiology and thermal sensitivities, along with cultural norms and preferences, can make it very challenging to attempt to universally satisfy thermal comfort and air quality. In addition, current design standards don't adequately address this complexity; as a result, they are often narrow or simplistic in scope, in order to satisfy the need for a uniform standard.

Studies by Povl Ole Fanger, an expert in the field of the health effects of indoor environments, focused on relating the overall heat balance of a person in steady-state conditions to his or her subjective experience of comfort. The industry standard for comfort in North America is ASHRAE Standard 55, which was derived from his research. The standard relates the following conditions to the experience of comfort:

- Metabolic rate
- Clothing level
- Air temperature
- Surrounding surface (radiant) temperature
- Humidity
- Air velocity
- Psychology (which cannot be controlled, so is typically dismissed)

Additionally, the standard identifies limits for cold air drafts and *radiant asymmetry*—when the surface temperatures on opposite sides of a person are significantly different. The standard focuses on limiting the number of people dissatisfied with a certain condition to an acceptable level, typically 20 percent.

Over the last few decades, our definition of comfort has broadened a bit; new models for thermal comfort have emerged, such as the UC Berkeley thermal comfort model, which more accurately represent the human physiological response to environmental conditions. These new models can take into account transient (not steady-state) conditions, which are fairly common in real-life conditions, and how each part of the body (local comfort) affects the overall experience of comfort; they also can account more accurately for nonuniform conditions within a space. This is particularly useful for considering comfort near windows, which create a relatively complex thermal geometry.

In 2004, a substantial addition was made to ASHRAE 55 to account for the psychological benefit of user control of operable windows. This addition is known as the *adaptive comfort model*. The provision applies to a fairly limited condition of naturally ventilated buildings, and does not allow the application to mixed-mode buildings that use a combination of natural ventilation and mechanical cooling. Although the new adaptive comfort model does not address all of the opportunities, nor the complexity, in achieving thermal comfort, it is a step in the right direction toward a more sophisticated and diverse approach.

Standards for ventilation and air quality in buildings are perhaps even more antiquated and arbitrary than those for thermal comfort. It is worth noting that standards developed for air quality were directed to silencing complaints about objectionable (body) odors, rather than to the more complicated issue of optimizing occupant health. ASHRAE Standard 62 is the primary standard for ventilation in North American commercial buildings, though it varies somewhat from requirements set forth in the International Codes.

In general, research on these basic issues requires broad and costly studies, and the current standards make the best out of the research that has already been done to bridge the gap between subjective human responses and hard-to-measure conditions that can be created in spaces. For buildings targeting net zero energy, interpreting what the standards really mean to the project is important. Making the case for the right standard (i.e., ASHRAE versus code default), as well as carrying out a more sophisticated calculation for comfort in specific locations within a building, may be necessary.

HVAC System Basics

To satisfy needs for comfort and air quality, a spectrum of components and systems has been devised over the last 100-plus years. Different systems have different benefits, and some will be better suited to particular climates, building types, building sizes, and sites. However, all these systems follow the same basic "architecture" for conditioning spaces. This high-level look at an HVAC system is presented in Figure 7.4.

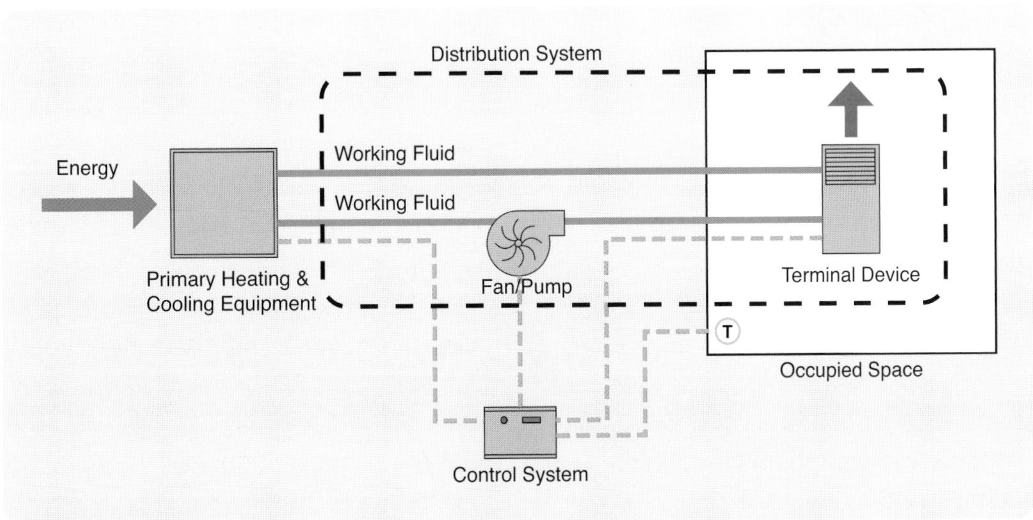

■ **FIGURE 7.4** An HVAC system simplified to its basic components.

Starting downstream, there is the occupied space that is being conditioned. From an energy perspective, conditioning the space means that the amount of heat entering the space is the same as the amount leaving the space. If the space is losing heat to the environment faster than it is gaining heat, the system must supply more heat, to prevent the temperature in the space from dropping. If the space is gaining more heat from internal sources and external sources (solar gain, etc.) than it is losing to the outside environment, then the HVAC system must remove heat from the space. This principle of balancing heat in the space is the basis of the load calculations, which are the foundation of sizing HVAC components and systems.

To control the thermal balance of a space, comfort conditions need to be measured. A temperature sensor or thermostat is required, and in some circumstances a humidistat is necessary as well. These components are part of the control system, which governs the operations of the components.

Upstream from the occupied space is a terminal device. The terminal device takes heat from the system and distributes it to the occupied space. Terminal devices can include variable air volume boxes, fin tube radiators, radiant panels, chilled beams, and distributed heat pumps.

Upstream of the terminal device is the working fluid. This is the medium that conveys heat to and from the occupied space. Common working fluids are air and water. For variable refrigerant flow systems, a refrigerant is the working fluid. There must be a means of circulating the working fluid. In modern buildings, this is typically done with a fan or pump. In variable refrigerant systems, a compressor drives the fluid circulation. In steam systems, distribution takes place based on the expansion of water into vapor form in the boiler; and the return of water takes place by gravity, or may be pumped.

Upstream of the fluid and its circulator is the primary heating and cooling equipment. For heating and cooling, this generally means a boiler, chiller, and associated equipment. It is also customary for these components to be integrated into packaged air-handling equipment, in the form of burners and direct expansion cooling. The primary equipment transfers energy between the HVAC system and a fuel source or the outside environment.

The same basic system components are used to maintain adequate air quality in the space for ventilation. In some cases, the air used for ventilation is also the working fluid for heating and cooling. However, in some cases, as discussed later in this chapter, ventilation air is a separate system.

Low-Energy System Design

The basic HVAC system architecture just described is the building block for conventional as well as innovative, low-energy approaches to HVAC design. The design of low-energy mechanical systems for net zero energy buildings is truly a creative and innovative design endeavor. The process is not just about selecting a highly efficient mechanical system; it is about designing the mechanical services as a whole system. (Refer to Chapter 3 for a discussion on design methods and system design thinking.)

The mechanical system selection and design for a net zero energy project will very likely include nonconventional components and systems. Quite simply, most of the conventional mechanical systems in wide use today are not efficient enough for a net zero energy building approach. Many of the higher-efficiency alternatives are summarized in this chapter. Note that many of these alternative systems are only nonconventional in the U.S. market; they are far more common in Europe and Japan.

It is important to reiterate that the whole system design is as important as the system selection. In fact, systems thinking can help lead to better, more integrated system selection. The principles that apply to a low-energy active system, discussed at the beginning of this chapter, can also be applied to HVAC system design.

Further, low-energy HVAC system methods can be divided into two main approaches: those that reduce energy through the distribution system, and those that reduce energy through the primary equipment. Examples of promising components and systems, which are likely to offer energy benefits to zero energy buildings, are presented in the following sections.

LOW-ENERGY DISTRIBUTION

Concepts and Guidelines

The services of HVAC—heating, cooling, and ventilation—need to be delivered effectively to each space within the building. There are nearly countless ways of accomplishing this—far too many, in fact, to fully discuss the merits and limitations of each here. This section, therefore, focuses on methods that represent significant energy benefits in many commercial buildings.

Low-Energy Distribution Strategies

- Avoid air for heat distribution.
- Decouple ventilation and temperature control.
- Use modest temperatures.
- Minimize reheat energy.

AVOID AIR FOR HEAT DISTRIBUTION

For a low-energy building, the energy efficiency and effectiveness of the thermal distribution system should be a fundamental design consideration. For many buildings, this means comparing water-based and air-based thermal energy transfer. The volumetric heat capacity of water is 4.1796 J/cm^3 · K, and the volumetric heat capacity of air is 0.0012 J/cm^3 · K. This means that for the same volume, water can hold almost 3,500 times more thermal energy than air. Therefore, a much smaller pipe can be used to distribute the same amount of heat as a much larger duct. Pumping the lower volume of water consumes less energy than blowing the higher volume of air. This presents a very compelling reason to consider water-based over air-based distribution.

DECOUPLE VENTILATION AND TEMPERATURE CONTROL

Water is great for transferring energy, but it does not help ventilate or dehumidify a space. We still need to provide air, but typically much less than we would for an all-air HVAC system. By separating the ventilation and dehumidification air from the temperature control water, we can actually control these better throughout the facility, reaping energy, thermal comfort, and air quality benefits (see Figure 7.5).

Kiel Moe makes an enlightening analogy in his book *Thermally Active Surfaces in Architecture*, where he compares the human body to a building. He points to the very effective decoupling of air (respiratory) and thermal (circulatory) systems in the human body, and suggests that building design can learn from this important biomimetic lesson.

This recommendation holds for buildings that are dominated by heating and cooling requirements, rather than ventilation or exhaust requirements. If the ventilation and exhausts require greater airflow than the heating and cooling for the space, there is no penalty for using this airflow for heating and cooling.

USE MODEST TEMPERATURES

Conventional HVAC systems use fairly extreme temperatures in the working fluid. Common air supply temperatures are 55°F for cooling and 90°F for heating. Chilled and hot water, which are often used to heat and cool the air, must be even more extreme. Chilled water is typically needed at about 45°F; heating hot water ranges from 160°F to 200°F. By using warmer water for cooling, and cooler water for heating, we can rely more often on natural sources for heating and cooling, and the primary equipment does not have to work as hard when it is in operation.

Using less extreme temperatures does mean that that you will need more of the working fluid to distribute the same amount of heat, which will lead to more pump/fan energy. This additional energy should be minimized by avoiding air as the working fluid, and can be outweighed by the use of free heating and cooling sources.

■ **FIGURE 7.5** The underfloor air distribution system at the DOE/NREL Research Support Facility is for delivery of ventilation air and is decoupled from the radiant heating and cooling system. The floor features several "truth" floor panels, made of glass to show the inner workings of the raised floor. *Image courtesy of RNL; photograph by Ron Pollard.*

If, based on project-specific constraints, the free heating and cooling sources are not available, it makes sense to turn the "modest temperature" philosophy on its head and maximize the temperature differences in the hydronic system in order to minimize pump power.

MINIMIZE REHEAT ENERGY

It may sound illogical, but a big energy consumer in commercial buildings is heating air that has already been cooled down. This is built into the operation of most air-based HVAC systems. Using modest distribution temperatures, and separating ventilation from temperature control, can minimize, or even prevent entirely, wasting energy for reheat.

Systems and Strategies

RADIANT HEATING AND COOLING WITH A DEDICATED OUTSIDE AIR SYSTEM

Radiant heating and cooling rely on surfaces exposed in the space to deliver heat and cooling. Typically, ceilings or floors are used as the heat exchange surfaces. Floors tend to be better suited for heating, and ceilings for cooling. This is because of both the natural human physiological response, which prefers warmth from below, and natural convection to enhance heat transfer in these configurations. Despite this ideal configuration, in many cases the not-ideal orientation may prove to be the better approach: for example, providing both heating and cooling from the ceiling because you do not want to pay for another set of pipes (see Figure 7.6).

For new construction, it is generally more cost-effective to use the structure itself as the radiant surface. In a concrete floor or ceiling, the slab itself is right in the middle of the heat transfer, between the surface and the working fluid. This means that the thermal mass will cause a "time" lag between when the working fluid starts running through the slab and when the effects are felt in the space. In this sense, radiant slabs are best suited for spaces where steady conditions are expected. Exposed slabs naturally integrate with passive strategies like night cooling and passive heating.

■ **FIGURE 7.6** Hydronic Piping for a Radiant Heating and Cooling Slab. *Image courtesy of RNL.*

Metal radiant panels suspended below the structure are another approach. While panels are more costly per square foot installed, they react much faster than slabs, and are well suited for retrofit applications and spaces where occupancy and other cooling loads may fluctuate widely. With either approach, space temperatures can be controlled in both heating and cooling during unoccupied hours, without turning on any fans at all. This is particularly valuable in heating-dominated climates.

Because the radiant system handles the heating and cooling, the air system can be devoted to ventilation and humidity control. This system will typically handle only outside air, and not recirculate air within the building. It is, therefore, referred to as a *dedicated outside air system* (DOAS). DOAS systems are much smaller than conventional air systems and consume less fan power.

A major limitation of the radiant approach is the amount of heat radiant surfaces can exchange. A floor in cooling may only be able to remove 13 Btuh/ft^2 from a space, and a ceiling roughly 25 Btuh/ft^2 of active surface. Fortunately, for a good low-energy design, architectural, lighting, and plug load reductions can make these limited capacities adequate for many applications.

Another limitation of the radiant approach is humidity. The cooling capacity is limited by the humidity in the space, in order to prevent condensation on the panels. For spaces with substantial internal humidity sources (e.g., high-occupancy conference rooms), radiant cooling may require very dry air to function adequately, making radiant impractical.

DISPLACEMENT VENTILATION WITH PERIMETER HEAT

Displacement ventilation is an approach to cooling and ventilating a space that was developed in Sweden in the 1970s. As opposed to a conventional American air system, which attempts to thoroughly mix the supply air with the air in the space, creating uniform conditions and diluting airborne contaminants, the idea of displacement ventilation is to create a pool of cooler cleaner air at the bottom of the room, where people are. This results in a stratified region high in the room that is warmer and moves contaminants up into this stratified zone, which are then removed (see Figure 7.7).

With displacement ventilation, air is introduced to the room around 68°F, at the low velocity of 40 feet per minute or less. This air sinks to the floor and spreads out. Heat sources like people and equipment generate a stack affect, described as *thermal plumes*, which draw the cooler, cleaner air up into the breathing zone, then up to the stratified level as the air is heated and "odorized." Depending on the balance between ventilation requirements and heat sources in the room, displacement ventilation commonly provides ventilation effectiveness 1.2 to 2.5 times that of an overhead mixing system. This means that the same air quality can be provided with a 15 to 60 percent reduction in outside air. This is highly beneficial in the summer and winter, when conditioning outside air can be a major energy draw. Because displacement ventilation uses such a mild supply temperature, it can often be achieved through lower-energy approaches.

As displacement ventilation is based on using natural buoyancy forces to create cleaner air in the occupied space, it does not work well for heating. In fact, providing warm air in a displacement approach will result in a ventilation effectiveness 30 percent worse than a mixing system. Because of this, it is good practice to combine displacement ventilation with hydronic perimeter heat. Perimeter heat can be in many forms, including radiant panels, or fin tube "radiators." Like the radiant/DOAS approach, nighttime heating can be provided with the air system fully off.

One of the limitations of the displacement ventilation system is that it uses air to cool working fluid—in fact, slightly more air than a conventional mixed-air system, in most cases. With careful design, the benefits of reduced outside air requirement and lower energy heating/cooling sources will outweigh the slight increase in fan energy.

CHILLED BEAMS

Chilled beams are a strategy that can provide some of the benefits of a radiant/DOAS system, but typically at a lower cost. Chilled beams come in two categories: passive and active.

Passive chilled beams are similar to a heating fin tube "radiator" (these "radiators" actually use convection) turned upside down. The beam consists of hydronic piping suspended high in the space, with metal fins along its length to increase the surface area for convection. The beam cools the surrounding air, which drops down into the occupied space by natural convection. Passive chilled beams don't work well for heating, as they would just cause warm air to pool at the top of the room. They are, however, well suited for interior locations that are not expected to need heating. Similar to radiant panels, passive chilled beams need a DOAS system for ventilation and dehumidification.

Active chilled beams use ventilation air to enhance the output of the fin tube. Nozzles

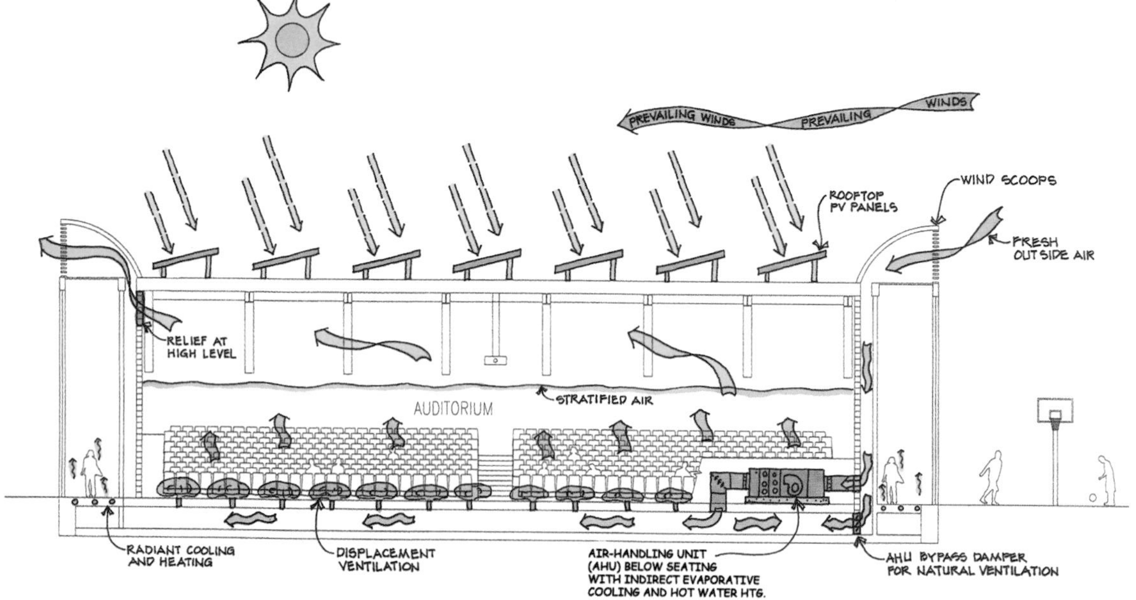

■ **FIGURE 7.7** Displacement ventilation diagram for an auditorium at the Science & Student Life Center at Sacred Heart School in Atherton, California. *Image courtesy of Stantec Consulting Services, Inc.*

within the beam shoot air at the fins, increasing heat transfer. These systems are well suited for spaces with relatively constant ventilation requirements. Because of the forced convection, active beams can be used for both heating and cooling, but require the air system to operate to condition the space after-hours. One drawback of the chilled beam system is that the nozzles in the beam cause a large additional pressure drop in the ventilation system, which must be overcome by additional fan power.

VARIABLE REFRIGERANT FLOW

Variable refrigerant flow (VRF), or variable refrigerant volume, systems are a relatively new approach that is coming to North America from Asia, where it is commonplace. A VRF system takes a refrigeration cycle (which is traditionally limited to the primary equipment in other HVAC approaches) and expands it throughout the entire building. The refrigerant itself becomes the heat transfer fluid for the building. This refrigeration cycle is a heat pump system that can provide either heating or cooling. Heat pump terminals distributed throughout the facility provide either heating or cooling by drawing heat from or rejecting heat to the circulating refrigerant (see Figure 7.8). In this way, heat moves around the facility from where there is excess to where it is needed. The net surplus of heating or cooling is drawn from outside via one or more outdoor heat pump units. The VRF is particularly well suited for applications that are likely to have many hours when some spaces are in heating while others are in cooling. Like some of the systems described previously, a DOAS system is required to provide ventilation.

One limitation of the variable refrigerant flow system is the large amount of refrigerants that are needed in the system. A design challenge for VRF systems is that common energy analysis software does not calculate their performance. Fortunately, design tools and resources, as well as education about these systems, are rapidly being developing in the U.S. market in response to the growing interest in the application.

LOW-ENERGY PRIMARY EQUIPMENT

The strategies just described lead to low-energy solutions by addressing how heating,

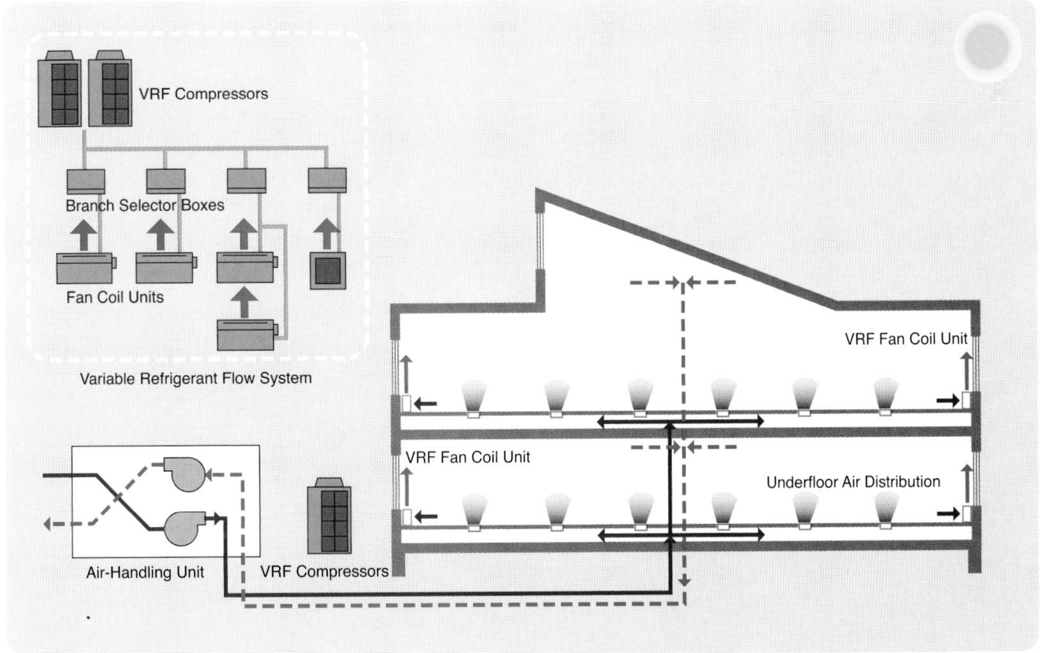

■ **FIGURE 7.8** VRF System Diagram for the Eastside Human Services Building. *Image courtesy of RNL and MKK Consulting Engineers.*

cooling, and ventilation are distributed from the primary equipment to the occupied space. The heat transfer medium used for a system has a major role in the efficiency and effectiveness of the system, as does the distribution system's temperature and volume.

Another important opportunity for low-energy HVAC systems is to address how the primary equipment generates heating and cooling energy. The starting point for low-energy primary equipment is to provide heating and cooling with limited or no generation of additional heating and cooling energy, or to look for systems that can take advantage of free energy. That is, can the free energy of the climate or the site be used to provide comfort? Another source of free energy is in waste energy. All HVAC systems have sources of waste energy in the form of waste heat. The question is, can this waste flow be directed back into the system for beneficial use? A common barrier to using waste heat is that it may not be readily usable at the specific time or place of its production. Can thermal energy storage be developed as a way of capturing waste energy for later use? Thermal storage concepts can be important means for capturing waste thermal energy, as well as using it to leverage free energy opportunities available from the climate and site.

The following strategies focus on low-energy primary equipment concepts. There are many opportunities to pair low-energy primary equipment strategies and systems with low-energy distribution systems. In fact, many low-energy and net zero energy buildings include a hybrid of low-energy and free-energy strategies, customized to meet the individual needs of a project.

Systems and Strategies

ECONOMIZER

The economizer operation, also known as free cooling, is an excellent strategy in many climate zones. The idea is that there are hours in the year when the outside air is cool enough to get significant cooling benefit—possibly, all the required cooling without needing to turn on the compressor-based cooling equipment. In many parts of the country, economizers are required by code.

The most common, and often most effective, economizer approach is the air-side economizer. In an air-side economizer, additional outside air above the ventilation requirement is brought into the air-handling unit during opportune conditions, when the outside air is at a temperature and a degree of humidity preferable to that of return air in the system. An air-side economizer operation pairs well with displacement ventilation, because with the warmer supply temperatures of the displacement approach, there will be many more economizer hours, particularly in relatively dry climates.

A water-side economizer, as the name suggests, produces cooling water for an HVAC system when outside temperatures are favorable. This is usually accomplished in systems with water-cooled chillers and cooling towers; it works by bypassing the chiller in cooler conditions when the cooling towers alone can produce the cooling water temperatures at the capacity that the facility needs. The water-side economizer is especially well suited to radiant cooling and chilled beam systems, where much warmer cooling water is desired. This greatly increases the number of hours in a year that the system can use economizer operation.

One clearly valuable opportunity for using economizers is in technology-heavy spaces such as data and server rooms. Historical approaches to cooling data centers have relied extensively on refrigeration equipment to distribute very cold air, which mixes with the warm air in the space being rejected by the electronic equipment. Current energy-saving strategies for cooling IT spaces rely on hot aisle containment, to keep the warm air from mixing with the cool air in the room, and allowing much warmer supply air temperatures to adequately cool the space. Research by companies such as Intel, Hewlett-Packard, and Microsoft has shown that modern IT equipment is far less vulnerable to high temperatures, humidity, and airborne particulates than previously thought by the IT and HVAC industries.

HEAT RECOVERY

Heat recovery is an extremely valuable strategy for zero energy buildings to reduce the heating and cooling requirements for ventilation. With heat recovery, heat is exchanged between fluid streams (typically, air) that are entering and leaving a building, preheating and precooling the air without any energy from the primary heating and cooling equipment (see Figure 7.9). Depending on the type of heat exchanger used and the airspeeds through the heat recovery device, 50 to 80 percent of the energy can be transferred from one airstream to the other. The drawbacks of heat recovery include the added pressure that these components put into the air system, the increases in air-handling equipment size, and the greater complexity of ducting.

There are a number of types of equipment that achieve heat recovery. Common types, listed in order of increasing performance, are run-around loops, cross-flow heat exchangers, heat pipes, and heat wheels. They provide different levels of heat exchange effectiveness; but they also escalate the chances of contamination between the outgoing and incoming airstream.

The energy recovery strategies just described transfer "sensible" heat—that is, no moisture. Enthalpy wheels are a modification to heat wheels that use a desiccant (water-absorbing) coating to transfer moisture between the airstreams, in addition to heat, in order to prehumidify and predehumidify the air. This approach can be beneficial in both cold dry and hot humid climates.

While it is typical to use the captured heat from the exhaust and return streams

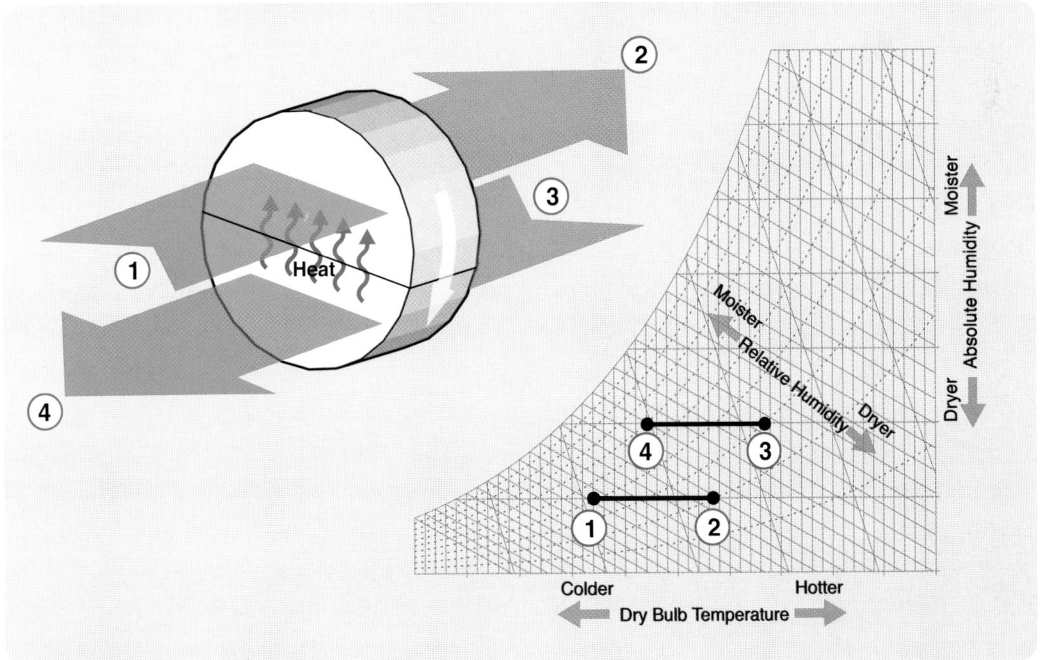

■ **FIGURE 7.9** Heat Recovery.

(see Figure 7.10), heat recovery can also be made from other fluid streams. Even kitchen exhaust has been successfully used in some applications.

EVAPORATIVE COOLING

Just as people sweat to help cool themselves, buildings can use the natural cooling effect of water-absorbing heat as it evaporates into moisture (vapor) in the air. Evaporative cooling is nothing new to the HVAC industry; it is, in fact, the principle on which all cooling towers operate.

The simplest form of evaporative cooling is called direct evaporative cooling (see Figure 7.11). With this approach, moisture is added to the air being supplied to a building, cooling down the airstream and making it more humid. The benefits of this process are limited by the outside humidity of the air, so while this is a promising strategy in dry climates, it is of little use in humid climates.

Indirect evaporative cooling, a modification of evaporative cooling, adds moisture to a "scavenger" airstream separate from the air entering the building (see Figure 7.12). The scavenger air is cooled and humidified and then passed through a sensible heat exchanger, where it absorbs heat from the outdoor airstream being used to ventilate the building. This way, the outdoor stream is cooled without adding humidity. Because of the limited effectiveness of the heat exchanger, and its associated pressure drop, indirect cooling has a more limited capacity to lower the outdoor air temperature, and comes with a higher fan energy penalty than direct evaporative cooling.

An interesting twist on the indirect evaporative cooling process is provided by a company called Coolerado. In the evaporative cooling medium developed by Coolerado, many stages of indirect evaporative cooling take place one after another. By doing this, it is possible to achieve better performance than with a typical indirect evaporative cooling arrangement.

There are a number of ways to add humidity to the air for evaporative cooling. The most common approach is to add water to a porous medium in the airstream. It can also be accomplished by adding water as a fine spray or mist directly to the airstream via ultrasonic vibrations or fine nozzles.

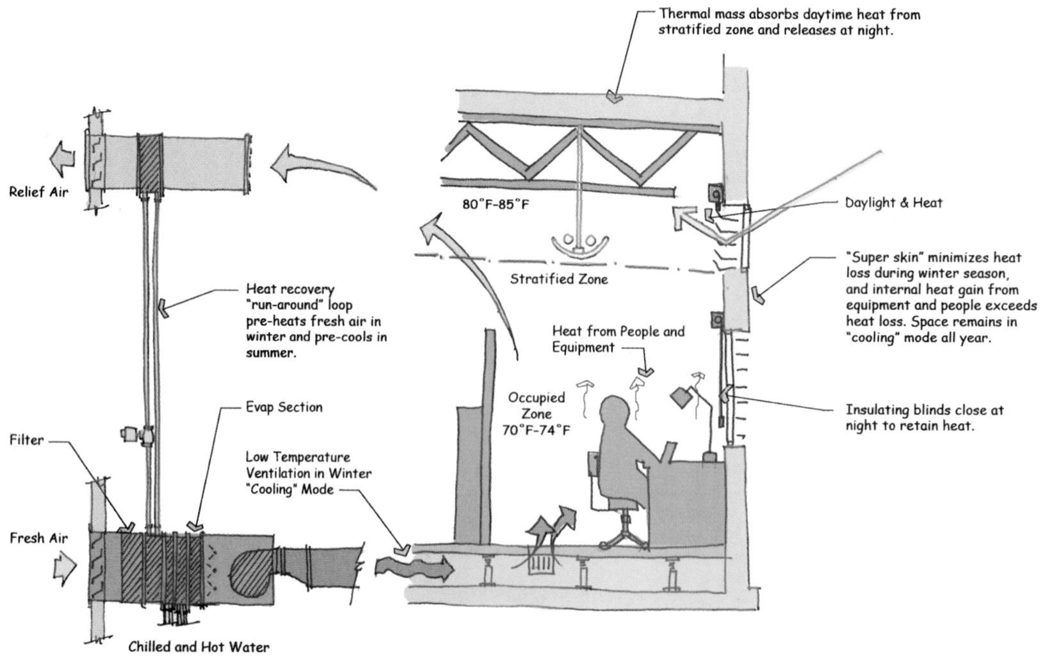

■ **FIGURE 7.10** Heat Recovery of a Return Airstream. *Image courtesy of Stantec Consulting Services Inc.; Drawing by Jim Burns*

Evaporative cooling also can be of benefit in places other than the air supply to the building. In some cases, it may make sense to apply evaporative cooling directly into the space, such as in downdraft cool towers. In other cases, evaporative cooling can be applied directly to condensers, the part of the air-cooled air conditioning system that rejects unwanted heat outside.

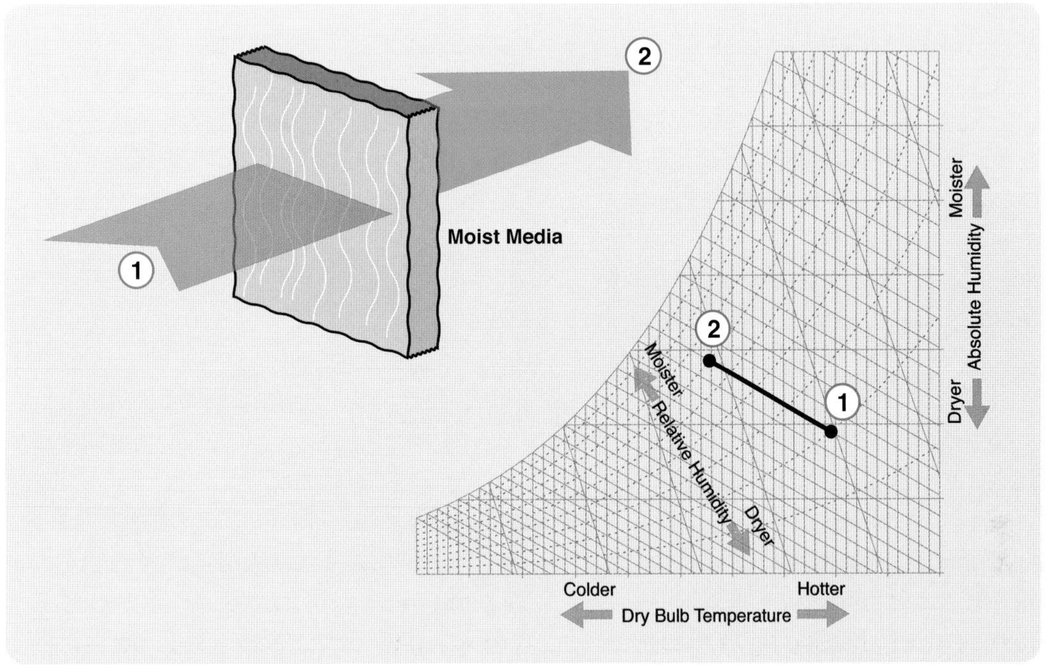

■ **FIGURE 7.11** Direct Evaporative Cooling.

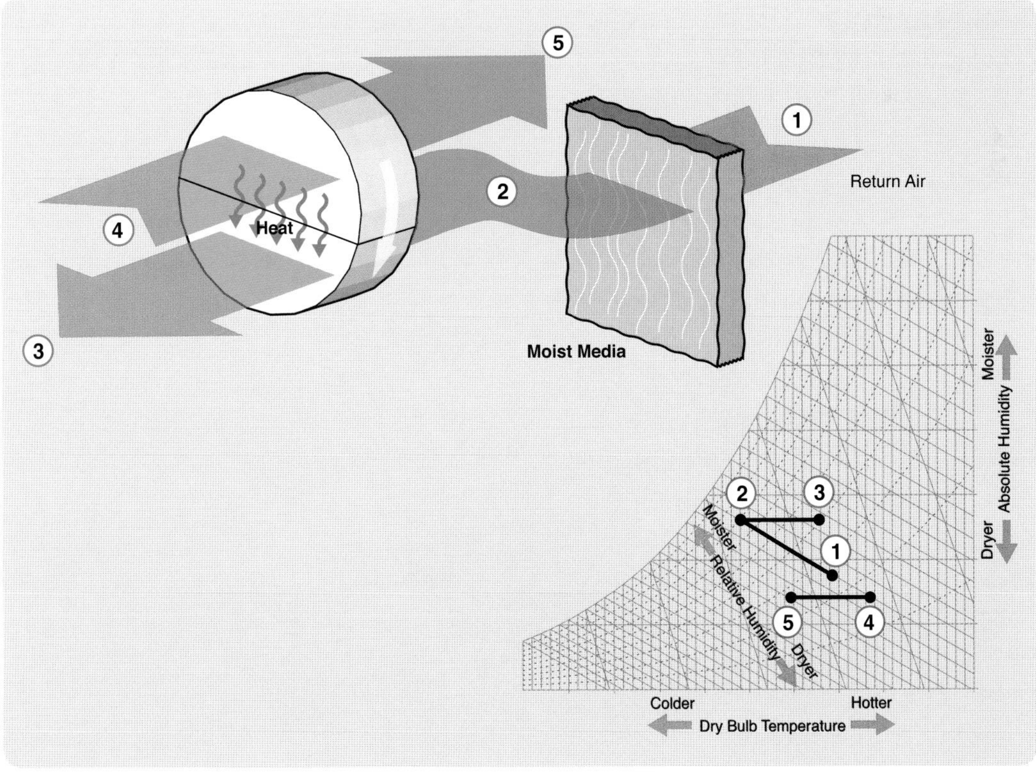

■ **FIGURE 7.12** Indirect Evaporative Cooling.

DESICCANT DEHUMIDIFICATION

Evaporative cooling and the economizer operation work well in dry climates, but what can you do to save energy in humid climates? In these climates, more cooling energy is used to wring moisture out of the air than to control space temperature. An effective low-energy approach for humid climates is desiccant dehumidification.

Desiccant dehumidification works similarly to the enthalpy wheel discussed previously. The key to this process is the use of a desiccant material that absorbs and releases moisture based on the temperatures of the airstreams it is in. When the desiccant is in the outside airstream, it absorbs moisture; it is then "regenerated" by exposing it to a hotter airstream that absorbs the moisture from the desiccant. So, opposite to the traditional refrigeration cycle, a desiccant system uses heating, not cooling, to extract moisture from the air. A major benefit of using heating is that there are typically more "free" sources of heating when dehumidification is required. Solar energy and rejected heat from the cooling equipment are rich sources of free heat, which can be used for desiccant dehumidification.

PASSIVE PREHEAT AND PRECOOL OF VENTILATION

As explained earlier in the discussion of the energy pie chart, a substantial amount of heating and cooling energy goes into conditioning outside air for most commercial buildings. Therefore, it is good practice to look for ways to heat and cool this air for free, as different projects will have unique opportunities. Preheat may come in the form of heat captured from waste sources in the building, so look for processes or spaces within the building that have consistent internal heat generation. Data centers, server rooms, IT closets, and electrical rooms with major transformers are examples of spaces to "mine" for heat.

Preheat can also be derived from integrating the air intake for the building with the building envelope, such that the envelope (using a solar air heat collector) absorbs solar energy and transfers that heat to the airstream. The optimal orientation of the collector will vary, based on the time of the heating need, the available direct solar resource, and the balance of the solar income between heat collection and electrical generation. A classic example of building-integrated solar air preheat is the Trombe wall concept, developed in France by an engineer named Félix Trombe, in the 1960s. Another example is the use of a transpired solar collector. (The case study in Chapter 12 discusses the operation of a transpired solar collector to preheat ventilation air.)

For cooling, a passive approach is to take advantage of the natural diurnal temperature swing. A night-purging strategy with thermal mass exposed in the occupied space is one way to take advantage of the diurnal swing; or, "remote" thermal mass introduced in the building air intake can be used to store the cool of the night to precool the air the following day. The East San Jose Carnegie Library Addition, shown in Figure 7.13, uses the mass of the crawlspace below the building to precool air before it enters the building.

Because the ground experiences a much steadier temperature than outside air, it can be a good source for both preheating and precooling ventilation air. The remote mass crawlspace can take advantage of ground coupling, in addition to the diurnal temperature swing. The earth tube concept, drawing air through uninsulated ducts or pipes in the ground, is another way to precondition the air, using the moderate temperature of the ground. The challenges inherent in employing this strategy at a commercial scale include a number of practical concerns regarding routing the ductwork from air-intake to air-handling

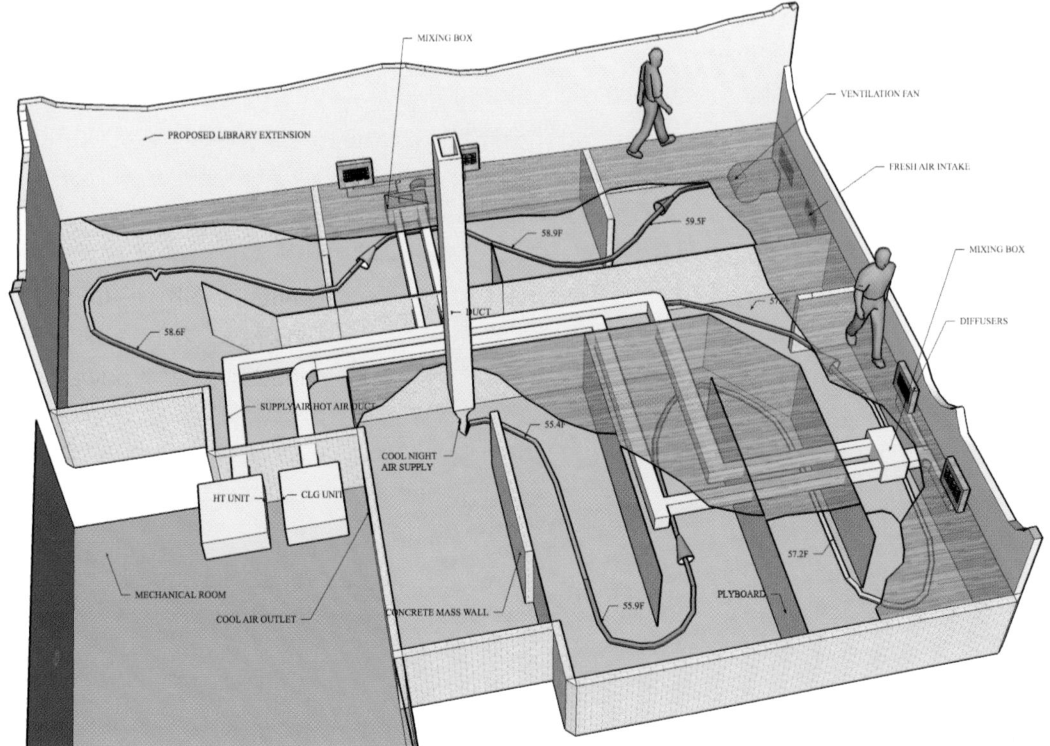

■ **FIGURE 7.13** The East San Jose Carnegie Library addition features a remote thermal mass for precooling ventilation air. *Image courtesy of Stantec Consulting Services Inc.; image by Porus Antia.*

equipment; having enough surface area of pipe in contact with the ground; balancing airflow to minimize the additional fan energy required to draw air through the earth tube; dealing with condensation; and preventing pest intrusion. Ground-coupled strategies are particularly promising in climates with substantial temperature swings throughout the year.

HEAT PUMPS

Heat pumps operate on the same principles as standard cooling equipment; but they can operate in reverse, as well, to produce heating. Whether the function is to provide cooling or heating, this vapor-compression refrigeration cycle draws heat from a cool source and rejects it at a warmer temperature (see Figure 7.14). In the process, energy is used to drive the cycle.

The cooling capacity of the cycle is equal to the amount of heat drawn into the evaporator. The heating capacity of the cycle is the heat rejected from the condenser, which is equal to (in fact, is the same as) the evaporator heat plus the compressor energy. Said another way, heat pumps convert low-quality heat to high-quality heat with a small investment of electricity.

Since more heat comes out of the heat pump than goes in as compressor energy, its efficiency is greater than 100 percent. Efficiency is measured as coefficient of performance (COP), where a COP of 1 would be 100 percent efficient. Typical COP values for refrigeration systems range from 3 to 6.

One of the advantages of heat pumps is their flexibility. They can draw heat from a variety of sources, such as outside air, or air from an indoor space that needs cooling, from a water tank, or from an outside body of water. The smaller the temperature difference between the condenser and the evaporator, the more efficiently heat pumps work, so they are especially well suited to moderate heat sinks/sources such as bodies of water and the ground (see Figure 7.15). Similarly, they are well suited to moderate indoor temperatures such as those required by radiant systems and displacement ventilation.

One consideration with heat pumps is that they typically represent a switch from on-site combustion of a fossil fuel source, like natural gas, to the use of electricity. Because of the many steps involved in the generation and distribution process for electricity, the source energy and emissions associated with 1 kW of delivered electricity can be significantly higher than the emissions associated with 1 kW worth of fossil fuel burned on-site. Heat pumps are

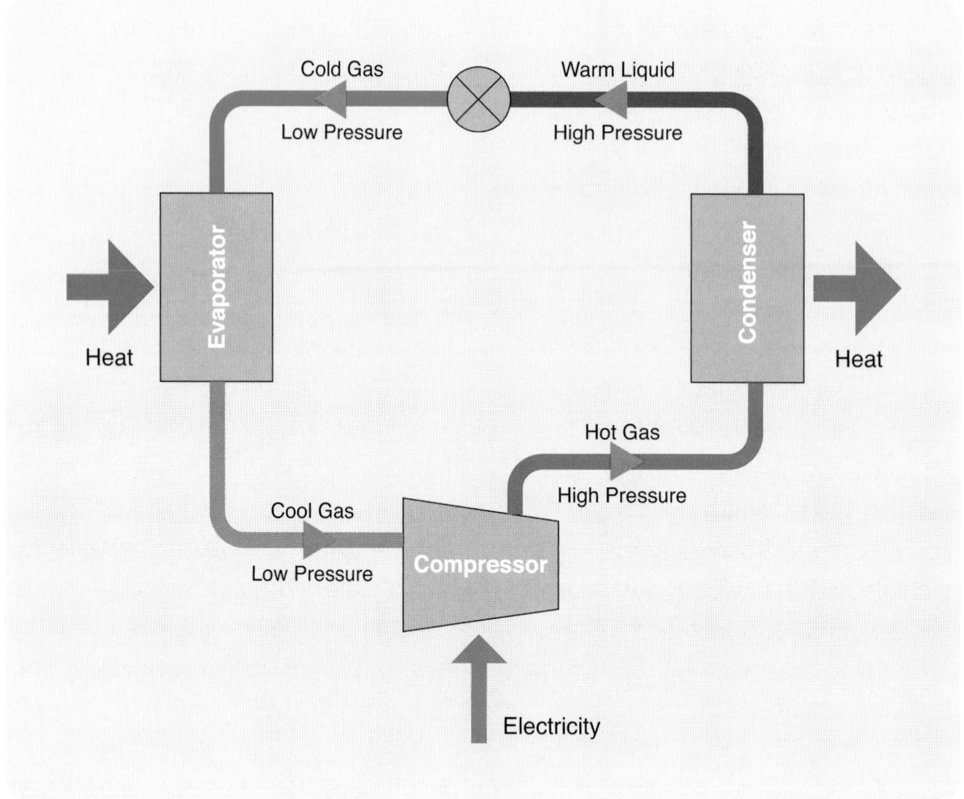

■ **FIGURE 7.14** Typical Refrigeration Cycle.

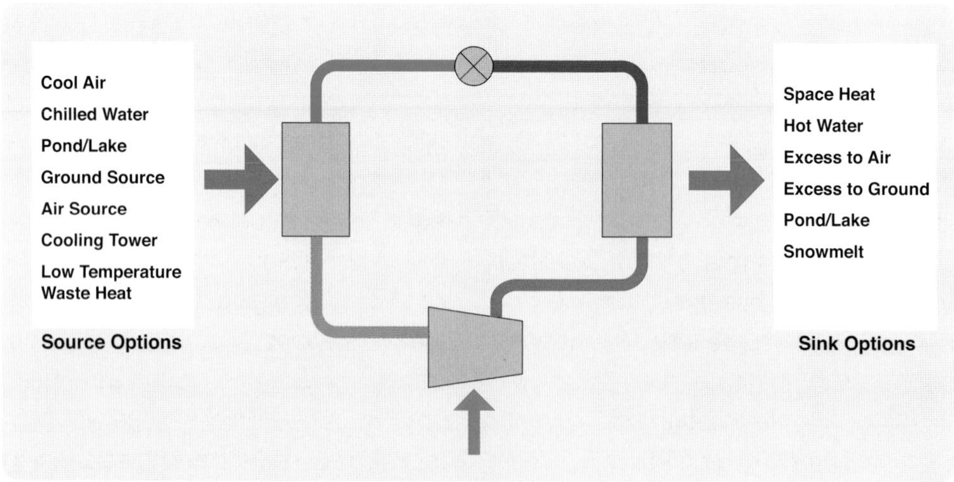

■ **FIGURE 7.15** Heat Pump Energy Sources and Sinks.

most favorable from a site energy perspective, which doesn't distinguish between electrical and gas energy source energy consumption. This concept (explored in detail in Chapter 4) highlights the benefit of on-site renewable electricity generation as a means of eliminating the source energy penalty and emissions from electricity-based primary equipment, such as heat pumps. For conventional buildings, there are plenty of circumstances where making this fuel switch produces a small or even negative effect; but for a net zero energy building, when on-site renewable electricity is being generated, this becomes a moot point.

GROUND-SOURCE THERMAL STORAGE

Earlier in the chapter ground-source heat pumps and passive ventilation preheating through ground coupling were introduced as two ways to take advantage of the earth's natural capability to store heat. It is because of the thermal storage capacity of the ground that its temperature is much steadier than the air, and essentially constant below about 30 feet in depth.

Ground-source heat pumps, sometimes called geothermal heat pumps, take advantage of both thermal transfer and thermal storage principles to become a low-energy system option. In this case, the ground is a passive thermal energy store that can be leveraged for cooling and heating year-round. The system is basically a thermal transfer process: It moves heat from the earth to provide heating in the building; and, conversely, it moves heat from the building to the earth to provide cooling in the building.

To accomplish this thermal energy exchange, a geoexchange system has three basic components: the ground-source loop, the heat pump, and the building distribution system. The ground-source loop is perhaps the most limiting factor in the application of ground-source heat pumps because the design is so site-specific. A geotechnical study should be conducted to determine the conductivity, or thermal transfer properties, of the soil. Having high conductivity will reduce the size needed for the ground-source loop. In addition, each site will have its own constraints on the area available for installation of the ground-source loop. The size and type of installation required for the ground-source loop have the greatest impact on the overall cost for a ground-source heat pump system.

There are two main types of ground-source loops, horizontal and vertical, and each has unique advantages and disadvantages, depending on the specific site. Vertical loops are very common because they require only a relatively small site footprint on which to install and develop the ground coupling through very deep piped wells. The drilling of the wells, particularly through rocky soil, is a significant factor in the overall cost of the system. In contrast, horizontal loops require a large surface area for installation; but they do not require drilling, because the loops are installed relatively close to the ground surface. The ground temperature is less consistent closer to the surface, so a horizontal loop may require a greater length of ground-coupled pipe, compared to vertical wells. To accomplish this, horizontal loops are often installed in "slinky" loops. If the site has an adequately sized pond or lake, the horizontal loop may be installed in the body of water, creating a water-source loop system. Water is more conductive than soil, and it is easier to install a horizontal loop in a pond or lake than it is to do the excavation and drilling required with ground-source loops.

Ground seasonal storage is another promising approach to ground-source thermal storage applications. It is, possibly, the purest example of using the ground as a thermal battery. Ground seasonal storage was pioneered as a technique for capturing solar energy from the sun when the resource is at its peak (and heating is unneeded), and saving that thermal energy until the winter when it is needed. Water-based solar thermal collectors absorb solar energy to heat water, which is then pumped through an array of pipes extending deep below the ground surface, heating a volume of the ground itself. Some of this heat will dissipate before the heating season, but the majority remains to be harvested throughout the heating season by circulating water through the ground piping and then to the conditioned buildings. Drake's Landing in Oktos Alberta, Canada, a neighborhood of 52 homes, is served by this type of seasonal ground thermal storage system. Constructed in 2007, the borehole thermal energy storage system required a five-year process of "charging up" to an operating temperature near 176°F (80°C).

WATER THERMAL STORAGE

Water has a number of amazing properties, one of which is a very high volumetric heat capacity. Not only is this heat capacity far higher than air, it is higher than almost every other substance. This means a given volume of water can be used to store more heat than any other substance, given a specific change in temperature.

One of the more common approaches to using water to store thermal energy is to generate cool water at night with a cooling tower or night-sky radiative approach, then store the water to be used throughout the following day to cool the space. Using these heat rejection approaches takes advantage of the diurnal temperature swing and the ability to cool the water below the dry bulb air temperature. To get the most out of the stored water, this approach pairs well with radiant cooling, which functions with higher supply-water temperatures.

When considering water storage, anticipate a substantial storage volume, even after measures have been taken to minimize heating and cooling requirements. Creating stratified conditions in the tank can maximize tank storage capacity, which includes a high height-to-width tank ratio. Heat pumps can be used to boost the capacity of these storage systems beyond what the outside environment can provide.

ICE THERMAL STORAGE

When water changes state from liquid to solid, it absorbs even more heat than when it changes temperature as a liquid. As with all phase changes, energy is absorbed in the freezing and thawing process at a constant temperature. Ice is a highly effective way to store cooling. A relatively common approach is to run a chiller at night to freeze water, then use that ice to cool the chilled water circulated the next day.

There are many potential benefits to ice thermal storage, one of the primary being as a way to reduce peak demand loads and charges and take advantage of low nighttime electricity prices. This may not be particularly important for a net zero energy, because during the summer days it will be producing its own on-site renewable energy; however, the cooler nighttime air temperatures allow the chillers to operate more efficiently, and so it may be possible to reduce the size of cooling equipment.

DOMESTIC HOT WATER

In plumbing systems, a significant energy use is for domestic hot water. In a typical office building, the energy used to provide hot water may add up to only a small proportion of the total building energy, but in athletic and recreation facilities, restaurants, and hotels, domestic hot water can consume a substantial amount of energy.

Low-Energy Hot Water

The following ideas can help save energy used to produce hot water.

MINIMIZE WATER CONSUMPTION

Minimizing hot water use is the best "downstream" approach to reducing energy use (and saving water). Installing low-flow hot water fixtures and appliances is a good way to reduce the amount of water consumed. Lavatory faucets should have 0.5 GPM aerators; showerheads should be "high-impact" designs, with 1 to 1.5 GPM flow.

REDUCE WAIT TIME FOR HOT WATER

If people have to wait too long for hot water, they will switch out the low-flow aerators and showerheads. To avoid this, it is important to consider that:

$$\text{Wait Time} = \frac{\text{gallons of cold water in the line}}{\text{flow rate}}$$

This means that reducing flow rate makes wait time longer, so the volume of cold water in the line must be reduced proportionally to make wait time reasonable. The volume of water in the line is based on the length of the pipe branch from the recirculation loop (or hot water heater if there is no recirculation loop) to the fixture and the size of the pipe. Both the pipe size and branch length should be minimized.

Shortening the branch length can be accomplished in a number of ways, each of which has practical benefits and drawbacks.

- Placing the heater close to the sink; using a point-of-use water heater.
- Using a hot water recirculation loop with a close connection to the point-of-use.
- Grouping hot water fixtures close to the heater location.

One interesting strategy is structured plumbing, or on-demand water circulation. This is an unusual approach to hot water recirculation whereby the recirculation pump operates at a high flow rate to quickly move water to the fixture when it is needed (based on an occupancy sensor or button operation).

Hot Water Source

Solar thermal hot water is an obvious approach to generate domestic hot water for a low zero energy building (see Figure 7.16). Solar hot water typically makes up some, but not all, of the heating requirements. Solar fraction, or the portion (0.0 to 1.0) of the total water heating load met with solar energy, is usually limited, for three reasons: The efficiency of the solar collector drops off at higher temperatures; rejecting excess heat becomes a bigger issue; and

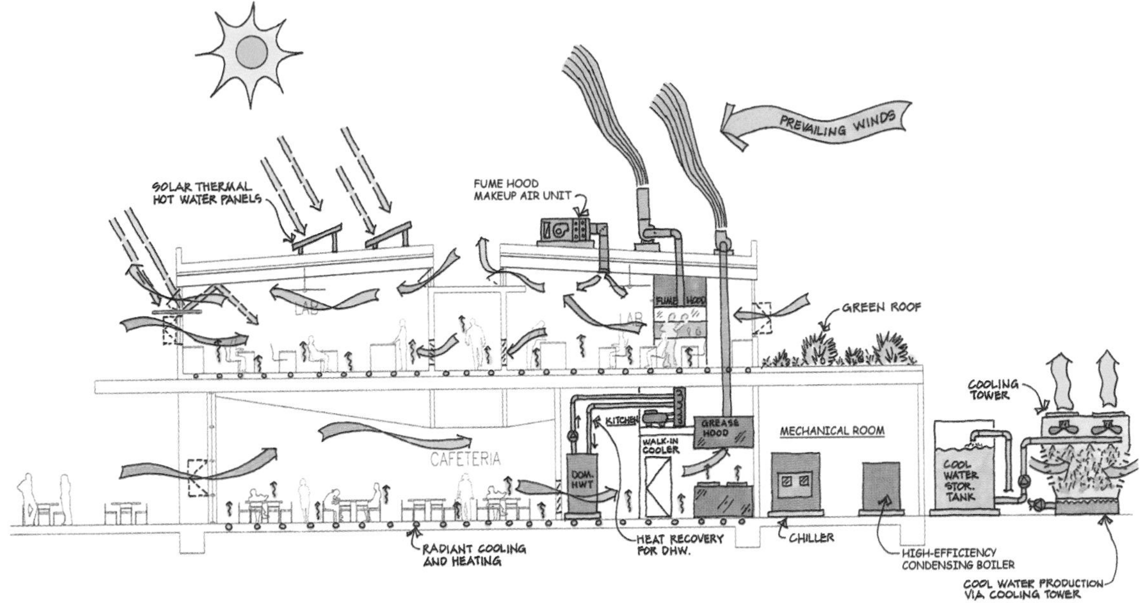

■ **FIGURE 7.16** Solar thermal and heat recovery from a walk-in cooler provide low-energy hot water at the Science & Student Life Center at Sacred Heart School in Atherton, California. *Image courtesy of Stantec Consulting Services, Inc.*

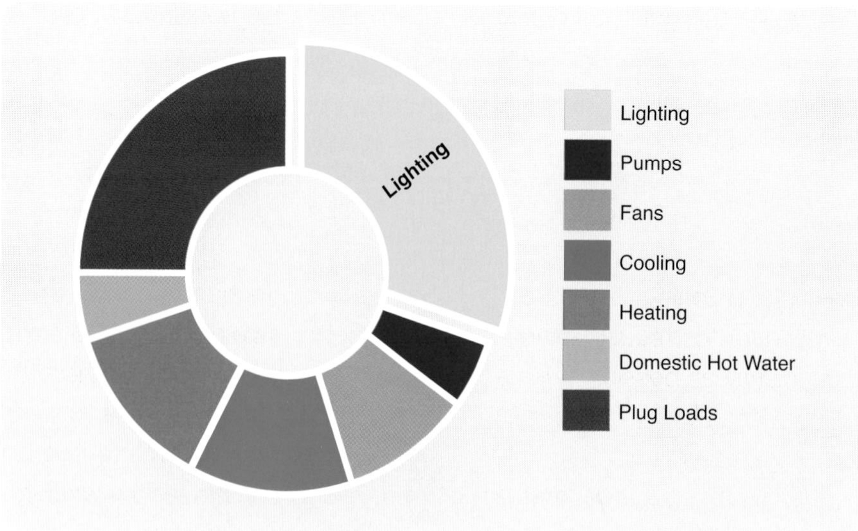

■ **FIGURE 7.17** Lighting is a large slice of a commercial building's energy pie.

storage requirements increase. The remaining energy is made up from a backup source, such as a natural gas or electric water heater.

Heat pumps can be a fruitful source of domestic hot water. They may be combined with heat pumps used for space heating, where excess heat is recovered with a desuperheater and used to preheat water. Alternately, a separate heat pump water heater, dedicated to domestic hot water production, may be the simplest and most effective approach for many applications. When combined with photovoltaics or other on-site energy generation, these units offer an overall efficiency that is on par with solar thermal. In addition, with some careful planning, they can provide useful space cooling as they produce hot water. Likewise, heat recovery using waste heat from cooling systems can be used to heat water (see Figure 7.16).

LIGHTING

Basic Concepts

Lighting is a major energy end use in almost all commercial building types (see Figure 7.17). The approach to the active systems for low-energy illumination of the environment is conceptually similar to the concepts that apply to low-energy active systems in general.

It is important that lighting be considered a holistic part of the design of the architecture, rather than as a set of components added to the architecture. Good lighting design works seamlessly with the architectural daylighting applications of the spaces and the functional requirements of the building's architectural program. The goal is to provide performance, quality, beauty, and energy efficiency to the visual environment.

Lighting starts with an understanding of the lighting performance requirements of the individual spaces. (The "Luminous Energy Design Science" section in Chapter 6 established a basic framework for using illuminance level requirements to guide daylighting performance.) A low-energy approach to lighting would be to design lighting as a supplement to daylighting. In this case, lighting would be off or dimmed in daylit spaces during daylight hours, and provide full lighting for nighttime hours, as well as for spaces that are not daylit. Further, because humans are biologically adapted to lower light levels at night, the light levels designed for nighttime lighting can be lower.

To achieve low-energy lighting, it is not enough to select energy-efficient technologies and light sources. The first priority is to reduce the need for artificial lighting through daylighting and the precise definition of illuminance-level requirements. The next step is to provide light only when and where it is needed through the use of controls and zoning. The third step is to provide lighting for the reduced illumination needs as efficiently as possible, with a low lighting power density. High-performance lighting is low energy, but it is also high quality. Lighting quality, functionality, visual interest, beauty, and design must not be sacrificed. Lighting design that meets this demanding definition of high performance is truly an art.

One concept essential to high-performance and low-energy lighting design is to separate ambient lighting level requirements from task lighting level requirements whenever practical. This approach has many benefits. It allows lower light level ambient conditions, which makes daylighting effective throughout more of the year, reducing lighting energy requirements from both daylight contributions and lower overall lighting power density. In addition, task conditions are optimized, which allows occupants to control the illumination levels to suit the needs of individual tasks. Light-emitting diode (LED) task light technology with very low power requirements is available.

Once the lighting performance and quality requirements are known, the objective is to meet them with the lowest-energy solution. Several design considerations work together to create a low-energy lighting system. Daylighting should be a foundation for the lighting design, and appropriate daylighting controls and zoning should be incorporated. Further, the overall control system should keep the lights off whenever they are not needed. The lighting itself should use energy-efficient technology that best meets the lighting application. One measure of the overall energy efficiency of the lighting design is the lighting power density. This important metric, discussed in Chapter 4, is a measure of the total connected lighting power (watts) per square foot of space served. Another important and related metric is the average *in-use* lighting power density after controls. This accounts for controls that keep the full installed lighting power from being used most of the year.

Integration with Daylighting

To save energy with daylighting, controls that "harvest" daylight must be successfully integrated with the lighting control system. It is also important that the daylighting control system

Key Principles for Low-Energy Lighting

- Integrate the lighting solution as part of the architecture.
- Daylight integration: Design as a supplement to daylight.
- High performance means maintaining high quality and low energy.
- Controls should work to keep lights off when not needed.
- Utilize a layered approach to lighting systems and controls.
- Separate task light from ambient light.
- Control both the interior and exterior lighting systems.
- Utilize high-efficiency lighting technology, with a focus on overall luminaire efficacy.
- The ultimate energy metric for a lighting system is its in-use lighting power density (LPD) or equivalent energy use intensity (EUI).

be automated and designed so that occupants cannot override it. This point cannot be overemphasized, because there are many examples of buildings that have good daylight design but do have not effective artificial lighting controls to actually save energy. The potential for energy savings is significant, in addition to counting the quality of light and the positive impact daylight has on occupant well-being.

In order to develop lighting design as a complete system of daylighting and artificial lighting, it is important to understand the daylight characteristics of the spaces being lit. This makes it possible for artificial lighting to effectively supplement and complement daylighting in a space throughout the year. The daylighting simulations completed for the spaces within the building will provide information about appropriate lighting control zones. The objective is to group areas with common daylighting characteristics into controlled lighting zones. The functional requirements of the space will also dictate specific zoning configurations. The daylighting zones of the space, at the most basic level, will differ based on the orientation of the sidelighting of exterior walls, or if toplighting is provided. Shading obstructions such as adjacent buildings or trees may also be cause for unique daylighting zoning requirements within the building.

Zones directly adjacent to south sidelighting exterior walls or toplighting zones will typically have daylighting levels consistently above illumination level requirements, and may be effectively controlled with simple bi-level stepped switching. South daylighting zones further from the exterior wall will likely benefit from dimming controls as the daylighting level drops off. This is also true for other daylighting zones within a building, which can frequently drop below required illumination levels.

The characteristics of the daylighting zones and the functional requirements of the space will also influence the type of daylighting sensor or photocell that is utilized. There are two basic types of photocells, local and global. Local photocells are located within the zones that they control and directly read the lighting levels in the space (see Figure 7.18). Global photocells are typically mounted on the roof of the building and capture exterior illumination levels. Spaces that can benefit from more exacting control should be fitted with local photocells. A global photocell, in contrast, can help make the overall daylighting controls system more cost-effective, because it can replace many individual local photocells. This can be effective for controlling many small zones such as private offices or other individual small rooms that have their own occupant

■ **FIGURE 7.18** Local Photocell Mounted Directly to Fluorescent Luminaire.

lighting controls. Global controls can be effective as well for controlling zones that only require bi-level switching for daylight harvesting.

Lighting Control Systems

Lighting controls provide for functionality, flexibility, and convenience in the operation of a lighting system. They also play a vital role in reducing lighting energy use. One way to design lighting controls to achieve energy savings is to make "off" the default position. This requires the engagement of occupants to turn on the lighting only when it is desired/needed. In practice, this is a very user-friendly approach. Good light control strategies allow for simple, direct, and easy-to-find "on and off" occupant control. Thereafter, the control system takes over, to ensure effective energy management. The occupant manages the demand for lighting, and the lighting controls manage the energy use of lighting by adjusting for a variety of control inputs or scenarios. This basic concept is part of a layered approach to lighting control.

The layered approach to lighting control includes manual occupant control and automated control, based on inputs such as daylight levels, time clocks, and occupancy/vacancy sensors (see Figure 7.19). The use of simple manual controls is important for functionality and to help prevent occupants from overriding the automated controls. Manual control can be more than an on and off switch; it can also feature dimming or multilevel switching capabilities, to further enable occupant customization and take advantage of the energy savings from dimmed lights. Automated controls work to keep the lights off or dimmed when they are not needed by occupants—an important benefit, for occupants are notoriously poor at turning the lights off.

Some commercial buildings, such as multifamily and lodging building types, have unique lighting control requirements for the individual dwelling or lodging units. A simple and effective approach to these types of spaces is the use of a master switch at the unit's main entry, which can easily activate or deactivate selected lighting and plug load circuits. The switch can even be used to control occupied versus unoccupied temperature set points. Depending on the complexity of the individual unit, additional controls such as daylight sensors, occupancy/vacancy sensors, and time clocks can be utilized to further enhance flexibility and energy savings while in occupied mode.

The use of vacancy sensors is an energy-saving improvement on the conventional occupant sensor. The goal with vacancy sensors is to turn off the light when vacancy is sensed. But the light should not turn on when occupancy is sensed; rather, the occupant should decide whether additional light is needed. The daylight levels may be adequate, or the illumination from a task light may be sufficient. This can save energy by preventing the light from turning on when it is unneeded. There are exceptions where occupancy detection is needed, such as spaces with no daylight or other light source.

Many commercial buildings have extended periods when they are unoccupied—most at night. The role of time clocks in lighting controls is to automatically turn off the lights during scheduled unoccupied periods (see Figure 7.20). A certain amount of manual, but temporary, override capability can be built in to allow for the occasional unplanned occupancy during unoccupied hours. In many commercial buildings, a few common building services are provided during unoccupied night hours, such as janitorial services, security services, and emergency lighting. These services can impact the ability to minimize and control lighting use at night.

One solution to nighttime janitorial service is to move to daytime cleaning, if possible. There

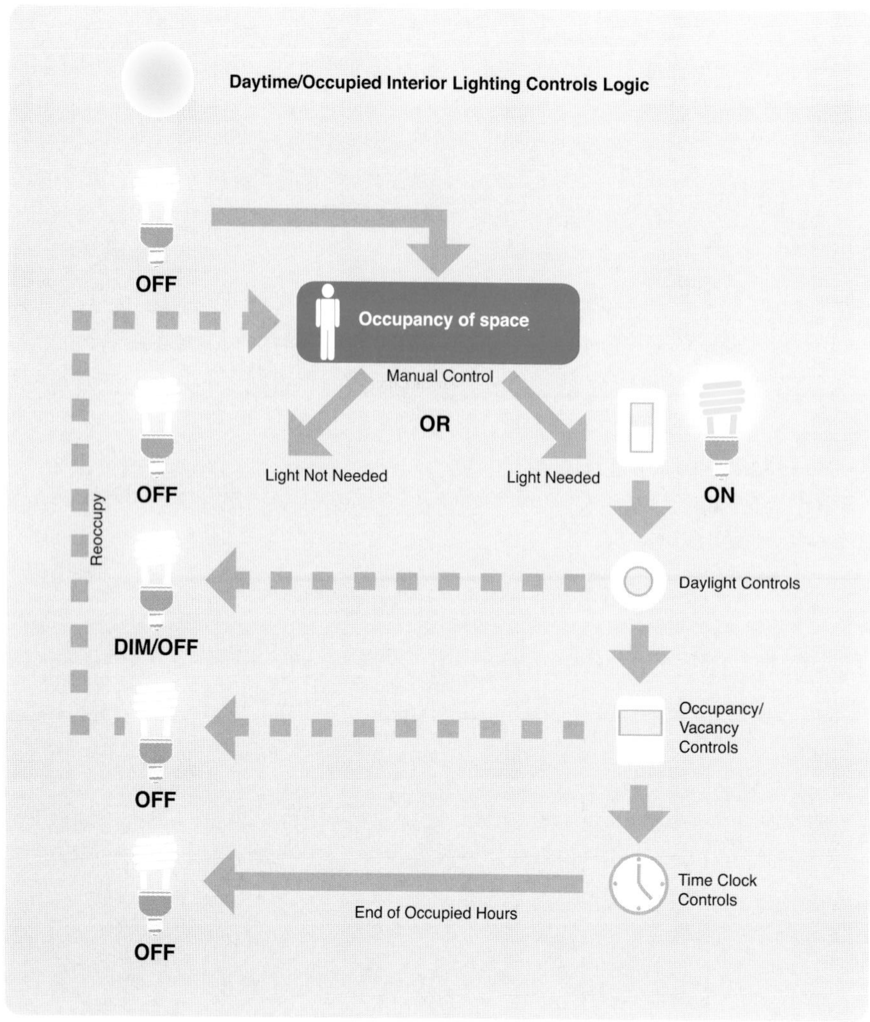

■ **FIGURE 7.19** Interior Occupied Hours Lighting Control Concept.

is a growing trend toward this type of arrangement, as it also makes better hours possible for janitorial service employees. If daytime cleaning is not feasible, then a time clock can be used to sweep lights off based on scheduled cleaning hours for the building.

Many buildings require regular security checks at night. These brief walkthroughs by security personnel can be controlled separately with their own light switches (enabled only at night), and designed so that the lights turn back off after a very brief period of time. Emergency lights are often left on continuously, and controlling them can represent additional energy savings. Emergency lights can be turned off with the main lights in each zone, based on the control sequences; but the emergency generator is required to activate the emergency lighting when power disruption is sensed.

Control of the exterior lighting also represents enhanced functionality and additional energy savings. The conventional practice of using photocells to activate and deactivate exterior lighting based on nighttime conditions is the most basic level of control; it does not control light levels based on nighttime needs. In fact, most exterior lighting does not need to be on all night.

A similar layered approach to lighting and controlling interior lighting can be applied to exterior lighting. Some of the primary exterior

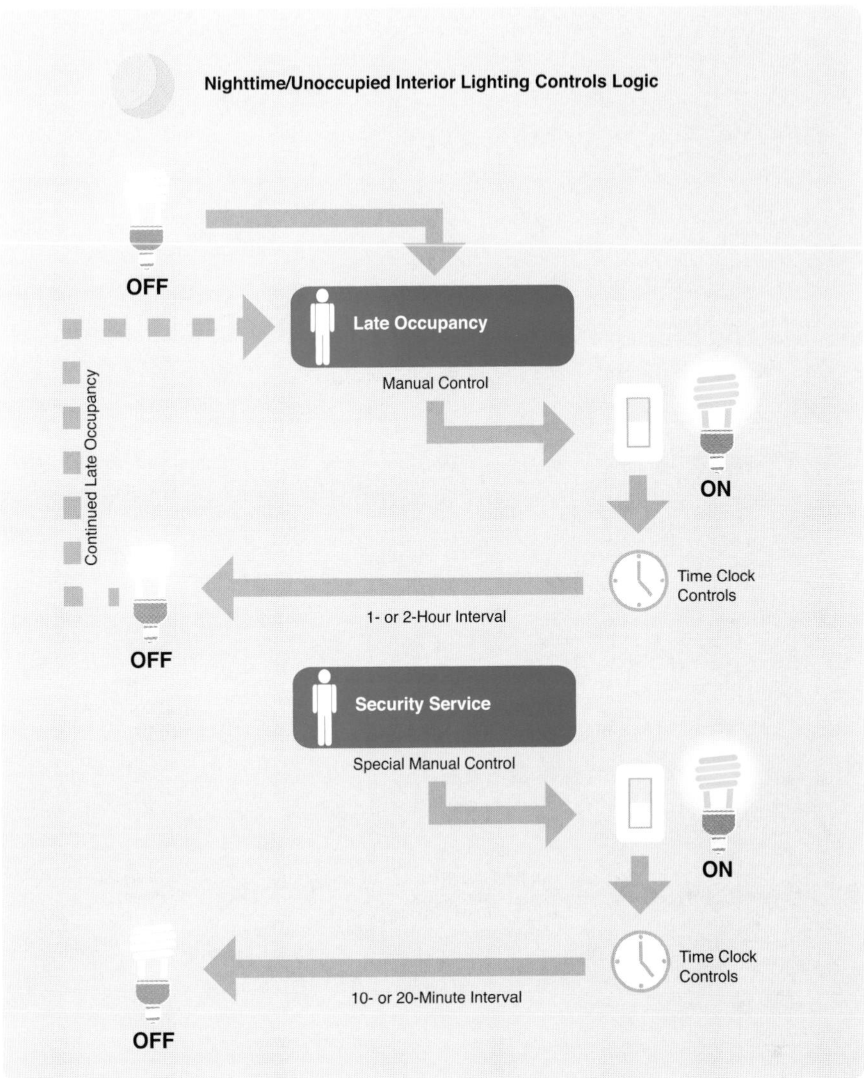

■ **FIGURE 7.20** Interior Unoccupied Hours Lighting Control Concept.

lighting functions include basic exterior area lighting, landscape and feature lighting, wayfinding, and security/safety lighting (see Figure 7.21). Landscape or site feature lighting should be controlled so that it is on only during scheduled occupied nighttime hours. This can be accomplished by setting the lighting to turn on with a photocell and off at a specific time based on building occupancy. Exterior area lighting and general wayfinding lighting can be set to turn on or step up based on occupancy sensors. In this way, only low-level safety lighting is on during all night hours, and other functional lighting is controlled based on occupant needs and the occupancy schedule of the building.

An important supplement to a well-integrated and layered lighting control approach to interior and exterior building lighting is to educate the occupants about the basic lighting control operation. The manual controls for occupants should be easy to find and intuitive to operate. With some simple instructions about how the manual controls work with the building's automated controls, the occupants will experience less frustration and be able to optimize lighting to meet their needs, while assisting the energy-saving features of the system.

From a control technology perspective, the advancement of digital distributed devices is changing the ability to optimize control

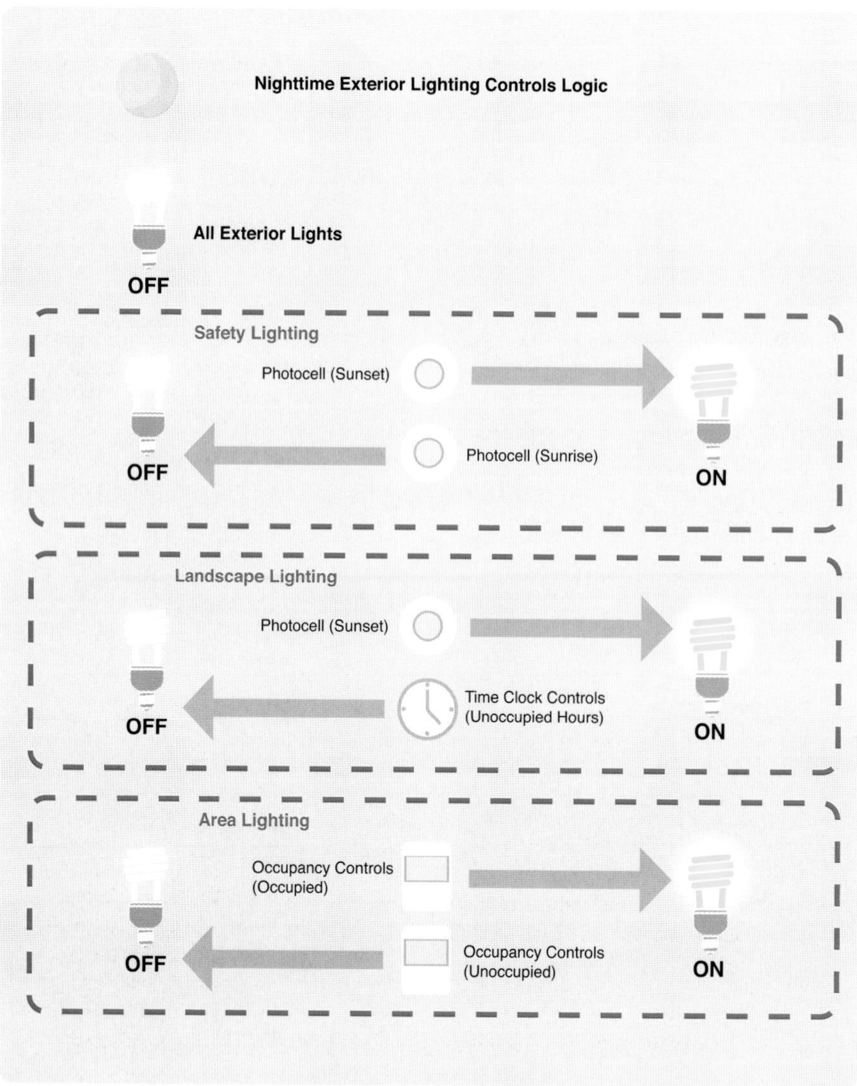

■ **FIGURE 7.21** Exterior Nighttime Hours Lighting Control Concept.

strategies. Digital distributed controls allow great flexibility with sensor and control functions within a space. Because they are digital and plug-and-play, these advanced control systems can allow any variation of control customization for any defined space. They can also allow for easy reconfiguration of zones and control sequences over the life of the building. While these devices make it possible to optimize lighting controls, issues of cost and complexity are currently trade-offs that need to be considered, especially with elaborate control configurations.

Low-Energy Light Source Technology

The technology and performance capability of light sources is rapidly advancing, allowing for greater control, longer lamp life, and significantly enhanced energy efficiency. There are many lighting source technologies that offer high efficacies, including high-intensity discharge (HID), compact fluorescent, linear fluorescent, light-emitting diode (LED), and organic light-emitting diode (OLED) (see Figure 7.22). Halogen and incandescent technologies, which have very low efficacy, are not appropriate for low-energy lighting solutions and net zero energy buildings.

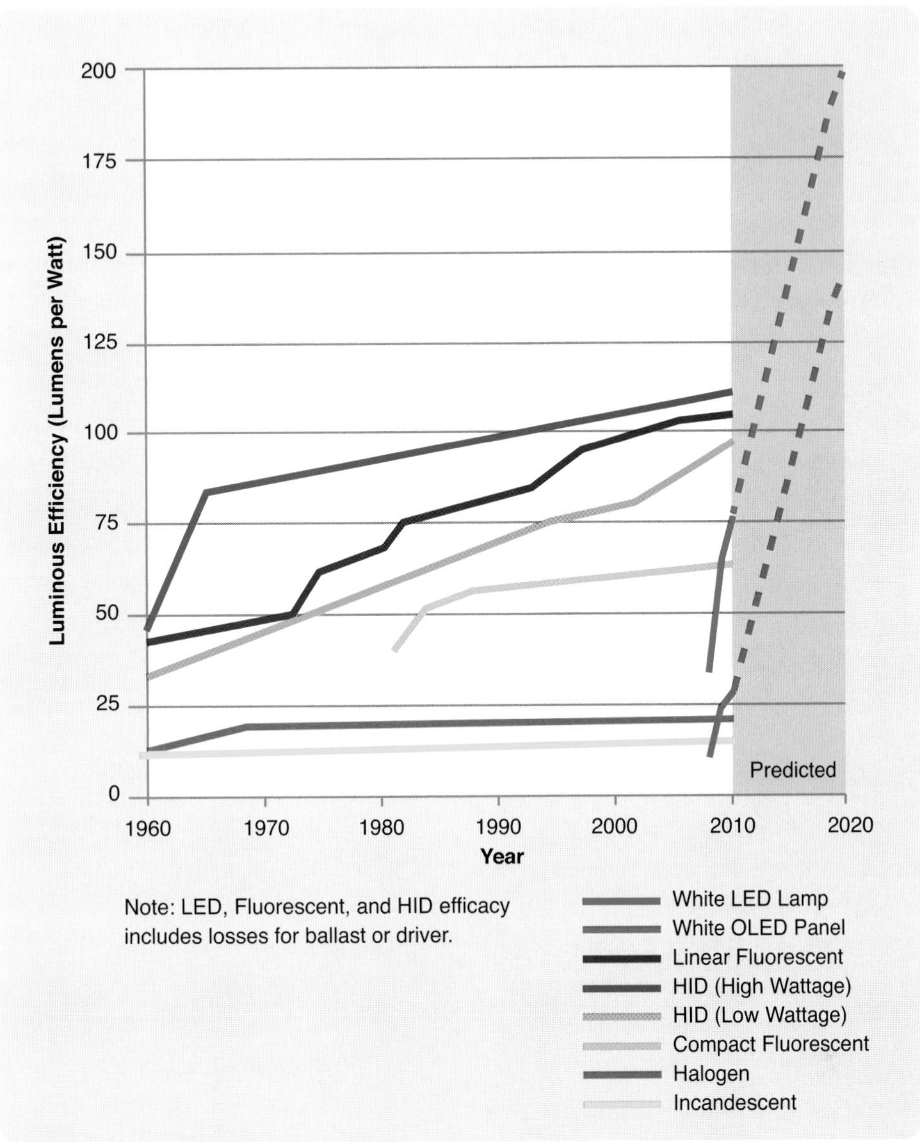

■ **FIGURE 7.22** Historical and Predicted Luminous Efficacy. *Data source: Department of Energy Solid State Lighting Research & Development: Multi-year Program Plan. www1.eere.energy.gov/buildings/ssl.*

The most striking technological advances are in solid-state lighting with both LED and OLED light sources. LEDs are small semiconductor devices that emit light in a narrow optical band under the presence of an electrical charge (see Figure 7.23). This property is known as *electroluminescence*. LEDs are, therefore, monochromatic and have been commonly used in lighting applications that utilize monochromatic light sources, such as traffic lights. A white light source is needed for general lighting applications. There are several approaches to making a white LED source. One is to use a phosphor coating on a blue LED to convert the emitted light to white light. Another approach is to use a combination of red, green, and blue LEDs to mix and create a white light. A hybrid combination of these two approaches can also be used to create a white LED source. Developing a quality white source has been one of the challenges in developing LED technology. The different approaches to creating quality white-light LED impact the efficacy of the light sources, which can vary dramatically.

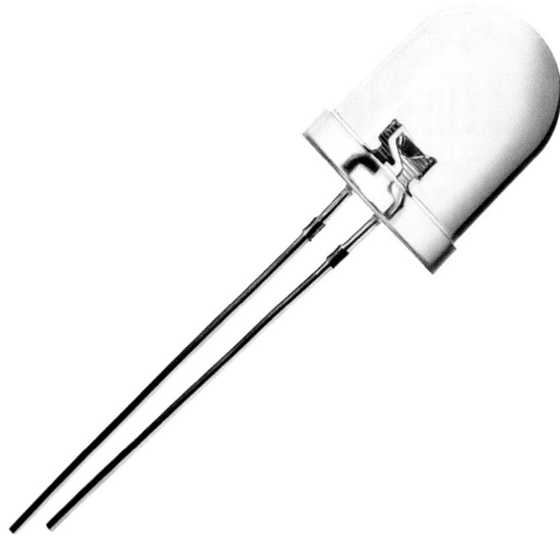

■ **FIGURE 7.23** Light-Emitting Diode.

OLEDs utilize a thin film organic material to create electroluminescence with an electrical charge. They are characterized by low-intensity light emitting from a whole surface, unlike LED, which is a compact source design. OLED technology is currently being used in consumer electronics, especially for displays that require general surface illumination. OLEDs are flexible and can be made into a variety of shapes and forms, allowing for many creative applications. This technology could introduce whole new ways of bringing lighting into the built environment.

LED technology has several unique advantages in addition to its energy efficiency. LEDs are compact and resistant to breakage. They perform well in cold temperatures. They have a long life and can be dimmed. They can be turned on instantly, and their long life is not affected by rapid cycling. LEDs are also a directional light, meaning all of the light emitting can be directed to the surface needing illumination. In contrast, luminaires for conventional light sources require surfaces to redirect much of the light to the surface needing illumination, which means a good portion of the light can be lost in the process.

LED performance is impacted by heat, and the design of LED fixtures includes heat sinks to reduce operating temperature. This sensitivity to heat can diminish energy performance; however, it can also make LEDs a very efficient application for exterior lighting, when outside air temperatures are low. LEDs operate with DC voltage and require a conversion from AC to DC. This conversion is completed with a driver, so the driver efficiencies must also be taken into consideration when examining the efficacy of LED light sources.

In fact, for all light source selections, the overall luminaire efficacy (lamp, ballast or driver, and luminaire) is far more important than the efficacy of the source. Currently, HID and linear fluorescent lamps can be combined with efficient ballasts and fixtures, and have the same or better overall efficacy as LED luminaires. Linear fluorescents with energy-saving lamping options offer lower wattage (25 W compared to 32 W) and further reduce energy use. The application, including what is illuminated and the way it is controlled, influences the ultimate lamp and luminaire selection.

Remember that the best technological solution should be optimized only after first reducing the need for lighting, as discussed earlier in this section. Further, the lighting power density and, ultimately, the in-use lighting power density or lighting energy use intensity are the measure of the energy effectiveness of a solution.

DISTRICT ENERGY

Basic Concepts

When considering energy independence, it is not necessary for every building to achieve net zero energy on its own. There are many benefits and synergies involved when addressing energy issues at the campus, community, and multiple building scales. Specifically, the energy ecosystem idea explored earlier in this chapter can be fully exploited at a multiple building scale. At this larger scale, high levels of efficiency and cost-effectiveness can be achieved. However, it is the inherent possibilities stemming from a diversity of energy loads and energy sources that can be leveraged for a very low energy system, or energy ecosystem.

One of the reasons for using a district energy solution is that different uses within a community may have complementary energy consumption profiles. When energy consumption, as well as heating and cooling requirements for multiple buildings occur at different times, the overall peak design load for all buildings will be smaller than the aggregate sum of the individual load requirements. This results in smaller central equipment, compared to the greater total capacity that would need to be installed on an individual building basis.

For example, a mix of typical multifamily residential and commercial office spaces would have complementary energy profiles. The office spaces would chart their highest energy use during the hours of the workweek. During this time a majority of the residents would be away from home, at work or school, meaning that the residential spaces would experience low energy use during the weekdays; their peak uses would be in the evenings and on the weekends, when the offices are largely unoccupied.

In addition to taking advantage of complementary energy use profiles, multiple building scale district energy systems can facilitate the sharing and reuse of waste energy. For example, an industrial process could export waste heat to be used to heat other buildings. There might even be thermal energy synergies between the residential and commercial offices described in the preceding example. Commercial offices are often in cooling mode because of high internal loads, whereas residential uses are often in heating mode because of low internal heat gain. In these cases, the heat generated from cooling the offices could be used to heat neighboring residential units.

Another reason to consider district energy is that some technologies for generating electricity, cooling, and heating are more appropriate for a larger application. They often don't scale down well to the demand of a single building. In addition, having more of the equipment located centrally means that it is easier to maintain; it may also mean that it is appropriate to use more sophisticated and diverse technologies, which would be difficult to maintain on a building-by-building level. In some cases, it is preferable to locate equipment further from buildings. For example, cooling towers generate noise and eject water vapor into the air. Noise and water vapor are two disturbances we typically want to separate from our buildings (especially operable windows) as much as possible.

Low-Energy District Systems

District energy systems can provide a wide variety of energy services to buildings. One traditional district energy solution is a steam-based central heating plant. District energy solutions can also offer hot water and chilled water to meet individual building heating and cooling needs. Numerous innovative, low-energy synergies and strategies can be considered to provide heating and cooling, based on the climate, site, and building types served. In addition to using efficient equipment, it may be feasible to use renewable energy fuels and systems to generate thermal energy. Good practice is to find ways to capture free energy from the site and reuse waste energy within the multiple building system. Thermal energy sinks and storage can be a significant opportunity at a large-scale system. Some projects have taken advantage of deep lake or deep sea water for cooling. Ground-source and seasonal ground-source systems may offer benefits for heating and cooling in a district energy solution. Another option is a moderate- or low-temperature central plant, which can lower infrastructure costs and energy use when coordinated with low-energy buildings designed with moderate-temperature systems.

Another service that district energy systems can provide is distributed generation of electricity with on-site generators or fuel cells or through renewable energy systems. District energy systems can include community-scale wind, hydro, geothermal, and solar, depending on the available resources. Some of these solutions will be far more feasible and cost-effective at larger scales. Biofuels or other renewable energy systems can be used to generate hydrogen for fuel cell electricity generation. This application will become increasingly more attractive as the technology continues to develop. (Chapter 8 provides guidance on a variety of renewable energy systems technologies, many of which can be optimized at a district energy scale.)

COMBINED HEAT AND POWER PLANT

There are many distributed generation applications that generate substantial amounts of waste heat. This is typical of all combustion-based generation using either biomass fuels or conventional fuels. Taking advantage of this waste heat can markedly increase the efficiency and usefulness of the district energy solution.

Combined heat and power, also called cogeneration, is the process of taking advantage of the inefficiency built into the process of generating electricity. When fuels are used to produce electricity, some of the energy is converted to electricity; the remainder—typically, 50 to 60 percent—is released to the environment as heat. Much of that heat can be put to use, producing a combined heating and electrical efficiency of 70 to 80 percent. Why use additional boilers for heating when good-quality heat is being rejected from the generators?

A combined heat and power plant is characterized by the type of technology used for distributed electricity generation; it may include gas turbines, microturbines, steam turbines, and reciprocating engines. Distributed generation through the use of fuel cells, rather than combustion, can also be used as a combined heat and power plant. Many, but not all, fuel cells operate at very high temperatures and can provide relatively high-grade thermal energy, appropriate for water heating and building heating applications.

ORGANIC RANKINE GENERATION AND ABSORPTION CHILLERS

Combined heat and power is just one way to take advantage of waste heat from distributed generation. Waste heat can also be used to generate additional electricity and to produce air conditioning.

An organic Rankine cycle is a technology that can use waste heat to generate electricity. Compared to conventional steam-driven turbines that require high temperatures, an organic Rankine cycle system uses a special low-temperature boiling point working fluid (see Figure 7.24). The cycle is the vapor-compression refrigeration cycle run in reverse. By applying heat (typically, above 160°F) to this cycle, it can produce electricity. This is the same process that drives the binary cycle system for low-temperature geothermal applications, as discussed in Chapter 8.

The earlier discussion of heat pumps touched on the vapor-compression refrigeration cycle, which uses electricity to move heat from a hotter energy source to a cooler energy sink. This is the most common refrigeration cycle; however, others exist as well, and some of these can actually use heat instead of electricity to drive the refrigeration cycle. The absorption cycle is one of these approaches (see Figure 7.25); it can use waste heat in a combined heat and power plant to provide cooling. In an absorption chiller, instead of a compressor, the difference in solubility of a refrigerant such as ammonia in another fluid (water) drives the system based on an additional heat source into the generator. The efficiencies of both the absorption cycle and the organic Rankine cycle technologies are closely tied to the difference between the driving heat source and the sink. The warmer the heat source provided, the greater the power output or cooling energy provided by the process.

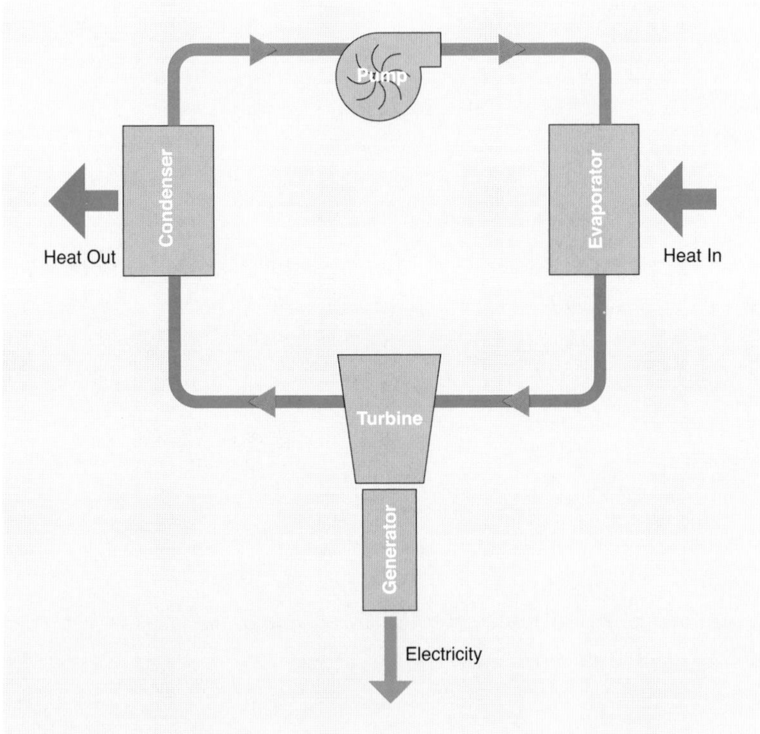

■ **FIGURE 7.24** Organic Rankine Cycle.

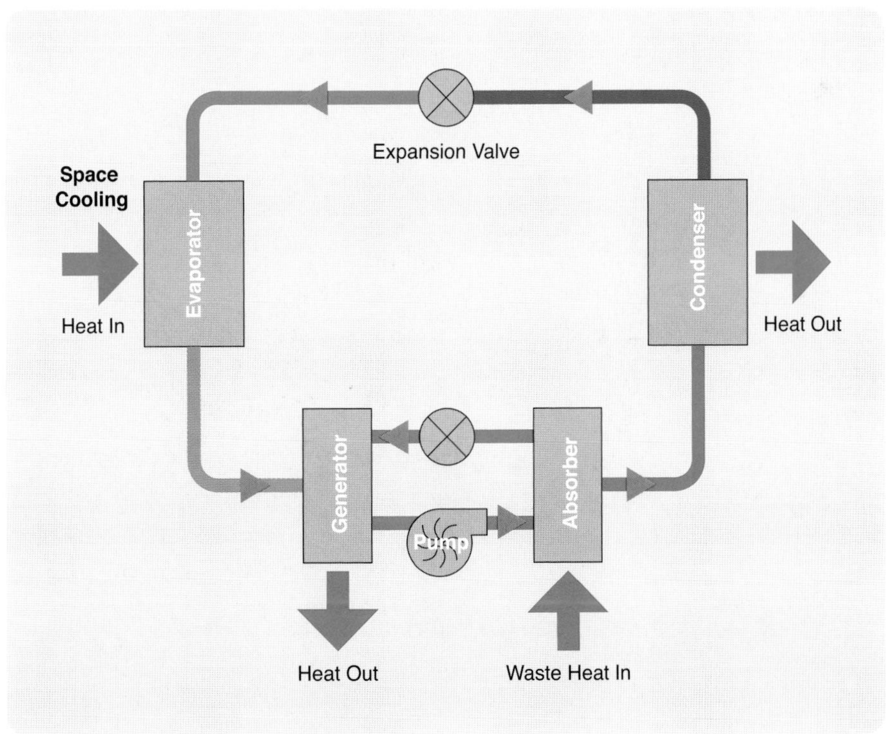

■ **FIGURE 7.25** Absorption Chiller.

RE

CHAPTER 8 RENEWABLE ENERGY

RENEWABLE ENERGY BASICS

There are many options for renewable energy integration for a net zero energy building. Which application or combination of applications is correct for any building is a complex question, one that involves variables such as available renewable energy resources, energy economics, and energy requirements, as well as building and site constraints. Planning for renewable energy systems for a net zero energy building can have dramatic impacts early in the project; as such, it should be part of the goal-setting, programming, and early concept phases, and be fully developed through to delivery of the project. (Chapter 4 takes a holistic view of renewable energy in the built environment. Chapter 9 sets up the economic framework for integrating renewable energy into a project.)

Net zero energy is the synthesis of passive strategies, efficient building systems, and renewable energy. The addition of significant renewable energy capacity is a highly distinguishing feature of a net zero energy building, and the design and implementation of renewable energy systems (see Figure 8.1) is highly specialized, requiring the capability of experienced consultants and integrators on the project delivery team. To that end, this chapter provides general guidance on planning renewable energy systems for net zero energy buildings, with a focus on early planning and the concepts needed to achieve effective integration into a net zero energy building.

This chapter—and for that matter, this book—leans heavily on solar electricity from photovoltaic systems as an important source of renewable energy for net zero energy buildings. Photovoltaic systems offer an integration technology and a modular design that make them very building-friendly. However, photovoltaics are not the answer for all projects, so it is

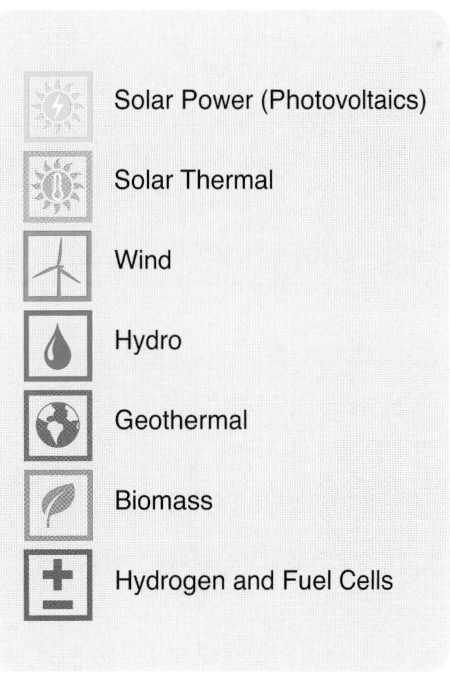

■ **FIGURE 8.1** Renewable Energy Systems.

good practice to consider all renewable energy system options when beginning a project. Evaluating a diversity of renewable energy systems can be a smart approach when matching available resources with energy needs, both thermal and electrical.

Solving our energy future and addressing climate change will require a broad and diverse approach to renewable energy solutions. Net zero energy buildings and communities are just one part of the solution, as they advance the objective of distributed renewable energy systems. But utility-scale energy also needs to be part of the solution, with a continual increase of the renewable energy proportion on the grid. The grid itself stands to play an important role in energy and demand management, in light of proposed smart grid systems that are being developed nationally and internationally. Most net zero energy commercial buildings will be grid-connected, using the grid like a battery—adding renewable energy when the building is generating a surplus of energy, and drawing from it when it has a deficit of renewable energy generation.

SOLAR POWER

Basic Concepts

Solar power derived through the use of photovoltaic (PV) technologies is the workhorse of the distributed, on-site renewable energy sector. It is the most common renewable energy resource for net zero energy buildings due to its versatility, cost-effectiveness, and capability for integration into projects at different scales. PV systems generate electricity, which is at the heart of their versatility. Most buildings use electricity more than any other energy source. Buildings can even be designed to be 100 percent electric, making PV a very complementary solution—although they may continue to use multiple energy sources and generate excess solar electricity to maintain their net zero energy position. Net metering enables the important function of importing and exporting electricity, which makes net zero energy buildings far more feasible. PV systems perform based on sunlight striking the surface of the module, and so tend to generate significantly more energy during the summer than in the winter, thus the need for net metering.

The photovoltaic process is highly reliable; photovoltaic cells, or solar cells, can generate electricity for decades. Moreover, they are free of moving parts and have low maintenance requirements, and their operation is quiet and pollution-free. They work based on a physical property called the photovoltaic effect, whereby certain materials produce an electrical current when exposed to light.

Solar cells are made from a semiconductor material, typically silicon. The molecular structure of silicon allows electrons to be freed by the incoming energy of photons from sunlight. This process is enhanced by "doping" the silicon cell with special atoms of a specific molecular structure that enhances silicon's ability to conduct electricity. The sunlit surface layer of the cell is doped with phosphorus atoms, creating extra electrons to break free. The bottom layer of the cell is doped with boron atoms, creating a molecular structure that is short of electrons, thus attracting the free electrons. The top layer with excess electrons is called the n-type semiconductor (negative); the bottom layer with a shortage of electrons is called the p-type semiconductor (positive). The flow from the n-type layer to the p-type layer is disrupted by an electric charge that occurs when the two types of semiconductors are joined. This charge prevents this flow but still allows electron flow in the opposite direction, from the p-type layer to n-type layer. By placing metal conductors on the top and bottom layers and connecting them, the solar cell conducts electricity through the applied conductor circuit, sending n-type layer electrons to the p-type layer. The electrons are free to move back to the n-type layer, thus completing the circuit (see Figure 8.2).

The solar cell is the basic building block in a PV module. The dark blue color typical of most solar cells derives from the antireflective coating added to the cell. The solar cells generate DC electricity, which, for most applications, needs to be converted to AC with the use of an inverter. There are a variety of solar cell types and manufacturing processes, each with its own level of efficiency and cost. A PV module is composed of many interconnected solar cells. Each manufactured module has a power rating, module area, module efficiency, and cost, among other specifications. The PV module is the basic planning and design unit for PV systems. Multiple PV modules can be connected into PV arrays, depending on the desired system size and energy generation goals.

Systems can be either off-grid or grid-connected. Grid-connected systems are very common in commercial buildings because of their size and because they are typically located in developed areas with access to grid-based electricity. Off-grid systems require energy storage for nighttime energy use and during lower solar-producing days. They also require larger PV systems that can keep the building fully operational during the winter months. One major consideration for off-grid net zero energy buildings is if backup energy systems are needed, in addition to batteries. Running a fossil fuel generator would have to be accounted for in a project's net zero energy balance, making net zero energy difficult to achieve, because off-grid PV systems have no way to export excess renewable energy to the grid as a means to offset this on-site fossil fuel use.

PV systems are composed of PV modules arranged in arrays and the *balance of system*. The balance of system is everything else that makes up the full functional system. A number of system components need to be considered and designed when implementing a PV system on a project. This section focuses primarily on the sizing and planning of the PV array because of its powerful influence on early design for a net zero energy project.

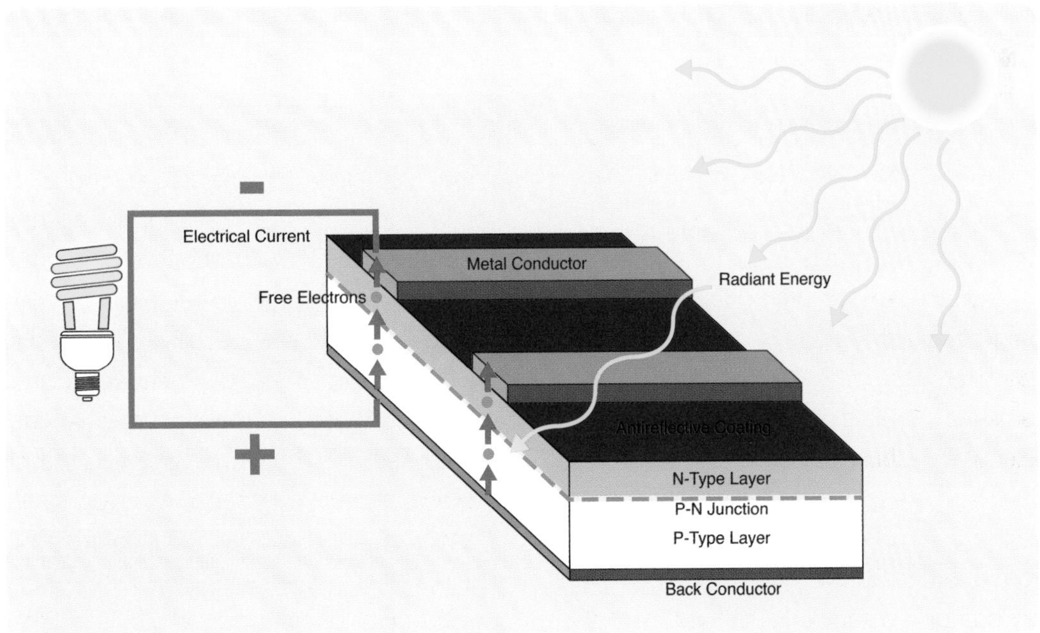

■ **FIGURE 8.2** Solar Cell Operation.

The key components that make up the balance of system include the mounting and racking, wiring and conduit, a PV disconnect for the array, and an inverter to convert the electricity to AC, which is connected to the building's electrical panel board. If the building is connected to the grid, ideally, the project will have a meter capable of net metering (see Figure 8.3). If the project is off-grid or grid-connected, and the intent is to have on-site energy storage, the system will also include storage batteries, a battery disconnect, and a battery charge controller. A PV system should also include a monitoring system that tracks system performance.

Technologies

CRYSTALLINE

There are two types of crystalline solar cells, monocrystalline and polycrystalline. Polycrystalline or multicrystalline cells are made from many smaller silicon crystals (see Figure 8.4); monocrystalline cells are made from single silicon crystals (see Figure 8.5). Polycrystalline cells are less efficient and less expensive than monocrystalline cells. Monocrystalline cells have a uniform appearance, whereas polycrystalline cells show some of the grain from the multiple silicon crystal process. Both polycrystalline and monocrystalline cells are made from thinly sliced wafers of the crystalline material.

A typical crystalline PV module is made up of rows and columns of connected solar cells that are encapsulated by two layers of laminated film. The PV module has a frame, backing panel, and front face of low-iron highly transparent glass.

Thin film modules cost less per watt than crystalline modules, but they are also considerably less efficient than the crystalline technology. Specifically, thin film systems require larger installation areas to generate the same amount of electricity, compared to a crystalline PV array. However, thin film PV is less affected by high temperatures and low light levels than crystalline PV.

NEW TECHNOLOGIES

The market is seeing many new approaches and advances to PV technology. Some are already available and established in the marketplace,

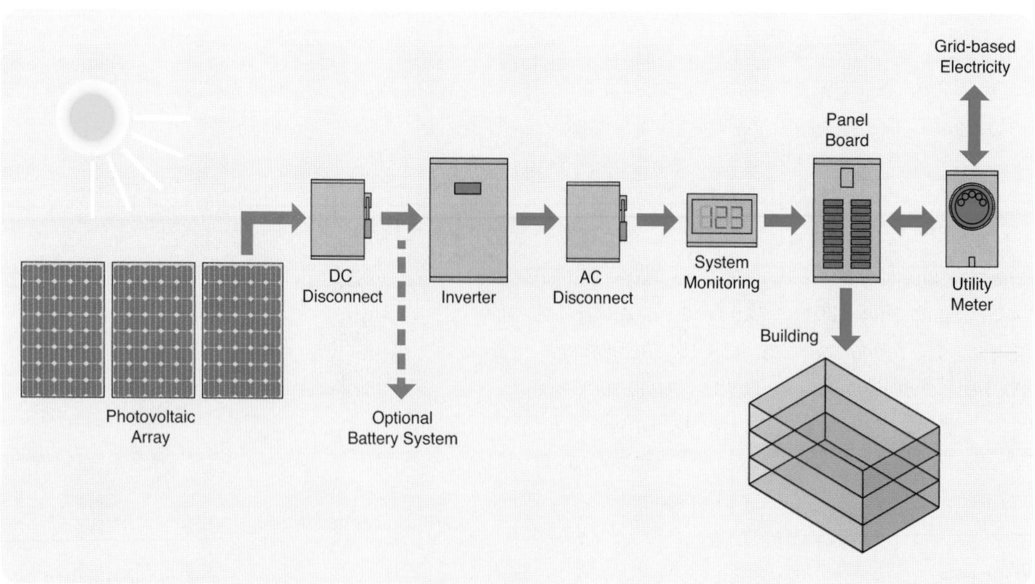

■ **FIGURE 8.3** Grid-Connected Photovoltaic System.

while others are in the research and development phase (R&D). Many of the promising advancements still in R&D are focused on new nanotechnologies and organic technologies. Some of the market-ready or near-market-ready improvements come from hybrid technology approaches.

■ **FIGURE 8.4** Polycrystalline Cells.

THIN FILM

There are a variety of thin film technologies that utilize different semiconductor materials, including amorphous silicon (a-Si), cadmium telluride (CdTe), and copper indium gallium diselenide (CIGS). Thin films are applied directly to a variety of rigid or flexible substrates, such as glass, plastic, or stainless steel. The resulting modules can take various forms, including rigid panels, similar to crystalline modules, or flexible sheets and rolls (see Figure 8.6).

■ **FIGURE 8.5** Monocrystalline Cells.

The thin film manufacturing process is the source of many of thin film PV's advantages: It is a low-energy and low-cost process, compared to crystalline PV manufacturing. The ability to create thin flexible sheets of any size makes thin film a good application for building-integrated PV (BIPV) materials, such as roofing, glazing, or wall panels.

Advanced PV Technologies

- ***Multijunction solar cells:*** *Multijunction cells use multiple junctions (compared to conventional cells that use a single n-type to p-type junction), thereby allowing greater efficiency because they can convert a wider spectrum of sunlight into energy.*
- ***Heterojunction solar cells:*** *Amorphous silicon thin film is layered onto a crystalline silicon wafer, improving its efficiency. The hybrid approach maintains the high efficiencies of crystalline cells while also offering some of the advantages of thin film, including higher efficiencies under high temperatures and lower light levels. Bifacial modules can be made that generate electricity from light striking both the front and back faces of the module.*
- ***Photovoltaic/thermal:*** *Photovoltaic and thermal hybrids (PV/T) combine solar cells and solar thermal collectors*

■ **FIGURE 8.6** Types of Thin Film Products. *NREL/PIX 13567; photograph by United Solar Ovonic.*

into a single module to generate both electricity and heat. The introduction of the solar thermal collector to the module captures waste heat from the photovoltaic process.

- ***Concentrating photovoltaics:*** *One approach to greater module efficiency is to increase the solar insolation striking the solar cell. Concentrating PV (CPV) modules feature a special lens design over the solar cell to either reflect or focus additional sunlight to the cell. This technology is different from concentrating solar power, which uses solar thermal energy technology to generate electricity.*

PV Module Efficiencies

One of the most important considerations when designing and selecting a photovoltaic system is the efficiency of the PV module. This is particularly true for net zero energy buildings, which require larger array sizes and are typically spaced-constrained. In addition to efficiency, the cost per watt, or kWh, is another important consideration, as it is closely related to efficiency. In general, more efficient modules are more expensive; however, they require less space to generate the same amount of electricity and will have corresponding lower installation-related costs.

Module efficiency refers to the efficiency of the assembled module, which takes into account solar cell efficiency and any other inefficiencies that are part of the module design. Module efficiencies diminish under higher operating temperatures, and with age, at a rate of about 1/2 to 1 percent per year. Manufacturers list module efficiencies along with other key module performance data, such as peak power (nameplate DC rating) and module size. The efficiency and peak power performance data are measured under standard test conditions (STC). STC is defined as 1,000 W/m^2 of irradiance, 25°C cell temperature, and 1.5 air mass (AM). So, at standard test conditions, a 15 percent efficient module with an area of 1 square meter would have a peak power rating of 150 watts.

The table in Figure 8.7 summarizes current efficiencies available in the market, based on solar cell technology, along with a potential near-term (10-year) efficiency range. The table also summarizes the peak power per square foot associated with each efficiency and the area of PV needed for a 500 kW system. Note how rapidly the area needed increases as the efficiency decreases.

Design Guidance

APPLICATION

Photovoltaic systems offer amazing flexibility for on-site renewable energy generation for net zero energy buildings. They can be sized to generate a great amount of energy, enough to supply all or a portion of a building's energy needs. PV systems can be incorporated into a wide variety of building types and site applications, and are adaptable to the many constraints imposed by a project and its site. PV systems also work in a wide variety of climates. They excel in regions like the southwest United States, with its clear skies and high solar irradiance levels, but they also perform well in more northern and overcast climates.

ESTIMATING THE LOAD

For a net zero energy building, the PV system is sized against the energy model or energy target for the project. If the only renewable energy system used on the project is PV, than it should be sized to accommodate the total annual predicted energy use, including any energy contingency. If other renewable energy systems are also incorporated, then the PV system can be designed for its portion of the annual energy use. For grid-connected net zero energy buildings with net metering, the annual energy use is the appropriate starting point. In an off-grid system or one that includes a battery, more analysis will be required to account for peak load and short-term energy cycle needs.

RESOURCE ASSESSMENT

The energy generated from a PV module is a function of the solar insolation striking the solar cells. Solar radiation data can be gathered as described in the "Solar Thermal" section, next in this chapter. Fortunately, there is a very user-friendly online tool that makes gathering solar resource data for a grid-connected crystalline PV design very straightforward. Called PVWatts, this resource is provided by the National Renewable Energy Laboratory (NREL) and can be found at http://www.nrel.gov/rredc/pvwatts/.

There are currently two versions of PVWatts online. The version 1 website has a simpler interface that displays a set of 239 locations in the United States and across the globe. The updated version 2 PVWatts allows customized location selections for the United States using a map with a 40 km-by-40 km grid. Selecting

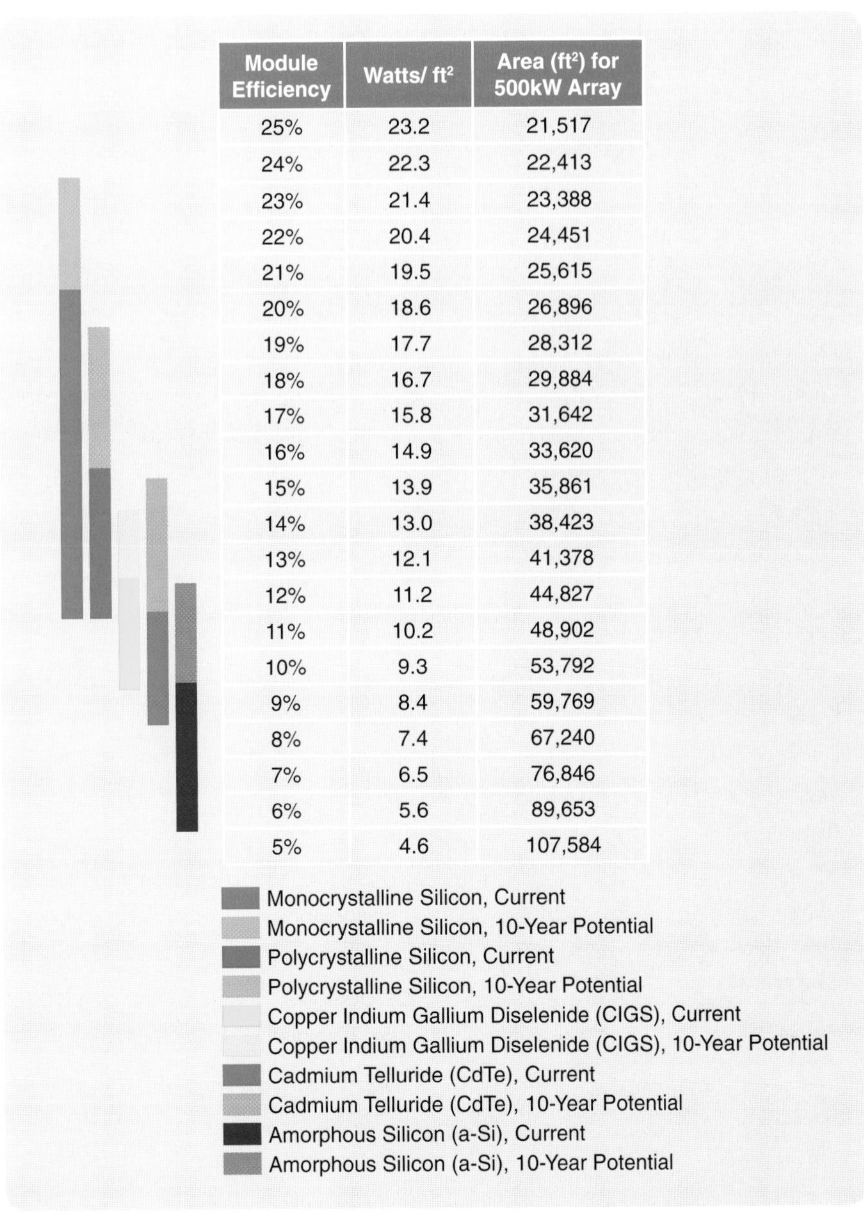

Module Efficiency	Watts/ ft²	Area (ft²) for 500kW Array
25%	23.2	21,517
24%	22.3	22,413
23%	21.4	23,388
22%	20.4	24,451
21%	19.5	25,615
20%	18.6	26,896
19%	17.7	28,312
18%	16.7	29,884
17%	15.8	31,642
16%	14.9	33,620
15%	13.9	35,861
14%	13.0	38,423
13%	12.1	41,378
12%	11.2	44,827
11%	10.2	48,902
10%	9.3	53,792
9%	8.4	59,769
8%	7.4	67,240
7%	6.5	76,846
6%	5.6	89,653
5%	4.6	107,584

■ **FIGURE 8.7** Typical PV Module Efficiencies Based on Solar Cell Technologies.

the location establishes site-specific information, such as solar insolation and utility rates, needed to calculate energy generation.

Once the location for the project is selected, the next step is to provide information about the PV system itself. The PVWatts calculator, which assumes a grid-connected crystalline PV module, has inputs for the PV system's nameplate DC rating (peak power), orientation, and tilt. When initially planning a system, a good technique is to use 1 kW as the system size, or nameplate rating, because the results can then be scaled up to any kW size system. It is also helpful to study a few tilt or orientation options, depending on the planned location for the PV array. In addition, the array can be selected as fixed, single-axis tracking, or dual-axis tracking. The calculator has a default derate factor that accounts for many system inefficiencies. The derate factor can be customized.

The PVWatts calculator results page provides average hourly solar insolation for the year and by month. Based on the system size, the monthly and annual energy produced and energy dollar value is given. If a 1 kW system is used, these results can be directly scaled to any system size. The key value needed from

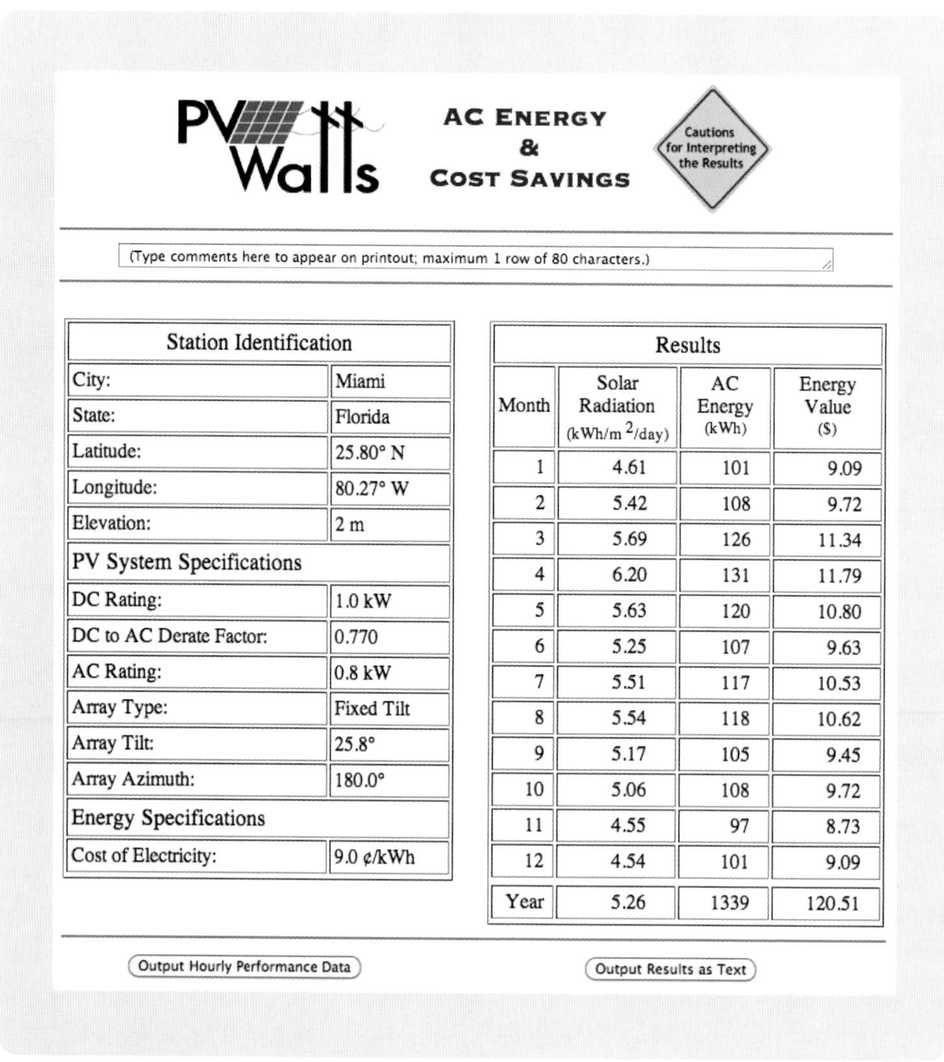

Station Identification	
City:	Miami
State:	Florida
Latitude:	25.80° N
Longitude:	80.27° W
Elevation:	2 m
PV System Specifications	
DC Rating:	1.0 kW
DC to AC Derate Factor:	0.770
AC Rating:	0.8 kW
Array Type:	Fixed Tilt
Array Tilt:	25.8°
Array Azimuth:	180.0°
Energy Specifications	
Cost of Electricity:	9.0 ¢/kWh

Results			
Month	Solar Radiation (kWh/m ^{2}/day)	AC Energy (kWh)	Energy Value ($)
1	4.61	101	9.09
2	5.42	108	9.72
3	5.69	126	11.34
4	6.20	131	11.79
5	5.63	120	10.80
6	5.25	107	9.63
7	5.51	117	10.53
8	5.54	118	10.62
9	5.17	105	9.45
10	5.06	108	9.72
11	4.55	97	8.73
12	4.54	101	9.09
Year	5.26	1339	120.51

■ **FIGURE 8.8** PVWatts Results Interface. *Data source and screen shots from NREL PVWatts website, accessed July 30, 2011.*

the PVWatts calculator to size the PV array is the annual kWh/kW of peak power, sometimes called a performance factor. For example, in Miami, with south-facing PV and a tilt equal to the location's latitude, this value is 1,339 kWh/kW (see Figure 8.8). The units for this value can be simplified to hours; and the result is conceptually similar to the annual peak sun hours for the PV system, except that the calculator factors in inefficiencies to account for any higher-temperature operation, and a customizable derate factor for the conversion of DC to AC power.

SYSTEM SELECTION

A PV array size can be determined using the results from PVWatts coupled with the annual design energy generation target for the PV system. For a net zero energy building with PV as its only renewable energy system, this would be equal to total annual energy use of the building, including any desired energy contingency.

To arrive at this figure, convert the required or targeted annual design energy generation (in kWh) to the design system size (in kW DC peak power) by dividing it by the annual kWh/kW performance factor from PVWatts. With the peak power system size, it possible to look at different PV module options and evaluate area needed based on their efficiency or watts per square foot, and begin to estimate cost based on module pricing or cost per watt. At early planning stages, it may be too early to settle on a specific module, so planning for installation space for a range of module efficiencies is an appropriate first step.

One of the most important reasons for doing early PV system sizing is to plan for the

PV Array Sizing and Selection Example

PV Array Sizing

- Annual design energy generation target: 5,000 MBtu, or 1,465,416 kWh
- Performance factor from PVWatts: 1,339 kWh/kW
- System size in DC peak power: 1,094 kW, or 1.1 mW

PV Module Option 1

- PV module: High-efficiency monocrystalline
- Peak power: 327 watts
- Module efficiency: 20.1 percent
- Module size: 1064 mm × 1559 mm, or 17.85 ft^2
- Number of 327 watt modules to provide 1,094 kW system: 3,346 modules
- Area of PV array to provide 1,094 kW system: Approximately 60,000 ft^2

PV Module Option 2

- PV module: High-efficiency polycrystalline
- Peak power: 315 watts
- Module efficiency: 14.4 percent
- Module size: 1320 mm × 1662 mm, or 23.62 ft^2
- Number of 315 watt modules to provide 1,094 kW system: 3,474 modules
- Area of PV array to provide 1,094 kW system: Approximately 82,000 ft^2

integration of the array during early design, either as roof-mounted, site-mounted, or some combination of the two. For space-constrained projects, panel efficiency will be a top priority; but when space is available, efficiency is less important. It may be useful to work from PV system size in watts-to-installed area by using a range of watts/ft^2 values before even looking at different modules in detail. If the amount of area available for installation is known, then a minimum watts/ft^2 and efficiency can be established for the PV modules.

BUILDING INTEGRATION

The orientation and tilt of the PV modules is a primary concern when integrating a PV array onto a building or site. For grid-connected systems, the goal is to maximize overall annual energy generation, which is typically a south-facing tilt equal to the project's latitude. For off-grid systems, it will be important to know the monthly differences and then design the system for lower solar resource days. Adjusting the tilt so it is 15 to 20 degrees greater than the latitude can even out the average daily solar insolation throughout the year. Both tilt and orientation relative to solar south have impacts on solar insolation, but usually not significant enough to prohibit less than optimal geometry. This is particularly valuable when working with building installations of PV modules, which will often impose some constraints on geometric options. See the tables in Figures 8.9 and 8.10 to see how tilt and orientation impact monthly and annual daily average solar radiation for a location in Boulder, Colorado.

Using roof-mounted PV arrays is a common approach for net zero energy buildings. A south-sloping roof can be a great asset for integrating PV with the roof design of a net zero energy building, and can be a benefit at any roof slope angle. Flat roofs are very common on commercial buildings and can easily accommodate a variety of PV array designs. Racking systems allow the flexibility to provide a variety of tilt angles for modules; they can even be made

Solar Insolation kWh/m²/day Based on Tilt Angle (South Orientation)
Boulder, Colorado
Latitude: 39° 43′ 59″

Month	Solar Altitude	0°	10°	20°	30°	40°	50°	60°	70°	80°	90°
Jan	27.31°	2.40	3.02	3.58	4.05	4.43	4.68	4.82	4.83	4.72	4.49
Feb	33.17°	3.13	3.72	4.22	4.61	4.89	5.05	5.09	4.99	4.77	4.43
Mar	42.69°	4.67	5.21	5.62	5.91	6.05	6.04	5.89	5.60	5.17	4.62
Apr	54.89°	5.68	5.99	6.17	6.20	6.09	5.84	5.46	4.96	4.37	3.69
May	65.41°	6.35	6.48	6.46	6.30	5.99	5.54	4.96	4.32	3.59	2.81
Jun	72.34°	6.81	6.86	6.74	6.49	6.08	5.53	4.88	4.15	3.34	2.55
Jul	73.34°	6.55	6.66	6.60	6.41	6.06	5.57	4.96	4.28	3.50	2.71
Aug	68.18°	6.03	6.31	6.44	6.42	6.24	5.90	5.42	4.83	4.13	3.35
Sep	58.47°	5.13	5.63	5.99	6.20	6.25	6.14	5.87	5.45	4.90	4.23
Oct	46.94°	3.81	4.46	5.00	5.40	5.67	5.79	5.76	5.58	5.26	4.79
Nov	35.65°	2.62	3.25	3.80	4.25	4.60	4.82	4.91	4.88	4.71	4.43
Dec	28.40°	2.19	2.82	3.40	3.89	4.29	4.58	4.75	4.81	4.74	4.55
Avg		4.62	5.04	5.34	5.52	5.56	5.46	5.23	4.89	4.43	3.89

Solar altitude at noon on the first day of the month.

Highest Insolation of the Month
Tilt Angle with the "Highest" Monthly Low Insolation
Tilt Angle with the Highest Annual Average Insolation

■ **FIGURE 8.9** Solar Insolation and Panel Tilt. *NREL PVWatts website, accessed October 16, 2011.*

Solar Insolation kWh/m²/day Based on Orientation (20° Tilt)
Boulder, Colorado
Latitude: 39° 43′ 59″

Month	Solar Altitude	180° South	190°	200°	210°	220°	230°	240°	250°	260°	270° West
Jan	27.31°	3.58	3.56	3.51	3.42	3.29	3.14	2.97	2.78	2.59	2.39
Feb	33.17°	4.22	4.19	4.12	4.02	3.90	3.75	3.59	3.41	3.22	3.03
Mar	42.69°	5.62	5.58	5.51	5.41	5.29	5.14	4.98	4.81	4.63	4.45
Apr	54.89°	6.17	6.12	6.06	5.98	5.90	5.81	5.70	5.59	5.47	5.35
May	65.41°	6.46	6.43	6.40	6.35	6.30	6.25	6.19	6.13	6.06	5.99
Jun	72.34°	6.74	6.71	6.68	6.64	6.59	6.55	6.50	6.45	6.41	6.36
Jul	73.34°	6.60	6.54	6.47	6.39	6.31	6.23	6.16	6.09	6.02	5.95
Aug	68.18°	6.44	6.39	6.31	6.23	6.13	6.04	5.93	5.82	5.70	5.58
Sep	58.47°	5.99	5.96	5.89	5.80	5.70	5.57	5.43	5.26	5.09	4.91
Oct	46.94°	5.00	4.96	4.89	4.78	4.65	4.48	4.29	4.10	3.89	3.68
Nov	35.65°	3.80	3.78	3.73	3.63	3.51	3.36	3.19	3.01	2.81	2.61
Dec	28.40°	3.40	3.38	3.32	3.22	3.09	2.94	2.76	2.57	2.37	2.18
Avg		5.34	5.31	5.24	5.16	5.06	4.94	4.81	4.67	4.53	4.38

Solar altitude at noon on the first day of the month.

■ **FIGURE 8.10** Solar Insolation and Panel Orientation. *NREL PVWatts website, accessed October 16, 2011.*

adjustable for each season. Ballasted mounts are popular, and much simpler than a racking system; they can provide a small tilt without racking or roof penetrations (see Figure 8.11).

While there are a variety of installation and mounting applications for roofs, it is important to make the roof PV-ready. Doing so requires installing conduits for the electrical connection of the modules. The structural capacity should allow for the extra roof load of the installed modules and be adequate to hold full pallets of modules, to aid installation staging. The roofing material should be ready to accept the installation, based on the desired mounting technique. Making a roof PV-ready can save labor and installation-related costs for the photovoltaic system.

Installing a horizontal or low-tilt angle ballasted PV array on a flat roof can be the simplest approach, and offers some unique advantages. When planning a large array with multiple rows of modules, the higher the tilt, the more shading that occurs on the next row of panels to the north. Therefore, tilted panels require wide spacing between rows to avoid self-shading. This means that for a fixed installation area, lower-tilt angles will result in narrower row spacing and more overall modules. It's worth studying because the additional module count can translate into more energy generation for a fixed installation area. This is a primary consideration for space-constrained installations. See the

■ **FIGURE 8.11** Close-up View of Ballast Mount System.

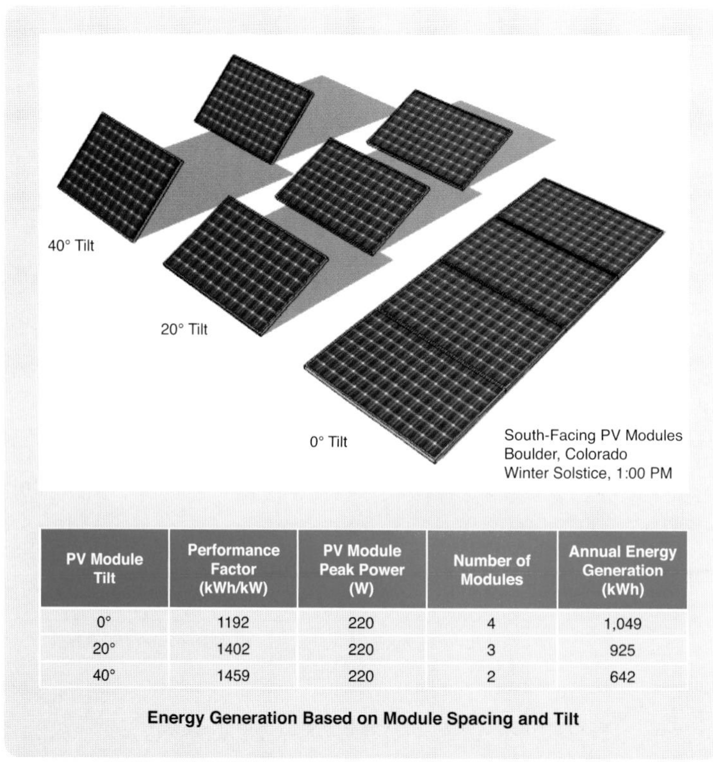

PV Module Tilt	Performance Factor (kWh/kW)	PV Module Peak Power (W)	Number of Modules	Annual Energy Generation (kWh)
0°	1192	220	4	1,049
20°	1402	220	3	925
40°	1459	220	2	642

Energy Generation Based on Module Spacing and Tilt

■ **FIGURE 8.12** PV Tilt Comparison Study. *Performance factor from NREL PVWatts website, accessed July 30, 2011.*

diagram in Figure 8.12 for an example that demonstrates this concept.

PV systems often are installed with a fixed tilt, but they can also be installed with single-axis or dual-axis tracking. With each step from fixed to single-axis tracking to dual-axis tracking, the energy generated by the system increases. See the table in Figure 8.13 for a comparison of fixed and tracking applications. With greater efficiency come increases in cost, complexity, and maintenance. Single-axis tracking allows the PV modules to track east to west, to follow the daily sun. Dual-axis tracking allows the PV modules to track the daily east to west movement of the sun, as well as the seasonal changes in sun altitude.

Shading studies should be conducted for all areas where PV is being considered for installation. The lowest sun angle, capable of casting the longest shadow, is on winter solstice, so a good rule of thumb is to prevent shading between 9:00 am and 3:00 pm on winter solstice. Consider all adjacent buildings, site elements, and trees. When a PV array is roof-mounted, it is important to take into account rooftop equipment (ideally, minimized or eliminated) and rooftop

Solar Insolation kWh/m²/day
Based on Tracking Type (South Orientation)
Boulder, Colorado
Latitude: 39° 43′ 59″

Month	Solar Altitude	40° Fixed	40° 1-Axis	40° 2-Axis
Jan	27.31°	4.43	5.21	5.59
Feb	33.17°	4.89	5.94	6.16
Mar	42.69°	6.05	7.64	7.83
Apr	54.89°	6.09	8.10	8.51
May	65.41°	5.99	8.14	8.95
Jun	72.34°	6.08	8.34	9.39
Jul	73.34°	6.06	8.07	8.92
Aug	68.18°	6.24	8.26	8.75
Sep	58.47°	6.25	8.04	8.25
Oct	46.94°	5.67	7.04	7.24
Nov	35.65°	4.60	5.54	5.84
Dec	28.40°	4.29	5.01	5.46
Avg		5.56	7.12	7.58

Solar altitude at noon on the first day of the month.

■ **FIGURE 8.13** Solar Insolation and Tracking Type. *NREL PVWatts website, accessed October 16, 2011.*

penetrations. Even small shadows can have an impact on energy production.

In a roof application, it is important to understand that the total roof area will typically not be used for PV installation because of potential shading obstructions; it is also important to allow spaces for walkways and other factors that might limit the installation area. All PV array installations benefit from a mounting standoff that allows for ventilation underneath the modules, to help dissipate heat and keep the modules running as efficiently as possible. For a roof, the standoff dimension can be small, with the goal of minimizing wind uplift forces. Incorporating cool roof systems or green roofs, in combination with PV modules, results in a positive synergy, because the cooler rooftop temperatures provided by these roof strategies can lead to more efficient module operation.

The roof of a net zero energy building is a prime location for PV array installation; but for some buildings, the roof area alone is not enough to provide the energy needed for a net zero energy building. Thinking creatively about the design of the façade and site elements of a project can lead to additional opportunities for PV array installations. The project site itself may enable ground-mounted PV arrays. Parking lots and parking structures, for example, are excellent opportunities for large-scale PV arrays (see Figure 8.14). The supporting structure for PV parking shade canopies is an additional cost, but there are additional benefits, as well: They shade vehicles and site pavement and reduce the heat island effect.

PV can be incorporated into wall panels, glazing systems, and shading devices on façades, in addition to roof applications. Façade orientation and tilt (vertical) should be carefully examined to determine the effectiveness of façade-integrated PV—it does not necessarily need to be applied vertically. PV-integrated shading elements can be horizontal or tilted, and PV-integrated façade elements can be inclined.

There is a growing market of building-integrated photovoltaic (BIPV) products that use both crystalline and thin film technologies. PV-integrated roofing is common for membrane roofing, standing seam roofing, and a number of shingle or tile roofing products. These products are typically thin film applications. Wall cladding and façade shading elements can be made of a variety of PV modules (see Figure 8.15). Rainscreen applications of PV cladding provide a ventilated cavity, helping to reduce PV operational temperatures. PV modules can be incorporated into framed glazing systems, and PV cells can be laminated into glazed units. Glazed PV modules are semitransparent because the integrated solar cells provide opaque regions, while light filters through the transparent regions of the unit.

The emergence of BIPV applications has provided new opportunities to address aesthetics in renewable energy building applications. It is important to design renewable energy

■ **FIGURE 8.14** PV arrays as Shade Canopies over Parking.

■ **FIGURE 8.15** BIPV Shading over Glazing.

Solar Power Resources and Design Tools

Industry Resources

- Solar Energy Industries Association (SEIA): www.seia.org

Climate and Solar Radiation Resources

- NREL PVWatts: www.nrel.gov/rredc/pvwatts
- METEONORM (commercial software by METEOTEST): www.meteonorm.com
- NREL Red Book: www.rredc.nrel.gov/solar/pubs/redbook
- NREL Map Search: www.nrel.gov/gis/mapsearch
- Solar and Wind Energy Resource Assessment (SWERA): www.swera.unep.net

Solar Power Design Software and Websites

- IMBY (In My Backyard; NREL's online simple PV and wind design tool with map interface): www.nrel.gov/eis/imby
- NREL PVWatts: www.nrel.gov/rredc/pvwatts
- System Advisor Model (SAM) (free software by National Renewable Energy Laboratory, Sandia National Laboratories and US Department of Energy): www.nrel.gov/analysis/sam
- RETScreen (free software by Natural Resources Canada): www.retscreen.net
- Polysun (commercial software by Vela Solaris): www.velasolaris.com

systems to be well integrated into the building, both aesthetically and functionally. Net zero energy architects should fully embrace the aesthetic possibilities of these new systems. Design and building integration is becoming a growing concern around the development of new PV modules and mounting systems. The availability of frameless PV modules offers new aesthetic possibilities, as do solar cells made in a variety of colors. However, colors other than the dark blue to black typical of the best antireflective coatings come at a price premium and performance reduction.

SOLAR THERMAL

Basic Concepts

Solar radiation is an abundant source of thermal energy and can be used to heat a fluid through a solar thermal collector, which can then be used to heat water or a building, or generate electricity (concentrated solar power). Solar thermal energy can also be used for solar cooling, by driving an absorption chiller. Solar thermal in cooling applications is a developing technology. Different solar thermal technologies provide water at different temperatures: High-temperature systems are used to generate electricity, while lower-temperature systems are used to heat water for pools, domestic hot water, process water applications, and building heating. This section deals primarily with solar thermal hot water applications for buildings.

Solar thermal systems can be open- or closed-loop. Open-loop systems heat the water directly through the solar thermal collector. A closed-loop system heats an antifreeze and water solution, which is then run through a heat exchanger, where it heats the end-use water. Closed-loop systems are important in climates when there is potential for freezing. Circulation of the water through the system can be achieved by gravity, conduction, or pumps. Thermosiphon systems use natural convection, via the heated water rising, to passively circulate the water. These systems store the heated water in a tank above the collector, which has the disadvantage of adding weight to roof-mounted applications. Closed-loop pressurized systems are common for commercial applications, while nonpressurized, passive systems can work for small, simple, commercial applications. A closed-loop drainback system can be considered for some commercial applications. A drainback system does not use an antifreeze mix to prevent freezing; rather, it allows the water to drain to a small drainback tank when the system is not active.

The components involved in a solar thermal system depend on the type of system used. For a closed-loop pressurized system, such as the one shown in Figure 8.16, the main components are the solar thermal collectors, mounting hardware, a solar storage tank with heat exchanger, expansion tank, pump, controls, valves, gauges, piping, and a backup water heater. The components in a closed-loop drainback system are similar, except that there is an added drainback tank and no expansion tank.

Technologies

For the production of solar hot water, there are two basic collector technologies: flat plate collectors and evacuated tub collectors. The primary objective of solar thermal technology is to allow as much solar energy as possible to be absorbed by the collector's fluid and to release as little thermal energy as possible back to the outside air. To accomplish this, some of the primary components in a solar thermal collector are the piping for the fluid, an absorber to collect heat, and insulation to retain heat.

FLAT PLATE COLLECTORS

Flat plate collectors are an established technology; they are versatile and cost-effective for many applications, and there are many manufacturers and options to choose from. Flat plate collectors are shallow framed panels with a glazed face. The panels are backed with rigid insulation, on which sits the coated absorber plate (see Figure 8.17). The dark

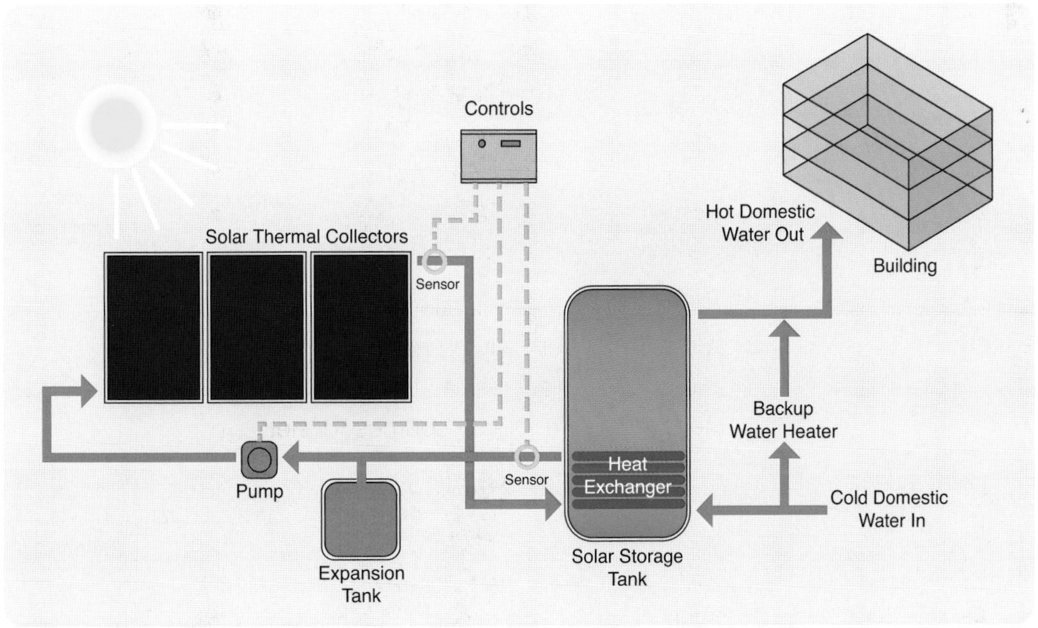

■ **FIGURE 8.16** Closed-Loop Pressurized Solar Thermal System.

color of the collectors is actually the coated absorber seen through the glazed face of the unit. The pipe risers form parallel runs in contact with the absorber plate, and are connected with inlet and outlet pipes. An air gap inside the glazed face of the unit provides additional insulation.

EVACUATED TUBE COLLECTORS

Evacuated tube collectors are much newer than flat plate collectors. They are immediately recognizable by the parallel run of exposed tubes. The key difference in evacuated tube technology is the way the collector is insulated. Instead of installing rigid insulation in the unit, the insulation is provided by a vacuum between the double-glazed tube. A vacuum is perhaps the ultimate insulator, and the technological concept is really no different from a thermos. The tubular shape provides the needed structural performance to withstand the vacuum. Within the glass tube is the absorber material and the heating pipe. Evacuated tube technology can be more effective at producing higher water temperatures than flat plate technology.

The collector tubes are modular and can be individually removed or installed into the header manifold. The heat pipes in the tubes are sealed; they contain a fluid that will vaporize when heated. This type of technology is known as a *heat pipe evacuated tube collector* (see Figure 8.18). The vapor rises to the top of the tube and transfers heat to the system's water or antifreeze solution running through the manifold. The vapor then condenses and falls back to the bottom of the heat pipe, where it is reheated and vaporized.

Another type of evacuated tube technology is a direct-flow technology, whereby the system's water or antifreeze mix is heated directly in the tube through a U-shaped pipe.

EFFICIENCIES

The two primary factors that influence solar thermal collector efficiency are the capability of the collector to absorb heat and to limit heat loss. Flat plate technology is more

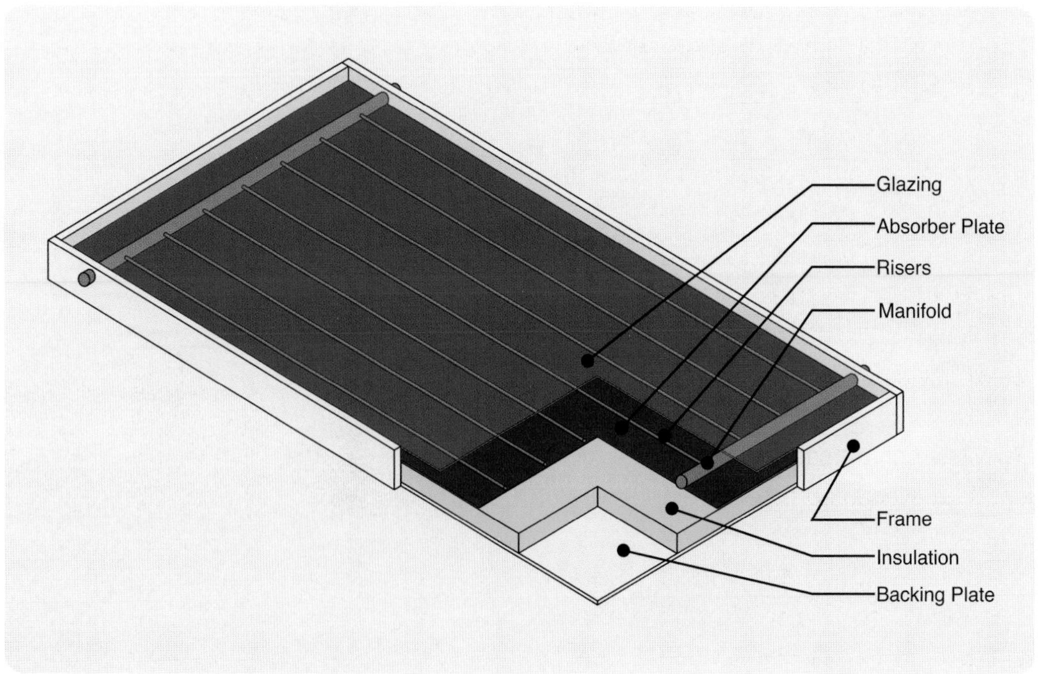

■ **FIGURE 8.17** Flat Plate Solar Collector.

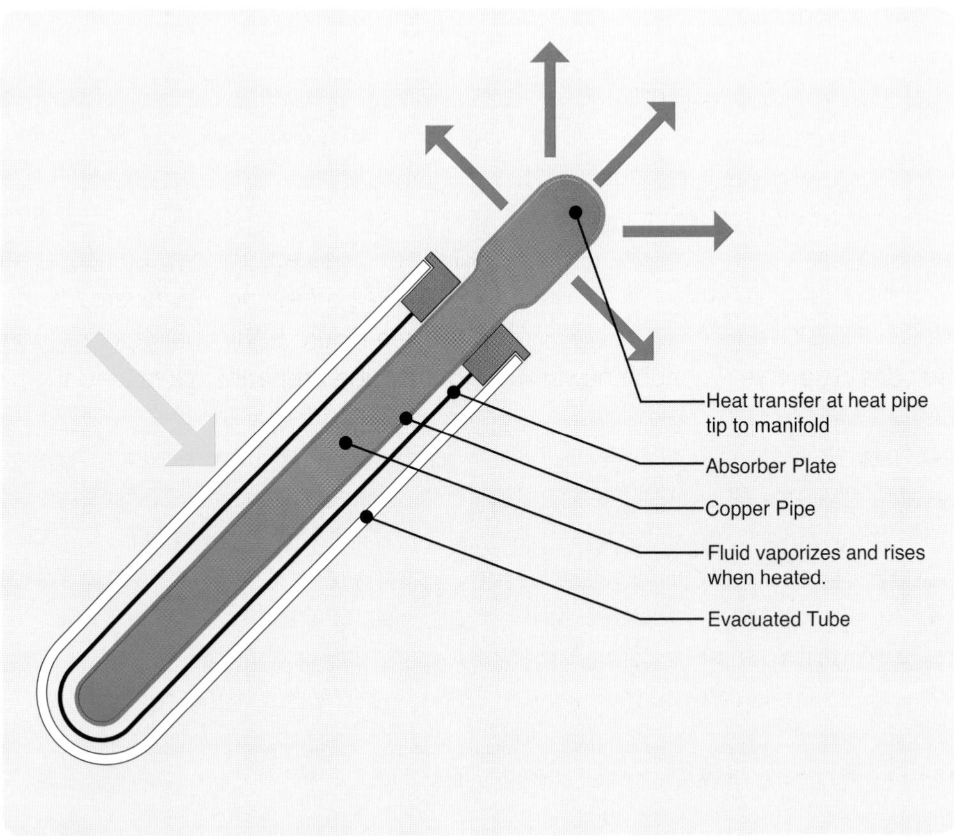

■ **FIGURE 8.18** Heat Pipe Evacuated Tube.

efficient at delivering heat gain, whereas evacuated tube technology is superior at retaining heat. The double-glazed evacuated tube is a superior insulator, but the two panes of glass reduce its solar transmission and capability to transmit solar radiation (see Figure 8.19). Heat pipe evacuated tubes also experience an efficiency loss because of the heat transfer process at the manifold.

Heat lost through the collector is a function of the outside air temperature and its relationship to the collector inlet temperature. All collectors lose efficiency as the difference between these two temperatures increases. Flat plate collectors, which excel at heat absorption, are more efficient than evacuated tube collectors when the difference between ambient air temperature and collector inlet temperature is not large. However, evacuated tube collectors, because of their capability to retain heat, do not lose efficiency as fast as flat plate collectors when the temperature difference increases. Once the temperature difference exceeds about 90°F, evacuated tube collectors are typically more efficient. As a generalized example, if the solar hot water inlet temperature is 120°F, and the ambient air temperature is 80°F, flat plate collectors would perform more efficiently. If the outdoor air temperature were significantly lower, such as 20°F, then the evacuated tube collector would provide more efficient performance. Evacuated tube

■ **FIGURE 8.19** Close-up of Evacuated Tube Collector.

collectors can be a good choice in cold climates and in applications where high-temperature water is needed for some commercial process water use.

Of course, the other measure of collector efficiency is their cost-effectiveness. Each collector has unique performance characteristics and price per collector. When selecting a solar thermal collector, it can be helpful to also look at the price per Btu offered by competing collector manufacturers.

Design Guidance

APPLICATION

Solar thermal is an efficient way to convert solar energy into useful energy. A solar thermal collector can be over three times more efficient than photovoltaic systems in converting radiant energy into useful energy. However, solar thermal generates hot water rather than electricity, so its applications are more limited than photovoltaics. In addition, electricity generated from a photovoltaic system can usually be exported to the grid when the system is overproducing. Solar hot water has no such advantage when the system is overproducing, so care should be exercised when matching a system size with the hot water load. To use solar thermal system effectively, it is important to match the system's strengths to the location's solar resources and the heating application and load.

Domestic hot water is one of the most effective and common uses for solar thermal, because the load is typically relatively small, and constant year-round. Note that solar insolation will vary throughout the year so the design can address worst-case or best-case scenarios, or split the difference and use annual average performance. Carefully selecting the collector tilt can minimize the seasonal variation. In either case, a backup water heater will be needed. Heating end-use water for commercial kitchens or other heated process water applications can also be effective. Higher end-use water temperatures may make for a good application for evacuated tube collectors. Heating water for a swimming pool is another effective application, because heating a swimming pool is a significant energy end use and would jeopardize a net zero energy building's energy use target. Special solar thermal collectors made specially for swimming pools, which lack the glazed face, are very effective at delivering lower-temperature hot water levels during conditions of warm ambient air temperatures.

Using solar thermal for building heat is challenging; it requires the right application, typically a hybrid approach with other heating or energy storage sources. It also helps to have a long heating season, to make the application cost-effective. The issue is that building heating is seasonal, so the collectors will sit unused much of the year. Further, systems are less efficient during the winter months because of the lower solar insolation and colder outside air temperatures. Some innovative systems include year-round thermal energy storage buried in the ground, which allows the solar thermal collectors to perform continuously. Another potential application is in climates with a very short heating season, where a system could be sized for domestic hot water and occasional building heating.

ESTIMATING THE LOAD

After identifying the appropriate applications for solar thermal, the first step is to estimate the thermal loads to be met by the system. To that end, itemize the needs in the building for hot water. For domestic hot water in a commercial building, this may include shower, lavatory and kitchen faucets, janitors' sinks, and other fixtures or equipment such as dishwashers. The hot water demand will need be estimated daily, as this is the typical cycle for solar thermal collection. It can be useful to conduct preliminary LEED water use reduction calculations very early in the process, based on building occupancy and desired fixture flow rates. This can help ensure reduced hot water consumption, as well as estimate daily water use. A mix rate of hot and cold water should be estimated for each fixture type; or an overall mix rate should be determined, as full hot water is rarely used at the fixture. Adjusting the daily hot water demands by the mix rate will result in the design daily gallon demand of hot water for sizing the system.

Next, using the equation below, convert the design daily gallon demand to a daily heating load (Q in the equation below), in Btu. Estimate the difference between the domestic supply temperature of the water and the desired hot water temperature at the tank. Multiply this temperature difference (Δt in the equation below) by 8.33 (Btu/gallon °F), which is the density of water (pounds/gallon) multiplied by the specific heat of water (Btu/pound °F). Then multiply the result by the gallons of heated water per day (*GPD* in the equation below). Using this equation, it takes 583 Btu to raise 1 gallon of water from 50°F to 120°F.

$$Q = 8.33 \times (\Delta t) \times GPD$$

CONDUCTING A RESOURCE ASSESSMENT

The first step in conducting a resource assessment is to gather solar radiation data to determine the solar resource available for the project location. There are many sources for solar radiation data, a number of which are listed at the end of this section (including Figure 8.20). With solar radiation data in hand, estimate the daily solar insolation in Btu/ft^2/day. (Note: If the value is in kWh/m^2/day, you can convert it by

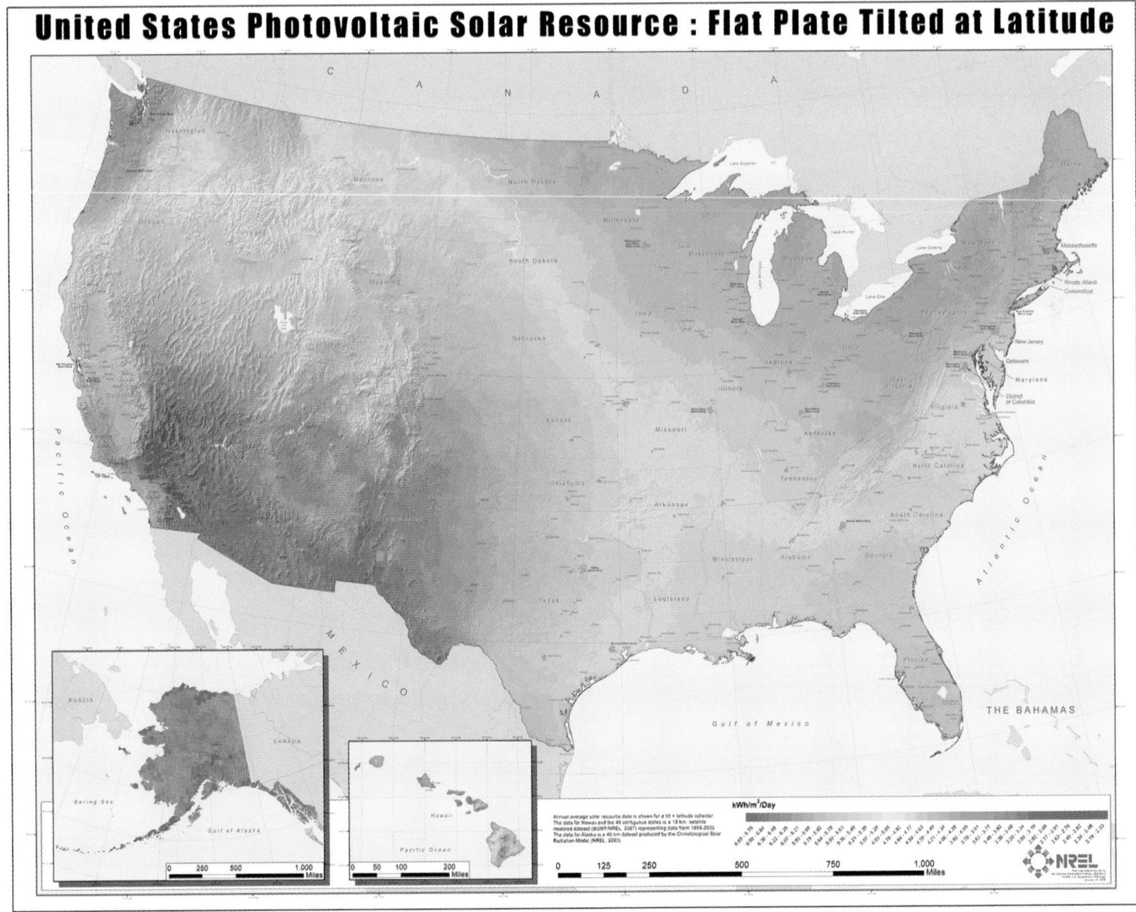

■ **FIGURE 8.20** Solar Insolation Map in kWh/m^2/day with Panel at a Tilt Equal to Latitude. *NREL.*

multiplying by 317.) A good starting point is to use average daily insolation. This will give you a good overall annual performance estimate. It may also be a good idea to look at the winter months and determine the average daily insolation for the worst-case condition. The tilt of the collector plays a role in the insolation values seasonally, so different scenarios can be run with different tilts.

In addition to collecting solar radiation data, an estimate of ambient air temperature is also needed. Nighttime lows are not used because the solar thermal system only operates under solar exposure. If an annual average for solar insolation is being used, then estimate annual average daytime temperature. When designing for winter conditions, estimate average winter daytime temperatures. The outside air temperatures play a role in thermal solar collector performance.

SYSTEM SELECTION

The Solar Rating & Certification Corporation (SRCC) is an independent third-party certification entity for the solar thermal industry. It is good practice to select collectors and systems that have been certified by the SRCC. It provides performance ratings for collectors in its OG-100 directory, and certifies and rates solar hot water heating systems in its OG-300 directory. The SRCC website (www.solar-rating.org) is an excellent resource, where climate data is combined with collector and system performance to serve as a guide to sizing systems.

The solar radiation and temperature data for the project can be used to select and size thermal solar collectors using the SRCC's performance data. The solar insolation in Btu/ft^2/day is used to classify the solar radiation resource in the SRCC performance rating system: It simplifies the daily insolation into three categories that typify three sky conditions as well as seasonal variation (see Figure 8.21).

As an example, according to the PVWatts website, Chicago, Illinois, has an average daily insolation on a south-facing 42° tilt of 1,401 Btu/ft^2/day. This would be equivalent to the SRCC's mildly cloudy weather classification of 1,500 Btu/ft^2/day.

The SRCC also categorizes the difference between inlet collector temperature and ambient air temperature, which relates to collector efficiency (see Figure 8.22). To determine this temperature difference, subtract the average daytime temperature for your application by the estimated collector inlet temperature, which in

	Clear Sky	Mildly Cloudy Sky	Cloudy Sky
Daily Solar Insolation	2,000 Btu/ft^2/day	1,500 Btu/ft^2/day	1,000 Btu/ft^2/day

■ **FIGURE 8.21** SRCC Weather Classification. *Data source: SRCC website, www.solar-rating.org/facts/collector_ratings.html. Accessed October 16, 2011.*

	A	B	C	D	E
Temperature Difference	-9°F	9°F	36°F	90°F	144°F

■ **FIGURE 8.22** SRCC Temperature Categories. *Data source: SRCC website, www.solar-rating.org/facts/collector_ratings.html. Accessed October 16, 2011.*

a closed-loop system will be near the temperature of the heated water in the storage tank.

From the table in Figure 8.22, choose the appropriate SRCC category for your application and climate. Categories A and B are for low-temperature applications such as swimming pool heating in the summer. Category E is for high-temperature applications such as some process water uses or building heating. Categories C and D cover most conventional uses, with D being used for cold weather conditions.

The SRCC's collector performance data provides a variety of data on individual certified collectors—such as collector type, collector size, collector dry weight, and other product data—helpful when designing and selecting the system. Each SRCC collector record also lists performance ratings in Btu per panel per day for each combination of weather classification and temperature category. This will allow for an estimate of the daily output and the number of collectors needed for the system. When estimating number of panels, it is important to also reduce the estimated daily output to account for overall system efficiency. An efficiency of 80 percent is usually a good assumption, but an even more conservative figure will provide an additional buffer in collector sizing. For demonstration purposes, the two tables in Figures 8.23 and 8.24 represent performance data extracted from two collector SRCC collector records. The first is a flat plate collector and the second is a direct pipe

SRCC Collector Performance Data
40ft² Flat Plate Collector Example
kBtu/panel/day

Temperature Category	Weather Classification		
	Clear Sky	Mildly Cloudy Sky	Cloudy Sky
A	59.9	45.6	31.5
B	51.0	36.8	22.7
C	38.4	24.5	11.2
D	14.9	4.8	0.0
E	0.5	0.0	0.0

■ **FIGURE 8.23** SRCC Flat Plate Example. *Data source: SRCC website, www.solar-rating.org. Accessed October 16, 2011.*

SRCC Collector Performance Data
37ft² Evacuated Tube Collector Example
kBtu/panel/day

Temperature Category	Weather Classification		
	Clear Sky	Mildly Cloudy Sky	Cloudy Sky
A	31.1	23.4	15.8
B	30.0	22.4	14.7
C	28.1	20.4	12.7
D	23.5	15.9	8.3
E	17.7	10.2	3.4

■ **FIGURE 8.24** SRCC Evacuated Tube Example. *Data source: SRCC website, www.solar-rating.org. Accessed October 16, 2011.*

evacuated tube collector. These are just two examples of the many collectors rated on the SRCC website.

It is possible to use this calculation method and estimate each season or month, and by doing so develop a better understanding when in the year the system is both underproducing and overproducing. Full solar thermal system design includes sizing all of the elements in the balance of system, including the storage tank and backup or supplemental water heater. It is also possible to implement software or other design tools to refine the collector sizing for final design.

BUILDING INTEGRATION

Solar thermal collectors can be roof-mounted or ground-mounted. Collectors need to be located in a nonshaded area and oriented south, with a tilt. The tilt can vary based on the mounting location and whether the collectors are optimized according to season. Low tilts optimize summer collection while high tilts optimize winter collection. To capture the most solar insolation over a year, a good rule of thumb to follow is a tilt equal to the location's latitude. If the goal is to minimize the seasonal differences, to provide a more uniform level of solar insolation, then a tilt of about 15° to 20° greater than the location's latitude should be selected. By studying solar insolation levels at different tilts, the optimal angle can be found for the application. Manufacturers typically publish recommended tilt ranges. Panels that rely on thermosiphoning, such as direct pipe evacuated tube collectors, require a tilt to function correctly.

Solar Thermal Collector Sizing Example

Basic Project Information

- Full-time occupants: 140
- Location: Chicago, Illinois
- Daily hot water demand: 250 gallons mixed at 55 percent = 138 gallons (at 120°F)
- Inlet temperature: 120°F
- Domestic water supply temperature: 50°F

Climate Data

- Average daytime temperature: 55°F
- Average daily solar insolation: 4.42 kWh/m^2/day or 1,401 Btu/ft^2/day (per PVWatts) at 42.0° tilt (= Latitude)

Thermal Load

$$Q = 8.33 \times (\Delta t) \times GPD$$

where:

$$Q = 8.33 \text{ Btu/gallons °F} \times (120°F - 50°F) \times 138 \text{ gallons}$$

$$Q = 80{,}468 \text{ Btu/day, or } 80 \text{ kBtu/day}$$

SRCC Performance Data

- SRCC weather classification: Mildly cloudy sky (1,500 Btu/ft^2/day)
- SRCC temperature category: D (120°F – 55°F = 65°F; use D at 90°F)

System Selection and Sizing

- Solar thermal collector selection: Evacuated tube collector (demonstrated in preceding example)
- Collector performance rating: 15.9 kBtu/day
- Overall system efficiency: 80 percent
- Number of collectors: 7 collectors (80 kBtu/day / (0.80 × 15.9 kBtu/day), rounded up
- Collector area = 259 ft^2

Solar Thermal Resources and Design Tools

Industry Resources

- Solar Rating & Certification Corporation (SRCC): www.solar-rating.org

Climate and Solar Radiation Resources

- Climate Consultant (free software by UCLA): www.energy-design-tools.aud.ucla.edu
- METEONORM (commercial software by METEOTEST): www.meteonorm.com
- NREL Red Book: www.rredc.nrel.gov/solar/pubs/redbook
- NREL PVWatts: www.nrel.gov/rredc/pvwatts
- NREL Map Search: www.nrel.gov/gis/mapsearch
- Solar and Wind Energy Resource Assessment (SWERA): www.swera.unep.net
- Solar Rating & Certification Corporation (SRCC): www.solar-rating.org

Solar Thermal Design Software

- RETScreen (free software by Natural Resources Canada): www.retscreen.net
- Polysun (commercial software by Vela Solaris): www.velasolaris.com

WIND

Basic Concepts

The kinetic energy of the wind is a powerful renewable energy resource that is available throughout the world—day or night, as long as the wind is blowing. Wind energy is an important complement to solar energy because although it, too, is an intermittent energy source, its availability is different from that of solar.

The kinetic energy of the wind is converted into useful energy through a wind turbine. The blades and rotor assembly of a wind turbine turn in the wind and rotate an alternator, which generates alternating current electricity. The energy generated by a wind turbine is a function of the energy collected by the blades, meaning that larger blades and higher wind speeds both contribute to greater energy generation. These two factors favor size. Large towers can support large blade spans, or the *swept area*. A large tower positions the turbine rotor hub at a position high above the ground to gain access to the greater wind speeds found at higher elevations above ground level.

Unfortunately, the principles of wind power do not scale down effectively. Certainly, small wind turbines produce less energy than large turbines, but not proportionally. The energy generated is a function of the rotor diameter squared and the wind speed cubed. For this reason, well-sited, utility-scale wind turbines can produce a significant amount of electricity at a very cost-competitive price. Utility-scale wind turbines range from 100 kW to 3 MW. Small wind turbines, ranging from less than 1 kW to 100 kW, are best suited to homes, farms, and small commercial buildings. To date, the wind energy industry has focused on these two scales, but because net zero energy commercial buildings will rely largely on an emerging medium-scale niche in the wind industry, the focus of this section is on larger-size small wind turbines and smaller-size utility-scale (medium-scale) turbines, for either individual net zero energy commercial buildings or net zero energy multiple building and campus settings.

A wind energy system comprises the turbine and the tower, which are both primary system decisions. Remember that the amount of energy generated is related to the rotor diameter squared and the wind speed cubed. The wind speed is greatly influenced by tower height. The wind turbine will include a braking mechanism so that the turbine can be stopped at any time. Wind turbines are also outfitted with a governing system, which prevents them from spinning too fast and protects them from strong winds.

A wind energy system can be grid-connected or off-grid. The balance of system for a grid-connected system will include a charge controller/rectifier, inverter, and wiring. Although the alternator in the turbine generates AC electricity, its voltage fluctuates with wind speed. It is converted to DC with a rectifier unit, and then to grid-quality AC with an invertor for building use at the electrical panel board, or grid connection through a meter capable of net metering (see Figure 8.25).

Off-grid systems include battery storage, which can be included in grid-connected systems if desired. The battery charge process is controlled through the charge controller unit. The battery system includes a disconnect switch in line with the connection to the invertor. In an off-grid system, some form of backup power may also be necessary. All wind energy systems should feature a monitoring device to track system performance and battery life.

Wind turbines should not run unloaded. In the case of a battery-based off-grid system, a ballast or dump load (typically, an appropriately sized heating element) can provide

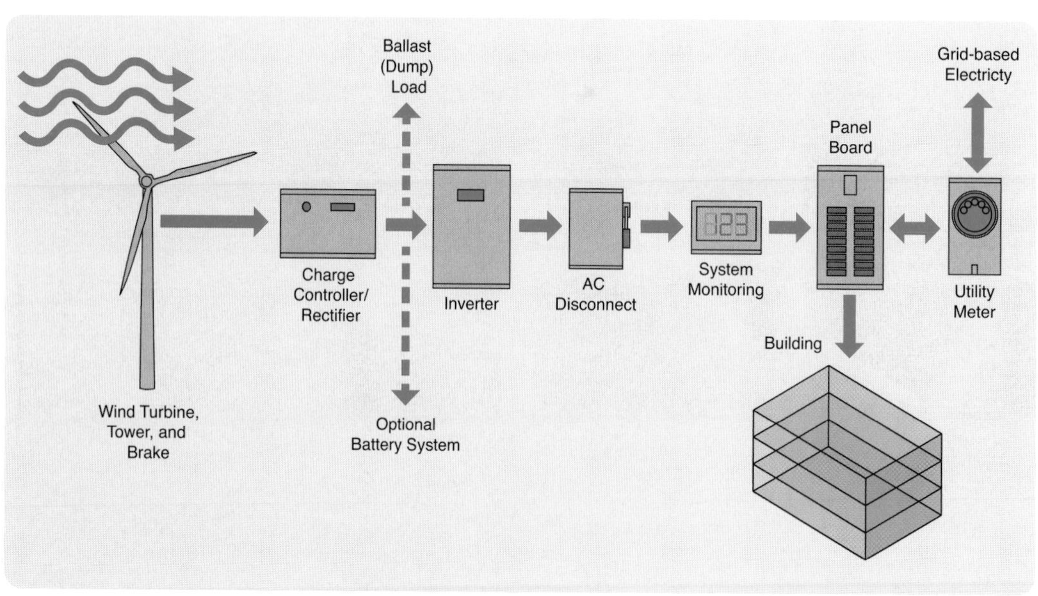

■ **FIGURE 8.25** Grid-Connected Wind Energy System.

an alternative load on the turbine when the batteries are fully charged. A ballast load can be used in grid-connected systems when the building does not provide full load or when the grid cannot accept the excess power.

Technologies

There are two main types of turbine technologies: vertical axis wind turbine (VAWT) and horizontal axis wind turbine (HAWT), shown respectively in Figures 8.26 and 8.27. The difference lies in the axis on which the rotor turns. HAWT is the most common and proven technology, featuring a horizontal rotor and, typically, three blades radiating form the hub. VAWT has a vertical rotor orientation and a wide variety of blade configurations. VAWT designs have no specific orientation to the wind and so can capture wind from any direction. HAWT designs, in contrast, are usually designed to face the wind and can track with the wind direction. Vertical axis turbines are generally very small-scale and, therefore, have proportionately limited energy generation capability. Horizontal axis turbines range in size from very small to very large utility-scale turbines and can be sized to meet a variety of applications.

All turbine technologies and scales require ongoing maintenance, because energy generation is through moving parts that function year-round, often in high winds and poor weather conditions. Also, turbines are mounted high off the ground, to optimize energy generation, making maintenance and turbine access a greater challenge.

PERFORMANCE

Wind turbines perform best under a specific range of average wind speeds. If the average wind speed is too slow, less than 7 or 8 mph, turbines produce very little energy. Small wind turbines have a minimum start-up speed, and cut-in speed near this lower end of the range. Most wind turbine manufacturers provide performance data for a range of average wind speeds, typically in the range of 8 to 19 mph (3.5 to 8.5 m/s). Too-high wind speeds can damage a wind turbine, so they are designed with a cut-out speed (or furling speed) and a governing system to protect the turbine. Wind

■ **FIGURE 8.26** Vertical Axis Wind Turbine (VAWT).

■ **FIGURE 8.27** Horizontal Axis Wind Turbine (HAWT).

turbine performance data assumes an air density based on sea level. At higher elevations, the air density decreases, and along with it the performance of the turbine. A 25 percent or more performance decrease can be expected at high elevations, above 7,500 feet. Wind turbines also do not perform well under turbulence, which can be caused by nearby obstructions such as trees and buildings.

Wind turbines have power ratings associated with them, typically measured in kW of power. The power ratings can give an indication of turbine size and capacity. However, to date, wind turbine power ratings published by manufacturers can be very misleading, as they may use different assumptions (such as average wind speed) to calculate their turbine power rating. Wind turbine manufacturers also supply estimated energy performance data in kWh per month or as annual energy output (AEO). This data can be a better guide to interpreting turbine performance, especially if it is provided under a variety of average wind speeds.

The small wind power industry only recently instituted a standard to certify power ratings, energy performance, and acoustical performance. In 2009, the American Wind Energy Association released the "AWEA Small Wind Turbine Performance and Safety Standard"; the Small Wind Certification Council is the independent certifier for small wind turbines based on the new standard. At the time of this writing, many wind turbines were in the application process or had temporary certifications.

Design Guidance

APPLICATION

Utility-scale wind is an extremely successful and well-understood renewable energy application. Small- and medium-scale wind technology for individual buildings and communities requires careful coordination to be successful—and it certainly can be, in the right application. Most wind energy experts agree that the key elements for a successful small wind application include a reliable wind resource and a properly sized horizontal axis wind turbine placed on a tall tower. This recipe for success favors rural project sites where there are fewer wind obstructions and tall towers are not expected to clear as many regulatory and zoning hurdles as in suburban and urban developments.

Scale matters for wind energy. Simply put, larger turbines and higher towers are more effective—although there is strong potential for medium-scale wind applications that serve multiple buildings and entire communities. The advantage of larger turbine and tower sizes is an increase in the cost-effectiveness of the solution. A community, campus, or multiple building application would also typically offer a wider range of siting options away from wind obstructions.

There are many different wind turbine options available in the small wind power market; in contrast, the medium-scale market, just below 100 kW and approaching 1 MW, offers fewer choices and a narrower range of turbine sizes, making it more challenging to optimize turbine size for a net zero energy project. This, in combination with the inherent variability of wind, means that a smart strategy for net zero energy buildings would be to supplement wind energy with another renewable energy source, such as solar. Alternatively, small- and medium-scale wind energy systems can serve as a good supplement to other primary on-site renewable energy systems.

Perhaps a shift in the commercial building industry toward net zero energy buildings and low-energy buildings with integrated on-site renewable energy will prompt the market in medium-scale wind energy systems to grow. Among the higher hurdles to overcome are the current limitations of zoning ordinances around the nation. By far, the most problematic is the lack of integration of language to address the unique aspects and opportunities of regulating and permitting. Tower heights and setback requirements are two of the most important issues to cover in zoning ordinances. Streamlining the regulatory process could help advance small- and medium-scale wind energy systems and make available more renewable energy options for projects pursuing net zero energy.

ESTIMATING THE LOAD

Wind energy can provide all or part of the energy requirements for a net zero energy building or for a net zero energy development. The ability to net-meter grid-connected applications is a necessary function because of the variability of wind and corresponding energy generation. This allows the project to import grid electricity when the turbine is underproducing, and export renewable electricity when the turbine is overproducing.

RESOURCE ASSESSMENT

Wind data for the site needs to be gathered. Average wind speed is the critical metric used in estimated annual energy generation. Many wind resource maps are published with average wind speeds data. NREL, for example, offers a number of global and U.S. wind resource maps, including individual state maps, such as the one shown in Figure 8.28. These maps contain wind data for different heights aboveground and at different resolutions. As such, they can be good starting points to learning about the wind resource availability at a project location.

Weather data files also can be mined for wind data. Climate analysis tools such as Climate Consultant can generate wind roses and tabulate average wind speeds based on the data compiled by weather stations. The quality of the data will, of course, be dependent on the weather station and its maintenance and

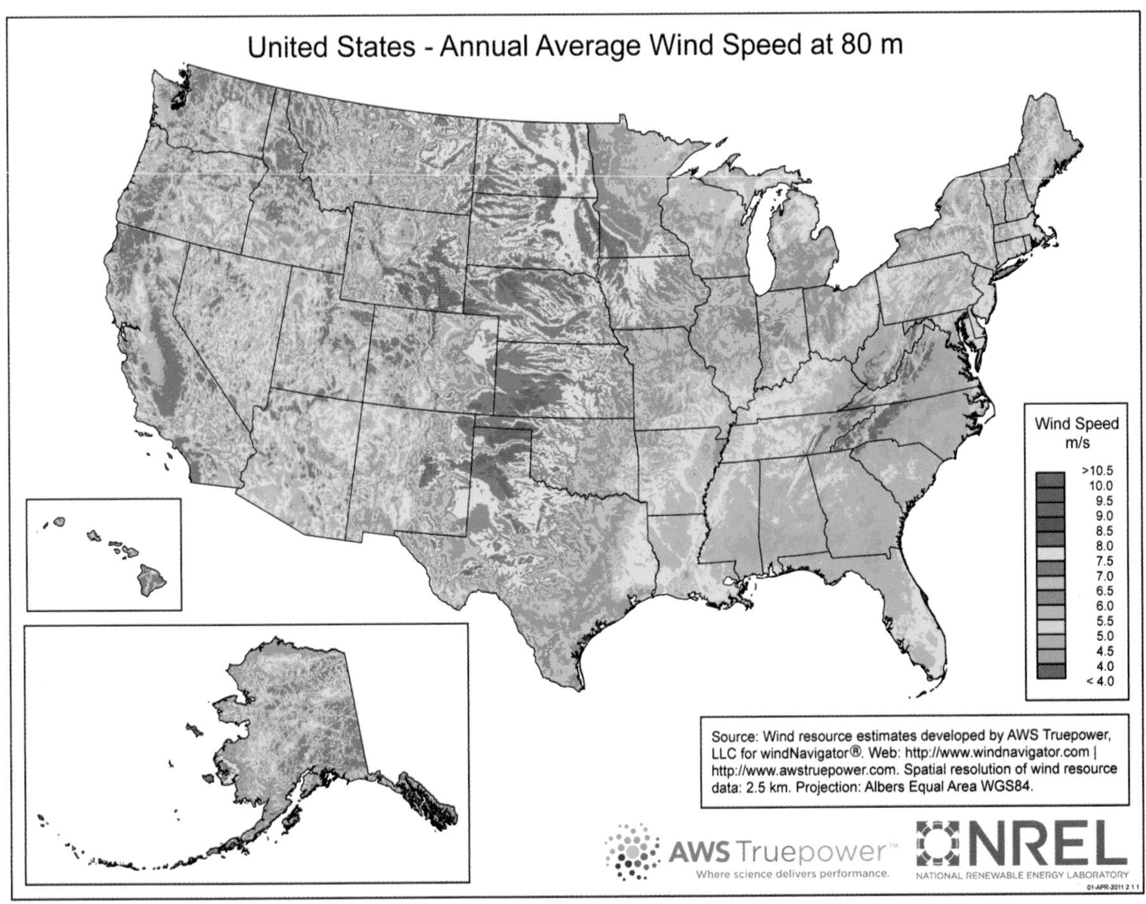

■ **FIGURE 8.28** Wind Speed Map. *Credit: NREL.*

positioning of the anemometer. More specifically, the height of the anemometer is an important consideration, because it will likely be lower than the proposed turbine mounting height, hence may have lower wind speeds reported. Anemometers are typically mounted at 10 meters above the ground (particularly at airports), but heights can vary. It is possible to interpolate wind speeds at heights above 10 meters; but, in general, wind speeds can be 15 to 25 percent higher at 24 meters than at 10 meters.

Wind Turbine Sizing and Selection Example

Site

- Elevation: Near sea level
- Terrain is open, with low-level campus buildings.

Wind Resource

- Average wind speed at 30 meters aboveground: 7.0 m/s (15.68 mph)
- Annual energy output required: 250,000 kWh (853 MBtu)

Solving for Rotor Diameter

$$AEO = 0.01328 \times D^2 \times V^3$$

where:

$D^2 = 250{,}000 / 0.01328 \times (15.68)^3$
$D^2 = 4{,}883$
$D = 69.9$ feet (21.3 meters)

Turbine Selection Option

- Northern Power 100
- Rotor diameter: 21 meters (69 feet)
- Rated power: 100 kW
- Manufacturer-estimated AEO for 7.0 m/s average wind speed: 300,000 kWh
- Tower height: 30 meters (98 feet)

Wind data is very site-specific and can be influenced by local topography, bodies of water, and nearby buildings and landscaping. Turbulence from adjacent buildings and landscaping also can affect wind data. Perhaps the best way to access wind data for a project is to install an anemometer at the site and record actual data at the proposed height of the wind turbine. At least a year's worth of wind speed data should be collected, to account for any seasonal differences. If a 12-month data collection period is not feasible, the site can be modeled and analyzed by an experienced wind consultant to substantiate the available wind resource.

SYSTEM SELECTION

It can be very challenging to estimate annual wind energy output for a wind energy system because of the many variables involved; system design and location are certainly factors, but the primary issue is the variability of wind over time. Ultimately, it is best to solicit system proposals from a few wind turbine manufacturers. Most publish estimated annual energy output based on a range of average wind speeds, and this information can be an effective way to compare turbines and size systems based on the project's estimated annual energy needs.

A simple equation for calculating annual energy output (*AEO*) in kWh for a small wind turbine is the following, where *D* is the diameter of the rotor diameter in feet and *V* is the average wind speed in mph. The equation is from "Small Wind Electric Systems: A U.S. Consumer's Guide," put out by the U.S. Department of Energy, Energy Efficiency, and Renewable Energy.

$$AEO = 0.01328 \times D^2 \times V^3$$

If the average wind speed and annual energy output required are both known, then this equation can be used to find the turbine rotor diameter that is sized to generally meet the project's energy needs.

The wind industry also uses a concept called capacity factor that accounts for the difference in actual annual energy output compared to the maximum theoretical energy output from the turbine operating the entire year at the peak power rating (power rating kW × 8,760 hours). Capacity factors, which range between 20 to 40 percent, are more commonly used in the utility-scale wind industry. If a 30 percent capacity factor is assumed for the 100 kW turbine in the preceding example, the result would be 262,800 kWh estimated annual energy output, which is close to estimate in the example.

BUILDING INTEGRATION

There have been recent examples and, consequently, growing interest in the integration of wind turbines directly on commercial buildings. The most common application is rooftop- or parapet-mounted turbines. To date, however, there is very little data available on how these projects are performing.

Installing a wind turbine directly on the building can be extremely problematic, for the following reasons: Most buildings cannot support the structural loads of a large wind turbine, and even small wind turbines have complex structural loads. Building-mounted turbine designs, therefore, need to carefully address structural loads and vibrations, as well as acoustics and sound-related problems caused by the turbine. Further, the mounting height of the turbines is typically limited to the roof height, which may or may not be at an appropriate height for the best wind resource. The building itself, and potentially any surrounding buildings or landscapes, can create turbulence. Turbulence is hard on wind turbines and is not conducive to effective energy generation. The larger issue, however, is that building-mounted turbines are often small and have very limited energy generation capacity because of restricted swept area of the blades.

Site-installed wind turbines mounted on high towers is the proven method to make effective use of wind energy technology. Not all sites are good candidates for a wind turbine and tower, however. Wind speeds are higher at higher elevations off the ground, and landscaping, terrain, and buildings all can cause turbulence. Good

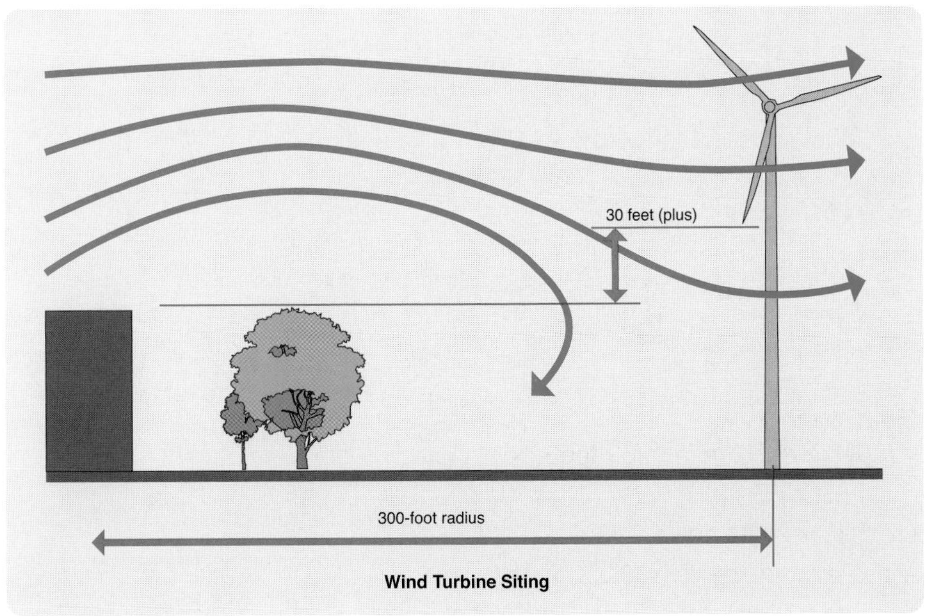

■ **FIGURE 8.29** Rule of Thumb for Siting a Wind Turbine around Obstructions.

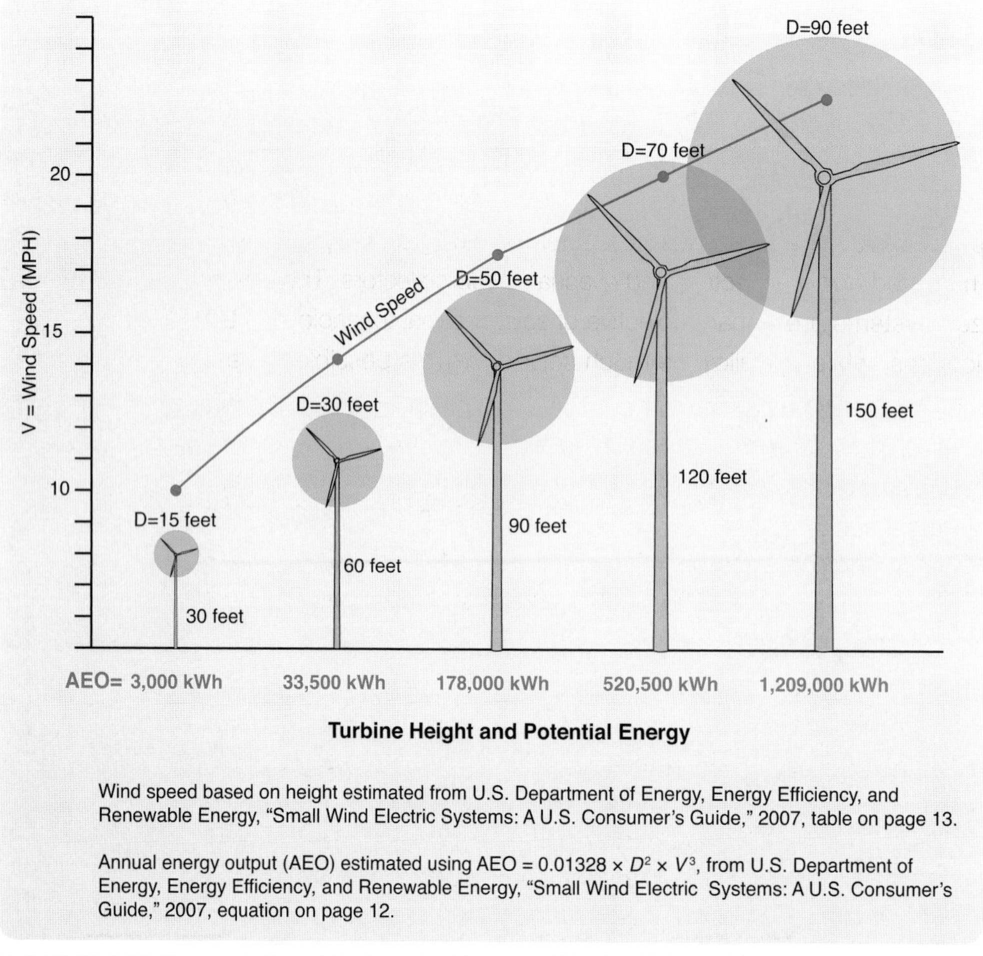

■ **FIGURE 8.30** Demonstration of the Impact of Increased Turbine Height (with Increased Wind Speed and Blade Diameter) on Potential Energy Generation.

project wind sites have open space and low-level buildings. Moreover, the turbulence zone can extend well above the height of buildings and trees, so a good rule of thumb, as illustrated in Figure 8.29, is to place the rotor height at least 30 feet above any obstructions within a 300-foot radius of the tower. Figure 8.30 shows the impact of increased turbine height, together with increased wind speed and blade diameter, on potential energy generation.

HYDRO

Basic Concepts

Water, together with the earth's global water cycle, is a source of tremendous energy. Its movement via gravity or waves is a source of kinetic energy. It is also a vital source of thermal energy stored from the sun. The earth's oceans are sources, too, of tidal energy, wave energy, and thermal energy, all of which can be harnessed to generate electricity. These ocean energy technologies are still maturing, however, but hold strong potential for adding to the world's mix of renewable energy solutions.

The focus of this section is on hydropower, and more specifically on micro hydropower and small hydropower as they relate to distributed renewable energy sources for net zero energy buildings and communities.

Hydropower refers to the capture of kinetic energy of flowing water and its transformation into useful energy—electricity. Hydropower is the largest source of renewable energy in the United States, comprising 70 percent of

Wind Energy Resources and Design Tools

Industry Resources

- American Wind Energy Association (AWEA): www.awea.org
- Small Wind Certification Council (SWCC): www.smallwindcertification.org

Climate and Wind Resources

- Climate Consultant (free software by UCLA): www.energy-design-tools.aud.ucla.edu
- NREL Map Search: www.nrel.gov/gis/mapsearch
- Solar and Wind Energy Resource Assessment (SWERA): www.swera.unep.net

Wind Design Software and Websites

- IMBY (In My Backyard; NREL's online simple PV and wind design tool with map interface): www.nrel.gov/eis/imby
- System Advisor Model (SAM; free software by National Renewable Energy Laboratory, Sandia National Laboratories and U.S. Department of Energy): www.nrel.gov/analysis/sam
- RETScreen (free software by Natural Resources Canada): www.retscreen.net
- *Polysun (commercial software by Vela Solaris):* www.velasolaris.com

all renewable energy generation. It is most common at a utility scale, and provides substantial amounts of electricity to regions with abundant hydro resources, such as the Pacific Northwest. Large-scale hydropower plants exceed 30 MW in capacity—with some plants exceeding 10 GW in capacity, globally. At this scale, the hydropower plant involves the construction of a large dam and reservoir to control the water resource in a river. There are drawbacks to this type of hydropower plant, however, which are becoming better understood; they center on the devastating destruction of natural habitats resulting from the construction of the dam and hydropower plant. According to the Department of Energy's Water Power Program website (http://www1.eere.energy.gov/water/index.html), new research and development is focusing on advanced hydropower technologies that are environmentally superior to those in use today.

Hydropower also can be applied at a small or micro scale on an individual property. Micro hydropower systems have capacities less than 100 kW in rated power; small hydropower systems range from 100 kW up to 30 MW in rated power. The range of scales is wide, with residential systems on one end and small municipal systems on the other. Systems at the high end of the micro hydro scale and small hydro systems have enough power capacity to provide all of, or a useful supplement to, the energy requirements of net zero energy commercial buildings. Having access to an appropriate waterway is the determining factor. In addition to finding a site with a quality water source, the established regulatory requirements have to be met, and water rights have to be secured.

Hydropower turbines convert the kinetic energy of water into electricity. Moving water turns a turbine and shaft, which spins a generator that produces electricity. The energy available through hydropower is a function of the water's head (elevation drop to the turbine) and flow. The taller the head height and the higher the flow rate, the greater the energy potential for the system. Hydro can be one of the most consistent renewable energy sources, because the stream or river flows day and night. The flow will experience seasonal variations, but the elevation change in a hydro system is fixed, based on the system design. Two other advantages of hydro are that it is one of the lowest-cost renewable energy systems available, and installations can generate energy for many decades.

Even though micro hydro and small-scale hydro are generally considered low-impact, care must still be taken to minimize the negative effects on the aquatic ecosystems and habitats. One way that micro hydro alleviates environmental impact is through the installation of a run-of-the-river system (see Figure 8.31). The goal of such a system is to have minimal or no impact on the waterway's course and flow. In this system, water is fed into a screened intake from the waterway and then piped (*penstock*) to the turbine located downstream. The water is then returned to the waterway through a *trailrace*. Only a small portion of the waterway's flow is temporarily diverted before being returned downstream. As the scale of the system increases, the intake is often incorporated with a diversion dam or weir. This type of run-of-the-river system is small in scale and does not include a reservoir, thus does not control the flow of the river. Nevertheless, even small dam structures should be carefully studied for their possible environmental impact. Retrofitting hydropower with existing dams is one low-impact alternative.

The Low Impact Hydropower Institute is a nonprofit organization that promotes and certifies low-impact hydropower facilities across the country. There is also a trend toward incorporating small hydro projects into urban or industrial waterways and water processes, such as canals and water treatment plant outfall, like the one shown in Figure 8.32. These types of waterways represent a much lower environmental impact for incorporation of hydro technology.

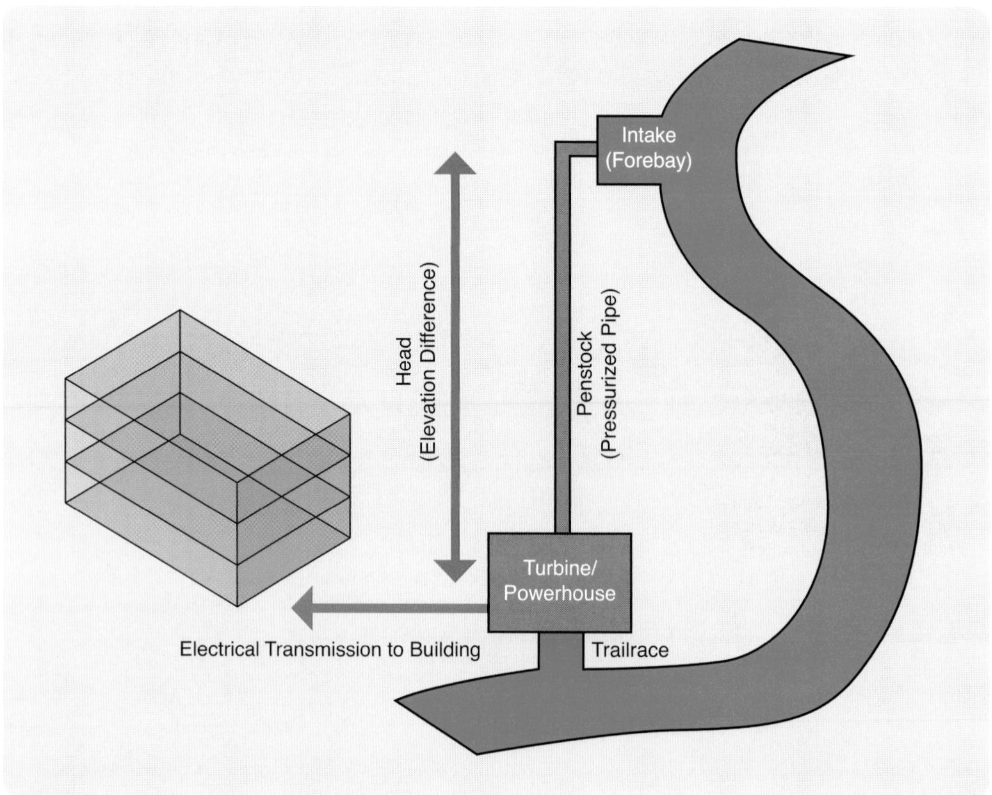

■ **FIGURE 8.31** Run-of-the-River Hydropower System.

■ **FIGURE 8.32** The 1.2 MW Hydropower System at Kankakee, Illinois, Provides Power for a Wastewater Treatment Plant. *NREL/PIX 00069; photograph by Warren Gretz.*

The basic parts of the electrical system for a grid-connected system are the turbine(s) and an AC controller connected to the building's electrical panel board (see Figure 8.33). A grid-connected system should include a meter capable of net metering. Battery storage can be added to a grid-connected or off-grid system. DC generators for charging batteries are usually found on small residential-scale micro turbines. These systems also include a charge controller and an inverter (with disconnect), to convert the DC electricity from the batteries to AC. Some systems require the inclusion of a ballast load (typically, a heating element) to absorb the full power capacity of the system when the energy generated is not used on-site, directed to batteries, or exported to the grid. Hydro turbines must operate under load to prevent damage.

Technologies

There are two main types of micro and small hydro turbine technologies: reaction and impulse. Each has its applications and benefits based on the characteristics of the waterway to be used for hydropower. It is important to work with a turbine manufacturer to carefully match the turbine technology and size to the waterway's energy potential.

A reaction turbine has its blades fully immersed in the water flow and is ideal for conditions with high flow and low to medium head. There are several types of reaction turbines, including the Propellor, Francis, and Kaplan, the latter shown in Figure 8.34. Each

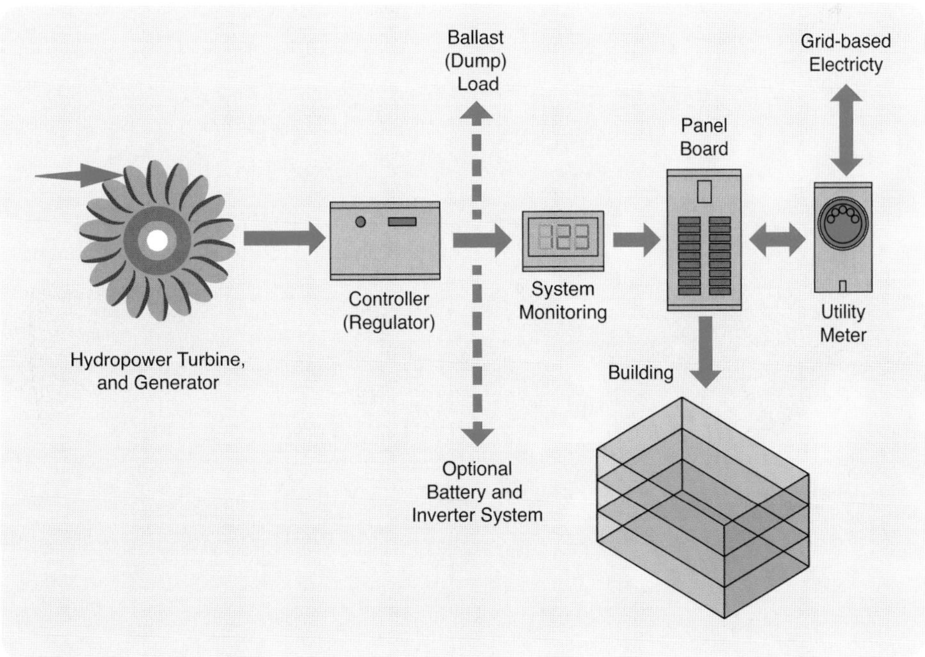

■ **FIGURE 8.33** Grid-Connected Hydropower System.

has a unique blade design to optimize high-flow water energy capture. The water flow acts on all blades simultaneously.

An impulse turbine has a runner (wheel) that is not immersed. Rather, water is piped into the turbine with a nozzle, or nozzles, at high velocity. Impulse turbines are ideal for high-head (high-pressure) and low-flow conditions. Among the types of impulse turbines are the Cross-flow, Turgo and Pelton, the latter shown in Figure 8.35. One or more nozzles direct high-velocity water at a spinning runner with multiple cup-shaded blades. The Turgo includes an enhanced blade design that allows the nozzle flows to strike more than one cupped blade at a time.

■ **FIGURE 8.34** Kaplan Turbine.

■ **FIGURE 8.35** Pelton Turbine.

EFFICIENCY

Hydro turbines can attain efficiencies as high as 90 percent, and most will operate in the 80 to 90 percent range if incorporated into a well-designed system. The smallest micro hydro turbines for residential applications will have lower efficiencies. However, the final water-to-wire efficiency will be less than the turbine efficiency because of other losses in the system. The water's path from the intake to the turbine can introduce friction through piping design of turns in the penstock. This friction reduces the total head of a system. Total system efficiencies run at 50 percent for micro hydro and 60 to 70 percent for small hydro.

Design Guidance

The use of hydropower is very site-specific. Under the right conditions, the resource may be available to generate all or a portion of a net zero energy building's energy use. If an appropriate waterway is available, the first step is to determine the system's head and flow, which will influence turbine selection and system design and lead to an estimate of the energy-generating capacity of the system.

System power can be estimated with the following simple equations. First, estimate the maximum potential of hydropower based on the flow (F) of water in cubic feet per second, and head (H) elevation in feet. The weight of water is 62.4 pounds per cubic feet.

$$P = H \times F \times 62.4$$

Power (P) in this equation is the units of foot-pounds per second. This can be converted to watts by multiplying the conversion of 1.36 watts to 1 foot-pound per second.

$$P(W) = H \times F \times 84.9$$

This equation can also be expressed for a flow rate in units of gallons per minute by dividing by the conversion of 1 cubic foot per second to 448.8 gallons per minute.

$$P(W) = H \times F \times 0.19$$

Next, to arrive at the design power for the hydro system, a total system efficiency (*e*) needs to be applied to the equation.

$$P(W) = H \times F \times 84.9 \times e \text{ (units of F is cf/s)}$$
$$P(W) = H \times F \times 0.19 \times e \text{ (units of F is gpm)}$$

With the design power of the system estimated, it is possible to estimate the annual energy generation. If the design flow for the system is conservative, and can be relied on year-round, even in the season of lowest flow, then simply multiply the power in watts or kilowatts by the hours per year to get annual kilowatt-hours. A capacity factor can be added in for estimating actual annual performance, to account for periods of lower flow and maintenance downtime.

Design integration for a micro hydro or small hydro system not only means complying with regulatory and legal requirements; it also requires careful assessment and mitigation of environmental issues, and close attention to the aesthetics of the system application and integration into the site. The aesthetic considerations will certainly be different for a site in a natural setting that utilizes a stream or river, versus an urban or industrial site, which has its own unique opportunities.

Small Hydropower System Size Example

Site available system head: 75 feet

Design flow: 15,000 gallons per minute

System efficiency: 70 percent

Power = 75 ft × 15,000 gpm × 0.19 × 0.70 = 149,625 watts, or 150 kW

Capacity factor: 75 percent

Energy = 150 kW × 8,760 hours × 75% = 985,500 kWh, or 3,363 MBtu

Hydropower Resources and Design Tools

Industry Resources

- National Hydropower Association (NHAA): www.hydro.org
- Low-Impact Hydropower Institute (LIHI): www.lowimpacthydro.org

Hydro Resources

Note: Resources are site-specific and require field measurements.

- U.S. Geological Survey (may have historical flow rates available): www.usgs.gov
- Virtual Hydropower Prospector (an online GIS hydro resource assessment tool by Idaho National Laboratory): http://hydropower.inel.gov/prospector/index.shtml

Hydropower Design Software and Websites

- RETScreen (free software by Natural Resources Canada): www.retscreen.net

Note: Consult turbine manufacturers when sizing and designing systems.

GEOTHERMAL

Basic Concepts

Geothermal energy comes from the heat or thermal energy stored within the earth. The earth's core temperature is extremely hot, believed to be almost 10,000°F, or about the same temperature as the surface of the sun. That is an enormous source of energy, and hot temperatures can be found relatively close to the earth's surface. In fact, the temperature generally increases based on the depth below the surface. The earth just below the surface stays at a relatively constant temperature, compared to air temperature, and in most areas it ranges between 50°F to 60°F. This shallow thermal resource is used in geothermal heating and cooling, sometimes known as geoexchange. This technology is generally categorized as an energy-efficient mechanical system, rather than a renewable energy system. (Refer back to Chapter 7 for a discussion of geothermal technology using ground-source heat pumps.)

Further below the earth's surface, pockets and reservoirs of hot water and steam can be found, especially in areas where recent volcanic activity has brought hot magma closer to the earth's surface. There are several geothermal power technologies used worldwide to generate renewable electricity from steam or hot water gathered from below the earth's surface. Compared to other renewable energy sources, geothermal is not intermittent and can provide baseload electricity 24 hours a day, 7 days a week.

Technologies

Although geothermal power supplies less than 1 percent of the energy to the United States, it has tremendous potential to supply a much larger portion. The nation's geothermal resources are considerable, especially the high-temperature resources found throughout the western United States, illustrated on the map in Figure 8.36. Furthermore, the technologies and techniques for harnessing geothermal energy are improving rapidly and will expand the available resources.

A suitable conventional geothermal site has heat, water, and a permeable geology that allows water to move through the heated rock. An emerging technology, known as enhanced geothermal systems, can modify once unsuitable sites for geothermal energy generation (also illustrated on the map in Figure 8.36). Many sites have the heated rock layers, but lack the water and permeable geology. Enhanced geothermal technology injects water deep into the rock layer, breaking it up and creating a water-filled, permeable geothermal reservoir. One of the potential risks of this technology is induction of seismic activity.

Google, as part of its RE<C initiative (Develop Renewable Energy Cheaper than Coal), has instituted a program aimed at advancing R&D and information about enhanced geothermal systems. A plug-in to Google Earth provides a state-by-state geothermal resource assessment that includes water temperatures at various depths and energy generation potential, compared to current total energy capacity in each state from all sources. The plug-in is available at www.google.org/egs.

Geothermal electricity generation has historically been at a utility scale, utilizing geothermal power plants located at the source of high-temperature geothermal reservoirs. Dry-steam power plants make use of steam directly from the earth to drive a turbine. This type of plant, the oldest established technology for geothermal, requires access to steam reservoirs, which thus can limit its application. The most common type of geothermal

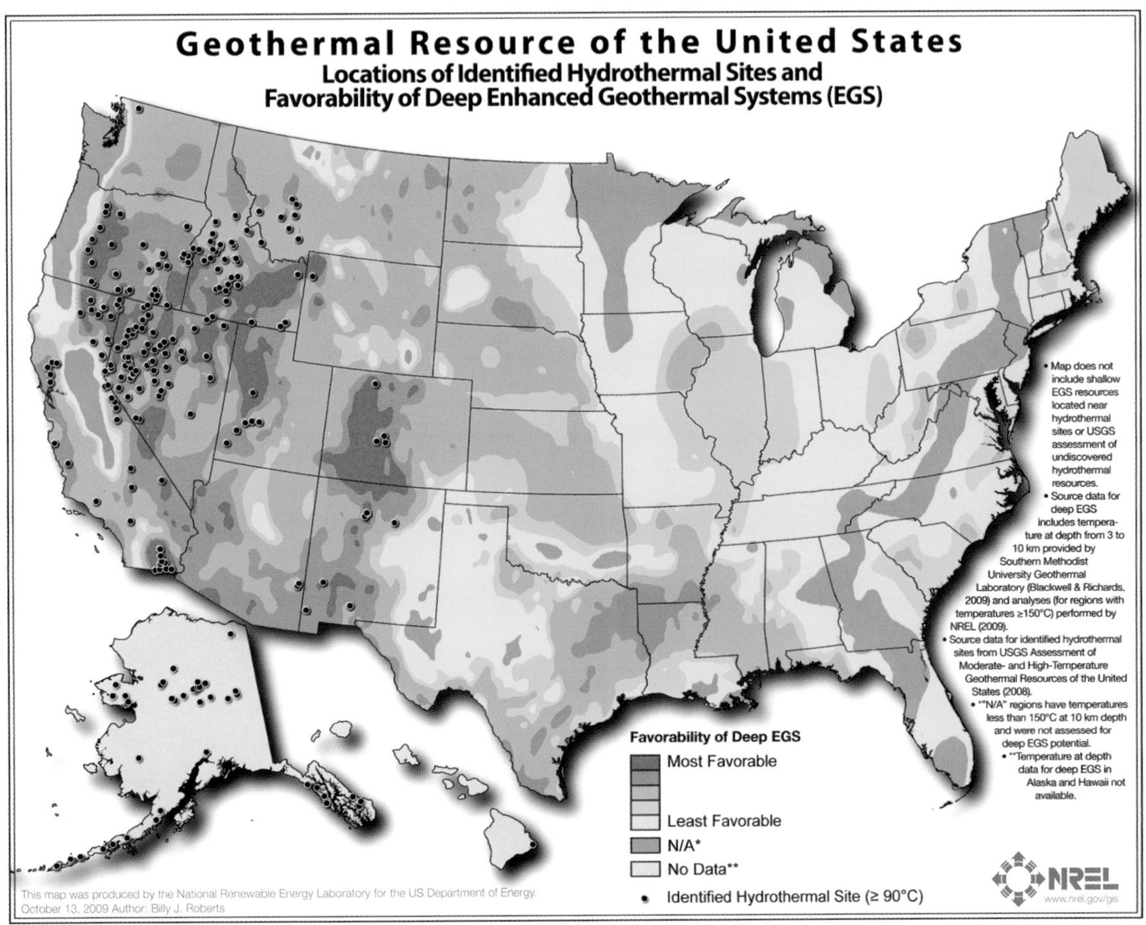
Geothermal Resource of the United States
Locations of Identified Hydrothermal Sites and Favorability of Deep Enhanced Geothermal Systems (EGS)
• Map does not include shallow EGS resources located near hydrothermal sites or USGS assessment of undiscovered hydrothermal resources.
• Source data for deep EGS includes temperature at depth from 3 to 10 km provided by Southern Methodist University Geothermal Laboratory (Blackwell & Richards, 2009) and analyses (for regions with temperatures ≥150°C) performed by NREL (2009).
• Source data for identified hydrothermal sites from USGS Assessment of Moderate- and High-Temperature Geothermal Resources of the United States (2008).
• *"N/A" regions have temperatures less than 150°C at 10 km depth and were not assessed for deep EGS potential.
• **Temperature at depth data for deep EGS in Alaska and Hawaii not available.
Favorability of Deep EGS
Most Favorable
Least Favorable
N/A*
No Data**
Identified Hydrothermal Site (≥ 90°C)
NREL
www.nrel.gov/gis
This map was produced by the National Renewable Energy Laboratory for the US Department of Energy.
October 13, 2009 Author: Billy J. Roberts

■ **FIGURE 8.36** Geothermal Resource Map. *NREL.*

power plant is a flash-steam plant that pulls hot water into a low-pressure tank where it vaporizes, or flashes, and provides the steam to drive a turbine.

The water temperature needed to run a flash-steam plant is 360°F or greater. This type of power plant is also location-specific, based on regions with high geothermal temperatures raised by volcanic activity along tectonic plate boundaries. But technology is advancing the application of low-temperature geothermal as well, utilizing temperatures of 300°F or less. Geothermal power technology using a binary-cycle technology is enabling low-temperature geothermal resources to also produce electricity (see Figure 8.37). Binary-cycle power plants use a heat exchanger to transfer thermal energy from the geothermal wells to a closed-loop (binary or secondary) fluid with a low boiling point that readily vaporizes and drives a turbine. This evolution in technology will make distributed geothermal energy systems for buildings or communities an increasingly feasible option. Currently, the lowest-temperature geothermal plant is located in Chena Hot Springs, Alaska. A 400 kW system with 165°F geothermal well water supplies all the energy needed for the resort year-round.

Low- to moderate-temperature geothermal water (68°F to 302°F) can be used directly to heat buildings or to meet other process heating needs. It can also be used in district central heating plants. This type of application is known as direct-use geothermal and has been used in many locations, including the Idaho State Capital in Boise, to provide a district-heating system. Low- to medium-temperature geothermal energy generation and direct-use heating broadens the potential for this type of renewable energy source to a variety of scales and locations, making it of growing interest for net zero energy buildings.

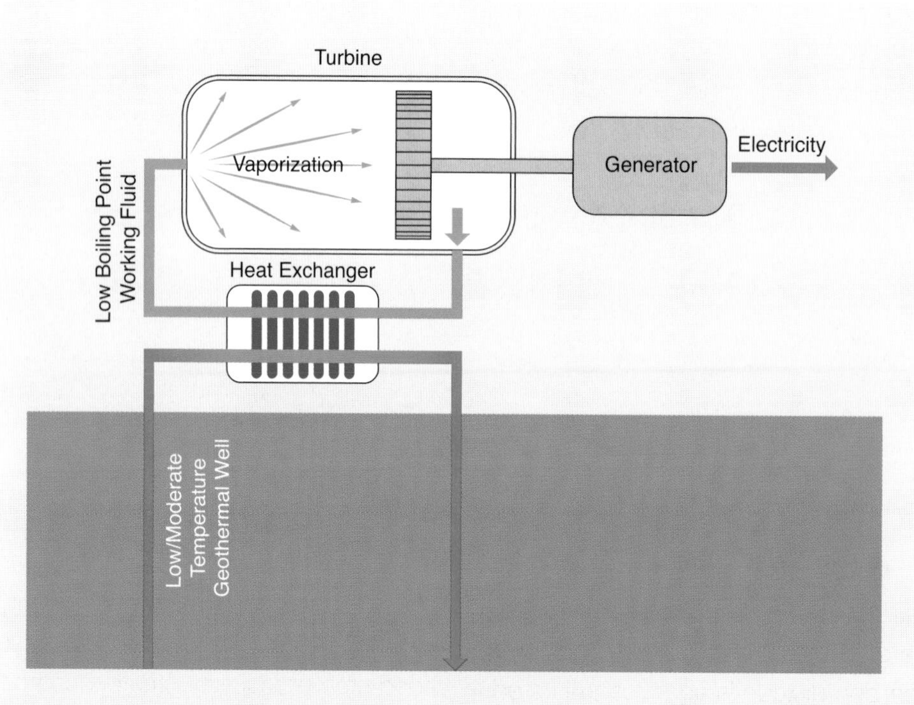

■ **FIGURE 8.37** Geothermal Binary Cycle Technology.

Geothermal Power and Direct-Use Resources and Design Tools

Industry Resources

- Geothermal Energy Association (GEA): www.geo-energy.org

Geothermal Resources

- Department of Energy, Energy Efficiency, & Renewable Energy Geothermal Technologies Program: www1.eere.energy.gov/geothermal/maps.html
- National Renewable Energy Laboratory, Geothermal Technologies: www.nrel.gov/geothermal/data_resources.html
- Google: www.google.org/egs

Geothermal Design Software and Websites

- RETScreen (free software by Natural Resources Canada): www.retscreen.net

Note: Consult turbine and system manufacturers and installers when sizing and designing systems.

BIOMASS

Basic Concepts

Biomass is a diverse source of renewable energy derived from biological or organic material. It is considered a renewable source of energy because it can be readily replenished. Typically plant-based, biomass material utilizes the stored energy from the sun through the photosynthesis process that converts solar energy into glucose. The glucose in plant-based material is an important biological energy source and part of the earth's carbon cycle.

The carbon cycle is the basic framework within which biomass can, at times, be considered carbon-neutral. As biomass crops grow, they sequester carbon dioxide as part of the photosynthesis process. When biomass is combusted to generate heat or electricity, the carbon dioxide is reemitted into the atmosphere. The crop can then be replanted, and the carbon dioxide is again sequestered, creating a carbon balance. Plant-based material also emits methane as it decays. Biomass technology can capture methane emissions and convert it to useful energy through combustion. This process results in carbon dioxide emissions, but prevents methane emissions, which is a much stronger greenhouse gas than carbon dioxide.

Currently in the industry there is uncertainty about and debate over the climate change impact of life-cycle greenhouse gas emissions for biomass energy, and research into the matter is ongoing. The actual life-cycle greenhouse gas emission that accounts for biomass includes many additional factors beyond the carbon cycle of plant carbon sequestering and plant combustion. Inputs related to land use changes, agricultural practices, fuel production, fuel transportation, and end-use application all affect life-cycle greenhouse gas emissions. Because of such inputs as converting forestland to biomass crops, and utilizing fertilizers in biomass crops, the life-cycle greenhouse gas emissions for many biomass applications are not carbon-neutral; nevertheless, they still can help to reduce greenhouse gas emissions significantly, when compared to fossil fuel use. In some cases, biomass energy can be carbon-neutral or represent a net decrease in life-cycle emissions. Applications that show the most promise for carbon neutrality or better are those that cause no land use change or have minimal to no agricultural production. Because of the many variables involved, there is wide variation in potential life-cycle emissions, and each biomass energy application should be considered on a project-by-project basis.

In addition to the greenhouse gas emission implications of using biomass energy, other environmental, economic, and social issues must also be addressed. The growing demand for biomass crops will impose pressure on food crop production, creating competition for irrigable land. These pressures may, over time, impact food prices and access to food for populations. Biomass crops also require substantial water resources, putting new demands on water supplies. The demand for biomass crops may also result in major land use changes that decrease biodiversity and compromise natural habitats.

Both the production and combustion of biomass for energy can result in large quantities of pollutants. The combustion of biomass can cause air pollution and smog, through the release of particulates and pollutants such as carbon monoxide and nitrogen oxides. The use of fertilizers in the agricultural production of biomass can lead to water pollution. The runoff of nitrogen and phosphorus from fertilizers can cause eutrophication of water bodies, which overstimulates plant and algae growth, thereby diminishing aquatic habitat and water quality.

It is critical to implement strict regulations and state-of-the-art pollution controls to mitigate the pollution risks of biomass energy. The negative ramifications of biomass energy are cause for heated debate in the industry, and they must be fully addressed to ensure successful and appropriate growth of the biomass industry.

There are many sources for biomass energy, including food crops, energy crops (nonfood crops planted specifically as biomass feedstock), aquatic crops (such as algae), and wood. An interesting source of biomass feedstock is waste by-products, among them municipal waste, landfill gas, industrial waste, animal manure, agricultural residue, and forest residue. Many applications that utilize waste by-products have great potential to be carbon-neutral, from a life-cycle perspective. Ironically, these applications also have the highest risk for causing air pollution, and so require tight pollution control measures.

Biomass, such as wood chips, can be used directly to generate energy. It can also be converted to a liquid or gas fuel for combustion. There are a number of biochemical and thermochemical conversion processes that break down biomass materials into liquid or gas form. Biochemical conversions involve the natural decomposition of organic material in a variety of processes, including fermentation into ethanol. Thermochemical conversions use heat to break down organic material, which can be combusted to generate energy or further refined into liquid biofuels. The two main thermochemical processes are called gasification and pyrolysis. Gasification uses a thermochemical conversion process to break down biomass feedstock with heat, and a small amount of oxygen to create a syngas (synthesis gas), composed of carbon monoxide and hydrogen. Pyrolysis uses a lower temperature than gasification, and no oxygen, to create a bio-oil.

Biomass replaces fossil fuels and petroleum for three main end uses: bioproducts, biofuels, and biopower. Bioproducts are products that formerly were made with petroleum but now are produced with one of the many forms of biomass; bio-based plastics are one example. The biofuels application involves making liquid or gas fuels from biomass feedstock. Two common types of biofuels are ethanol and biodiesel. Biofuel applications are primarily used in the transportation industry, to replace and/or supplement a variety of fuels. Biopower, which uses biomass to generate electricity and/or heat, is the application of interest for net zero energy buildings, and so is the focus of this section.

Biopower system technologies include direct-firing, co-firing, anaerobic digestion, gasification, and pyrolysis. Biopower energy systems can be used at a utility or a distributed scale for individual buildings or communities. One advantage of biomass, compared to solar or wind, is that it can provide baseload electricity generation, as long as a supply of feedstock is available.

Technologies

Biopower at the utility scale has been developed as direct-fired biomass power plants in the 20 to 50 MW range. These power plants typically use wood and agricultural residues as feedstock. Biomass is also used at some coal-fired power plants that have been converted to co-firing technologies that allow both coal and biomass feedstock to be combusted for electricity generation.

Biopower technologies come in a number of forms that have applications for commercial buildings. This scale is often called modular biopower systems. In a modular direct-firing biomass system, solid biomass is combusted to create steam that drives a turbine and generator to produce electricity. This process can also be used to heat a building or water, or for some process heating use. An efficient application of biomass is to generate both electricity and heat, or cogeneration (also called combined heat and power). The process to generate electricity through combustion is not, however, very efficient (20 to 40 percent), and this inefficiency is regarded as waste heat. But the waste heat can be captured in a cogeneration application and used for a variety of heating purposes. In some applications, trigeneration can be achieved where cooling is also provided. Waste heat can be used to drive an absorption chiller, in addition to providing heating energy. In cogeneration or trigeneration systems, high efficiencies of 70 to 90 percent can be achieved. The main barrier to effective utilization of cogeneration systems is matching the annual heat energy generation with year-round building loads.

A technology that is just beginning to be commercialized is integrated gasification. Instead of direct combustion of the biomass feedstock, the feedstock is converted to a syngas, which is a mixture of hydrogen and carbon monoxide. The use of syngas as a fuel makes it possible to use more efficient electricity generation technologies. A wide variety of generation technologies can be employed, including combined steam and gas turbines, Stirling engines, microturbines, and fuel cells. This technology can incorporate an assortment of feedstocks, such as wood, agricultural residues, and energy crops. It is also a scalable technology, often referred to as modular biopower systems, like the one shown in Figure 8.38.

Another method of utilizing a gas-fired biopower system is to create biogas using an anaerobic digester. Anaerobic digesters use bacteria to break down or digest the organic material. The process is considered anaerobic because it is completed without the presence of oxygen. The resulting biogas is a renewable form of natural gas comprising 50 to 80 percent methane. Anaerobic digesters use wet biomass feedstock, including animal and human waste, organic landfill waste, and a variety of organic wastes such as food waste.

There can be viable synergies between some industrial processes that involve organic waste and on-site biomass power. A consistent supply of organic waste, if not recycled back into the industrial process, can be converted into biogas via an anaerobic digester and then be used to generate electricity and/or heat. Farms and ranches, for example, can install anaerobic digesters to convert animal manure into biogas; a similar process has been applied to waste water treatment plants. Waste heat from electricity generation can be used to heat the anaerobic digestion process, optimizing the conversion temperature. The organic waste in landfills releases methane into the atmosphere as it decomposes. A landfill gas collection system features a series of wells piped into the landfill and a piped collector system to capture the biogas.

An assortment of organic waste by-products can be incorporated into an on-site biopower system. Pulp and paper mills are examples of using wood waste to produce heat and electricity, typically through gasification. An industrial process such as this can combine the production of bio-based products, the creation of biofuels, and the generation of its own electricity and heat.

■ **FIGURE 8.38** Modular Biopower System. *NREL/PIX 11913; photograph by Jim Yost.*

One of the most important factors in analyzing the applicability of a biopower system for a net zero energy building is the availability of appropriate feedstock. For some industrial processes, the feedstock is on-site and part of the process. In other cases, the feedstock will need to be delivered to the site. This makes biomass a regionally specific solution, as the feedstock should be locally available and have a reliable distribution system in place. The map in Figure 8.39, from NREL, shows both the availability of biomass resources in the United States and the composite availability of a wide range of biomass resources. NREL also publishes resource availability maps for specific individual feedstocks.

WOOD CHIP BOILERS

One of the simplest biomass technologies for commercial buildings is the wood chip boiler, which can generate thermal energy for both building and water heating. This technology can be applied to a small commercial building and as district hot water for an entire campus. The basic components of a wood chip boiler system include fuel storage, a fuel-handling system, a wood chip boiler with emission controls technology, an ash collection bin, and a water loop to heat the water. For larger systems, fuel handling can be automated with conveyors, to minimize operator time. For small systems, manual feeding of a day bin hopper can be a cost-effective materials-handling option.

Wood chip boilers require a consistent and reliable source of wood chips. Appropriate project sites are usually located in regions with extensive forestland and reliable access to wood through sustainably managed forest practices. Urban sites may have access to wood chips through urban waste wood

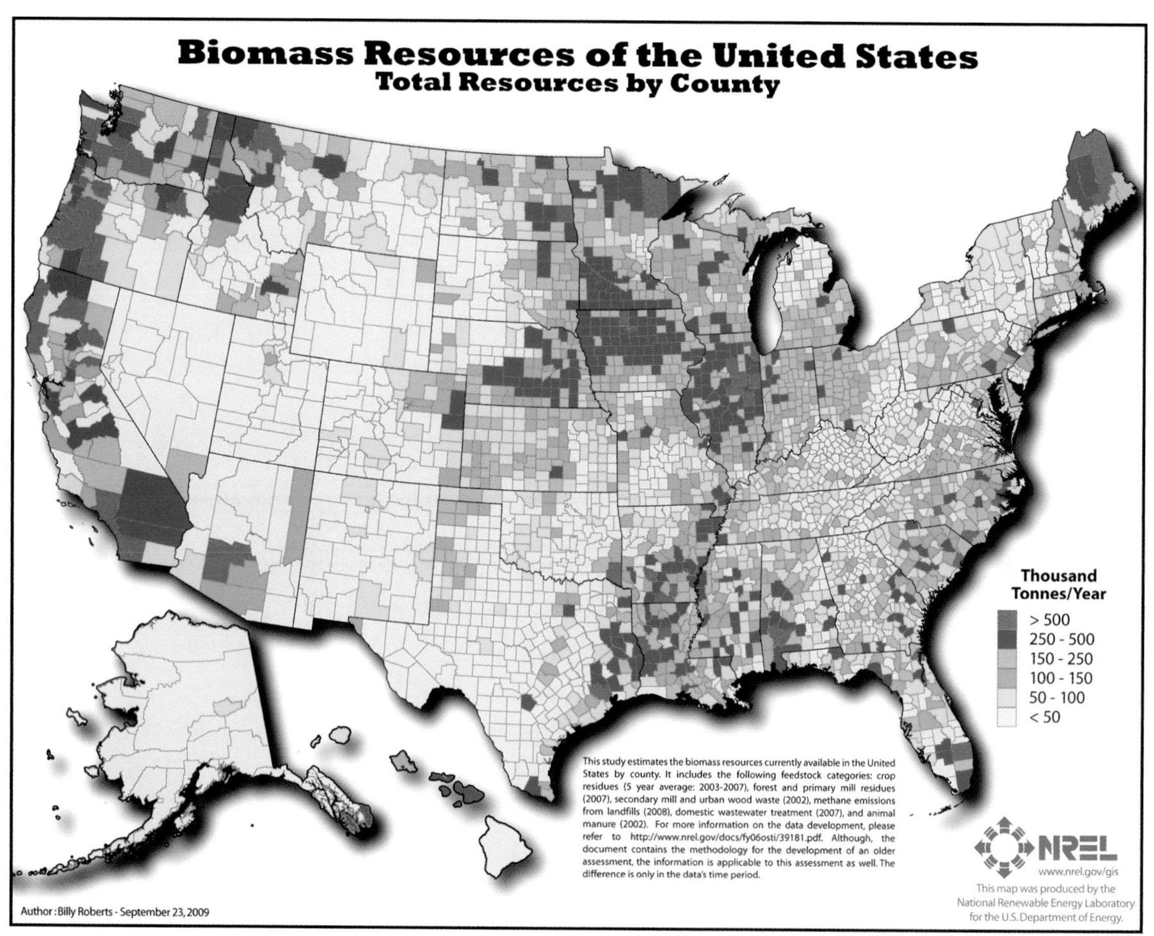

Biomass Resources of the United States
Total Resources by County
Thousand Tonnes/Year
> 500
250 - 500
150 - 250
100 - 150
50 - 100
< 50
This study estimates the biomass resources currently available in the United States by county. It includes the following feedstock categories: crop residues (5 year average: 2003-2007), forest and primary mill residues (2007), secondary mill and urban wood waste (2002), methane emissions from landfills (2008), domestic wastewater treatment (2007), and animal manure (2002). For more information on the data development, please refer to http://www.nrel.gov/docs/fy06osti/39181.pdf. Although, the document contains the methodology for the development of an older assessment, the information is applicable to this assessment as well. The difference is only in the data's time period.
NREL
www.nrel.gov/gis
This map was produced by the National Renewable Energy Laboratory for the U.S. Department of Energy.
Author: Billy Roberts - September 23, 2009

■ **FIGURE 8.39** Biomass Resource Map. *NREL.*

resources. Wood chips are typically supplied as green wood, meaning they contain moisture. The wood chips are dried before combustion, as part of the overall process. The energy from wood is measured based on dry wood; bone-dry wood has an energy content of about 8,000 Btu per pound.

The map in Figure 8.40 shows wood-related biomass resources in the United States for forest residues.

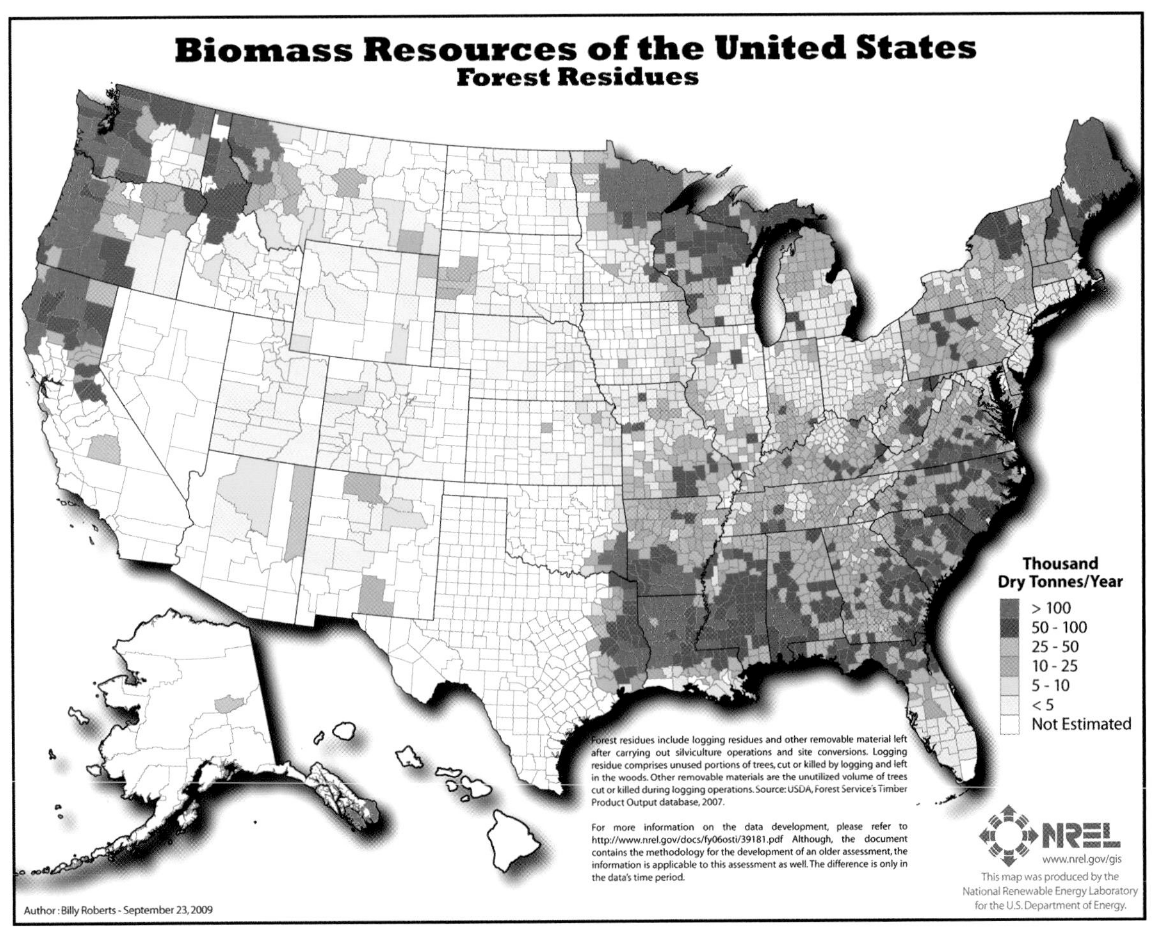
Biomass Resources of the United States
Forest Residues
Thousand
Dry Tonnes/Year
> 100
50 - 100
25 - 50
10 - 25
5 - 10
< 5
Not Estimated
Forest residues include logging residues and other removable material left after carrying out silviculture operations and site conversions. Logging residue comprises unused portions of trees, cut or killed by logging and left in the woods. Other removable materials are the unutilized volume of trees cut or killed during logging operations. Source: USDA, Forest Service's Timber Product Output database, 2007.
For more information on the data development, please refer to http://www.nrel.gov/docs/fy06osti/39181.pdf Although, the document contains the methodology for the development of an older assessment, the information is applicable to this assessment as well. The difference is only in the data's time period.
NREL
www.nrel.gov/gis
This map was produced by the
National Renewable Energy Laboratory
for the U.S. Department of Energy.
Author: Billy Roberts - September 23, 2009

■ **FIGURE 8.40** Biomass Forest Residues Resource Map. *NREL.*

Biomass Resources and Design Tools

Industry Resources

- Biomass Energy Resource Center (BERC): www.biomasscenter.org
- Biomass Thermal Energy Council (BTEC): www.biomassthermal.org

Biomass Resources

- NREL Map Search: www.nrel.gov/gis/mapsearch
- U.S. DOE Biomass Program: www.eere.energy.gov/biomass
- U.S. Forest Service Woody Biomass Utilization: www.fs.fed.us/woodybiomass

Biomass Design Software and Websites

- RETScreen (free software by Natural Resources Canada): www.retscreen.net

FUEL CELLS AND HYDROGEN

Basic Concepts

A fuel cell is a device that generates electricity, without combustion, through an electrochemical process involving a fuel (hydrogen) and oxygen. The process is more efficient than conventional engines and turbines. The by-products of fuel cell electricity generation are heat and water. Hydrogen is an energy carrier or fuel that can be manufactured at small or large scales. It can be made locally and stored, used at point of service, or manufactured at central locations and transported. Hydrogen can be used to generate electricity through a fuel cell in a number of applications. The technology can provide base-load electricity or supplement other renewable energy systems. Fuel cells can play an important role in net zero energy buildings because of their versatility and clean operation. However, it is critical to ensure that the hydrogen fuel is not produced using fossil fuels.

Hydrogen

Hydrogen as a fuel is gas made up of hydrogen molecules (H_2) composed of two bonded hydrogen atoms. Hydrogen is the simplest atomic element—number 1 on the periodic table—composed of one proton and one electron. It is extremely abundant throughout the universe and on earth; however, hydrogen molecules in gas form do not readily exist on earth, because hydrogen combines easily with other elements; and as a gas, it is so light it rises out of the atmosphere. Therefore, hydrogen gas has to be produced. There are a number of methods to produce hydrogen. Currently, the most common, and cost-effective, is called steam methane reforming, which uses high-temperature steam to separate hydrogen from the methane molecules in natural gas. This method does, however, have a major disadvantage: It results in greenhouse gas emissions.

Fortunately, other emerging methods are being developed to generate hydrogen without emitting greenhouse gases. One, water splitting, uses an electric charge to split hydrogen from water. This process, called electrolysis, can be completed with the use of electricity from a renewable energy source, such as solar or wind. Biomass conversions to syngas or liquid biofuels can be further processed into hydrogen. The carbon neutrality of this approach would be based on the life-cycle greenhouse gas emissions of the biomass feedstock. Other promising technologies to split hydrogen atoms from water include the use of certain microorganisms and sunlight or special semiconductor materials and sunlight.

Fuel Cells

A fuel cell is composed of a stack of many individual fuel cells, called a *fuel cell stack* (see Figure 8.41). Each individual fuel cell has three thin layers: a negative electrode face (anode), a positive electrode face (cathode), and an electrolyte membrane center to facilitate the flow

■ **FIGURE 8.41** A 5 kW Fuel Cell Stack. *NREL/PIX 12506; photograph by Warren Gretz.*

of positively charged protons from the anode to the cathode (see Figure 8.42). Hydrogen enters the fuel cell and the anode of each cell, coated with a catalyst, separates the electron and proton of the hydrogen atoms. While the protons are conducted through the electrolyte to the cathode layer, the freed electrons are directed into a separate circuit that goes around the electrolyte membrane and connects back to the cathode and generates an electrical DC current. When the hydrogen electrons and protons reunite in the presence of oxygen, water and heat are produced. Several fuel cell technologies operate in this manner; others operate in a similar manner, but have a flow that results in water being produced on the anode side.

Fuel cell technologies are distinguished by the type of electrolyte used in the cell. Some are already commercially available, while others are still in development. There are several different technological approaches, each with advantages and disadvantages. Fuel cells have to be designed to manage fuel, temperature, humidity, and water. One of the most daunting design challenges is to develop a cost-effective technology that is also durable, with a long service life. The fuel cell technologies

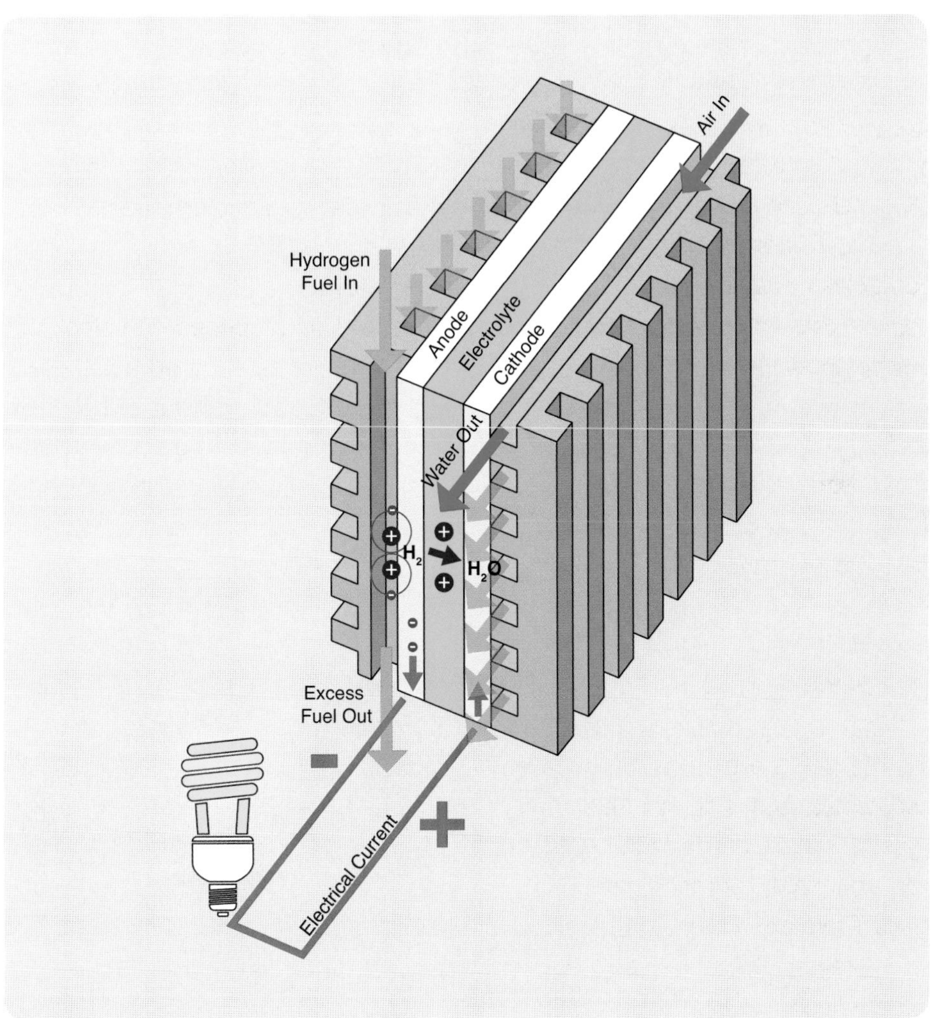

■ **FIGURE 8.42** PEM Fuel Cell Operation.

listed here have potential application in a distributed energy system.

One of the fuel cell components that has a dramatic impact on cost is the use of a platinum catalyst. PEMs and PAFCs utilize a platinum catalyst but have lower operating temperatures than MCFC and SOFC technologies. Lower operating temperatures allow quicker start-up times and make temperature management easier; they also make it easier to manufacture durable and safe units. Conversely, high operating temperatures offer different advantages, such as the capability to operate in combined heat and power mode, and for the fuel cell to directly reform fuel into hydrogen as part of its process, meaning that hydrogen will not have be stored on-site.

A recent breakthrough in commercial fuel cell technology is Bloom Energy's Energy Server (see Figure 8.43). This fuel cell, often called a "Bloom Box," is based on advances in solid oxide technology and offers a high-efficiency and cost-effective solution. The system is based on a 100 kW modular unit that can run on natural gas or biogas as the primary fuel being reformed in hydrogen.

Fuel Cell Technologies

Polymer Electrolyte Membrane (PEM) Fuel Cells

- Operating temperature: 50°C to 100°C
- Typical stack size: 1 kW to 100 kW
- Efficiency: 35 percent for stationary applications

Phosphoric Acid Fuel Cells (PAFC)

- Operating temperature: 150°C to 200°C
- Typical stack size: 400 kW/100 kW module
- Efficiency: 40 percent

Molten Carbonate Fuel Cells (MCFC)

- Operating temperature: 600°F to 700°F
- Typical stack size: 300 kW to 3 MW/300 kW module
- Efficiency: 45 to 50 percent

Solid Oxide Fuel Cells (SOFC)

- Operating temperature: 700°F to 1,000°F
- Typical stack size: 1 kW to 2 MW
- Efficiency: 60 percent

Data source: Department of Energy, Energy Efficiency, and Renewable Energy, Fuel Cell Technologies Program. www.hydrogenandfuelcells.energy.gov.

■ **FIGURE 8.43** Bloom Energy Server Installed at Fireman's Fund. *Image courtesy of Bloom Energy.*

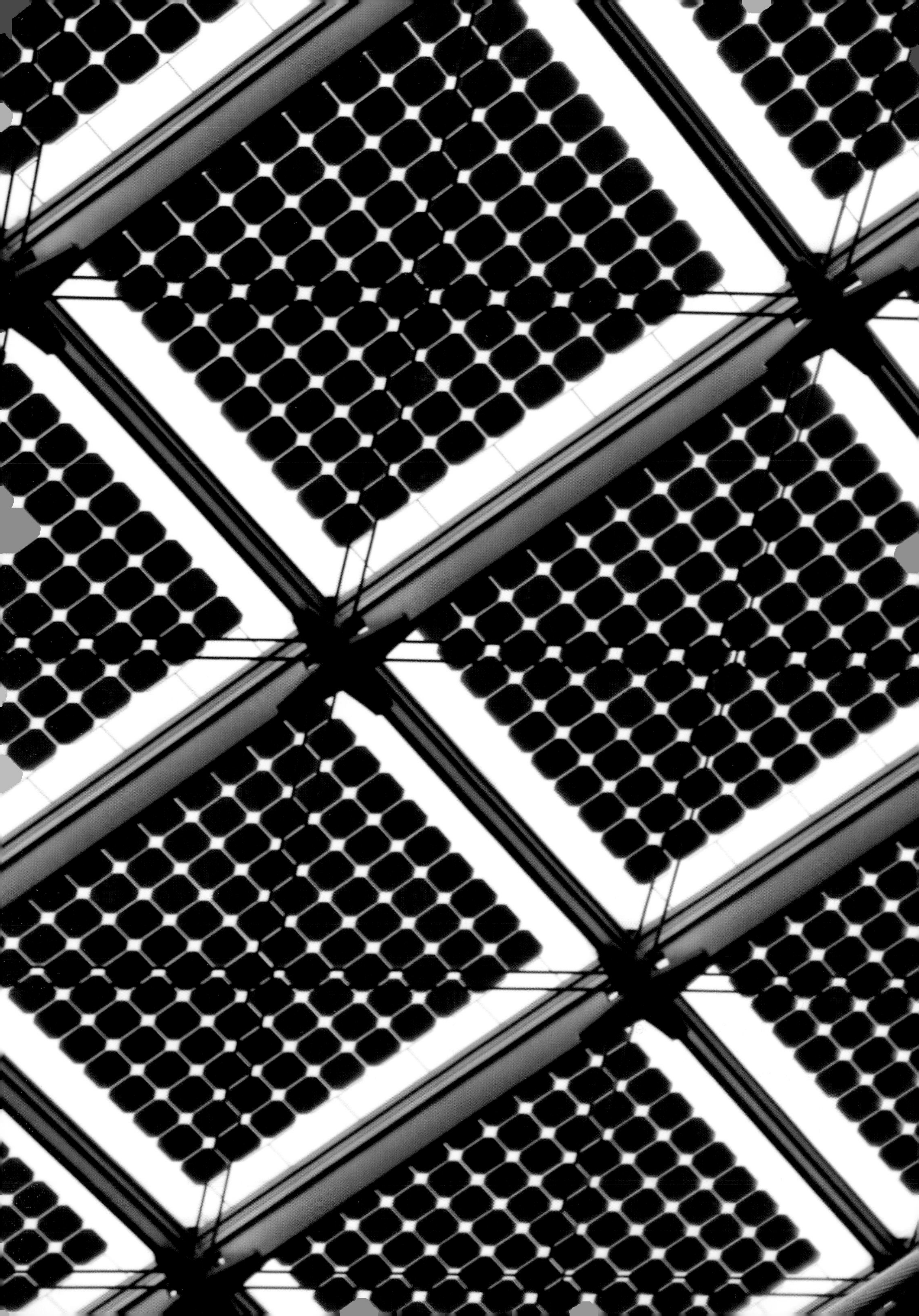

CHAPTER 9

ECONOMICS

FINANCIAL CONSIDERATIONS

Most construction budgets are developed without renewable energy systems in mind. After all, renewable energy systems do not have the conventional functions of typical construction elements and are not considered part of the program or performance requirements for most projects. In addition, renewable energy systems represent a sizable investment, not easily added in any sizable quantity to a conventional construction budget.

Investing in renewable energy systems is like paying your entire utility bill up front. A high-quality net zero energy building will have a very long service life, but it is unlikely that initial renewable energy systems will provide lifetime energy. Most photovoltaic systems have a warranty of 20 to 25 years, and a potential service life of up to three to four decades. Investing in a photovoltaic system is like paying your utility bills up front for the next 25 to 30 years—a sizable investment but also an important value proposition.

One of the most tangible value propositions for net zero energy buildings is the energy cost savings. The value of this investment is a function of future energy prices. A higher rate of energy escalation will yield a higher return on investment. Further, the introduction of carbon emission regulation, such as a cap-and-trade or a carbon tax, will likely yield even greater returns. Also note that a net zero energy building is more than just the addition of renewable energy; it is a low-energy high-performance building—an investment in its own right. So, in truth, the return on investment is the combination of energy cost savings, based on a hedge against escalation, and the energy cost savings through conservation—a compelling combination. The analysis of net zero energy buildings financially and as an investment is explored throughout this chapter.

Budget Considerations

Budget considerations for a net zero energy building involve both construction and renewable energy system costs. It is important to address each of these budget items independently. At the same time, it's important to recognize that they also have a powerful interdependence. As a general rule, energy efficiency is more cost-effective than renewable energy. An investment in a more energy-efficient net zero energy building will result in a smaller renewable energy system size and lower cost.

The renewable energy budget is closely tied to the operational budget for a building. Every building has an operational budget, and it can be leveraged in several ways to finance the cost of a renewable energy system. From a creative standpoint, the operational budget can be thought of as the built-in renewable energy budget for any project. Typically, the long-term energy operational costs are leveraged to finance the up-front capital cost in renewable energy. Alternatively, the renewable energy system can be leased or financed through a power purchase agreement (PPA), which pays for the renewable energy as it is generated, using the operational budget with no up-front capital cost. (The "Financial Models" section of this chapter provides more details on procurement methods.)

The next level of energy budget planning is to consider both building energy efficiency and renewable energy systems as a linked decision. If the project's operational energy budget is established and then consolidated in terms of up-front capital, this budget, along with the construction budget, can be used for energy investment in the form of renewable energy and energy conservation. This technique allows the leveraging of both the operational and construction budgets to find the most cost-effective way of meeting operational energy needs.

Renewable Energy System Costs

Many variables come into play when determining cost for renewable energy systems. The type and scale of the renewable energy system are both primary factors. The cost of renewables also changes over time, on a downward trend, as the technology improves and the industry increases market share.

There are two primary financial parameters to address when planning the renewable energy system for a net zero energy building. The capital investment is the overall up-front cost to implement the project. This is particularly important for building owners who plan on directly owning the renewable energy system. The second parameter is the estimate of the levelized cost of energy for the system. This takes the total cost of the system as a function of the total energy produced over the service life of the system. This financial metric can be a clear indicator of how competitive the renewable energy system will be over time compared to energy rates of the local utility, and accounting for energy escalation.

The capital costs for photovoltaic systems have two primary components: the cost of the modules and the cost of the balance of system. The balance of system excludes the module but includes all other hard and soft costs for the system. The balance-of-system costs have typically been about half the total system costs, but they fluctuate based on market conditions. As module prices decrease, the balance-of-system costs—in particular, the installation cost—could become a larger factor in the overall cost of installation. Installation costs are also highly project-specific; but they can be minimized by designing and prepping the installation area, such as the roof, to ease installation and make it PV-ready.

Photovoltaic modules are becoming commoditized; industry research groups such as Solarbuzz maintain pricing indices that reflect average as well as lowest module technology cost on a price-per-watt basis. The scale of renewable energy systems also plays a key role in total system cost. According to the "U.S. Solar Market Insight First Quarter 2011" report by the Solar Energy Industries Association and GTM Research, first-quarter 2011 total photovoltaic system costs for residential averaged $6.41 per watt; nonresidential averaged $5.35 per watt; and utility scale averaged $3.85 per watt.

Another source for customizable searches on photovoltaic installed cost information is NREL's Open PV Project, at http://openpv.nrel.gov. Here, PV system owners around the nation can upload basic project data on individual systems, thereby adding to a vast searchable catalog of PV systems, with data points including location, date of installation, installation cost (before incentives), and system size. A search for all systems installed in the first half of 2011 yielded 42 systems with a total of 45.03 MW of capacity and an average installed cost of $5.30 per watt, without incentives (see Figure 9.1).

In planning for a renewable energy system, it is valuable to examine the system costs in a number of ways. It may be helpful, for example, to know the installed cost per watt, which is related to the installed cost of the system and its rated power output (typical for photovoltaic and wind systems). The cost per kilowatt-hour is another cost metric and is related to energy costs and allows a comparison to utility bills. This measure, which needs to be calculated over a time period, can be taken in the range of from one year to the life of the system. The system cost per square foot provides a cost metric similar to other construction assemblies. The system cost per square foot of gross building area makes it possible to compare the renewable energy system budget with the construction budget. Related to system cost per square foot of building is the installed watts per square foot of the building; it is a measure of energy efficiency in terms of renewable energy requirements.

To illustrate the different cost and related energy metrics, the table in Figure 9.2 offers a simple example with some typical values for photovoltaic systems, and assumes a system size for achieving net zero energy. The example is based on the square footage of the building and square footage of PV modules, so it is independent of total building size

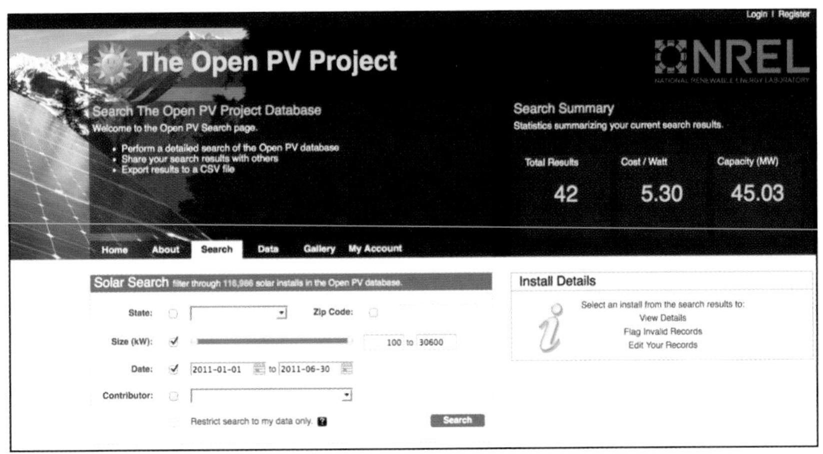

■ **FIGURE 9.1** NREL Open PV Website Screen Capture.

Building EUI (kBtu/ft²/year)	Building EUI (kWh/ft²/year)	Solar Radiation (kWh/m²/day)	Solar Radiation (kWh/ft²/year)	PV Module Eff.	DC/AC Derate Factor	PV Generation (kWh/ft²/year)	PV Module W/ft²	PV Watt / ft² (Bldg) W/ft²	Cost per Watt $/W	Cost per kWh (30 year) $/kWh	Cost per ft² (PV) $/ ft²	PV Generation /EUI Ratio	Cost per ft² (Bldg) $/ ft²
15	4.4	5.0	169.6	17%	80%	23.1	15.8	3.0	$4.00	$0.09	$63.21	5.25	$12.05
20	5.9	5.0	169.6	17%	80%	23.1	15.8	4.0	$4.00	$0.09	$63.21	3.94	$16.06
25	7.3	5.0	169.6	17%	80%	23.1	15.8	5.0	$4.00	$0.09	$63.21	3.15	$20.08
30	8.8	5.0	169.6	17%	80%	23.1	15.8	6.0	$4.00	$0.09	$63.21	2.62	$24.09
35	10.3	5.0	169.6	17%	80%	23.1	15.8	7.0	$4.00	$0.09	$63.21	2.25	$28.11
40	11.7	5.0	169.6	17%	80%	23.1	15.8	8.0	$4.00	$0.09	$63.21	1.97	$32.12
45	13.2	5.0	169.6	17%	80%	23.1	15.8	9.0	$4.00	$0.09	$63.21	1.75	$36.14

■ **FIGURE 9.2** Photovoltaic Cost and Energy Metrics: Example 1.

or specific PV module size. The table can be developed in a spreadsheet and customized. The shaded cells represent those that require data to be input and variables that can be tested. The other cells use relationship equations to develop the desired metrics. A spreadsheet similar to this table would allow the testing of different building energy use intensities (EUIs), average annual solar radiation, PV module efficiency, and installed system cost, in terms of a variety of cost metrics as just described.

In this example, an average annual solar radiation value of 5 kWh/m^2/day for a south-facing tilted panel is used. The photovoltaic module specification also remains constant, using an efficiency typical of a very high-quality module. The installed cost per watt for the photovoltaic system is assumed to be \$4.00 per watt after incentives. In the example, notice how working to reduce the EUI of the building pays off when budgeting for the renewable energy system. The last column in the table expresses the approximate cost per square foot added to the project budget for a renewable energy system sized to achieve net zero energy based on the assumptions in this example. Remember that these values are independent of building size. The metric of PV generation per square foot to EUI is a measure of the approximate number of stories that can be supported based on the ratio of floor area to PV area (which simply assumes a full roof area).

This example could be run a number of different ways by changing different variables. For example, the table in Figure 9.3 uses the same input as the table in Figure 9.2 but fixes the EUI of the building, tests a range of installed photovoltaic system costs on a cost-per-watt basis, and analyzes the impact of system price independent of the energy efficiency of the building.

Using a sampling from these two examples to represent a wide range of installed photovoltaic system costs per building floor area, it is possible to develop a relationship between photovoltaic system costs and construction costs for a net zero energy building. The table in Figure 9.4 compares three photovoltaic system costs (low, medium, and high) to a wide range of commercial building construction costs per square foot, also from low to high. For planning purposes, a photovoltaic system budget ranges from 3 to 20 percent of the construction budget. The average and median photovoltaic system budget is 8 percent of the construction budget. The lower construction costs have the greatest sensitivity to photovoltaic costs, whereas the higher construction costs show a much narrower range of photovoltaic system budgets as a percent of construction budget.

Building EUI (kBtu/ft²/ year)	Building EUI (kWh/ft²/ year)	Solar Radiation (kWh/m²/ day)	Solar Radiation (kWh/ft²/ year)	PV Module Eff.	DC/AC Derate Factor	PV Generation (kWh/ft²/ year)	PV Module W/ft²	PV Watt / ft² (Bldg) W/ft²	Cost per Watt \$/W	Cost per kWh (30 year) \$/kWh	Cost per ft² (PV) \$/ ft²	PV Generation /EUI Ratio	Cost per ft² (Bldg) \$/ ft²
25	7.3	5.0	169.6	17%	80%	23.1	15.8	5.0	\$5.00	\$0.11	\$79.01	3.15	\$25.10
25	7.3	5.0	169.6	17%	80%	23.1	15.8	5.0	\$4.50	\$0.10	\$71.11	3.15	\$22.59
25	7.3	5.0	169.6	17%	80%	23.1	15.8	5.0	\$4.00	\$0.09	\$63.21	3.15	\$20.08
25	7.3	5.0	169.6	17%	80%	23.1	15.8	5.0	\$3.50	\$0.08	\$55.31	3.15	\$17.57
25	7.3	5.0	169.6	17%	80%	23.1	15.8	5.0	\$3.00	\$0.07	\$47.40	3.15	\$15.06
25	7.3	5.0	169.6	17%	80%	23.1	15.8	5.0	\$2.50	\$0.06	\$39.50	3.15	\$12.55
25	7.3	5.0	169.6	17%	80%	23.1	15.8	5.0	\$2.00	\$0.05	\$31.60	3.15	\$10.04

■ **FIGURE 9.3** Photovoltaic Cost and Energy Metrics: Example 2.

Module efficiency has an important role in planning and budgeting for systems. Typically, higher-efficiency modules are more expensive than lower-efficiency modules on a cost-per-watt basis. However, efficiency drives down the overall area of photovoltaic array, which reduces racking, cabling, and other balance-of-system costs, including installation. Module efficiency is important for net zero energy buildings because it can reduce area and improve performance. A 1 percent difference in module efficiency from 12 to 13 percent can result in an over 8 percent increase in watts-per-square-foot performance. This is demonstrated in the next table, in Figure 9.5. For each 1 percent gain in efficiency, a module can gain 0.93 watts per square foot in capacity. While this is a direct relationship with efficiency, it is important to note that as module efficiencies go up, the percent increase in production capacity gradually decreases (refer to the last column in the table). This is a very important relationship to keep in mind when considering modules with lower efficiency, especially in a space-constrained installation location. Note that panel efficiency is based

PV Cost per Building Area	Construction Cost					
	$150/ft²	$200/ft²	$250/ft²	$300/ft²	$350/ft²	$400/ft²
$10/ ft²	7%	5%	4%	3%	3%	3%
$20/ ft²	13%	10%	8%	7%	6%	5%
$30/ ft²	20%	15%	12%	10%	9%	8%

■ **FIGURE 9.4** Renewable Energy Budget as Percent of Construction Budget.

PV Module Efficiency	PV Module W/ft²	Incremental % Increase in W/ft²
25%	23.2	4.17%
24%	22.3	4.35%
23%	21.4	4.55%
22%	20.4	4.76%
21%	19.5	5.00%
20%	18.6	5.26%
19%	17.7	5.56%
18%	16.7	5.88%
17%	15.8	6.25%
16%	14.9	6.67%
15%	13.9	7.14%
14%	13.0	7.69%
13%	12.1	8.33%
12%	11.2	9.09%
11%	10.2	10.00%
10%	9.3	

■ **FIGURE 9.5** Module Efficiency and Increase in Watts per Square Foot.

on standard test conditions (STC) and is the percentage of power output from 1,000 watts per square meter of solar irradiance at 25°C.

Net Zero Energy Construction Costs

The financial considerations for net zero energy buildings are more than just those for renewable energy systems. The foundation for a net zero energy building is energy efficiency. The investment in construction and design costs to enhance energy performance is the first priority, and leads to an enhanced feasibility for the addition of renewable energy systems.

Any cost difference or premium that improves energy efficiency for a net zero energy building should be thought of as an investment, rather than a cost. The investment can lead to substantial returns in energy cost savings over a very long building life, and far outweigh the initial investment. And for net zero energy buildings, an additional benefit is the opportunity to "buy energy" as energy-efficiency at a lower price, which means that less of the more expensive renewable energy has to be purchased. In other words, a kilowatt-hour saved is a kilowatt-hour earned.

GREEN BUILDING COST STUDIES

As noted in Chapter 2, a net zero energy building should cost no more, or only slightly more, than a conventional high-quality building (excluding the cost of renewable energy systems). In many cases, a net zero energy building need not cost any more, and can be managed within the total construction budget. Unfortunately, the notion that it will cost substantially more tends to become a self-fulfilling prophecy. If the owner or team expects it to cost more, it likely will. Many recent studies on the cost of building green prove this out. The most recent and extensive study to date is by Greg Kats, a senior director at Good Energies and a leading authority and researcher on the cost of green building. In his 2010 book, *Greening Our Built World: Costs, Benefits, and Strategies*, he outlines key results from his latest costs and benefits study on a group of 170 green buildings in the United States. The median cost premium identified for the 170-building set was 1.5 percent.

A subset of 18 buildings in Kats's study were identified as advanced energy-reducing buildings, saving 50 percent or more energy than their baseline buildings. This group would represent the net zero energy level of energy performance. One of the 18 buildings is, in fact, a net zero energy building—the Aldo Leopold Center by The Kubala Washatko Architects (see Figure 9.6). Interesting to note is that further analysis of Kats's advanced energy savings group reveals that the 8 of 18 buildings that include renewable energy have a median premium of 8 percent, whereas those in the group that do not include renewable energy have a median premium of 2 percent. The higher premium (8 percent compared to 2 percent) is related to the inclusion of the renewable energy system cost in the premium.

The distinction between including and not including renewable energy is dramatic. If on-site renewable energy is treated as an energy generation system, rather than an energy-efficiency measure that is part of the building, then the renewable energy system costs should be treated separately. As cited earlier in this chapter, the cost of a photovoltaic system as a percentage of the construction cost has a median value of 8 percent. Although the subgroup of advanced energy buildings with renewable energy in Kats's study are not all net zero energy buildings, and their green premiums likely include strategies in addition to renewable energy, there is still a strong correlation between the higher premiums seen in this sampling and the cost of photovoltaic systems as a percentage of construction

■ **FIGURE 9.6** Photovoltaic System at the Aldo Leopold Legacy Center. *The Kubala Washatko Architects, Inc./Mark F. Heffron.*

cost. It is clear that the inclusion of renewable energy systems distorts the green premium. To understand the green premium as related to making a building highly energy-efficient, Kats's study would suggest that the premium is small; on average, in the 2 percent range.

It is worth noting that it is challenging to determine the extent to which cost premiums exist for higher-performing buildings. Cost premiums for performance are, essentially, educated estimates, which usually combine several of the key performance-enhancing strategies compared to some lower-performing but less expensive options. Only occasionally are high-performing and conventional options bid side-by-side for accurate comparison. Yet the inclusion of a few higher-performance alternatives does not always lead to overall higher construction costs. In the larger scheme of the whole construction budget, adequate cost transfers and trade-offs may be made to adhere to the same budget, while increasing performance. It is the whole-building cost comparison that really matters.

Comparing whole-building costs is another way to analyze the cost question regarding green buildings. In the landmark study, "Cost of Green Revisited," completed in 2007 by the firm Davis Langdon, authors Lisa Fay Matthiessen and Peter Morris show, by comparing the costs of LEED-certified buildings of various levels of certification to nongreen buildings, that statistically there is no difference in average cost between green buildings and nongreen buildings.

BUILDING INTEGRATED PHOTOVOLTAICS

The use of building integrated photovoltaics (BIPV) is an interesting cost control strategy for net zero energy buildings; it gives net zero energy buildings additional creative options for augmenting renewable energy generation. *Building integrated photovoltaics* refers to the integration of photovoltaic technology into a building material or assembly. This is distinctly different from the application or mounting of a photovoltaic system onto a building. Cost efficiencies can be gained from buying and installing a single material or assembly, compared to buying and installing a material or assembly and then a separate photovoltaic system on top of that.

Building integrated photovoltaics are available in a wide variety of forms and applications, and

BIPV Applications

- Roofing (membrane, metal, shingles, etc.)
- Glazing (windows, skylights)
- Cladding (see Figure 9.7)
- Shading

■ **FIGURE 9.7** BIPV Wall Cladding on the German Entry for the 2009 Solar Decathlon. *NREL/PIX 17356; photograph by Jim Tetro.*

the choices will continue to grow as this still relatively new technology trend gains momentum. BIPV can incorporate crystalline silicon and thin films; so, accordingly, efficiencies will vary. In addition, BIPV provide many options that may be installed in nonoptimized orientations, such as vertical wall applications, which will decrease their energy generation. However, they do offer unique economic and aesthetic benefits, and provide net zero energy buildings more surface area for energy generation. Each application should be analyzed on a case-by-case basis to assess the suitability of BIPV for a project.

Incentives

Economic incentives are commonly employed to move new and desirable markets into more economically sustainable positions. Incentives enable new markets to capture enough share so that their scale of production can yield financial efficiencies and continue to make the new market more cost-competitive. Incentives have played a role in the advancement of green building practices, as well as renewable energy technologies and applications. Incentives are generally designed to taper down as the new market takes hold. Currently, incentives remain strong for both energy-efficient buildings and renewable energy systems, but that may change over time, to follow government budgets and policy direction. Fortunately, there is a comprehensive web-based guide to green building and renewable energy incentives called DSIRE, for Database of State Incentives for Renewables & Efficiency, at www.dsireusa.org. DSIRE is a project of the North Carolina Solar Center and the Interstate Renewable Energy Council, with funding from the Department of Energy. It lists federal and local incentives, and is searchable by state.

Current incentives for renewable energy have a powerful impact on the cost of systems. Thus, incentives should be researched early in the planning for renewable energy systems and energy-efficient measures. Incentives are typically based on either initial cost, ongoing production, or performance. The federal government currently offers significant tax deductions for energy efficiency in commercial buildings (up to $1.80 a square foot) and investment tax credits up to 30 percent for installations of qualifying new renewable energy systems. The federal government also offers a production tax credit per kWh for renewable energy production over a specific number of years. And many states and local utilities offer rebate and loan programs for both energy efficiency and renewable energy. Some states offer tax credits for renewables as well.

Another form of incentive that has been successful in spurring the renewable energy markets in regions around the world is the feed-in tariff (FIT). Feed-in tariffs are used widely in Germany, and are largely responsible for making that country the photovoltaic capital of the world. Feed-in tariffs do not provide up-front incentives in the form of rebates or tax incentives; rather, they offer long-term contracts to compensate for renewable energy generation that feeds into the grid. The tariff price paid per kWh can be designated in a FIT policy in a number of ways, but the price is usually set to compensate for the cost of generation, plus a reasonable return for investors. In this way, each renewable energy technology can be targeted with an appropriate feed-in tariff price to stimulate investment in new renewable energy projects. There has been growing interest and experimentation in—and debate over—feed-in tariffs in the United States in the last several years. California and Florida have been early adopters of feed-in tariff programs.

As incentives are powerful tools to manage costs and spur innovation, it is important to also look at those offered by local governments and utilities. Many local governments offer a variety of tax benefits, rebate programs, and financing options; and many utilities offer valuable rebates programs. Some even offer free or incentivized energy modeling to promote energy efficiency and an integrated design approach. The aforementioned DSIRE website is a great tool for researching local incentives, as well as local policies and regulations.

Energy Cost Escalation

A very important consideration when conducting a financial analysis of the future benefits of energy efficiency and renewable energy is how these investments will fare against future energy prices. Since estimating future energy prices is speculative, the customary approach is to use historical energy price escalation rates as the basis for assumed future escalation. Every year the Energy Information Administration publishes an "Annual Energy Review" that contains decades of historical pricing data for a variety of fuels, including natural gas and electricity for the commercial sector.

Perhaps the most surprising observation from historical energy price data is how dramatically energy prices fluctuate. Energy fluctuations can be as much of a building operational budget issue as energy price escalation is. The not-so-surprising observation is that, over the long haul, energy prices have risen. Historically, natural gas prices have risen at a faster rate than electricity prices for the commercial sector. The average commercial energy escalation, blending both electricity and natural gas, has been about 5 percent over the last four decades. This 5 percent escalation rate is commonly used in the industry, although lower, more conservative rates are also used. It is also common to use low, average, and high escalation rates to bracket the financial analysis between worst-case and best-case scenarios.

GRID PARITY

Within the renewable energy industry, a concept known as grid parity signifies an important economic inflection point. As energy prices continue to escalate over time, and renewable energy system costs continue to decrease over time, at some point, renewable energy will be the lowest-cost energy alternative. Grid parity is market-specific, as it depends on local commercial market rates for electricity and the relative abundance of renewable energy resources, such as wind or solar. While this is a rapidly evolving set of economics, grid parity can be reached today in certain locations with high electricity rates and excellent solar and wind resources. The more important point is that grid parity will become commonplace over time, certainly within the lifetime of buildings being designed and constructed today. That means net zero energy buildings will be able to take advantage of this important economic shift.

IMPLICATIONS OF CARBON REGULATION

One of the primary goals of shifting to renewable energy is to reduce global carbon emissions. However, renewable sources and fossil fuel sources compete financially without incorporating the full cost of externalities such as carbon emissions and climate change. Carbon regulations through mechanisms such a carbon tax or carbon cap-and-trade are potential ways to account for the externalities in energy generation. Carbon regulation can have a major impact on fossil fuel energy prices, and increase demand for renewable energy sources, thereby dramatically changing the economic position of renewable energy.

Renewable Energy Certificates

Currently in the United States, voluntary carbon markets and renewable portfolio standards in many states (see Figure 9.8) have helped advance renewable energy markets. The primary market mechanism has been the buying and selling of renewable energy certificates, or RECs. Most people involved in LEED and green building are familiar with the purchase of RECs to satisfy the LEED Energy & Atmosphere credit for green power.

The EPA defines a REC as the property rights to the environmental, social, and other nonpower qualities of renewable electricity generation. With a REC, power is not purchased; instead, the benefits of clean energy generation are purchased. Therefore, RECs can be sold independent of the purchase of electricity. RECs can also be purchased *with* electricity. When a REC is bundled with the electricity purchase, it is often known as renewable electricity. A REC is equal to 1,000 kWh (or 1 MWh) of renewable energy generation.

The use of RECs is a means of valuing renewable energy in the marketplace. RECs are regularly sold in the voluntary markets to those wanting to minimize the environmental impact of and carbon emissions from their electricity use, and to be able to make environmental claims regarding these purchasing preferences. The purchase of RECs in the voluntary market stimulates an increased demand for new renewable energy projects. Nonvoluntary markets such as those driven by renewable portfolio standards have the same and potentially even greater impact on the demand for new renewable energy projects in the market. When a state has adopted a renewable portfolio standard, it obligates the electric utilities to have a minimum percentage of renewable energy generation as part of their portfolio by a specific date. Many states with renewable energy portfolios have

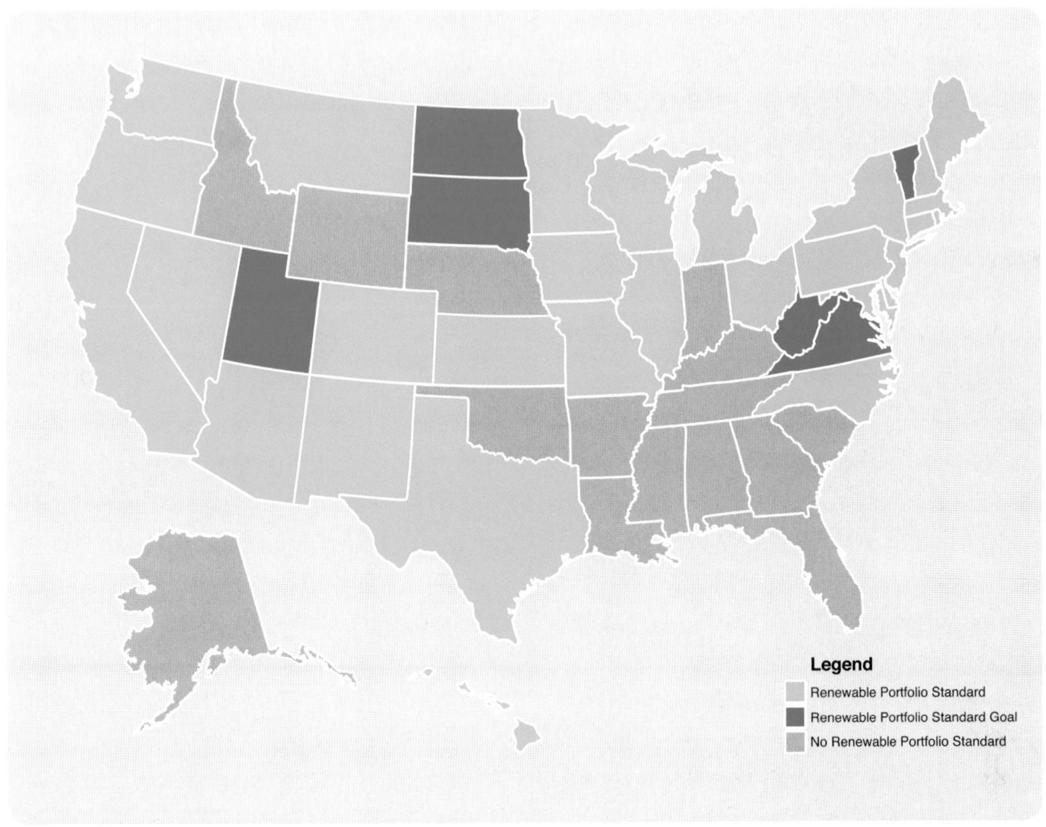

■ **FIGURE 9.8** States with Renewable Portfolio Standards. *Database of State Incentives for Renewables & Efficiency, www.dsireusa.org, May 2010.*

a special set-aside for distributed solar energy projects. This provides a regulatory mechanism for utilities to purchase solar renewable energy certificates, or SRECs, from customer-sited solar projects. SRECs are typically valued at a higher rate than a voluntary-market REC, and SREC purchases are often part of the incentive programs offered by utility companies.

Ironically, although RECs have a positive impact on market penetration for renewable energy technologies, they often add a complication to net zero energy buildings. Because the incentives offered in states with renewable portfolio standards can be financially necessary for the purchase of renewable energy systems, many projects give up of their RECs as part of the process of taking the financial incentives. The complication lies in the right to claim the environmental attributes of the energy produced with the project's renewable energy system. In this case, the RECs are transferred to the utility company, which claims them against the renewable portfolio standard requirement. In order to maintain a claim for a net zero energy building, the building owner must either maintain all the project's RECs or replace them with the purchase of an equal number of new RECs. This REC "swap" can often be beneficial financially, as it is often feasible to find lower-cost voluntary-market RECs to replace the premium-priced SRECs sold to meet renewable portfolio standards.

FINANCIAL MODELS

The purchase of a renewable energy system for a net zero energy building is a significant investment, one that often requires specialized financial tools and methods to make the system purchase feasible. Fortunately, renewable energy systems have a built-in revenue stream that can be leveraged to finance the system. Many of the financial models available for building owners take advantage of the financial gains of renewable energy generation.

Procurement Methods

Renewable energy systems are often procured through specialized vendors known as integrators or developers who offer a full range of services to support the delivery of systems, including design, installation, and financing. When financing is provided, it is often through a third party that has an established business partnership with the developer and expertise in renewable energy finance. The procurement method and choice of developer will be influenced by many factors, such as how the renewable energy system asset will be owned and how the renewable energy system will be integrated into a building owner's net zero energy project scope.

There are two basic ownership models for renewable energy for net zero energy buildings. The building owner can directly own the system and power, or a third party can own the system and sell the power to the building owner. For a net zero energy building, it is assumed that the building owner will use the power generated by an on-site renewable energy system, whether the system is owned by the building owner or not. There are some financial models where the purpose of the investment in the renewable energy system is to sell the renewable energy rather than use it on-site. These types of financial models are excluded from this discussion.

Direct ownership of a renewable energy system requires up-front capital from the building owner. The capital investment can come from a building owner's assets or may be financed. Direct ownership enables a high level of control over how the renewable energy system is procured and how the asset is managed. In some scenarios, it may also offer the best financial performance. However, not all building owners have the ability to make the size of initial capital investment required for the purchase of a system. In addition, not all building owners are in a position to take advantage of the tax benefits through government incentives. These two constraints have led to the popularity of third-party ownership models. The most common third-party models are discussed in more detail later in this chapter.

The building owner can include the renewable energy system as part of a construction project, or contract with a renewable energy developer independent of the construction project. There are pros and cons to both approaches. Including the renewable energy system as part of the overall delivery of a net zero energy building offers the best opportunities for integration. After all, a net zero energy building is one with a precisely balanced position of energy use and energy generation. The farther removed the renewable energy system design and installation are from the overall delivery of the project, the higher the risk of upsetting that delicate energy balance. In addition to energy integration, the actual design and construction integration require careful coordination of mounting, conduits, equipment location, and other details that can be optimized when covered under a single contract.

The building owner may want more control over the selection and procurement of the renewable energy system. In the case where the system will be owned by a third party, rather than the building owner, a long-term contractual relationship will need to be established, and the selection of the renewable energy developer is a decision that can transcend the procurement of design and construction services.

Power Purchase Agreements

Power purchase agreements (PPA) are the most common form of third-party ownership and financing for renewable energy systems. PPAs are very common for solar electric systems, but they are applicable to other renewable energy technologies as well. With a third-party ownership structure, the renewable energy system is provided as a turnkey project, which includes financing, design, installation, monitoring, and maintenance for the service length of the agreement. The system is financed through the purchase of energy from the system at a negotiated rate per kWh of production. The rate can be fixed over the life of the agreement, or it can incorporate a set escalation schedule. PPAs may include provisions for the purchase of the system by the building owner, which typically occurs at any point after six years under the agreement.

The market viability of PPAs is based on their ability to compete with grid-based electricity prices. Substantial value and appeal are added for the building owner, who does not require up-front capital. The long-term fixed energy price is a valuable hedge against future energy price escalation and fluctuation. The range of incentives available influences the viability of PPAs in markets across the United States. Currently, the combination of federal and local incentives has made PPAs very cost-competitive in many markets. The PPA market is also affected by the availability of investment capital. In turn, the creditworthiness of building owner customers will influence their ability to get financing; it will also have an effect on the competiveness of their PPA rates. The combination of market forces and quality of regional renewable energy resources can influence the feasibility of a PPA for any given project. Larger systems are often the most attractive to PPA providers, but smaller systems can be viable under the right market conditions.

Power purchase agreements can work for off-grid as well as grid-connected systems. The latter are more complicated because of the interface with the local utility; but they also make the project eligible for utility-based incentives. In a grid-connected project, the building receives and purchases power from the utility when the on-site system does not provide 100 percent of its electricity needs; conversely, it exports energy to the grid when the on-site system generates more energy than the building needs. To accomplish this, an interconnection agreement must be in place with the utility company, stipulating the terms for connecting an on-site system to the grid. An important feature of the interconnection agreement is the ability to net-meter. Net metering allows the electricity meter to run forward and backward, depending on whether the building is drawing electricity from the grid or exporting excess electricity from the on-site system to the grid. Every state has its own set of requirements for net metering, though not all states and utility companies have net-metering policies in place (see Figure 9.9).

Leases

The leasing of renewable energy equipment is another form of third-party ownership. Many aspects of a lease structure may be similar to a power purchase agreement. The main difference with a lease is that instead of paying on a kWh basis for the energy generated by the system, a monthly or periodic lease payment is made for the equipment, and any energy generated by the equipment is used by the building owner. The lease terms are typically 15 years, and an option to purchase the system at the end of the lease is generally available to the building owner.

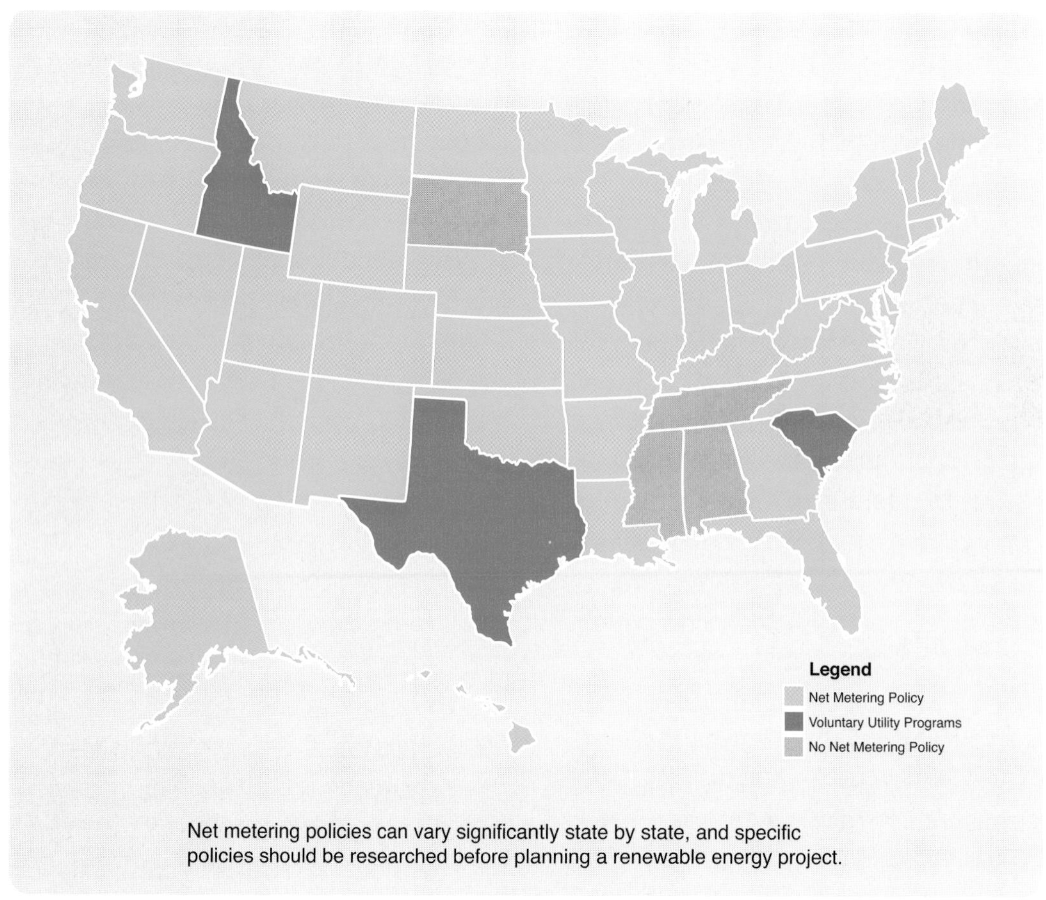
Legend
Net Metering Policy
Voluntary Utility Programs
No Net Metering Policy
Net metering policies can vary significantly state by state, and specific policies should be researched before planning a renewable energy project.

■ **FIGURE 9.9** States with Net-Metering Policies. *Database of State Incentives for Renewables & Efficiency; www.dsireusa.org, October 2011.*

Performance Contracting

A number of performance contracting models are available. The most common is an energy performance contract through a third party known as an energy service company (ESCO). Energy performance contracts can fund and implement energy-efficiency and renewable energy projects. Traditionally, energy performance contracts have been used for existing buildings, to provide energy-efficiency retrofits, but the model can also be used on new projects. ESCOs provide turnkey projects, and may include financing, energy audits, design, installation, monitoring, and maintenance as part of their services.

This contract model works by leveraging the energy cost savings—or, in the case of renewable energy, the energy generation—to fund the initial investment. Therefore, the building owner is not required to provide the initial capital for the project, but agrees to a long-term contract with the ESCO and uses the energy savings to finance the project. An important consideration is that the ESCO guarantees the energy savings and/or energy generation performance of the project, which assures that actual energy savings are realized and put toward the energy performance contract. This also shifts some risk from the building owner to the ESCO. After the contract terms have been met, the building owner then benefits from future energy savings from the project. A similar method is available through some utilities, where it is called a utility energy service contract.

FINANCIAL ANALYSIS

Time Value of Money

The element of time is important for determining the value of money and evaluating financial alternatives. The principle of the time value of money is, simply, that a specific sum of money today is worth more than the same sum of money at some point in the future. As the saying goes, a dollar today is worth more than a dollar tomorrow—that dollar today can earn interest over time. If a dollar is borrowed today, it is paid back with interest over time. Factoring the time value of money into financial analyses, to guide project- and energy-related decisions, will raise the quality and level of sophistication of the evaluation.

The two main concepts for time value are present value and future value. Future value is the worth of a current sum of money over a specified time frame using a specified interest rate. For example, $1,000 invested for one year at a 5 percent interest rate will have a future value in one year of $1,050. Present value is the same concept but working backwards from a future value of money and discounting it back using a specified time frame and interest rate (or discount rate).

Payback

Payback analysis is one of the simplest financial analyses that can be made on a project investment decision. In terms of an energy-efficiency investment, it is a measure of the number of years' worth of energy savings it would take to pay back the initial first-cost investment. The investment is typically the difference in cost between the base-case solution and the proposed energy-efficient solution. The following equation can be used to calculate simple payback in years (SP), where I is the initial investment and S is the cost savings per year. The initial investment is not always the entire initial cost. Often, the analysis compares the benefit of an added cost to some baseline condition; in this case, the added cost is the investment.

$$SP = \frac{I}{S}$$

Payback analysis has many critics. While it might be a rough gauge of risk and the relationship of an investment to its benefits, it does not consider the time value of money. It also does not measure the value of the investment. Further, many use payback with a very low threshold, such as just a few years, in evaluating a project investment, and so potentially miss out on excellent financial returns. There are many other preferred methods, presented next, for making a financial analysis that includes the time value of money and expresses the value of an investment.

Return on Investment

Investing in improved energy performance is, well, an investment. The word *investment* is key here, because an investment is expected to generate a return; an investment is not just an added cost. Return on investment (ROI) or rate of return (ROR) is a measure of the annual gain or loss as a percentage of the initial investment. The following equation calculates simple return on investment (ROI) as a percentage, where S is the cost savings per year and I is the initial investment.

$$ROI = \frac{S}{I} \times 100\%$$

Return on investment is also equal to 1 divided by the simple payback, taken as a percentage.

$$ROI = \frac{1}{SP} \times 100\%$$

Although return on investment is related to simple payback, it offers some distinct advantages. The main one is that it can be compared to a threshold interest rate to determine whether it is a better investment than a baseline investment choice. For example, if an energy-efficiency investment results in an annual return on investment of 15 percent, and the threshold interest rate is 5 percent, then the energy-efficiency project is a wise investment. Incidentally, a 15 percent return on investment equates to a payback of six years and eight months, a payback period that some may dismiss as too long.

Return on investment does not stipulate how long the investment will continue to produce a return. For most energy-efficiency or renewable energy projects, the investment period can be determined. Further, return on investment does not measure the total value of the investment over the investment period, and in its simple form assumes that the annual savings are constant. This is where net present value comes into play.

Net Present Value

Net present value (NPV) is directly tied to the concept of the time value of money. NPV is the total present value of future cost savings over a specified time period subtracted from the initial investment. It is the net value of all costs and gains expressed as present values. With the time value of money, future money flows must be discounted to express it in terms of present value. The discount rate is typically the threshold interest rate used to evaluate the investment against an alternative investment. If the investment's return is equal to the discount rate, then the net present value will be zero. Investments that exceed the discount rate will generate positive net present values.

The calculation of NPV is more complex than the simple payback and return on investment, but nevertheless can be easily accomplished with a spreadsheet using built-in net present value functions. The following equation is used to calculate present value (*PV*), where S_t is the future value of savings cash flow during the time period (*t*) being analyzed, and *d* is the discount rate.

$$PV = \frac{S_t}{(1+d)^t}$$

The present value over multiple time periods can be calculated by adding the net present value of each time period.

$$PV = \frac{S_1}{(1+d)^1} + \frac{S_2}{(1+d)^2} + \frac{S_3}{(1+d)^3} \cdots$$

Or stated as:

$$PV = \sum_{t=1}^{n} \frac{S_t}{(1+d)^1}$$

The equation is to be expanded to include the total number of time periods being analyzed. For a 10-year present value, the equation would be expanded until $t = 10$. The present value of the initial time period is the initial investment. Subtract the initial investment from the present value of all summed future savings or gains to get the net present value (NPV).

$$PV_0 = I$$
$$NPV = PV - PV_0$$

Knowing how to calculate the present value of future energy savings and renewable energy generation is an important skill for conducting the financial analysis of a net zero energy building. Because the metric allows for annual adjustment of the cost savings, the energy cost savings can be increased over time using an appropriate energy escalation rate. A helpful metric to calculate is the present value for all energy savings using the whole building's energy savings over periods of 10, 20, 30, and more years. These present values can be normalized against the square footage of the building so they can be compared to the initial cost of the project on a dollar-per-square-foot basis. The same present value calculation should be run for the value of the energy generated by the renewable energy system.

Life-Cycle Cost Analysis

Life-cycle cost analysis (LCC) is an effective way of determining the true cost impact of any project decision, and it is particularly valuable when making energy-efficiency and renewable energy decisions. LCC is the total cost over the life of a product, material, system, or building, from cradle to grave. Considerations include initial cost and operational, maintenance, replacement, and end-of-life costs. LCC analysis is one of the best tools to compare project alternatives, because it is focused on overall cost-effectiveness.

> **NOTE**
>
> Life-cycle cost analysis is a distinctly different process from life-cycle assessment (LCA). LCA is a measure of the environmental impact of a project decision over the life of the alternative. Embodied energy is often a measurable output of a life-cycle assessment. This section deals strictly with life-cycle cost analysis as a financial analysis tool.

The use of present value is important in LCC analysis, as all future values need to be discounted to present values. The following equation is used to calculate life-cycle cost (LCC). Note there are multiple approaches and versions of this basic equation, based on the parameters included in the analysis. Also note the time period is for the estimated service life of the system under evaluation.

$$LCC = C + E_{pv} + M_{pv} + R_{pv} + O_{pv} - S_{pv}$$

where:

C is the initial capital cost or investment.

E_{pv} is the present value of the energy costs. The cost should include energy escalation rates. For renewable energy system analysis, the energy generation can produce a negative value or credit for energy costs.

M_{pv} is the present value of maintenance costs.

R_{pv} is the present value of replacement costs. Typically, this includes replacement of parts, which can be added optionally to the maintenance costs. If the time period of analysis is longer than the life of the system under evaluation, the replacement costs should include the entire replacement cost.

O_{pv} is the present value of other optional costs or added value, which can include finance or other costs.

S_{pv} is the present value of end-of-life salvage value.

Using life-cycle cost analysis is standard practice for the federal government. To that end, the government has developed many tools and resources to aid federal agencies, as well as those working with the federal government on building projects. The U.S. Department of Commerce, Technology Administration, National Institute of Standards and Technology (NIST) has published the *Life-Cycle Costing Manual for the Federal Energy Management Program*, or *NIST Handbook 135*, authored by

Sieglinde K. Fuller and Stephen R. Petersen. This manual offers detailed guidance on utilizing life-cycle cost analysis.

One of the challenges of completing an LCC analysis is being able to estimate future values over the analysis time period. For example, it may be difficult to determine replacement costs of parts over the analysis time period. In such a case, a range of values for that specific parameter can be input to determine how sensitive the final result is to that parameter—this technique is called a *sensitivity analysis*. It is also a way to test a number of scenarios to determine best-case and worst-case potential outcomes.

The various financial analysis methods available to delivery teams offer a wide diversity of financial filters through which to examine project design decisions. It is good practice to engage in multiple analysis methods to gain a broad perspective. To that end, in the next section, several of the financial analysis methods are described in example form to help illustrate their application to net zero energy buildings.

Financial Analysis Examples

The basic examples featured here demonstrate the financial analysis tools just discussed. Each one builds on the same hypothetical example project, a 70,000-square-foot net zero energy office building in Boston, Massachusetts. To keep the examples simple, the facility is assumed to be an all-electric building, with no other energy sources to account for in the calculations. Further, demand charges and other variables in electricity costs are simplified via a single blended electricity rate. Also note the following:

- Boston permits full net metering, and credits its excess generation at retail rates. Credit can accumulate and be carried into future utility billing cycles.
- Massachusetts has a renewable portfolio standard that includes set-asides, also called carve-outs, for solar renewable energy certificates (SRECs). These solar carve-outs provide a market for the SRECs, created by qualifying distributed solar energy projects with a minimum price of $300 per MWh and a maximum price of $550 per MWh. Because the SRECs are sold in this example, the project replaces the SRECs with less expensive Green-e certified RECs.
- The only two incentives assumed in these examples are the performance-based incentives for the SRECs and the federal government's business energy investment tax credit of 30 percent. The examples do not include other incentives or tax implications.

The simple payback and return on investment examples could also be extended to include a combined energy efficiency and renewable energy analysis to evaluate the aggregate financial impact. The next example for calculating net present value is more complex because it accounts for the time value of money. In fact, in these calculations, there are three interacting time-based factors:

- The first is energy escalation, which will incrementally increase energy costs each year. In this example, energy cost increases 4 percent each year.
- The second time-based factor is the discount rate, which will incrementally decrease costs to convert them to present-day dollar values. The example includes a discount rate of 3 percent. Higher discount rates will result in lower net present values.
- The third time-based factor, unique to photovoltaics, includes the gradual decrease in performance due to age.

Project Data for Financial Analysis Examples

Basic Project Information

- Building Type: Office
- Location: Boston, Massachusetts
- Building area: 70,000 ft^2
- Construction cost: \$225/ft^2, or \$15,750,000
- Energy-efficiency premium: 2 percent of cost, or \$315,000

Financial Information

- Analysis period: 25 years
- Energy escalation: 4 percent
- Discount rate: 3 percent

Renewable Energy System

- Photovoltaic system: 500 kW
- Photovoltaic base cost: \$5.30/W, or \$2,650,000
- Federal tax credit: 30 percent, or \$795,000
- Photovoltaic final cost: \$1,855,000 (\$3.71/W)
- Performance factor: 1,244 kWh/kW (per PVWatts: 42.2° tilt, and 0.77 derate factor)
- Renewable energy generation: 622 MWh
- Photovoltaic age losses: 1 percent per year
- Maintenance costs: Assumed to be 0.10 percent of photovoltaics installed cost
- Replacement costs: Assumed that inverter will be replaced at year 15 at a cost of \$0.71 per watt of photovoltaic system size
- Other costs: Assumed insurance cost of 0.25 percent of photovoltaics installed cost
- Salvage value: Assumed a 20 percent salvage value at year 25 (end of warranty)

Energy Use

- Baseline case energy use: 55 kBtu/ft^2/year, or 1,128 MWh
- Design case energy use: 28 kBtu/ft^2/year, or 574 MWh
- Energy efficiency/reduction: 49 percent, or 554 MWh

Energy Costs

- Electricity rate: \$0.12/kWh
- Baseline annual energy cost: \$135,404
- Design annual energy cost: \$68,933 (without renewable energy)
- Design annual energy cost: –\$5,707 (credit with renewable energy)
- Total first-year renewable energy generation value: \$68,933 + \$5,707 = \$74,640

Solar Renewable Energy Certificates (SREC)

- SREC credit: \$300/MWh for 10 years
- Green-e REC replacement: \$5/MWh for 10 years
- Net SREC credit: \$295/MWh for 10 years
- Annual net SREC credit: (\$295 × 622 MWh) = \$183,490

Simple Payback

Simple Payback for Energy Efficiency

$$SP = \frac{I}{S}$$

where:

I = \$315,000

S = \$135,404 – \$68,933 = \$66,471

SP = 4.7 years

Simple Payback for Renewable Energy

$$SP = \frac{I}{S}$$

where:

I = \$1,855,000

S = \$74,640 + \$183,490 = \$258,130

SP = 7.2 years

Return on Investment

Return on Investment for Energy Efficiency

$$ROI = \frac{1}{SP} \times 100\%$$

where:

SP = 4.7 years

ROI = 21.1%

Return on Investment for Renewable Energy

$$ROI = \frac{1}{SP} \times 100\%$$

where:

SP = 7.2 years

ROI = 13.9%

Because of the performance losses over time, this example project would cease performing at a net zero energy level sometime in the middle of the 25-year analysis period. In reality, additional renewable energy or energy-efficiency projects could be added to the project over time to maintain the net zero energy balance. These additional projects are excluded from this example.

Energy escalation and photovoltaic age losses are both simple percentage base adjustments. The discount rate is applied using the equation for calculating present value. It can be helpful to compile a table of present value factors for each year in the analysis period based on the net present equation, where S is 1, t is the year value (in this example, 1 through 25), and d is the discount rate.

$$PV = \frac{S_t}{(1 + d)^t}$$

The tables in Figures 9.10 and 9.11 show the present value calculations in the form of spreadsheets. The resulting present values are used to calculate the net present value of the investment, as shown in the next example, which is the sum of all future gains converted to present dollar values less the initial capital costs.

The preceding net present value calculation example on page 342 uses an energy escalation rate of 4 percent and a discount rate of 3 percent, which may be enough to account for inflation. These two rates are used to develop the example of an LCC analysis on page 342 for the renewable energy system in the example project. Additional present value calculations are made to include the life-cycle costs (LCCs) of the photovoltaic system, such as maintenance, replacement, insurance, and end-of-life salvage value. The table in Figure 9.12 details the background calculations for the additional LCCs as present values. In this example, the LCC of renewable energy is compared to the LCC of using conventional grid-based electricity.

Year	Present Value Factor	Electricity Rate	Baseline Energy Use (kWh)	Baseline Energy Cost	Baseline Energy Cost (PV)	Design Energy Use (kWh)	Design Energy Cost	Design Energy Cost (PV)
1	0.971	$0.120	1,128,370	$135,404	$131,461	574,443	$68,933	$66,925
2	0.943	$0.125	1,128,370	$140,821	$132,737	574,443	$71,691	$67,575
3	0.915	$0.130	1,128,370	$146,453	$134,026	574,443	$74,558	$68,231
4	0.888	$0.135	1,128,370	$152,312	$135,327	574,443	$77,540	$68,894
5	0.863	$0.140	1,128,370	$158,404	$136,641	574,443	$80,642	$69,563
6	0.837	$0.146	1,128,370	$164,740	$137,967	574,443	$83,868	$70,238
7	0.813	$0.152	1,128,370	$171,330	$139,307	574,443	$87,222	$70,920
8	0.789	$0.158	1,128,370	$178,183	$140,659	574,443	$90,711	$71,608
9	0.766	$0.164	1,128,370	$185,310	$142,025	574,443	$94,340	$72,304
10	0.744	$0.171	1,128,370	$192,723	$143,404	574,443	$98,113	$73,006
11	0.722	$0.178	1,128,370	$200,432	$144,796	574,443	$102,038	$73,714
12	0.701	$0.185	1,128,370	$208,449	$146,202	574,443	$106,119	$74,430
13	0.681	$0.192	1,128,370	$216,787	$147,621	574,443	$110,364	$75,153
14	0.661	$0.200	1,128,370	$225,458	$149,055	574,443	$114,779	$75,882
15	0.642	$0.208	1,128,370	$234,477	$150,502	574,443	$119,370	$76,619
16	0.623	$0.216	1,128,370	$243,856	$151,963	574,443	$124,145	$77,363
17	0.605	$0.225	1,128,370	$253,610	$153,438	574,443	$129,111	$78,114
18	0.587	$0.234	1,128,370	$263,754	$154,928	574,443	$134,275	$78,872
19	0.570	$0.243	1,128,370	$274,305	$156,432	574,443	$139,646	$79,638
20	0.554	$0.253	1,128,370	$285,277	$157,951	574,443	$145,232	$80,411
21	0.538	$0.263	1,128,370	$296,688	$159,484	574,443	$151,041	$81,192
22	0.522	$0.273	1,128,370	$308,555	$161,033	574,443	$157,083	$81,980
23	0.507	$0.284	1,128,370	$320,898	$162,596	574,443	$163,366	$82,776
24	0.492	$0.296	1,128,370	$333,733	$164,175	574,443	$169,901	$83,580
25	0.478	$0.308	1,128,370	$347,083	$165,769	574,443	$176,697	$84,391
Total					$3,699,497			$1,883,380

Energy Escalation = 4%
Discount Rate = 3%
Abbreviations: PV = present value

■ **FIGURE 9.10** Example: Present Value Calculations for Energy Efficiency.

Net Zero Energy Economics

The economics for net zero energy buildings are a departure from the economics and analysis of conventional energy-efficient buildings. While the financial analysis methods discussed in this chapter provide useful tools for the owner and team, their greatest value lies in helping to make the business case, or the initial decision, on whether to pursue net zero energy as a project objective. Once an energy goal and construction budget is set, many project decisions need to be made to support this larger goal. Individual measures can be analyzed to compare alternative solutions but, ultimately, the solution that best meets the overall project objectives must be implemented. In this sense, calculating an individual payback or other financial analysis for any individual design decision is less important, because the goal is to meet the overall cost and energy requirements.

An entirely new economic analysis comes into play when planning and delivering a net zero energy project. One of the primary financial concerns implicit in any project decision is whether an energy-efficiency measure is more or less cost-effective than the alternative: to add renewable energy capacity. Most often, energy-efficiency strategies are significantly

Year	Present Value Factor	Renewable Energy Generation	RE Net Energy Use (kWh)	RE Net Energy Cost	RE Net Energy Cost (PV)	RE Net SREC (per MWh)	RE SREC Net Credit	RE SREC Net Credit (PV)
1	0.971	622,000	-47,557	-$5,707	-$5,541	$295	$183,490	$178,146
2	0.943	615,780	-41,337	-$5,159	-$4,863	$295	$181,655	$171,227
3	0.915	609,622	-35,179	-$4,566	-$4,179	$295	$179,839	$164,578
4	0.888	603,526	-29,083	-$3,926	-$3,488	$295	$178,040	$158,186
5	0.863	597,491	-23,048	-$3,235	-$2,791	$295	$176,260	$152,043
6	0.837	591,516	-17,073	-$2,493	-$2,087	$295	$174,497	$146,139
7	0.813	585,601	-11,158	-$1,694	-$1,377	$295	$172,752	$140,463
8	0.789	579,745	-5,301	-$837	-$661	$295	$171,025	$135,008
9	0.766	573,947	496	$81	$62	$295	$169,314	$129,765
10	0.744	568,208	6,235	$1,065	$792	$295	$167,621	$124,726
11	0.722	562,526	11,917	$2,117	$1,529	$0	$0	$0
12	0.701	556,900	17,543	$3,241	$2,273	$0	$0	$0
13	0.681	551,331	23,112	$4,440	$3,024	$0	$0	$0
14	0.661	545,818	28,625	$5,720	$3,781	$0	$0	$0
15	0.642	540,360	34,083	$7,083	$4,546	$0	$0	$0
16	0.623	534,956	39,487	$8,534	$5,318	$0	$0	$0
17	0.605	529,607	44,836	$10,077	$6,097	$0	$0	$0
18	0.587	524,311	50,132	$11,718	$6,883	$0	$0	$0
19	0.570	519,068	55,376	$13,462	$7,677	$0	$0	$0
20	0.554	513,877	60,566	$15,312	$8,478	$0	$0	$0
21	0.538	508,738	65,705	$17,276	$9,287	$0	$0	$0
22	0.522	503,651	70,792	$19,358	$10,103	$0	$0	$0
23	0.507	498,614	75,829	$21,565	$10,927	$0	$0	$0
24	0.492	493,628	80,815	$23,902	$11,758	$0	$0	$0
25	0.478	488,692	85,751	$26,377	$12,598	$0	$0	$0
Total					$80,147			$1,500,282

Energy Escalation = 4%
Discount Rate = 3%
Abbreviations: PV = present value, RE = renewable energy

■ **FIGURE 9.11** Example: Present Value Calculations for Renewable Energy.

more cost-effective than renewable energy. Nonetheless, it is an important consideration to keep in mind.

It is also very informative to ascertain the cost of renewable energy systems for each installed watt of equipment in the building. This metric can be arrived at by first calculating the annual energy use of one continuous watt of power over a full year of 8,760 hours, which is 8.76 kWh. Based on the cost per installed watt of the renewable energy system, and the project energy generation per watt, a cost of renewable energy per watt of installed equipment can be calculated.

For the project example just used, the cost of installed photovoltaics is $3,170 per kW, and the energy generation for the first year for 1 kW is 1,244 kWh. This results in $2.55/kWh and a cost of $22 per continuous watt of installed equipment. This metric can be used when comparing equipment costs and efficiencies. It is important to note that this is not a life-cycle assessment; it is an assessment of the first-cost implications of installed equipment power.

Year	Present Value Factor	Mainte-nance Costs	Mainte-nance Costs (PV)	Replace-ment Costs	Replace-ment Costs (PV)	Insurance Costs	Insurance Costs (PV)	Salvage Value	Salvage PV
1	0.971	$1,855	$1,801	$0	$0	$4,638	$4,502	$0	$0
2	0.943	$1,855	$1,749	$0	$0	$4,638	$4,371	$0	$0
3	0.915	$1,855	$1,698	$0	$0	$4,638	$4,244	$0	$0
4	0.888	$1,855	$1,648	$0	$0	$4,638	$4,120	$0	$0
5	0.863	$1,855	$1,600	$0	$0	$4,638	$4,000	$0	$0
6	0.837	$1,855	$1,554	$0	$0	$4,638	$3,884	$0	$0
7	0.813	$1,855	$1,508	$0	$0	$4,638	$3,771	$0	$0
8	0.789	$1,855	$1,464	$0	$0	$4,638	$3,661	$0	$0
9	0.766	$1,855	$1,422	$0	$0	$4,638	$3,554	$0	$0
10	0.744	$1,855	$1,380	$0	$0	$4,638	$3,451	$0	$0
11	0.722	$1,855	$1,340	$0	$0	$4,638	$3,350	$0	$0
12	0.701	$1,855	$1,301	$0	$0	$4,638	$3,253	$0	$0
13	0.681	$1,855	$1,263	$0	$0	$4,638	$3,158	$0	$0
14	0.661	$1,855	$1,226	$0	$0	$4,638	$3,066	$0	$0
15	0.642	$1,855	$1,191	$355,000	$227,861	$4,638	$2,977	$0	$0
16	0.623	$1,855	$1,156	$0	$0	$4,638	$2,890	$0	$0
17	0.605	$1,855	$1,122	$0	$0	$4,638	$2,806	$0	$0
18	0.587	$1,855	$1,090	$0	$0	$4,638	$2,724	$0	$0
19	0.570	$1,855	$1,058	$0	$0	$4,638	$2,645	$0	$0
20	0.554	$1,855	$1,027	$0	$0	$4,638	$2,568	$0	$0
21	0.538	$1,855	$997	$0	$0	$4,638	$2,493	$0	$0
22	0.522	$1,855	$968	$0	$0	$4,638	$2,420	$0	$0
23	0.507	$1,855	$940	$0	$0	$4,638	$2,350	$0	$0
24	0.492	$1,855	$913	$0	$0	$4,638	$2,281	$0	$0
25	0.478	$1,855	$886	$0	$0	$4,638	$2,215	$371,000	$177,192
Total			$32,301		$227,861		$80,753		$177,192

Energy Escalation = 4%
Discount Rate = 3%
Abbreviations: PV = present value

■ **FIGURE 9.12** Example: Present Value Calculations for Life-Cycle Costs.

NET ZERO ENERGY AND THE REAL ESTATE MARKET

Designing net zero energy buildings is a very new trend in the construction industry, and early adopters have primarily been on owner-occupied projects. The financial investment in energy efficiency and renewable energy holds a strong position in long-term building ownership. In addition to the long-term value of net zero energy buildings, there is an exciting value opportunity in the real estate market. The value proposition is similar to the phenomenon started with LEED, which created a powerful market differentiator for LEED-certified properties. The higher performance and marketability of LEED buildings raised their value over non-LEED buildings. Now, net zero energy buildings represent a level of building performance markedly higher than LEED buildings. How will net zero energy buildings be perceived in the commercial real estate market?

Net Present Value

Net Present Value for Energy Efficiency

$$NPV = PV - PV_0$$

where:

PV = \$3,699,497 – \$1,883,380 = \$1,816,117

PV_0 = \$315,000

NPV = \$1,501,117

Net Present Value for Renewable Energy System

$$NPV = PV - PV_0$$

where:

PV = (\$1,883,380 – \$80,147) + \$1,500,282 = \$3,303,515

PV_0 = \$1,855,000

NPV = \$1,448,515

Net Present Value for Combined Energy Efficiency and Renewable Energy

$$NPV = PV - PV_0$$

where:

PV = \$1,816,117 + \$3,303,515 = \$5,119,632

PV_0 = \$315,000 + \$1,855,000 = \$2,170,000

NPV = \$2,949,632, or \$42/ft^2

Life-Cycle Cost Analysis

Life-Cycle Cost Analysis for Renewable Energy System

$$LCC = C + E_{pv} + M_{pv} + R_{pv} + O_{pv} - S_{pv}$$

where:

C = \$1,855,000

E_{pv} = \$80,147 – \$1,500,282 = –\$1,420,135

M_{pv} = \$32,301

R_{pv} = \$277,861

O_{pv} = \$80,753

S_{pv} = -\$177,192

Life-cycle cost (LCC) = \$598,590

Levelized life-cycle cost of energy = \$0.04/kWh

Life-Cycle Cost Analysis for Project without Renewable Energy System

$$LCC = C + E_{pv} + M_{pv} + R_{pv} + O_{pv} - S_{pv}$$

where:

C = \$0

E_{pv} = \$1,883,380

M_{pv} = \$0

R_{pv} = \$0

O_{pv} = \$0

S_{pv} = \$0

Life-cycle cost (LCC) = \$1,883,380

Levelized life-cycle cost of energy = \$0.13/kWh

Result: Over a 25-year period, it would cost \$1,284,791 less to operate the building with the proposed renewable energy system (photovoltaics) than it would to operate the building with the renewable energy system excluded from the project.

Net Operating Income

Net zero energy new construction or renovations can serve as a solid real estate investment that can add value in terms of higher rental rates, higher occupancy rates, and greater asset value, as well as lower monthly operating expenses through energy efficiency and on-site renewable energy generation. Asset value for commercial real estate is based largely on its ability to produce income—or net operating income (NOI). Reducing operating expenses is an effective way to produce more operating income.

For commercial real estate assets, energy is typically the single largest expense. According to the EPA's ENERGY STAR program, energy accounts, on average, for one-third of a building's operating expenses. Net zero energy buildings allow more control, and offer more opportunities, to lower the energy expense of buildings. This can directly raise net operating income and asset value. An average real estate asset may have annual energy costs exceeding $2 a square foot. However, because a net zero energy real estate asset is, first and foremost, a very energy-efficient building, it can result in energy costs under $1 a square foot. Lowering annual energy costs by $1 a square foot adds $10 a square foot in asset value, assuming a capitalization rate of 10 percent. For a 100,000-square-foot building, this is a $1 million boost in asset value. (Note that asset value is equal to the net operating income divided by the capitalization rate.)

A net zero energy real estate asset is also one that generates its own renewable energy. This provides additional means to control and capitalize on the energy expenses and, therefore, produce income. On-site renewable energy fixes the energy costs for the building and acts as a hedge against future energy cost escalation. It is often the lowest-cost energy option, especially over time. For many projects, on-site renewable energy systems can generate a steady flow of income from solar RECs for many years.

The investment in renewable energy is a substantial initial cost that must be accounted for in the pro forma for any new or existing real estate project. The addition of on-site renewable energy systems is an investment in an energy-producing asset, one that must be carefully analyzed based on current technology costs, incentives, tax implications, utility rates, and other concerns, as outlined earlier in the "Financial Analysis" section of this chapter. A building owner may also choose to use a third-party ownership structure in lieu of owning the system outright, which has its own financial implications. One of the most important financial considerations when conducting an analysis on the energy cost savings advantages of a net zero energy building is to identify who makes the investment and who benefits—building owner(s) or tenants. This gets into one of the more challenging aspects of leveraging energy efficiency in a building: the commercial lease.

Green Lease

The green lease concept emerged in response to the need to define the relationship of building owners and tenants around the operation and benefits of a green building. With the building owner and tenants working together to maximize the environmental, social, and economic sustainability performance of the building and its operation, a green lease can address the myriad aspects of operating a green building, including transportation management, water conservation, interior environmental quality, and recycling, among others. The green lease also addresses energy use in the building.

As net zero energy buildings maintain a net zero energy balance in actual operation over the course of each year, energy management in a multitenant building can be a significant challenge. The green lease is the vehicle to address the energy management responsibilities of both the owner and tenants. It is also the vehicle to share and maximize the economic benefits of a net zero energy building. The fact is that both the owner and tenants have an important role in achieving net zero energy. The building owner is responsible for the energy efficiency and operation of the building systems, whereas tenant improvements and behavior drive a large portion of the energy use in a building. (The role of building occupants is explored in more detail in Chapter 10.)

One of the greatest challenges to implementing a net zero energy green lease is the way most commercial leases are structured around the cost of energy. In a gross lease, the tenant does not pay a separate energy bill. The cost of energy, along with taxes, insurance, and operating costs, is incorporated into the rental rate. The building owner has the potential to maximize the value of energy savings in this scenario, and so may look for ways to invest in additional energy-efficiency measures. However, the energy savings is always relative to the tenant's actual energy use (particularly plug loads), even with very efficient building systems. The lack of accountability in energy use discourages energy conservation on the side of the tenant.

Under the terms of a net lease, the tenant pays a separate energy bill based on metered data or, more typically, its pro rata share of energy use based on leased building area. This can create an incentive for individual tenant energy use reduction, because it will directly impact their bottom line. However, for an individual tenant, the energy savings may not always be prioritized over other more pressing business expenses. In addition, the building owner has less of an incentive to operate the building as efficiently as possible and to invest in additional energy efficiency measures.

These problems inherent in conventional leases are often called split-incentives, and they are amplified in the case of net zero energy buildings. In a multitenant net zero energy building, both the tenant and the building owner need to commit to their roles in the energy performance of the building; there also must be a way to allow both parties to share in the benefits. Perhaps some form of hybrid commercial lease is the answer. One possibility would be a modified gross lease or a form of fixed-base lease, following an energy budget concept. This concept could consolidate the energy costs to the owner. The tenants' lease rate would then include energy costs up to a predetermined energy budget, with overages being charged directly to the tenants. In this scenario, the gross lease rate would have to be attractive enough for tenants to accept the responsibility and risk of increased energy use. The energy budget would also have to be aligned with the net zero energy target of the building. The energy budget would enhance the tenants' understanding of and participation in the net zero energy goal.

Another lease structure to incentivize energy efficiency and manage a net zero energy goal is to split the energy costs between the building owner and tenants, based on their ability to invest in efficiency and their ability to manage energy. For example, the building owner would be responsible for energy in common areas, as well as energy for heating, cooling, and ventilation. These costs would be rolled into the modified gross lease of the tenants, who would then be responsible for their plug and process load and lighting energy costs. However, the tenants would have access to a prorated share of the building's renewable energy as part of their leases. Anything over this amount would need to be paid, in addition to the base rent. Ideally, the on-site renewable energy generation would provide an energy cost savings compared to current utility-based rates. If the tenants stay within their share of renewable energy, they will operate with a net zero energy balance and save in energy costs. If tenants operate outside of the energy budget, RECs would need to be purchased to maintain a net zero energy status—at least a classification D level (refer back to Chapter 1 for a description of NREL's net zero energy classification system).

One of the most important tools in managing a multitenant building and associated green leases is the ability to submeter tenant spaces and energy end uses (see Figure 9.13). Submetering provides the data needed to effectively manage the energy costs of any building, and allows for accountability of energy use between building owners and tenants. Also keep in mind that the green lease sets up the legal framework for the landlord/tenant relationship in a net zero energy building, and as such should cover the requirements and the remedies when requirements are not met. With a proper green lease in place, numerous "soft" requirements, agreements, or understandings can be arranged in the landlord/tenant relationship to further optimize the quest for net zero energy.

■ **FIGURE 9.13** The Bullitt Center, under construction in 2011, will become one of the first multitenant net zero energy office buildings. The owner is considering a cap-and-trade system to manage an energy budget between tenants. *Image courtesy of The Bullitt Foundation, Seattle, Washington, Miller Hull and Point32.*

Considerations and Ideas for a Net Zero Energy Green Lease

- Institute strict guidelines on the energy-efficiency requirements for tenant improvements.
- Submeter individual tenant spaces as well as energy end uses in each tenant space.
- Provide visual displays of real-time and average energy use in each tenant space and in the lobby of the building, to help maintain a culture of energy awareness and friendly competition among tenants.
- Make provisions for how energy reporting and energy audits are to be addressed, and how the costs are to be handled.
- Provide tenant education on building energy features, green occupant behavior, and meeting thermal comfort performance.
- Introduce provisions defining an acceptable range of interior temperature set points that change with the seasons.
- Incentivize energy savings by making tenants accountable for their energy use.

Image courtesy of RNL; photograph by Ron Pollard.

OO

CHAPTER 10
OPERATIONS AND OCCUPANCY

BUILDING OPERATION

Net zero energy is a challenging objective, which influences the entire delivery process for buildings. In fact, it has far-reaching implications for the entire building industry. That said, net zero energy is ultimately an owner goal, which is met in actual operation—a year of measured net zero energy operation. The operation and occupancy of a building is the critical, final piece of the net zero energy solution.

Bridging Design Intent and Operations

One of the challenges the building industry has faced recently is translating projected energy performance during design into real energy performance during building operation. This obstacle has to be overcome if net zero energy buildings are to be successfully implemented. The integrated delivery process is a key part of the solution. Specifically, the integrated delivery process should, from the outset, involve the participation of the building's facility management staff. This helps assure buy-in and understanding of the proposed systems and strategies; it also permits the vetting of proposed strategies against operational constraints and realities.

The integrated delivery process for a net zero energy building should also involve the delivery team in enhanced postoccupancy services. This can be a win-win for both the building owner and the delivery team. The building owner and facility management can benefit from the continued expertise of key delivery team members to help make the transition to building operation; and the delivery team will get direct and valuable feedback on the design solution.

There are several common areas where design intent does not effectively translate into actual operations. The most common problems with high-performance buildings are building controls. Control-related problems are diverse; they may include software programming and setup, sensor hardware errors, operator errors, and intentional override of controls by operators. Proactive and early collaboration between mechanical engineers, control vendors, and facility management staff can help improve control system and sequence design, ensure shared understanding of the design intent of controls, and improve troubleshooting and optimization during operation.

Energy-efficient technologies or strategies that are new or unfamiliar to occupants and facility management staff can also be problematic in the effort to translate design intent into actual operation benefits. Occupant and operator education and training on essential building technologies can help form reasonable expectations and build knowledge on the proper operation of the technologies. By establishing a good working relationship between the delivery team and the building's occupants and operators early in the process, this education process can be relatively seamless. It also assures that the delivery team will reach a comprehensive understanding of how the building will be used by its occupants, which impacts assumptions used in the energy model of the building. A disconnect between occupant behavior and actual building use, compared to the building and occupancy schedules assumed for the energy model during design, has the potential to open a gap in predicted versus actual energy performance.

Stewardship Services

To support an integrated delivery process, it is important to plan for delivery team involvement beyond occupancy. The goal is to emphasize that delivery of a net zero energy building is neither at substantial completion nor at the end of the warranty period; rather, it is at the achievement of net zero energy in operation. The delivery team can make a valuable contribution during postoccupancy by providing energy stewardship services targeted at meeting the net zero energy goal and assuring building performance. Refer to the "Net Zero Energy Performance Plan" at the end of this chapter for related services and activities.

Traditionally, postoccupancy activities and services have been treated as add-on services, rather than seen as a continuation of the delivery process. An effective way to follow through on the delivery of a net zero energy project is to strategize a customized and comprehensive scope for the delivery team's postoccupancy activities. The stewardship services would ideally be part of the primary delivery contract and fee structure. They could also be paid for appropriating a portion of utility energy-efficiency rebates or other energy incentives earned by the project. They might also be tied to incentive award fees for meeting net zero energy or other project performance objectives.

Commissioning

Commissioning is an important transitional step between delivery and building occupancy and operation. It is a documented quality assurance process that ensures that the basis of design and the owner's project requirements are met. The commissioning agent, also known as the commissioning authority, is an independent party who operates as an advocate for the owner in the delivery process. The commissioning agent is in a key position, between the design team, contractor, building owner, and the facility management staff. The role the agent plays is part of the process of bridging design and occupancy. The commissioning process is also a value quality assurance process for net zero energy building, where there is little room for error and improperly performing systems.

Two essential documents within the commissioning process are intended to help bridge design and occupancy: the Owner's Project Requirements (OPR) and the Basis of Design (BOD). These two complementary documents should make explicit the net zero energy goal and how it will be met. Drafting the OPR offers an important opportunity for the building owner to define net zero energy in terms of the building functionality and performance, and in terms of the owner's role in meeting net zero energy. The BOD is the design team's response to the OPR; it communicates the technical concepts, strategies, systems, and methods used to achieve net zero energy and other owner project requirements. For a net zero energy project, special attention should be given to crafting these two documents, as they assist in delineating how net zero energy will be met.

The commissioning process has become a common requirement for green buildings because of LEED and the perquisite for fundamental commissioning, as well as the credit for enhanced commissioning. In fact, the requirements for LEED have become the de facto scope of work for most commissioning projects. A net zero energy building would benefit from a commissioning process that builds on the LEED commissioning scope requirements, but then expands on it to address its unique needs.

Facility Management

Facility management and building engineers are responsible for a diverse array of building-related services, including the operation and maintenance of the building and its systems. At the building system level, facility managers balance building conditions, such as thermal comfort and lighting, with overall building energy use. Two of the main activities to accomplish this

Commissioning Issues for Net Zero Energy Buildings

- **Envelope:** Because the building envelope is a critical part of a net zero energy building's energy system, the building envelope should be commissioned. The full commissioning process should be applied to all elements of the building envelope. (Refer to NIBS Guideline 3–2006, "Exterior Enclosure Technical Requirements for the Commissioning Process.") Thermal photography and pressurization tests are important additions to the building envelope commissioning process. (Note: Building envelope commissioning is currently being proposed as part of enhanced commissioning for the upcoming 2012 version of LEED.)
- **Renewable Energy Systems:** Renewable energy systems for net zero energy buildings are typically substantial in scale, and optimal operation is vital to meeting the energy goal. These systems may require special expertise by the commissioning agent. If a renewable energy system is owned by a third party, the system will generally be commissioned through the system owner, but the activity should be coordinated with the overall building commissioning process.
- **Submeters:** Submeters are an important part of the energy management system, but not usually part of the commissioning process. Submeter installations would benefit from the quality assurance and functional performance testing of commissioning.
- **Controls:** Controls are part of the typical commissioning process, yet can dominate the issue logs for high-performing buildings. Being proactive around commissioning building controls can help alleviate control-related issues. Develop high-quality, project-specific control sequences in advance of the commissioning agent's construction document review.
- **Training:** While training of facility management staff is part of the usual commissioning process, focusing especially on exemplary training practices and including the facility management staff as active participants in the commissioning process will better prepare staff for some of the unique characteristics of systems of a net zero energy building.
- **Recommissioning:** The initial commissioning process is only the beginning of an ongoing commissioning process. Facility managers should integrate recommissioning into their maintenance and operation plan to assure that building operation preserves the net zero energy design intent and works to accommodate changes in building use or operation over time.

are the monitoring and control of building systems and the maintenance of building systems. Facility managers are aided by building automation systems (BAS), which provide a centralized interface and control over the various connected building systems and their control systems. Building automation systems allow for a wide range of system management, including energy, demand, and load management functionality.

Energy management is becoming an increasingly important part of the facility management role—and is vital for net zero energy buildings. Traditionally, however, the energy management role has been not been prioritized within facility management; instead, the focus has been on building maintenance, system controls, and addressing building services complaints. Energy management has a few other hurdles to overcome. First, standard facility management budgets often do not support the scope and services for effective energy management. Second, there is a need for additional training and education, to prepare existing and new facility management professionals for their enhanced roles in energy management. When the International Facility Management Association (IFMA) introduced its Sustainability Facility Professional (SPF) credential, in 2011, it was an important step in providing the needed tools and training to the facility management profession.

Energy management for a net zero energy building is not just the facility manager's job; it is everyone's job. For it to be successful it has to have strong organizational leadership support and commitment. The leaders of an organization set the example for all involved, and can change its culture around the net zero energy goal. It is also important to have the commitment of organizational leaders with regard to applying resources and institutionalizing policies that aid in the goal.

Energy management impacts departments across an organization. The information technology group, for example, needs to be fully supportive of the commitment to net zero energy, in order to effectively manage the energy use of IT equipment and data centers. Likewise, food service departments have a key role in a net zero energy building's energy performance because of the energy intensity of commercial kitchens. And the human resources department needs to help train staff, both new and existing, to take on their roles in the energy use of the building.

Energy Information System

To fulfill the energy management requirements for the operation of a net zero energy building, a comprehensive energy information system (EIS) should be integrated as a complement to a commercial building's BAS. An EIS is a complete system; it includes the hardware and software to collect, store, analyze, and display energy data. The main components of an EIS are a variety of sensors and meters, data loggers, server, and analysis and visualization applications (see Figure 10.1).

The technologies needed for energy information systems are readily available today through a number of vendors; in contrast, integration of a complete and comprehensive EIS is a relatively new undertaking and still under development. Therefore, it is important to integrate the components of the EIS into the design and specifications of a net zero energy building, which can benefit from a robust set of data inputs and analytical tools. To develop a project-customized EIS, consider what data needs to be collected and what analysis needs to be completed.

METERS AND SENSORS

The ultimate goal of data collection for a net zero energy building is to determine whether it is meeting its net zero energy goal. This requires, at a minimum, whole building energy use metering (typically, for each utility) and renewable energy generation metering. However, achieving net zero energy requires attention to the details; unfortunately, the measured data from building-level metering is not detailed enough to provide meaningful ongoing guidance in operating the building to meet its net zero energy goal. Operating the building so that it hits its overall net zero energy target means that all of the individual energy end uses need to stay on target as well. The submetering installation and measurement should match the energy end uses from the as-built energy model for the project. Submeters can also be used to capture energy data for specific spaces or zones of a building, such as different tenant spaces.

Submetering should be capable of time-interval recording of at least 60-minute intervals or less, depending on the application. This will allow for the analysis of daily load and energy profiles. The data can also be compared to the as-built energy model run, based on hourly simulations. Using short intervals of 15 minutes or less can enhance the resolution of load profiles and make real-time energy dashboard displays more dynamic.

Capturing a variety of sensor data in conjunction with the submetered energy data collection can improve the evaluation and understanding of building performance. Sensors can be installed in a number of locations and for diverse inputs, including interior temperature, humidity, carbon dioxide, various other indoor environment quality (IEQ) measures and weather conditions, solar radiation, levels of illuminance, and occupancy.

ANALYSIS

Currently, in the building industry, one of the common analysis outcomes for measured performance data is the comparison of the building against a baseline building, in order to verify predicted savings or efficiencies. This analysis process is used to check performance contracts against energy service contracts, and is the basis for performance measurement and verification activities for LEED buildings. The protocol for performance

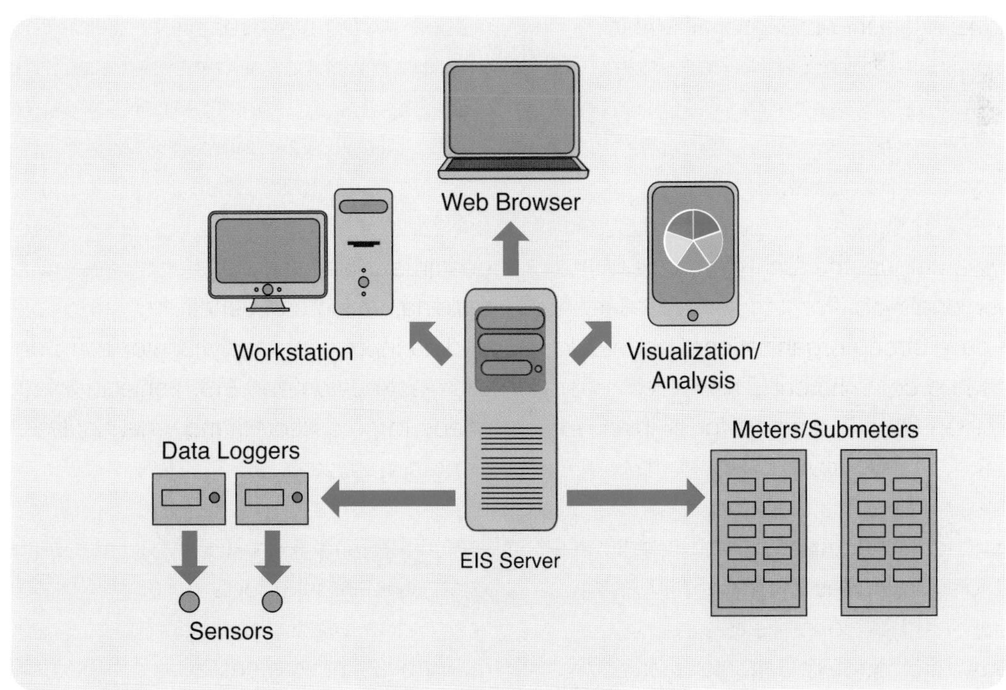

■ **FIGURE 10.1** Energy Information System (EIS) Concept Diagram.

measurement and verification is governed by the International Performance Measurement and Verification Protocol (IPMVP), a series of industry guidance documents for measurement and verification (M&V) best practices developed by the international nonprofit, Efficiency Valuation Organization.

The analysis of a net zero energy building is a unique case because its purpose is not to compare the building performance with a calibrated baseline energy model performance; rather, it is to determine whether the building is meeting net zero energy in operation. What is measured is the actual energy use and energy generation, and the resulting net zero energy balance over time. This eliminates the added complexity of developing a calibrated as-built baseline energy model. It also removes the ambiguity that may occur when defining an appropriate baseline for comparison.

In addition to comparing energy use and energy generation, it is important to compare the energy performance with the project's final as-built energy model. The as-built model is a valuable guide to assess whether the operation of the building is meeting the design intent, because it can be used to assess sub-yearly performance periods, such as monthly or seasonally. This gives the building operators important interim feedback, and can be used to track energy performance against the net zero energy goal.

The as-built energy model should also be maintained and calibrated to match changes to the building operation over time. It is particularly important to incorporate changes in occupancy and building schedules. Capturing actual weather data for use in the calibrated energy model, to validate past metered building performance, will provide better accuracy in the assessment. An on-site weather station for recording project-specific weather conditions may be an appropriate part of a net zero energy building's energy information system. In addition, there is a growing technological trend toward model-predictive control capabilities that enable a building control system to use real-time and short-range forecasted weather data to better manage building systems.

Verifying energy performance against design intent, and using submetered data with end-use energy model runs from a calibrated as-built energy model, can serve as a valuable diagnostic tool for troubleshooting ongoing operations and maintenance. This diagnostic capability is especially important in the first year or two of building operation. Even with a quality delivery and commissioning process, it is still possible to discover resolvable system issues and continue to optimize performance. (Refer to Chapter 12 for examples of the DOE/NREL Research Support Facility performance data.)

PLUG LOADS

Plug and Process Loads

Plug and process loads are the energy loads *not* related to heating, cooling, lighting, and ventilation, but they typically account for about one-quarter of U.S. commercial building energy use. They are the loads specific to the function of the building's organization and include items such as computers, office equipment, electrical devices and chargers, server rooms, data centers, appliances, vending machines, ATM machines, elevators, and water coolers. Some building types have specialized and heavy process loads, such as hospitals, manufacturing facilities, and buildings with foodservice operations.

For low-energy and net zero buildings that effectively and dramatically reduce energy related to heating, cooling, lighting, and ventilation, the remaining plug and process load can grow to be a high percentage of the building's energy use if it, too, is not effectively managed.

Careful attention to plug and process load management has the additional benefit of lowering internal heat gains, which has the potential of greater energy savings on space cooling.

The process for documenting energy cost saving for LEED treats plug and process loads as unregulated, meaning these loads traditionally do not come under the influence of design decisions, as do the main building systems. LEED assumes a 25 percent process load for both the baseline and design case. For a net zero energy building, all loads need to be regulated. There is tremendous energy savings potential and plenty of opportunity to reduce plug and process load use in a building through careful planning and working with the building owner to develop a comprehensive plug and process load management plan.

Plug and Process Load Management

SECURE BUILDING OWNER COMMITMENT

Plug and process load management begins during the project planning and design process. It is crucial that the building owner engage in plug and process load management and planning, and designate an internal leader to follow it through, from project programming to building operation. The project delivery team can be a valuable resource for plug and process load reduction and for integrating the strategies into the project.

BENCHMARK EXISTING LOADS

Many organizations have an existing plug and process use pattern based on equipment procurement practices, internal policies, and specialized operational energy requirements. Benchmarking existing plug and process load use is the best place to start when planning for a new net zero energy project, and is even more relevant when the project is a renovation of an existing building into a net zero energy building.

There are several strategies for benchmarking existing plug and process loads. If submeters are installed, or can be installed, to isolate plug loads, the metered data can be used to quantify existing patterns. Alternatively, plug load meters can be used to systematically measure sample sets of major equipment. Here are some guidelines:

- Use plug meters with a 30-second recording interval and with the capacity to handle the largest equipment loads.
- Measure each equipment load for a week to determine energy use during occupied and unoccupied times.
- Inventory the equipment currently used by the organization, and record its power rating of the equipment.

Once a thorough plug and process load audit is complete, management strategies can be developed for the project.

ASSESS PLUG LOAD NEEDS

A good plug and process load management strategy starts with identifying the actual needs of the organization's operation within the building (see Figure 10.2). The next step is to meet and, ideally, optimize those needs in the most energy-efficient manner possible. Unnecessary equipment should be eliminated, and redundant equipment consolidated. For example, occupants may feel that a personal printer is necessary even though a shared multifunction printer will meet the organizational needs and provide additional quality, functionality, and energy efficiency. Personal appliances at workspaces are most often redundant and thus represent a substantial use of energy. Items such as personal space heaters and minirefrigerators should be disallowed per organizational operational policy. A minirefrigerator, specifically, can use as much energy as a full-size model, whereas a shared refrigerator tends to be filled closer to capacity, which allows it to run more efficiently.

CHOOSE EFFICIENT EQUIPMENT

Choosing the most energy-efficient equipment requires conducting research to evaluate differences between options. Using ENERGY STAR-rated equipment is a good way to start, but it is essential to compare power requirements in watts (or if watts are not given by the manufacturer, then multiply voltage by amperage). Also compare standby power requirements, if provided by the manufacturer.

When working toward a net zero energy building, every watt counts. In particular, to leverage energy efficiency, it is important to choose carefully equipment such as computers and phones that must be purchased in large numbers for a commercial building; the impact can be multiplied by the number of installed devices—which, for some devices, can easily number in the hundreds. For example, an average desktop computer uses approximately 100 watts, compared to an average laptop, which uses approximately 30 watts. A CRT monitor on average consumes about 70 watts, whereas a fluorescent backlit LCD monitor consumes around 30 watts. Better still is an LED backlit LC monitor, at about 15 watts. See Figure 10.3 for a comparison of a conventional workstation and a low-energy workstation.

Clearly, the energy effects of these equipment choices can add up fast. Take, for example, the phone selected for the DOE/NREL Research Support Facility (RSF). A new 2-watt phone replaced the 15-watt phone installed previously. There are approximately a thousand 2 watt phones in the RSF, which results in an energy

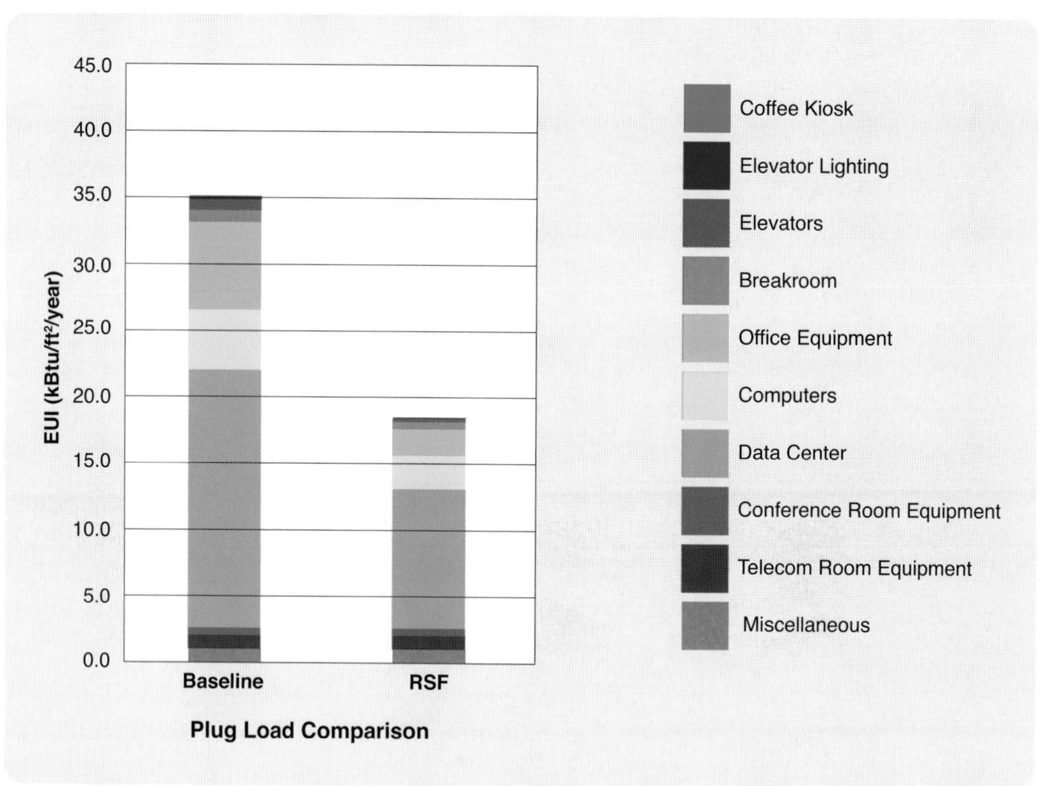

■ **FIGURE 10.2** Baseline plug load assessment compared to actual plug load at the DOE/NREL Research Support Facility. *Data source: DOE/NREL, Chad Lobato, Shanti Pless, Michael Sheppy, ad Paul Torcellini, "Reducing Plug and Process Loads for a Large-Scale, Low-Energy Office Building: NREL's Research Support Facility," ASHRAE conference paper, February 2011.*

savings of 1.51 kBtu/ft^2/year. This savings also meant that approximately $375,000 of photovoltaics would not need to be installed.

In addition to equipment that is installed repeatedly throughout a building, it is also important to identify high-power equipment or uses. Elevators, vending machines, fitness equipment, and breakroom appliances all present opportunities for choosing energy-efficient alternatives. To make the most energy-efficient choices for special uses, such as foodservice operations, laboratories, medical services, and data centers, will require a strong focus on design strategies and equipment by the delivery team and building owner. In fact, these loads will be among the primary energy drivers for facilities with these types of loads.

CONTROL EQUIPMENT POWER SETTINGS

Turning off equipment when it is not in use is another key plug and process load management technique. There are numerous opportunities to manage the power settings and controls for equipment. Equipment and appliances often have energy-efficiency settings that can, and should be, optimized. Even then, most equipment will still draw a "phantom load" in power-saving standby modes; and some equipment will continue to draw power even when switched off, unless completely

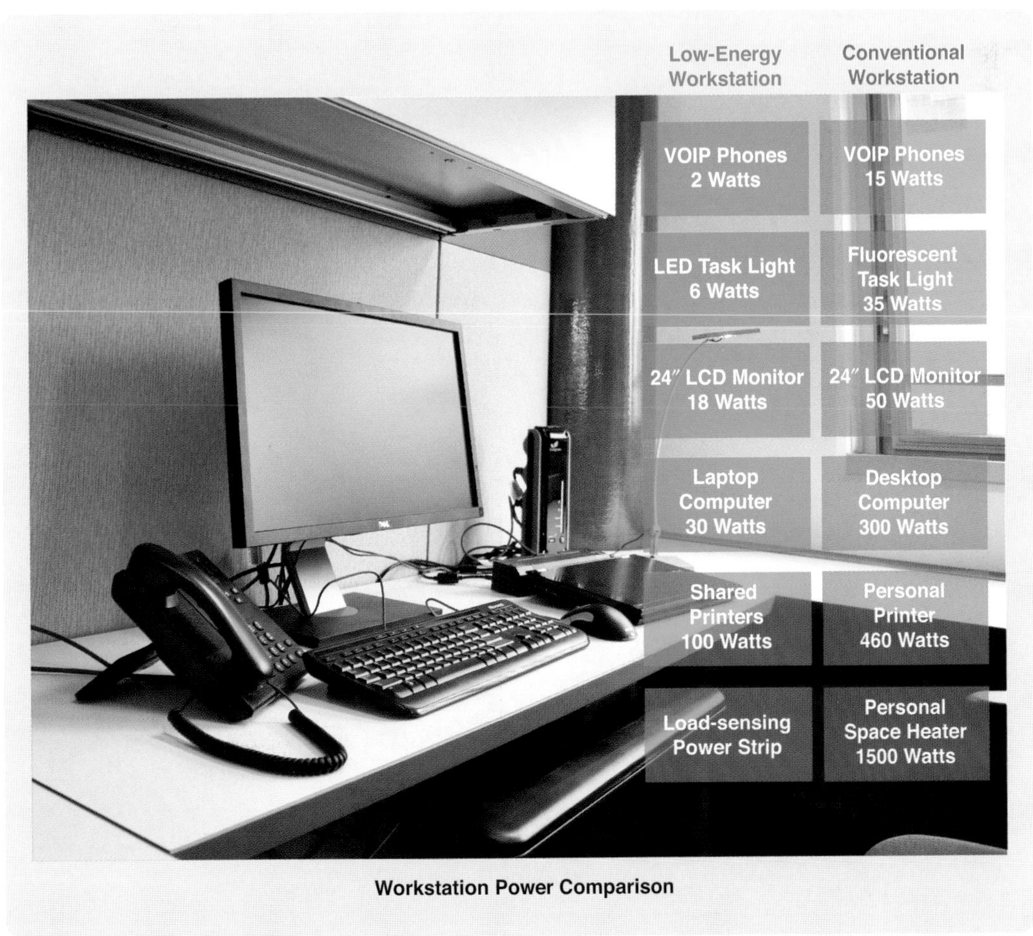

■ **FIGURE 10.3** Comparing a low-energy workstation at the DOE/NREL Research Support Facility to conventional workstation power requirements.

unplugged or deenergized. Conducting the plug and process load audit with a plug meter can help determine the phantom load component of individual pieces of equipment.

There are several ways of disconnecting power from appliances when they are not in use. One simple method is to install an electrical outlet timer for equipment, such as coffee makers, that is "on" for a certain period and then turned off for extended lengths of time. Sophisticated plug control outlets and power strips are available for managing equipment power. These devices are ideal for workstations where multiple devices are powered. They control power via simple manual switches or automatic switching through occupancy sensors, timer controls, or load-sensing controls that manage phantom loads. The design of the electrical system can also integrate substantial control for plug load circuits, including manual occupant switches for outlet control, occupancy/vacancy controls, and timer or time clock controls. Plug load circuits can also be managed and integrated with the building automation system.

Computers present unique control challenges, compared to desk lamps, cell phone chargers, monitors, and so on, because computers cannot simply be turned off or deenergized; they need to be shut down through the operating system's shutdown procedure. For managing computer-related plug loads, institute energy-saving standby settings and instruct occupants to shut down their computers at the end of each workday or during periods of nonuse.

For commercial buildings that have no night occupancy or regular unoccupied periods, turning off connected plug loads can save large quantities of energy. The controls just mentioned can automate this process, or at least make it easier for occupants to manage. The matrix in Figure 10.4 illustrates the magnitude of plug loads during unoccupied hours and occupied hours. The matrix converts a range of plug load densities for 8,760 occupied and unoccupied hours into a resulting energy use intensity (EUI) for the building. It is based on a typical commercial office building, but it can be applied or adapted to other commercial building types. It is important to

Occupied Hours Power Density (W/ft²)	Unoccupied Hours Power Density (W/ft²)														
	0.10	0.20	0.30	0.40	0.50	0.60	0.70	0.80	0.90	1.00	1.10	1.20	1.30	1.40	1.50
0.10	3.0	5.2	7.4	9.7	11.9	14.1	16.3	18.6	20.8	23.0	25.2	27.4	29.7	31.9	34.1
0.20	3.8	6.0	8.2	10.4	12.7	14.9	17.1	19.3	21.5	23.8	26.0	28.2	30.4	32.7	34.9
0.30	4.5	6.8	9.0	11.2	13.4	15.6	17.9	20.1	22.3	24.5	26.8	29.0	31.2	33.4	35.6
0.40	5.3	7.5	9.7	12.0	14.2	16.4	18.6	20.9	23.1	25.3	27.5	29.7	32.0	34.2	36.4
0.50	6.1	8.3	10.5	12.7	15.0	17.2	19.4	21.6	23.8	26.1	28.3	30.5	32.7	35.0	37.2
0.60	6.8	9.1	11.3	13.5	15.7	17.9	20.2	22.4	24.6	26.8	29.1	31.3	33.5	35.7	38.0
0.70	7.6	9.8	12.0	14.3	16.5	18.7	20.9	23.2	25.4	27.6	29.8	32.1	34.3	36.5	38.7
0.80	8.4	10.6	12.8	15.0	17.3	19.5	21.7	23.9	26.2	28.4	30.6	32.8	35.0	37.3	39.5
0.90	9.1	11.4	13.6	15.8	18.0	20.3	22.5	24.7	26.9	29.1	31.4	33.6	35.8	38.0	40.3
1.00	9.9	12.1	14.4	16.6	18.8	21.0	23.2	25.5	27.7	29.9	32.1	34.4	36.6	38.8	41.0
1.10	10.7	12.9	15.1	17.3	19.6	21.8	24.0	26.2	28.5	30.7	32.9	35.1	37.3	39.6	41.8
1.20	11.4	13.7	15.9	18.1	20.3	22.6	24.8	27.0	29.2	31.4	33.7	35.9	38.1	40.3	42.6
1.30	12.2	14.4	16.7	18.9	21.1	23.3	25.5	27.8	30.0	32.2	34.4	36.7	38.9	41.1	43.3
1.40	13.0	15.2	17.4	19.6	21.9	24.1	26.3	28.5	30.8	33.0	35.2	37.4	39.7	41.9	44.1
1.50	13.7	16.0	18.2	20.4	22.6	24.9	27.1	29.3	31.5	33.8	36.0	38.2	40.4	42.6	44.9

■ **FIGURE 10.4** Annual Plug and Process Load EUIs Based on Day and Night Power Densities. *Source: Chad Lobato, Shanti Pless, Michael Sheppy, and Paul Torcellini, "Reducing Plug and Process Loads for a Large-Scale, Low-Energy Office Building: NREL's Research Support Facility," Table 2.*

stress that the resulting EUI is only for the plug load component of energy use. Many net zero energy targets for the entire energy use of the building will be lower than many of the values listed on this matrix, just for plug load energy. It is easy to see that managing plug and process loads is absolutely essential to net zero energy performance.

SET POLICIES, EDUCATE, AND RAISE AWARENESS

Many aspects of plug and process load management may be relatively transparent to the occupants, from selecting energy-efficient equipment to providing automated controls. For example, computers and equipment can be upgraded to more energy-efficient options, and occupancy or vacancy controls can be added to lighting. There is quantifiable benefit to making energy reductions effortless. However, to fully benefit from the potential of plug and process load management, it is critical to engage the occupants.

Instituting plug and process load policies is the first step in coordinating operational procedures and occupant behavior with equipment choices and load management strategies. But policies can only make explicit the expectations and requirements; it is occupant education and awareness about his or her role in the energy use of a net zero energy building that drive meaningful behavioral changes. After all, an occupant who is not aware or invested in the energy goal of the building may easily override automated controls and/or ignore policies.

GREEN BEHAVIOR

Occupant Behavior

As challenging as the design, delivery, and operation of a net zero energy building may be, engaging the building occupants in the net zero energy goal is the important, and demanding, final step. It is worth noting that directing occupant behavior around building energy use is considered one of the next frontiers for high-performance buildings. Among the lessons learned about actual energy performance of buildings is that energy-efficient building systems are not enough, because it is the occupants who control a major portion of the overall energy use of the building. As stated previously, but it bears repeating here, buildings do not use energy; people do.

Occupants have an impact on a wide range of energy end uses within a building. Energy is used to provide thermal comfort, quality lighting, and ventilation; and it powers all the equipment occupants need to complete their tasks—computers, equipment, appliances, and many other devices. In a typical commercial building, the occupants are relatively passive; they are, simply, users of the equipment, lights, HVAC systems, and so on. But occupants do not generally think of of themselves as consumers of energy. And this speaks to two fundamental issues about energy and occupant behavior: expectations and awareness.

Living and working in a net zero energy building should not mean sacrificing function, quality, or environment. If anything, the mantra should be: "How can we do more at a higher quality with fewer resources?" The main priority is, simply, to eliminate waste. There are significant opportunities for energy savings without sacrificing function or quality. Many of the plug and process load management strategies discussed earlier in this chapter demonstrate how to optimize both efficiency and effectiveness. Further, many of the passive and low-energy strategies to provide heating, cooling, and air can offer occupant benefits while lowering energy use. In short, occupant behavior has an effect on building energy in a wide range of circumstances, sometimes in positive ways, sometimes in negative ways.

Green behavior can be defined as a condition whereby building occupants understand and work toward the energy and sustainability objectives of the building. The notion of participating in a net zero energy building may be inspiring to and meaningful for many occupants. A heightened awareness and sense of purpose can make it easier for people to change the way they use a building. And for their part, designers of net zero energy buildings have the opportunity to consider how their efforts can influence and shape occupant expectations of and behavior around energy use in commercial buildings.

Occupant Feedback

One way to encourage green behavior is to provide mechanisms for feedback—both from and to occupants. Feedback loops are important, to reinforce what is working and to identify and correct what needs improvement. There are a number of reasons and opportunities to gather feedback from occupants regarding issues that impact energy.

When starting a new building project, where the future occupants are known, it can be very beneficial to conduct preoccupancy surveys to learn what their expectations, preconceptions, and behaviors are in regard to energy use and thermal comfort. Preoccupancy surveys also can help identify areas for occupant education, and influence design decisions.

At the other end, postoccupancy surveys should be conducted to evaluate how effectively the building is fulfilling the design intent in terms of occupant energy use, occupant thermal comfort, and occupant behavior. Results can be used to first identify and then address issues that are uncovered during the evaluation. Conducting regular surveys can be part of an ongoing improvement process.

There are multiple methods of gathering preoccupancy and postoccupancy information from occupants. Surveys, as just mentioned, are one of the most common; web-based surveys especially have notable advantages—ease of distribution, compilation, and analysis. A disadvantage of surveys is that it can be difficult to collect valuable data and meaningful responses from participants, who may rush through a survey or treat it as the platform from which to air all of their complaints. One approach would be to administer short surveys more frequently, and at random or periodically throughout the year.

NREL is researching and developing an occupant-focused desktop application that will serve as an interface between the occupant and energy and thermal comfort data about the building. Called the Building Occupant Agent (BOA), it will be prototyped at the DOE/NREL Research Support Facility (see Figures 10.5 and 10.6). BOA is a two-way interface that collects thermal comfort and energy behavior survey data from occupants throughout the year, and provides details to them about the energy use of the building and recommended operation of operable windows. USB-based environmental sensors will retrieve workstation temperature and light levels, along with survey information. BOA is supported by a web service that collects data for analysis and interfaces with the building's systems.

SOCIAL NETWORKING

There is tremendous opportunity to incorporate occupant feedback mechanisms into social networking. Social media applications can be designed to gather data in a number of compelling and interactive ways. And the feedback mechanisms can work both ways, making it possible to "push" energy performance feedback to users on the social network and to "pull" feedback from users. Furthermore, social media can go beyond collecting occupant data, to actually create a

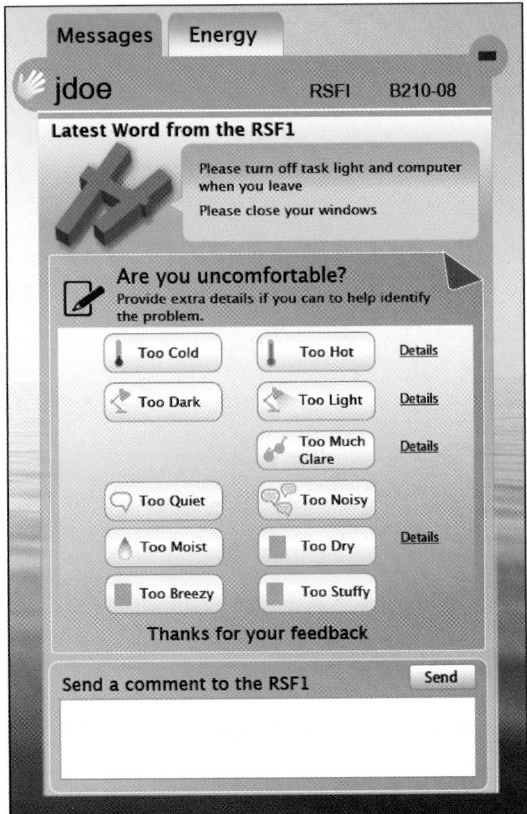

■ **FIGURE 10.5** NREL's Building Occupant Agent (BOA) can survey occupants. *NREL.*

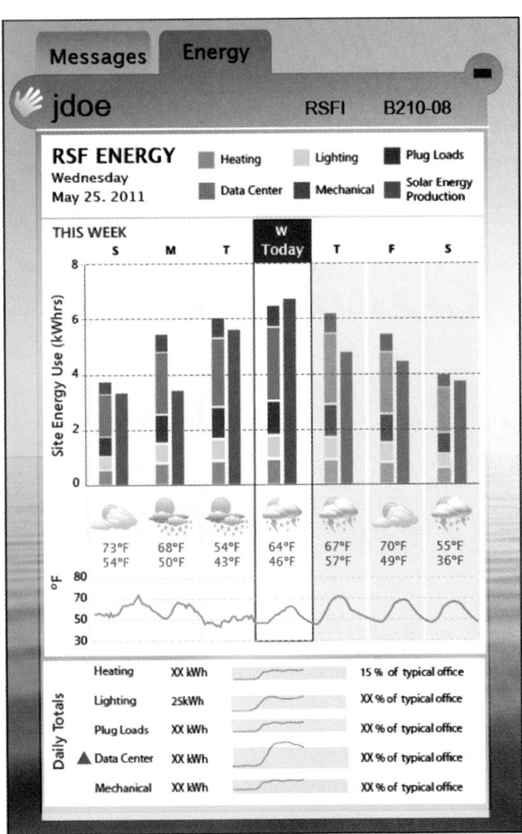

■ **FIGURE 10.6** NREL's Building Occupant Agent (BOA) can provide a detailed look at building energy use. *NREL.*

culture around energy performance. Such an application can be leveraged for other green occupant behaviors, such as water use, paper use, recycling, and commuting.

The Center for the Built Environment at the University of California, Berkeley, tested a prototype interface, called Green NetWork, that incorporated building energy and operations features into a social media application (see Figures 10.7 and 10.8).

VISUALIZING ENERGY

Giving occupants feedback on the energy performance of the building, and even direct feedback on the impact of their behavior on energy use, can be a powerful tool to manage energy use. Keep in mind, however, that energy is invisible. To provide feedback to occupants about energy use, it is important to find ways to visualize energy.

Social Media Application Features for Building Occupants

- Individual and organizational goal setting and tracking
- Interorganizational energy competitions
- Coworker and group benchmarking
- Self-reporting
- Reward systems
- Sharing stories, tips, and questions
- Surveys
- Building operation/occupant information
- Energy and building features education
- Energy information visualization
- Group and individual energy performance metrics

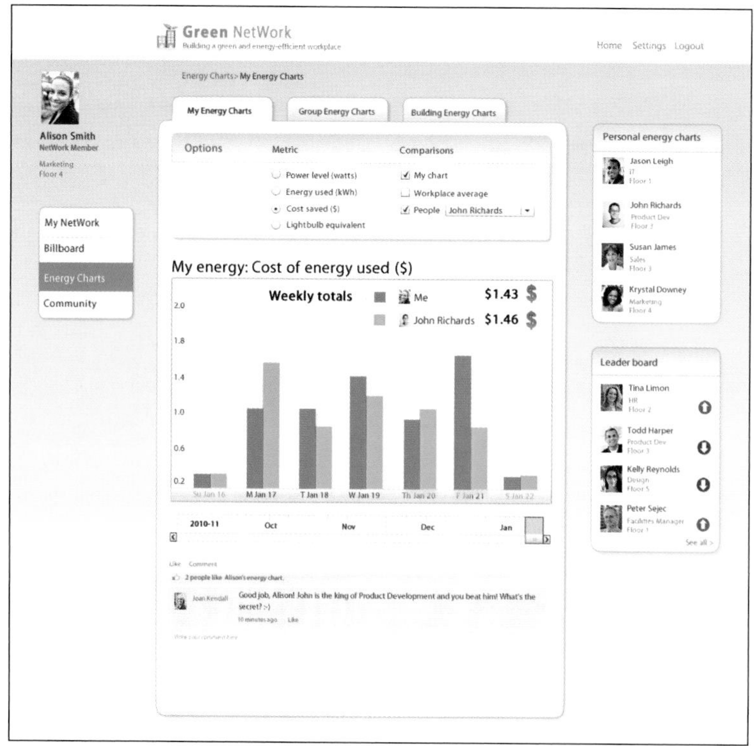

■ **FIGURE 10.7** The Center for the Built Environment's Green NetWork, showing the ability to compare energy use among members. *Center for the Built Environment (CBE), University of California, Berkeley, concept and design by David Lehrer and Janani Vasudev.*

■ **FIGURE 10.8** The Center for the Built Environment's Green NetWork, showing the ability for a member to set and track goals. *Center for the Built Environment (CBE), University of California, Berkeley, concept and design by David Lehrer and Janani Vasudev.*

One good way is through digital dashboards, which are connected to the project's energy information system; they can provide real-time, daily, and annual energy use, and display it as meaningful visual information (see Figure 10.9). These displays can be made into kiosks or shown on display monitors, where they are visible to occupants and visitors alike. The information can also be distributed through an internal computer network so that it can be accessed by any computer and occupant on the network. This type of feedback is most effective when it provides easy-to-understand information that can influence future action. The graphics, images, and interface are key to enhancing understanding. It is also effective when the feedback becomes part of the social structure of occupants, when internal competition or social awareness becomes integral to energy usage—as with the growing popularity of social media as a building occupant and energy engagement tool.

Education

Educating building occupants is a central part of the process of engaging them in the energy performance of a net zero energy building. Smarter occupants is a more important outcome than smarter buildings. We are all occupants and users of buildings—meaning there are a lot of people who need to be educated on how to be smarter building occupants. How is it possible to get everyone to think and behave differently about the way they use energy in a building? For the most part, it has to be done one building at a time, one occupant at time. That said, there is potential to leverage the public's interest in green building—specifically, net zero energy buildings—by using general media to get the message out.

Educating and engaging with the occupants should be a process that continues over the course of project delivery. The responsibility for education is shared between the delivery team and the owner's project leadership. Each design milestone, where progress is presented to building occupants, is an opportunity to discuss the net zero energy goal, the design features that support it, and what it will mean to the occupants. These three issues are core components of occupant education. Sharing information about the net zero energy goal can

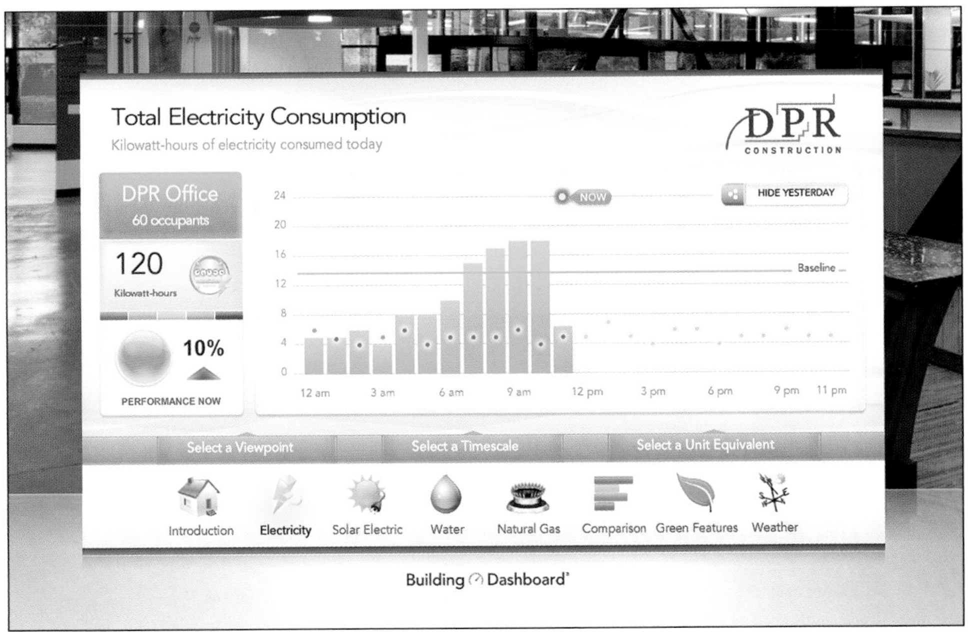

■ **FIGURE 10.9** Energy dashboard at DPR's San Diego office, which is pursuing net zero energy.
Credit: Building Dashboard by Lucid.

give occupants the big picture, and inspire a high level of interest and commitment. Some of the technology and systems in a net zero energy building may be new to many occupants, so introducing them to details about how the building works will help them learn to use the building effectively. The final step is to set expectations about the role occupants play.

The entire education process should be undertaken with awareness that change can be hard for people. It is important to identify the new features or expectations of a net zero energy building that will represent the greatest change for occupant groups, and then target those proactively. Providing opportunities for feedback from occupants, in conjunction with the educational elements, can help address and manage change-related issues.

Another effective way to help people transition into a new net zero energy building is through hands-on experience. This can also be effective for showcasing exciting new features, as a way to build interest and gain commitment from occupants. Hands-on experience is important, as well, for features about which occupants have concerns or reservations. One way to offer hands-on experience is by visiting other buildings with similar features. Or specific features can be mocked up or replicated within existing occupant spaces. For example, prototyping a new open workstation that is integral to the daylighting and natural ventilation strategies of a building may offer valuable hands-on experience for occupants who are reluctant to give up their cubicles. This was the technique used at NREL's Research Support Facility.

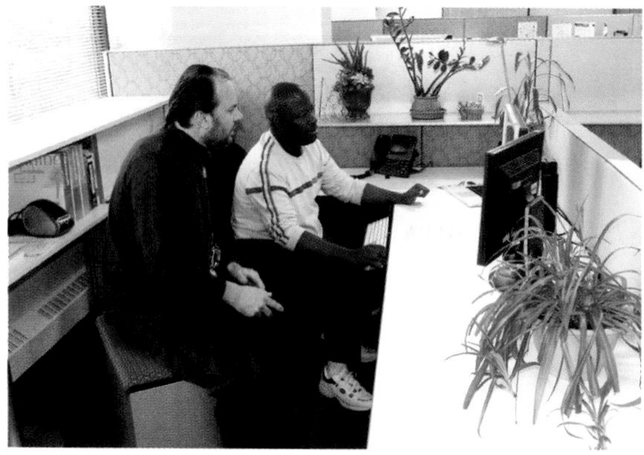

■ **FIGURE 10.10** Prototyping new open workstations prior to moving into the Research Support Facility. *NREL/PIX 16864; photograph by Heather Lammers.*

The proposed workstations for the Research Support Facility were very open, to allow for daylighting and natural ventilation. However, the new workstations did represent a major change from the private offices and high cubicle walls of the staff's current spaces. The NREL Information Services department was fitted out as a prototype with the new furniture to solicit feedback about it (see Figure 10.10). Initial concerns about noise and privacy soon gave way to acceptance, especially upon experiencing the new ease of collaboration. The test also served to help alleviate concerns and set expectations across other NREL departments before the organization moved into its new office building.

Training can be another effective tool for educating building occupants, and can be given in-person or online. Furthermore, training can be targeted to specific functions and operations of the building, or integrated with broader workforce training components. Training is best conducted upon the move into the new building, or for new occupants as part of their orientation. A companion to training is the development of an occupant's manual. This can be a simple document that explains the key building features and how they operate; how the occupant controls the building; and expectations for occupant behavior.

Posting educational signage about the sustainable features of a net zero energy building can help promote ongoing education. Education signage is also very beneficial on buildings tours, helping visitors learn how a net zero energy building works. But the ultimate form of education is to engage occupants themselves as educators for newcomers and visitors, and as leaders of tours through the net zero energy building. Teaching is, after all, an excellent means of learning.

Indoor Environmental Quality

Indoor environmental quality (IEQ) is strongly tied to energy and the heating, cooling, ventilation, and lighting systems of a building. Net zero energy buildings are high-performance energy buildings and can also excel at IEQ (see Figure 10.11). The passive strategies and low-energy mechanical and lighting systems may differ significantly from conventional building systems. To provide energy performance and high-quality indoor environments, it is important that occupants understand the fundamental principles of how these systems work and how they are controlled. Occupants also need to be aware that passive strategies are dynamic and are more difficult to precisely control. Passive strategies such as daylighting are also natural, beautiful, and often promote health and well-being.

■ **FIGURE 10.11** The interior design at the DOE/NREL Research Support Facility has many IEQ features such as daylighting, natural ventilation, dedicated outside air system with an underfloor air distribution system, thermal mass, and radiant heating and cooling. The design of the space also successfully addresses the acoustical challenges of these IEQ features. *NREL/PIX 17904; Dennis Schroeder.*

Daylighting

- Daylighting is high-quality, full spectrum light.
- Daylighting provides high-quality environments, but is more dynamic and may provide lower ambient light levels than conventional artificially lit spaces.
- Glare control is important for occupant satisfaction with daylit spaces.
- Daylighting is linked to occupant well-being and productivity.
- Daylighting is enhanced with high ceilings, light to white finishes, and an open space plan with few obstructions.

NET ZERO ENERGY PERFORMANCE PLAN

The transition from project delivery to building operation and occupancy is a critical juncture in a net zero energy project. Certainly the realities of building operation and occupancy add many new variables and complexities to the process of meeting a net zero energy goal. Then there are the many coordinated activities that need take place to manage the goal. For a net zero energy building, a more formal and comprehensive plan for net zero energy performance should be developed, to itemize the key steps and identify the procedures necessary to follow to meet the net zero energy goal in operation.

Thermal Comfort

- A range of seasonal temperature set points can save energy and be seasonally acceptable to occupants.
- Encourage occupants to dress based on seasons.
- Operable windows allow fresh air and air movement, which can have a desirable cooling effect.
- Operable windows allow occupants control to adapt the environment to their thermal needs.
- Thermal mass and radiant heating and cooling systems are effective through radiant energy transfer with the occupants and are often more comfortable than air-based heating and cooling, but they are also controlled in a different manner.

Acoustics

- Passive and low-energy strategies can present challenges for the design of acoustical environments:
  - Daylit and naturally ventilated spaces are often open and can impact acoustical privacy.
  - Many low-energy mechanical systems do not require the circulation of large quantities of air, and the lack of mechanical noise can make spaces very quiet.
  - The raised floor plenums of underfloor air distribution systems can allow sound to travel and impact acoustical privacy.
  - Thermal mass and thermally active surfaces are acoustically reflective (typically concrete or masonry) and are often sizeable in area.
  - Operable windows can introduce exterior noise.
- There are many solutions to the acoustical challenges in net zero energy buildings:
  - Sound masking can provide an important but low-level background noise that will not be present with many low-energy mechanical systems.
  - Sound-masking systems can address acoustical privacy issues.
  - Sound-masking systems can be installed in raised floor plenums.
  - Utilize high-quality acoustical panels and surfaces strategically to reduce the reverberation time in the room.
  - Landscaping can help reduce exterior noise intrusion.

The net zero energy performance plan includes the actions of the building owner, occupants, facility managers, delivery team, and commissioning agent. The plan overlaps the operation and maintenance plan for the building and engages the delivery team in postoccupancy or stewardship services, as discussed earlier in this chapter. One important benefit of a net zero energy performance plan is that it can identify the gaps in the building owner's capability, and then utilize the full capacity of the owner, design team, contractor, and commissioning agent in support of the net zero energy goal. The plan should be customized according to the energy management capabilities of facility management; to that end, continued focus should be placed on project transfer knowledge and information sharing between the delivery team and the facility management staff.

Elements of a Net Zero Energy Performance Plan

1. Coordinate with commissioning activities:
   A. Ensure all energy-related systems are commissioned.
   B. Plan for comprehensive facility management training.
   C. Begin preparation and review of controls design early, and work proactively with the control vendors to coordinate the work.
2. Coordinate with the building's operation and maintenance plan:
   A. Plan for energy management activities.
   B. Develop strategies for addressing thermal comfort complaints while maintaining energy goals.
   C. Institute operational policies and procedures for enhanced energy savings.
   D. Secure organizational leadership support for achieving the net zero energy goal.
   E. Coordinate energy-related procedures with other groups and departments in the organization.

3. Plan the energy information system, to include:
   A. Implement building-level metering.
   B. Implement a submetering plan, including energy end uses and any zones or spaces to be submetered.
   C. Plan sensor types and locations (interior environment and weather, at a minimum; coordinate with BAS).
   D. Plan the data server for the EIS (consider size, hosting, and web access).
   E. Determine the building's energy analysis needs and applications.
   F. Integrate visual energy displays, dashboards, and feedback mechanisms for occupants.
4. Plan for periodic energy data analysis and reporting:
   A. Calibrate as-built model, as needed, during building operation.
   B. Prepare minimum monthly reports for all energy end uses, total energy use, and energy generation.
   C. Determine supplemental weekly and daily load profiles.
   D. Track net zero energy goal trend, showing progress toward goal and estimated schedule for achieving net zero energy. Using trending data to guide corrective actions and overall system optimization.
5. Develop a plug and process load management plan:
   A. Identify an internal champion.
   B. Conduct a plug load audit, and benchmark existing loads.
   C. Access actual needs, and eliminate or consolidate loads where possible.
   D. Organize equipment procurement around high levels of energy efficiency.
   E. Develop a plan to control and manage all types of equipment and loads.
6. Develop occupant education, training, and feedback programs:
   A. Plan education and user input during development of the design.
   B. Find opportunities to prototype solutions or visit other buildings implementing similar solutions.
   C. Develop a building owner's manual.
   D. Develop a training program prior to occupancy, and ongoing for new occupants.
   E. Incorporate visual feedback and data on energy use that is accessible to occupants and visitors.
   F. Solicit occupant feedback through surveys or other web-based vehicles such as social media to track thermal comfort and green behavior around energy use and energy features of the building.
7. Plan for future changes:
   A. Track age degradation of photovoltaic systems (if present) and plan for additional renewable energy installations or additional energy-efficiency measures over time to maintain net zero energy balance.
   B. Evaluate new equipment or changes in building loads against renewable energy capacity. Develop a procurement process that includes the purchase of new renewable energy systems, to compensate for new equipment purchases and loads that exceed current capacity.
8. Celebrate success when one year of net zero energy operation is achieved and share lessons learned with the building industry.

NZ CHAPTER 11
NET ZERO ENERGY

NET ZERO ENERGY BALANCE

Managing a net zero energy commercial project requires tracking the objective from the initial goal-setting session through design and into actual operation. Goal tracking is not unlike maintaining a balance sheet; in fact, a relatively simple spreadsheet can be an effective tool for keeping the balance in check. This chapter describes the methods for calculating a building's net zero energy balance. It also discusses a related but more comprehensive issue, that of measuring carbon neutrality. A project team and owner may opt to track their total carbon balance in concert with the net zero energy measures.

A project team and owner can pursue and track one or all four of the net zero energy measures: site energy, source energy, energy emissions, and energy costs. These four measures, as defined by NREL, are of equal importance, though prioritizing them can be done on a project-by-project basis. If, for example, carbon emissions are of primary importance to the owner, then the energy emissions measure may be prioritized. If cost is a priority, then the energy cost measure may be prioritized. That said, in practice, the energy cost measure may prove to be the most complicated and challenging measure to achieve. The economic benefit of renewable energy and energy efficiency can and should be validated with or without a net zero energy cost balance. From a purely practical point of view, I would recommend always including a site energy measure, because it the simplest to calculate, even though it may be the most difficult to achieve in terms of the renewable energy needed to maintain the balance. The source energy measure is a valuable way of quantifying the total energy balance; and while it is a bit more complicated to calculate than site energy, it may be easier to achieve in terms of renewable energy capacity. Simply put, considering all four measures is always a good place to start.

NET ZERO ENERGY MEASURES

Chapter 1 discussed in detail the approaches to net zero energy buildings and defined relevant terms. Chapter 4 addressed in depth on-site and source energy, as well as energy sources. This section focuses on bringing together all of the chapters of the book, and offers specific guidance on how to calculate the four different net zero energy measures.

Calculations made during the design phase will factor in the results of the project's energy model, to include the annual energy use of the project, renewable energy generation, and energy sources for the project. Calculations made during actual operation should include metered data for annual energy use, renewable energy generation, and the project's energy sources. The calculation methods described here include itemizing the building's energy baseline (typically, based on CBECS 2003) and the building's energy reduction. Note: These steps are optional, but are included to emphasize the importance of energy efficiency in the net zero energy balance.

Furthermore, these calculation methods allow for reasonably complex net zero energy building configurations, including multiple nonrenewable energy sources and multiple offsetting renewable energy systems. The calculation methodology is, basically, an accounting approach, one that balances renewable energy resources with the annual energy use of the building. The building's energy use is first quantified as if it were supplied 100 percent by a utility; thereafter, renewable energy resources are added to the mix and then deducted from the utility-provided energy baseline to determine whether a net zero energy balance has been achieved. The project's location and utility company determine the factors that influence the source energy, energy emissions, and energy costs measures.

The method also incorporates NREL's net zero energy building classification system. (Refer to Chapter 1 for details on that system's levels.) Note that it is possible to achieve different classification levels for different net zero energy definitions. For example, a project may be both a Classification B net zero source building and a Classification C net zero site energy building.

NET ZERO ENERGY UNITS

When tracking a project's net zero energy balance, take care to track energy units closely. In the United States, building energy use is often given in terms of the British thermal unit (Btu). For building energy use intensity (EUI), the units are kBtu/ft^2/year; and for annual energy use, the units are usually MBtu. The majority of renewable energy systems generate electricity and use the units kWh or MWh, depending on the overall size of the system. Renewable energy systems that provide thermal energy use the units of kBtu or MBtu. The calculation methodology described in this section often includes both watt- and Btu-based units, to allow for input of the energy values in their "native" units. It is easy to convert the units back and forth: 1.0 watt equals 3.412 Btu.

The methodology for site and source energy converts values for the net zero energy balance calculation to MWh; however, MBtu could just as easily be used instead, as long as the units are consistent. For energy emissions and energy cost calculations, it is important to keep electrical energy in MWh and thermal energy in MBtu so that the appropriate carbon emission factors and energy rates may be applied. For the energy emissions calculation, the units used to determine the net zero energy balance are metric tons of CO_{2e}; for the energy costs calculation, the units are in dollars. Once the base net zero energy calculations are complete, the value can be converted to an intensity value per square foot of space, with units that are appropriate to that measure. For example, an annual metric ton of CO_{2e} value for the entire project can be converted to a carbon intensity measure of pounds of CO_{2e} per square foot.

Net Zero Site Energy

A net zero site energy building produces at least as much renewable energy as it uses over the course of a year, when accounted for at the site. The net zero site energy measure is the most straightforward calculation of all of the net zero energy measures. It can also be one of the most difficult to achieve, depending on the fuel mix of the project. Site energy must be calculated first, as it serves as the basis for the other net zero energy calculations.

Net Zero Site Energy Balance Method

1. **Baseline:** Establish the annual site energy baseline for the project.
2. **Energy use reductions:** Take credit for energy-efficiency measures.
3. **Design or operational site energy use:** Indicate either the design site energy use or the actual measured energy use, depending on the phase of the project (design/construction or occupancy). If an energy contingency for design energy data is desired, then escalate the design site energy use by the desired contingency amount.
4. **Energy sources:** Break out the annual design or operational site energy use based on each energy source/fuel used for the project. For this step, it is assumed that the project uses energy sources provided by the local utility company. This breakout is necessary to calculate the additional three net zero energy measures.
5. **Renewable energy systems:** For each renewable energy system used for the project, indicate the annual renewable energy generation. Systems can include different renewable energy sources, such as a photovoltaic installation and a wind installation; it can also include an off-site purchase of renewable energy through RECs.
6. **Renewable energy classification level:** As part of the net zero energy classification system developed by NREL, the location of the renewable energy system determines the classification ranking of the net zero energy building. Indicate the location and the relationship of the renewable energy system to the building and site. (Refer to Chapter 1 for a detailed explanation of the classification system.)
7. **Net zero energy balance:** To determine which classification of net zero energy building is achieved, begin with Classification A and check the building site energy use against A-level renewable energy systems. Move through each level of classification incrementally, adding the next level of renewable energy systems to the mix. For example, the net zero energy balance for Classification C would include renewable energy system levels A, B, and C. The highest classification to achieve a zero or negative balance is the net zero energy classification for the project. If net zero energy is not achieved, or not achieved at the level desired, look for additional energy use reductions or sources of additional renewable energy.

The example in Figure 11.1 shows the net zero site energy balance calculations in a spreadsheet format to illustrate the workflow of the calculations. A similar spreadsheet could be developed in Excel and adapted to meet project needs. The example is hypothetical but incorporates values typical of commercial net zero energy buildings. It is assumed that the building is grid-connected with net metering, and that the building has a natural gas connection.

Multiple renewable energy systems are shown in a variety of locations in relation to the building and site to illustrate multiple classification levels. Two types of renewable electricity sources are provided: a roof-mounted photovoltaics system and a site-mounted wind turbine and tower. Both of these renewable energy sources are net-metered. The project is assumed to have a biomass boiler to supply the majority of the heating demand. Natural gas supplements the biomass boiler.

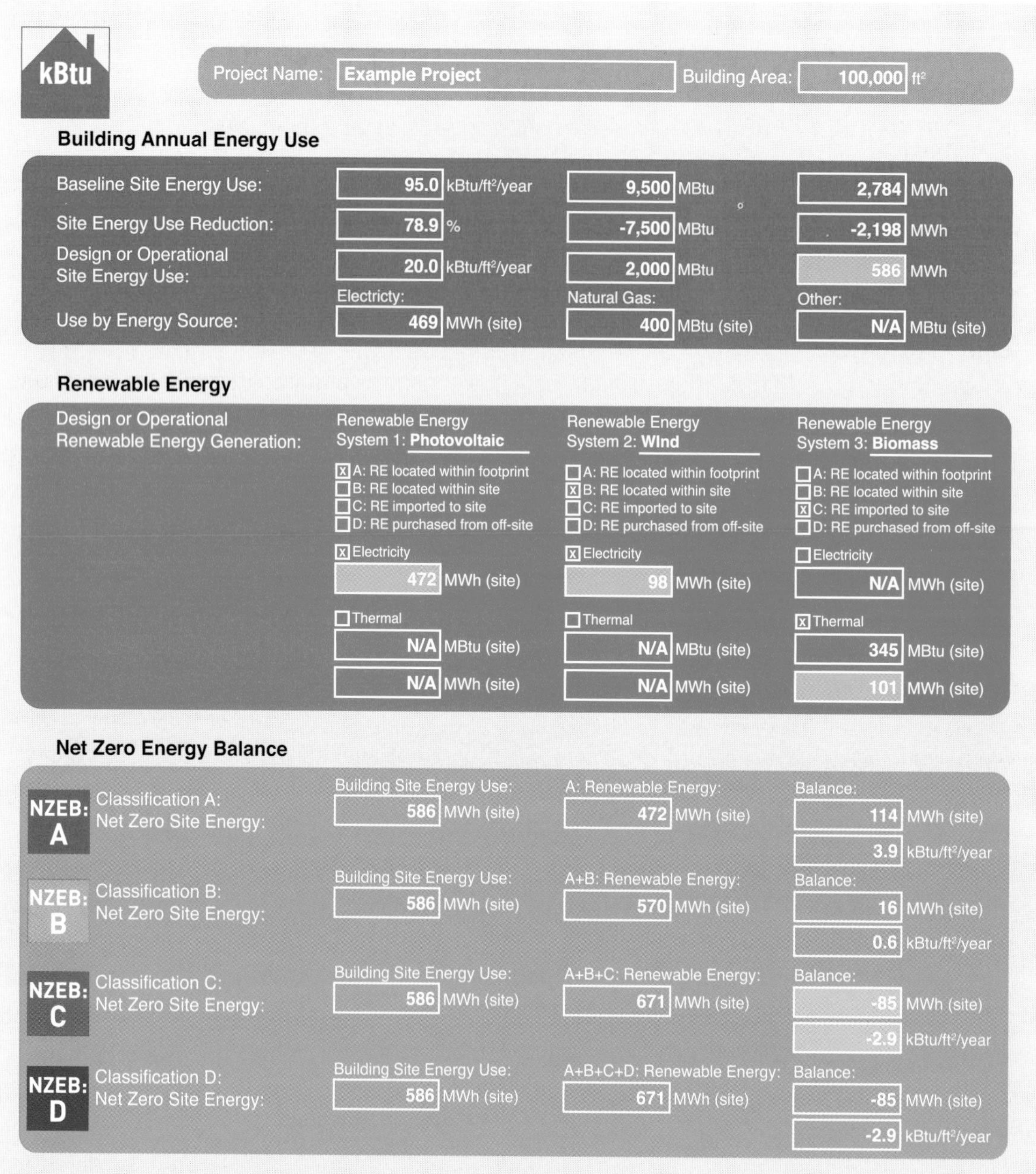

■ **FIGURE 11.1** Net Zero Site Energy Balance.

It is further assumed that RECs are maintained for all renewable energy systems. It is not assumed in the example that additional RECs are to be purchased, but they could be; in which case, they would constitute a level D renewable energy system and be used in the Classification D balance calculation. For this example, the project achieves a Classification C net zero site energy balance. Note that the example achieves a Classification A for net zero electricity, because the photovoltaic system located within the building footprint (level A) generates more electricity than it consumes.

Net Zero Source Energy

A net zero source energy building produces or purchases at least as much renewable energy as it uses over the course of a year, when accounted for at the source. Source energy calculations are based on the site energy modeling or measurements. Source energy cannot be measured or modeled directly, so it is estimated using source energy factors. (For more on source energy factors, refer to Chapter 4.)

With a site-to-source energy relationship of approximately one to three for grid-based electricity, it would seem that source energy would be the most challenging definition to meet for a net zero energy building. The reason that site energy is often a more difficult net zero measure to meet, compared with source energy, lies in the way renewable energy is accounted for in these definitions. Taking the example of electricity again, electricity generated with renewable energy on-site will have the same source and site energy value, or a source energy factor of 1.0. However, when used in a net zero source energy calculation, electricity generated via renewable energy is given a value based on the source energy factor of grid-based electricity so that it offsets grid-based electricity at a one-to-one ratio. In this way, a grid-connected all-electric building has the same position as a net zero energy building, whether measured at the site or at the source. Interestingly, this can make renewable electricity a powerful source energy when offset against other fuels with a low site-to-source factor such as natural gas.

The example in Figure 11.2 shows the net zero source energy balance calculations in a spreadsheet format to illustrate the workflow of the calculations. It builds on the hypothetical project described for the site energy calculation (refer back to Figure 11.1). The source energy factors to convert site energy to source energy can be found in Chapter 4. Those entered into this example are from the Source Energy Factors for EPA's ENERGY STAR Program table in Chapter 4 (see Figure 4.9). A national average for the electricity source energy factor is used. Chapter 4 also contains a map of electricity source energy factors by state (see Figure 4.11).

Net Zero Source Energy Balance Method

1. **Net zero site energy balance:** Complete the site energy calculations as a prerequisite to calculating source energy.
2. **Source energy factor:** Determine the appropriate source energy factor for each utility-based energy source used on the project.
3. **Design or operational source energy use:** Multiply the source energy factor for each utility-based energy source by the annual site energy use for each energy source, respectively. Convert the individual source energy values to a common energy unit (MWh and/or MBtu) and sum the values for the total source energy use.
4. **Renewable energy:** The renewable energy generation for each of the project's systems also needs to be multiplied by the appropriate source factor. For renewable electrical energy, multiply by the same source energy factor used for grid-based electricity. For renewable thermal energy, insert the same source energy factor used for the utility-based source tapped to generate thermal energy for the project. The default is the energy source factor for natural gas.
5. **Net zero energy balance and classification:** Once both the building energy use and the renewable energy generation values are converted to source energy, follow the same methodology used for the site energy calculation to determine the net zero source energy balance and the net zero energy classification.

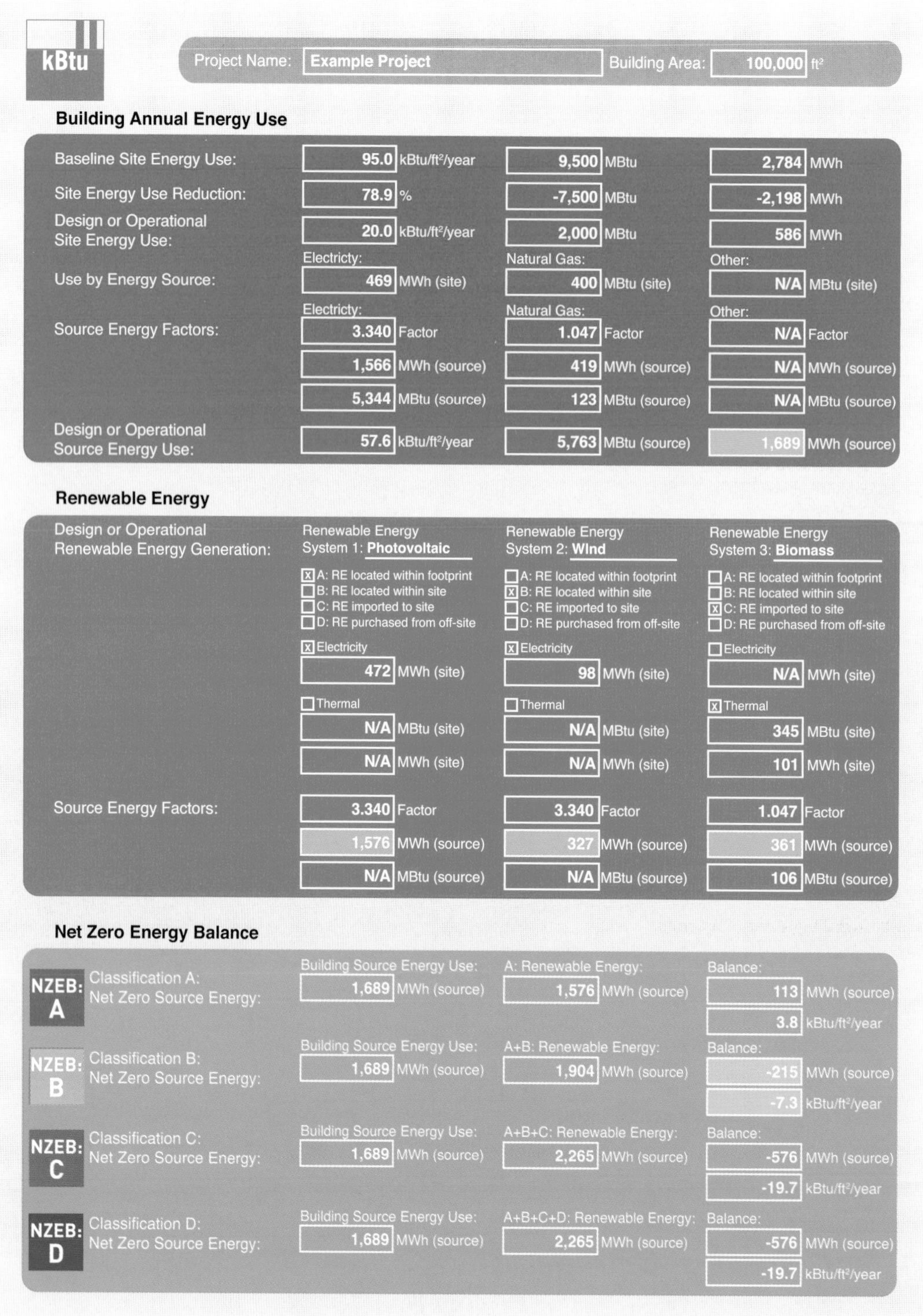

■ **FIGURE 11.2** Net Zero Source Energy Balance.Figure 11.3 Net Zero Energy Emissions Balance.

Note that the biomass renewable energy system in the example uses the natural gas source energy factor because its thermal energy offsets natural gas used for thermal energy. The project in this example achieves a Classification B net zero source energy balance.

Net Zero Energy Emissions

A net zero energy emissions building produces or purchases at least enough emissions-free renewable energy to offset emissions from all energy used in the building, over the course of a year. In this case, the CO_{2e} offsets from the

CO_{2e} | Project Name: Example Project | Building Area: 100,000 ft²

Building Annual Energy Use

Baseline Site Energy Use:	95.0 kBtu/ft²/year	9,500 MBtu	2,784 MWh
Site Energy Use Reduction:	78.9 %	-7,500 MBtu	-2,198 MWh
Design or Operational Site Energy Use:	20.0 kBtu/ft²/year	2,000 MBtu	586 MWh
Use by Energy Source:	Electricty: 469 MWh (site)	Natural Gas: 400 MBtu (site)	Other: N/A MBtu (site)
Carbon Emission Factors (CO_{2e}):	Electricty: 0.689 Mtons/MWh	Natural Gas: 0.066 Mtons/MBtu	Other: N/A Mtons/MBtu
	323.1 Mtons	26.4 Mtons	N/A Mtons
Energy Emissions before Renewable Energy (CO_{2e}):		7.7 lb/ft²/year	349.5 Mtons

Renewable Energy

Design or Operational Renewable Energy Generation:	Renewable Energy System 1: **Photovoltaic**	Renewable Energy System 2: **Wind**	Renewable Energy System 3: **Biomass**
	[X] A: RE located within footprint [ ] B: RE located within site [ ] C: RE imported to site [ ] D: RE purchased from off-site	[ ] A: RE located within footprint [X] B: RE located within site [ ] C: RE imported to site [ ] D: RE purchased from off-site	[ ] A: RE located within footprint [ ] B: RE located within site [X] C: RE imported to site [ ] D: RE purchased from off-site
	[X] Electricity: 472 MWh (site)	[X] Electricity: 98 MWh (site)	[ ] Electricity: N/A MWh (site)
	[ ] Thermal: N/A MBtu (site)	[ ] Thermal: N/A MBtu (site)	[X] Thermal: 345 MBtu (site)
Carbon Emission Factors (CO_{2e}):	[X] Electricity: 0.689 Mtons/MWh	[X] Electricity: 0.689 Mtons/MWh	[ ] Electricity: N/A Mtons/MWh
	[ ] Thermal: N/A Mtons/MBtu	[ ] Thermal: N/A Mtons/MBtu	[X] Thermal: 0.066 Mtons/MBtu
Energy Emissions offset with Renewable Energy (CO_{2e}):	325.2 Mtons	67.5 Mtons	22.8 Mtons

Net Zero Energy Balance

NZEB: A	Classification A: Net Zero Energy Emissions:	Building Energy Emissions: 349.5 Mtons	A: Renewable Energy: 325.2 Mtons	Balance: 24 Mtons; 0.5 lb/ft²/year
NZEB: B	Classification B: Net Zero Energy Emissions:	Building Energy Emissions: 349.5 Mtons	A+B: Renewable Energy: 392.7 Mtons	Balance: -43 Mtons; -1.0 lb/ft²/year
NZEB: C	Classification C: Net Zero Energy Emissions:	Building Energy Emissions: 349.5 Mtons	A+B+C: Renewable Energy: 415.5 Mtons	Balance: -66 Mtons; -1.5 lb/ft²/year
NZEB: D	Classification D: Net Zero Energy Emissions:	Building Energy Emissions: 349.5 Mtons	A+B+C+D: Renewable Energy: 415.5 Mtons	Balance: -66 Mtons; -1.5 lb/ft²/year

■ **FIGURE 11.3** Net Zero Energy Emissions Balance.

renewable energy systems are greater than or equal to the CO_{2e} production from utility-based energy use. Energy emissions calculations are based on the site energy modeling or measurements. Energy emissions cannot be measured or modeled directly and so are estimated using carbon emission factors (which can be found in the "Carbon Neutrality" section at the end of this chapter).

The example in Figure 11.3 shows the net zero energy emissions balance calculations in a spreadsheet format to illustrate the workflow

Net Zero Energy Emissions Balance Method

1. **Net zero energy emissions balance:** Complete the site energy calculations as a prerequisite to calculating source energy.
2. **Carbon emission factor:** Determine the appropriate carbon emission factor for each utility-based energy source used on the project.
3. **Design or operational energy emissions:** Multiply the carbon emission factor for each utility-based energy source by the annual site energy use for each energy source, respectively. This will result in a mass of CO_{2e} for each utility-based energy source, and the sum of these values will equal the total energy emissions for design or operational energy use.
4. **Renewable energy:** The renewable energy generation for each of the project's systems also needs to be multiplied by the appropriate carbon emission factor. For renewable electrical energy, multiply by the same carbon emission factor used for grid-based electricity. For renewable thermal energy, insert the same carbon emission factor used for the utility-based source tapped to generate thermal energy for the project. The default is the carbon emission factor for natural gas.
5. **Net zero energy balance and classification:** Once both the building energy use and the renewable energy generation values are converted to energy emissions, follow the same methodology used for the site energy calculation to determine the net zero energy emissions balance and the net zero energy classification.

of the calculations. This example, too, builds on the project described for the site energy calculation. The carbon emission factors to convert site energy to energy emissions can be found later in this chapter; the carbon emission factor for electricity can be found in the Carbon Emission Factors for Electricity by State map, shown in Figure 11.9. Although a national average for the electricity source energy factor is used, the map also contains carbon emission factors by state. The carbon emissions factor for natural gas is found in the Carbon Emission Factors for On-site Combustion table, provided in Figure 11.7. To derive the carbon emission factor for thermal energy, this project example assumes natural gas, with a commercial boiler. The project here achieves a Classification B net zero energy emissions balance.

Net Zero Energy Costs

A net zero energy cost building receives at least as much financial credit for exported renewable energy as it is charged for energy and energy services by the utility, over the course of a year. In this definition, the monetary credit from the renewable energy systems is equal to or greater than the monetary cost for utility-based nonrenewable energy use.

The project's utility rate structure can make the calculation of net zero energy costs complex and very challenging to achieve. Utility rates for electricity are based on both a use charge for each kWh consumed and a peak demand charge based on the project's peak demand. Some utilities combine the use and demand portions into a single time-of-use rate that varies based on demand. The use charge is relatively easy to account for, whereas the peak demand charge can vary widely. In addition, utility rates will vary over time, impacting the calculation into future years of net zero energy operation. Utility bills also include a number of fees and taxes that need to be accounted for in the net zero energy cost balance.

Ultimately, this measure should be based on actual utility bills during building operation, rather than a calculation. Estimated energy cost calculations can be made during the design phase, or if the building does not receive an individual utility bill. However, it is difficult to quantify the many complex variables involved in the calculation. The methodology proposed here is a simplified one that mirrors the calculation methods for the source and emissions measure; specifically, the many variables associated with utility costs and renewable energy credits are broadly estimated, and a blended utility rate is assumed. Furthermore, in lieu of tracking separate peak demand charges, fees, and taxes, in addition to use charges, this methodology requires the calculation of a blended rate for each utility that accommodates an estimate for all charges.

More rigorous calculation methods can be developed and used by the project delivery team if deemed appropriate, especially if peak demand can be estimated from the energy model. Further, to estimate the renewable energy credit from exporting to the grid, on-site renewable electricity generation will have to be multiplied by a discounted blended utility rate. The rate should be discounted to account for net-metering policies and the net effect that the renewable energy generation will have on demand and other utility charges.

The example in Figure 11.4 shows the simplified net zero energy cost balance calculations in a spreadsheet format to illustrate the workflow of the calculations. This example, too, builds on the project described for the site energy calculation. The blended utility rates to convert site energy use to energy costs are hypothetical but typical of national averages. Here, the blended utility rate for electricity is discounted by 10 percent to approximate the effective credit for

Net Zero Energy Cost Balance Method

1. **Net zero energy cost balance:** Complete the site energy calculations as a prerequisite to calculating energy costs.
2. **Utility rates:** Determine the appropriate blended utility rate for each utility-based energy source used on the project.
3. **Design or operational energy costs:** Multiply the blended utility rates for each utility-based energy source by the annual site energy use for each fuel energy source, respectively. This will result in a dollar value for each utility-based energy source, and the sum of these values will equal the total energy cost for design or operational energy use.
4. **Renewable energy:** Multiply the renewable energy generation for each of the project's systems by an appropriately discounted blended utility rate.
5. **Net zero energy balance and classification:** Once both the building energy use and the renewable energy generation values are converted to monetary values, follow the same methodology used for the site energy calculation to determine the net zero energy cost balance and the net zero energy classification.

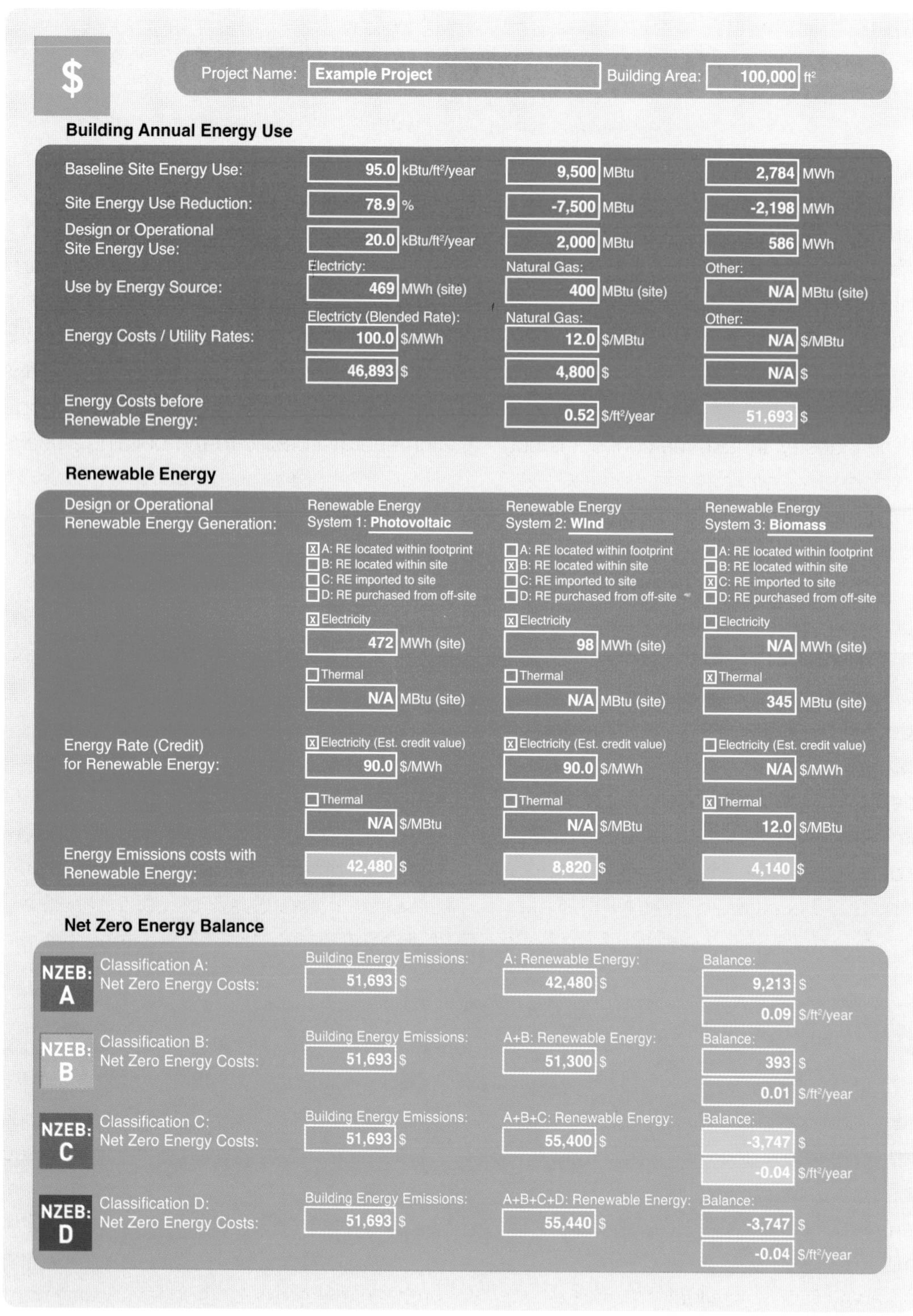

$

Project Name: Example Project | Building Area: 100,000 ft²

Building Annual Energy Use

Baseline Site Energy Use:	95.0 kBtu/ft²/year	9,500 MBtu	2,784 MWh
Site Energy Use Reduction:	78.9 %	-7,500 MBtu	-2,198 MWh
Design or Operational Site Energy Use:	20.0 kBtu/ft²/year	2,000 MBtu	586 MWh
Use by Energy Source:	Electricty: 469 MWh (site)	Natural Gas: 400 MBtu (site)	Other: N/A MBtu (site)
Energy Costs / Utility Rates:	Electricty (Blended Rate): 100.0 $/MWh	Natural Gas: 12.0 $/MBtu	Other: N/A $/MBtu
	46,893 $	4,800 $	N/A $
Energy Costs before Renewable Energy:		0.52 $/ft²/year	51,693 $

Renewable Energy

Design or Operational Renewable Energy Generation:	Renewable Energy System 1: **Photovoltaic**	Renewable Energy System 2: **Wind**	Renewable Energy System 3: **Biomass**
	[X] A: RE located within footprint [ ] B: RE located within site [ ] C: RE imported to site [ ] D: RE purchased from off-site	[ ] A: RE located within footprint [X] B: RE located within site [ ] C: RE imported to site [ ] D: RE purchased from off-site	[ ] A: RE located within footprint [ ] B: RE located within site [X] C: RE imported to site [ ] D: RE purchased from off-site
	[X] Electricity 472 MWh (site)	[X] Electricity 98 MWh (site)	[ ] Electricity N/A MWh (site)
	[ ] Thermal N/A MBtu (site)	[ ] Thermal N/A MBtu (site)	[X] Thermal 345 MBtu (site)
Energy Rate (Credit) for Renewable Energy:	[X] Electricity (Est. credit value) 90.0 $/MWh	[X] Electricity (Est. credit value) 90.0 $/MWh	[ ] Electricity (Est. credit value) N/A $/MWh
	[ ] Thermal N/A $/MBtu	[ ] Thermal N/A $/MBtu	[X] Thermal 12.0 $/MBtu
Energy Emissions costs with Renewable Energy:	42,480 $	8,820 $	4,140 $

Net Zero Energy Balance

NZEB: A — Classification A: Net Zero Energy Costs:	Building Energy Emissions: 51,693 $	A: Renewable Energy: 42,480 $	Balance: 9,213 $ 0.09 $/ft²/year
NZEB: B — Classification B: Net Zero Energy Costs:	Building Energy Emissions: 51,693 $	A+B: Renewable Energy: 51,300 $	Balance: 393 $ 0.01 $/ft²/year
NZEB: C — Classification C: Net Zero Energy Costs:	Building Energy Emissions: 51,693 $	A+B+C: Renewable Energy: 55,400 $	Balance: -3,747 $ -0.04 $/ft²/year
NZEB: D — Classification D: Net Zero Energy Costs:	Building Energy Emissions: 51,693 $	A+B+C+D: Renewable Energy: 55,440 $	Balance: -3,747 $ -0.04 $/ft²/year

■ **FIGURE 11.4** Net Zero Energy Cost Balance.

on-site renewable energy. If peak demand is not effectively managed and reduced, the discount might need to be greater.

Because these factors are approximate, it may also be helpful to run the calculation bracketed within a range of discounted rates. The biomass thermal energy offset is simpler to account for because it is not net-metered, and it directly offsets natural gas, which has no peak demand charges. In this example, the project achieves a Classification C net zero energy cost balance.

CARBON NEUTRALITY

Net Zero Energy and Carbon Neutrality

The terms *net zero energy* and *net zero energy emissions* have been well defined by the National Renewable Energy Laboratory; they apply specifically to the net zero fossil use of annual building energy use. *Carbon neutrality* is a broader term and so is less well defined within the industry. In fact, the concept is not building-industry-centric; it accounts for carbon emissions from all sources. But in terms of commercial architecture projects, carbon neutrality can be considered to include operational energy carbon emissions as well as embodied carbon emissions from the construction of the project, and carbon emissions related to the transportation energy intensity of a project. Note that *carbon* is used here to mean carbon-dioxide-equivalent greenhouse gases.

It is important to note that the definition used by the 2030 Challenge for carbon neutrality by 2030 is different from NREL's net zero energy emissions measure. The goal of the 2030 Challenge is complete carbon neutrality, and does not account for a "net" zero result; rather, it is seeking an absolute zero result. To meet this definition, a building would need to be off-grid or grid-connected to a 100 percent renewable energy grid. We are a long way from having grid-based power that is 100 percent renewable, but it does call attention to the importance of moving our electricity generation away from fossil fuels.

Carbon Footprint

Carbon neutrality requires the delineation of a carbon footprint boundary, to define the scope of carbon emissions for a project. The time frame for a carbon footprint can be for the construction scope or annual or lifetime carbon emissions of a project. To calculate a carbon footprint for a project, carbon accounting principles are applied to carbon emission activities and renewable energy or carbon sequestering activities that offset total carbon emissions.

A typical carbon footprint for a building project would account for the annual carbon emissions from energy use, embodied carbon construction and land use changes (annualized over the life of the project), and annual carbon emissions related to the transportation energy specific to the building's use (see Figure 11.5). The site boundary can generally be taken as the operation and construction carbon footprint boundary; but the carbon emission scope extends beyond this boundary. For example, the manufacture and transportation carbon related to the construction materials brought to the job site produce emissions outside the site boundary.

Carbon Accounting Basics

The globally accepted method for carbon accounting has been developed through the Greenhouse Gas Protocol Initiative, a joint effort of the World Resources Institute (WRI) and the World Business Council for Sustainable Development (WBCSD). The protocols for carbon accounting are comprehensive and apply to a wide range of industry sectors. The Greenhouse Gas Protocol Initiative provides specific guidance for sectors such as agriculture, products, greenhouse gas reduction projects, and corporations. While specific guidance for carbon accounting for architectural projects in general is limited, the principles can be applied to commercial architectural projects.

The core principle for carbon accounting is to organize the carbon emission activities into three distinct carbon emission scopes: scope 1, scope 2, and scope 3 (see Figure 11.6). The division into scopes allows for carbon accounting

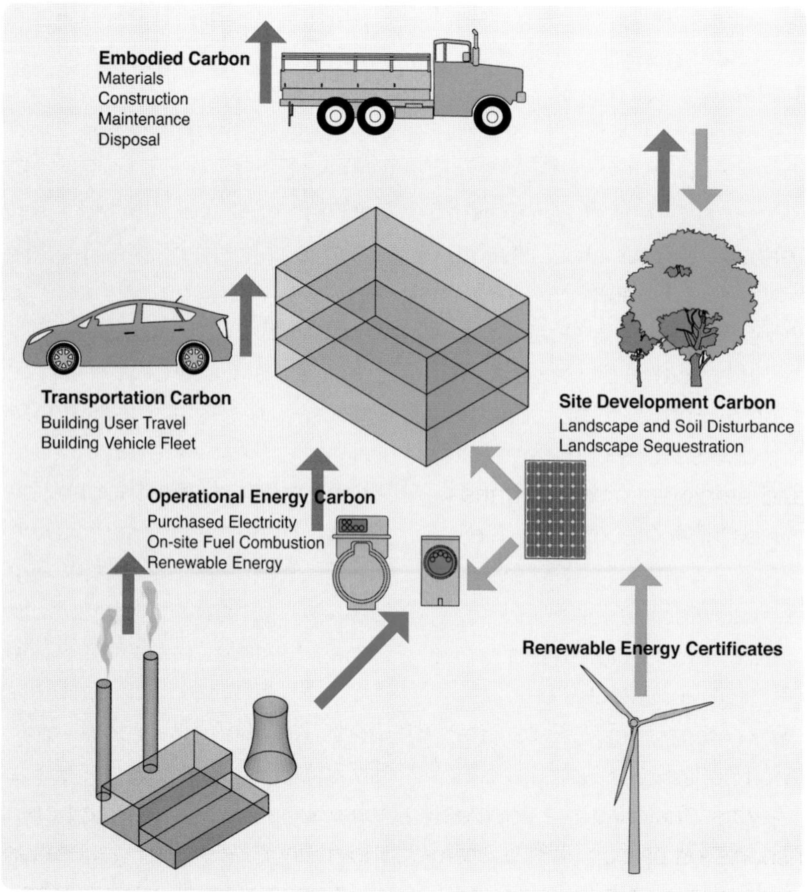

■ **FIGURE 11.5** Building Carbon Footprint.

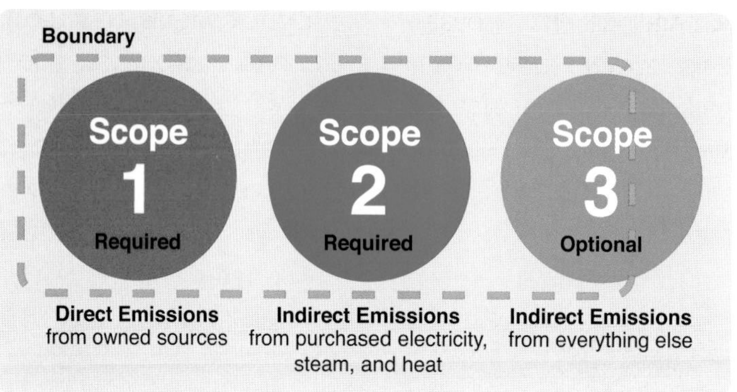

■ **FIGURE 11.6** Greenhouse Gas Emission Scopes.

without double-counting emissions; it also serves to define the relationship of the project and project owner to the various emissions.

- Scope 1 emissions are those related to owned sources of carbon emission activities. For example, a natural gas boiler onsite would be a direct emission activity, hence be considered scope 1.
- Scope 2 emissions are indirect emissions from purchased energy sources such as electricity or steam. In the case of electricity, the power company accounts for the emissions as scope 1, and the building owner claims their electricity use as scope 2.
- Scope 3 emissions are a broad category, inclusive of all other indirect emissions.

According to the aforementioned greenhouse gas accounting protocol, scope 3 emissions are voluntary. This allows a great deal of flexibility in defining the carbon footprint boundary for a project. By including more activities in scope 3, a project team and owner can influence a broader reduction in total carbon emissions. Some of the emission activities that can come under the category of scope 3 of an architectural project include the embodied carbon from construction, the carbon emissions and sequestering from site development, and employee or visitor transportation energy related to traveling to and from the building.

Carbon neutrality for scope 1 and scope 2 emissions is generally equivalent to the net zero energy emissions definition and can be readily achieved with a net zero energy building. In contrast, full carbon neutrality is far more challenging to achieve when factoring in embodied carbon and transportation carbon. It may, therefore, be useful to develop a carbon emission baseline for the same carbon footprint boundary as the design case. Operational energy baselines are relatively straightforward to establish, by following the same energy use baseline for the project and converting to carbon emissions using the appropriate carbon emission factors. Creating baseline carbon emissions for scope 3 requires developing baseline assumptions for the building construction or transportation patterns. There is no common set of requirements for these assumptions, and they should be developed on a project-by-project basis to help inform decision making and increase the potential for additional carbon emission reductions.

Operational Carbon

A building's operational energy carbon is the carbon-dioxide-equivalent emissions resulting from its annual energy use. These emissions fall into scope 1 for any owned, on-site combustion equipment for thermal or electrical energy generation, and into scope 2 for energy purchased through a utility. The operational energy carbon is calculated using a carbon emission factor specific to the energy source, and converts site energy use into the mass of CO_{2e} emitted. Carbon emission factors vary widely, depending on the fuel and the method of energy generation.

For commercial projects with on-site combustion for electrical or thermal energy generation, the table in Figure 11.7 summarizes carbon emission factors for on-site combustion, as calculated in the NREL paper, "Source Energy and Emission Factors for Energy Use in Buildings," by Michael Deru and Paul Torcellini. These factors include both precombustion

Fuel Delivered to Building	On-site Combustion Equipment		
	Commercial Boiler	Stationary Reciprocating Engine	Small Turbine
Coal (Bituminous)	0.107	–	–
Coal (Lignite)	0.158	–	–
Natural Gas	0.066	0.073	0.067
Residual Fuel Oil	0.094	–	–
Distillate Fuel Oil	0.088	0.088	0.088
LPG	0.079	–	–
Gasoline	–	.077	–

■ **FIGURE 11.7** Carbon Emission Factors for On-site Combustion. *Source: M. Deru and P. Torcellini, "Source Energy and Emission Factors for Energy Use in Buildings," Table 6 and Table 10.*

emissions associated with the fuel choice and combustion emissions. Precombustion effects include the emissions related to extracting, processing, and delivering the fuel to the building. The units for the factors are in metric tons of CO_{2e} per MBtu of site energy.

Carbon emission factors for electricity generation are complex and far more difficult to estimate. The emissions are tied to the energy source used to generate the electricity, such as coal, natural gas, wind, and hydro, among others. Renewable energy sources and nuclear energy have no carbon emissions, unlike fossil fuel sources, which do produce emissions. Each utility and each region of the grid blends a unique mix of fuel to generate electricity. That said, the nation's grid is dominated by fossil fuel use for electricity generation. However, some regions, such as the Pacific Northwest, have a significant amount of hydropower; others, nuclear energy (see Figure 11.8). The adherence to renewable portfolio standards by many states has begun to increase the amount of renewable energy on the grid. The relationship of carbon emissions to energy generation is similar to that of source energy factors and energy generation. (Refer to Chapter 4 for an overview of source energy and source energy factors as they relate to the nation's electrical grid.)

The map in Figure 11.9 provides carbon emission factors by state in units of metric tons of CO_{2e} per MWh of electricity, as summarized from data in the aforementioned NREL paper, "Source Energy and Emission Factors for Energy Use in Buildings," by Michael Deru and Paul Torcellini. These factors include both precombustion emissions associated with the fuel choice and combustion emissions. Because electricity is often imported and exported between states, carbon emission factors for states with high import levels should be used with some caution.

Another source of carbon emissions information is the EPA's eGRID, available through a user-friendly web interface called eGRIDweb at http://cfpub.epa.gov/egridweb/index.cfm. eGRID is a well-maintained database of greenhouse gas emissions related to electricity generation in the United States (www.epa.gov/egid). The eGRID dataset is available in a variety of formats and regions, including national average, states, grid regions, utility companies, and individual power plants. (A related EPA web-based tool called Power Profiler, found at www.epa.gov/powerprofiler, provides carbon emission factors

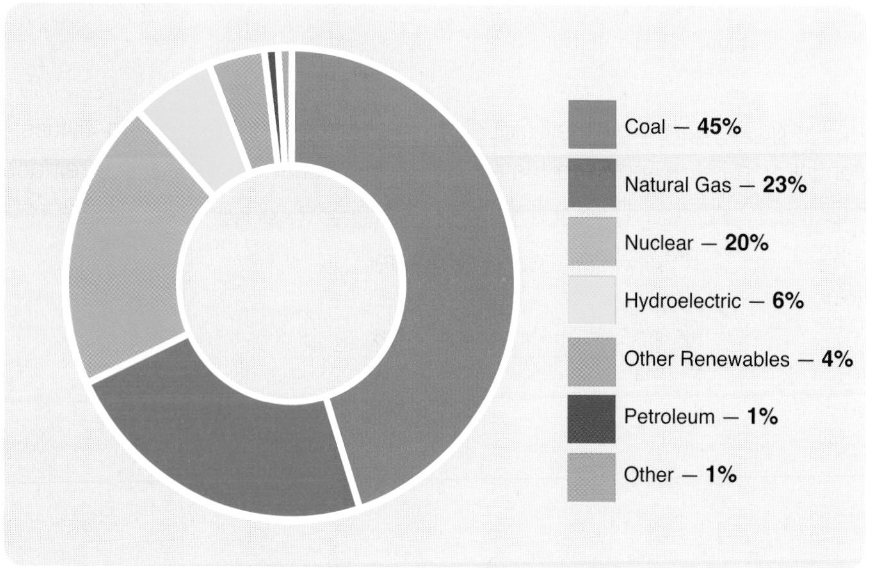

■ **FIGURE 11.8** U.S. Electricity Generation by Fuel (2010). *Data source: U.S. Energy Information Administration.*

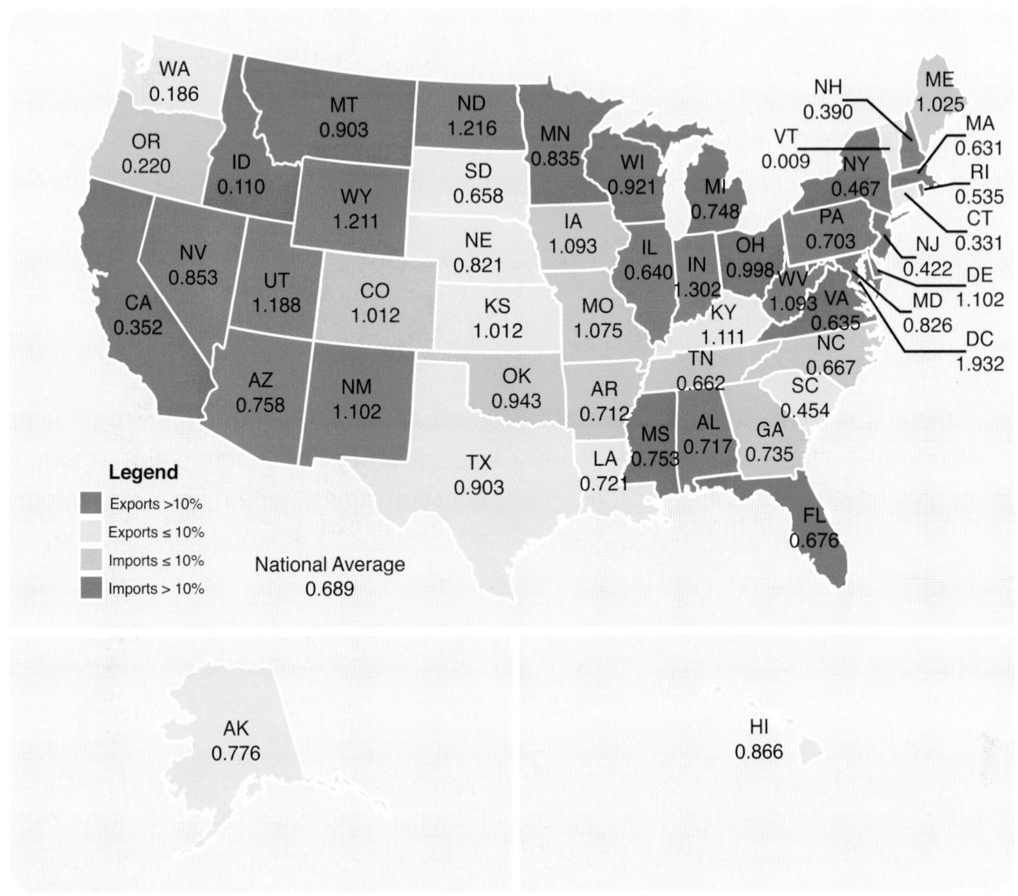

■ **FIGURE 11.9** Carbon Emission Factors for Electricity by State (2004): Metric Tons CO_{2e}/MWh. *M. Deru and P. Torcellini, "Source Energy and Emission Factors for Energy Use in Buildings," Table B-3, Table B-5, and Table B-10.*

and such data as local fuel mix used for electricity generation based on zip code.) While eGRID represents the most current data for carbon emission factors, they are not recorded in terms of CO_{2e}; rather, individual greenhouse gas emissions are recorded. These cannot simply be added because CO_{2e} is a weighted factor that includes other greenhouse gases based on their global warming potential, and is converted to the equivalent mass of CO_2. Further, eGRID data does not account for precombustion effects, which can account for 10 percent of CO_{2e} emissions.

Embodied Carbon

Embodied carbon is gaining importance in the overall discussion about carbon neutrality. According to the United Nations Environment Programme (UNEP), operational energy use accounts for 80 to 90 percent of a building's life-cycle emissions, with the remaining 10 to 20 percent in embodied carbon emissions. However, as buildings become quantifiably more energy-efficient, the percentage of embodied carbon will increase. For a net zero energy building, the embodied carbon can be the largest remaining source of emissions.

Embodied carbon for a building encompasses the initial construction activities; the ongoing maintenance, repair, and replacement of the building and building components; and the final demolition or deconstruction of the building. The construction-related embodied carbon involves the individual materials and products that make up the construction, as well as the actual construction activity at the job site. Materials and products that arrive at the job site produce carbon emissions related to raw material extraction, manufacturing, and transportation.

Calculating embodied carbon is complex. Life-cycle assessment (LCA) is a method for

Embodied Carbon Resources and Tools

- Construction Carbon Calculator (www.buildcarbonneutral.org): A free and simple online carbon calculator to compute a general estimate of carbon emissions related to construction.
- Athena Institute (www.athenasmi.org): A nonprofit focused on advancing life-cycle assessment within the North American building community by developing resources and tools and offering consulting services.
- ATHENA EcoCalculator for Assemblies: A free life-cycle assessment calculator for common commercial and residential building assemblies, developed by the Athena Institute.
- ATHENA Impact Estimator for Buildings: A commercially available life-cycle assessment program for whole buildings and assemblies, developed by the Athena Institute.
- U.S. Life Cycle Inventory Database (www.nrel.gov/lci): A publicly available life-cycle assessment database of materials developed by NREL.
- Simapro (www.simapro-lca.com): Commercially available life-cycle assessment program developed by Sustainmetrics; available in the United States and the United Kingdom.
- Ecoinvent (www.ecoinvent.org): A subscription-based comprehensive life-cycle inventory database developed by the Ecoinvent Centre.
- Inventory of Carbon and Energy (ICE) (www.bath.ac.uk/mech-eng/sert/embodied): An embodied carbon and energy database developed by the University of Bath.
- DOE Building Energy Data Book (http://buildingsdatabook.eren.doe.gov): Includes tables of embodied energy and carbon for common building assemblies.

calculating the whole life-cycle impact of a project; it is different from the life-cycle cost analysis (LCC) discussed in Chapter 9. LCA can provide a range of analyses on environmental impacts, including greenhouse gas emissions. The focus on net zero energy and carbon-neutral buildings, coupled with the emergence of tools and data, should help to mainstream this evaluation.

Site Development Carbon

Calculations of embodied carbon focus on construction materials, but it is important to keep in mind that a project's soil and vegetation also sequester and release carbon. Site construction activities can disturb soil and vegetation and contribute to carbon emissions. In addition, site development choices for new landscape installation or existing landscape preservation can provide opportunities to sequester carbon.

The role of the landscape in carbon emissions is part of the larger global carbon cycle of the earth, specifically, the photosynthesis and respiration process of plant life. Vegetation and soil help sequester fossil fuel carbon emissions, in addition to the natural carbon cycle. According the EPA, of the 6.3 gigatons of carbon emitted from fossil fuel combustion, 2.3 gigatons of carbon are sequestered by the earth's vegetation and soils. Subsequently, land use changes and deforestation release 1.6 gigatons of carbon back into the atmosphere (see Figure 11.10).

Forestlands play a large role in terrestrial carbon sequestering, too, as do urban trees and forests (see Figure 11.11). In the report "Carbon Storage and Sequestration by Urban Trees in the USA," authors David J. Nowak and Daniel E. Crane estimate that the trees in the continental United States store 700 million tons of carbon, and sequester 22.8 million tons

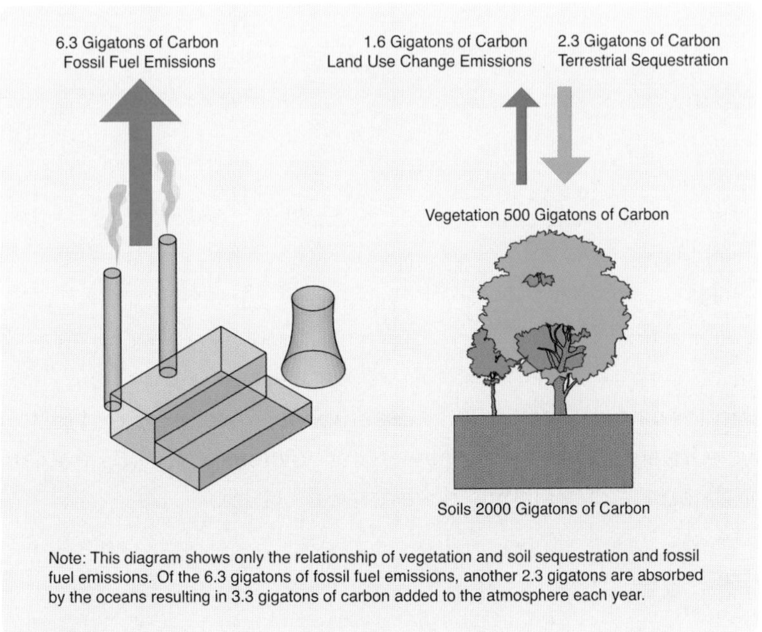
6.3 Gigatons of Carbon
Fossil Fuel Emissions
1.6 Gigatons of Carbon
Land Use Change Emissions
2.3 Gigatons of Carbon
Terrestrial Sequestration
Vegetation 500 Gigatons of Carbon
Soils 2000 Gigatons of Carbon
Note: This diagram shows only the relationship of vegetation and soil sequestration and fossil fuel emissions. Of the 6.3 gigatons of fossil fuel emissions, another 2.3 gigatons are absorbed by the oceans resulting in 3.3 gigatons of carbon added to the atmosphere each year.

■ **FIGURE 11.10** Terrestrial Sequestration of Fossil Fuel Emissions. *EPA, "Carbon Sequestration in Agriculture and Forestry," www.epa.gov/sequestration/index.html. Accessed October 16, 2011.*

per year. The EPA estimates that one urban coniferous tree sequesters 0.039 metric tons of CO_2 during its first 10 years of growth from a seedling, and that an acre of pine or fir forest sequesters 4.69 metric tons of CO_2 per year.

Carbon sequestration in vegetation and soils is generally a function of biomass density. High-biomass-density landscapes, such as forests and wetlands, can sequester more carbon than lower-density landscapes. Landscapes such as prairie grasslands have limited woody biomass; they sequester primarily in the soils. Most of the research on terrestrial carbon sequestration is in relation to large land uses changes and forestry practices. There are few tools developed specifically for use on architectural and site development projects. The exception is the Construction Carbon Calculator, at www.buildcarbonneutral.org, an online tool that accounts for landscape considerations.

The carbon balance contribution to landscape installations or preservations for commercial projects is typically small, compared to the embodied carbon of buildings and their annual operational energy carbon emissions; nevertheless, there is still an opportunity to leverage landscape design in the overall planning for net zero energy projects and carbon-neutral projects. Projects with large sites or master plan and campus or community projects offer good opportunities. A strategy for site-constrained projects is to make preservation or restoration of off-site forestland or other high-biomass-density lands a part of project planning and implementation.

■ **FIGURE 11.11** New York's Central Park is a beautiful urban amenity, but also a major source of carbon sequestration.

Transportation Carbon

Many site selection and building and site design decisions impact the transportation energy and carbon emissions associated with a commercial building. The location of a building has major implications for the transportation energy intensity of a project. Is the site centrally located and close to public transit and bike paths? Is it in a walkable neighborhood? Or is it remotely located and without access to public transit, bike paths, and pedestrian connections? These types of location considerations influence, first, whether people have to drive to access the building, and second, how far they will have to go to do so. Building and site design and program decisions, such as parking capacity, distance to bike or pedestrian connections, and access to changing facilities for cyclists, also influence people's transportation choices.

According to the DOE's *Transportation Energy Data Book*, Edition 30, 2011, the average fuel economy of light trucks and cars is 20.2 miles per gallon. According to the same study, the average commute to work is 12.2 miles each way, and the average vehicular trip for all types of trips is 9.7 miles. The average round-trip commute to work is then 24.4 miles at 20.2 miles per gallon, or 1.21 gallons of gas. A gallon of gas produces 19.4 pounds of CO_2 when combusted. For a 24.4-mile round-trip commute, that comes to 23.4 pounds of CO_2, or almost a pound a mile.

The transportation carbon linked to a building can rival the operational carbon in energy buildings. In low-energy buildings, the transportation carbon can be substantially greater. Take, for example, a low-energy office building with an energy use intensity of 30 kBtu/ft^2/year. Using the national average carbon emission factor for grid electricity of 1.52 pounds of CO_2 per kWh, the carbon intensity of the office building would be 13.36 lb CO_2/ft^2/year. If the office has an occupancy density of 250 ft^2 per person, the carbon intensity per person for operational energy would be 3,341 lb CO_2/person/year. Using the average fuel efficiency and round-trip commute as just discussed for a 260-workday year, and assuming everyone drives a single-occupancy vehicle to work, the carbon intensity per person for transportation energy would be 6,093 lb CO_2/person/year (see Figure 11.12).

For projects wishing to include transportation carbon as a scope 3 component in their carbon footprint, an estimate can be made using the national averages for vehicle miles traveled and average fuel efficiency. If the occupants can be surveyed on their traveling patterns associated with the project and the fuel efficiency of their vehicles, greater accuracy can be achieved. A baseline case can then be developed, and part of the project objective can be to find ways of reducing vehicle miles traveled, through incentive programs, site location, and design features that promote alternative transportation. If the

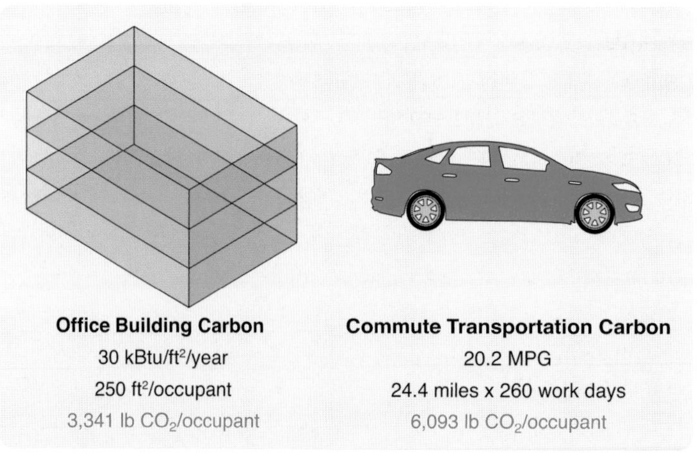

■ **FIGURE 11.12** Example comparing carbon intensity of building energy with transportation energy for an office building.

project will have a fleet of vehicles owned by the building owner, these vehicles will be considered scope 1 emissions for the owner, and can be included in the carbon footprint analysis.

Carbon Offsets

The on-site renewable energy generation for net zero energy buildings offsets carbon emissions related to building operational energy, as defined in the "Net Zero Energy Emissions" section earlier in the chapter. The carbon emissions related to embodied energy, site development, and transportation energy can be effectively reduced with careful planning, though they can be more challenging to offset completely.

One approach to offset the embodied carbon in a net zero energy building is to incorporate a surplus of renewable energy capacity that can act as a contingency for operational energy; it may also be applied to offsetting the embodied carbon over the service life of the building. This would require adding to the budget for renewable energy, in concert with careful planning to reduce the embodied carbon. As a word of caution to this approach, it is important to consider the net-metering policy of the local utility company. If the building exports excess energy to the grid on an annual basis, most utility companies will pay only a wholesale rate, rather than a retail rate, for the excess generation. This would have to be incorporated into the financial analysis of the renewable energy system.

For example, if a net zero energy project has an embodied carbon of 2,000 metric tons, and using the national average carbon emission factor of 1.52 pounds of CO_2 per kWh for grid-based electricity, it would require 58,016 kWh of additional renewable energy generation per year for a 50-year building life to offset the embodied carbon. Depending on the project's location, this could result in approximately 40 to 50 kW of additional installed PV.

Another approach to addressing embodied carbon, site development carbon, and transportation carbon is for the owner or the project to purchase carbon offsets. Carbon offsets should, however, be applied only after efforts have been made to reduce the overall carbon footprint of the project. One type of carbon offset that a net zero energy building team will already be familiar with is the use of renewable energy certificates (RECs). The project must retain or purchase replacement RECs for on-site renewable energy generation to claim net zero energy status. There are many other types of carbon offset that can be purchased. The purchase of a carbon offset allows building owners to claim the carbon reduction against their project footprint; it also spurs investment in carbon reduction projects, locally and globally.

There are many types of carbon reduction projects that provide offset credits for purchase through retailers. Projects fall into two distinct types: emission reduction and carbon sequestration. Emission reduction projects can include renewable energy generation projects of all types. Emission reduction projects can also include energy-efficiency projects and projects that destroy industrial pollutants that cause climate change. Sequestration projects are land use and forestry projects that increase terrestrial carbon sequestration.

If considering carbon offsets as part of a project's carbon neutrality strategy, note that it is important to purchase them through credible retailers and organizations, and ensure that the credits comply with a globally accepted third-party standard. One of the characteristics that defines a quality carbon offset is the issue of additionality. Additionality means that the offset is funding a carbon reduction project that creates additional benefit, which would not have been possible otherwise. Another consideration when evaluating an offset for a project is to choose one that is meaningful to the project or owner. Perhaps it helps fund a local carbon reduction project, or is tied to a type of carbon reduction project that is meaningful to the owner's mission.

Image courtesy of RNL; photograph by Ron Pollard.

CS CHAPTER 12
CASE STUDY: DOE/NREL RESEARCH SUPPORT FACILITY

INTRODUCTION

The U.S. Department of Energy's Research Support Facility (RSF) at the National Renewable Energy Laboratory (NREL) campus in Golden, Colorado, is a 222,000-square-foot federal office building housing more than 800 people who support and conduct important research work at this national laboratory (see Figures 12.1 and 12.2). The building also houses a data center that serves the entire NREL campus. The project was designed to replace leased office space, located outside of the NREL campus, with a government-owned facility located on-site, next to the laboratory buildings the facility supports.

The goal of NREL and DOE is to transform innovative research in renewable energy and energy efficiency into market-viable technologies and practices. The RSF building serves as an example of these ideas and is a living laboratory for the staff of the RSF to learn from and work by. The resulting project is one of the most energy-efficient buildings in the world, providing a high-performance workplace, one that is on track to operate at net zero energy on an annual basis. One of the aspirations of the project was to create an industry prototype that demonstrates a replicable net zero energy approach for large-scale commercial buildings.

■ **FIGURE 12.1** The DOE/NREL Research Support Facility; view of east façade and main entry. *Image courtesy of RNL; photograph by Frank Ooms.*

■ **FIGURE 12.2** The DOE/NREL Research Support Facility; view of west façade. *Image courtesy of RNL; photograph by Frank Ooms.*

Project Data

Project Name: National Renewable Energy Laboratory Research Support Facility

Location: Golden, Colorado, 80401

Building Type: Federal Office Building

Building Area: 222,000 ft^2

Owner/Client: U.S. Department of Energy and National Renewable Energy Laboratory

M&O Contractor: Alliance for Sustainable Energy, LLC

Design-Build RFP Consultant: Design Sense, Inc.

Owner's Representative: Northstar Project Management

PROCESS

One of the key process innovations for the DOE/NREL Research Support Facility was the use of a performance-based design-build delivery method. This delivery approach was set in motion in an innovative RFP and acquisition process. An RFQ process, which resulted in a short list of three firms, preceded the RFP. The short-listed firms were composed of design-build teams, and responded to the RFP in the form of a competition. The competition included the development of a concept design that best met the RFP requirements, including the performance requirements and the firm fixed price for the project. The performance requirements differed from prescriptive requirements by focusing on *what* the project should do, not *how* it should do it. A performance-based approach basically involves defining the requirements and budget, and asking for the design solution, rather than providing the design and asking for the price.

The owner believed that the scope and objectives might exceed the budget. So instead of reducing the scope, the RFP prioritized it and the objectives of the project. This resulted in a prioritized performance objective list of 26 items, categorized according to three priority tiers: *mission-critical*, *highly desirable*, and *if possible*. The performance objectives defined requirements, such as LEED Platinum certification (mission-critical); accommodate up to 800 staff (highly desirable); an absolute energy use target for the building of 25 kBtu/ft^2/year (highly desirable); and follow a net zero energy design approach (if possible).

DOE and NREL's procurement process was aimed at gaining the most value from a fixed-budget project and creating a contractual structure that supported integrated design and leveraged the innovation of the private sector. The resulting integrated delivery process was driven by performance yet constrained by budget and schedule.

The delivery process included many best practices of integrated delivery. The delivery team readily aligned around the goal of net zero energy and began the process with a multiple-day charrette, to develop a concept design and take a competitive approach. The delivery team quickly reached the conclusion that to win the competition it was critical to find a way of delivering all the project objectives, even the challenging (and lower-ranking) net zero energy design objective. In fact, aligning around net zero energy became a strong catalyst for pulling all of the objectives together.

Energy modeling was used extensively throughout the process as both a design decision-making tool and an assessment tool, to gauge how the team was doing with respect to the energy target and the net zero energy goal. The energy modeling began on day one of the charrette; it continues to be used to this day for building operations. At the charrette were representatives of the whole delivery team, including contractors, designers, engineers, and consultants, all of whom brainstormed and integrated

Project Team

General contractor: Haselden Construction

Architect: RNL

MEP engineer: Stantec

Structural engineer: KL&A

Civil engineer: Martin/Martin

Interior design: RNL

Landscape architect: RNL

Energy modeling: Stantec

Daylight modeling: Architectural Energy Corporation

LEED consulting: Architectural Energy Corporation

Commissioning: Architectural Energy Corporation

Measurement and verification: Architectural Energy Corporation

Renewable energy consultant: Namaste Solar

Process Data

Procurement Method

- Request for Qualifications (RFQ) to short-list three firms
- Request for Proposal (RFP) with design competition and firm fixed price

Delivery Method

- Performance-based design-build; fast-track

Schedule

- Owner planning and beginning of RFP development, including the building program and performance specifications: April 2007
- RFP issued: February 2008
- Oral presentations by short-listed design-build firms: April 2008
- Design-build contract awarded: July 2008
- Preliminary design completed: November 2008
- Construction: February 2009 to June 2010
- Substantial completion and occupancy: June 2010
- Final completion: July 2010

potential solutions, to arrive at a general scheme and a favorable energy model by the end of the first week. The entire delivery process was influenced by the initial competition charrette, and maintained the same interdisciplinary approach to problem solving and decision making.

PROJECT ECONOMICS

The RSF was funded through a series of appropriations by Congress to a total project cost of about \$80 million. Of the \$80 million, \$64.3 million was allocated as the firm fixed price for the design-build contract for the RSF, meaning that only the owner could generate change orders, and that the design-build team had to manage risks and potential cost overruns within the budget. This price included the complete building, site, and infrastructure work; furniture and appliances; and all fees and associated soft costs for the design-build team. The price did not include the photovoltaic systems or the owner-provided equipment such as data center and IT equipment.

Of the \$64.3 million design-build contract amount, approximately \$57.4 million was the construction cost, after subtracting the cost of furniture, and appropriate soft costs. The resulting cost per square foot was \$259. This amount is highly competitive for government office buildings, but more problematic to compare to the private commercial office building market, because it tends to be divided into two separate costs—core and shell—and the various tenant improvement costs for the interior fit-outs.

The value of the energy savings of the RSF, compared to the energy use of the leased office, was substantial, at over $275,000 in the first year. Assuming a discount rate of 6 percent, and an energy escalation of 4 percent, the net present value of energy savings over 20 years is over $4.3 million, or approximately $20 per square foot. Over 30 years, the net present value is nearly $6.0 million, or approximately $27 per square foot.

The owner procured the renewable energy systems, comprising several photovoltaic systems, using two different procurement methods. The first system acquired was a 449 kW photovoltaic system for the roof of the RSF (see Figure 12.3), which was procured using a power purchase agreement (PPA). The remainder of the 1.6 MW system was purchased directly, using American Recovery and Revinvestment Act (ARRA) stimulus funding. The contract details of the PPA are confidential to the solar developer; and the final cost of the ARRA-funded arrays have yet to be determined, as the final photovoltaic system phase awaits installation at the time of this writing. It was not possible to take advantage of the federal tax credit for the ARRA-funded arrays. The market price at the time for photovoltaic systems at this scale is approximately $5 per watt, before incentives. In a September 2011 press release, issued by the Lawrence Berkeley National Laboratory, large-scale commercial photovoltaic projects were benchmarked at $5.20 per watt. For a 1.6 MW system, this would be approximately $8 million dollars.

■ **FIGURE 12.3** Installation of the roof-mounted photovoltaic system at the DOE/NREL Research Support Facility. It was acquired with a power purchase agreement. *NREL/PIX 17842; photograph by Dennis Schroeder.*

The economic feasibility for net zero energy was driven by the big picture, rather than incremental life cycle cost analysis (LCC) of multiple design options. The firm fixed price and the absolute energy target were important constraints. The budget could not be increased to enhance performance, nor could performance be reduced to meet the budget. What drove the solution was the integration of systems and strategies and the continual feedback loops of the cost and the energy models.

A unique aspect of the project's procurement method and economics was the use of an incentive award fee by DOE/NREL. The award fee totaled $2 million, and was outside of the original contract award. It was used to incentivize superior performance on the part of the delivery team and was awarded in six stages throughout the life of the project, based on team performance and monthly team performance assessments conducted by the owner.

Project Economic Data

Design-build contract firm fixed price: $64.3 million

Construction cost: $57.4 million (excludes furniture, interior design fees, and insurance)

Construction cost per square foot: $259/ft^2

Incentive award fee: $2 million

CLIMATE, SITE, AND PROGRAM

Climate

The climate for Golden, Colorado, is ideal for passive strategies. The location experiences wide seasonal variation, including hot summers and cold winters. The climate is heating dominated, but charts seasonal differences of over 100°F between the summertime highs and the wintertime lows. It is dry, as well, with low relative humidity year-round. The year-round sunshine is a tremendous asset for passive solar heating and solar electric power generation. And situated as it is next to the foothills of the Rocky Mountains, the location amplifies typical wind patterns; a site-specific wind study was conducted to assure pedestrian comfort in the building's courtyards and functional natural ventilation. Select climate data are diagrammed in Figures 12.4 to 12.7.

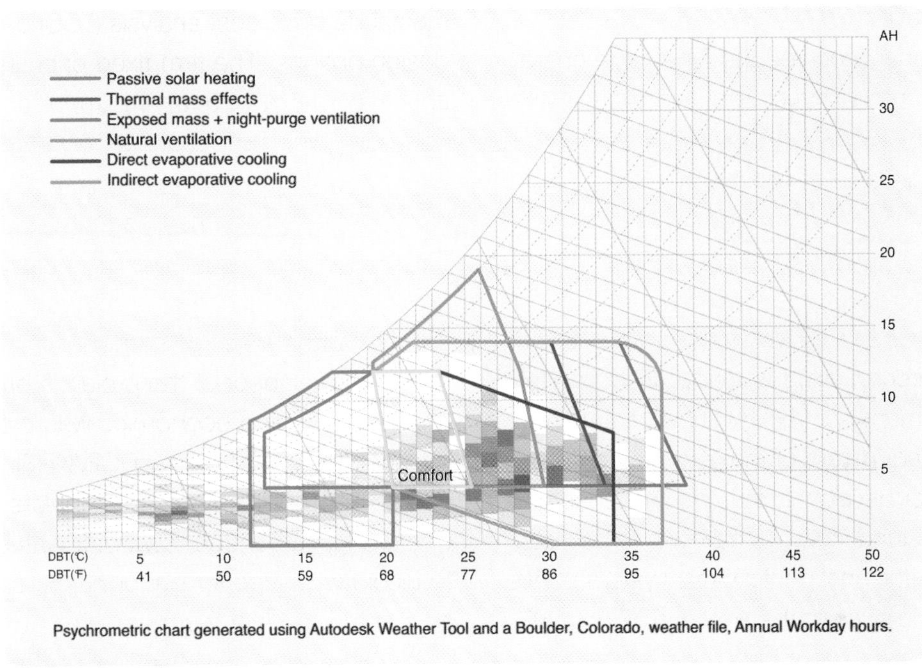

■ **FIGURE 12.4** Psychrometric Chart.

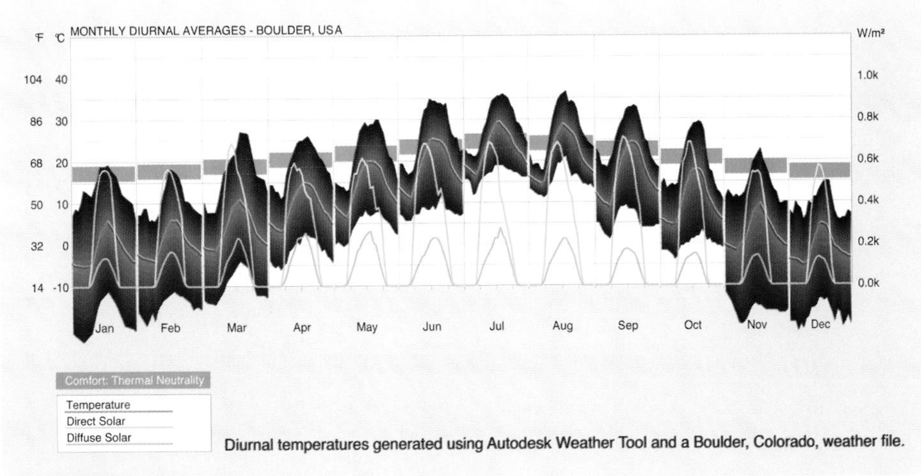

■ **FIGURE 12.5** Average Diurnal Temperatures.

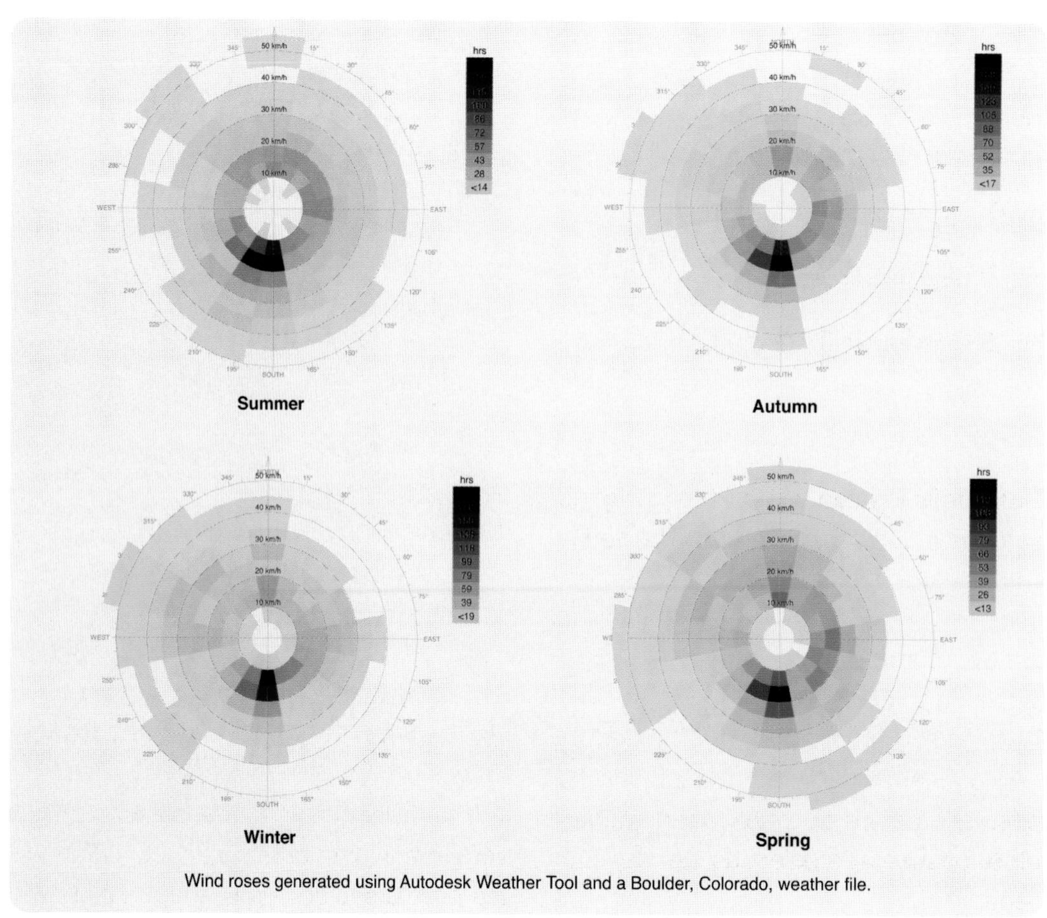

■ **FIGURE 12.6** Seasonal Wind Roses.

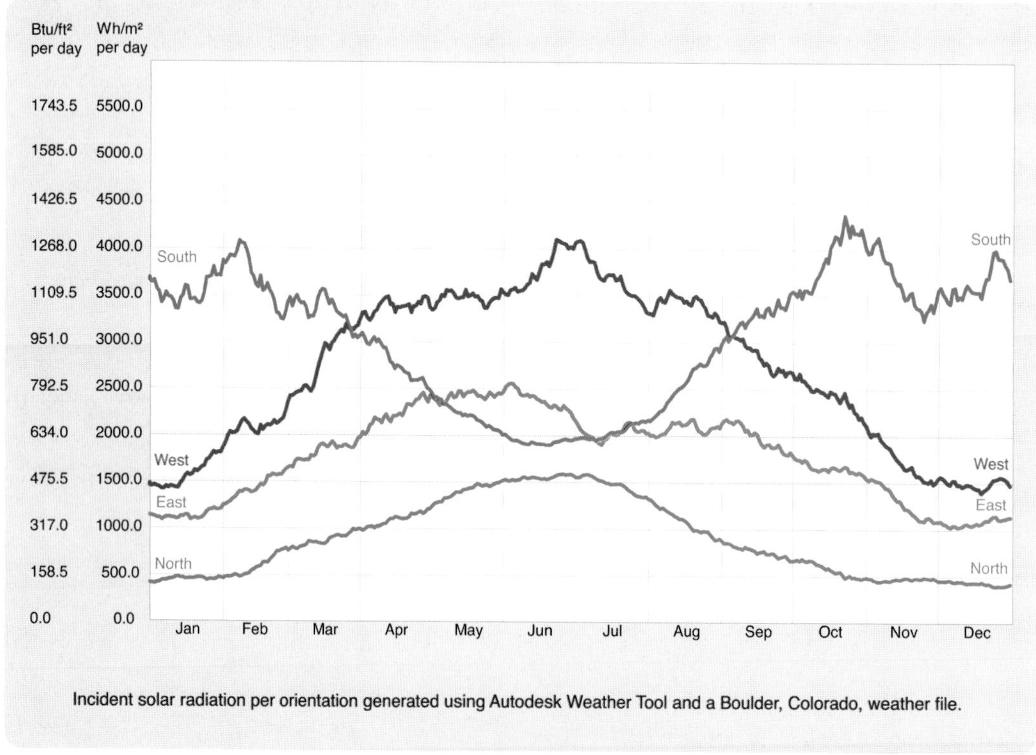

■ **FIGURE 12.7:** Annual Incident Solar Radiation on Exterior Walls.

Climate Data

Köppen climate classification: B, Arid-Steppe; cold

Climate zone: 5B; cool, dry

Heating degree-days base 65: 6,220

Cooling degree-days base 65: 1,154

Site Data

Latitude and longitude: 39°44′28″N; 105°10′16″W

Site area: 4.25 acres (no defined property line; campus setting)

Site context: Suburban

Building footprint area: 65,600 ft^2

Site

The RSF site is located within an existing federal campus in Golden, Colorado. The setting is a suburban context; the buildings on the campus are surrounded by naturally landscaped open space (see Figure 12.8). The RSF site has no defined property lines, but responds to the master plan of the campus. This campus setting allowed building massing and orientation to be optimized for daylighting and other passive strategies, as well as for solar energy.

The building's lazy-H shape has two wings that are 15° from being parallel to each other. The south wing of the RSF is located with a true east-west axis. The north wing of the RSF is 15° off-axis, at the same angle as the adjacent laboratory buildings and sloping topography of the toe of South Table Mountain to the north.

■ **FIGURE 12.8** Aerial view of the RSF, showing the third wing expansion under construction. *NREL/PIX 19089; photograph by Dennis Schroeder.*

Program

The RSF is primarily an office building. A small portion of the building program is dedicated to a data center, serving 1,200 staff members campuswide, at 65 watts per person. While relatively small in area, the data center energy use alone is about one-third of the entire energy use of the building.

The building has sizable conferencing facilities, to aid in its collaborative function with the private sector. The H-shaped plan, which optimizes passive energy, provided a unique opportunity to optimize the program. In the connector space between the two main office wings is the main building entry and lobby (see Figure 12.9); this is also where the main conference facilities are situated, creating a centralized and secure collaboration zone. Visiting collaborators and partners can conduct all their business with DOE/NREL without entering the main office wings.

The design of the RSF accommodates a population of 822 staff members, larger than the RFP requirements. The owner saw this increase in occupancy density as a benefit, even though it would heighten the energy use intensity. The RFP energy use intensity goal from the RFP was 25 kBtu/ft^2/year based on 650 occupants in 200,000 square feet. The energy use goal was adjusted to 35.1 kBtu/ft^2/year to account for higher occupancy density and an increase in the data center loads.

■ **FIGURE 12.9** View of the Building Lobby at the DOE/NREL Research Support Facility. *Image courtesy of RNL; photograph by Frank Ooms.*

Program Data

Occupants: 822

Occupied hours per week: 50

Visitors per week: 60

Program/primary space types:

- Open office
- Private office
- Conference facilities
- Common areas (copy rooms, breakrooms, lobby, storage)
- Data center
- Building support

DESIGN RESPONSE

The design was a specific response to the project site, program, and climate, to solve the multifaceted problem of cost, schedule, scope, and performance—with a particular focus on energy performance. At the foundation of the design's net zero energy approach was the introduction of a diverse and integrated set of passive strategies. The passive strategies, itemized in Figure 12.10, allowed for the effective use of very low-energy active systems, which, taken together as a whole-building energy solution, resulted in a building with an energy position low enough that on-site renewable energy can be used to generate all of its energy.

The first drawing completed at the initial design charrette was of the primary building section. It proved ideal for identifying the bioclimatic opportunities for the design (see Figure 12.11). The section resolved the main building footprint depth of 60 feet, in order to assure a 100 percent daylit space and to permit natural cross ventilation. The section also allowed for a column-free space, making the office wings very flexible. The section ultimately influenced the final form and plan of the building, joining the passive energy strategies with the functional planning of programmed space. The site plan and plan of the RSF are illustrated in Figures 12.12 and 12.13.

Passive Design

DAYLIGHTING

Daylighting is the keystone strategy for the RSF (see Figure 12.14). When fully developed as an integrated part of the lighting system, daylighting can save substantial energy. Overall, 92 percent of the regularly occupied spaces at the facility are daylit, per LEED requirements. Daylighting provides the primary ambient lighting in most of the building, with dimmable or stepped lighting on daylight controls supplementing the light levels when daylighting falls below the daylight sensor set point (typically, 25 footcandles). When the lights are on, generally they are at dimmed levels. The lighting design is very efficient to begin with, and the building has an installed lighting power density of 0.56 watts per square foot.

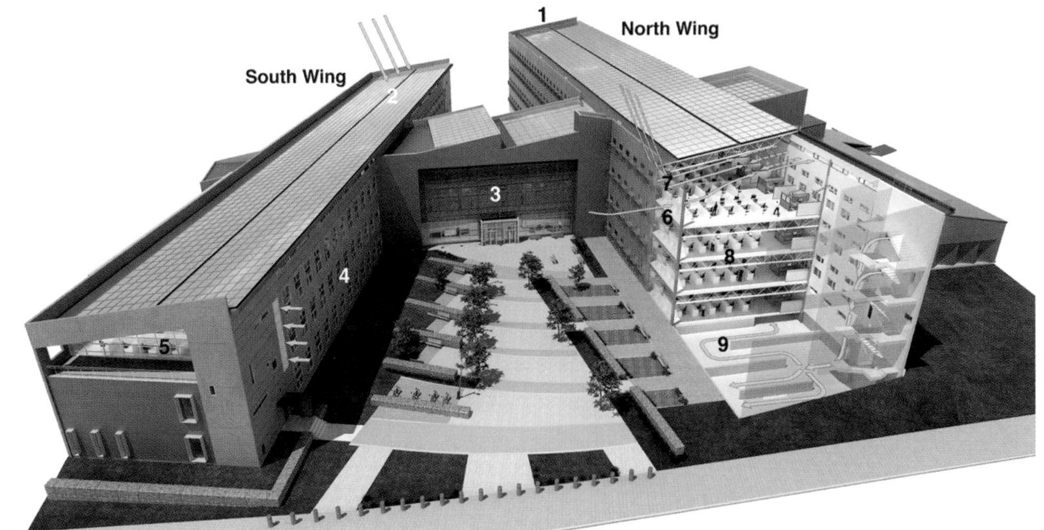

■ **FIGURE 12.10** Net Zero Energy Strategies: (1) 60-foot-wide office wings; (2) 1.6 MW on-site photovoltaics; (3) louvered sunshade at entrance; (4) low window to wall ratios; (5) electrochromic glazing and shaded balconies; (6) manual and automatic operable windows; (7) daylighting devices to redirect daylight; (8) radiant slabs for heating and cooling; (9) crawlspace thermal labyrinth to store heat from the data center and transpired solar collector. *Image courtesy of RNL and VStudios.*

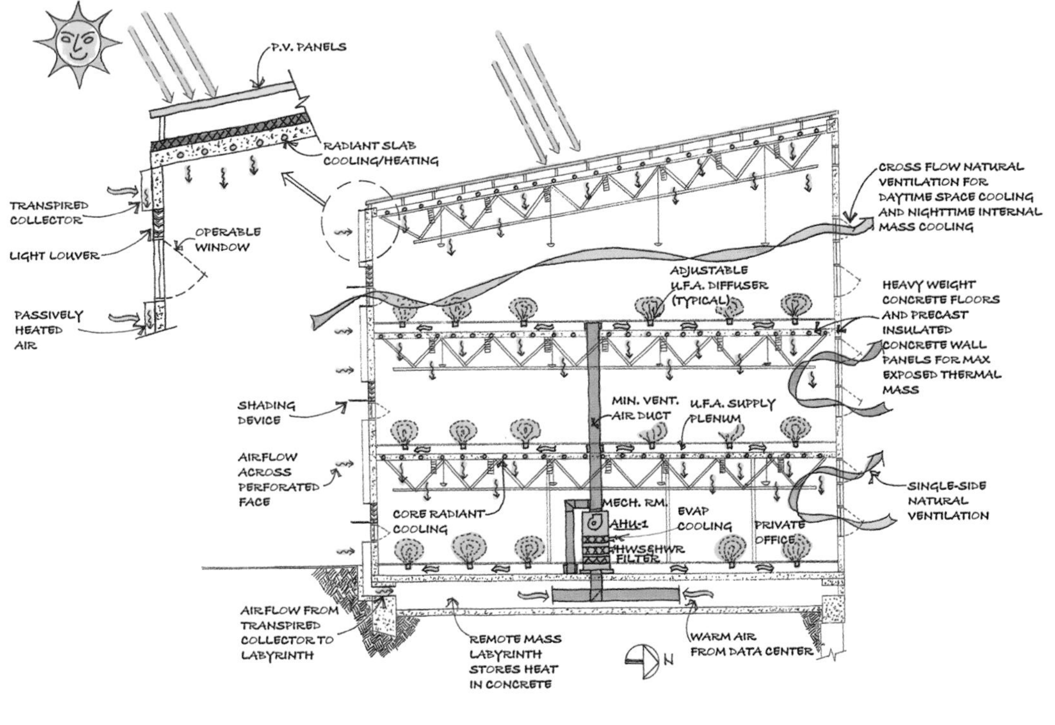

■ **FIGURE 12.11** Bioclimatic Section of the RSF Design. *Image courtesy of Stantec Consulting Services Inc.*

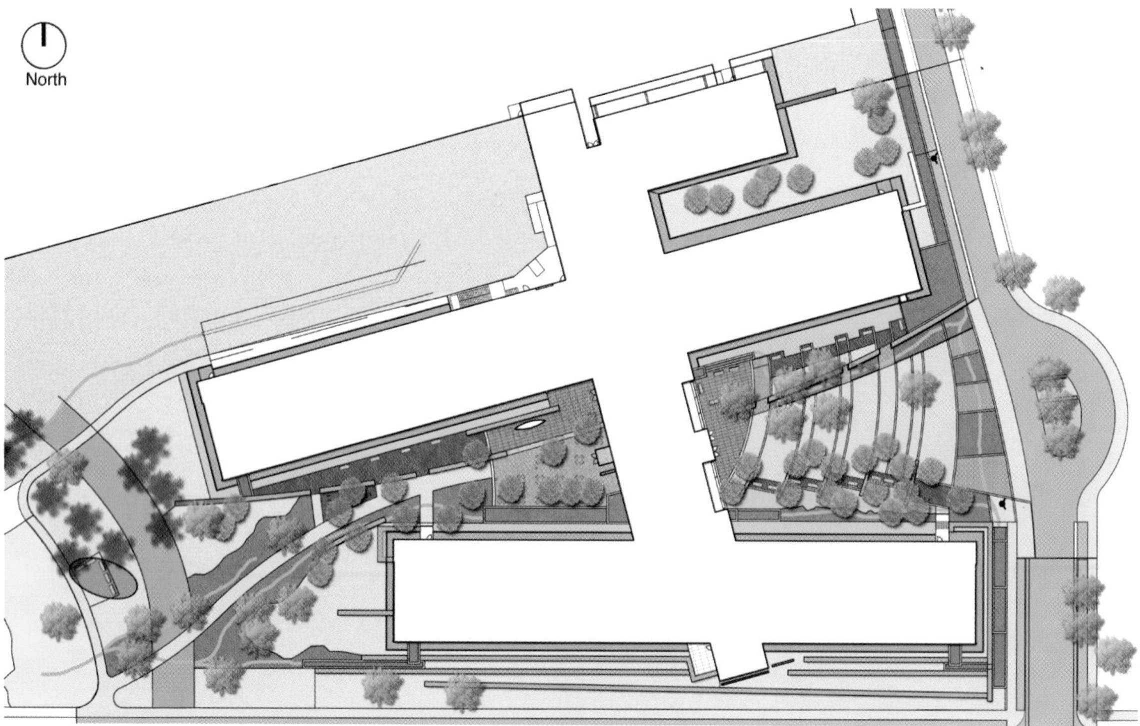

■ **FIGURE 12.12** Site Plan. *Image courtesy of RNL.*

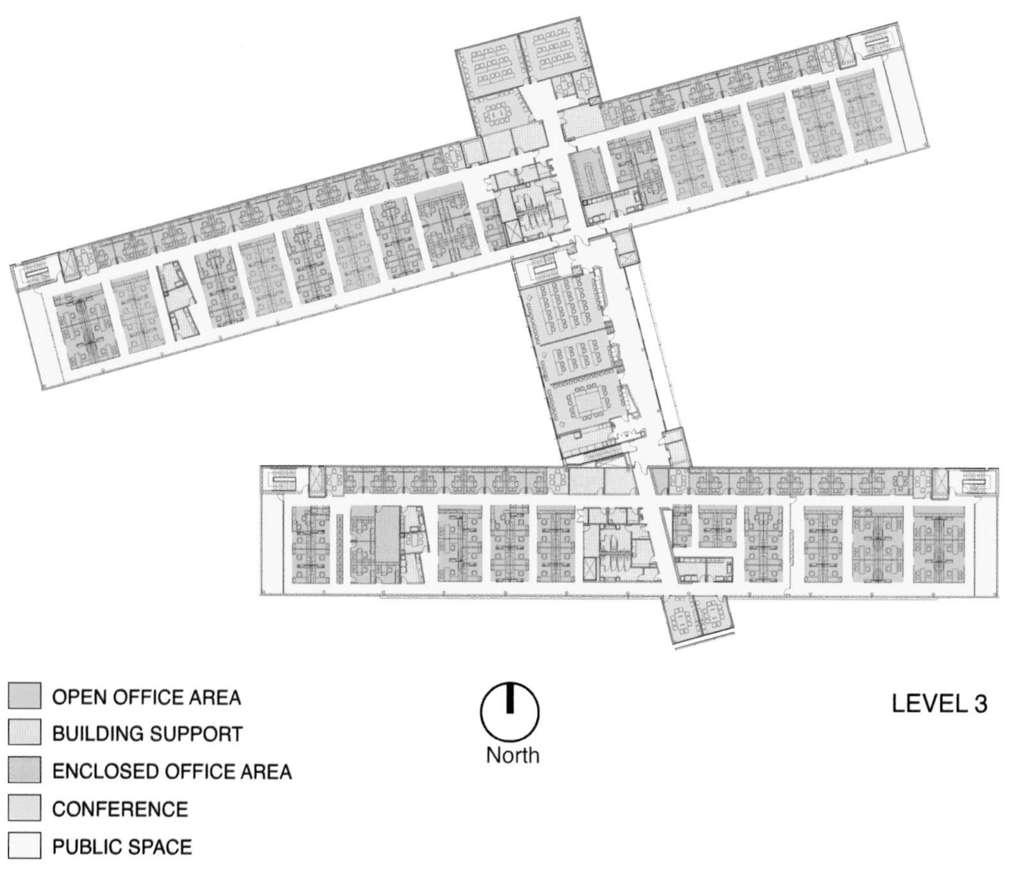

■ **FIGURE 12.13** Level Three Plan. *Image courtesy of RNL.*

With the daylighting controls, the effective lighting power density is 0.12 watts per square foot in the winter, under full sun, and 0.18 watts per square foot in the summer, under full sun. It turns out that the LightLouver daylighting devices installed in the daylighting windows are effective all year long, and are extremely effective with the lower sun angles during the winter months.

The window shown in Figure 12.15 illustrates the design employed on the south-facing

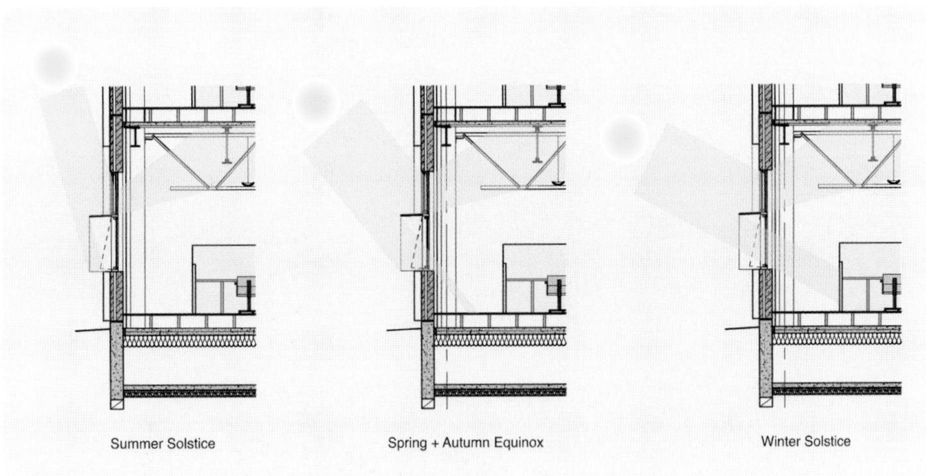
Summer Solstice
Spring + Autumn Equinox
Winter Solstice

■ **FIGURE 12.14** Seasonal Variation of Daylighting. *Image courtesy of RNL.*

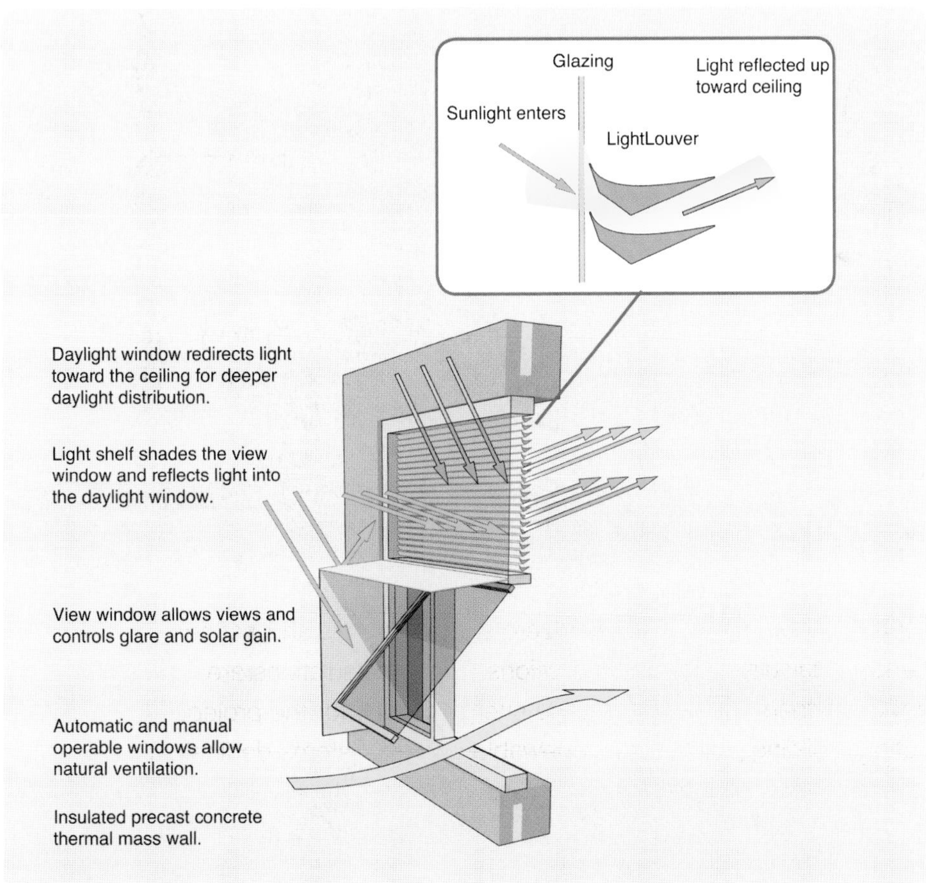
Glazing
Light reflected up toward ceiling
Sunlight enters
LightLouver
Daylight window redirects light toward the ceiling for deeper daylight distribution.
Light shelf shades the view window and reflects light into the daylight window.
View window allows views and controls glare and solar gain.
Automatic and manual operable windows allow natural ventilation.
Insulated precast concrete thermal mass wall.

■ **FIGURE 12.15** South Window Function. *Image courtesy of NREL and RNL.*

NREL RSF South Façade Window Design

View Window

- Primary function is view.
  - Triple-pane low-e glazing installed in thermally broken aluminum frame.
  - Exterior three-sided 18-inch-deep sunshade controls solar heat gain and glare.
  - No interior window treatment is needed for glare control, solar heat gain, control or privacy
  - Low solar heat gain coefficient (SHGC) = 0.23
  - Low thermal transmittance, U-factor winter = 0.17, U-factor summer = 0.17
  - Visible light transmittance (VLT) = 43 percent
- Secondary function is natural ventilation.
  - Operable window portion is located for easy access by occupants.
  - The ground-level operable windows do not open past 4 inches, to enhance security, as the windows are sometimes opened automatically at night.

Daylighting Window

- Primary function is daylighting.
  - Double-pane low-e glazing installed in thermally broken aluminum frame.
  - Located at the highest portion of the window.
  - High visible light transmittance (VLT) of 70 percent maximizes the daylight entering the daylight window.
  - Solar heat gain coefficient (SHGC) = 0.38
  - Thermal transmittance, U-factor winter = 0.29, U-factor summer = 0.26
  - Fitted with a LightLouver daylighting device that redistributes the daylight toward the ceiling and deep into the space.
  - The daylighting window has no external or internal shade (therefore, daylighting is always "on").

façades at the RSF. The window's most prominent feature is the separation of the view portion from the daylighting portion. This is key, because it allows the daylight window to be optimized for daylighting, and the view window to be shaded for solar and glare control. The window is repeated uniformly across the south façade and results in a window to wall ratio of 29 percent.

PASSIVE HEATING

The first line of defense for heating is prevention of heat loss. This is particularly important for the RSF because the building envelope area is two times larger than it would be for a conventional, more compact form. The window areas are optimized to all orientations for complete daylighting of the space and to provide good views, but they are not oversized. The north façade windows represent a heat loss liability during the winter. On the north façades, the basic window to wall ratio for a typical office bay is 27 percent, with an overall window to wall ratio of 21 percent for all north façades. Most of the windows, with the exception of the southern daylight window, are highly insulated (center of glass U-factor = 0.17), triple-pane glass in thermally broken frames. Note that the whole window U-factor is considerably higher. The wall assemblies are a precast concrete sandwich panel, with 3 inches of exterior concrete, 2 inches of continuous rigid insulation, and 6 inches of interior concrete with an R-value of 15. The roof has an R-value of 33. The primary goal was to minimize thermal bridging in the envelope. Thermal imaging photography reveals that the thermally broken aluminum frames are the weakest point in the thermal envelope.

The south façade is a key aspect of the passive heating strategy; it has a transpired solar collector installed over a portion of the precast concrete panels (see Figure 12.16). The transpired solar collector, a technology co-developed at NREL in the 1990s, is composed of dark-colored perforated corrugated metal panels. The heated air behind the transpired solar collector is drawn into the crawlspace of the RSF, which houses the central element to the passive heating system, the building's thermal labyrinth.

The thermal labyrinth is a large remote thermal mass that acts like a large thermal battery for the building, which stores heat from the transpired solar collector to preheat ventilation air. The thermal labyrinth is also heated using waste heat from the data center—a primary cooling strategy for the center. The thermal labyrinth under the north wing is dedicated to accepting waste heat from the data center, while the thermal labyrinth under the south wing is dedicated to accepting heat generated from the transpired solar collector (see Figure 12.17).

PASSIVE COOLING/VENTILATION

The cooling load for the RSF is quite small for a large office building, even considering that it is located in a heating-dominated climate.

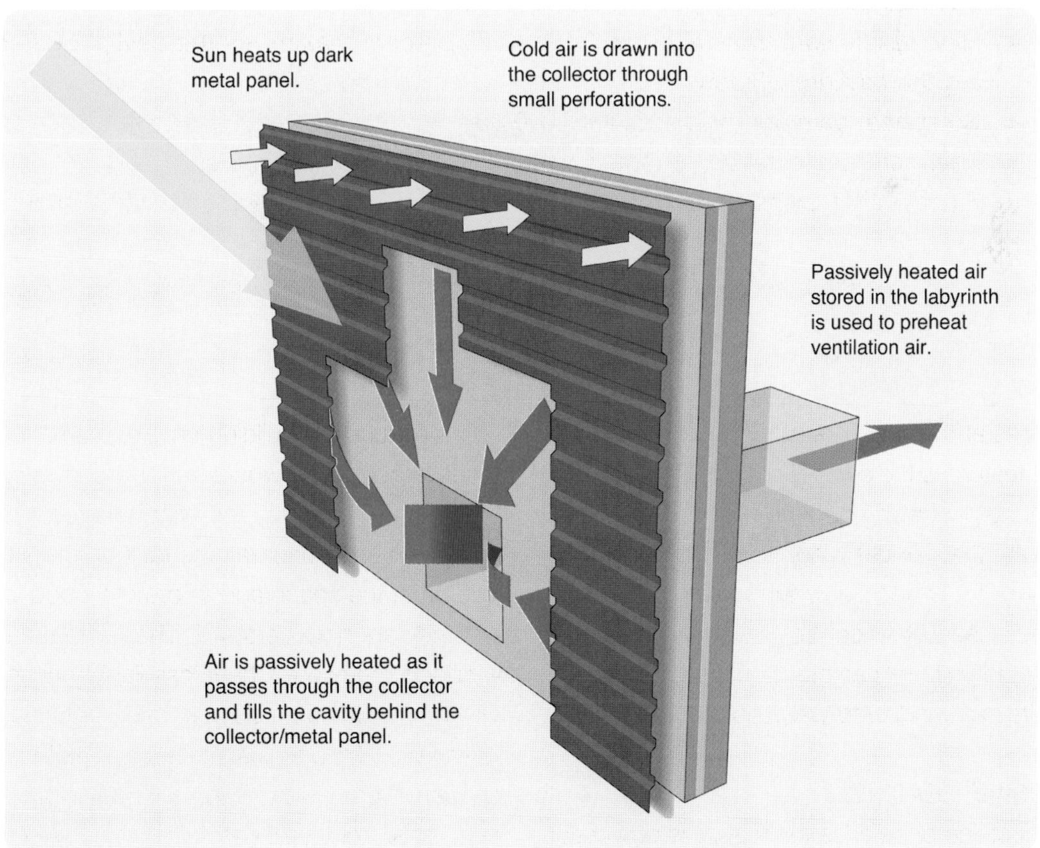
Sun heats up dark metal panel.
Cold air is drawn into the collector through small perforations.
Passively heated air stored in the labyrinth is used to preheat ventilation air.
Air is passively heated as it passes through the collector and fills the cavity behind the collector/metal panel.

■ **FIGURE 12.16** Transpired Solar Collector Operation. *Image courtesy of NREL and RNL.*

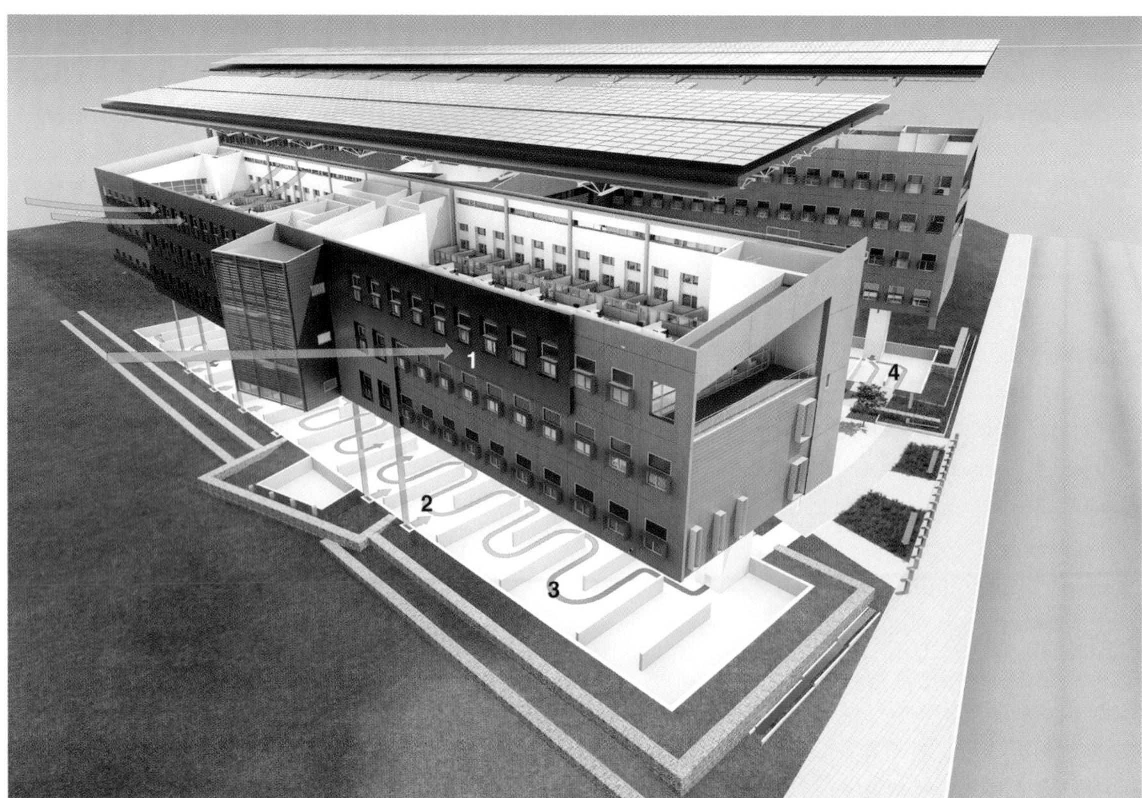

■ **FIGURE 12.17** Thermal Labyrinth: (1) Transpired solar collectors passively heat outside air. (2) Passively heated air is pulled though inlets into the labyrinth. (3) The south wing thermal labyrinth is heated using air from the transpired solar collector. (4) The north wing thermal labyrinth is heated using air and waste heat from the data center. *Image courtesy of RNL and VStudios.*

The cooling load is reduced through reduced internal gains, specifically, reduced lighting and equipment loads. The cooling load is also reduced because of the skin-dominated form of the building and the effective use of passive cooling strategies. The climate permits free cooling much of the year.

The operable windows allow the building and occupants to take advantage of this free cooling opportunity (see Figure 12.18). Two-thirds of the operable windows are manually operated, enabling a high degree of occupant control of the thermal environment The RSF's computer network facilitates communication about appropriate times to open a window, by displaying an icon on everyone's computer to indicate when weather conditions are favorable for window operation. One-third of the operable windows are automated and controlled by the building automation system, to allow for the automatic night-purge function of the building.

The night purge passive cooling strategy takes advantage of the thermal mass of the building's interior and the wide diurnal temperature swings of the climate. The interior face of the exterior walls has 6 inches of concrete exposed to the interior. This thermal mass absorbs internal heat gains during the day. The mass can be purged of this stored heat by allowing cool nighttime air to flush the building during the cooling season.

The ventilation air for the building is cooled using evaporative cooling, taking advantage of the dry climate and the relatively low wet bulb temperature. With evaporative cooling, the dry outside air can be cooled simply by adding moisture. The evaporative cooling strategy is also one of the cooling strategies for the data center.

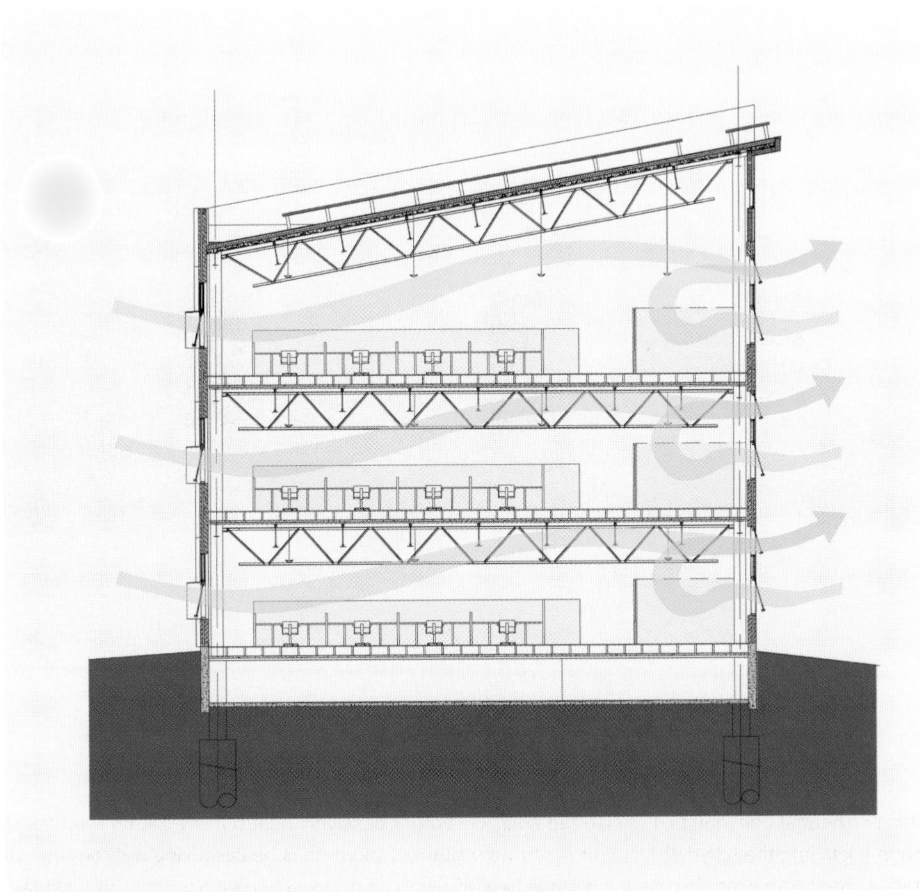

■ **FIGURE 12.18** Section Showing Basic Natural Ventilation Scheme. *Image courtesy of RNL.*

The data center cooling strategy begins with allowing the space to run warmer, with temperatures reaching the higher levels of equipment manufacturer operating requirements. The data center equipment is organized into hot aisles and cold aisles so that the hot aisles can be contained (see Figure 12.19). The data center equipment is organized into racks so that all of the equipment dissipates heat into the hot aisle. The heated air from the hot aisles is then pulled into the thermal labyrinth as waste heat that can be reused for building ventilation air preheating (see Figure 12.20). Air coming into the data center is direct from the outside, when conditions allow, or direct from the outside but tempered with heated return air during colder winter periods. During the summer, evaporative cooling is used to condition the space. The data center can also use chilled water to maintain space and equipment temperatures, even during the hottest summer days.

■ **FIGURE 12.19** The RSF Data Center with Hot Aisle Containment. *Image courtesy of RNL; photograph by Frank Ooms.*

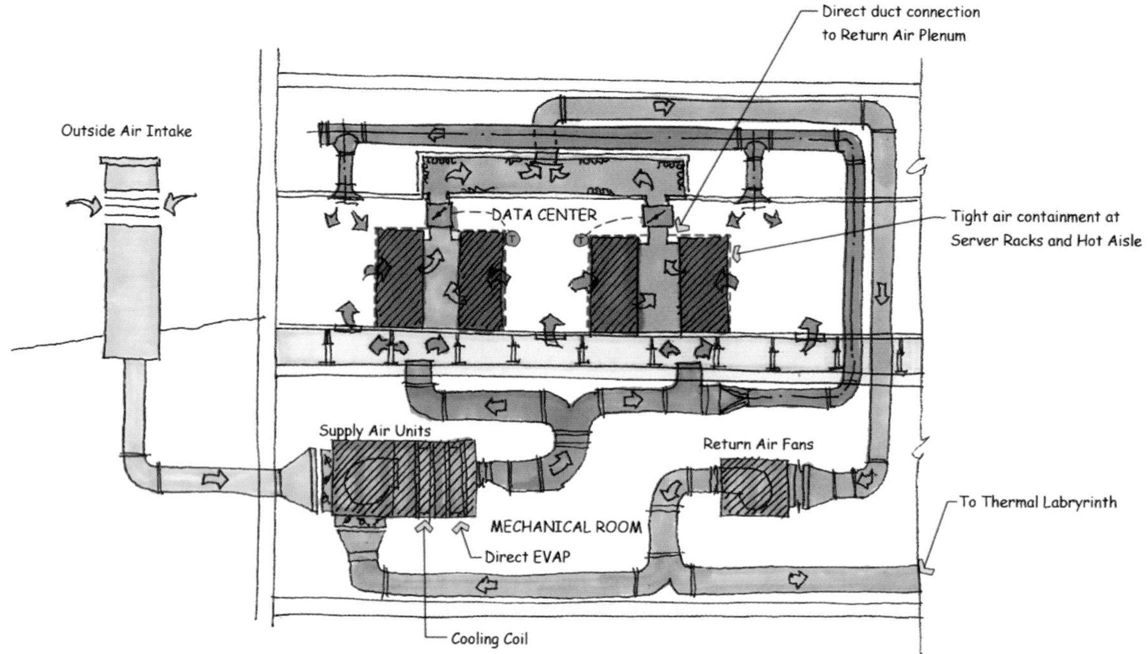

■ **FIGURE 12.20** Data Center Waste Heat Reuse. *Image courtesy of Stantec Consulting Services Inc.; drawing by Jim Burns.*

Energy-Efficient Building Systems

An NREL campus-central plant, supplying chilled water and heated water, serves the RSF. The cooling plant consists of water-cooled chillers and a cooling tower with a high coefficient of performance (COP). The heating plant is a wood chip burner with natural gas backup. The chilled and heated water are used in the hydronic radiant heating and cooling system that serves a majority of the RSF building program. The hydronic tubing is embedded in the concrete floor and roof decks and is designed to radiate down to the space below (see Figure 12.21). This requires the use of exposed floors and roof decks. Carefully coordinated high-performance acoustic panels are incorporated into the exposed decks.

The building's ventilation system, supplied with an underfloor air delivery system, is decoupled from the space heating and cooling function (see Figure 12.21). A dedicated outside air system is an important energy-efficiency measure of the RSF. Ventilation-only air systems require dramatically less air volume and less extreme temperatures than do air-based heating and cooling systems. This reduces both thermal energy and fan energy requirements. It also allows the implementation of a water-based radiant system, which gains considerable efficiency by moving heat through water, rather than air. The use of CO_2 sensors in the space controls the supply of ventilation air so that the system can respond to periods when the operable windows are open and lowering CO_2 levels through natural ventilation.

The conference facilities in the RSF's central collector space (connecting the two main wings) are served by a variable air volume (VAV) system. The conference room program is small and isolated from the main office zones. Further, the conference rooms have highly fluctuating schedules; they can sit empty for long stretches and then suddenly be densely occupied for a period of time. Thus, they are better served by an air-based system that can quickly escalate air exchanges and address changes in internal heat gain. The system remains efficient because it uses demand-controlled ventilation triggered by CO_2 sensors in the room.

The RSF lighting systems are an effective combination of fluorescent and LED

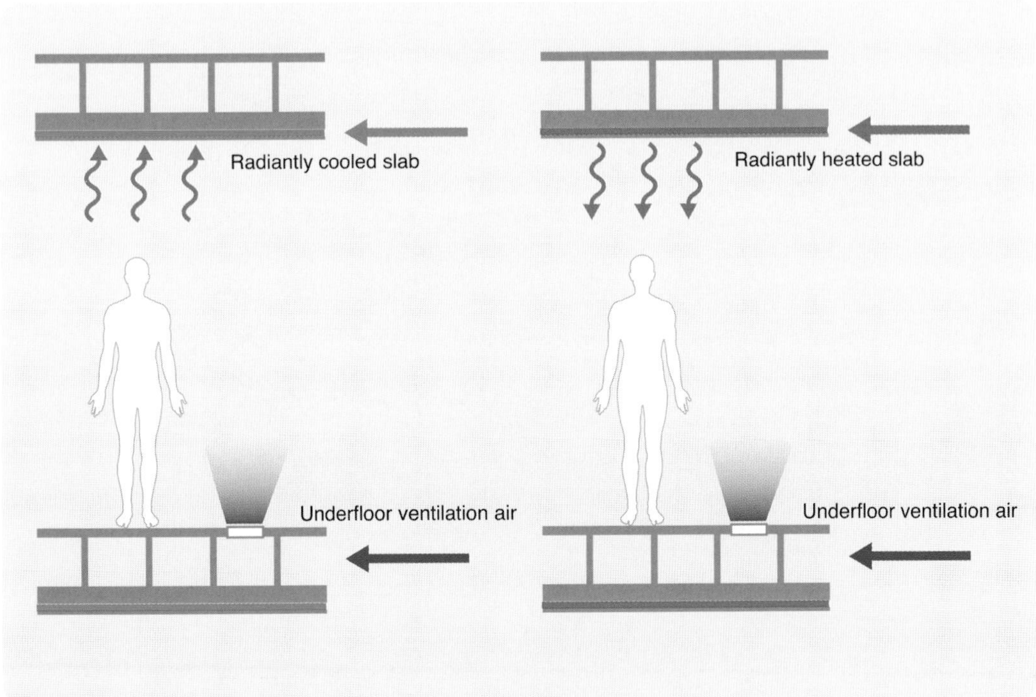

■ **FIGURE 12.21** Radiant Floor and Underfloor Ventilation Air.

fixture types. The primary light fixture used throughout the RSF for open offices and over ceilingless private offices is a custom direct/indirect fluorescent fixture utilizing two 25-watt T8 lamps (see Figure 12.22). Each workstation and office is outfitted with a 6-watt LED task lamp. There are two main lighting control approaches. The first is to keep the lights off when they are not in use (i.e., nighttime or unoccupied). Instead of occupancy sensors that turn on the lights when they sense occupancy, the controls are vacancy-based. The lights are always off unless manually turned on by an occupant, and turn off when vacancy is sensed. The vacancy controls are used in conjunction with daylight controls that allow the lights to be dimmed, stepped down, or turned off in response to daylight conditions.

Renewable Energy

There are several types of renewable energy sources utilized at the RSF, primary among them, solar electric from on-site photovoltaic (PV) systems. The PV systems are sized to meet net zero energy without any other renewable energy source. In this case, the renewable electricity offsets the fuel energy for hot water used for building heating and domestic hot water.

■ **FIGURE 12.22** High-Efficiency Custom T8 Direct/Indirect Fixture (now known as the Corelite Element).

The hot water for the building is supplied from a central renewable fuels heating plant that burns wood chips from forest wood waste, to provide a heated water loop for campus buildings. The plant's campuswide capacity is 10 MBtu per hour, or 600 gallons of hot water per minute. The central heating plant is estimated to provide nearly 2,000 MBtu of heating energy each year to the RSF. Of this, about 75 percent comes from biomass; the remainder comes from supplemental natural gas. This biomass renewable energy contribution is not needed to achieve the net zero energy goal. The owner and delivery team wanted a net zero energy solution that was replicable by others, and it was deemed that a biomass central heating plant would be easy to replicate for most commercial buildings.

The building's photovoltaic system was designed in three phases, totaling just over 1.67 MW of installed PV. The first-phase PV system, which is on the roof of the RSF, is a 449 kW system installed through a power purchase agreement. The second-phase PV system, of 524 kW, comprises shade canopies over the visitor's parking lot. Shade canopies also make up the third-phase system, these installed at the top level of the adjacent staff parking garage; it is a 706 kW system. The two parking canopy systems were procured using ARRA funding, which made possible the direct purchase of a total of 2,088 kW in photovoltaics. This additional PV provides on-site renewable energy for an expansion of the RSF, extending the net zero energy boundary to include the RSF, the RSF II (the expansion), the parking garage, and the visitor's parking lot (see Figures 12.23 and 12.24).

■ **FIGURE 12.23** The RSF Roof-Mounted PV System.

■ **FIGURE 12.24** The RSF Visitor's Parking Lot PV System.

Design Data

Exterior wall area: 112,700 ft^2

Roof area: 69,950 ft^2

Exterior wall area to gross floor area: 0.51

Floor to roof area: 3.33

Floor-to-floor height: 14 feet 6 inches; top stories are sloped higher

Ceiling height: Most spaces have no ceilings

Window to Wall Ratio

- North: 21 percent
- South: 30 percent
- East: 32 percent
- West: 31 percent
- Overall: 27 percent

Percent skylight area of roof area: No skylights

Window Assembly Energy Performance

- North
  - Triple-pane
  - Center of glazing U-factor: 0.17

- Assembly U-factor: 0.41 (using Window 5 output)
- SHGC: 0.23
- VLT: 0.43

- South Daylighting
  - Double-pane
  - Center of glazing U-factor: 0.29
  - Assembly U-factor: 0.44 (using Window 5 output)
  - SHGC: 0.38
  - VLT: 0.70
- South View
  - Triple pane
  - Center of glazing U-factor: 0.17
  - Assembly U-factor: 0.41 (using Window 5 output)
  - SHGC: 0.23
  - VLT: 0.43
- East and West View
  - Triple pane
  - Center of glazing U-factor: 0.18
  - Assembly U-factor: 0.38 (using Window 5 output)
  - SHGC: 0.22
  - VLT: 0.43

Opaque Wall U-factor

- Precast wall assembly: 0.065 (before any derating for thermal bridges)
- Steel stud wall assembly: 0.053
- Roof U-factor: 0.030

Key Passive Strategies

- Daylighting
- Natural ventilation
- Thermal mass
- Remote thermal mass
- Night purge
- Solar shading
- Transpired solar collector

Lighting Controls

- Daylight controls: stepped and continuous dimming
- Time clock controls
- Occupancy and vacancy controls

Lighting Systems

- Primary fixture: Cooperatively designed Corelite luminaire (93 percent efficiency) with energy-saving reduced-wattage 25 watt T-8 linear fluorescents (now a standard product)
- Typical downlight and accent lighting: Compact fluorescent lamps and LEDs
- Task lighting: 6 watt LED desk lamps
- Design illuminance levels: 25 fc (after accounting for light loss factors) ambient and 50 fc with additional task lighting
- Exterior lighting: Stepped LED with occupancy and time clock control

Mechanical Systems

- Radiant cooling and heating
- Decoupled ventilation with underfloor air delivery
- VAV system in grouped conference room area
- Central plant using water-cooled chillers, cooling towers for chilled water, and wood chip burner (natural gas backup) for hot water

Renewable Energy Systems

- Photovoltaic
  - Roof-mounted: 449 kW, Solon 230 watt modules, 14.0 percent, monocrystalline
  - Parking canopies: 524 kW over visitor parking and 706 kW over staff parking, SunPower 315 watt modules, 19.3 percent, monocrystalline
- Biomass woodchip central plant boiler (Note that the biomass woodchip central plant is excluded from the RSF's net zero energy calculation shown later in this chapter.)

OPERATION AND OCCUPANCY

The RSF project is a good example of the successful continuation from design and construction into operation and occupancy. The project benefited from internal owner expertise and a deep commitment to operating the building to achieve net zero energy. Having an internal understanding of the energy strategies and design intent enabled the owner to use the final as-build energy model as a guide for building operation. This expertise was also central to managing the plug loads and developing the internal standards for IT equipment. Although a small group of energy experts are very focused on learning from the building, the vast majority of staff regard the RSF simply as their workplace, rather than a learning lab (see Figure 12.25). The owner and delivery team implemented a comprehensive education and training program to prepare staff for the new building. The building includes real-time energy displays in the lobby to add in the occupant feedback loop and to serve as a demonstration for visitors to the facility (see Figure 12.26).

The RSF workplace represented a marked change from the one DOE/NREL staff were accustomed to in their leased office space. That space was typical of many office environments across the nation, dominated by private offices and high-partitioned cubicles. In contrast, the new office environment at the RSF is a collaborative high-performance workplace that is tuned for energy performance; to that end, it is dominated by open-office workstations and a minimal number of hybrid-designed private offices (see Figure 12.27). The new open-workplace design was part of the integration of daylighting, natural ventilation, and radiant heating and cooling.

The occupant engagement process helped transition staff into the new environment. By and large, the results have been very positive, with a noted improvement in collaboration and interaction among all staff. One of the primary concerns about the new workplace was acoustic privacy. The solutions to address this have been successful, resulting in an acoustically tuned space that also features plenty of planned programmed spaces for making private phone calls and holding meetings.

■ **FIGURE 12.25** A Typical RSF Open Workstation. *Image courtesy of RNL; photograph by Frank Ooms.*

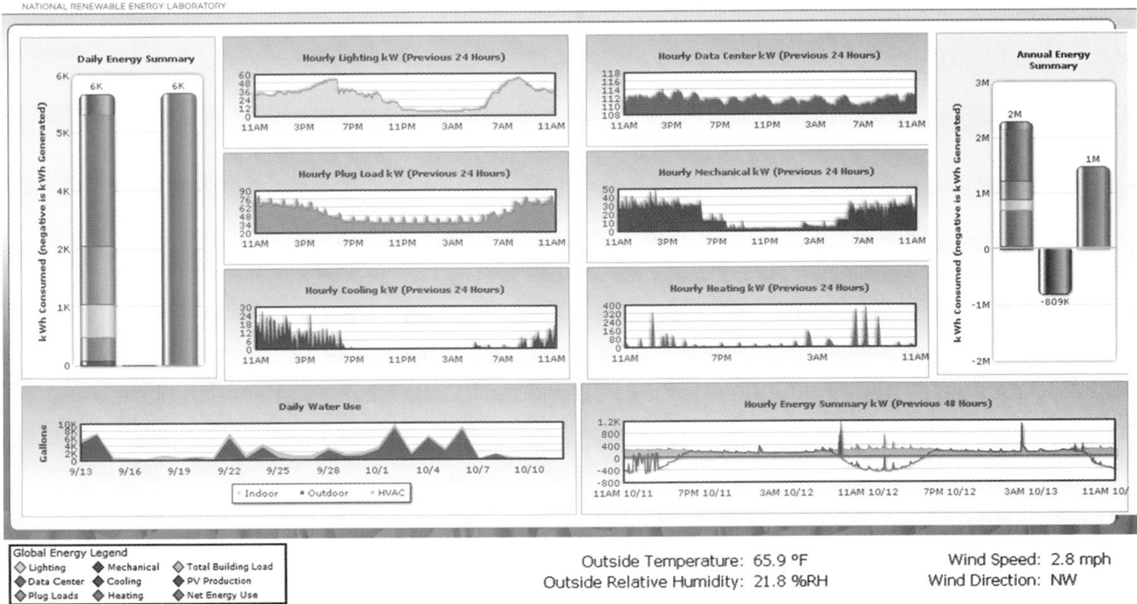

■ **FIGURE 12.26** The energy display showing real-time and trending data in the lobby. *NREL.*

Operational Energy Data

At the time of this writing, the project had one full year of energy operational data. However, the project had not completed its first year of measured net zero energy operation, due to the phased installation of the photovoltaic systems. Energy use has been intensely measured and regularly compared to the energy model and energy target for the building. Actual energy use for the first year tracked very closely with the energy model and overall energy target, and it is fully anticipated that the project is well on its way to meeting its net zero energy goal. The project achieved net zero operation during the month of July 2011 with only two of the three photovoltaic systems in place. The winter months are more challenging because of the reduced solar resource. The final photovoltaic system should be fully operational in 2012. This final photovoltaic system includes additional capacity for the extension of the RSF, as well as extra capacity for a small renewable energy generation contingency.

■ **FIGURE 12.27** A typical RSF private office has no ceiling, so it can be conditioned by the radiant slab above. *Image courtesy of RNL; photograph by Frank Ooms.*

Figures 12.28 to 12.35 are operational performance charts showing many energy end uses, as well as whole building energy use for one year compared to the final energy model. The first year of operational data resulted in an energy use intensity of 35.4 kBtu/ft²/year, very close to the project's energy target of 35.1 kBtu/ft²/year.

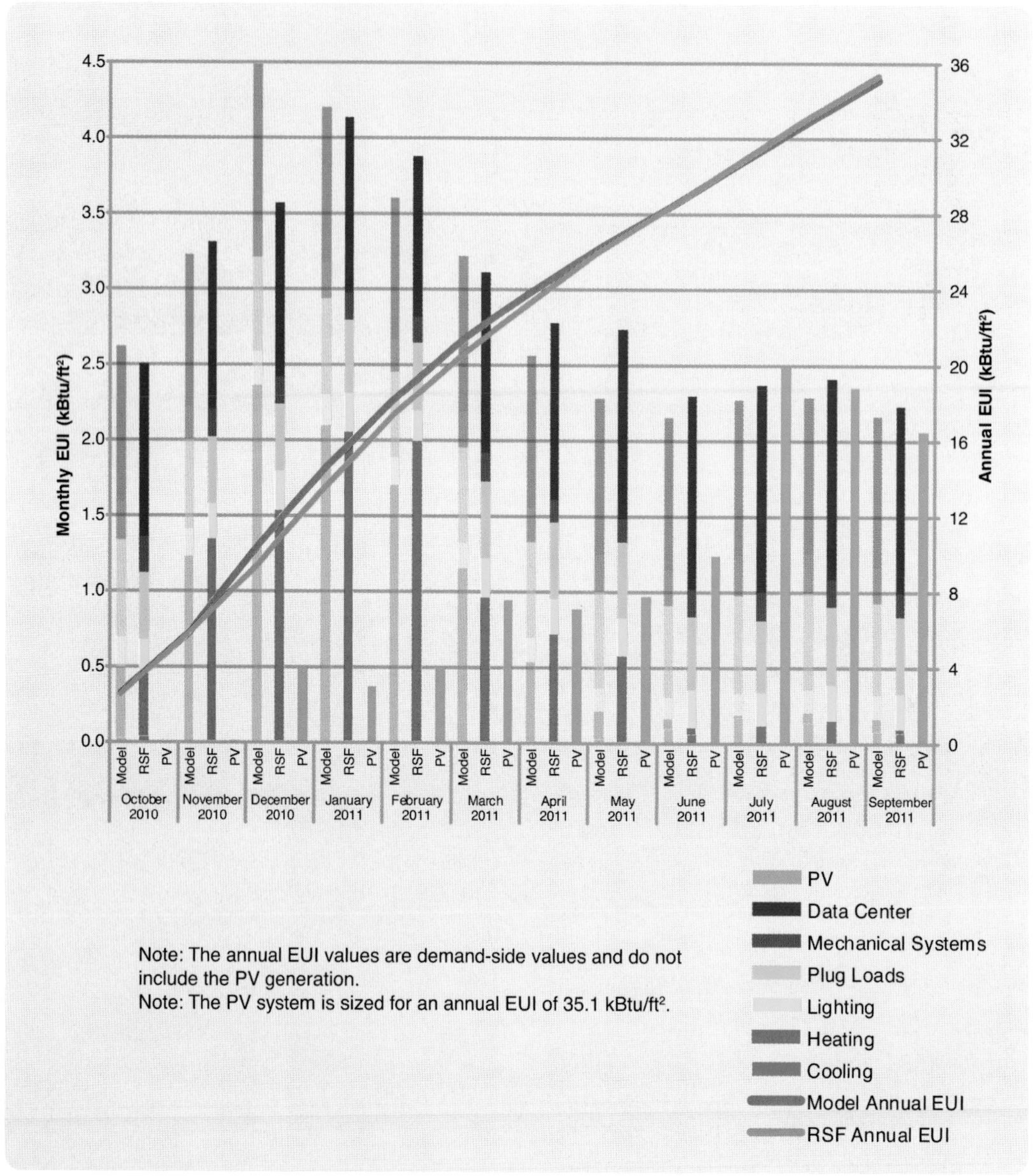

■ **FIGURE 12.28** Measured versus Modeled Monthly and Cumulative EUI: October 2010 to September 2011. *Chad Lobato/NREL.*

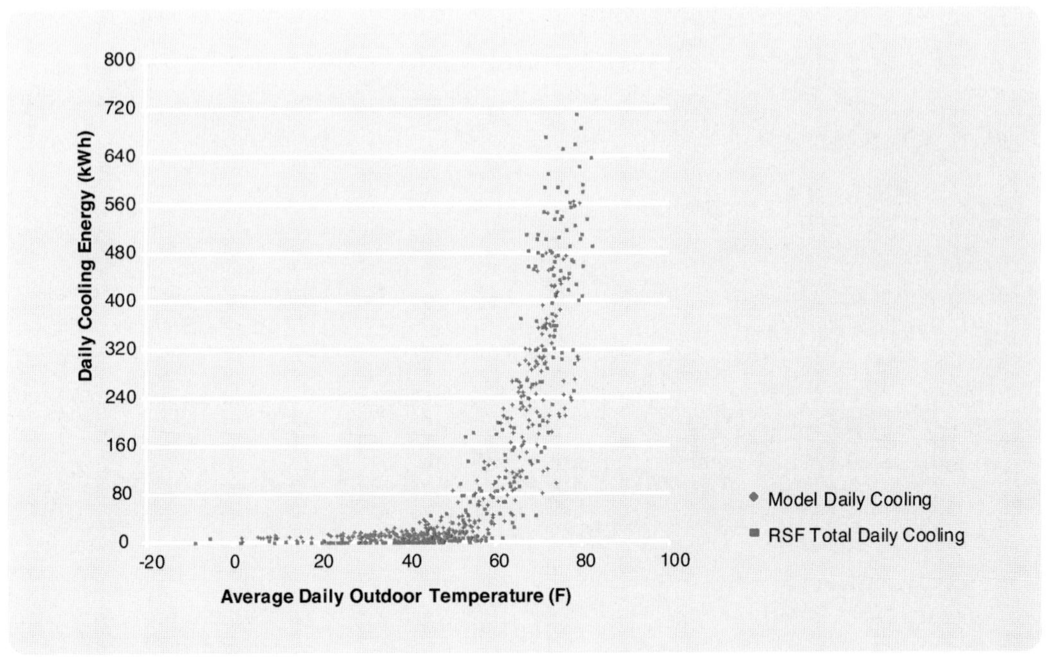

■ **FIGURE 12.30** Daily Cooling Energy: January 2011 to September 2011. *Chad Lobato/NREL.*

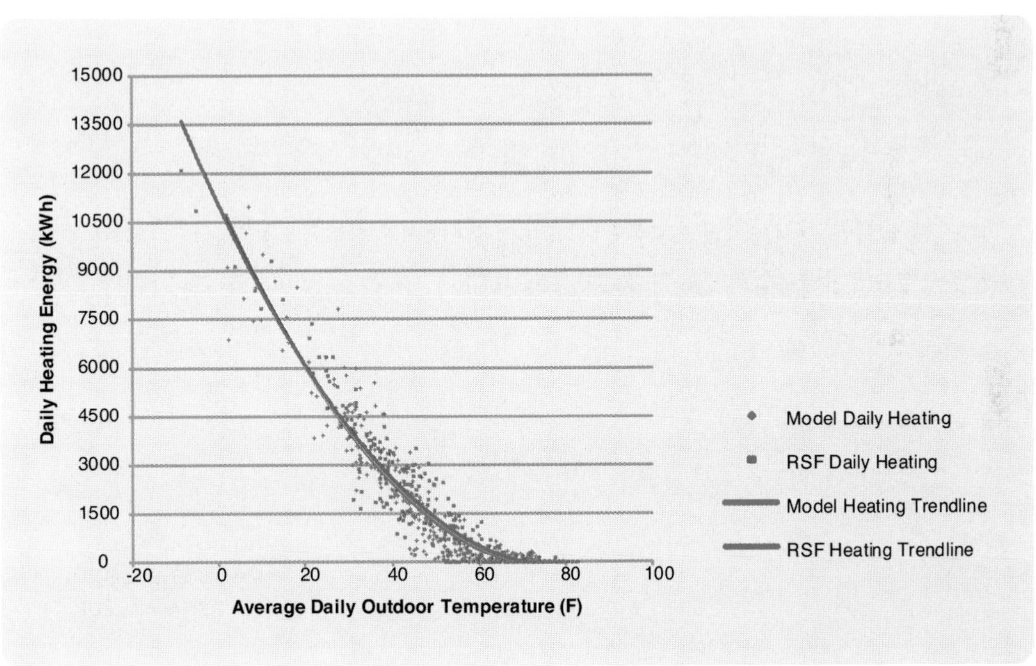

■ **FIGURE 12.29** Daily Heating Energy: October 2010 to September 2011. *Chad Lobato/NREL.*

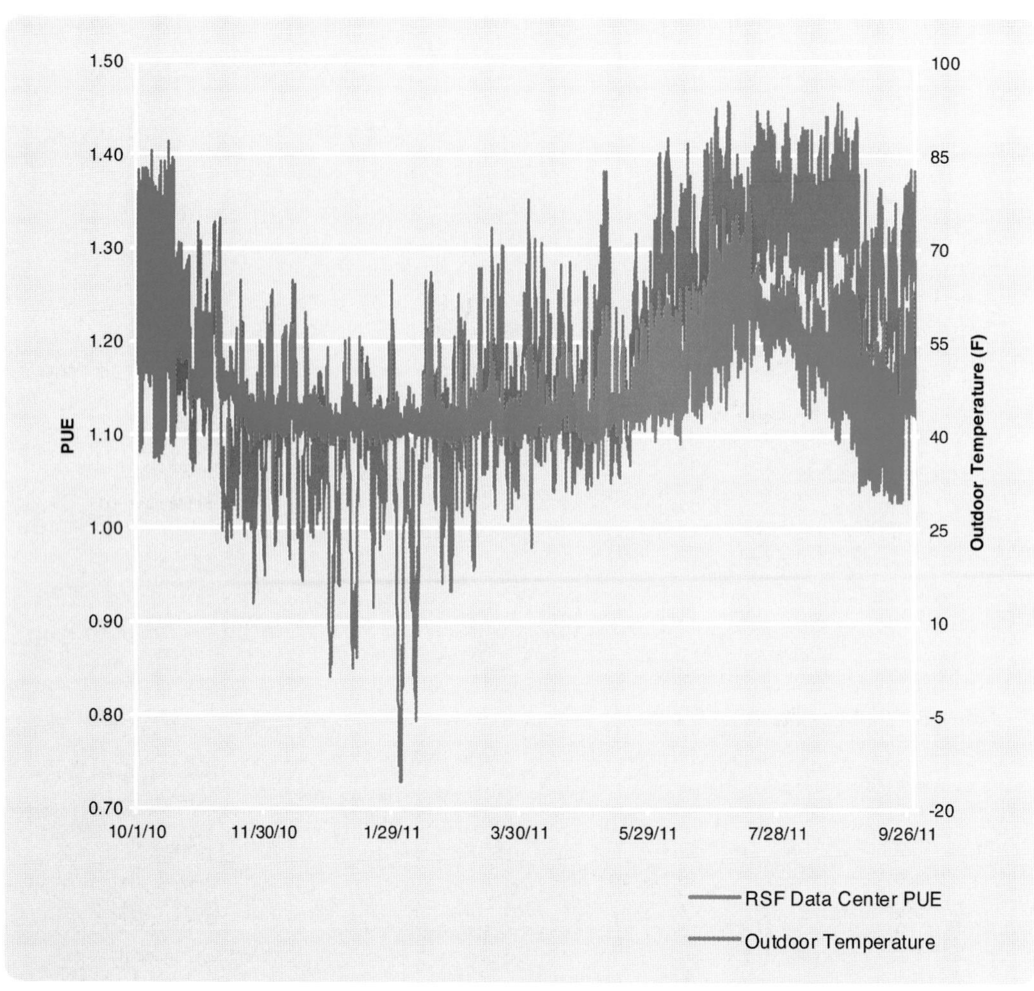

■ **FIGURE 12.31** Data Center Power Usage Effectiveness (PUE): October 2010 to September 2011. *Chad Lobato/NREL.*

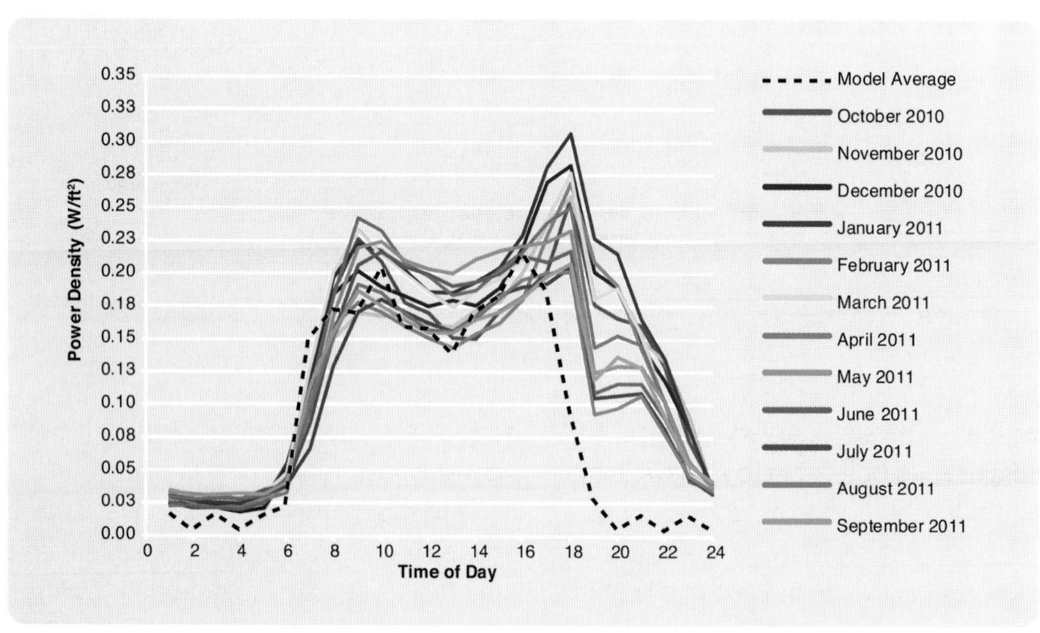

■ **FIGURE 12.32** Lighting Power Density: October 2010 to September 2011. *Chad Lobato/NREL.*

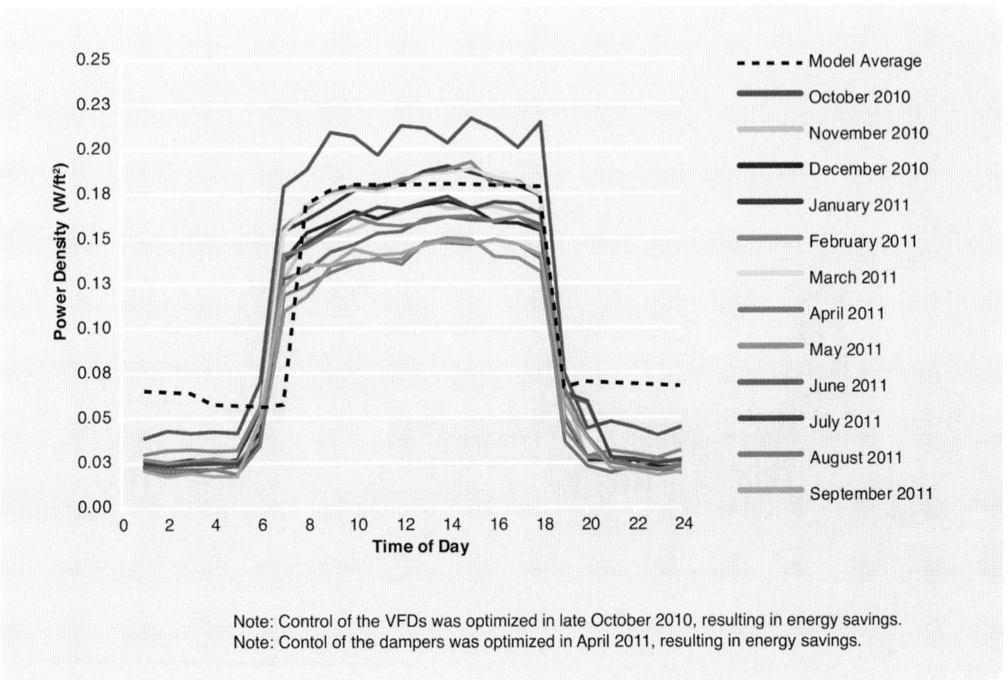

■ **FIGURE 12.33** Mechanical Power Density: October 2010 to September 2011. *Chad Lobato/NREL.*

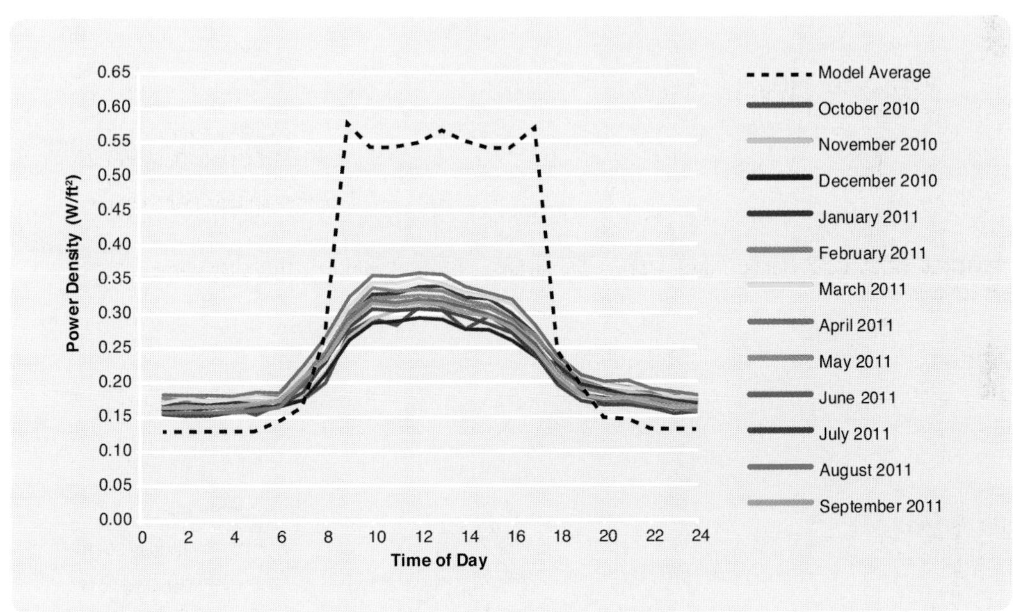

■ **FIGURE 12.34** Plug Load Power Density: October 2010 to September 2011. *Chad Lobato/NREL.*

PERFORMANCE METRICS

Through an integrated delivery process, the RSF project has been able to achieve some very high levels of performance. The project was registered for LEED-NC 2.2 and achieved Platinum certification in the summer of 2011, earning 59 of 69 points, placing it among the highest-scoring projects certified to date, and the highest scoring project by the federal government.

The final design, as-built model, showed the project at 33.2 kBtu/ft2/year, just below the project's energy target of 35.1 kBtu/ft2/year. The energy pie chart in Figure 12.36 shows the breakdown by energy end uses,

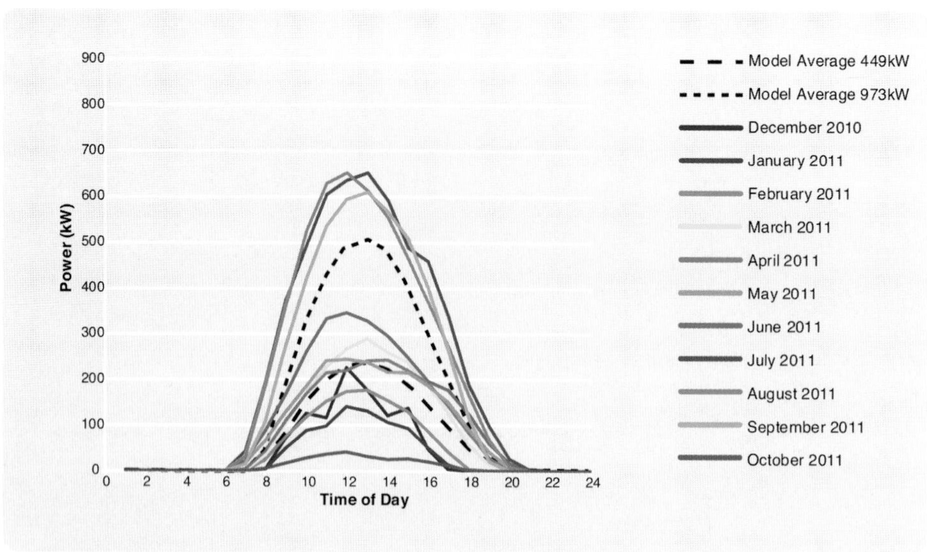

■ **FIGURE 12.35** PV System Power Output: October 2010 to September 2011. *Chad Lobato/NREL.*

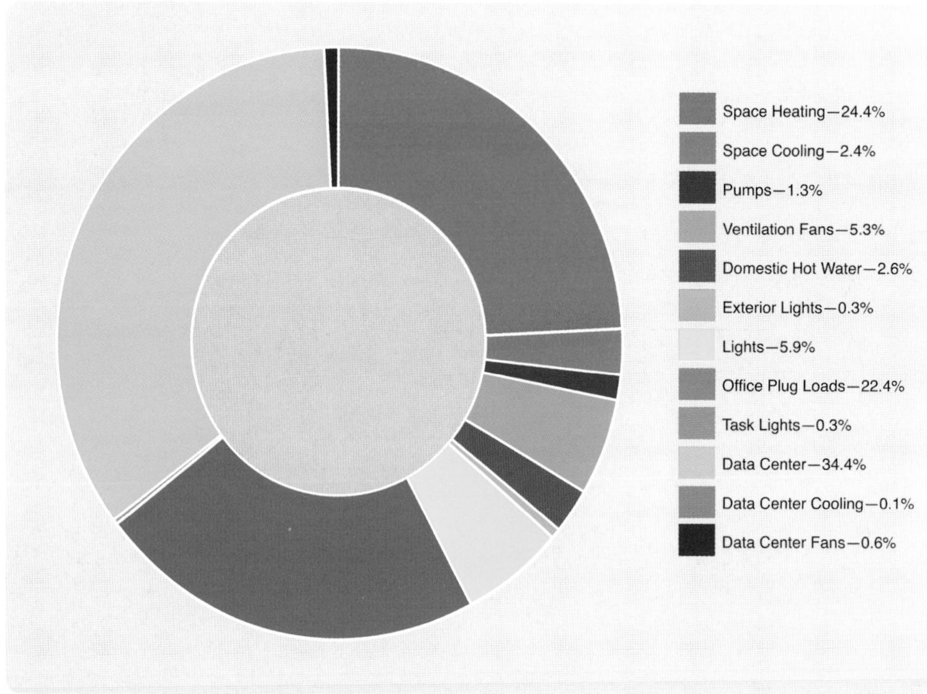

■ **FIGURE 12.36** Energy End Use Breakdown for the RSF. *Chad Lobato/NREL.*

and the graph in Figure 12.37 shows the EUI comparison to other building benchmarks. The building area used in the energy calculations is slightly smaller, at 219,105 ft2, than the basic gross building area of the building, at 222,000 ft2. For the purposes of energy calculations, the energy model building area was used.

The net zero energy balance calculations show that the building, as designed, should achieve a Classification B for net zero site energy, net zero source energy, and net zero energy emissions. These calculations are based on the energy budget for the project and the renewable energy systems dedicated to the system (less the small photovoltaic contingency). The cost measure was not calculated because the project does not receive a separate utility, as it is part of a larger campus.

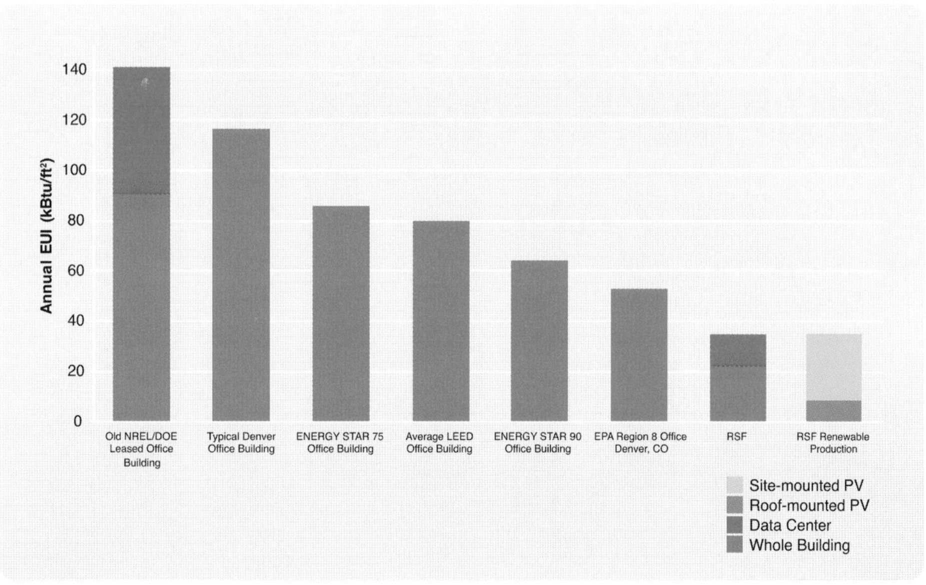

■ **FIGURE 12.37** Energy Use Intensity Comparison. *Chad Lobato/NREL.*

Performance Data

LEED rating: LEED-NC 2.2 Platinum

LEED score: 59/69 (17/17 Energy & Atmosphere points)

Project energy target/budget: 7,691 MBtu

Energy target EUI: 35.1 kBtu/ft^2/year

Final design (as-built) annual energy: 7,281 MBtu

Final design energy use intensity: 33.2 kBtu/ft^2/year

Baseline energy use intensity (2030 Challenge): 137 kBtu/ft^2/year (based on ENERGY STAR Target Finder)

Data center energy: 65 watts/person for 1,200-occupant campus, or 683,280 kWh/year

Renewable Energy System Performance

- Photovoltaic system on roof: 633,539 kWh
- Photovoltaic system over parking: 1,620,440 kWh
- Total anticipated annual renewable energy generation: 2,254 MWh (7,691 MBtu)
- Lighting power density: 0.56 w/ft^2 installed (0.16 w/ft^2; typical with daylight controls) (Task lights are part of plug load density.)
- Daytime plug load density: 0.55 w/ft^2 (measured data averaging under 0.35 w/ft^2)

Carbon Intensity

- Without renewable energy: 18.4 lb $CO2_e$/year
- With photovoltaic renewable energy: −4.6 lb $CO2_e$/year
- Baseline: 67.6 lb/year (based on ENERGY STAR Target Finder)

Net Zero Energy Measures (annual based on project's energy target)

- Site energy balance: 0 MWh (Classification B) (See Figure 12.38.)
- Source energy: –1,307 MWh (Classification B) (See Figure 12.39.)
- Energy emissions: –453 metric tons (Classification B) (See Figure 12.40.)
- Energy cost: Not calculated; utilities are paid as a campus.

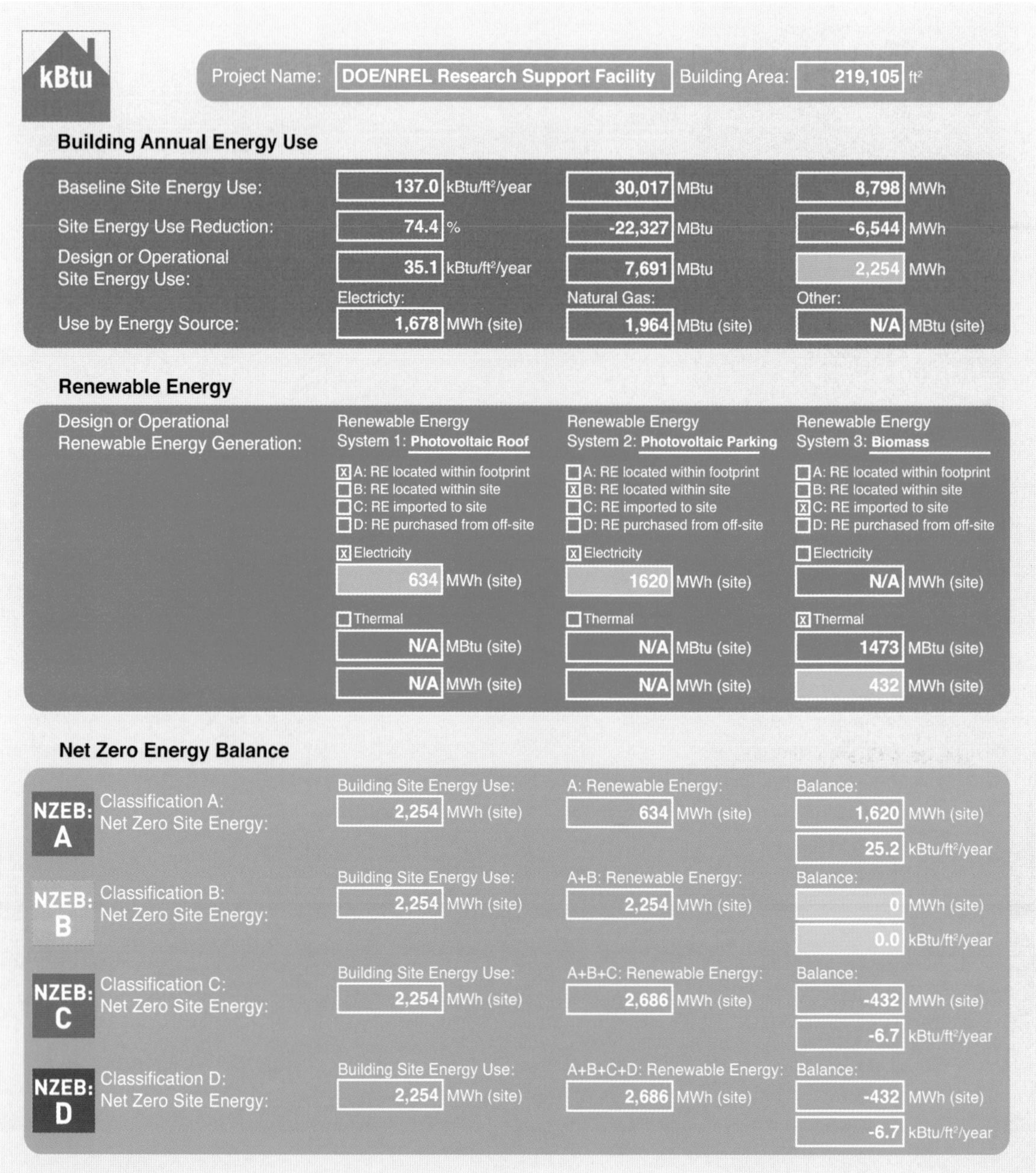
kBtu

Project Name: DOE/NREL Research Support Facility | Building Area: 219,105 ft²

Building Annual Energy Use

Baseline Site Energy Use:	137.0 kBtu/ft²/year	30,017 MBtu	8,798 MWh
Site Energy Use Reduction:	74.4 %	-22,327 MBtu	-6,544 MWh
Design or Operational Site Energy Use:	35.1 kBtu/ft²/year	7,691 MBtu	2,254 MWh
Use by Energy Source:	Electricty: 1,678 MWh (site)	Natural Gas: 1,964 MBtu (site)	Other: N/A MBtu (site)

Renewable Energy

Design or Operational Renewable Energy Generation:	Renewable Energy System 1: Photovoltaic Roof	Renewable Energy System 2: Photovoltaic Parking	Renewable Energy System 3: Biomass
A: RE located within footprint	[x]	[ ]	[ ]
B: RE located within site	[ ]	[x]	[ ]
C: RE imported to site	[ ]	[ ]	[x]
D: RE purchased from off-site	[ ]	[ ]	[ ]
Electricity	[x] 634 MWh (site)	[x] 1620 MWh (site)	[ ] N/A MWh (site)
Thermal	[ ] N/A MBtu (site)	[ ] N/A MBtu (site)	[x] 1473 MBtu (site)
	N/A MWh (site)	N/A MWh (site)	432 MWh (site)

Net Zero Energy Balance

	Building Site Energy Use:	Renewable Energy:	Balance:
NZEB: A — Classification A: Net Zero Site Energy:	2,254 MWh (site)	A: 634 MWh (site)	1,620 MWh (site); 25.2 kBtu/ft²/year
NZEB: B — Classification B: Net Zero Site Energy:	2,254 MWh (site)	A+B: 2,254 MWh (site)	0 MWh (site); 0.0 kBtu/ft²/year
NZEB: C — Classification C: Net Zero Site Energy:	2,254 MWh (site)	A+B+C: 2,686 MWh (site)	-432 MWh (site); -6.7 kBtu/ft²/year
NZEB: D — Classification D: Net Zero Site Energy:	2,254 MWh (site)	A+B+C+D: 2,686 MWh (site)	-432 MWh (site); -6.7 kBtu/ft²/year

■ **FIGURE 12.38** Net Zero Site Energy Balance.

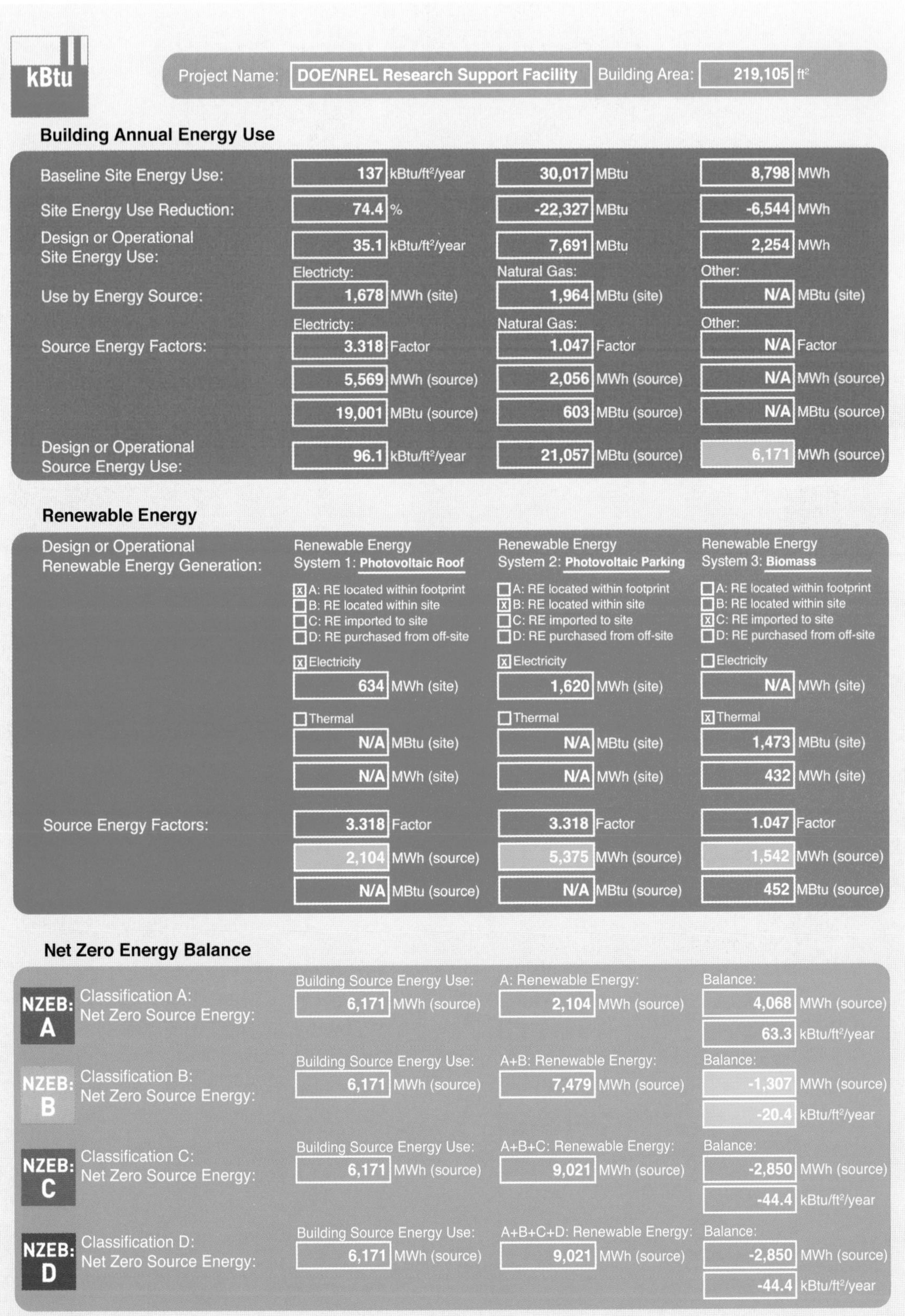

kBtu

Project Name: DOE/NREL Research Support Facility | Building Area: 219,105 ft²

Building Annual Energy Use

Baseline Site Energy Use:	137 kBtu/ft²/year	30,017 MBtu	8,798 MWh
Site Energy Use Reduction:	74.4 %	-22,327 MBtu	-6,544 MWh
Design or Operational Site Energy Use:	35.1 kBtu/ft²/year	7,691 MBtu	2,254 MWh
	Electricty:	Natural Gas:	Other:
Use by Energy Source:	1,678 MWh (site)	1,964 MBtu (site)	N/A MBtu (site)
	Electricty:	Natural Gas:	Other:
Source Energy Factors:	3.318 Factor	1.047 Factor	N/A Factor
	5,569 MWh (source)	2,056 MWh (source)	N/A MWh (source)
	19,001 MBtu (source)	603 MBtu (source)	N/A MBtu (source)
Design or Operational Source Energy Use:	96.1 kBtu/ft²/year	21,057 MBtu (source)	6,171 MWh (source)

Renewable Energy

Design or Operational Renewable Energy Generation:	Renewable Energy System 1: Photovoltaic Roof	Renewable Energy System 2: Photovoltaic Parking	Renewable Energy System 3: Biomass
	[X] A: RE located within footprint	[ ] A: RE located within footprint	[ ] A: RE located within footprint
	[ ] B: RE located within site	[X] B: RE located within site	[ ] B: RE located within site
	[ ] C: RE imported to site	[ ] C: RE imported to site	[X] C: RE imported to site
	[ ] D: RE purchased from off-site	[ ] D: RE purchased from off-site	[ ] D: RE purchased from off-site
	[X] Electricity	[X] Electricity	[ ] Electricity
	634 MWh (site)	1,620 MWh (site)	N/A MWh (site)
	[ ] Thermal	[ ] Thermal	[X] Thermal
	N/A MBtu (site)	N/A MBtu (site)	1,473 MBtu (site)
	N/A MWh (site)	N/A MWh (site)	432 MWh (site)
Source Energy Factors:	3.318 Factor	3.318 Factor	1.047 Factor
	2,104 MWh (source)	5,375 MWh (source)	1,542 MWh (source)
	N/A MBtu (source)	N/A MBtu (source)	452 MBtu (source)

Net Zero Energy Balance

NZEB: A — Classification A: Net Zero Source Energy:	Building Source Energy Use: 6,171 MWh (source)	A: Renewable Energy: 2,104 MWh (source)	Balance: 4,068 MWh (source); 63.3 kBtu/ft²/year
NZEB: B — Classification B: Net Zero Source Energy:	Building Source Energy Use: 6,171 MWh (source)	A+B: Renewable Energy: 7,479 MWh (source)	Balance: -1,307 MWh (source); -20.4 kBtu/ft²/year
NZEB: C — Classification C: Net Zero Source Energy:	Building Source Energy Use: 6,171 MWh (source)	A+B+C: Renewable Energy: 9,021 MWh (source)	Balance: -2,850 MWh (source); -44.4 kBtu/ft²/year
NZEB: D — Classification D: Net Zero Source Energy:	Building Source Energy Use: 6,171 MWh (source)	A+B+C+D: Renewable Energy: 9,021 MWh (source)	Balance: -2,850 MWh (source); -44.4 kBtu/ft²/year

■ **FIGURE 12.39** Net Zero Source Energy Balance.

CO_{2e}

Project Name: **DOE/NREL Research Support Facility** Building Area: **219,105** ft²

Building Annual Energy Use

Baseline Site Energy Use:	**137** kBtu/ft²/year	**30,017** MBtu	**8,798** MWh
Site Energy Use Reduction:	**74.4** %	**-22,327** MBtu	**-6,544** MWh
Design or Operational Site Energy Use:	**35.1** kBtu/ft²/year	**7,691** MBtu	**2,254** MWh
Use by Energy Source:	Electricty: **1,678** MWh (site)	Natural Gas: **1,964** MBtu (site)	Other: **N/A** MBtu (site)
Carbon Emission Factors (CO_{2e}):	Electricty: **1.012** Mtons/MWh	Natural Gas: **0.066** Mtons/MBtu	Other: **N/A** Mtons/MBtu
	1698.5 Mtons	**129.6** Mtons	**N/A** Mtons
Energy Emissions before Renewable Energy (CO_{2e}):		**18.4** lb/ft²/year	**1,828.1** Mtons

Renewable Energy

Design or Operational Renewable Energy Generation:	Renewable Energy System 1: **Photovoltaic Roof**	Renewable Energy System 2: **Photovoltaic Parking**	Renewable Energy System 3: **Biomass**
	[X] A: RE located within footprint [ ] B: RE located within site [ ] C: RE imported to site [ ] D: RE purchased from off-site	[ ] A: RE located within footprint [X] B: RE located within site [ ] C: RE imported to site [ ] D: RE purchased from off-site	[ ] A: RE located within footprint [ ] B: RE located within site [X] C: RE imported to site [ ] D: RE purchased from off-site
	[X] Electricity **634** MWh (site)	[X] Electricity **1,620** MWh (site)	[ ] Electricity **N/A** MWh (site)
	[ ] Thermal **N/A** MBtu (site)	[ ] Thermal **N/A** MBtu (site)	[X] Thermal **1,473** MBtu (site)
Carbon Emission Factors (CO_{2e}):	[X] Electricity **1.012** Mtons/MWh	[X] Electricity **1.012** Mtons/MWh	[ ] Electricity **N/A** Mtons/MWh
	[ ] Thermal **N/A** Mtons/MBtu	[ ] Thermal **N/A** Mtons/MBtu	[X] Thermal **0.066** Mtons/MBtu
Energy Emissions offset with Renewable Energy (CO_{2e}):	**641.6** Mtons	**1,639.4** Mtons	**97.2** Mtons

Net Zero Energy Balance

	Building Energy Emissions:	Renewable Energy:	Balance:
NZEB: A — Classification A: Net Zero Energy Emissions:	**1,828.1** Mtons	A: Renewable Energy: **641.6** Mtons	**1,187** Mtons **0.5** lb/ft²/year
NZEB: B — Classification B: Net Zero Energy Emissions:	**1,828.1** Mtons	A+B: Renewable Energy: **2,281.0** Mtons	**-453** Mtons **-4.6** lb/ft²/year
NZEB: C — Classification C: Net Zero Energy Emissions:	**1,828.1** Mtons	A+B+C: Renewable Energy: **2,378.3** Mtons	**-550** Mtons **-5.5** lb/ft²/year
NZEB: D — Classification D: Net Zero Energy Emissions:	**1,828.1** Mtons	A+B+C+D: Renewable Energy: **2,378.3** Mtons	**-550** Mtons **-5.5** lb/ft²/year

■ **FIGURE 12.40** Net Zero Energy Emissions Balance.

BIBLIOGRAPHY

7 Group, and Bill Reed. *The Integrative Design Guide to Green Building: Redefining the Practice of Sustainability.* Hoboken, NJ: John Wiley & Sons, Inc., 2009.

Adrian Smith + Gordon Gill Architecture. *Toward Zero Carbon: The Chicago Central Area DeCarbonization Plan.* Victoria, Australia: Images Publishing, 2011.

AIA California Council and the American Institute of Architects. "Integrated Project Delivery: Case Studies," January 2010.

Aldous, Scott, Zeke Yewdall, and Sam Ley. "A Peek Inside a PV Cell." *Home Power*, 121, October and November 2007, 64–68.

The American Institute of Architects. 50 to 50 Wiki, last accessed July 7, 2011, http://wiki.aia.org.

———. Carbon Neutral Design Project, last accessed October 29, 2011, www.architecture.uwaterloo.ca/faculty_projects/terri/carbon-aia/index.html.

———. "AIA Contract Documents: Contract Relationship Diagrams," June 2010.

The American Institute of Architects and AIA California Council. "Integrated Project Delivery: A Guide," 2007.

American Lung Association. "Public Policy Position, Energy," June 11, 2011.

American Wind Energy Association. "FAQ for Small Wind Systems," last accessed August 3, 2011, www.awea.org/_cs_upload/learnabout/publications/factsheets/9464_1.pdf.

Ander, Gregg D. *Daylighting Performance and Design*, 2nd ed. Hoboken, NJ: John Wiley & Sons, Inc., 2003.

Anis, Wagdy, and William Wiss. "Air Barriers: Walls Meet Roofs." *Journal of Building Enclosure Design*, Summer 2007, 29–32.

Architecture 2030 website, last accessed November 9, 2011, http://architecture2030.org/2030_challenge/the_2030_challenge.

Architectural Energy Corporation. "Daylight Metric Development Using Daylight Autonomy Calculations in the Sensor Placement Optimization Tool: Development Report and Case Studies." CHPS Daylighting Committee, March, 2006.

ASHRAE (American Society of Heating, Refrigerating and Air-Conditioning Engineers). "Advanced Energy Design Guide for K-12 School Buildings: Achieving 30% Energy Savings Toward a Net Zero Energy Building," 2008.

———. "Advanced Energy Design Guide for Small to Medium Office Buildings: Achieving 50% Energy Savings Toward a Net Zero Energy Building," 2011.

———. "Advanced Energy Design Guide for Small Retail Buildings: Achieving 30% Energy Savings Toward a Net Zero Energy Building," 2006.

———. *ASHRAE Handbook Fundamentals.* Atlanta, GA: ASHRAE, 2009.

———. "ASHRAE Vision 2020," January 2008.

———. "Energy Standard for Buildings Except Low-Rise Residential Buildings, ANSI/ASHRAE/IESNA Standard 90.1–2007," 2007.

———. "Standard for the Design of High-Performance Green Buildings Except Low-Rise Residential Buildings, ANSI/ASHRAE/USGBC/IES Standard 189.1–2011," 2011.

———. "Thermal Environmental Conditions for Human Occupancy, ANSI/ASHRAE Standard 55–2004," 2004.

———. "Ventilation for Acceptable Indoor Air Quality, ANSI/ASHRAE Standard 62.1–2004," 2004.

Associated General Contractors of America. "Qualifications Based Selection of Contractors," August 2009.

Barbose, Galen, Naïm Darghouth, Ryan Wiser, and Joachim Seel. "Tracking the Sun IV: An Historical Summary of the Installed Cost of Photovoltaics in the United States from 1998 to 2010." Lawrence Berkeley National Laboratory, September 2011.

Barley, D., M. Deru, S. Pless, and P. Torcellini. "Procedure for Measuring and Reporting Commercial Building Energy Performance." National Renewable Energy Laboratory, Technical Report NREL/TP-550–38601, October 2005.

Bayon, Ricardo, Amanda Hawn, and Katherine Hamilton. *Voluntary Carbon Markets: An International Business Guide to What They Are and How They Work.* London: Earthscan, 2007.

BC Green Building Roundtable. "Roadmap for the Integrated Design Process Part One: Summary Guide," 2007.

Behling, Sophia, and Stefan Behling. *Solar Power: The Evolution of Sustainable Architecture.* Munich: Prestel, 2000.

Biomass Energy Resource Center. "Wood Boiler Systems Overview," 2011.

Bony, Lionel, Stephen Doig, Chris Hart, Eric Maurer, and Sam Newman. "Achieving Low-Cost Solar PV: Industry Workshop Recommendations for Near-Term Balance of System Cost Reductions." Rocky Mountain Institute, September 2010.

Brickford, Carl. "Sizing Solar Hot Water Systems." *Home Power,* 118, April and May 2007, 34–38.

Briggs, Robert S., Robert G. Lucas, and Z. Todd Taylor. "Climate Classification for Building Energy Codes and Standards." Pacific NW National Laboratory, Technical Paper Final Review Draft, March 26, 2002.

Brown, Carl, Allan Daly, John Elliott, Cathy Higgins, and Jessica Granderson. "Hitting the Whole Target: Setting and Achieving Goals for Deep Efficiency Buildings." ACEEE Summer Study on Energy Efficiency in Buildings, 2010.

Brown, G. Z., and Mark DeKay. *Sun, Wind & Light: Architectural Design Strategies*, 2nd ed. Hoboken, NJ: John Wiley & Sons, Inc., 2001.

Brown, Robert, D. *Design with Microclimate: The Secret to Comfortable Outdoor Space.* Washington, DC: Island Press, 2010.

Building Design + Construction. "Zero and Net-Zero Energy Buildings + Homes, Eight in a Series of White Papers on the Green Building Movement," March 2011.

Carlise, Nancy, Otto Van Geet, and Shanti Pless. "Definition of a 'Zero Net Energy' Community," National Renewable Energy Laboratory, Technical Report NREL/TP-7A2-46065, November 2009.

Carmody, John, Stephen Selkowitz, Eleanor S. Lee, Dariush Arasteh, and Todd Willmert. *Window Systems for High-Performing Buildings.* New York: W.W. Norton & Company, 2004.

Commercial Buildings Consortium. "Analysis of Cost & Non-Cost Barriers and Policy Solutions for Commercial Buildings." Zero Energy Commercial Buildings Consortium, February 2011.

———. "Next-Generation Technologies Barriers & Industry Recommendations for Commercial Buildings." Zero Energy Commercial Buildings Consortium, February 2011.

Congressional Research Service. "Energy Independence and Security Act of 2007: A Summary of Major Provisions." CRS Report for Congress, December 21, 2007.

Crawley, Drury, Shanti Pless, and Paul Torcellini. "Getting to Net Zero." National Renewable Energy Laboratory, NREL/JA-550–46382, *ASHRAE Journal*, September 2009.

Cunningham, Paul, and Ian Woofenden. "Microhydro-Electric Systems Simplified." *Home Power*, 117, February and March 2007, 40–45.

Database of State Incentives for Renewables & Efficiency Solar portal website, last accessed November 16, 2011, www.dsireusa.org/solar.

Davis, Stacey C., and Susan W. Diegel. "Transportation Energy Data Book: Edition 30." Prepared by the Oak Ridge National Laboratory for the U.S. Department of Energy, June 2011.

Del Vecchio, David. "Optimizing a PV Array with Orientation and Tilt." *Home Power*, 130, April and May 2009, 52–56.

Deru, Michael, and Paul Torcellini. "Performance Metrics Research Project—Final Report." National Renewable Energy Laboratory, Technical Report NREL/TP-550–38700, October 2005.

———. "Source Energy and Emission Factors for Energy Use in Buildings." National Renewable Energy Laboratory, Technical Report NREL/TP-550–38617, June 2007.

———. "Standard Definitions of Building Geometry for Energy Evaluation." National Renewable Energy Laboratory, Technical Report NREL/TP-550–38600, October 2005.

Deru, M., N. Blair, and P. Torcellini. "Procedure to Measure Indoor Lighting Energy Performance." National Renewable Energy Laboratory, Technical Report NREL/TP-550–38602, October 2005.

Elvin, George. *Integrated Practice in Architecture: Mastering Design-Build, Fast-Track, and Building Information Modeling.* Hoboken, NJ: John Wiley & Sons, Inc. 2007.

Engage 360. "California Energy Efficiency Strategic Plan, Net Zero Energy Action Plan: Commercial Building Sector 2010–2012," 2010.

European Council for an Energy-Efficient Economy. "Steering Through the Maze #2, Nearly Zero Energy Buildings: Achieving the EU 2020 Target," February 8, 2011.

The European Parliament and the Council of the European Union. "Directive 2010/31/EU of the European Parliament and of the Council of 19 May 2010 on the Energy Performance of Buildings (recast)." *Official Journal of the European Union*, 2010.

Fernández–Galiano, Luis. *Fire and Memory: On Architecture and Energy.* Translated by Gina Cariño. Cambridge, MA: MIT Press, 2000.

Field, Kristin, Michael Deru, and Daniel Studer. "Using DOE Commercial Reference Buildings for Simulation Studies." National Renewable Energy Laboratory, Conference Paper NREL/CP-550–48588, August 2010.

Fuller, Sieglinde K., and Stephen R. Petersen. *Life-Cycle Costing Manual for the Federal Energy Management Program* (NIST Handbook 135). U.S. Department of Commerce, 1995.

Gardner, Ken, and Ian Woofenden. "Hydro-electric Turbine Buyer's Guide." *Home Power*, 136, April and May 2010, 100–108.

Garnderson, Jessica, Mary Ann Piettem, Girish Ghatikar, and Phillip Price. "Building Energy Information Systems: State of the Technology and User Case Studies." Lawrence Berkeley National Laboratory, LBNL-2899E, November 2009.

General Services Administration, Public Buildings Service. "Energy Savings and Performance Gains in GSA Buildings: Seven Cost-Effective Strategies," March 2009.

Gevorkian, Peter. *Alternative Energy Systems in Building Design.* New York: McGraw-Hill, 2010.

Gonchar, Joann. "Zeroing in on Net-Zero Energy." *Architectural Record*, December 2010.

Griffith, B., N. Long, P. Torcellini, R. Judkoff, D. Crawley, and J. Ryan. "Assessment of the Technical Potential for Achieving Net Zero-Energy Buildings in the Commercial Sector." National Renewable Energy Laboratory, Technical Report NREL/TP-550–41957, December 2007.

———. "Methodology for Modeling Building Performance across the Commercial Sector." National Renewable Energy Laboratory, Technical Report NREL/TP-550–41956, March 2008.

Grondzik, Walter T., Alison G. Kwok, Benjamin Stein, and John S. Reynolds. *Mechanical and Electrical Equipment for Buildings*, 11th ed. Hoboken, NJ: John Wiley & Sons, Inc., 2010.

Gowri, K., D. Winiarski, and R. Jarnagin. "Infiltration Modeling Guidelines for Commercial Building Energy Analysis." Pacific Northwest National Laboratory, September 2009.

Guglielmetti, Rob, Jennifer Scheib, Shanti Pless, Paul Torcellini, and Rachel Petro. "Energy Use Intensity and Its Influence on the Integrated Daylight Design of a Large Net Zero Energy Building." National Renewable Energy Laboratory, Conference Paper NREL/CP-5500–49103, March 2011.

Guglielmetti, Rob, Shanti Pless, and Paul Torcellini. "On the Use of Integrated Daylighting and Energy Simulations to Test-Drive the Design of a Large Net-Zero Energy Office Building." National Renewable Energy Laboratory, Conference Paper NREL/CP-5500–47522, August 2010.

Hassett, Timothy G., and Karin L. Borgerson. "Harnessing Nature's Power: Deploying and Financing On-Site Renewable Energy." World Resources Institute, 2009.

Hausladen, Gerhard, Michael de Saldanha, and Petra Liedl. *ClimateSkin: Building-Skin Concepts That Can Do More with Less Energy.* Basel, Switzerland: Birkhäuser, 2006.

Hawkens, Paul, Amory Lovins, and L. Hunter Lovins. *Natural Capitalism: Creating the Next Industrial Revolution.* Boston: Back Bay Books, 2008.

Helms, Robert N. *Illumination Engineering for Energy-Efficient Luminous Environments.* Englewood Cliffs, NJ: Prentice-Hall, 1980.

Heschong, Lisa. *Thermal Delight in Architecture.* Cambridge, MA: MIT Press, 1979.

Hirsch, Adam, Shanti Pless, Rob Guglielmetti, Paul A. Torcellini, David Okada, and Porus Antia. "The Role of Modeling When Designing for Absolute Energy Use Intensity Requirements in a Design-Build Framework." National Renewable Energy Laboratory, Conference Paper NREL/CP-5500–49067, March 2011.

International Energy Agency. "Biomass for Power Generation and CHP." IEA Energy Technology Essentials, January 2007.

———. "Technology Roadmap: Solar Photovoltaic Energy," 2010.

International Living Building Institute. "Documentation Requirements, Living Building Challenge 2.0: Renovation, Landscape + Infrastructure, and Building Typologies," December 2010.

———. "Living Building Challenge 2.0: A Visionary Path to a Restorative Future," April 2010.

———. "Net Zero Energy Building Certification, Documentation Requirements," 2011.

International Performance Measurement & Verification Protocol. *Concepts and Practices for Determining Energy Savings in New Construction, Volume III, Part O*, January 2006.

Jewell, Mark T. "Energy-Efficiency Economics: What You Need to Know." *HPAC Engineering*, January 2003, 38–46.

Kats, Greg. *Greening Our Built World: Costs, Benefits, and Strategies.* Washington, DC: Island Press, 2010.

Klein, Gary. "Hot-Water Distribution Systems—Part III." *Plumbing Systems & Design*, May/June 2005, 12–15.

Kosny, Jan. "A New Whole Wall R-Value Calculator: An Integral Part of the Interactive Internet-Based Building Envelope Materials Database for Whole-Building Energy Simulation Programs." Oak Ridge National Laboratory, August 2004.

Kwok, Alison G., and Walter T. Grondzik. *The Green Studio Handbook: Environmental Strategies for Schematic Design*, 2nd ed. Oxford: Architectural Press, 2011.

Lawrence Berkeley National Laboratory, EnergyIQ website, last accessed March 12, 2012, http://energyiq.lbl.gov.

Leach, Matthew, Chad Lobato, Adam Hirsch, Shanti Pless, and Paul Torcellini. "Technical Support Document: Strategies for 50% Energy Savings in Large Office Buildings." National Renewable Energy Laboratory, Technical Report NREL/TP-550-49213, September 2010.

Lechner, Norbert. *Heating, Cooling, Lighting: Sustainable Design Methods for Architects.* Hoboken, NJ: John Wiley & Sons, Inc., 2009.

Lehrer, David, and Janani Vasudev. "Evaluation a Social Media Application for Sustainability in the Workplace." Center for the Built Environment, University of California, Berkeley. CHI2011, May 7–12, 2011, Vancouver, BC, Canada, May 2011.

Lerum, Vidar. *High-Performance Building.* Hoboken, NJ: John Wiley & Sons, Inc., 2008.

Lobato, Chad, Shanti Pless, Michael Sheppy, and Paul Torcellini. "Reducing Plug and Process Loads for a Large-Scale, Low-Energy Office Building: NREL's Research Support Facility." National Renewable Energy Laboratory, Conference Paper NREL/CP-5500-49002, February 2011.

Lobato, Chad, Michael Sheppy, Larry Brackney, Shanti Pless, and Paul Torcellini. "Selecting a Control Strategy for Miscellaneous Electrical Loads (draft)," August 2011.

Lund, John W. "Development of Direct-Use Projects." National Renewable Energy Laboratory, Conference Paper NREL/CP-5500-49948, January 2011.

Massachusetts Department of Energy Resources. "An MPG Rating for Commercial Buildings: Establishing a Building Energy Asset Labeling Program in Massachusetts," December, 2010.

Massachusetts Zero Net Energy Buildings Task Force. "Getting to Zero: Final Report of the Massachusetts Zero Net Energy Buildings Task Force," March 11, 2009.

Mazria, Edward. *The Passive Solar Energy Book, Expanded Professional Edition.* Emmaus, PA: Rodale Press, 1979.

McConahey, Erin. "Mixed Mode Ventilation: Finding the Right Mix." *ASHRAE Journal*, September 2008, 36–48.

McLennan, Jason. "Burning Questions—The Role of Combustion in Living Buildings: Why Prometheus Was Wrong." *Trim Tab*, Summer 2010.

Mehalic, Brian. "Flat-Plate & Evacuated-Tube Solar Thermal Collectors." *Home Power*, 132, August and September 2009, 40–46.

Miller, Rex, Dean Strombom, Mark Iammarino, and Bill Black. *The Commercial Real Estate Revolution: Nine Transforming Keys to Lowering Costs, Cutting Waste, and Driving Change in a Broken Industry.* Hoboken, NJ: John Wiley & Sons, Inc., 2009.

Moe, Kiel. *Thermally Active Surfaces in Architecture.* Princeton, NJ: Princeton Architectural Press, 2010.

Moorefield, Laura, Brooke Frazer, and Paul Bendt. "Office Plug Load Field Monitoring Report." *Ecos*, December 2008.

Morris, Peter, and Lisa Fay Matthiessen. "Cost of Green Revisited: Reexamining the Feasibility and Cost Impact of Sustainable Design in the Light of Increased Market Adoption," July 2007.

National Association of State Facilities Administrators, Construction Owners Association of America, The Association of Higher Education Facilities Officers, Associated General Contractors of America, and the American Institute of Architects. "Integrated Project Delivery for Public and Private Owners," 2010.

National Building Controls Information Program. "NBCIP Roundtable Summary: What's Wrong with Building Controls?" Iowa Energy Center, 2002.

National Institute of Building Sciences. "Exterior Enclosure Technical Requirements for the Commissioning Process, NIBS Guideline 3–2006." November 27, 2006.

National Renewable Energy Laboratory. "Assessing and Reducing Plug and Process Loads in Office Buildings," June 2011.

———. *A Handbook for Planning and Conducting Charrettes for High-Performance Projects*, 2nd ed., September 2009.

———. "Information Technology Settings and Strategies for Energy Savings in Commercial Buildings," August 2011.

———. "Integrated Design Team Guide to Realizing Over 75% Lighting Energy Savings in High-Performance Office Buildings," June 2011.

———. Open PV Project website, last accessed August 17, 2011, http://openpv.nrel.gov.

———. PVWatts website, last accessed October 16, 2011, www.nrel.gov/rredc/pvwatts.

———. *Solar Radiation Data Manual for Buildings*, September 1995.

———. "Where Wood Works: Strategies for Heating with Woody Biomass." Flexible Energy Communities Initiative, 2008.

———. NREL Newsroom. "Green Computing Helps in Zero Energy Equation," April 14, 2010.

———. "Solar System Tops Off Efficient NREL Building," September 29, 2010.

National Resources Canada. "Micro-Hydropower Systems: A Buyer's Guide," 2004.

National Science and Technology Council, Committee on Technology. "Federal Research and Development Agenda for Net-Zero Energy, High-Performance Green Buildings," October 2008.

New, Dan. "Intro to Hydropower, Part 1: Systems Overview." *Home Power*, 103, October and November 2004, 14–20.

———. "Intro to Hydropower, Part 2: Measuring Head & Flow." *Home Power*, 104, December 2004 and January 2005, 42–47.

———. "Intro to Hydropower, Part 3: Power, Efficiency, Transmission & Equipment Selection." *Home Power*, 105, February and March 2005, 30–35.

New Buildings Institute. Advanced Lighting Guidelines website, www.algonline.org.

———. "Getting to Zero 2012 Status Update: A First Look at the Cost and Features of Zero Energy Commercial Buildings," March 2012.

Nicol, Fergus J., and Michael A Humphreys. *Adaptive Thermal Comfort and Sustainable Thermal Standards for Buildings*. Oxford Centre for Sustainable Development, School of Architecture, Oxford Brookes University, March 2002.

Nowak, David J., and Daniel E. Crane. "Carbon Storage and Sequestration by Urban Trees in the USA." *Environmental Pollution*, 116, 2002, 381–389.

NYS Energy Research & Development Authority. "Wind Energy Model Ordinance Options," October 2005.

O'Brien, Sean M. "Thermal Bridging in the Building Envelope: Maximizing Insulation Effectiveness Through Careful Design." *The Construction Specifier*, October 2006.

Olson, Ken. "Solar Hot Water: A Primer." *Home Power*, 84, August and September 2001, 44–52.

———. "Solar Hot Water for Cold Climates." *Home Power*, 85, October and November 2001, 40–48.

Peel, M. C., B. L. Finlayson, and T. A. McMahon. "Updated World Map of the Köppen-Geiger Climate Classification." *Hydrology and Earth System Sciences*, 11, 2007, 1633–1644.

Peterson, Kent, and Hugh Crowther. "Building Energy Use Intensity." *High Performance Buildings*, Summer 2010, 40–50.

Petro, Rachel. "Countdown to Zero." *LD+A*, February 2011.

Phillips, Duncan, Meiring Beyers, and Joel Good. "How High Can You Go? Building Height and Net Zero." *ASHRAE Journal*, September 2009, 26–36.

Pless, Shanti, and Paul Torcellini. "Controlling Capital Costs in High-Performance Office Buildings," NREL Webinar, October 31, 2011.

———. "Net-Zero Energy Buildings: A Classification System Based on Renewable Energy Supply Options." National Renewable Energy Laboratory, Technical Report NREL/TP-550–44586, June 2010.

Pless, S., M. Deru, P. Torcellini, and S. Hayter. "Procedure for Measuring and Reporting the Performance of Photovoltaic Systems in Buildings." National Renewable Energy Laboratory, Technical Report NREL/TP-550–38603, October 2005.

Pless, Shanti, Paul Torcellini, and David Shelton. "Using an Energy Performance-Based Design-Build Process to Procure a Large-Scale Low-Energy Building." National Renewable Energy Laboratory, Conference Paper NREL/CP-5500–51323, May 2011.

Presidential Documents. "Executive Order 13514 of October 5, 2009, Federal Leadership in Environmental, Energy, and Economic Performance." *Federal Register Vol. 74, No. 194*, Thursday, October 8, 2009.

Preus, Robert. "Thoughts on VAWTs: Vertical Axis Wind Generator Perspectives." *Home Power*, 104, December 2004 and January 2005, 98–100.

Price, Derek. "Structuring the Deal: Funding Options and Financial Incentives for On-site Renewable Energy Projects." Johnson Controls, Inc., 2008.

Putt del Pino, Samantha, and Pankai Bhatia. "Working 9 to 5 on Climate Change: An Office Guide." World Resource Institute, December 2002.

Rawlinson, Simon, and David Wright of Davis Langdon. "Sustainability: Embodied Carbon." *Building Magazine*, October 2007, 88–91.

Reinhart, Christoph F., John Mardaljevic, and Zach Rogers. "Dynamic Daylight Performance Metrics for Sustainable Building Design." National Research Council Canada (NRCC-48669).

Roberts, Simon, and Nicolò Guariento. *Building Integrated Photovoltaics: A Handbook.* Basel, Switzerland: Birkhäuser, 2009.

Rocky Mountain Institute. "Collaborate and Capitalize: Post-Report from the Building Energy Modeling Innovation Summit," 2011.

Rothschild, Susy S., Cristina Quiroz, Manish Salhorta, and Art Diem. "The Value of eGRID and eGRIDweb to GHG Inventories." E.H. Pechan & Associates, Inc., U.S. EPA, December 2009.

Sanchez, Justine. "2010 PV Module Guide. *Home Power*, 134, December 2009 and January 2010, 50–61.

Sanchez, Justine, and Ian Woofenden. "PV Systems Simplified." *Home Power*, 144, August and September 2011, 70–78.

Sheppy, Michael, Chad Lobato, Otto Van Geet, Shanti Pless, Kevin Donovan, and Chuck Powers. "Reducing Data Center Loads for a Large-Scale, Low-Energy Office Building: NREL's Research Support Facility," December 2011.

Sherwood, Larry. "U.S. Solar Market Trends 2010." Interstate Renewable Energy Council, June 2011.

Solar Energy Industries Association and GTM Research. "U.S. Solar Market Insight, First Quarter 2011, Executive Summary," 2011.

Solar Rating & Certification Corporation website, last accessed October 16, 2011, www.solar-rating.org.

Speer, Bethany, Michael Mendelsohn, and Karlynn Cory. "Insuring Solar Photovoltaics: Challenges and Possible Solutions." National Renewable Energy Laboratory, Technical Report NREL/TP-6A2–46932, February 2010.

The Sustainable Sites Initiative. "Guidelines and Performance Benchmarks, 2009."

———. "The Case for Sustainable Landscapes," 2009.

Szokolay, Steven V. *Introduction to Architectural Science: The Basis of Sustainable Design*, 2nd ed. Oxford, UK: Architectural Press, 2008.

Torcellini, Paul, and Drury Crawley. "Understanding Zero-Energy Buildings." *ASHRAE Journal*, September 2006, 62–69.

Torcellini, P., M. Deru, B. Griffith, K. Benne, M. Halverson, D. Winiarski, and D. B. Crawley. "DOE Commercial Building Benchmark Models." National Renewable Energy Laboratory, Conference Paper NREL/CP-550–43291, July 2008.

Torcellini, Paul, Shanti Pless, Michael Deru, and Drury Crawley. "Zero Energy Buildings: A Critical Look at the Definition." National Renewable Energy Laboratory, Technical Report NREL/TP-550-39833, June 2006.

Torcellini, Paul, Shanti Pless, Chad Lobato, and Tom Hootman. "Main Street Net-Zero Energy Buildings: The Zero Energy Method in Concept and Practice," July 2010.

United Nations Environment Programme (UNEP). Sustainable Buildings & Climate Initiative. "Common Carbon Metric for Measuring Energy Use & Reporting Greenhouse Gas Emissions from Building Operations."

———. International Panel for Sustainable Resource Management. "Towards Sustainable Production and Use of Resources: Assessing Biofuels," 2009.

U.S. Army Corps of Engineers, Engineer Research and Development Center. "U.S. Army Corps of Engineers Air Leakage Test Protocol for Measuring Air Leakage in Buildings."

U.S. Department of Energy. "U.S. Billion-Ton Update: Biomass Supply for a Bioenergy and Bioproducts Industry," August 2011.

U.S. Department of Energy, Energy Efficiency, & Renewable Energy. *2009 Building Energy Data Book*, October 2009.

———. *2009 Renewable Energy Data Book*, August 2010.

———. *2010 Building Energy Data Book*, March 2011.

———. "2010 Wind Technologies Market Report," June 2011.

———. *Biomass Energy Data Book, Edition 3*, 2010.

———. "The Design-Build Process for the Research Support Facility" (draft), July 2011.

———. "High-Performance Home Technologies: Solar Thermal and Photovoltaic Systems," June 2007.

———. "Operations & Maintenance Best Practices: A Guide to Achieving Utility Resource Efficiency," October 2007.

———. "Metering Best Practices: A Guide to Achieving Operational Efficiency, Release 2.0," July 2004.

———. "M&V Guidelines: Measurement and Verification for Federal Energy Projects, Version 3.0," April 2008.

———. "Small Wind Electric Systems: A U.S. Consumer's Guide," August 2007.

———. "Small Hydropower Systems," July 2001.

———. "Solid-State Lighting Research and Development: Multi-Year Program Plan," August 2010.

———. "Research Support Facility—A Model of Super Efficiency," May 2011.

U.S. Department of Energy, Energy Information Administration International Energy Statistics website, last accessed December 6, 2010, www.eia.gov/countries.

———. "Annual Energy Outlook 2010 with Projections to 2035," April 2010.

———. "Annual Energy Review 2009," August 2010.

———. "Historical Natural Gas Annual 1930 through 2000," December 2001.

———. "International Energy Outlook, 2010," July 2010.

———. "Method for Calculating Carbon Sequestration by Trees in Urban and Suburban Settings," April 1998.

U.S. Environmental Protection Agency. Carbon Sequestration in Agriculture and Forestry website, last accessed October 16, 2011, http://www.epa.gov/sequestration/index.html.

———. "ENERGY STAR Performance Rating Methodology for Incorporating Source Energy Use," August 2009.

———. ENERGY STAR Target Finder website, last accessed April 10, 2011, www.energystar.gov/targetfinder.

———. "EPA's Green Power Partnership: Renewable Energy Certificates," July 2008.

U.S. Green Building Council. "LEED Reference Guide for Green Building Design and Construction: For the Design, Construction and Major Renovations of Commercial and Institutional Buildings Including Core & Shell and K-12 School Projects, 2009 Edition," 2009.

———. "LEED Reference Guide for Green Building Operations and Maintenance: For the Operations and Maintenance of Commercial and Institutional Buildings, 2009 Edition," 2009.

———. "LEED Building Design & Construction Rating System, 3rd Public Comment Draft," March 2012.

Utzinger, Michael, and James H. Wasley. "Building Balance Point." Vital Signs Project, University of California–Berkeley, August 1997.

Watson, Donald, and Kenneth Labs. *Climatic Building Design: Energy-Efficient Building Principles and Practice.* New York: McGraw-Hill, 1983.

Welch, Michael. "Architectural PV Design Considerations." *Home Power*, 142, April and May 2011, 44–51.

Weliczko, Erika. "Solar-Electric Options: Crystalline vs. Thin-Film." *Home Power*, 127, October and November 2008, 98–101.

Wells, Malcolm. *Gentle Architecture*. New York: McGraw-Hill, 1981.

Woofenden, Ian. "Understanding Wind Speed." *Home Power*, 143, June and July 2010, 106–108.

———. "Wind-Electric Systems Simplified." *Home Power*, 110, December 2005 and January 2006, 10–16.

Woofenden, Ian, and Hugh Piggott. "Anatomy of a Wind Turbine." *Home Power*, 116, December 2006 and January 2007, 52–55.

Woofenden, Ian, and Mick Sagrillo. "2010 Wind Generator Buyer's Guide." *Home Power*, June and July 2010, 137.

———. "Is Wind Electricity Right for You?" *Home Power*, 143, June and July 2011, 52–61.

ABOUT THE AUTHOR

Tom Hootman, AIA, LEED AP BD+C, is the Director of Sustainability and an Associate Principal at RNL, a global design firm and industry leader in sustainable design. He is also an architect and LEED Accredited Professional with over 19 years of experience. As Director of Sustainability, Tom provides leadership and guidance to RNL's sustainable project work, design standards, staff education, research, and outreach. He is currently working on several net zero energy buildings, and has recently completed the 222,000-square-foot National Renewable Energy Laboratory Research Support Facility. He regularly speaks and writes on a variety of sustainable design topics, both nationally and internationally.

CONTRIBUTING AUTHORS

Shanti Pless, LEED AP, is a Senior Energy Efficiency Research Engineer for the National Renewable Energy Laboratory's Advanced Commercial Buildings Research Group. His work at NREL is focused on applied research and design processes for commercial building energy efficiency and building-integrated renewable energy. He facilitates the numerous integrated design processes required to realize low- and zero-energy commercial buildings. More recently, he has been working to develop a classification and energy optimization modeling system for zero energy buildings. He is also conducting research to determine how to provide technical support for zero energy building and research projects, including the NREL's new zero energy office building projects.

David Okada, PE, LEED AP, is a leader in the field of high performance green design, focusing his mechanical engineering experience on projects achieving the highest levels of sustainability. With over a decade of experience, his projects include three LEED Platinum certifications, two AIA COTE Top Ten awards, and three projects tracking net zero energy performance. David is passionate about this work and presents regionally and nationally on the topic of net zero energy buildings. David currently leads Integral Group's Seattle office after ten years of delivering high-performance projects with Stantec and Keen Engineering.

INDEX

C

D

F

G

H

I

Q

R

S

T

U

V

W

Z